MARRIAGE AND THE FAMILY
Studying Close Relationships

KAREN KAYSER KERSTEN
University of Michigan

LAWRENCE K. KERSTEN
Eastern Michigan University

HARPER & ROW, PUBLISHERS, New York
Cambridge, Philadelphia, San Francisco, Washington,
London, Mexico City, São Paulo, Singapore, Sydney

A list of text and illustration credits can be found on pages 618–622.

Sponsoring Editor: Alan McClare
Project Editor: Carla Samodulski
Text and Cover Design: Lucy Krikorian
Cover Illustration: 37.375; Dance at Bougival; Pierre Auguste Renoir; French, 1841–1919; Oil on Canvas; 181.8 × 98.1 cm. (71⅝ × 38⅝ in.); Picture Fund; Courtesy, Museum of Fine Arts, Boston.
Text Art: Fineline Illustrations, Inc.
Photo Research: Mira Schachne
Production Manager: Jeanie Berke
Production Assistant: Paula Roppolo
Compositor: Ruttle, Shaw & Wetherill, Inc.
Printer and Binder: R. R. Donnelley & Sons Company
Cover Printer: Lehigh Press

Marriage and the Family: Studying Close Relationships

Library of Congress Cataloging in Publication Data

Kersten, Karen Kayser.
  Marriage and the family.

  Bibliography: p.
  Includes indexes.
  1. Marriage. 2. Family. 3. Love. 4. Sex (Psychology) 5. Intimacy (Psychology)
I. Kersten, Lawrence K. II. Title.
HQ728.K445 1988   306.7   87-17715
ISBN 0-06-043641-7

87 88 89 90 9 8 7 6 5 4 3 2 1

Brief
Contents

Contents

Preface

TO THE INSTRUCTOR

In the 1980s there has been an explosion of interest in intimacy, both within and outside of marriage. Increasingly, emotional intimacy is a goal of marriage in American society, both for those building new marriages and those seeking to improve existing ones.

When studying marriage and the family, we believe it is important to examine how individuals strive to achieve emotional closeness in their relationships. Early in the book—in Chapter 2—we present a model for the development of intimate relationships. We use the theme of human intimacy to unify all the chapters and provide a framework that helps students learn to analyze and interpret what occurs in interpersonal relationships.

This text provides theoretical explanations of how and why individuals seek intimacy or emotional closeness through marriage, family, and friendship. It is an interdisciplinary text. While sociological research predominates, we have also included findings from the fields of social psychology, anthropology, human development, and history. Each of these perspectives offers insights into the study of close human relationships. Increasingly it is recognized that marriages and families are best understood through the combined knowledge of many disciplines.

The text is also unique in bridging the gaps among theory, research, and practical application. It presents material that is personally meaningful to the student as well as specifically connected to research on and theories of interpersonal relationships. We believe in promoting students' abilities to think scientifically about families, while at the same time helping them to become aware of their own interpersonal abilities.

Some of the topics of current interest discussed in the text include:

the ongoing controversy between family liberals and family conservatives

the study of friendships

a clear conceptual distinction between love, sex, and intimacy

the concept of illusionary intimacy

a new typology of marriages

dual-income marriages

sexual difficulties and sex therapy

violence and abuse in families

marriage and family in the middle and later years

the process of uncoupling

PEDAGOGICAL AIDS

The text provides chapter outlines, chapter reviews, a glossary, appendices, and easy-to-read illustrations, graphs, and tables. Each chapter also includes several boxes containing practical applications of the topics discussed in each chapter. In addition, most chapters include at least one cross-cultural box. Family research methods, with examples, are discussed in the first appendix.

An instructor's manual is available. Test questions emphasize analytical thinking and not simply the memorization of names, dates, and statistics. In addition, a supplementary paperback text, *Seeking Closeness,* is available from Harper & Row. This book helps students understand themselves and their own potentials for intimacy, and suggests ways of making changes and building intimate relationships in their lives.

TO THE STUDENT

This book was written with two important goals. The first was to acquaint you with the most recent scientific research in the field of marriage and the family. The second was to make the material meaningful for your personal life. We hope to help you think more scientifically and become more competent in your interpersonal relationships. These goals are closely related: Making informed choices in your life requires thoughtfulness and scientific awareness.

There is now a new emphasis on intimacy. Most individuals no longer form groups only for basic survival needs. Instead, they enter into human relationships for the purpose of meeting their needs for closeness. As our society as a whole becomes increasingly impersonal, most people turn toward their families and friendships to obtain emotional and social support. This need for emotionally close relationships occurs throughout the life cycle. In order to better understand intimate relationships, we develop a model of intimacy in this text and use it throughout the entire book. This theoretical model provides a basis for analyzing *all* interpersonal relationships. It will help you to understand the many dimensions of close relationships and learn important ideas and concepts.

ACKNOWLEDGMENTS

We are especially indebted to Shari Jackson, an expert on family abuse, who provided us with valuable suggestions for our chapter on family violence. We are grateful as well to Linda Acitelli, Sandy Richards, and Kathy Pursell for their contributions to many of the boxes, and to Clare Holden, who did much of the word processing. We also appreciate the many helpful comments and suggestions made by our students, who played vital roles in the development of the manuscript. Larry Kersten is particularly grateful to Eastern Michigan University for providing him with released time and a grant to work on the early stages of this book. We appreciate the comments of the following reviewers, which helped to guide the development of this text and gave us encouragement that this was indeed a worthwhile endeavor:

Stephen Bahr, Brigham Young University
Betsy Bergen, Kansas State University
Darla Botkin, University of Kentucky
Peter Chroman, College of San Mateo
M. Donnelly, Lehman College
Rollie E. Dorsett, Austin Community College
Constance Shehan, University of Florida
Janice Stroud, University of North Carolina—Charlotte
Kenrick Thompson, Northern Michigan University
Charles Varni, Allan Hancock College
Rebecca Smith, University of North Carolina—Greensboro
Bill Brindle, Monroe Community College

This book would not have been possible without the fine staff at Harper & Row. We would particularly like to thank Alan McClare, who provided us with enthusiastic encouragement and support throughout every stage of the publishing project. Our thanks also to Carla Samodulski for her superb job as our project editor. Their patience and guidance made the whole project much more enjoyable.

Karen Kayser Kersten
Lawrence K. Kersten

Close
Relationships

1

The Search
for Closeness

Most of us do not desire to go through life alone. Human relationships are important throughout our lives. We want contact with people, and we are dependent on others from birth to death. Human needs tend not to be met in isolation.

Relationships vary in degrees of closeness; some are little more than acquaintances while others are intimate connections. To understand various relationships better, specific types can be identified and compared on a continuum. As you move along the continuum of relationships (see Figure 1.1) from left to right—as you move toward greater closeness—the number of persons with whom you will have these relationships will likely decrease.

It's possible for a relationship to develop starting at one end of the continuum and leading to the other. For instance, people may originally meet at work and so pattern their meeting within certain particular hours of the day, talking about a relatively narrow set of topics (the boss, the company, the news in the day's papers) and doing a very restricted set of things together (eating lunch, chatting). As the relationship grows, however, they may meet outside work, at different times of the day or evening, do a wider range of things together (for example, playing a sport, going to a movie), and talk about a wider range of topics. Many other aspects of their activities can also change. For instance, the intensity of their actions will increase; where they used to greet each other with a simple "Hi," they may now hug each other; where they used to smile politely, they may now smile affectionately; where they used to share superfi-

cial chitchat, they may now share values and feelings (Duck, 1983).

Kinship relations can fall anywhere on this continuum from mere acquaintances to intimate others. Obviously many kinship ties lack any real feelings of closeness, and this characteristic generally increases the farther removed the kin is from the nuclear family. Even sibling contacts among a majority of adults do not typically manifest the characteristics of strong social companionship or intimacy (Adams, 1970). Rather, contact is limited to home visiting, telephone communication, and occasions of family ritual.

When one looks at relationships with cousins and other secondary relatives, one is hard pressed to find much significance in the vast majority of them today. Among poor black families, however, extended kin provide a significant source of strength and stability. The cooperation and mutual aid among the kin network enables these families to meet their basic needs for survival (Queen, Habenstein, and Quadagno, 1985). There is some tendency to use distant kin as substitutes for missing relationships. For example, a childless couple may be close to their nephews and nieces; and an only child may be close to his or her cousins (Adams, 1970).

As we move across the continuum, the *quality* of the relationship also changes. Several factors that help to define relationships include the degree of self-disclosure, the degree of commitment, the degree of exclusivity, the amount of time spent together, the type of rewards expected, the degree of consensus of values, and the degree of closeness—physical and emotional. Figure 1.2

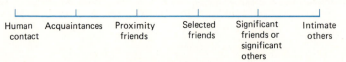

Figure 1.1   Continuum of human relationships.

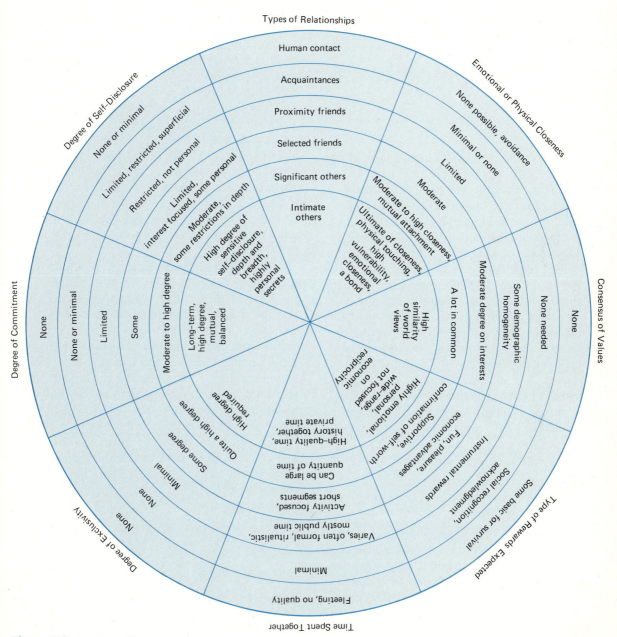

Figure 1.2 Analysis of human relations.

compares these seven factors with the six types of relationships shown on the continuum of human relationships.

TYPES OF RELATIONSHIPS

Human Contact

Since humans are social beings, if there is no contact with other people, infants will actually die and adults will have difficulty functioning. In modern American society there is a lot of superficial interaction, which may be grouped into this human-contact category. In most of our daily activities we are thrust into at least some contact with others, even if it's very marginal. Students experience human contact as they walk across campus and pass by a large number of other students, many of whom they may not know or even recognize. This contact is public and very fleeting and involves no commitment. Self-disclosure is minimal—if any takes place at all—and the benefits from any particular contact may also be minor. Typically, we make great efforts to avoid physical contact in such circumstances—so much so that if we do have contact we usually say "Excuse me" or "I'm sorry."

Acquaintances

Acquaintances may have a little more meaning for us, although interaction with them is usually still quite superficial and restricted. But it differs from simple human contact in that there is some recognition and acknowledgment of the other person. Perhaps a smile, eye contact, a greeting, or a name may be used—there is some affirmation of the other person's existence. Still, at this level very little of oneself is revealed, there is little or no commitment, the time spent together is minimal, and there is little, if any, closeness.

Proximity Friends

Some of our relationships are the result of the mere fact of physical proximity. Friendships arising out of proximity are not initially "chosen" but exist merely because others live near us, sit next to us in class, or work next to us at the office or factory. Recurrent interaction does occur and friendship can develop. Proximity friends could include neighbors, professional colleagues, students in the same class. The workplace is a natural setting where this type of friendship can develop. When one is working with someone closely and continually, there is considerable opportunity to talk to each other.

Usually disclosures between proximity friends are not about very private matters; the amount of personal information shared and the degree of emotional closeness typically are not great. Only rarely do proximity friends confide in each other or discuss personal problems in their lives; if they did, it would become another type of friendship. Interactions are often restricted to certain formal ritualistic activities—the "block" party, condominium association meetings, school classes, union meetings, or office business. The rewards from such proximity relations are typically of a practical rather than an emotional nature; for example, services or information or perhaps some sense of community.

Selected Friends

From these proximity relationships or from many other interactions closer types of friendships can develop. One such type is selected friends—people who are actually chosen or selected to be friends. They may be individuals with whom we prefer to work or play. Often particular activities become the primary focus—bowling together, playing poker, attending bingo games, carrying on a business partnership. Persons may be chosen because of similar interests, shared backgrounds, mutual commitments, shared religion, or shared political orientation. In addition, particular life-cycle phases may bring these friends together, such as Lamaze classes for pregnant women, Parent-Teacher Association (PTA) meetings, high school booster clubs, or senior-citizens' groups.

Selected friendships tend to be quite segmented in that contact is usually restricted to certain activities, and people are seen only in connection with certain roles. Bowling partners, for example, typically do not go to the movies or have dinner together. Again, these relationships usually are not characterized by deep emotional bonds, but they do provide for a moderate degree of social support. Self-disclosure is typically limited to common interests and is less focused on personal information. Many of the activities with selected friends are carried out in groups, which to a meaningful degree hinders emotional closeness.

Significant Friends or Significant Others

Significant friends are also chosen, but they are not restricted to particular activities or time periods. These are friends with whom a *breadth* of personal information is shared, although the relationship may not be as deep as with intimate others. There is more of a commitment with significant others than with proximity friends or selected friends; these are people who certainly do not involve just temporary contacts.

These individuals are chosen as friends because they are likely to share concerns, common values, or similar problems. Also they tend to be people who we expect will be there when we need them. We hope we can rely on them in a crisis and that they will provide assistance and support when and if needed. The benefits from significant friendships extend beyond social support or practical activities to include also emotional support. Here friendship is viewed more as an end in itself and not as a means to an end—these people are not "used" for particular services. This type of relationship involves a high level of reciprocity and mutuality.

Intimate Others

Most of us want at least one of our relationships to be characterized by emotional closeness, or intimacy. We define an intimate relationship as one involving an emotional bond with proven mutual commitment and trust between two people that provides personal and relationship security and rewards. Intimate others, then, are people who provide us with emotional closeness. While the development of intimacy is a process, intimacy itself can also be viewed as an end result. Particular couples may achieve degrees of intimacy, but it is a process that will always have to be worked on. The opposite of intimacy is human isolation.

The concept of emotional intimacy in this book does not coincide with the popular usage of the term *intimacy*, which implies sexual behavior. The meaning of intimacy in this discussion is much broader. It is possible to be sexually involved without any emotional intimacy at all. It is also possible to be intimate with someone—say a close friend—and not be sexually involved with that person.

The definition of intimacy here suggests that it takes place only between two people, what is called a *dyad*. Of course, one can be involved in more than one intimate dyad. For example, a woman could be emotionally close to her husband and also close to a female friend. If individuals within a larger group are intimate, this closeness will exist between pairs of people. Thus it's possible for all members of a nuclear family—mother, father, and children—to be emotionally close to one another. A detailed discussion of intimate relationships is found in Chapter 2. Various theoretical perspectives used by social scientists in explaining family relationships are discussed in Box 1.1.

WHERE INTIMACY CAN BE FOUND

When people in America think of an intimate couple they usually think of a husband and wife. But that is only one of many possible types of intimate relationships. For example, there can be an emotionally close relationship between any family members, including a parent and a son or daughter, two siblings, or any combination of extended family members including grandparents, aunts, uncles, nieces, nephews, cousins, stepparents or stepchildren. In actuality the word *family* is often used as a metaphor for closeness (L. Rubin, 1985). When we want to emphasize how close we are to a friend, we may say, "They're like family." These words then indicate a quality of closeness.

In general, two women are more likely to be in an intimate relationship than two men. Females seem much more determined to seek out close connections than men. Women not only actively search for more intimacy but they are, according to Carin Rubenstein and Phillip Shaver (1982), the undisputed "intimacy specialists." In fact, the word *intimacy* itself may sound overly feminine to many men.

Studies of children's friendships consistently show that girls, in comparison to boys, tend more to develop close, loyal friendships and to practice interpersonal relating. The result is, for a number of possible reasons, that in adult relationships women are ready and

prepared for emotional closeness but are shocked and discouraged to discover that their marriage partners know almost nothing about intimacy (Rubenstein and Shaver, 1982).

This does not mean that men do not have a need to be emotionally close to others: "Both sexes have a biologically based need for intimacy" (Rubenstein and Shaver, 1982, p. 25). Rather, it seems that men often do not know how to satisfy this need. If a man wants to learn the details about intimacy, he would do well to take lessons from a woman.

Thus, intimacy is "feminine" only in the sense that women are the major intimacy providers. Most likely, men and women need intimacy to the same degree. Ironically, fewer women than men get their needs met, despite women's expertise, because so many men are intimacy-takers rather than givers. (p. 26)

THE FEAR OF CLOSENESS

As mentioned, most people indicate that they want meaningful human closeness in their lives. Furthermore, research suggests that those human beings who experience intimacy are less lonely and much more content with their lives (Freedman, 1978). Extensive loneliness exists, however, in our rather anonymous and impersonal American culture. At any given time as many as 25 percent of all adults report that they have no friends, or that they are "lonely," "bored," or "depressed" (R. R. Bell, 1981; Freedman, 1978). It appears that people want emotional closeness, but they also fear it. They fear the tasks involved in attaining intimacy, namely, among other things, the admission of one's dependency, the ability to allow oneself to become vulnerable, the making of a commitment, a willingness to take on obligations and

(Text continued on page 12.)

BOX 1.1

FAMILY THEORETICAL PERSPECTIVES

Theories are used by social scientists for explaining research data. Theories can also be used to help stimulate new research. The research process can begin with a hunch, an idea, or an existing theory, out of which hypotheses are formed. To test hypotheses, subjects are observed or asked questions; data are collected. The research findings are ultimately interpreted in terms of theory. Theories therefore are end products, as well as serving as the basis for further research.

Each theory views the world from a particular perspective and organizes a set of interrelated assumptions, principles, and concepts, which are used to explain relationships among facts. Theories and facts need each other. Theories without facts are empty, and facts without theories to explain them are meaningless. Theories of marriage and the family, therefore, provide understanding and meaning to family life. Most family scientists are guided in their research by particular theoretical perspectives. Discussed below are five major theoretical orientations. These theories are utilized throughout the rest of the text.

FUNCTIONALISM AND SYSTEMS THEORY

Functionalism and systems theory have contributed significantly to explanations of family life. A *function* is the contribution that something makes for the maintenance of either the family institution in society as a whole or for an individual in a particular family. The institution of the family is looked at as one of many systems needed in an ongoing society, and each individual family is viewed as a system in itself. The family as a system has boundaries that define and separate it from the outside world. The system is under constant pressures to change both from within and outside.

Families exist because they perform certain necessary functions. These functions include the following: reproducing the next generation, providing nurturant socialization for children, regulating the sexual activity of family members, maintaining and providing for the family's physical needs, and providing for emotional and intimacy needs for the husband, wife, and children. These functions are all interrelated in a system, and a change in one function affects all the others. Over the years the family has been losing functions, such as, being the economic production unit, the protection unit, the education unit, and the social-security unit. The function of providing for nurturance and intimacy is increasingly viewed as the major function of the family today, both for adults and children. It is generally agreed that the nurturant socialization of children is best carried out in a small kinship-structured group such as the family.

Functionalists also place importance on relationships within a family. They are concerned, for example, with the purposes of the incest taboo in

(Continued)

maintaining the family system. They also analyze traditional male and female roles in terms of a family division of labor. *Instrumental roles* are connected with the outside world, such as the good-provider role. *Expressive roles*, in contrast, are roles within the family, such as providing for nurturance, affection, and emotional satisfaction. The *structure* of a family refers to the way that positions or roles in the family are organized. Examples of family structural arrangements include nuclear, matriarchal, single-parent, and childless. Particular roles that do not help the family system to maintain itself are said to be *dysfunctional* and will cause the system to change or even break up.

SYMBOLIC INTERACTIONISM

Whereas functionalism emphasizes *purpose*, symbolic interactionism focuses on *process*. The family itself is defined as personalities involved in ongoing interaction processes. The basic point of analysis is the processes involved in the internal workings of small family groups. Interactionists argue that we cannot study family behavior by external observations alone. We must, in addition, understand the thought processes and how people "feel" about certain actions. People's feelings depend upon the *meaning* attached to behavior, not just the behavior itself. Human beings interpret meanings through interactive thought processes that take place within themselves. Individuals develop their own *definition of the situation* through ascertaining the meaning of other people's actions.

Meaning is interpreted through the use of *symbols*—words, gestures, body language, facial expressions. So symbolic interactionism stresses the fact that people interact with each other through symbols. Humans learn the shared symbols of a culture through the *process of socialization*. The unique way in which we respond to symbols is part of our *personality*. Both socialization processes and the development of personality are analyzed by interactionist theorists.

Communication processes within the family are one of the chief concerns of symbolic interactionists. Individuals must be able to interpret symbols correctly if effective communication, and ultimately intimacy, are going to exist. Some other types of family-related issues that interactionists study include the processes involved in mate selection, marital interaction, child-rearing patterns, and sexual interaction. Additional concepts utilized by interactionists include ''*significant other,*'' ''*generalized other,*'' ''*role taking,*'' and ''*reference group.*''

EXCHANGE THEORY

Many theorists see exchange theory as having significant explanatory power in family studies. Humans are seen as seeking relationships for self-interested reasons. People look for rewarding exchanges and try to avoid costly ones. All human interaction involves exchanges. The idea of exchange allows for the *evaluation of interations in terms of rewards and costs*. Relationships will more than likely cease when the costs exceed the rewards or when more rewards are perceived as coming from another relationship. Most people believe that kindnesses should be *reciprocated*, and they are naturally interested in another individual's response when they do something for that person.

The exchange between two persons can be either largely positive or negative. *Positive exchange* involves the reciprocal giving and receiving of rewards. *Negative exchange* involves the reciprocal giving and receiving of costs. The rewards and costs that are given or received in the exchange process can be either *extrinsic* (given from the outside, externally) or *intrinsic* (given to oneself, internally).

Exchange theory is utilized to analyze many aspects of family relationships. The way *different personalities* exchange is one area of study. Some people do not reciprocate whatever is given to them and therefore are *exploitative*. Others are focused on giving and *pleasing* most of the time. Still others do not see themselves as worthy to *accept* anything from individuals. Furthermore, many people do not know how to exchange in-depth confidences in an intimate relationship. Other ways in which exchange theory has been utilized include mate selection, marital decision making, the analysis of power, conflict resolution, reasons for falling out of love, sexual interaction, parent-child problems, marital satisfaction, and the development of emotional closeness.

DEVELOPMENTAL THEORY

The developmental, or *life-span*, approach is based on the reality that human beings change physically, emotionally, and cognitively over the *life cycle*. The focus then is on changes in family relationships and patterns over time. But just as an individual family member develops and ages while experiencing a series of adjustments in life from birth to death, so does a marriage and a family have developmental sequences from the initial beginnings through expansion, contraction, and dissolution. Each stage of the life cycle is influenced by preceding events. The family is looked at as a group of interacting persons. At each stage of life new challenges emerge, and through reciprocal interaction the family attempts to deal with the continually changing needs of the family members.

Development tasks are *role expectations* that arise at various stages of the life cycle. The changing tasks result from biological needs, cultural norms, and personal goals. Dealing adequately with a task will have an influence on later task successes and also on the potential for personal happiness in later stages of life. Examples of particular family stages include (1) marrying, (2) having children, (3) living with teenagers, (4) the empty-nest situation when the children are gone, (5) living as retired family members, and (6) living as a widowed person.

Obviously there will be changes in family relationships over time. Family life is dynamic, not static. Each stage will have its unique problems, and some stages may be more difficult than others. Conflicts more often arise between children and parents and between husbands and wives at particular stages. Crises may arise and successful adjustments may be difficult, such as

(Continued)

to the arrival of an unexpected child. Husband and wife relationships change over time; sometimes the couple grows apart, and at other times they become more intimate with age. Individuals must be ready to accept new responsibilities and changes in their life-styles as stages develop if they expect to achieve personal happiness.

CONFLICT THEORY

In the conflict-theory orientation, conflict is viewed as a natural part of human interaction. Instead of emphasizing consensus and equilibrium (as in functionalism) this theory focuses both on the negative and positive aspects of conflict. There is ongoing change in family life, as in all human interactions, and change often stimulates conflict. In fact, conflict is considered to be inevitable. Change disrupts old patterns and leads to disagreements over values and decisions. Individuals will fight for their own self-interested needs or for what they themselves perceive is best for the family as a whole.

Conflict itself is not good or bad. One advantage of conflict is that it brings disagreements out into the open. Once in the open there is the possibility for constructive *conflict resolution* through negotiation, compromise, and collaboration. Thus, conflict is not necessarily disruptive; without conflict there is often no chance for the resolution of an issue. Not dealing with or ignoring conflict is bad. Married couples who have never had a fight often end up divorcing because problem issues were swept under the rug until one day there was an "explosion." Prolonged battles and struggles, however, particularly those involving physical or verbal abuse, are certainly damaging to emotional closeness and may cause irreparable harm to a relationship.

Marriage and the family are the setting for the most heightened emotions. Power struggles from competing interests are common. Conflict theorists focus on such matters as the following: conflicts involving male and female roles, decision making, communication problems, parent-child conflicts, spouse and child abuse, marital happiness, and the causes of divorce.

---

a willingness to put restrictions on one's freedom.

Individuals who do not want to take on the obligations and responsibilities of a relationship are unwilling to put restrictions on their freedom and independence. But according to social psychologist Judy Bardwick, over the past two decades many writers and therapists judged the "need for security in a relationship as evidence of a lack of independence; furthermore they believed that autonomy, not needing anyone else, was the

hallmark of adult psychological health" (Bardwick, 1979, p. 122). Bardwick thinks that Americans came to the point in the 1970s of an exaggerated denial of people's dependence so that emotional well-being was often described in fact as autonomy (1979).

In reality, people who are able to admit their dependence and their vulnerability are emotionally healthy. As Bardwick indicates, "without the sense of belonging and thus of commitment—without the knowledge that you are terribly important to someone else—

you can feel that nothing you do is important because there is no one to do anything for'' (1979, p. 124). Bardwick indicates that all of us have feelings of inadequacy and fears of being abandoned, ''and this is part of the human condition'' (p. 125). But she states:

If we do not love or permit intimacy but interact by surface charm, social ritual, and recreational sex, we behave as though we were intimate while we retain the barriers that protect us from our own vulnerability. (p. 126)

Bardwick thinks that people are probably better able to experience successful and fulfilling lives in *all* ways ''when they are in a mutually committed relationship because, feeling secure, they are better able to take risks'' (1979, p. 127). If we try always to avoid vulnerability and we need always to feel in *total control*, we will fear and avoid meaningful commitment and intimacy. ''Without commitment and real obligations, now and extending into the future, it is difficult to have a firm sense of who or what we are, a sense that it matters that we lived. Without commitment one is free from obligation, but without obligation there is too little that matters'' (p. 127).

Thus the idea of interdependence recognizes that human beings need each other. Marriage is the relationship ''in which the dependent needs of interdependent people can be met'' (Bardwick, 1979, p. 129). ''The most important feelings—that one exists, that one's existence is a good thing, that the future has promise—come from long-term commitment'' (p. 129). Thus when we speak of the fear of closeness we speak of the apprehension that humans have to admit their dependency, to become vulnerable, and to make commitments. It is a fear that reduces

a person's potential for decreasing loneliness and achieving happiness.

Schopenhauer's parable about the porcupines which drew together for warmth but separated when their quills pricked each other illustrates the pull-and-push interplay of intimacy and vulnerability. Pained, the animals move apart; then, feeling the chill of the air they move close again, only to be hurt once more in the act of sharing warmth. We are often told that hate is the opposite of love, remoteness the reverse of intimacy. But it appears the real antagonist of both is the fear of being vulnerable to hurt, rejection, or disillusionment. (Quoted in Lasswell and Lobsenz, 1976, p. 182)

TRENDS IN THE SEARCH FOR CLOSENESS

At various times in history and in various parts of the world, cultural norms have either encouraged or discouraged the seeking of human closeness. Norms not only regulated how close people should be to each other but also to whom, in particular, one could be close. The expectations were often different for men and women.

This section traces various patterns of emotional closeness in marriage and the family and in friendship. It begins with early America and continues through the twentieth century, when the most dramatic changes in family life have occurred. While the changes are striking, marriage and the family remain strong institutions still today.

Premodern America to the Industrial Revolution

Many myths and misconceptions about close relationships in history have been exposed by research done since 1970. Exposure has been

Premodern families focused largely on physical survival rather than emotional closeness. Husband, wife, and children often worked together as a team.

accomplished through the careful study of official government records, church records, and private letters and diaries. For a brief description of various research methods and techniques on the family see Appendix A.

Premodern American families focused largely on physical survival rather than emotional closeness. The husband, wife, and children worked together as a team on farms, in family shops, or in businesses. Wives performed a provider role as much as husbands in an economic partnership. The family also took care of the functions of education, recreation, health care, religious training, protection, and social security. People without a family were taken in as boarders. Furthermore, orphans and the indigent and even criminals were "placed" by local officials in particular households (Demos, 1974). Everybody—it was thought—needed to be part of a family.

A common belief held today is that premodern families were organized into "extended households"—large kin groups including several husbands and wives and extended kin from all sides of the family spanning three or more generations. In fact, such groups appear never to have existed, and families like the Waltons on television are nostalgic myths. The nuclear family—

husband, wife, and children—did not just appear with the rise of the Industrial Revolution more than a century ago. Research shows that nuclear households have been the norm in America throughout history (Demos, 1974).

Children were seen as needing strict discipline from early life on. A "spare the rod, spoil the child" philosophy was applied. Young persons were thought to have a natural stubbornness and pride, which had to be "broken." The child was seen as being totally depraved when he or she was born—having an original sin involving an inherent corruption and a selfish nature. It was considered literally necessary at times to "beat the devil" out of the child (Demos, 1974). Little parent-child emotional closeness existed.

The earliest Puritan settlers had a strict moral code regarding sexual relations outside of the marital bond. They condemned premarital and extramarital sex. They had a positive view, however, of sexual pleasure within marriage. Sexual activity was viewed as "God's way of encouraging a harmonious and companionate relationship between husband and wife" (Clanton, 1984, p. 15). Sexual activity in marriage was seen as strengthening the nuclear family. Thus husband-wife closeness was encouraged through sexuality.

The Industrial Revolution to World War I

The first third of the nineteenth century marked a turning point in the history of American family life; narrower, more specific roles were defined for both men and women. A sentimentalized image of women developed as they were separated from the expanding world and as their role was confined to the care of home and children. While the male was becoming more deeply involved in competitive work out in the world, he held an ever more morally idealized image of the lady in his life.

> *Women could no longer be permitted to work outside the home (except among the poorest classes where it was a matter of simple survival). Their position in life was defined in terms of a purity directly opposed to everything characteristic of the larger world. (Demos, 1974, p. 433)*

A woman's greatest virtue was "submissiveness" and "obedience" to the will of her spouse. Her central role was now an "expressive" one, to be a "comforter." Her function was morally to uplift everyone with whom she came into contact, but chiefly her husband and children (Demos, 1974).

It was in the nineteenth century, and particularly in the period 1880–1920, that the concept of the "ideal" middle-class family came into its own. The characteristics of this family were high moral standards, particularly regarding sexual matters; an extreme interest in the welfare and protection of children; religious faith; a sense of obligation to change conditions perceived as morally offensive; and distinct and separate roles for men and women (Berger and Berger, 1983, p. 7). It is this "ideal family" that many people with conservative life orientations are hoping to create or recreate in the late 1980s. Ironically, family life around the turn of the century was probably quite different than it is currently idealized to have been (see Box 1.2).

THE GOOD-PROVIDER ROLE. Sociologist Jessie Bernard (1981) has described the growth of the male, breadwinning role or the good-provider role in the nineteenth century. This male role arose when men moved out of the home into the world of work, a move accelerated by the Industrial Revolution. It emerged around the 1830s and it had wide

BOX 1.2

"TILL DEATH DO US PART"
EARLIER MORTALITY MEANT LESS INTIMACY IN 1900

Many of the significant changes in the American family cannot be adequately understood without recognizing the impact of changes in death rates.

> At the beginning of this century about 140 infants out of every 1,000 born died in the first year of life; now only 14 out of 1,000 born die. In this same period the average life span has increased from less than 50 to 73. (Uhlenberg, 1983)

Today the loss of an immediate family member is a relatively rare occurrence. But in 1900, the loss of a parent, a child, a sibling, or a spouse was a "pervasive aspect of life" that disrupted established family patterns (Uhlenberg, 1983).

As a result of higher mortality rates in 1900, intimacy between family members was much less likely to be initiated and, obviously, maintained. The amount of emotional investment that one person was willing to put into another person was greatly influenced by the likelihood of that other person's death. People "could not allow themselves to become too attached to something that was regarded as a probable loss" (Aries, 1962, cited in Uhlenberg, 1983).

Parent-child relationships, for example, had a much lower potential for intimacy in 1900 than they do today. Not only were parents facing the grim reality of the possible loss of a child, but children were also more likely to lose their parents. Sibling relationships may have been affected as well. (See Table 1.)

Table 1 **PROBABILITIES OF PARENTS AND SIBLINGS DYING BEFORE A CHILD REACHED AGE 15: 1900; 1940; 1976**

Year	Probability of 1 or more parents dying	Probability of 1 or more of 2 siblings dying	Probability of death to member of nuclear family
1900	.24	.36	.51
1940	.10	.12	.21
1976	.05	.04	.09

SOURCE: *U.S. Public Health Service.*

Moreover, contact between children and their grandparents was much less likely in 1900. Only one-fourth of the children had all grandparents alive at birth; by 1976 the proportion increased to almost two-thirds (Uhlenberg, 1983).

Marital intimacy may have also been affected by mortality. Marriages in 1900 were much more likely to end in early death than divorce. The likelihood of couples experiencing time together after the children have left home was much less than it is today. (See Table 2.)

Table 2   PROBABILITY OF MARITAL DISRUPTION DUE TO DEATH OR DIVORCE WITHIN THE FIRST 40 YEARS: 1900; 1940; 1976

Year	Broken by death[a]	Broken by death or divorce[a]
1900	.67	.71
1940	.50	.63
1976	.36	.60

[a] Assuming husband is 25 and wife is 22 at the time of marriage.

SOURCE: *U.S. Public Health Service.*

In conclusion, then, the current lower death rates could mean greater intimacy for many family relationships—parent-child, grandparent-grandchild, sibling-sibling, husband-wife. Going back to the "good old days," therefore, may not be as good as it sounds.

ramifications. Bernard says it marked the beginning of a new type of marriage, and it did not have good effects on women.

Since women were discouraged from participating in the outside labor force, they were deprived of opportunities to achieve power and competence. Women were not allowed to acquire productive skills, and they were not reimbursed for their contributions to the family. Women "dedicated themselves instead to winning a good provider, who would 'take care of them.' The wife of a more successful provider became for all intents and purposes a parasite, with little to do except indulge or pamper herself" (Bernard, p. 2).

The new industrial order fixed the site of the work that the two sexes engaged in. Each sex had its own turf. This resulted in "the identification of gender with work site as well as with work itself. The very nature of maleness and femaleness becomes embedded in the sexual division of labor" (p. 3). The spatial separation of the work site also reduced the amount of time available for personal interaction, spontaneous emotional give-and-take, and intimacy within the family. In contrast, in the premodern period—when men and women worked in an economy based in the home—frequent opportunities for interaction were available. Bernard writes:

When men and women are in close proximity, there is always the possibility of reassuring glances, the comfort of simple physical presence. But when the division of labor removes the man from the family dwelling for most of the day, intimate relationships become less feasible. (1981, p. 3)

Certainly the spatial separation of the two sexes did nothing to help men become emotionally expressive. What was important to men was their new "enormous drive for achievement, for success, for 'making it'" (p. 3). A real man was not only a provider but a *good* provider. Bernard says that "success in the good-provider role came in time to define masculinity itself. The good provider had to achieve, to win, to succeed, to dominate. He was a bread *winner*" (p. 4). A man's family became a display case for his success as a good provider. One person took on the responsibility for the whole family's support. In the middle class, if a wife worked, the man was humiliated—it admitted to everybody that the husband was a failure as a good provider (Bernard, 1981).

A man was usually so busy that he had little time even to talk to his wife or children.

Emotional expressivity was not included in the good-provider role. . . . [But,] if in addition to being a good provider, a man was kind, gentle, generous, and not a heavy drinker or gambler, that was all frosting on the cake. Loving attention and emotional involvement in the family were not part of a woman's implicit bargain with a good provider. (Bernard, 1981, p. 3)

To be sure, some men disliked the role that was forced upon them. Some took it out on their families and punished them for the heavy burden they had to carry. The money a man earned was considered to belong to him; members of the family often had to beg

for money. Some men only knew how to "love" by buying expensive gifts—"the fur coat became more important than the affectionate hug" (p. 5).

Bernard argues that the good-provider role lasted a century and a half, until the 1980 census, when men were no longer considered automatically the head of the household. In reality, however, much of the good-provider role still exists, particularly in the lower class and to a somewhat lesser degree in the middle class.

INTIMACY BETWEEN WOMEN. It's apparent—at least up until World War I—that American husbands and wives did not experience much intimacy in their marriages. But it appears that there was indeed some meaningful emotional closeness between women. Evidently strong patterns of friendship existed between women but not between men in the nineteenth century. Historian Carroll Smith-Rosenberg (1975) describes the significance of numerous diaries and thousands of letters that women wrote to each other from adolescence to old age.

For most of these women their affection for each other remained strong their entire lives, emphasized by their loneliness and their desire to spend time together. Female friendship was the only real behavioral and emotional option socially available during this period. Single-sex, or homosocial, networks were facilitated and supported by severe social restrictions on intimacy between men and women generally, and particularly between young men and women. The distinctly male and female spheres in the world were assumed to be determined by the laws of God and nature. Contacts between men and women were usually formal and stiff (Smith-Rosenberg, 1975).

Middle-class and upper-class women of the nineteenth century "lived within a world bounded by home, church and the institution of visiting—that endless trooping of women to each others' homes for social purposes" (Smith-Rosenberg, 1975, p. 10). Theirs was a world encompassed by children and other women. "Women helped each other with domestic chores and in time of sickness, sorrow, or trouble" (p. 10). Women at suppers huddled together sharing and comparing the letters received from other close women friends. Secrets were exchanged and cherished. Women held communities and kin systems together. They exchanged news letters with almost any female extended kin and through such letters gradually formed deeply loving and dependent ties. Smith-Rosenberg writes:

> *Especially when families became geographically mobile women's long visits to each other and their frequent letters filled with discussions of descriptions of growing children, and reminiscences of times and people past provided an important sense of continuity in a rapidly changing society. (1975, p. 11)*

Within this close-knit female world, sorrows, anxieties, and joys could be shared by women who were confident that other women had experienced similar feelings. Women gave one another inner security and self-esteem. Talking helped to relieve troubles—troubles that apparently most men could not understand. The woman's world was an emotional one to which men had little access (Smith-Rosenberg, 1975).

Married life, also, was organized around a host of female rituals. "Sisters, cousins, and friends frequently accompanied newlyweds on the wedding night and wedding trip, which often involved additional family visiting" (p. 22). Childbirth—particularly the birth of the first child—involved "a lengthy seclusion of the woman before and after delivery, severe restrictions on her activities, and

finally a dramatic reemergence. Death, like birth, was structured around elaborate unisexed rituals" (p. 23). Women turned "to each other for comfort when facing the frequent and unavoidable deaths of the 18th and 19th centuries" (p. 24). A man was barred from the deathbed of his wife. "Women relatives and friends slept with the dying woman, nursed her, and prepared her body for burial. . . . Intense bonds of love and intimacy bound together those women who, offering each other aid and sympathy, shared such stressful moments" (p. 24). Nineteenth-century American society did not place taboos on close female relationships but rather recognized them as a valuable form of human contact throughout a woman's life (Smith-Rosenberg, 1975). Lower-class wives of necessity often had to work outside the home, and they did not have the extensive leisure that middle-class and upper-class wives had. "Other women," however, still made up the emotional support system of lower-class women—not their husbands.

Marriage resulted in a major problem of adjustment. Much of the emotional stiffness and distance that was associated with marriage during this time was a consequence of gender-role differentiation. "With marriage both women and men had to adjust to life with a person who was, in essence, a member of an alien group" (Smith-Rosenberg, 1975, p. 28). Also, sexual desire in the nineteenth century and early twentieth century, particularly the 1880–1920 era, was regarded as exclusively male. Women were supposed to be passionless and not interested in sex. It is hard to imagine that many married couples were either emotionally or physically close during this period. Sexuality merely reflected the distant pattern that existed in the entire relationship. Same-sex companionship seemed preferable to what was available between husband and wife at home.

In the nineteenth century, emotional intimacy was more likely to develop between two women than between a man and a woman.

Between the World Wars

Between the two world wars there continued to be a sharp division of gender roles in the family. In the 1920s and 1930s, sociologists Robert and Helen Lynd found a similar pat-tern to that which had existed in the previous hundred years in their studies of the families in Middletown—a small Midwestern com-munity (Lynd and Lynd, *Middletown*, 1929, and *Middletown in Transition*, 1937). The hus-band's responsibility was still to be a good

According to the Middletown studies, the typical marriage in the 1920s was dreary. Women continued to seek emotional intimacy with other women.

provider; the wife was primarily responsible for keeping the house and raising the children.

But there were some meaningful rumblings of change—in part brought about by the crisis of World War I—which challenged the traditional gender-role pattern. Twenty-five percent of working-class wives worked full time outside the house in 1920. In addition, some husbands of working wives "were beginning to help clean the house, cook the meals, shop for groceries, do the laundry and care for the children" (Caplow et al., 1982, p. 112). Nevertheless, the role of the full-time homemaker and mother was still the ideal and the most highly respected role for women (Caplow et al., 1982).

The Lynds' account of the typical marriage in the 1920s was a dreary one, particularly for the working class. For most families the primary concern was economic survival. Happy marriages were rare, and the majority of couples appeared to lead a depressing existence. Most married partners were pressured to remain together by community values discouraging divorce. "Married life was disappointing, but the prospect of a divorce was even more painful" (Caplow et al., 1982, p. 117).

Marriages involved very limited companionship. Social and recreational activities were usually separated by gender; men talked about business, sports, and politics, and women discussed children, dress styles, and local gossip.

> About the only activity men and women shared together was playing cards—but even here the married couple did not have "fun" alone. In fact there were few activities shared alone together as a couple. The separation of men and women was reflected in the widely held view that the two sexes were quite different species. Women were seen as emotional, illogical and incapable of sustained thought, and as being morally superior to men. (Lynd and Lynd, 1929, p. 118)

Working-class females in particular had little time, energy, or money to spend on family leisure. But even when couples spent time at home together, there was little pleasant or stimulating conversation. When they were not "bickering" over family problems, they often lapsed into "apathetic silence." Many of the wives were so lonely they did not want the Middletown researchers' interviews with them to end.

> "I wish you could come often. I never have anyone to talk to," or "My husband never goes anyplace and never does anything. In the evenings he comes home and sits down and says nothing. I like to talk and be sociable, but I can hardly ever get anything out of him." (Lynd and Lynd, 1929, p. 120)

Their sexual relations also were troubled. Lack of knowledge about birth control and religious beliefs opposing its use made babies the inevitable consequence of physical closeness. On the one hand, women were so emotionally separated from their husbands that they felt they could not even ask the men in their lives what they thought about birth control—let alone how they felt about practicing it. The fear and worry of having unwanted children often made wives resentful—they felt that their husbands were selfish and insensitive. Other women just "kept away" from their husbands, which certainly did nothing to strengthen their marriages (Caplow et al., 1982).

On the other hand, husbands felt rejected by their wives' avoidance of sexual activity, which was the only form of closeness they knew. The fact that prostitution flourished in Middletown during the 1920s may be attributed to the limited marital sex. In any event, husband-wife relationships were neither physically nor emotionally close. This is demonstrated by the responses of 69 working-class wives to the question, "What are the thoughts and plans that give you courage to go on when thoroughly discouraged?" Not a single wife mentioned her husband as a source of emotional support (Caplow et al., 1982)!

Business-class wives, in addition to "making a home" for their husbands and children, played a more active and meaningful social role in the world. Besides having traditional skills, a business-class wife was to be physically attractive and well dressed. In general, "brains" were not regarded as important in a wife. The key thing that girls should learn from high school was the ability to pick a good provider.

The depression of the 1930s didn't really change marriages that much, except perhaps to make life harder. While husbands and wives did spend more time together—partly because outside activities were unaffordable—the quality of their interaction was still poor. Norms discouraging open self-disclosure continued to exist; spouses were not supposed to be frank with each other, particularly regarding emotional matters. The partners did a lot of mutual tearing down, as wives blamed their husbands for failing to "bring home the bacon" and husbands defended their wounded egos by lashing out at their wives and children. "Despite these mounting tensions, the typical marital relationship during the depression was similar to that of the 1920's" (Lynd and Lynd, 1937, p. 145). The depression, however, seemed to have had more devastating effects on men than on women. A number of men who "lost everything" in the depression, and therefore failed in the good-provider responsibility, committed suicide.

The divorce rate actually decreased in the 1930s and early 1940s. Marriages were not really better, but rather many couples were forced to stay together out of poverty. Many did not have the $60 needed to pay for a divorce. However, the economic upheaval of the 1930s hit the working class the hardest, and this situation was reflected in the large number of desertions that took place.

Child care in the 1920s and 1930s continued to involve "coldness" and "stiffness." John B. Watson, one of the child-training experts of the obedience school, said the following:

> There is a sensible way of treating children, treat them as though they were young adults. Never hug and kiss them, never let them sit in your lap. If you must, kiss them once on the forehead when they say good night. Shake hands with them in the morning. Give them a pat on the head if they have made an extraordinary good job of a difficult task. (1928, pp. 81–82)

In the 1920s and 1930s dating became the accepted method of checking out possible mates. This practice gave young people more freedom than ever before in their search for a marriage partner. But dating served additional functions for many individuals. It did not necessarily lead to marriage but became just a way of having a good time, a way of gaining status and prestige, and a way of learning about different types of human beings.

Petting became popular beginning in the 1920s. It emerged as a compromise between new opportunities to engage in sexual intercourse and old, internalized values that declared such behavior wrong. "Although petting included most of the sexual activities that often precede intercourse, it stopped short of actual intercourse" (Caplow et al., 1982, p. 165). It allowed sexually active girls to preserve their "technical" virginity while "petting to orgasm" (Hunt, 1974).

Most individuals, however, still attempted to hide their true feelings in this period of history, and dating was no exception to this pattern. Dating appeared, at least among college students, to involve play acting rather than the honest sharing of emotions. Sociologist Willard Waller, who studied dating patterns during the 1930s and 1940s, described the concept of "light love," which involved little vulnerability or emotional dependence among young people. It emphasized a lot of game playing as a way of avoiding emotional hurt (Waller, 1937). Unfortunately this pattern also prevented the partners from really getting to know each other.

The bargain being struck in the search for a marriage partner was a practical, economic one for women—to have a good provider. The man, in turn, focused on the search for a "beautiful object." An attractive woman was regularly looked upon as a symbol of a successful man. In general, the search for intimacy between men and women was not a prime concern during this period between the

BOX 1.3

THE GREAT RUSSIAN FAMILY EXPERIMENT

Between the two world wars one of the most dramatic family experiments ever recorded was initiated in Soviet Russia. The Communists, gaining control after the Russian Revolution in 1917, thought that they must abolish the traditional family, as well as the church and the capitalist economic system. Since it is the nature of the family to preserve tradition, it had to go. A Soviet authority in 1919 indicated: "The family has ceased to be a necessity, both for its members and for the State."

The goal was to destroy the traditional patriarchal family, where husbands were superior to wives and where parental authority was strong. Prior to the revolution, marriage was a religious institution and could only be put together or broken up by the church. One objective of the new regime was to liberate marriage from the bonds of religion. Therefore, church weddings were made illegal. All couples had to do was "register" their marriages with the government, and no ceremony about the significance of marriage was allowed. Beginning in 1917, divorce was made available simply for the asking. No reasons had to be given, and one's spouse could even be notified by postcard.

But the antifamily campaign focused on other aspects of life also. Incest and adultery were no longer criminal offenses. Abortion became legal in 1920. Inheritance rights ceased to exist. The distinction between legitimate and illegitimate children was dropped. Parental authority became weakened, and children no longer had to obey their parents if they did not follow strict Marxist teachings. Children could turn their parents in to government authorities. There were numerous family tragedies resulting from the state backing the children against the parents.

In 1925 a new Family Code was developed to help facilitate the destruction of the family. Now couples no longer had even to register their marriages. This in essence, led to the legalization of bigamy, a condition in which a man or woman could have many spouses. Promiscuity was common. At this same time, a new labor law made it a requirement that a person must accept any job assigned, and often husbands and wives were sent to live and work in different towns.

By 1930 the antifamily policies were largely successful—family ties were indeed significantly weakened. But there were a number of unforeseen problems, detrimental effects that were so strong that the very stability of the society was threatened. The birth rate dropped dramatically as a result of divorce and abortions. There were almost three times as many abortions as live births, and the divorce rate neared 40 percent. A nation on the verge of war with Germany saw its strength declining fast.

The whole society began to disintegrate; with the decreasing quality of parent-child ties, young hooligans roamed the streets. Juvenile delinquency, sadistic crimes, and gang wars and killings were not uncommon. In addition, the development of a "free love" philosophy and the "liberation" of women ended with females being exploited sexually by Russian Don Juans. Millions of children were born without knowing who their fathers were.

The price paid for the decline of the family became unbearable. So what did the Communist leadership do? They reinstituted the family as the "pillar of society." Marriage was made important again, and young people were encouraged to consider it "as the most serious affair in life." An official Soviet journal made the following amazing statement in 1939:

> The State cannot exist without the family. Marriage is a positive value to the Socialist Soviet State only if the partners see in it a lifelong union. So-called free love is a bourgeois invention and has nothing in common with the principles of conduct of a Soviet citizen. Moreover, marriage receives its full value for the State only if there is progeny, and the consorts experience the highest happiness of parenthood. (*Sotsialisticheskaya Zakonnost*, 1939, No. 2, cited in Timasheff, 1946)

Marriage was glorified again; marriage certificates began to be issued, and wedding rings became available once more. In 1936 divorce became difficult to obtain and also very expensive. Irrefutable evidence was needed. The concept of legitimate and illegitimate children reappeared. Mothers of illegitimate children no longer received state support. Abortion, once again, became a crime punishable with prison. Parents were given back authority over their children and were allowed to restrict their freedom. By 1944 marriages had to be registered, and they came to be the only legally recognized union. The great experiment to get rid of the family had failed miserably.

SOURCE: *Timasheff, 1946, pp. 192–203.*

---

two world wars. In Soviet Russia during this time still other norms existed that contrasted sharply with the scene in the United States (see Box 1.3).

The Period 1945 to 1965

MIDDLE-CLASS MARRIAGES. The norms in the period after World War II to 1965 were strongly family centered, and young people rushed into marriage as soon as possible. Marriage seemed more like a duty or an obligation; there were few other acceptable options. Marriages, however, continued to be

governed by rigid gender roles. Men were primarily concerned with experiencing success through their jobs and making money. The key to upward mobility for females was to marry up in social class or at least to marry better than their mothers. Women were attracted to men who gave the appearance of being the best of the good providers (Schnall, 1981). Women were accused of going to college to get their MRS. degree—something we don't hear as much about anymore.

Dating continued to be a rather formal situation of going somewhere and "making out" afterward. Mutual, in-depth self-disclosure and the sharing of real feelings continued to be rare during the courtship and marriage. Couples generally had children soon after they were married (Schnall, 1981).

Child rearing changed dramatically during the baby-boom period after World War II. The modern psychology movement brought with it new suggestions. Children were catered to and given more emotional affection; there was a change in attitude toward child care away from the stiffness and coldness of the past. A more pleasure-oriented view of child rearing existed both for the parent and child, which, by past standards at least, was permissive. Many parents looked to Dr. Benjamin Spock's *Baby and Child Care* (1946) as their parenting bible (Schnall, 1981).

Most of the women who worked during World War II gave up their jobs and returned to the world of children. Parenting was considered in such a positive light in this period that in a study conducted by Gurin, Veroff, and Feld (1960), parents seldom responded negatively to the parenting experience. "It was apparently not possible in the normative climate of that time for a parent to say she/he was dissatisfied or unhappy with her/his experience of parenthood" (Veroff, Douvan, and Kulka, 1981, p. 203).

Between the husband and wife there was little togetherness other than eating and sleeping and occasionally doing things together with the children. Seldom did couples carry out activities jointly, separate from their children. Work seemed to provide all the excitement that men needed. The husband typically believed that his marriage would take care of itself. Financial security was considered to be much more important than emotional closeness—loving was shown through material things (Schnall, 1981).

Women in the 1945–1965 period were expected to be completely fulfilled through marriage and child rearing. But more often

than not this idealistic view of domestic life was found lacking, particularly in the isolation of middle-class suburbia. Wives usually found that their husbands did not have much sympathy or understanding for the loneliness they were experiencing. Men escaped by focusing on their work. In reality, husbands were seldom available physically or emotionally (Schnall, 1981).

What added to women's frustrations during this period of so-called nuclear-family togetherness was the idealistic depiction of families on television. Such shows as "Father Knows Best," "Leave It to Beaver," and "Ozzie and Harriet" presented an image of the typical American family as being largely conflict free, stable, and intimate—except for little problems that were solved in half an hour. The women in these shows were found happily engaged in full-time homemaking, and they were married to caring, sensitive husbands. Even though this image of the typical family was inaccurate, people still believed in it, developed expectations about it, and compared their families to it. The discrepancy between image and reality only contributed to the wives' feelings of inadequacy and failure.

Despite an individual's marital status—whether married, widowed, divorced, or separated—women in the 1950s were always more negative about marriage than men. "Only among those who had never been married were women *more positive* about marriage than men. And they were extraordinarily positive—more so than married women, and more than any group except widowed men" (Veroff, Douvan, and Kulka, 1981, p. 148). Single women idealized marriage because they wanted to achieve the closeness they fantasized about and that they saw in family television shows. In this era, marriage was often seen as the only legitimate status for a woman. But women were more likely than men to report problems in their marriages. They seemed to be looking for something different from their husbands than their husbands were looking for from them. What women appeared to be seeking was intimacy, which they seldom obtained (Veroff, Douvan, and Kulka, 1981).

A random sample of wives in the early 1950s was asked to choose the most important aspect of marriage in a study conducted by the sociologists Robert Blood and Donald Wolfe (1960). The largest percentage chose "companionship in doing things together with the husband." This suggests that women in general desired to share activities closely with their husbands. The lowest level of companionship was found in the traditional type of marriage, where the wife "sticks to her knitting" while the husband is focused on his job. Couples that were most egalitarian had the highest level of companionship, and couples where one partner had much more power over the other had the least.

Two key elements of intimacy mentioned by Blood and Wolfe were "understanding and emotional well-being." They saw these elements as the primary emerging function of marriage. These authors were among the first to argue that emotional security was not just something that parents give to children but, in addition, it is needed in the exchange between husbands and wives. Adults have emotional needs too—"needs for acceptance as a person, for a sense of belonging, for knowing someone understands how they feel, and for sympathy and empathy" (1960, p. 176). These needs can be met through "intimate others."

American marriages had traditionally provided only limited opportunities for such emotional support. The dominant male was expected to depend on his own competencies. The traditional husband was not really expected to rely upon his wife for emotional sustenance, even though he covertly did. "A

real he-man does not depend on petticoat encouragement. He gets it—to be sure—but only because it is his due, not because he needs it" (Blood and Wolfe, 1960, p. 178). A really good provider is not supposed to have problems and he even denies their existence. To turn to "the weaker sex" for help in time of trouble would be disgraceful and admitting to defeat.

Blood and Wolfe argue, however, that the American tradition has also discouraged the wife from relying on her husband for help with emotional problems. "Her right to have problems was fully accepted—for the weaker sex by definition is subject to limitations. To cry was an acceptable symbol of her inability to cope with difficulties, and the appropriate place for crying was on her husband's brawny shoulder. Yet the difference between a good wife and a troublesome wife was whether she 'bothered her husband'" (1960, p. 179). In reality, the "ideal woman" was a mother who could cope with the problems of the children on her own, without giving her mate undue worry about her sphere of things. After all he was much too busy to be bothered with such matters.

In fact, very few wives in the 1950s reported obtaining emotional support from their husbands. Only 8 percent of the city wives and 3 percent of the farm wives specifically mentioned their spouses as a source of help when they were tense, upset, or just having a bad day. The husbands, however, were often the target of the wives' growing anger. The result was that the husband was even less likely to respond sensitively and empathetically after being attacked (Blood and Wolfe, 1960).

BLUE-COLLAR MARRIAGES. Among blue-collar husbands and wives we find the greatest separation of the sexes and the least amount of intimacy of any social class (Komarovsky, 1962). Particularly prominent is the lack of self-disclosure. For example, a common complaint of the women in Komarovsky's research on blue-collar marriages was that their husbands didn't talk enough. Here's what one man had to say.

> One thing that gets my wife mad is that I don't talk enough. She wants to sit down and talk. And there is nothing to talk about. I have been married to her for thirteen years and I am talked out. I can't find anything to talk about. The kind of things that she wants to talk about are kidstuff and trivial. (1962, pp. 149–150)

Most of the men felt that there was really nothing that they had to say. They found their jobs monotonous and felt that there was little to elaborate about their work; their jobs were not fun and they just wanted to get away from them. They wanted merely to come home and rest. Men felt that talking about the job carried the connotation of "griping," which was thought to be unmanly; it was considered masculine not to bring one's job home. In the working class the male's view was that work and home should be separate. Not only did men not want to share their daily experiences, they also did not want to hear about their wife's day. The working-class situation stands in sharp contrast to the frequently reported involvement of the "corporation wife" in her husband's career (Komarovsky, 1962).

A major trait found among blue-collar men is a "trained incapacity to share." "The ideal of masculinity into which they were socialized inhibits expressiveness both directly, with its emphasis on reserve, and indirectly, by identifying personal interchange with the feminine role" (1962, p. 156). Of the 23 qualities of a good husband that women were asked to rank, "speaks his mind

when something is worrying him" came out second most important (p. 157). This reflects the desire of women to know their husbands, to share in their lives, and to become closer couples. But the ideal of masculinity accepted by the men is a key factor in their meager disclosure of stressful feelings.

The working-class wives of the 1945–1965 era ended up seeking emotional closeness—just as women did in the nineteenth century—from other women. "Two-thirds of the wives have at least one person apart from their husbands in whom they confided deeply personal experiences" (Komarovsky, 1962, p. 208). In most instances they shared significant segments of their lives *more fully* with female confidantes than with their husbands. But, like women in other social classes, blue-collar wives wanted to be closer to their husbands, although they lacked the power and know-how to get this message across.

The Period 1965 to 1975

THE MODERN WOMEN'S MOVEMENT. A key stimulus to the feminist movement was the publication of Betty Friedan's book *The Feminine Mystique* in 1963, but the full impact of the book was not evident until years later. "This book was an indictment of the middle-class housewife's imprisonment in domesticity" (Berger and Berger, 1983, p. 24). The problem was that women had been told throughout the years after World War II that their only dream should be to be perfect wives and mothers and that their highest ambition should be to have four or five children and a beautiful house. "Occupation: housewife" was something women should be proud to announce (Friedan, 1963).

Women throughout the 1945–1965 period increasingly complained of not being happy. They knew something was missing

During the decade of 1965–1975, women struggled to achieve equality with men and freedom from traditional female roles. This equality increased the possibility for intimacy in marriage—as well as the possibility for divorce.

from their lives, but most could not verbalize specifically what they wanted. They went to doctors by the tens-of-thousands and were given tranquilizers. A new mental illness was created called ''housewife syndrome'' (Friedan, 1963).

The solution, according to Friedan, was clear—women should get out of the household and into the world of work, where they could create a new, positive self-image. In the 1960s women entered the work force in record numbers, with mothers of young children making up the bulk of the rise. With success outside the home, women became more equal to men. This achievement, along with their increased assertiveness and confidence, allowed for the greater possibilities of

intimacy in their marriages—as well as greater possibilities for divorce. The modern feminist movement was largely a middle-class force.

THE PERSONAL-FULFILLMENT MOVEMENT. Values of ''personal fulfillment,'' ''self-realization,'' ''self-actualization'' and ''human potential'' became the ultimate goals for some people in the period 1965 to 1975. With the emphasis placed on ''self,'' in-depth commitments and close relationships apparently took a back seat. In fact, some individuals went to great lengths to avoid attachments.

There was enthusiasm for ''new experiences.'' People challenged each other to try different patterns of behavior. Pressures on people existed to experiment with various drugs and to try almost anything sexual. The mere experiences of homosexuality, a one-night stand, group sex, group living, and non-marital cohabitation were all considered to be important forms of "growth." Having an open marriage, a variety of sexual partners, multiple orgasms, a marriage contract, or even a divorce—to get back into the singles action—was considered to be "where it was at."

The 1965–1975 decade saw people struggling to achieve a measure of autonomy and independence away from the restricted and traditional nuclear family of the 1945–1965 era, even at the cost of isolation. There arose a proliferation of self-help books guaranteeing people happiness. Weekend encounter groups—dressed or nude—promised to remake personalities and provide "instant intimacy."

Watching out for yourself, or "number one," was the ethic of the times. Self-proclaimed gurus came out of nowhere and became prophets to thousands of unhappy individuals. Encounter groups, T-groups, sensitivity training, est, psychodrama, and primal-scream therapies all were focused on the personal self. Being "open," or "totally honest," "getting it together," "letting yourself go," "hanging loose," "never being afraid to try anything once," became part of the "psychobabble" slang. Whatever else, the personal-fulfillment movement gave people the right to focus on themselves and to seek individual happiness. It also brought to the forefront the importance of the self-disclosure of personal feelings. Finally, it broke the traditional emphasis on rigid roles and made alternative life-styles more acceptable. In total, the personal-fulfillment movement, like the feminist movement, helped to contribute to more intimacy found in marriages of the later 1970s.

SEXUAL BEHAVIOR. There is ample evidence to describe the 1965–1975 time period as the most sexually permissive decade in Amerian history. The traditional, committed, monogamous marriage coexisted along with sexual activity without commitment, open marriages, adultery, high rates of divorce, high rates of remarriage, significant numbers of unmarried couples living together, and many married couples living separately. Some people became obsessed with the goal of maximizing pleasure through sexual activity without responsibility or obligation. The saying went, "If it feels good, do it."

It was the younger generation who seemed to be able to enjoy sexual acts without investing them "with any heavy significance or rules of participation based on obligations, expectations, and commitment" (Bardwick, 1979, p. 85). It was also among this group that the double standard of sexual behavior was challenged. There was an attempt to develop an identical morality for both sexes, a morality based on a fundamental revision of ideas about female sexuality. "The new ideas about female sexuality legitimated women's assertion that they owed themselves maximum sexual pleasure" (p. 85). Magazines, books, and sex therapists encouraged women to become orgasmic, to masturbate, to use vibrators, to engage in fantasy, and to enjoy pornography. But most significantly, in this decade of rootlessness, sexual activity "became a means to fill the void of not touching and not feeling; the act of sex was used as a symbol of connecting, even though there was no true connection with the other or with the self" (p. 84).

A major shift that occurred in the 1965–1975 era was the growing acceptance of nonmarital sex when there was mutual affection. This value change had been slowly evolving since the 1920s, but it was helped along by the extensive use of the birth-control pill.

"The partners, especially the women, no longer need to assume that they will ultimately marry this lover to justify the sexual relationship" (Bardwick, 1979, pp. 87–88). While the number of virgins was still considerable in this era—30 percent at the time they left college—the trend was to define sexual activity as "morally acceptable outside of marriage if the partners are in a continuing relationship" (p. 88).

The sexual permissiveness of the 1965–1975 period had some positive impacts on intimacy in marriage. As women became sexual equals, their desires and feelings became more accurately understood; sexual openness probably influenced openness in other respects. Compared to the past, sex now served a function of the husband and wife having "fun" together. There was considerably less guilt about sexual activity than in previous times. Certainly women enjoyed sex more, which made the interaction more exciting for both partners. It was even possible for the improved physical closeness—in touching, caressing, and orgasm—to carry over and broaden into emotional intimacy.

1975 to the Present

MARRIAGE. Despite all of the media attention given to "self-fulfillment," the human-potential movement, and alternative lifestyles, marriage was still of central importance to the vast majority of people in the 1970s. This importance, however, was now based more on the interpersonal support that marriage provided. In a study done in 1976, family relationships (marital and parental) were almost uniformly rated higher in fulfilling personal values than work or leisure roles for both men and women. This seems to suggest what is really at the core of a meaningful life. In addition, comparing the 1976 respondents to an earlier sample interviewed in 1957, there was an increase in reported marital happiness. Two factors, "frequency of chatting" and "physical affection," were highly correlated with marital happiness (Veroff, Douvan, and Kulka, 1981).

Ironically, the greater marital happiness in the later 1970s is partly accounted for by a very high divorce rate. People who were really unhappy in the 1970s were much less likely to stay in their marriages than people were in the 1950s. Thus the modern institution of divorce may not just be a force weakening marriage but may ultimately increase the potential for quality marriages in American society. But in 1976, compared to the 1950s, most people thought that an unmarried person could have a happy life also. Marriage, by 1976, had come to be seen as only one potential mechanism for increasing happiness. Veroff, Douvan, and Kulka also found that people in 1976 were more open about the negative, as well as the positive, aspects of marriage. Individuals in the 1970s were more likely to say that marriage both enlarges *and* restricts life, a more realistic view of marriage.

Marriages in 1976, as compared to 1957, were more likely to involve a close, interpersonal relationship between partners and less likely to involve a rigid arrangement of interacting roles. The growth of *female power*, the greater concern for *personal feelings*, and the new *sexual openness* coming out of the 1965–1975 decade all helped to account for this trend. When Veroff, Douvan, and Kulka restricted their analysis to those factors that specifically have to do with intimacy—e.g., thoughtfulness, sensitivity, responsiveness to the spouse—a change from 1957 to 1976 was definitely apparent. Moreover, people *want* even more closeness in their marriages. The majority of individuals interviewed in the

1976 study indicated that they "often" or "sometimes" wished that their spouse understood them better.

The results from the 1976 study clearly show that women still see more problems in marriage than men do. "Women are much more likely than men to say that their marriage problem stems from some characteristic or problem behavior of their husbands whereas men more often attribute the problem to themselves" (Veroff, Douvan, and Kulka, 1981, p. 175). Men attribute their own inadequacy as spouses to their lack of sensitivity and responsiveness, while women attributed men's inadequacy to their dominance or bossiness. Women still also wished that their husbands would talk more about their thoughts and feelings. "In marriage, then, women talk and want verbal responsiveness of the kind they have had with other women, but their men are often silent partners, unable to respond in kind" (Veroff, Douvan, and Kulka, 1981, p. 178).

Similar findings of more closeness in marriage were discovered in a repeat study of Middletown (Caplow et al., 1982). Major changes were found in the style of communication between husbands and wives from that existing in the 1920s and 1930s. Contributing to these changes were assertiveness-training programs, marriage-enrichment programs, and the growth of marital therapy. These programs helped contribute to the possibility of "more equal marriage relationships in which the needs and wishes of the wives are considered to be at least as important as those of the husbands" (Caplow et al., 1982, p. 124).

Theodore Caplow et al. found that husbands and wives were talking more to each other than couples did 50 years ago, but they were also engaging in more leisure activity together. Overall the study indicates a very high level of marital satisfaction and much improvement over the marriages of 50 years earlier. More wives reported their husbands as a source of strength and comfort in 1982 than did in 1929. Caplow concludes that "the marital relationship has deepened since the 1920's and that husbands and wives share each other's burdens and provide emotional support to a greater degree now than then" (1982, p. 128). Indeed interpersonal intimacy has become more of a "vehicle for personal

cathy®   **by Cathy Guisewite**

CATHY © 1984, Universal Press Syndicate. Reprinted with permission. All rights reserved.

fulfillment'' and emotional well-being in contemporary society (Veroff, Douvan, and Kulka, 1981).

THE WAR OVER THE FAMILY. The period 1975 to the present has seen two opposing groups, the family liberals and family conservatives, involved in a major controversy over the family. Enlightening summaries of this deep division are found in Brigitte and Peter Berger's book *The War over the Family* (1983) and in John Scanzoni's book *Shaping Tomorrow's Family* (1983). Although there are many subgroups within each of these two camps, these subgroups clearly lean toward one major orientation or the other.

The conservatives began to join together in the late 1970s and came to be known as the pro-family group. Among those involved were antifeminists, anti-ERA (Equal Rights Amendment) groups, people who were concerned about homosexuality and pornography, people opposed to sexual permissiveness, people concerned with growing secularism in American life, and, most significantly, the pro-life antiabortionists. These various groups developed a remarkably strong working relationship and exerted powerful political pressure in the national elections of 1980 and 1984. The Moral Majority, consisting mostly of fundamentalist and evangelical religious groups and led by media personalities such as Jerry Falwell, came to be a meaningful force in the public debate over the above issues (Berger and Berger, 1983).

The original stimulus for the conservatives came with the 1973 Supreme Court decision that allowed abortions during the first three months of pregnancy. Fuel was added to the fire in 1976, when the Supreme Court further decided that abortion was a right solely of women—neither husbands nor parents had a veto. The conservatives viewed this decision as challenging the very basis of the family as a group entity over and beyond individual interests.

Scanzoni (1983) suggests that the conservatives' concept of society is a ''static'' one—stable, unchanging, and rigid. This traditional view looks upon the husband as the head of the family and as a good provider. The wife's responsibilities are focused on domestic activities and child care. It is this traditional image of *the family* as a harmonious and stable nuclear group that the conservatives are determined to bring back. Although in the past the quality of life in such families has often been highly questionable, the *image of the family* has extraordinary influence on people and their expectations (Skolnick, 1979, p. 19).

The family conservatives, in essence, stand in opposition to a pluralistic society. They want public affirmation only for their moral values—values which are no longer *generally* held in the larger society (Berger and Berger, 1983). They feel so intensely about these matters that they see themselves as engaged in a moral battle with pagans. Research shows that the so-called Moral Majority actually makes up about one-fourth of the population of the United States and is, in fact, a moral *minority* (Connecticut Mutual, 1981). This group, however, is vocal and powerful well beyond its actual numbers. The power of the conservatives cannot be underestimated, as evidenced by their political clout in helping to defeat the Equal Rights Amendment.

Among family liberals the biggest opposition to traditional norms has come from feminism and its allies in other liberationist movements. Emotional moral issues such as abortion are again crucial. Feminists want women to be able to get out of the household and into the world of paid work. Women's freedom, to the greatest extent, means having the choice to be free from family obligations or at least to share these obligations more equally. What has remained into the 1980s among militant feminists is the theme of total liberation and a view of the traditional family "as the major obstacle to this liberation" (Berger and Berger, 1983, p. 25). Many in the women's movement have called for new bonds of "sisterhood" to meet intimacy needs, replacing the "confining" bonds of the family.

The conservatives see the liberals as "anti-family" and hostile to children. The liberals' enthusiasm for abortion and for day care has strengthened this impression, "suggesting that here are people who want to prevent children from being born . . . and, failing this, to dump children so that mothers can pursue their selfish programs of self-realization" (Berger and Berger, 1983, p. 27). While many liberals have denied such sentiments, the perceptions remain real nonetheless (Berger and Berger, 1983). Box 1.4 discusses the Family Protection Act—legislation introduced by the family conservatives to "protect" *the family*.

The liberals view the family as focused on change, not the status quo. They see the decline, or even the disappearance, of the family as it was in the past to be a good thing because of the harmful effects of the traditional nuclear family. One of their goals is the elimination of fixed gender roles. Liberals also want marriage to provide for the interests and goals of both spouses. According to Scanzoni, marriage "takes on the possibility of being shaped to fit the interests of the participants, rather than [as in the conservative model] the participants 'shaping up' to fit unremitting marital demands" (1983, p.159). With marital equality, liberals see intimacy as more

possible. "People in a superior-subordinate relationship rarely become as deeply intimate as genuine peers or equal partners" (p. 161). Between these two opposite poles on a continuum (liberal to conservative) is a more moderate view which is *"probably held by the majority of the population"* (Berger and Berger, 1983, p. 86).

The 1980s find the family liberals and family conservatives in a political deadlock. The liberals and conservatives agree that there have been tremendous changes in family life from the past. But the conservatives regard these changes as a dramatic demise of the family that is harmful both to the individual and to society. Conservatives view the changes negatively and consider them to be leading to decadence (Berger and Berger, 1983).

In reality, the standard image of the family, consisting of husband, wife, and children, applies to only a minority of families in our society today. American families are indeed far more diverse than the traditional view suggests. For example, legally married couples have made up a declining percentage of the total of all households since 1960. In 1960 they were 75 percent, in 1975, 65 percent, and the projection for 1990 is 55 percent. Male-headed households (with children but no female adult present) were 8 percent in 1960, 11 percent in 1975, and are projected to be 16 percent by 1990. Female-headed households were 17 percent in 1960, 24 percent in 1975, and are projected to reach 29 percent by 1990. In addition, growing numbers of men and women are living alone (Masinch and Bane, 1980). The once usual household of two parents and children—with a husband-breadwinner and a wife-homemaker—is fading from prominence (Masinch and Bane, 1980). We can no longer speak meaningfully about "the American family,"

BOX 1.4

THE FAMILY PROTECTION ACT—WILL YOU BE PROTECTED?

The efforts to enshrine publicly the old, ideal view of the family reached a climax in the Family Protection Act, introduced by Senator Paul Laxalt of Nevada in 1979. What is to be "protected" here, of course, is precisely the old normative definition of the family (Berger and Berger, 1983, p. 64). Proponents argued that "homosexuality, unsanctioned sexual cohabitation, and promiscuity—have been elevated to family status by a simple semantic change" (p. 64).

The Family Protection Act begins with this warning: "A reversal of Government policies which undermine the American family is essential if the United States is to enter the Twenty-first century as a strong and viable nation." The following are aspects of the act as discussed by Letty Cottin Pogrebin in *Family Politics* (1983, pp. 13–15):

> Protect the right of parents and other authorized individuals to use corporal punishment against children.
>
> Repeal federal laws relating to child abuse and wife beating and discontinue intervention programs that treat or shelter their victims.
>
> Repeal all federal laws that grant educational equity to both sexes.
>
> Require that marriage and motherhood be taught as the proper career for girls, and deny federal funds to schools whose textbooks show women in nontraditional roles.
>
> Prohibit the "intermingling of sexes" in any sport or other school-related activities.
>
> Provide for parents unlimited classroom visits, review of courses, and censorship of textbooks.
>
> Impose prayer in the schools.
>
> Provide tax incentives that discourage women's employment and promote wives' economic dependence on husbands.
>
> Give a $1,000 tax exemption for the birth or adoption of a child, but only to a married couple.
>
> Require that parents be notified before their daughters can receive counseling on or medical help for venereal disease, contraception, or abortion.
>
> Prohibit federal funded legal services for abortion, divorce, homosexual rights or school segregation complaints.

but must speak more realistically about "American families" (Berger and Berger, 1983).

Scanzoni argues that the advantage of a "changing" model of the family, as compared to a "static" model, is that it can include the growing numbers of single-parent families and nonmarried couples. These groups also constitute families—a fact recognized by the U.S. Census in 1980 (Scanzoni, 1983). Since families can take different forms, we have to look for additional characteristics to define them rather than just relying on structural or legal considerations. Instead of describing families only by their biological or legal memberships, we want to emphasize also *the function of the emotional bonds linking individuals together*. These emotional connections help to define a family unit. Of course, we still have the legally defined families, but to them we are adding individuals who share housing and who are involved in emotionally close relationships.

CHAPTER REVIEW

1. Human relationships can range from relatively fleeting human contact to those very personal relationships characterized by intimacy. While kinship relationships may fall anywhere along our continuum of relationships, for the most part, nuclear family members strive to attain a meaningful degree of closeness, hoping to be either significant others or intimate others.

2. Premodern America found families working together as a team and the family fulfilling almost every necessary function. But these families focused primarily on physical survival rather than emotional closeness.

Families organized in large kin groups, including kin from several generations, were rarely found in America.

3. The Industrial Revolution separated the home from the world of paid work, and women and men began to take on very separate and narrow roles. Hers was taking care of the personal and emotional needs of the family. His was the good-provider role, supporting the physical needs of the family. With this separation of the sexes, women often sought emotional closeness with other women.

4. The picture of family life during the 1920s and 1930s was dreary. Economic survival was primary, and separation of the sexes was typical. Most couples were pressured to stay together by community values and the unacceptability of divorce as an option. The infrequent use of effective birth control produced tensions regarding sexual relations between spouses.

5. The period after World War II brought more economic security and a major interest in "family togetherness." Rigid gender roles continued to persist, however. But slowly individuals began to indicate verbally that they wanted more from their marriages, looking to their spouses for companionship and emotional support. Even child rearing changed, with child-care experts stressing more emotional affection and a pleasure orientation.

6. An emphasis on personal fulfillment and individual happiness pervaded American society during the 1965–1975 period. Feeling restless and unfulfilled by their marital and child-rearing roles, women started their movement for equality, both at home and in

the work place. The growth of female power, the greater concern for personal feelings, and the new sexual openness all helped to account for the trend toward the search for intimacy in marriage. Some groups, however, namely the "family conservatives," view these changes as threats to the stability of *the family*.

2

Intimate
Relationships

An intimate relationship involves an emotional bond characterized by proven mutual commitment and trust between two individuals that provides personal and relationship security and rewards. Intimate bonds are not givens in any family, marriage, or friendship; they develop as a result of particular feelings, thoughts, and behaviors. Before intimacy can possibly be realized, however, individuals first must have certain personal characteristics, which are the building blocks of such a relationship. Second, particular forms of interactions need to occur between the two people. And third, certain situational components involving time, space, and cultural norms relating to intimacy will have an im-

pact on emotional closeness (see Figure 2.1). The model outlined in this chapter is an ideal conceptualization; not every intimate relationship will necessarily include all these elements.

INDIVIDUAL PREREQUISITES TO INTIMACY

Human beings bring their personalities into relationships. Individual behaviors, attitudes, values, feelings, and perceptions are crucial in determining whether intimacy is possible. Such characteristics, however, are not fixed or static but can change dramatically throughout a person's lifetime. The following

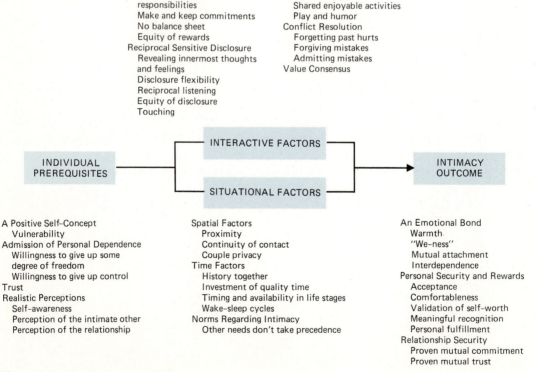

Positive Exchange
   Enlightened self-interest
   Fulfill obligations and
   responsibilities
   Make and keep commitments
   No balance sheet
   Equity of rewards
Reciprocal Sensitive Disclosure
   Revealing innermost thoughts
   and feelings
   Disclosure flexibility
   Reciprocal listening
   Equity of disclosure
   Touching

Mutual Empathy
Exclusivity
Companionship
   Shared enjoyable activities
   Play and humor
Conflict Resolution
   Forgetting past hurts
   Forgiving mistakes
   Admitting mistakes
Value Consensus

INDIVIDUAL PREREQUISITES → **INTERACTIVE FACTORS** / **SITUATIONAL FACTORS** → **INTIMACY OUTCOME**

A Positive Self-Concept
   Vulnerability
Admission of Personal Dependence
   Willingness to give up some
   degree of freedom
   Willingness to give up control
Trust
Realistic Perceptions
   Self-awareness
   Perception of the intimate other
   Perception of the relationship

Spatial Factors
   Proximity
   Continuity of contact
   Couple privacy
Time Factors
   History together
   Investment of quality time
   Timing and availability in life stages
   Wake-sleep cycles
Norms Regarding Intimacy
   Other needs don't take precedence

An Emotional Bond
   Warmth
   "We-ness"
   Mutual attachment
   Interdependence
Personal Security and Rewards
   Acceptance
   Comfortableness
   Validation of self-worth
   Meaningful recognition
   Personal fulfillment
Relationship Security
   Proven mutual commitment
   Proven mutual trust

Figure 2.1   The development of intimacy.

traits are individual prerequisites to developing intimacy.

A Positive Self-Concept

All individuals, through socialization and social interaction, develop a sense of self, a fairly definite notion of who and what they are. This conception of self consists primarily of a subjective view of how we feel about ourselves. Our sense of self develops as a result of our personal experiences with other people, the manner in which others act toward us and our impression of others' views about us (Cooley, 1902; G. H. Mead, 1934). The family is the initial setting for the formation of our self-concept. The more positively we evaluate ourselves, the more we will see ourselves as deserving care and positive behaviors from others and the more capable we will be of participating in close relationships.

Thus an individual needs to possess at least a moderate degree of self-esteem in order to take part in an intimate relationship. *Self-esteem* involves a personal assessment of the extent to which one is worthwhile, lovable, capable, and confident, among other things. It is nourished by recognizing one's own strengths, abilities, and accomplishments and by having these traits acknowledged, particularly by significant others early in life. A person's childhood family experiences do not, however, preclude his or her developing a different level of self-esteem at other times in life.

Those with high self-esteem feel sure and confident of themselves in human interaction. Such individuals do not try to build themselves up by tearing other people down. Positive self-esteem should not be confused, however, with arrogance, acting superior, bragging, or attempting to hide negative feelings about oneself.

People with low self-esteem sometimes attempt to gain a better self-image through "connecting" themselves with a more impressive person. By "clinging" to another and identifying closely with the accomplishments and achievements of the other, they hope to share in the other's positive well-being. In this situation, self-esteem is built by or through the other person. Sometimes, however, because they invest too much in that person, they suffocate the other individual.

Since individuals with low self-esteem feel inadequate in most ways and do not feel that they have much of value to give to another human being, they find it difficult to *accept* positive evaluations from other people. In fact, negative remarks and actions from others may be more easily accepted. Thus, because of their feelings of inferiority, these individuals do not see themselves as worthy of loving behavior from others. Even receiving compliments becomes difficult for them. This nonaccepting attitude prevents others from getting close to them.

Individuals with a positive self-concept can permit themselves to become *vulnerable*; that is, they can allow themselves to be open to the possibility of getting hurt. Vulnerable people disclose personal feelings, initiate investments, and make commitments—all with the possibility of being rejected by other people. Many people who lack self-esteem avoid becoming truly known to others in order to avoid rejecton. Also, some people never totally, emotionally commit themselves to, or invest themselves in, a relationship, even though they may marry. Such individuals often cover up faults, weaknesses, fears, and shortcomings, and hide their real selves behind masks, facades, and pretenses. In addition, they may be unable to express negative feelings about conflicts in a relationship for fear of evoking hostile responses from their partners. They may remain in empty-shell or pseudo-intimate relationships (see Chapter 7), which are perhaps unsatisfying but are worthwhile because they help to avoid the risk of disapproval, hurt, or rejection. Even those who have been hurt by love, however, typically do not regret the experience of having loved. In the final analysis it appears "better to have loved and lost than to never have loved at all."

Admission of Personal Dependence

Another important prerequisite to intimacy is the admission of the emotional need for other human beings. Social scientists agree that we are social beings and that we need other people; complete independence is an illusion. If one could be a truly independent person, he or she would not really need anyone. In reality, the actual price of attempted complete independence is almost always loneliness.

Dependence is not "good" or "bad" but rather just part of being human. Thus to acknowledge our dependence or interdependence is simply to recognize our humanness. The individual who cannot admit personal dependence will never let himself or herself become vulnerable and thus will never experience closeness. The admission of dependence further functions to make one's partner feel needed. Also, when two people admit their dependence on each other, the relationship becomes more equal.

In addition, the obligations and commitments of a relationship set limits on one's freedom. Perhaps one of the most difficult tasks for some individuals in American society is to be *willing to give up some degree of freedom* when entering a potentially close relationship. It is a mistake to think that we can have as much freedom in a committed relationship as we have as unattached individuals (Crosby, 1976). Intimate partners need to limit some of their freedom for the

I AM A ROCK

A winter's day
In a deep and dark December
I am alone
Gazing from my window
To the streets below
On a freshly fallen silent
*   shroud of snow*
I am a rock
I am an island.

I built walls
A fortress deep and mighty
That none may penetrate
I have no need of friendship
Friendship causes pain
Its laughter and its loving I
*   disdain*
I am a rock
I am an island.

Don't talk of love
Well, I've heard the word
*   before*
It's sleeping in my memory
I won't disturb the slumber
Of feelings that have died
If I'd never loved I never
*   would have cried*
I am a rock
I am an island.

I have my books
And my poetry to protect me
I am shielded in my armor
Hiding in my room
Safe within my womb
I touch no one and no one
*   touches me*
I am a rock
I am an island

And a rock feels no pain
And an island never cries.

PAUL SIMON AND ART GARFUNKEL

sake of the other person and the relationship. And the cost of giving up some freedom and independence is replaced by feelings of security and attachment.

Intimacy is not likely when one person dominates another. Rather, emotional closeness requires some sense of human equality (Martinson, 1981). Some people, however, feel the need always to be in control. Such individuals derive most of their rewards in life through being the person who is in charge. For example, a person concerned with control is usually unwilling to share feelings of weakness, since he or she attempts to maintain an image of superiority and strength. Sharing true feelings is perceived as a risk of losing control. A *willingness to give up control* may be too high a price to pay for those who feel their security lies in their own power. In reality, self-disclosure and vulnerability are signs of a "strong" person, in the sense that the individual is willing to take some risks.

Thus power imbalances make closeness difficult, even though power is an elusive and difficult concept to define in close relationships. One definition of power is an individual's ability to induce another person to do what he or she wants the person to do. It is not easy to observe directly or measure objectively this form of power. But most partners seem to make a subjective overall assessment of the balance of power in their relationships. This evaluation is usually based on both general experience and specific confrontations in the relationship.

Even with a balance of power, however, the actual roles played within a relationship may be quite different. For example, responsibilities and decisions could be divided in quite traditional ways—with highly segregated roles—but the partners may still *treat each other as equals*. Two individuals do not have to *do exactly the same things* for a rela-

tionship to be considered fair and equal. Thus it is possible for a traditional marriage to be quite intimate, as long as the partners see their roles as having relatively equal power.

Nevertheless, in a traditional marriage in which the relationship is structured to preserve the husband's sense of superiority over his wife, the man is typically inhibited from becoming vulnerable and expressing his deepest feelings and desires to the wife. Revealing personal fears and weaknesses usually does not "measure up" to the husband's perception of the masculine ideal. Feeling a strong need to maintain a controlling position, men in particular are often on guard and remain silent. But a "master" and a "slave" will never be emotionally close.

Trust

Trust implies a confidence in, reliance on, and faith in particular human beings. Trust is one of the most, if not *the* most, important traits that will determine how we interact with other human beings. Without trust there can be no meaningful relationships. When we say we trust someone, we imply two things. First, trust means that we can predict how the other person will behave, or, in other words, we expect consistency in actions. Second, trust involves a faith that that person will not purposely try to hurt us.

The ability to trust varies among individuals from the extremes of those who are overly trusting to those who trust hardly anyone—even, or maybe we should say particularly, family members. Trust is a learned trait. The foundation for it is consistent, nurturing care in the earliest years of life. Individuals who are extremely nontrusting usually had very unstable and disruptive experiences in childhood. Examples include the separation, divorce, or death of parents or physical, emotional, or sexual abuse.

There is no assurance, however, that trust will remain a lifelong personal pattern just because we have learned to trust as a child. Our trust in other people must be positively reinforced throughout life. Recurring breaks of trust tend to diminish our tendency, and even our desire, to trust others. If we have a continuous sense of trust, most of us are willing to make emotional investments in others. The ability to trust is obviously a crucial precondition to intimacy.

Overly trusting persons usually hold very idealistic and optimistic views of human beings. Because these individuals trust almost everyone, they do not use much discretion when disclosing personal information about themselves or when investing themselves in others. These are people who are "too open" and, hence, too vulnerable. A few overly trusting individuals remain this way their whole lives, but most change as a result of the "school of hard knocks." Indeed not every person should be, or can be, trusted.

Realistic Perceptions

"Know thyself" is an appropriate maxim for the development of any close relationship. *Self-awareness* of our feelings, thoughts, and behaviors allows us more accurately to communicate ourselves to another person. This does not mean a total focus on self that preoccupies one's every moment, but rather, when needed, individuals having available realistic information about their own strengths and weaknesses.

People vary considerably in the amount of accurate self-data they are aware of. Those with high quantities of information are often thought to be "emotionally healthier" (Culbert, 1968). Individuals who are not conscious of their feelings and are unable to identify them will not be able to disclose their emotions to another person. Hence, unless individuals have a significant awareness of

themselves, it will be very difficult for other people to come to know them intimately.

Intimacy also requires that partners have a *realistic perception of each other*. An individual who lacks an accurate perception, for example, may view the other person in quite idealistic ways. Perceiving the other idealistically may involve glossing over negative behaviors and actions that the individual feels may jeopardize the relationship. Sweeping annoying behaviors under the rug only postpones disappointments and dissatisfaction that will surface when the partner's actions are finally realistically acknowledged. An undercurrent of anger and resentment may also result from the glossing over process. In sum, one cannot relate intimately with a fantasy.

Likewise there needs to be a *realistic awareness of the relationship*. Individuals need to recognize the necessary mutuality required in an intimate partnership and the time, effort, and thought necessary for the development of intimacy. The partners need realistically to evaluate their interactive individual personalities, the comfortableness of their exchange patterns, and their commitment to each other—in essence, their potential to be a close couple. False views of what it takes to create a meaningful connection will only hinder the development of intimacy. Ignoring relationship problems may serve to deny, extend, and compound inevitable hurt. For example, a drug addiction can distort a person's perceptions of a relationship (see Box 2.1). Also, expectations for happiness that are too high and too unrealistic may result in disillusions and dissatisfactions with the relationship and ultimately obstruct the possibility for meaningful closeness.

INTERACTIVE FACTORS AFFECTING INTIMACY

The previous discussion has provided a good idea of the individual characteristics that are

BOX 2.1

WARNING: DRUG ADDICTION MAY BE HAZARDOUS TO INTIMACY

Addictions to alcohol and other drugs hinder a person's ability to develop intimate relationships. Drugs alter one's sensations, mood, consciousness, and thinking processes; an addicted individual functions with a distorted picture of the world. Hence, it is very difficult for an individual on drugs to be attuned to and sensitive to another person and what he or she is feeling or doing.

Problems also exist for the partner of the alcoholic or drug addict. Intermittent drug-induced highs and lows make it almost impossible really to know that person or to trust him or her. For example, with alcoholism there may be quite a difference between the behavior of the alcoholic when drunk and the behavior of the same person when sober.

Other family members of the addicted personality, such as his or her children, may also develop problems with intimacy. In order to survive in the alcoholic family, children form a special set of personality traits (Policoff, 1985). For example, children of alcoholic families are often not allowed to express their emotions and needs. "Strong emotions are taboo—they too often lead to anger, parental battles, a tremendous despair" (Brown, quoted by Policoff, 1985, p. 56). Therefore, disclosing deep feelings in later relationships becomes very difficult for them. Intimacy problems of adults who grew up in alcoholic families center around four particular issues: "a strong need for control, a chronic inability to trust, a tendency to suppress needs and feeling, and a sense of personal responsibility for all of life's troubles" (Policoff, 1985, p. 56).

A chemical dependency is often an escape from the reality of the world. It can also be an escape from intimacy, both for the addicted individual and ultimately for those persons around him or her.

prerequisites to the development of an intimate relationship. The next section moves to the interacting couple and looks at behaviors that are conducive to the development of emotional closeness.

Positive Exchange

Exchanging involves the giving and receiving of rewards and costs in our interactions with others. In any type of relationship, one person's actions typically have an impact on another person's actions. Exchange can be eval-uated on the basis of such cultural norms as fairness and justice, reciprocity, social responsibility, and intimacy.

Individuals differ in their skills to exchange in relationships. Some, for example, focus on "giving," while others focus on "taking." Those individuals who know how to exchange positively—both to give and to receive fairly—have internalized the concept of *"enlightened self-interest"* (Lenski, 1966). That is, to satisfy their own self-interests, individuals take the self-interests of others into account and cooperate with these individuals. Thus, "good" exchangers recognize that (1) other people are just as reward seeking as they are; (2) rewards may be obtained through, or from, other individuals; and (3) cooperation with these individuals is advantageous (Kersten and Kersten, 1981).

A person's ability to exchange positively is also based upon how reliably he or she can *fulfill obligations and responsibilities*, as well as *make and keep commitments*. Individuals who have difficulty in these areas will have problems with close relationships. For example, exploitative individuals who do not follow through on commitments—who take advantage of others—are going to be impossible as partners in an intimate relationship. We cannot easily allow ourselves to be vulnerable when there is a high risk of exploitation and untrustworthiness.

To develop any close relationship, a large quantity of rewards must be exchanged between the partners, and the rewards must greatly exceed the costs for both individuals. Human beings try not to enter into relationships, or to sustain patterns of interaction, that they find unrewarding. Rewards can be defined as pleasures, satisfactions, and gratifications that a person enjoys (Thibaut and Kelley, 1959). The meanings attached to particular actions are not the same among all individuals. In fact, one person's reward might even be another person's cost. But in an emotionally close relationship, individuals can often simultaneously gratify their own desires as well as those of the intimate other. That is, it is rewarding to one person to see his or her partner receive certain rewards. So rewards for oneself and for the other become highly intertwined and even inseparable.

Not only do two people evaluate rewards within a relationship but they also look at alternatives, particularly in the early stages of relationships. John Thibaut and Harold Kelley (1959) have coined the term "comparison level of alternatives" to describe the situation in which a person compares the level of current rewards from a partner with perceived potential rewards from an alternative relationship. As partners begin to feel that each has the potential to reward the other in ways that few people can and/or that others who could possibly offer such special rewards are unavailable, intimacy can develop (Huston and Burgess, 1979).

Closeness is dependent to a large degree on the type of exchange taking place. In the beginning of a relationship this cooperation could be more of a "tit for tat"—"I'll do something good for you *if* you'll do something good for me." But as the relationship continues and becomes closer, the "if" no longer applies. Thus with greater commitment and stability, less attention is paid to precise or immediate reciprocity. Partners move beyond literal, exact exchange and are less likely to keep *a balance sheet* of what is owed them by the other. Now, each person can recall countless instances where the other has already done something good for him or her or is likely to do so again (Levinger, 1979).

A willingness to put up with temporary lower returns implies a confidence in the other person. Whereas casual relationships more likely would end if imbalances are not redressed, intimates committed to long-range interaction are more likely to be tolerant of imbalances. They know they have ample time to set things right. Individuals who "must" keep a balance sheet, at least mentally, of the exchange taking place will have difficulty tolerating imbalances in the relationship. They may become disillusioned when an imbalance occurs and choose to end the relationship.

Relationships are more likely to be close where an *equity of rewards* prevails. A person seeking emotional closeness would be better off finding someone with whom he or she can give and receive equally. Although the calculation of equity can be a mind-boggling task, most people in their personal relationships have some notion of what is fair and equitable. It is easier to calculate equity in casual, rather than in close, relationships, since casual acquaintances are usually involved in the exchange of resources of a set value and are limited to specific kinds of interaction. But even in close relationships, partners have a sense of whether they are overbenefited, underbenefited, or receive and give equally (Walster, Walster, and Berscheid, 1978). Research shows that individuals tend to be happier when the exchange is equitable, rather than when the reward giving is unbalanced (Hatfield, Utne, and Traupmann, 1979).

Reciprocal Sensitive Disclosure

The extent to which intimacy develops in a relationship is greatly influenced by the amount of personal information the partners are willing to share. Self-disclosure can involve special knowledge selectively revealed to particular persons. Much of the information disclosed in close relationships is "personally private"—that is, it is of such a nature that it would not be shared with most other people (Culbert, 1968). Particular information revealed about the self can include personal feelings, moods, events from the past, and goals for the future, to name a few possibilities. The types of information disclosed by people vary according to how personal and private they are to the discloser. Adler and Towne (1984) distinguish four levels of self-disclosure (see Figure 2.2).

Superficial disclosures tend to include *clichés*, such as, "Hi, how are you doing?" "We'll have to get together sometime." "Have a nice day." These clichés serve some useful

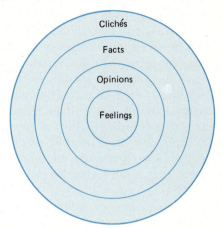

Figure 2.2 Levels of self-disclosure. (*Source:* Adler and Towne, 1984.)

functions. They allow each person some time to size up the other and to decide whether to carry the conversation further. They also acknowledge the person's presence.

Facts may be impersonal, but they can also reveal a great deal about a person and in doing so form the basis for further conversation. Included under facts would be such things as one's name, place of residence, marital status, major in college, and occupation. Facts can be a good clue as to whether a relationship with the other person is worth pursuing, simply on the basis of the kinds of facts selected for sharing. In other words, facts may give some hint about the person's deeper values and feelings.

Opinions, however, are disclosures that are even closer to the core of an individual's personality. Every time a personal opinion is offered, valuable information for the listener is revealed. Opinions also provide material to which other people can respond, and this allows for the opportunity to keep the conversation flowing.

The fourth level of disclosure—the one that is the most personal—is the realm of *feelings*. Sharing feelings is usually the most private and subjective form of self-revelation. Although the levels of disclosure of the outer rings may be appropriate for certain situations, such as work and business relations, self-disclosure in close relationships must be characterized by the inner rings, especially the center ring of feelings. Thus, as an emotionally supportive connection develops, the persons involved move from the outer ring to the inner ring of self-revelation (Adler and Towne, 1984).

Probably the *depth* of feelings is one of the most important elements in the development of intimacy. Closeness, therefore, is brought about by *revealing innermost thoughts and feelings* and sharing secrets. Of course, as the self-disclosure increases in depth, more risk is involved. Hence, while it is true that as more is revealed, more chance exists for understanding, sensitivity, and empathy between the two partners, there is also more chance for disagreements and conflicts. Possible hurts are the primary reason many people refuse to open up. In-depth disclosures may end up revealing that the partners don't have that much in common and that they share different values and expectations. To some people the need for security in just having a relationship may override the need for depth. "Rocking the boat" becomes more costly than maintaining a low-level, superficial relationship.

Appropriate self-disclosure also requires flexibility; that is, the ability of an individual to adjust his or her disclosure levels according to the interpersonal and situational demands of the moment (Chelune, 1978). The revealing of private information will not enhance a relationship if it is too personal, too soon, in the interaction. To say "I love you" on a first date would probably only serve to scare a person off. In the early stages of the development of a relationship—when disclosure is typically more superficial—it is certainly not

wise to "spill all the beans" or to bring the family skeletons out of the closet.

Disclosure flexibility also demands that the revealer be a good listener. One needs to be able to listen accurately to what another person is saying so that one's own disclosure is relevant to the topic at hand. Not actively listening may result in self-revelation that is out of context, out of bounds, or inappropriate to the conversation. *Reciprocal listening* is just as important as reciprocal revealing. Obviously, disclosure at the wrong time may involve insensitivity to the partner's feelings. Thus, hearing and understanding are as crucial in building closeness as speaking is.

Disclosure is reciprocal when both partners disclose at approximately similar rates and amounts. While the absolute amount of self-disclosure is important in close relationships, what appears to be even more significant is each partner's perception of the *equity of disclosure*. If each person feels that he or she is revealing similar amounts of self-information, he or she will be more satisfied with the relationship (Davidson, Balswick, and Halverson, 1983). Great dissatisfaction is likely to exist when the partners perceive an imbalance in the amount of information revealed.

There is considerable debate over the amount of self-revelation necessary for emotional closeness to develop. In general, research shows that high amounts of disclosure are beneficial to the enhancement of intimacy. Several social scientists, however, agree that there exists a point at which too much disclosure actually reduces satisfaction with the relationship. According to sociologist Georg Simmel (1950), too much disclosure results in the relationship slipping into a "matter of factness" that no longer has any room for surprise. It is important that a certain degree of discretion in self-revelation is maintained. Thus, it is found, for example, that the relationship between the amount of

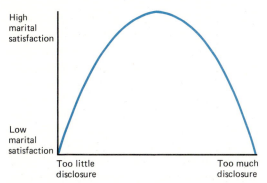

Figure 2.3   Relationship between self-disclosure and marital satisfaction. (*Source:* Gilbert, 1976.)

disclosure and marital satisfaction is curvilinear—too much or too little is not good (see Figure 2.3).

Another way we express ourselves and communicate our feelings is through touch. *Touching* is a nonverbal means of expressing warmth and sensitivity, just as verbal expres-

sions can. In fact, a single instance of body contact can often express more than words can. Touch is probably one of the most important of all of the human senses. People in Western societies, however, have traditionally relied on the "distance senses"—sight and hearing—for communication. This has changed somewhat in recent years, probably partly as a result of the self-fulfillment movement of the 1965–1975 era.

Of all the senses, touch can be one of the most personal experiences; for many people, it is associated with life's most intimate interactions. Intimate touching involves satisfying mutual contact, the enjoyment of feeling another's skin or of having one's own skin touched. Touching may take the form of caressing, cuddling, holding, kissing, stroking, or patting with the fingers or whole hand, or varying forms from simple body contact (such as holding hands) to whole

Body contact can often express more than words.

body contact (such as in sexual intercourse) (Montagu, 1971). Comfortableness with touch varies among individuals and how tactually expressive a person is depends in part on early experiences of tactile affection with those who cared for the person. In any event, touching provides reassurance to human beings, the feeling that they are wanted and valued. The different ways in which individuals express themselves tactually can be seen when comparing various cultures. (See Box 2.2.)

Unfortunately, for many members of Western societies, touch, or bodily contact, implies only sexual interest. This social attitude tends to inhibit closeness by encouraging many people to refrain from touching.

There certainly is nothing necessarily sexual about a hug between a parent and child. Similarly, touching between two men or two women need not be perceived as sexual.

Mutual Empathy

Empathy literally means "feeling inside." It is the ability to understand how someone else feels by putting oneself subjectively into his or her shoes. An empathetic person has the disposition to set aside for the moment his or her own concerns, attitudes, and values and consider those of the other person. This is especially difficult when the other person is radically different from oneself (Adler and Towne, 1984).

Empathetic people have the ability to set aside their concerns and consider those of others.

One of the most rewarding of human experiences is "to understand another person's thoughts and feelings thoroughly, with the meanings they have for him, and to be thoroughly understood by this person in return" (Rogers, 1961). In trying to be open-minded, however, people sometimes confuse *understanding* another's position with *accepting* it. These are two distinct conditions. To understand a friend's feelings on an issue that may differ from one's own feelings on the issue doesn't mean that one has to give up one's position and accept the friend's.

A person who holds rigidly to certain beliefs and is quite resistant to differing views will have difficulty empathizing. Some people view the world in "absolute terms" from their own perspectives and cannot see it from another's point of view. Often individuals with this rather closed-mindedness will attempt to change other people's behaviors and opinions to be more consistent with their own. They may even try to change or deny another's feelings as expressed in the statement, "You *shouldn't* feel that way." Hence, empathy is very difficult for such a person; he or she is unable really to listen to the feelings of another individual and refuses even to try to understand them.

Nonempathetic individuals tend to be preoccupied with their own needs and feelings. This makes it difficult for them simply to listen and really hear someone else. An individual who is wrapped up in his or her own problems may not be able to supply the empathy expected or desired by a partner. Couples lacking *mutual empathy* will not have an accurate understanding of each other and therefore will not be emotionally close.

Exclusivity

One of the defining characteristics of an intimate relationship is that there are elements of that particular interaction that are restricted to the two individuals. For example, the fact that a married individual restricts certain aspects of behavior to a specific person, and to no one else, helps to define the relationship as potentially intimate. Also, particular secrets held between two persons tie them together in a special way (Simmel, 1950). Sometimes an intimate couple even develops some exclusive terms of endearment or nicknames such as "Snuggles," "Wonder Buns," or "Love Chunks."

Zick Rubin (1973) also emphasizes the important role of exclusivity in terms of self-disclosure.

> *For a disclosure to serve as a demonstration of trust and affection, it must single out the recipient as a confidant. People who are willing to tell anyone their personal strengths or weaknesses do not find it easy to establish intimate relationships. Because their feelings and experiences are available to all, they cannot serve as a basis for an intimate and unique bond. (1973, p. 169)*

The number of intimate relationships a person can have is of necessity somewhat limited. While it is indeed possible to have more than one intimate other, a person is not likely to have more than a handful at most.

Exclusivity may also be an indication of a mutual commitment to the development of intimacy. As an individual focuses his or her interactions and disclosures on a specific person, he or she is showing a commitment to the further development of emotional closeness. In order for this closeness to grow, both partners need to make such a commitment. Intimacy cannot be achieved if only one person is committed to its development. Frustrations emerge where one partner is pushing for greater connectedness and the other wants to keep the relationship at a more superficial level. Until one of the two changes

BOX 2.2

"A TOUCH OF CULTURE"

"Just as there are wide differences between individuals in their ability to express" feelings through touch, so there also exist variations among societies (Montagu, 1979, p. 98). People with Anglo-Saxon roots—the English, Germans, Scandinavians, and Americans descended from them—are much less demonstrative in their expression of affection than are the people of the Romance-language group—Italians, French, and Spanish. These tactile variations stem from socialization occurring over generations. "In Victorian times, for example, upper-class boys were taught that demonstrations of affection were 'unmanly.' " In addition, "a virtuous woman never allowed a man to touch her, unless she was married to him or, at least, engaged" (p. 98). So extreme was this phobia of touching that an accidental touch was considered a trespass upon one's person and privacy. "The offender was expected to apologize for it, even to members of his own family" (p. 98).

"The conditioning received by many Anglo-Saxons . . . produced a virtual negative sanction against touch. . . . The sense of touch and the act of touching came to be culturally defined as vulgar" (p. 99). Only men who were quite outside the Anglo-Saxon society—such as Latins, Russians, and the like—"would ever dream of putting their arms around each other, not to mention indulging in such effeminacies as kissing each other on the cheek" (p. 99).

"In England the National Guidance Council on Marriage, in one of its publications some years ago, suggested that the rising divorce rate was due largely to a lack of physical contact in the English family" (p. 99). The article encouraged small boys to embrace their mothers during some little crisis instead of trying to remain manly by maintaining "a stiff upper lip." The Council's advice to the English: "[they] need to touch, stroke, and comfort one another more often" (p. 99).

Even more phobic about touch than the English are the Germans. The traditional emphasis on warrior virtues, the hard-headed, authoritarian father, and the submission of mothers and other females in the German family made for a "rigidified, unbending character that has rendered the average German, among other things, a not very tactile creature" (p. 99).

Americans of Anglo-Saxon origin may not be quite as untouching as the English or Germans, but they do not lag far behind. Unlike the Latin Americans, Anglo-Saxon "American boys neither kiss nor embrace their friends." The only occasion when American males will spontaneously shed their inhibitions, joyfully embrace, and even kiss one another is when an athletic contest has been won.

Examples of "touch phobia" appear in the behavior of members of the noncontact cultures in a variety of social situations. "In a packed bus, subway, or elevator, the Anglo-Saxon tends to remain stiff and rigid, with a blank facial expression which seems to deny the existence of the other passengers" (p. 102). Although crushed against other human beings, the person pretends that he or she is alone. A scene on the French Metro or an Italian train offers a striking contrast. "Here passengers will lean and press against one another, if not without reserve, at least without embarrassment or apology" (p. 102). No attempt is made to avoid meeting the eyes of other passengers, and often the leaning and lurching give rise to good-natured laughter and joking (Montagu, 1979).

Does the touching behavior between men in Latin countries indicate more intimacy between them? According to Lillian Rubin (1983), the embraces and touching of men in Latin countries are not necessarily signs of affection. Her own interviews and observations over a period of years of men in Mexico, Spain, and Italy suggest that these gestures are as ritualized and stylized as a dance, with "no greater emotional meaning or content than the handshake between American men" (1983, p. 137). American men, unfamiliar with these ritual forms, often express discomfort with their encounters in these countries, such as when they are openly hugged by other men. Rubin contends that although such touching may be associated with what Anglo-Saxons usually think as of being intimate, there is nothing else about these Latin men's relationships that is intimate, no expression of innermost thoughts, frailties, or vulnerabilities.

---

his or her goal, there will be a continual push-and-pull within the relationship. On the one hand, the person who doesn't want closeness may feel smothered and restricted. On the other hand, the person who wants to develop closeness will feel hurt and rejection as his or her attempts for closeness are shunned.

Companionship

Companionship involves *doing* things together in *shared enjoyable activities*. But it involves more than merely spending time together. It means *being* together both physically and emotionally, sharing each other's world of feelings, hopes, anxieties, and dreams (Clinebell and Clinebell, 1970). But activities in themselves are important also.

The quality of a relationship, whether friendship, courtship, marriage, or work, depends very largely upon the quality of the activities that take place within it. Feelings and activities are not independent: feelings about the partner come from the activities that are performed together—or, more importantly, come from the way that people look at what they do together. If they see themselves enjoying one another's company, they believe more firmly that they like one another. When the activities are enjoyable, feelings about the partner reflect that; when they are not, the feelings change. It is not as simple as we used to believe; that the feelings dictate the activities that we perform; the reverse is equally true. (Duck, 1983, p. 93)

Three out of four Americans consider it "very important" to do things as a family group. But, sadly enough, what many families do when they're together is to spend their time in front of the television set.

Television watching is the most frequently mentioned family activity, and 35 percent of the families are total television house-

holds, meaning that their television sets are turned on all afternoon, at dinner time, and all evening. . . . A large number of families do little more than watch television together. . . . Thus, they watch TV side by side, mesmerized, unspeaking, unengaged. It is not the television itself that depersonalizes parent-child time, but our generation's use of television as an escape from intimacy. (Pogrebin, 1983, p. 231)

Many married couples find it a challenge to share in activities that they both find enjoyable. Often the repetition of certain activities makes them routine, the partners' interests develop in different directions, or child-rearing and work-related responsibilities compete with the time available to be together. To develop intimacy, the couple, separate from the rest of the family, needs to

continue to find and share pleasurable events and mutual interests. These enrich the relationship by introducing enjoyment and novelty (Margolin, 1982). Discovering new interests may prevent the relationship from a debilitating trend toward dullness and indifference, or from having one of the partners seek gratification primarily outside of the relationship. But emotional closeness can diminish as previously rewarding interactions become stale and boring. In such a situation, behaviors that have once provided great benefits and rewards produce gradually diminishing returns. (See Figure 2.4.)

Light-hearted and humorous situations experienced together by the couple help to promote intimacy. It is impossible to live happily in a family without *a sense of humor and playfulness.* Research indicates that the "ca-

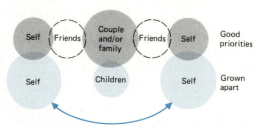

Figure 2.4   The three-ring-circus view of marriage and the family.

The three-ring circus offers one way of viewing good and poor relationships. In a good marriage, for instance, the focus is on the center ring in terms of time and priorities. It is here that the couple makes great investments in each other and in the relationship—including their children if they have any. The couple should not, however, just totally focus on their children but rather retain a strong focus on each other. In addition, each individual also has time for himself or herself, although these rings will be smaller than the main-event ring. Furthermore, typically there are friendships brought in by both partners (more typically couple friends) connecting the center ring and each person's own self ring.

In a relationship that has become unbalanced the self rings grow very large. For example, if a man is a workaholic or is nonintimate in his personality, then his ring becomes very large. He may also encourage his wife to be more independent and develop her own larger ring. Or she, because of her loneliness, may develop her own network of friendships and a largely separate life. One day the couple wakes up to find that they have grown apart—he has a big self ring and she has a big self ring, and the center ring is quite small, sometimes just focused around a child or two. A similar disruption to a relationship can take place if a friend's ring becomes extraordinarily large.

Playfulness and a capacity for acting goofy are characteristics of many intimate relationships.

pacity for playfulness'' is a characteristic that many good marriages have in common. Research also shows that "the common factor in intimate play of all kinds is its ability to stabilize a relationship'' (Cole, 1982). Play helps couples to keep a balance between too much distance, which of course alienates them from each other, and extreme clingingness, which is apt to be threatening and smothering.

Absurd and idiotic things that happen must be laughed at; humor has a way of breaking up the tension of living (Zerof, 1978). Humor is also a means of defusing conflict. Sometimes it's easier for a couple or

family to face some conflict or problem after having a humorous experience together. Humor and spontaneity also allow individuals to "let loose" and to reveal parts of themselves that are rarely seen by others. The inability to interact in such a way—the inability to let one's hair down and be "goofy"—creates an atmosphere of uneasiness and a reluctance of others to reveal themselves. Subjects in a study conducted by Betcher (1981) indicated that sharing a sense of humor is an important bond in marriage. Betcher states that laughing together implies shared values and gives one a feeling of being in sync with another person and on the same wavelength.

Conflict Resolution

If much of the time that families spend together consists of continuous conflict and negative exchange, intimacy cannot develop. Hurts, resentments, and anger obviously do not provide a fertile soil for the growth of emotional closeness. If the time spent in conflict outweighs the time spent in nonconflict situations, certainly the partners will begin to avoid each other and create emotional or physical distance or both. Unfortunately, a small number of couples seem to find negative exchange quite rewarding. "Revenge is sweet" to these people in that they receive rewards from "hurting back." They thrive on tearing each other down. Needless to say, a close relationship could not develop from such exchange.

But some conflict is inevitable in all relationships. The real question is how to handle conflict in order to enhance intimacy instead of hindering or destroying it. If conflict is appropriately dealt with and resolved, couples can be left with a feeling of closeness, sometimes even greater closeness. Partners who develop a pattern of dealing openly and directly with differences of opinion and who then make necessary compromises and collaborations can foster intimacy in a marriage. Those who can resolve their problems successfully are not only able to discuss and pinpoint the issues but can also take specific actions that result in desired behavior changes (Margolin, 1982).

In any relationship, there will be occasions when people hurt each other by their actions or words. Insults may be spoken, unreasonable demands made, or insensitive thoughts expressed. It takes a certain level of personal security and self-esteem for family members to *forget past hurts, forgive mistakes*, and go on with the relationship. Swallowing some pride in order to *admit mistakes* and to say one is sorry also goes a long way toward resolving conflicts.

Value Consensus

Similar values, goals, expectations, and priorities help to foster ease of communication, empathy, and sensitivity between partners. Such commonalities serve as a base from which the partners relate. It is easier to understand and to interact with a person who shares values similar to one's own. When two people come from different social classes or ethnic backgrounds, behavioral expectations are often quite dissimilar. Empathy will be much more difficult under such conditions.

Researchers have concluded that having shared attitudes and values may be *more* important to the success of a relationship than the particular nature of the attitudes held (Hill, Rubin, and Peplau, 1976). When comparing dating couples who held traditional gender-role attitudes with couples holding liberal attitudes, Hill et al. (1976) found that there was no difference in the level of satisfaction in the relationship or in the rate at which they broke up. What was more important was the consensus of the partners' attitudes.

SITUATIONAL FACTORS AFFECTING INTIMACY

There are other factors that need to be examined because of their impact on intimate relationships. Time, space, and cultural norms are among the situational factors affecting interpersonal relationships, over which individuals may have relatively little control. For example, societal expectations and cultural norms encourage or discourage intimacy and help to determine the persons with whom we may be intimate and how we should conduct ourselves in close relationships. These situational factors are not sufficient in themselves to create intimacy, particularly if there are deficits in the individual prerequisites or interactive factors.

Spatial Factors

Proximity is a spatial factor that can be viewed on a couple of levels. First, there is physical proximity between persons, with the distance ranging from living in the same house to living on opposite sides of the world. With technological advances in communication and travel, physical distances between people appear to be growing smaller. Hundreds of miles can be only an hour away by plane. There is an important difference, however, between living with someone in close proximity and living a distance apart, a difference that can influence the development of intimacy. A certain *continuity of contact* is typically lacking in long-distance relationships.

Although physical closeness is desirable to facilitate intimacy, severe overcrowding or too much spatial closeness in the home often makes it difficult to develop quality personal relationships. Stumbling over each other is not on a par with a loving embrace (Morris, 1973). Forced contact is anti-intimate, in that, paradoxically, we need more space to give body contact greater meaning. "To cramp the home-space is to convert the loving touch into a suffocating body proximity" (Morris, 1973, p. 255).

Another aspect of an intimate relationship connected to proximity is the need for *couple privacy*. Since intimacy depends to a large degree on exclusivity—on what each person discloses or shows only to the other—relationship privacy is an important factor. It is necessary for the dyad to have private space in order to develop and enjoy intimate interactions fully. Couples may feel restricted in revealing their innermost feelings and desires with their parents, their children, or a lot of other people hanging around.

Alternative family systems, such as communes, where a large number of people are continually present, tend to inhibit, and in many instances prohibit, intimate relationships. The commune by itself is meant to be a large family group. Intimacy and emotional commitment within dyads may compete with the time and energy available for sharing within the larger group (Kanter, 1973). The privacy between two individuals may threaten their commitment to the group as a whole. Today in various non-Western cultures, including modern China, privacy is often difficult to obtain. (See Box 2.3.)

Time Factors

A *history together* in a relationship provides the partners with a common base of experience that they can draw upon to help build an emotional bond. Short-lived interpersonal relationships lack a history upon which intimacy can thrive. To have emotional closeness we need partners who have shared significant segments of our adult lives with us—both crises and successes. From past experiences our partners know the kind of approval we need and what makes us happy, because they know the kind of people we were in the past and the kind of people we are now. Spending time recalling the positive aspects of the past, "the time that we did such and such together," reinforces mutual images and validates the commitment to the relationship. The many years invested in an ongoing relationship provide continuity to the dyad. Separations or significant periods of time spent apart are usually obstacles to intimacy.

There is no "instant intimacy." Lasting emotional closeness is slowly, and sometimes painfully, attained. For many, it is a difficult journey. The mobility patterns and the high

BOX 2.3

NEIGHBORHOOD WATCH IN CHINA— AN INVASION OF PRIVACY?

If a major aspect of intimacy is the sharing of private and personal information, what happens when personal secrets become public knowledge? In China the "nosey neighbor," "tattletale," or "busybody" is an integral part of an all-encompassing surveillance system. These people are members of neighborhood committees set up by the Chinese government for the purpose of "supervision by the masses."

Usually run by tough, older men and women, these committees work closely with local government officials and the police. The committee is well versed on everyone's personal and family histories. These "watchdogs" take pride in their diligent work in reporting and investigating their neighbors' private lives. Every little detail of family life is supervised with pervasive precision. Such information as the following is reported to the committee: an account of each woman's menstrual cycles, daily birth-control use in each family, domestic disputes, unauthorized pregnancies, and any visitors to households. Such actions as the following are commonplace:

> In the Old Curtain neighborhood a woman didn't go to work for two days and her courtyard watchdog immediately became suspicious. Then he overheard her telling her 5-year-old son to buy her guodanpi, a sweet-sour fruit candy craved by pregnant women.
>
> Then he knew her secret, but he didn't confront her with her impending violation of China's rigid one-child policy. Instead he reported her to the neighborhood committee. The clinic sent a nurse but the woman gave it no thought since the committee regularly checks every married woman's menstrual cycle every three months, questions her about birth control and sometimes delivers contraceptives.
>
> The committee then called the woman's work unit and the unit sent a delegation to persuade her to have an abortion. ("In China, someone is always watching, and often informing," *Ann Arbor News,* April 20, 1983, p. F5.)

The neighborhood committee serves many useful functions—caring for the elderly, counseling wayward youths, finding the unemployed jobs, and mediating disputes. But the effects of such intrusiveness on intimate relationships can be negative. People under constant surveillance by the government and police are less likely to be totally honest, open and free to disclose innermost thoughts and feelings. Even disclosing with spouses carries the fear that one could be overheard and reported. Family secrets that in most societies are thought to be private are now at the public's disposal. Fears of being reported prompt people to be on their "good behavior" at all times.

China's concern for the welfare of the group or community as a whole has come at the expense of privacy for the dyad. The Chinese society is just one example of how cultural norms influence the development of intimate relationships.

divorce rate in American society force some people to develop short-lived and temporary relationships. Brief love, to these people, is probably better than no love at all. But it is doubtful whether such temporary love systems will ever completely eliminate the desire for intimacy.

Chronic "busy-ness" can also be a barrier to developing closeness—in fact, it can serve as an escape from intimacy for some people. Intimacy requires the *investment of quality time*, and if one of the partners or both are workaholics and regularly busy with other activities, intimacy will have less of a chance to develop. When a potential intimate other is not available, an increasing number of persons in our society are seeking "pet intimacy" (see Box 2.4).

There are times during each person's life when he or she may be more accessible for a close relationship than at other times. Unless two individuals are *available* to each other— unless the *timing* is right—closeness may not be a possibility. For example, if one or both of the persons are married to other individuals or committed to another relationship, they are not likely to be available to develop an intimate relationship. Also, an individual who has recently experienced a loss as a result of a death or divorce may not be as ready to make a commitment to a new relationship as someone who has been without a partner for several years. The extremely low success rate of "rebound" relationships supports this fact. Also, people at *discrepant levels of maturity, age levels, or life stages* may experience tension when attempting closeness; one partner might be ready for it and the other might not. If both parties are immature—for example, two teenagers in American society— emotional closeness is highly unlikely.

Another time element that could relate to the development of intimacy involves the *wake-sleep cycles* of the individuals in the dyad.

When people lack intimacy in their human relationships, they may turn to other sources.

A definite obstacle exists for couples in which one person is a "morning person" and the other is a "night person." Since the amount of time that couples have to spend together is usually limited in modern "busy" society, the differences in time periods when individuals are going to bed or waking up can make for even less available time together.

A "night person" may enjoy in-depth conversations, sexual activity, or watching television as the evening wears on, while a "morning person" would rather be sleeping so that he or she can be up at 6:00 A.M. to go jogging. Other tensions that arise between partners who are on different time schedules include such things as deciding on the time

BOX 2.4

PET LOVE

When people lack intimacy in their human relationships, they may turn to other sources. If it is far too dangerous for some people to seek closeness with others—and family cannot supply it—for a small sum they can buy a piece of "animal intimacy" (Morris, 1973).

> For pets are innocent; they cause no questions and they ask no questions. They lick our hands, they rub softly up against our legs, they curl up to sleep on our thighs, and they nuzzle us. We can cuddle them, stroke them, pat them, carry them like babies, tickle them behind the ears, and even kiss them. (Morris, 1973, pp. 184–185)

In the United States, more than $5,000 million are spent on pets every year. Although true intimacy cannot develop with a pet, scientists are finding that some emotional, mental, and physical benefits are provided by pets to their owners. A pet will reduce stress and lower blood pressure in hypertensives. A pet greeting a person when he or she comes home eliminates that coming-home-to-an-empty-house feeling. Pet ownership can also provide the well-being that comes from knowing that somebody—a dog, a cat, or even a bird or a turtle—needs you, depends on you for sustenance. "People talk to pets in the same way that they talk to infants and other intimates. This comforting style of expression is associated with distinct patterns of facial expression, rate and tone of speech, and a measurable decrease in blood pressure and other signs of tension" (Jones, *Detroit Free Press,* 1984). Thus, though animals cannot totally fulfill a person's need for intimacy, the beneficial effects of pet ownership demonstrate that pets can be a good substitute.

Reprinted with permission of United Press International, copyright 1984.

to leave parties, scheduling recreational activities, and doing housework. This is a difficult problem to resolve since many people have biological clocks that make them night owls or early birds (Adams and Cromwell, 1978). A lot of resentment can arise over this issue.

Norms Regarding Intimacy

When developing an intimate relationship, we often tend to underestimate the part that cultural or subcultural values and social roles play in determining whom we come close to and how we conduct ourselves with that person. Norms within a culture, however, can either encourage or discourage the development of intimacy. Norms regarding touching, the balance of power between men and women, interpersonal communication, privacy, who is a legitimate intimacy partner, and so on, influence dyadic closeness. Even though it is possible for particular *individuals* to transcend cultural expectations, such patterns would not be widespread among *groups of people*. The norms themselves, however, can change over time.

Societal norms that support the concept of male superiority and that indicate that a woman should look up to the significant man in her life certainly have an impact on the potential for closeness between a man and a woman. Patriarchal norms die slowly. Not only does male domination exist in business, education, religion, and politics, but it also extends to personal relationships within the family. Traditional gender roles prescribe that men should be in control. Today in American society, however, the trend is for marriages to involve a balance of power that is closer to being equal.

Marriage in our society ordinarily involves a certain amount of intimacy and sharing between husband and wife. . . . This degree of togetherness is usually not *found in other* societies. . . . *Traditional barriers frequently stand between husband and wife, curtailing their intimacy, sharing, and togetherness. They usually observe avoidance customs while in public; they may sleep in separate beds, live in separate houses, own separate property, eat separately, go separately to community gatherings, and . . . usually work at separate tasks. . . . In our present-day American society, for some reason, these traditional barriers have largely disappeared. (Stephens, 1963, pp. 270, 278)*

Lee Rainwater (1980) found that the lower-class subculture has norms that are more likely to prohibit intimacy in family relationships, especially between spouses. The traditional pattern in this subculture is for highly segregated role relationships in marriage. Men and women do not share many joint activities; there is a sharp separation of men's and women's play. The traditional low value placed on intimacy in the marital relationship is probably in part an extension of the more generalized division of men's and women's worlds. Since the spouses in this class are more likely to be isolated from each other, they do not seem to be dependent on each other emotionally, though each performs important instrumental services for the other (1980). Women in these subcultures often look to other kin relations and female friends for intimacy.

Lillian Rubin (1976) makes a similar observation:

Earlier descriptions of working-class family life present a portrait of wives and husbands whose lives were distinctly separate, both inside and outside the home—the wife attending to her household role, the husband to his provider role. He came home at night tired and taciturn; she kept herself and the children out of his way. For generations, it was enough that each did their

*job adequately—he, to bring home the ba-
con; she, to cook it. Intimacy, companionship, sharing—these were not part of the
dream. (p. 120)*

Lillian Rubin discovered, however, that
working-class women were starting to desire
more intimacy, companionship, and sharing
from their husbands but that they could not
always verbalize what they wanted. The following response was typical in her interviews.

*I'm not sure what I want. I keep talking to
him about communication and he says,
''Okay, so we're talking; now what do you
want?'' And I don't know what to say
then, but I know it's not what I mean.
(1976, p. 120)*

The degree to which a society places
value on close relationships and encourages
their formation will affect the ease or difficulty of forming intimate bonds. For example,
on the one hand, in societies that place a high
value on friends, kinship or family ties may
be minimized as individuals look more to
their friends for closeness. On the other hand,
if strong kinship ties exist in a society, it may
be assumed that individuals can meet their
emotional needs through marriage and the
family and, therefore, they will not need
friends for such a purpose (Robert Bell,
1981). In this instance, friendship may be
viewed as a threat to the family, as is reflected
in the words of the following respondent in
Robert Bell's (1981) research:

*I can tell at various times that my mother
doesn't want to hear me talk about my
friends. Especially if I mention help or advice that my friends give me she will get
uptight and often say something sarcastic.
What it is is that she thinks I should always
turn to her. To my mother that's what fam-*

*ilies are for—not friends! She believes that
just about all needs can be met within the
family and to go to friends is to put down
the family. My mother and I often have
conflict because I don't see it that way.
(p. 11)*

Mexican-Americans, or Chicanos, are
unique in the sense that there is not a clear
line separating friends and relatives; ''they
are often one and the same. Not only are
relatives included as friends, but friends are
symbolically incorporated into the family,''
writes sociologist Alfredo Mirande (1977, p.
752). Dating back many centuries is the custom of *compadrazgo,* which is a form of ritualized kinship and friendship involving the
linking of friends. One form of *compadrazgo* is
the relationship between godparents and
children, who *are not* related to each other.
The godparents are co-parents (*compadres*)
with the child's real parents. The godparents
function as an additional set of parents, primarily to care for the child in emergencies or
to take care of him or her should the parents
die. The interaction between the child and
the co-parent is rather formal and one of mutual respect (Queen, Habenstein, and Quadagno, 1985).

Among adults however, the *compadrazgo*
relationship is one of mutual ''helping.'' But
traditionally this relationship has not been a
very intimate one, often specifically excluding
joking and the discussion of subjects of a personal nature (O. Lewis, 1960). Favors and
advice are exchanged, and borrowing is common. A *compadre* (co-parent) is expected to
contribute toward the funeral expenses of the
other *compadre* when he or she dies (O. Lewis,
1960). *Compadres* are formal social friendships that remain intact in Chicano culture
today. One study found that nearly every
adult had at least one such friendship, and
some had two, three, or more (Goodman and

In some ethnic groups the extended family is still very important.

Beman, 1971). At the same time the traditional husband-wife relationship among Mexicans tends to be quite formal, with no deep intimacy. Also the direct confrontation of marital problems is uncommon. "Respect, consideration, and curtailment of anger or hostility are highly valued" (Falicov, 1982, p. 140).

The members of some societies cluster together in larger family groups in order to meet basic survival needs; the traditional Eskimos are one example of this. Their days are filled with activities to provide food, clothing, and shelter for the larger group beyond the nuclear family. Needless to say, the fulfillment of dyadic intimacy is not a primary concern among these people. Human contact is important, but it centers around the provision of instrumental support.

Similarly in American society other needs may negatively affect emotional closeness. Survival needs always have—and always will—come first. Feeding one's family comes before intimacy on a hierarchy of needs. Unemployment, the illness of a family member, children with special problems—all may reduce the concern for intimacy. But some couples and families can, in fact, be brought even closer as the result of a family crisis. In general, however, intimacy becomes more of a possibility where *other needs don't take precedence*.

According to Abraham Maslow's theory of a hierarchy of needs (1970), the social and economic factors of one's environment determine to what degree the need for love and intimacy will become a priority. Once a person's basic physiological and safety needs have been met, then and only then will he or she be able to seek to satisfy the need for intimacy. It has only been in the last generation or so that Americans have experienced greater satisfaction of survival needs and therefore have come to focus on the needs of personal happiness and intimacy.

Still, many people attempt to avoid intimacy. Often they do this without even being aware of how their behavior functions to keep other people at a distance. Box 2.5 lists ten rules to follow to *avoid* intimacy. Perhaps this list will help to sensitize you to the ways that your behavior prevents others from getting close.

INTIMACY OUTCOME

An Emotional Bond

The development of intimacy is dependent upon individual, interactive, and situational factors. One result of this process is that the couple in the intimate dyad experiences a *warmth* and closeness described as an emotional bond. The bond means that each person no longer typically thinks or speaks in terms of "you" and "me" but in a deep sense of *"we."* Through identification with each other and mutual empathy, the partners come to define themselves as a unit, as one couple, a partnership (Hatfield, 1979). It is an *emotional bond* because the satisfaction of emotional needs is primary. We are not emphasizing "instrumental" needs, that is, physical or basic survival needs. Rather we are focusing on the satisfaction of the desire for emotional support, care, and affection.

In an intimate relationship the attachment is joint; it certainly is not a situation of one-sided attachement where only one person needs or loves another. Intimacy cannot evolve in situations where only one person is

committed, trusting, giving, and self-disclosing. There has to be a mutuality in all of these interactions in order for a *mutual attachment* to result.

The reliance of two individuals on each other for valued rewards, benefits, and emotional gratifications creates a time-tested *interdependence*. Close relationships themselves create an even stronger mutual dependence. Partners who are interdependent find that their shared activities are mutually rewarding. Individuals sense that their own well-being and that of their partners are inextricably tied together. Each person finds it rewarding when the other receives certain rewards. Interdependence, however, does not mean the loss of an individual's own self-concept or identity.

As partners grow increasingly closer, the following characteristics of interdependence exist:

1. They begin to synchronize their goals and behavior and develop stable interaction patterns.

2. They increase their investment in the relationship, thus enhancing its importance in their life space.

3. They begin increasingly to feel that their separate interests are inextricably tied to the well-being of their relationship.

4. They more and more relate to others as a couple rather than as individuals (Huston and Burgess, 1979).

Personal Security and Rewards

An intimate relationship offers individuals a significant degree of security, an inner feeling of stability and safety that comes from feeling acceptance, belonging, and being wanted (Clinebell and Clinebell, 1970). The feeling of being understood by another person also contributes to personal security. It's a tremen-

BOX 2.5

TEN RULES TO AVOID INTIMACY

1. Don't tell the people you love about your needs, desires, and expectations. It's better if they find out for themselves—besides it's no good if they do something just because you asked them to.

2. Always protect yourself from potential hurt by avoiding commitments and not getting too obligated to others.

3. Never admit that you're angry over an issue. Suppress your negative feelings; get even in other ways.

4. Never admit that you are really dependent on another human being.

5. In a conflict, stand firm with your point of view; people respect individuals who don't compromise or back down.

6. Hold to the philosophy that "variety is the spice of life" when it comes to relationships and sexuality.

7. Point out people's mistakes as much as you can to try to change these people.

8. Don't be afraid to get high on alcohol or other drugs; it helps people let go and get to know each other.

9. Don't let people around you know of any past or present pain; the message might be "you can't take it."

10. Never state that you like someone directly to his or her face—or any other strong feelings of loving, caring, loneliness, or sadness.

dous experience to find that one's dreams, hopes, mistakes, and failures can all be understood by another person. This feeling of understanding and *acceptance* results in a *comfortableness* with the relationship; one is relaxed and does not have to put up defenses to hide feelings and thoughts.

With intimacy what evolves for the individual is a *validation of self-worth*. Self-worth as a human being continues to grow as the relationship grows and is affirmed by the intimate other's *meaningful recognition*. "Self-esteem of each partner can be enhanced by the other—the awareness that one is valued, recognized, and affirmed by others can be steadily strengthened by one's spouse" (Clinebell

and Clinebell, 1970, p. 71). The end result is a feeling of *personal fulfillment*.

Relationship Security

Besides individual security, relationship security also comes with intimacy. Throughout the developmental process toward emotional closeness there is proven commitment to the other person. The commitment to the relationship is continuously reaffirmed as the partners avoid competitive alternative relationships. Each partner feels dedicated to the current relationship and no longer considers alternatives. There is true and final commitment where both partners have stopped counting rewards and costs, where both care for the other's pleasure as well as their own, and where satisfaction is considered less in terms of "mine" than in terms of "ours" (Levinger, 1979a).

Mutual commitment implies a total dedication of the partners. If conflicts arise, there is a willingness to work them through. Thus there is a sense of stability, permanence, and duration with *proven mutual commitment*.

Related to mutual commitment is *proven mutual trust*, also an outcome of intimacy. There is now a confidence that each person will behave in consistent ways, that each will follow through on promises, responsibilities, and obligations. There is a history, a track record, of having the partner's best interests at heart and making every effort to avoid hurting the intimate other.

CHAPTER REVIEW

1. The potential for an intimate relationship begins with each person's unique personality—characteristic behaviors, attitudes, values, and feelings. Individual prerequisites for intimacy include a positive self-concept, the admission of personal dependence, the ability to trust, and realistic perceptions of self, others, and the relationship.

2. Intimacy will be fostered if the specific interactions between two individuals include such factors as positive exchange, reciprocal sensitive disclosure, mutual empathy, exclusivity, companionship, conflict resolution, and value consensus.

3. The potential for intimacy can also be influenced by situational factors experienced by the couple. Such aspects include spatial and time factors as well as cultural or subcultural norms.

4. Many rewards can result from building an intimate relationship. There will be an emotional bond characterized by warmth and closeness. Also, an individual's personal security—feelings of acceptance and belonging—is facilitated by an intimate relationship. Finally, emotional closeness brings a sense of security and stability to the relationship itself.

3

Gender Differences and Intimate Relationships

Many stereotypes and beliefs exist as to what males and females are "really" like. But to what extent are these feelings accurate and supported by research evidence? This chapter describes and analyzes several behaviors in terms of gender differences. We are particularly concerned with those factors that impinge upon intimate relationships.

We know that there are many more similarities than differences between men and women. Our primary concern here, however, is with any differences that complicate and interfere with developing closeness and the way such differences do so. Once any differences are recognized, the obvious question follows: What causes them? Are the differences in the innate nature of males and females? Or are they more simply products of culture or socialization? Or is the growing moderate view more correct—that both biological and cultural factors contribute to existing gender differences?

It must be stressed that as social scientists studying gender differences, we are making *generalizations* about the sexes. Of course, there are individual variances that do not fit the generalizations. In reality, there is considerable overlap between the sexes, and at times as much variation can exist within each sex as between the sexes (see Figure 3.1)

MALE AND FEMALE DIFFERENCES IN INTERPERSONAL BEHAVIOR

Assertiveness and Aggressiveness

Intimate relationships require that both partners assert their feelings and desires. *Assertive* behavior involves simply making one's self-interests and wishes known without degrading or putting down the other person. Assertiveness may be forceful and determined, but

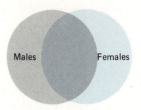

Figure 3.1   The similarities and differences between males and females on most behaviors can be viewed as two intersecting circles.

it is not necessarily aggressive, hostile, or domineering.

The lack of assertiveness lies at the root of many unresolved problems, tensions, and misunderstandings in relationships. "I don't know what she wants!" complains a husband married to a passive, accommodating, and nonassertive woman. The voluminous self-help books, seminars, and training groups on assertiveness for females attest to the fact that many women tend to be less assertive than men. A woman may hold back from expressing her desires for fear of sounding controlling and demanding, which she perceives would result in a negative reaction from others. But only when people can firmly assert feelings, thoughts, and behaviors can they understand each other and respond according to each other's needs.

Gender differences in assertiveness do not hold true across all situations or in terms of what specifically is being asserted. For example, while men are more likely to initiate social contacts and to assert themselves in public settings, women tend to be more assertive in expressing love and affection to close friends. In general, however, women seem to have a greater fear of confrontation than men and seem to be more reserved in problem-solving situations (Mathison and Tucker, 1982).

Since the mid-1960s there has been increased social pressure on women to express themselves more boldly. Females today, however, may still find themselves in a bind when they do try to be assertive.

> *If she's direct in defining her needs, her likes and dislikes and her limits, he sees her as demanding, pushy, shrewish and possibly even castrating.*
>
> *If she's reluctant to define her needs and to express her likes and dislikes and tries to avoid conflict by giving in, he sees her as being passive and unexciting and tells her that they will get along much better if she would only tell him how she* really *feels, what she* really *wants and what she really* likes and dislikes. (Goldberg, 1979, p. 129)

Aggression, in contrast to assertiveness, is the tendency to harm a person either physically or verbally. Males, in general, have consistently been found to show more aggres-

Males are more likely to behave aggressively than females.

siveness than females. At every age and in almost every situation, men tend to be more physically aggressive (MacCoby and Jacklin, 1974). From preschool years through adulthood, males are more likely than females to inflict pain on others (Doyle, 1983). When females do show aggression, it is usually verbal, such as through yelling and screaming. Or it can involve nonverbal gestures, such as glaring and frowning.

Obviously, continuous physical aggression will annihilate the potential for intimacy. Verbal aggression also interferes with closeness. Inflicting any kind of physical or emotional hurt only results in anger, resentment, and bitterness in the other person. Both from fear and lack of trust, the person being attacked creates distance from, rather than desiring closeness to, the other individual. Unless interpersonal aggression can be eliminated completely, intimacy will be difficult to build or rebuild.

In summary, aggressiveness and assertiveness must be conceptually distinguished; they are two quite different traits. In addition, they differ in their impact on the development of emotional closeness. Assertiveness, in contrast to aggressiveness, will usually have a positive effect on a relationship, assuming the partner has some degree of security and self-esteem. In many respects, assertiveness training has helped individuals to express their real needs and feelings, to the betterment of their marriages.

Admission of Dependence

Basic to intimacy is a healthy dependence that each person has on the other for meeting certain emotional needs. When we admit our dependence, we can ask another human being for support, encouragement, a hug, or just a listening ear. When two individuals expose their needs, there develops a bond of interdependence. By not admitting one's dependence on another individual, one is saying directly or indirectly "I don't really need you." This implies indifference—an attitude of "You're not really important or valuable to me."

The admission of dependence seems to be especially difficult for many males in American society. Asking a female for support contradicts the socialization of most males to dominate and to be the more powerful person in the relationship. Maintaining control seems to be a more important concern to males than to females. The socializing of males to control and of females to please begins early in life as dominance and submissiveness are stressed in the play patterns of boys and girls (Lever, 1976).

A denial of dependence, or of any weaknesses, is particularly evidenced among men in the workplace. A man will quickly learn to avoid admitting personal failings for fear that a competitive co-worker could capitalize on them. "Men are not supposed to show their vulnerability for it implies weakness—a dreaded characteristic in a man" (Eichenbaum and Orbach, 1983, p. 63). In order to maintain an image as a "pillar of strength" a man is taught to project power, confidence, and independence at the expense of admitting his dependence on others.

So where does that leave women? Are women more "needy" and dependent than men? For most of history the myth has existed that women are the more dependent creatures, that they need men more than men need them. Certainly in the economic area, women have traditionally needed men for instrumental security. But when it comes to emotional needs, women have been the primary providers. In reality, women are not more dependent than men; they are just more willing to admit their dependence. They

are not as concerned with maintaining a dominant position; on the contrary, they are much more concerned about building emotional closeness based on an equal status with men.

In addition, the fact that women are socialized to take care of others and to be nurturers also plays a role in male-female differences in terms of dependence. Many women may be so adept at, and sensitive to, meeting men's needs that it's not really necessary for men to express these needs. "Whatever a man's dependent needs are, therefore, they simply won't be as obvious as a woman's because there's usually a woman quickly and easily available to help obscure them" (L. Rubin, 1983, p. 127).

It's possible that some women themselves encourage men to hide their dependence. Women may be putting men into a no-win situation. A man who openly shares his wants, dependence, and weaknesses with a woman could elicit a response of a lack of respect or disgust from the woman. "Women help perpetuate the myth of the strong man, for if there is a strong man a woman can imagine that she is safe, that she is being cared for and looked after" (Eichenbaum and Orbach, 1983, pp. 63–64). So even women have a stake in maintaining this image of male "invincibility" and independence.

The denial of a man's dependence on a woman can be so strong that often he will not recognize his neediness until the relationship falls apart. Faced with being alone, the male finally consciously realizes how dependent he was on her. Whereas the woman often has close female friends to whom she can turn if a relationship breaks up, the male typically does not.

Most men sat silently for a long while when I asked, "Who (sic) would you turn to if you came home one night and your wife announced she was leaving you?" When they finally spoke, it was with great hesitation as the realization came to them that there would be no friend to whom they could turn in that moment of pain and shock. (L. Rubin, 1983, p. 132)

Positive Exchange

Human beings also differ in their ability to exchange, that is, to give to and receive from others; to make investments in other people; to make and keep commitments; and to fulfill obligations that have built up. The authors have found in their research that females are significantly more likely than males to exchange positively with others (Kersten and Kersten, 1981). In addition, women are more likely to behave according to the concept of enlightened self-interest. That is, they believe that in order to attain their own self-interests, they need to take the self-interests of others into account and to cooperate with these people. Not so preoccupied with competition or control over others, women are more inclined to cooperate, compromise, and collaborate—to take others' needs into consideration.

Society appears to have been more successful in teaching women how to relate interpersonally. Certainly the socialization of males to be competitive, aggressive, and independent hinders them in developing the capacity to exchange positively with others. It's difficult for a person to exchange warmly with another individual while still trying to maintain power and dominance over that person.

Self-Disclosure

To be open and honest with personal feelings in a close relationship is not easy for a lot of people. For many men, in particular, revealing personal information about themselves is

a risk they're not often willing to take. The result is a large group of women who feel emotionally shut out by men. In a recent survey, 400 therapists were asked why marriages fail. By far the largest single reason given for the cause of divorce was the husband's inability to communicate his feelings (cited in Naifeh and Smith, 1984).

An exhaustive review of the research on self-disclosure arrives at the same conclusions (Cozby, 1973). Women are more revealing of their personal feelings than men. When men do disclose, they reveal themselves to fewer people and are more likely to disclose to women than to other men—usually to mothers, wives, or female friends. The main disadvantage of a male friend as a confidant was explained by a college senior: "A guy means competition. . . . I have competed with guys in sports and for girls. Once you let your guard down, the guy can hurt you and take advantage of you. Your girl has your interest at heart" (Komarovsky, 1976).

This gender difference in self-disclosure may not be as strong in the beginning of a relationship when men might appear to be just as self-disclosing as women. Researchers have found that if there is an interest in developing a relationship with a particular woman, males will disclose very personal information. "Males may selectively self-disclose as a tool to cultivate a relationship with their female partner, reflecting a cultural prescription that males are supposed to make the first direct move in developing a male-female relationship" (Derlega et al., 1985, p. 41). Most of the literature on self-disclosure and gender, however, has found that women tend to exceed men in self-disclosure in ongoing relationships. Possibly men are using self-disclosure as a strategic function in the development of an encounter, but as Valerian Derlega (1985) warns, this cannot be directly inferred from the data. During marriage counseling, it is not uncommon to hear wives claim that their husbands were quite disclosing during their courtship but that the women can't understand why the husbands don't talk now. It is apparent that self-disclosure can be influenced by the timing and stage of the relationship.

Men and women also differ in terms of which emotions or behaviors they control or express (Montagu, 1974). For females, crying is considered to be an appropriate and proper behavior, but women have been socialized to refrain from losing their tempers or swearing; it isn't "ladylike," at least in public. Males, in contrast, have traditionally seen crying as sissy behavior; it is more acceptable for them to lose their tempers, show anger, or swear. So when researchers speak of the "inexpressive male," they are referring primarily to the sharing of personal feelings such as affection, sadness, and weakness. Feelings such as loneliness, inferiority, fear, embarrassment, and worry are also more likely to be disclosed by women than men (Derlega et al., 1981; Hacker, 1981). Revealing these types of feelings allows for emotional closeness; it therefore appears that women have a big advantage in these terms in building intimacy.

Although male inexpressiveness is a common complaint of women, still many females are attracted to the strong, silent, "John Wayne" type of man. They cringe at the sight of their husbands or lovers crying and feel more comfortable when they keep a stiff upper lip. They feel let down when "the cowboy who won their hearts with a steady gaze and choice words unexpectedly exposes a soft heart filled with unromantic anxieties. . . . Many women want a man to be strong and silent one minute, warm and emotional the next. They want men to be vulnerable *and* invincible" (Naifeh and Smith, 1984, p. 82).

Empathy

If men tend to have difficulty being aware of and expressing their own feelings, it should not be surprising that they also have a difficult time listening to and identifying with the feelings of other people. This is indeed the situation for a large percentage of men. Women tend to have a significant advantage over men in the ability to empathize; that is, to recognize emotions and feelings in other people, "to put themselves in their shoes."

This gender difference is found quite consistently in research, and its tendencies appear very early in life. Studies reveal that female infants are more responsive than male infants to the cry of another infant, although there is some question as to whether this is really empathy (Barfield, 1976). Research indicates that women tend to be better than men in tuning in to and labeling other people's feelings. Rosenthal and his colleagues measured men's and women's reactions while they watched and listened to a 45-minute film of a person portraying different emotions. Females were reliably better than males at determining the correct emotion depicted in the film. This particular finding appears to hold true from third grade—the earliest age tested—through adulthood (Rosenthal et al., 1974).

Patiently spending time with someone when that person is upset, and listening and trying to understand what it is he or she is going through, are behaviors much more common among women than men. Men in their problem-solving approach to life do not do well in just "feeling." In addition, many men may act bewildered, confused, or even helpless about what they're supposed to do when demands are made of them to respond to another's emotional needs. A husband may dismiss his wife's feelings by saying, "It's just one of her moods," "That's just the way women are," or "I'll never understand women" (Fasteau, 1975). Many men tend to simply withdraw from such uncomfortable situations.

Even in times of crises—a death of a parent, an illness, a rape, or an abortion—a woman's feelings are often ignored, denied, or avoided by her husband. Males have been socialized to jump in to "fix" problems and take control of the situation. But the offering of suggestions or practical solutions to the problem is usually not what the woman wants. The husband may be confused and frustrated that his attempts at helping his wife are rebuked. One husband states,

No matter what I do it's never the right thing. When Alice is upset she tells me I make her feel worse. I try to make suggestions about how she can get out of feeling

depressed and she says I'm all wrong and that I don't understand anything. It's infuriating. (Eichenbaum and Orbach, 1983, p. 82)

What most women want is someone to listen, to be attentive, to understand, and to care about what is going on inside her. A woman who is lucky enough to have a man who is empathetic will be envied by many other females.

Tactile Expressiveness

Gender differences in touching behaviors are very marked in all cultures; females are much more apt to engage in almost every form of human touching than males. Overall, women appear to be much more sensitive to tactile properties (Montagu, 1971). Even at birth, female babies respond more to touch (R.

Women tend to respond more tactually than men.

cathy

by Cathy Guisewite

CATHY © 1983, Universal Press Syndicate. Reprinted with permission. All rights reserved.

Schaffer, 1977). Women continue to respond more tactually than men throughout life. For example, females are more likely than males to walk barefoot, to dangle their feet in the water from the side of a pool, to run their hands over fabrics, and to touch and hug members of the same sex. Fondling and caressing are largely feminine activities. Back-slapping and handshaking are specifically masculine forms of touching (Montagu, 1971).

The vast majority of the wives we see in counseling complain that their husbands do not give them enough holding, touching, and cuddling. Only rarely do we find men who complain about such deprivations. When men do touch women, however, it often implies a desire for sex. A common request of wives is for their husbands to hold them and touch them without it necessarily leading to sexual intercourse.

Many women complain of primarily being sexual objects to men, although some men say that they show their love best through sexual activity. For many men, however, holding and caressing with no purpose or goal is discomforting, as well as often incomprehensible. While being touched by a woman may be a prelude to sexual activity

for a man, being touched by another man usually arouses extreme anxiety. Touching between men often takes forms such as a slap on the back, a punch on the arm, or a pat on the butt after scoring the winning touchdown in an intensive athletic contest.

THEORIES OF EXPLANATION

How can we account for gender differences in close relationships? Are they the result more of biology or of culture, or of a combination of the two? If biology contributes at least to some degree, is it possible then to bring about changes in the behaviors of males and females?

The Influence of Biology

The debate over whether "nature" or "nurture" explains gender differences has become meaningless over time. As most social scientists now agree, the interactive effects of both biology and culture together determine human behavior. The distinction between what is specifically the result of biology and what is specifically the result of culture is rarely clear. Hence, it is impossible to attribute behavior to biological processes without considering cultural or environmental factors. Likewise, looking solely at environmental influences neglects other possible contributions. To complicate the issue even further, the relative importance of biology and culture varies significantly at different points of the life cycle. For example, biological processes have a greater influence on a human being before birth, during puberty, before menstruation, or during pregnancy than at other times in a person's life. Women suffering from premenstrual syndrome (PMS) can testify to its physiological effects on their behavior during the days prior to their menstruation (see Box 3.1).

In order to attempt to ascertain the relative importance of biological influences on behavior, as compared to cultural influences, those specific biological mechanisms responsible for certain gender differences in behavior must be identified. Evidence—hardly complete—of such biological influences comes from five sources:

1. patterns of behavior varying according to the quantity and proportion of *sex hormones*

2. behavioral patterns among *infants or very young children* who have not yet experienced much socialization from their environment

3. similar behavior *across cultures*

4. consistent patterns of behavior *across species*, especially among higher primates (sources 1 through 4 are taken from Parsons, 1982)

5. biological *abnormalities*

Biological processes can have an impact on behavior either directly or quite indirectly. An example of a direct influence is the level of the hormone testosterone, which directly influences aggression. An indirect influence exists when parents engage in more active play patterns with boys than with girls just because of the boys' larger size and greater muscle mass.

The influence of biology on gender differences can be located at any point on a chain of human development. This chain has four links, which involve *chromosomes, gonads, hormones,* and *neural, or brain, organization* (Rossi, 1984). Ordinarily, all of these links are highly interrelated, and the overall result is the differentiation of males and females. Thus, the genetic sex, a consequence of chromosomes, normally results in the same gonadal sex, which, in turn, normally results in the same hormonal sex, which normally results in a sex-typed brain organization.

Occasionally there are inconsistencies among the various sex links. For example, as a consequence of hormonal imbalances, a genetic female (XX chromosomes) may be born with masculine-appearing genitals. Such instances provide the scientist with an opportunity to explore the distinct and separate influences of various biological factors on the differentiation of males and females (Frieze et al., 1978, p. 83).

CHROMOSOMES.   At the moment of conception, the fertilized egg contains one pair of sex chromosomes, which determines genetic sex. Mothers always contribute an X to the sex-regulating pair, so that everybody receives at least one X. Fathers contribute either an X or a Y. If it is an X, the baby is a chromosomal female; if it is a Y, the baby is a chromosomal male.

Although the XX or XY chromosome pattern is duplicated in every cell of the human body, the influence of the sex chromosomes ends once their sex-determining message is sent to the gonads. If some chromosomal abnormality occurs, the result can be underdeveloped gonads—ovaries or testicles. These

(Text continued on page 80.)

BOX 3.1

PMS AND INTIMACY

In the first half of this century, menstruation was considered a biological "curse" and the price paid for being a woman. In the 1960s and 1970s it was argued that any symptoms of menstruation were the result of social conditioning—an "it's all in your head" type of approach. But research in the past decade suggests that premenstrual symptoms are real, not imaginary, and that there is indeed a physiological basis. "The monthly cycle of about 85 percent of menstruating women causes them to experience bodily or psychological changes" (Andrews, 1985, p. 52). Up to 10 percent of all women experience reactions that are severe enough to interfere with and disrupt their activities and interpersonal relationships.

Although more than 150 different symptoms have been linked to premenstrual syndrome (PMS), the most common are tension, depression, irritability, crying spells, anxiety, fatigue, clumsiness, swelling and tenderness in the breasts, headaches, backaches, abdominal bloating, and cravings for sweet and salty foods. The symptoms of PMS usually occur anywhere from two weeks to three days before the onset of menstruation. They generally cease shortly after menstruation has begun and are followed by a symptom-free phase in each cycle. In fact, during this symptom-free part of the cycle, a woman may experience high self-esteem, and many feel especially creative and productive (Andrews, 1985). But if a woman understands her body, she can actually enhance good days and alleviate bad days.

THE DARK SIDE OF PMS

The hormonal changes experienced by PMS sufferers can cause a range of problems.

> Her tolerance for pain is decreased so she notices joint pain and backaches that otherwise would not bother her. Her resistance to infection is lowered: hospital admissions . . . occur more often at premenstrual times.
>
> Before her period a woman may go on food binges, especially craving salty foods and chocolate. Yet eating salty foods increases water retention, enhancing the bloating she feels. . . .
>
> A woman's coordination may be affected as well. Some women report feeling clumsy right before their period. . . . Accidents are more likely to occur in the 48 hours before menstruation. . . . The most troubling aspects of PMS are depression, tension, and anxiety. (Andrews, 1985, p. 53)

TAKING CONTROL OF PMS

Most women can eliminate much of their PMS suffering with (1) communication and support from family members, (2) exercise, (3) changes in their diet, and (4) modification of vitamin intake (Andrews, 1985, p. 54).

Recommendations include specific exercises, eating small amounts of food at regular intervals rather than two or three large meals a day and avoiding salt, sugar and caffeine. Frequently, vitamins and minerals are recommended since good nutrition can help put your body in balance and thus influences the production of hormones.

The minerals that have been found to minimize the severity of various PMS symptoms are calcium, magnesium, zinc, iron, and the electrolyte potassium. The B vitamins and vitamins D, E, A, and C are important to the body's internal balance and they, too can diminish the intensity of PMS. In fact, some doctors use vitamin B-6 along with vitamin B complex, as the main treatment for PMS. (Andrews, 1985, p. 55)

If stronger medical treatment is advised, progesterone therapy is used. Although this approach is highly controversial and is without scientific support, some PMS sufferers have found their symptoms alleviated. It is very possible that no *one* solution will be found for all of the various types of PMS, but women are becoming innovative.

Many women today are learning to anticipate and utilize or control the effects of their hormones. Some professional women adjust their schedules so that they perform more analytical tasks before ovulation and undertake tough negotiations just prior to their periods. (Andrews, 1985, p. 54)

THE POSITIVE SIDE OF THE STORY

Although most research has focused on the negative side of women's monthly cycles, there are also benefits to the changing constellation of female hormones.

Around the time of ovulation some women have more energy, feel they accomplished a lot, and experience greater self-esteem and optimism. The majority of female athletes perform best at mid-cycle and during the two weeks after menstruation. Some women report feeling increased sexual desire premenstrually. (Andrews, 1985, p. 56)

THE EFFECT OF PMS ON INTIMACY

PMS can be a very real barrier to achieving an intimate relationship. A woman may suffer both physical and psychological symptoms. For example, the physical symptom of water retention can cause a woman to feel fat and ugly, which in turn may cause her to experience lowered self-esteem and doubt about her attractiveness. Most importantly, the emotional side effects of PMS can inhibit closeness right from the beginning of a relationship. Sometimes there are emotional outbursts—attacking of the person who is loved—causing anger and frustration between the couple. Some PMS suffer-

(Continued)

ers report feeling out of control during their premenstrual phase. This feeling often causes them to avoid interactions and withdraw, hoping to bypass situations of negative exchange (Roelofs, 1985).

During the premenstrual phase a woman's perceptions are sometimes distorted. Therefore, she may feel justified in her exaggerated feeling of anger over minor things. These reactions and rationalizations of her feelings confuse those around her and also serve to create distance in relationships. Her exaggerated responses to stressful situations serve to alienate the woman from others and cause her to incur feelings of guilt. The guilt feelings experienced can have a negative impact on potential intimacy. When a woman feels guilty for her moodiness or outbursts, her self-esteem suffers further. She might not even feel worthy of love and affection (Roelofs, 1985).

> The guilt may throw a woman into days or weeks of remorse and the cyclic depression and moodiness of PMS may continue into the symptom-free phase. Even though the hormonal basis for the emotional symptoms becomes normalized when the woman begins to menstruate, her poor self-concept and guilt can cause her to continue behavior and feelings similar to the PMS phase. Some women can accept comfort and understanding from a man at this time, but if a couple does not know what is happening, anger and distance usually result. (Roelofs, 1985)

It is therefore important that couples talk about and understand PMS. Unfortunately, many men see the women in their lives as unpredictable from month to month, and therefore they are wary of getting too close to them. A man may desire to be emotionally and physically close but be fearful of her "moods" and afraid of her anger. On the one hand, his commenting on her mood is often interpreted negatively by the woman. On the other hand, he is often rebuffed when he approaches her positively, and repeated rejection may cause him to lose feelings for her. He may then give up trying to be closer. A cycle develops where the woman feels unwanted and hurt and the man frustrated and angry; and distance grows as they do not really understand the possible basis for their conflicts. Men need factual knowledge about PMS and training in how to react to, and deal with, this situation (Roelofs, 1985).

---

abnormalities include *Turner's syndrome* (second X chromosome is defective or missing), *Klinefelter's syndrome* (a surplus of X or Y chromosomes), and the *Double-Y syndrome* (an extra Y chromosome).

GONADS AND HORMONES.   As the fertilized egg grows, cells cluster to form rudimentary organs. Some of these include sexual organs, called gonads. The gonads can develop into either testicles or ovaries. For six weeks after conception, XX and XY embryos continue to develop along the same neutral path. At the end of six weeks, the XY embryo develops in the male direction; the Y chromosome sends a message to the two gonads, ordering them to develop testicles. If no Y chromosome exists, the embryo continues for another six weeks before the gonads begin to develop into ovaries.

When the ovaries and testicles have differentiated, the gonads start to manufacture sex hormones. The male and female organs produce the same hormones but in different quantities and proportions. Chemically, all the hormones are closely related, but each hormone has its specific functions.

Testosterone (a type of androgen) is known as the masculinizing hormone, *estrogen*, the feminizing hormone. At puberty these two hormones determine such secondary characteristics as facial hair, voice level, and different body proportions. *Progesterone* is known as the pregnancy hormone because a woman's progesterone level goes up during pregnancy. It also increases after ovulation during the course of the menstrual cycle in preparation for a possible pregnancy. All of the sex hormones are normally circulating in every individual throughout life. Testicles produce enough testosterone to dominate the estrogen in a male, while ovaries produce enough estrogen to dominate the testosterone in the female.

The level of each sex hormone that is produced and the relative proportion among the sex hormones will differ somewhat among individual men and women. Neither do they remain at a constant level within a particular person. Normally there is variation within certain limits. However, variation beyond the normal limit—especially at a critical period such as in prenatal life—can have dramatic consequences (Money and Tucker, 1975).

One example of the many syndromes that can result from such deviations is the *adrenogenital syndrome* (AGS). Research on this syndrome has provided some clues as to how sex hormones affect behavior. Cases of

AGS have resulted from the administration of hormones to women during pregnancy, a common medical treatment during the 1940s to prevent miscarriages. This practice resulted in the fetus experiencing high concentrations of androgen, masculinizing hormones, of which testosterone is most significant.

Genetically female infants with this disorder are often born with fully or partially masculinized genitalia, even though their gonads are normal and female. But AGS can affect both male and female infants. If untreated, such children will continue to have high concentrations of androgen, resulting in premature puberty for boys and continuing development of masculine characteristics for girls. Cortisone therapy is now used, however, to control androgen levels, and the females' external sexual organs can be surgically "corrected."

June Reinisch (1981) studied a sample of children who were exposed early in their prenatal development to the same synthetic hormones that were administered to their mothers during pregnancy. When the AGS females were compared to their unexposed sisters on a measure for the potential for aggressive behavior, their scores were significantly higher. A significant difference in aggression was also found between exposed boys and their brothers.

Another study has shown that AGS girls, in comparison to a group of girls without AGS, preferred active outdoor games, including sports; they preferred boys as playmates; they preferred masculine toys; and they preferred pants to dresses. They were less interested in play and fantasy relating to maternalism (doll play, interest in infants, daydreams of pregnancy and motherhood) and marriage (Money and Ehrhardt, 1972). These findings support the hypothesis that behavior is influenced by exposure to hormones during early stages of development.

Another hormonal abnormality is the *androgen insensitivity syndrome*, which is an extreme abnormal hormonal condition affecting some males. The person who suffers from this syndrome is a genetic male who usually grows up female because the embryonic sex tissue did not respond to the masculinizing effects of the androgens. These individuals have what appear to be external female sex structures at birth but are lacking normal internal sex structures (Doyle, 1985).

NEURAL ORGANIZATION: THE BRAIN. A new area of research focuses on the brains of men and women. Scientists are trying to find out if differences between the sexes in the organization and functioning of their brains cause them to think and behave in different ways. A number of animal studies have indicated that hormone levels at a particular time early in development have a direct impact on the brain (Gorski et al., 1978; Goy, Bridson, and Young, 1964; McEwen, 1976).

Recent research on humans has indicated that early levels of sex hormones affect the pattern of nerve connections in specific parts of the brain, resulting in a characteristically male or female pattern of nerve circuits (McEwen, 1976). The brain, as it develops, follows a female pattern when there is an absence of high levels of testosterone. When testosterone is available to the brain to any marked degree, it then becomes more or less masculinized (Durden-Smith and de Simone, 1983).

Another area of brain research involves looking at each of the two brain hemispheres and comparing how they differ in their functioning between males and females. The human brain is divided into the right and the left hemispheres with some fibers connecting the two sides. Recent studies on split-brain subjects (individuals whose hemispheres have been separated with no remaining connecting fibers) suggest that each hemisphere

of the brain specializes in certain abilities: the left hemisphere specializing in verbal abilities and the right hemisphere specializing in spatial-visual perception (Sperry, 1982).

Epileptics who have had part of their right hemisphere removed to ease their seizures have also been studied. Since the visual center was believed to be located in this hemisphere, it was hypothesized that the epileptics with this part of the brain removed would do poorly on an abstract design test. Men did but the women, who had the same surgery, did not do as poorly.

Other studies have shown that if a particular mental function is localized in a particular hemisphere of the brain, men show more deficits than women. A woman's verbal and spatial abilities are less likely to be specialized on a particular side of the brain, while a man (for example, a right-handed man) is more likely to have his speech center on the left and spatial skills on the right (Goleman, 1978). Thus, most evidence suggests that males have *more specialization within each hemisphere* and *less processing activity between the hemispheres* than females.

But how do these differences in the way the hemispheres work affect interpersonal behavior? In particular, they may affect those interpersonal activities that combine linguistic and spatial skills.

Because women's hemispheres may be less specialized for spatial and linguistic functions, it may be easier for them to perform tasks which combine the two in a single activity, such as reading or understanding a person's behavior from his or her facial expression, body language, and words. (Witelson, 1976)

Because more processing between the hemispheres occurs in women, they may be better at doing things that require the activity of both hemispheres. For example, perceiving facial emotion, which is generally a right-hemisphere talent, is not hampered in women by activity of the left hemisphere's verbal centers occurring at the same time (Goleman, 1978). This finding could help explain the tendency for women to be better than men at empathizing; they can both recognize a person's emotion and respond verbally at the same time.

How these differences in brain symmetry are exactly translated into many of the behavioral differences in close relationships is still unclear. At this point there is only speculation. Moreover, critics of this research argue that any conclusion about the role of hemispheric specialization in the development of gender differences is premature (Huston, 1983).

In summary, evidence suggests that there may be some biological bases for gender differences in behavioral patterns. In particular, aggressive and dominant behaviors in males and empathy and nurturance in females appear to have biological links. But does the acceptance of biological factors imply that the behavior is stable, inevitable, and resistant to change? By no means. As we learn more about specific biological mechanisms and about their interaction with social forces, we find that behavior with a biological base can indeed be changed. For example, brain specialization patterns that result in gender-differentiated spatial-visual skills can be largely eliminated with appropriate training (Parsons, 1982). So to conclude that some trait or social behavior is biologically influenced *does not mean that it is resistant to change* via some environmental influences.

The Socialization of Gender Differences

Although biological processes seem to influence some behavioral differences between the sexes, society and its cultural norms probably play the more significant role. So strong is the impact of socialization that almost all biological tendencies can be changed by altering the social or cultural conditions. The research of anthropologist Margaret Mead illustrates the force of different cultural norms on gender behavior. (See Box 3.2.) It is through the process of *socialization*—that is, an internalizing of society's norms, values, and expectations—that males and females learn particular gender-typed behavior. *Gender norms* are the particular prescriptions of behaviors, goals, and attitudes for each sex. Behavior that is consistent with gender norms comprises *gender roles*. Thus, gender norms are considered as guidelines for gender roles (Doyle, 1985).

Two examples of traditional female gender norms are the *motherhood mandate* and the *marriage mandate*. The motherhood mandate is the expectation for women to have babies and become mothers (Russo, 1976). At an early age, girls are encouraged and reinforced for motherhood by playing with dolls ("What a cute little mommy you are!"). Motherhood can become a central feature of a woman's self-concept. The *marriage mandate* is the expectation for women to marry. For many women marriage becomes a *"rite de passage,* an entrance into the world of adults, freedom from parental control, and a means for fulfilling a basic tenet of womanhood" (Doyle, 1985, p. 89).

Male gender norms are not so closely related to the family roles of spouse and parent as the female norms. James Doyle (1985) has categorized five male gender norms.

1. *Antifeminine:* Men must be the opposite of women to prove themselves manly or masculine in the ideal sense, that is, unemotional, independent, and assertive.
2. *Successful:* By performing better than others at work, sports, or whatever else men do, a man proves his manhood.

BOX 3.2

LOOKING ACROSS CULTURES

Dramatically different gender roles have been found for men and women in various societies of the world. Among the best-known research is that of anthropologist Margaret Mead in her book *Sex and Temperament in Three Primitive Societies* (1935). As a result of her fieldwork in New Guinea, Mead argued that cultural learning—not anything biologically innate—was responsible for the roles that males and females played. Mead studied three small groups—the Arapesh, the Mundugamor, and the Tchambuli—all existing within a hundred miles of each other.

Both men and women of the Arapesh displayed personalities that in American society would be described as "feminine." The two sexes were said to be nonaggressive, nurturant, cooperative, gentle, compliant, and responsive to the needs of others. In contrast, among the Mundugamor, the two sexes were mostly "masculine" in their behavior, at least from the point of view of American society. Both men and women, in this tribe of headhunters and cannibals, were described by Mead as aggressive, ruthless, and violent. Compared to the Arapesh, the Mundugamor were very sexual individuals. The Tchambuli were again different from the other two groups. Here Mead found the exact reversal of the gender roles that have traditionally existed in American society. The women were dominant, controlling, impersonal, and not adorned. The men were more emotional, more dependent, and less responsible, and had decorated and adorned bodies as well.

Mead's studies provide evidence for the argument that probably any behavior can be learned. If there are biological predispositions for gender-role behavior, it appears that these can be overriden by cultural experiences. But it should be pointed out that males still held the power in all three groups studied by Mead. Even among the Tchambuli, where women held significant economic influence, they still had to participate in a tribal ritual that celebrated the inferiority of women. Recently, Mead's work has come under criticism. She is accused of doing incomplete research and of finding what she wanted to find to prove previously held theories (Freeman, 1983). In any event there is considerable cross-cultural evidence that cultural learning has a major impact on gender roles.

---

3. *Aggressive:* Men are expected to use force in dealing with conflict rather than using nonviolent—"feminine"—means.

4. *Sexual:* Sexual conquest is proof of one's manhood.

5. *Self-reliant:* Males should be "cool," in control, and tough in most situations.

The male gender norms, in particular, hinder the development of intimacy by discouraging males from expressing emotions, admitting dependence and weaknesses, and allowing themselves to be vulnerable. Females, to the extent that they expect their male partners to behave according to these gender norms, will discourage the development of intimacy also. Although all males and females do not fulfill these gender norms, that in and of itself does not deny their presence and influence (Doyle, 1985).

Adherence to gender norms can differ according to the social class, race, and ethnicity of families. Lower-class white children demonstrate a greater degree of traditional gender stereotypic behaviors than middle-class or upper-class white children (Nadelman, 1974). It appears that black children in general may not learn as rigid a distinction between male and female roles (White, 1972). A role flexibility between black males and females in child rearing and household responsibilities discourages black children from learning rigid gender role distinctions (R. Hill, 1972). More specifically, husbands and wives may even reverse roles regarding child care. Nontraditional female roles, such as women working full time, seem to be more widely accepted by black males than by white males (Axelson, 1970). Black females also appear to hold less stereotypic attitudes toward gender roles in general than do white females (Gold and Ange, 1974).

Male gender norms similar to those generally found in the United States are evidenced in other cultures also. For example, the traditional Mexican ideal of *machismo* (manliness or virility) expects men to be "aggressive, sexually experienced, courageous, and protective of their women (who include mother, sisters and wives) and their children." To complement this role is the female ideal of a "humble, submissive, and virtuous woman, devoted to her home and children" (Falicov, 1982, p. 139).

SOCIALIZING AGENTS. A *socializing agent* is "any person or social institution that shapes a person's values, beliefs, or behaviors" (Doyle, 1985). A child learns gender norms from primary socializing agents such as the family. This group communicates in subtle or overt ways messages of how boys and girls should act.

Starting at birth, parents treat the sexes differently. Researchers have found that parents view their children more according to gender stereotypes than according to their children's actual behaviors (Lamb, Owen, and Chase-Lansdale, 1979). In one study of fathers, they saw their one-day-old male infants as firmer, having larger features, better coordinated, more alert, stronger, and hardier. Fathers of daughters in the study saw their newborn daughters as softer, having finer features, more awkward, more inattentive, weaker, and more delicate (Rubin, Provenzano, and Luria, 1974). Gender-related differences were perceived by these fathers even though there were no differences in actual behavior. Beginning at a child's birth, parents play a socializing role, which continues throughout childhood into adulthood. Starting with the way they play with their toddlers, to the way they assign household chores, parents are reinforcing gender roles.

Two areas in which parents in particular reinforce the two sexes for different behaviors are dressing them differently and encouraging them toward certain interests, toys, and play activities thought to be appropriate for their own sex. Adults encourage children to play with sex-typed toys and strongly discourage them from engaging in play activities they consider appropriate only for the other sex. For the most part, boys receive more pressure than girls not to engage in sex-inappropriate behavior. The activities that girls are not suppose to engage in are much less clearly defined and less firmly enforced. Tomboyish behavior for a daughter is more acceptable than sissy behavior for a son.

Even when parents try not to impose gender-role norms on their children, often

Through socialization, males and females learn particular gender-typed behaviors.

the actual behavior of the parents will contradict their stated expectations for their sons' or daughters' behavior. Fathers in one study stated that they would like their sons to be able to experience and express a fuller range of feelings, including affection, intimacy, and vulnerability. The majority of fathers, however, were not modeling the kinds of behavior they said they would like their sons to be able to exhibit. For example, 90 percent of the fathers surveyed reported that they wanted to communicate to their child that it was acceptable for men to show emotion—"It is good for men to cry." But most did not ever express their own feelings through tears (Martinson, 1981).

Parents may be significant socializing agents in children's lives, but many other influential people teach gender-role behavior as well. Preliminary results of a major ten-year study (Jacklin and Maccoby, 1984) indicate that it's not only parents who convince their children that boys and girls behave in different ways; it is also society—teachers, neighbors, relatives, and the media—who treat children according to gender stereotypes. Children have an entire "smorgasbord of models" to copy, with the result that each of us is a unique composite of many influences (*Marriage and Divorce Today*, April 30, 1984).

Television is a storehouse of gender stereotypes. The average child spends more time watching television than in any other single activity, except sleep (Comstock et al., 1978; Gross and Jeffries-Fox, 1978). From the 1960s to the late 1970s, the proportion of adult women TV characters who were employed outside their homes gradually increased, but it remained well below the actual percentage of women who were employed in the American population (DeFleur, 1964; Tedesco, 1974). When female TV characters were shown working outside the home, the majority held occupations associated with traditional "women's work" such as nursing and teaching (Kalisch and Kalisch, 1984). Male TV characters still projected independent, strong, silent "macho" images, as, for example, the detective who never breaks under pressure, who is emotionless and independent from needing anyone. Female characters are often seen as being dominated by a man, "hysterical," or helplessly clinging to a man for support.

Identification Theory

A child's relationship with the same-sex parent can have a tremendous impact on the learning of behavior typical of that particular gender. Through the process of identification, the child takes the same-sex parent as a model. Thus, *identification* is seen as a means by which a child acquires the behaviors that society expects of him or her as an adult.

Identification theory is one of the few theories that outline two distinct pathways by which males and females are socialized into their gender roles. Sociologist Nancy Chodorow (1978) uses this theory to explain how males are socialized to be "independent" and females are socialized for "interdependence." She proposes: "Girls and boys develop different relational capacities and senses of self as a result of growing up in a family in which women mother" (p. 173). So the differences between males and females in their intimate behavior is said to be based on the simple fact that *a woman* is usually a child's primary caregiver—the one who feeds, nurtures, and comforts the infant. A woman is the first person to whom an attachment is made and with whom a bond is formed.

The development of gender differences then begins with the handling of the infant's dependence on, and attachment to, the mother. For a girl, her attachment is to the same person with whom she identifies in terms of her sex. Hence, it is fairly easy for her to learn behavior appropriate to her sex from this person with whom she has a close relationship. Her sense of herself as a female then develops through this personal connection with her mother. "She experiences herself always as more continuous with another; and the maintenance of close personal connections will continue to be one of life's essential themes for her" (L. Rubin, 1982, pp. 58–59).

It's a different and more complicated story for a boy. He must deny his attachment to his mother and repress his dependence on her in order to identify with a person of the same sex, his father. Hence, the boy tries to separate himself from his mother. Also, the mother usually is encouraging her son to separate from her, at least more so than her daughter. She wants him to be more independent and to take on "male behaviors." Thus, learning what it means to be a male involves the denial of attachment and dependence on the mother.

The gender-role socialization of the young boy is further complicated by the fact that a deep attachment and identification with his father is often difficult to obtain. His father, with whom he is expected to identify, has, until this time, usually been of secondary importance in his life. If a father is rarely at home or even totally absent, the boy may shift his primary identification from a woman to any man or perhaps even to an idealized representation of the absent father.

Unlike boys, girls are not required totally to sever their ties to their mothers in order to develop and learn appropriate social behavior. It is argued that women "cultivate" the qualities of nurturance and intimacy because they grow up identifying with and imitating their mothers. The girl finds herself in connection with and close to another human being; she doesn't need to fear closeness with another.

How does this process of identification more specifically affect male and female differences in terms of intimate behavior? As adults—when both sexes are trying to achieve closeness—that closeness resembles in many ways the physical and emotional bond they first had with their mothers. As a man attempts to build such a bond with another woman, feelings of dependence for emotional needs on another woman become threatening to his ideal of masculinity. He may continually defend himself against the dependence he once had on his mother, a mother who later "pushed him away."

An adult woman, on the other hand, does not have to repress her feelings of dependence. She can more easily form an emotional bond with a man and, in addition, usually with other women and with her children as well. Therefore, she is generally less threatened by intimate relationships than men are (K. Schaffer, 1981).

According to this theory, men's social behavior is characterized by a forced independence and the denial of a need for close relationships. Women, in contrast, develop certain qualities consistent with their mother's behaviors—nurturance, emotional support, and empathy, among others. For men, however, independence and disconnection dominate their early development and inhibit the growth of more intimate traits.

Chodorow (1978) reminds us that these different socialization pathways for males and females occur within the context of a society that encourages a woman to define her identity primarily in terms of her family roles (mother and wife) and relates a man's identity to a nonfamilial role (occupation). This situation has traditionally resulted in the mother doing practically all the parenting

while the father spends most of his time working outside the home. Chodorow's view (1978) is that parenting done solely by the mother is "bad for mother and child alike. . . . Mothers in such a setting are liable to overinvest in and overwhelm the relationship. . . . The current organization of parenting separates children and men" (p. 217). Her strategy to change gender roles involves a "fundamental reorganization of parenting, so that primary parenting is shared between men and women" (p. 215). Equal parenting would result in children being dependent from the outset on people of both genders and in establishing a sense of self in relation to both. "In this way, masculinity would not become tied to denial of dependence and devaluation of women" (p. 218). By having strong emotional attachments to both mother and father, children will learn behaviors of both genders instead of adhering to extreme and rigid gender roles.

The Biosocial Perspective

The biosocial explanation of gender behavior attempts to integrate the biological and social theories. It suggests that the differences in behavior between the sexes are a result of a genetic propensity as well as cultural learning. Alice Rossi (1984), a sociologist and prominent proponent of this theory, states that

> . . . my assumption is that persistent differences between men and women, and variations in the extent to which such differences are found along the life line, are a function of underlying biological processes of sexual differentiation and maturation as well as social and historical processes. (p. 2)

A major proposition of this theory is that modern men and women are still equipped with certain innate behavior predispositions passed down through history. These innate differences then influence the ease with which men and women can learn certain behavioral patterns.

Proponents of this theory suggest that numerous gender differences in social and cognitive skills are the result of "precultural influences." Rossi (1984) notes the following such differences:

> *Females are more sensitive to context, show greater skill in picking up peripheral information and process information faster; they are more attracted to human faces and respond to nuances of facial expression as they do to nuances of sound. Males are better at object manipulation in space, can rotate objects in their mind, read maps and perform in mazes better, and show a better sense of direction. Males are more rule-bound, less sensitive to situation nuance. (p. 13)*

These differences appear and can be observed at very early ages. Rossi states that male infants are more likely to be attracted to the movement of objects, and females are more likely to be attracted to changing expressions on human faces. In addition, girl babies are startled by sound more easily than boy babies and are soothed by a human voice, while boys respond to physical contact and movement (p. 13).

Taking these traits altogether, we are left with the impression that females are predisposed to be more responsive to people and better at receiving, interpreting, and giving back communications than males are. Males have an edge in dealing with the physical world through better spatial visualization and the manipulation of physical objects. The label "female intuition," which carries a somewhat derogatory overtone, may be the result of the tendency for females to be more sensitive to sound and face and to process peripheral information rapidly and make quick judgments of emotional nuance. "It also suggests an easier connection between feelings and their expression in words among women" (Rossi, 1984, p. 13).

Are men and women then predestined to behave differently? Most proponents of the biosocial perspective do not assume a "genetic *determination*" of behavior for either men or women. Rather they argue that there are simply certain "constitutional propensities" that may shape behaviors, but these behaviors are not necessarily fixed and are amenable to change through socialization.

Do biosocial theorists conclude that the sexes should not try to change in a direction different from their biological predispositions? On the contrary, Rossi stresses that society may benefit from the "blending" of traditional masculine and feminine traits. Research has found that scientists *high on both* masculinity and femininity scales were the *most* scientifically productive. The highest scientific attainment was among those *high* in subject mastery and work commitment and *lowest* in competitiveness, a profile that again combines both traditionally feminine with traditionally masculine characteristics. Rossi concludes, "No individual and no society can benefit from a circumstance in which men fear intimacy and women fear impersonality" (1984, p. 15).

"Compensatory training"—additional training to compensate for certain biological tendencies—will be required if changes are to be made in each gender, since biological predispositions make certain things easier for one sex to learn than the other (Rossi, 1984). Unisex socialization of education in itself will not eliminate the differences between the sexes. "Compensatory training" is needed for the particular weaknesses in certain areas for each gender. For example, merely putting men in a child-care situation will not dramatically enhance their capacity to be nurturing, empathic, and sensitive fathers. Some extra training will be necessary to prepare them for this role. Many women have already become more successfully assertive through assertiveness training classes.

The Functionalist Explanation

The *functionalist* orientation to gender differences arises out of societal "needs" that are said to serve a purpose for society as a whole. Functionalists argue that it is useful for a society to divide work along sex lines. Talcott Parsons and Robert Bales (1953), the orginators of this theory, have argued that the family works best when the father assumes the *instrumental role* of physically supporting the family and dealing with the outside world. The mother serves in an *expressive role,* providing the love, emotional support, and service that sustains the family. Since women, on the one hand, bear and nurse children, it is argued that they need to spend much of their time near home, and they should take on most of the domestic duties. Men, on the other hand, being physically stronger, more dominant, and less nurturant, are more useful in the world of work outside the home.

Funtionalism represents a conservative approach to understanding gender differences. It is primarily concerned with those social structures, roles, and processes that contribute to the maintenance of an equilibrium in the social system. Forces that encourage change in the status quo—including those that result in any type of conflict—are often viewed as deviant and dysfunctional.

An underlying assumption of this approach is that any activity or role that has traditionally existed over time has a function and that "if it exists, it is good." In applying this to gender roles, if males do not accomplish the instrumental goal of working and making money, and if females do not fulfill the expressive function of emotional support and caring for the husband and offspring, the pattern is considered to be disruptive and, hence, "pathological" (Chafetz, 1974).

Functionalism has been under attack since the 1960s, particularly by feminists. Perhaps in some societies of an earlier era, it was functional for men and women to have specifically assigned tasks. In modern society, however, the rigid assignment of roles by gender is no longer necessary. Physical strength is not a factor in most occupations today. Also, smaller families and childless families eliminate many household tasks. In spite of such criticism, however, the functional approach is still frequently used in marriage and family textbooks, and some instructors continue to teach these traditional views as "scientific truths."

MALES AND FEMALES IN TRANSITION

Societal influences since the 1960s have indeed changed the ways in which males and females view their roles. The women's movement in particular has opened new opportunities for females in terms of education, jobs, and income. In an attempt to avoid what was perceived as an unhappy life-style of their homemaking mothers, the majority of women are now opting for part-time or full-time careers, many in areas that were previously dominated by men.

More opportunities involve more decisions for women regarding career, marriage, and family. Although these choices allow females a certain amount of control over their lives, particular decisions are not always that easy to make. Most young women today express a desire to have it all—a career, husband, and children (Spanier, 1986). In reality a woman's overall sense of well-being is de-

A woman's sense of well-being is dependent on both her work and her close relationships. Women today attempt to combine both mastery and intimacy in their lives.

pendent *both* on her work—usually paid work—and her intimate relationships (Baruch, Barnett, and Rivers, 1983).

Hence, women want both a sense of mastery (work in one's society) and a sense of pleasure (feeling intimate with others). Figure 3.2 illustrates that those married women who are employed rank the highest on both the mastery and pleasure scales of well-being. Groups of working women are all in or near the top half of the mastery scale, all higher than the groups of homemakers. Homemakers with children appear to be doing well in terms of pleasure (intimacy), but a feeling of mastery is mostly absent from their lives.

Those homemakers with no children experience neither mastery or pleasure (Baruch, Barnett, and Rivers, 1983).

Can a women take on all the roles of wife, mother, and worker without excessive stress? Won't strain result from trying to juggle these roles? The findings of a study by Grace Baruch and her colleagues (1983) indicate that involvement in multiple roles has a strengthening effect, rather than a negative result, on the well-being of women. This is especially true if the woman had a highly prestigious job. According to the researchers, the number of roles a woman occupies has little to do with her level of role strain. What

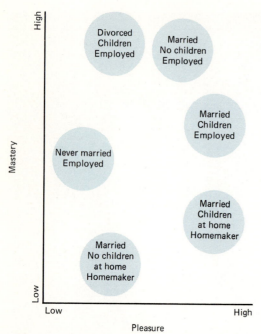

Figure 3.2   Women's rankings on mastery and pleasure. (*Source:* Adapted from Baruch, Barnett, and Rivers, 1983, p. 37.)

is more important is the nature of her job and her support network. The researchers also conclude that husbands are not doing much more work around the household, but that women are doing less, giving up "dispensable household tasks" and spending some leisure time for themselves.

No one life pattern fits all women equally well, but it would appear to be to the advantage of women to design, as much as possible, combinations of roles that fit them. This process of finding a satisfying life pattern can be exciting but also frightening for women.

It's risky, but essential, for a woman to look at her own life and make her own choices. Just because there are so many choices, today's women probably face more conflict

than women did in past generations. But the old way was hardly problem-free. There was only one acceptable life pattern for women, and for the many women whose talents and personalities were an imperfect fit with that pattern, the cost was depression and lack of self-esteem. The new cost may be periods of struggle and conflict. (Baruch, Barnett, and Rivers, 1983, p. 149)

As women carve out new frontiers for their lives, men are also forced to examine and reevaluate their life-styles and roles. Many men are slowly recognizing their desire for emotional closeness and are therefore beginning to place their interpersonal relationships at a higher priority level. They are also expressing more of a desire to be intimate with their children (Veroff, Douvan, and Kulka, 1981). Nevertheless, the extent to which men have been successful in establishing such intimacy is still well below this desire. Women still consistently score higher than men on measures of interpersonal communication, empathy, and the expression of feelings and affection (Rubenstein and Shaver, 1982). But there is pressure on men to change their personalities to include those traits and qualities traditionally thought of as feminine.

In the process of changing behaviors, men and women find themselves in various dilemmas as they try to adjust to each other's change. On the one hand, women degrade the "sexist macho" ideal but sometimes find it hard to respect men who are emotionally expressive and vulnerable. Although demanding that husbands be involved in child raising, some wives show signs of resenting it. On the other hand, a man's desire to see his wife change and become an equal partner conflicts with his reluctance to lose a sense of the power and control in the relationship. A man wants a woman to be strong, independent, and assertive, but he becomes romantically attracted to the woman who plays the traditional feminine role of being passive, dependent, and submissive (Goldberg, 1982).

In order for a man and a woman to attain intimacy, individuals need a blending of the positive traits of both genders. This doesn't mean rejecting certain qualities typical of one's own sex, but adding on and expanding to include other desirable traits. For women, this means pursuing a sense of achievement and learning to be assertive; for men, it means learning to become expressive, sensitive, and warm. Some women over the past 20 years have felt that they have had to deny their dependence, emotions, and fears and become "macho females." Driven to attain successful careers, these women actually developed a new fear of intimacy (Marshall, 1984).

How we accomplish this blending of traits to achieve intimacy begins with identifying the sources of various attributes in biology and culture. Biological predispositions may make certain things easier for one sex to learn than for the other sex. With knowledge of this predisposition in advance, some compensatory training for each sex could be provided in families, in schools, and in the workplace. Change may be slow, but we must first understand and respect the qualities of each sex and actively encourage children to absorb the socially desirable attributes of both sexes (Rossi, 1984).

CHAPTER REVIEW

1. In studying the complexities of close relationships it is crucial to have an understanding of how gender differences impinge on a couple's ability to develop intimacy. Males, in general, rank higher than females on assertiveness and aggressiveness. Women are more likely than men to admit dependence, to disclose their feelings, to exchange positively, to be emphatic, and to be tactually expressive.

2. Evidence suggests that there may be some biological bases for gender differences in behavior—in particular, aggressive and dominant behaviors in males and empathy and nurturance behaviors in females. Biology can influence gender at any point on the chain of human development involving chromosomes, gonads, hormones, and neural organization.

3. Society exerts its greatest influence on gender differences through the process of socialization. Socializing agents such as parents, teachers, and television models facilitate the learning of gender roles.

4. According to the identification theory, a child's relationship with the same-sex parent can have an impact on the learning of behavior typical of a particular gender. The development of gender differences is said to begin with the infant's dependence on and attachment to the mother.

5. A biosocial explanation suggests that gender differences result from a genetic propensity as well as cultural learning. A major thesis of this theory is that males and females today are still equipped with certain innate behavior predispositions passed down through history.

6. The functionalist orientation states that gender differences arise out of societal "needs" that serve a purpose for society as a whole. Rather conservative in their approach, functionalists argue that it is useful for society to divide work along sex lines—for example, males assuming an instrumental role and females playing an expressive role.

7. Contemporary society is becoming more accepting of a wider variety of behaviors for men and women, including behaviors that have traditionally been assigned to one or the other sex. But the full acceptance of such changes has yet to be realized. Some women still cringe at the sight of a man showing feelings of weakness and dependence. And many males may still have difficulty accepting females as assertive, equal partners in their marital relationships.

Love, Sexuality, and Close Relationships

4

The Meanings
of Love

Love may indeed, as the song suggests, "make the world go around," but when people are really pressed to explain just what love is, their answers are quite varied. Some say, "You just *feel* it." "It's *giving*," according to many individuals. Others say, "It's just something that you *know* when it comes along." Another response is that love exists "when another person meets *your needs*." Still other people indicate, "It's when you are *attached* to a person." And finally there are always some individuals who insist that "love can't really be defined," and they become angry if anyone tries to analyze it too much.

If we check the dictionary we find 24 definitions under the word *love* (*Random House Dictionary of the English Language*, 1973, p. 849). So one word—love—is used to describe many types of human emotions, thoughts, and behavior. *Love* is also one of the most often used words in Western society. But still confusion reigns. And, to compound the problem even more, we also love our dogs, apple pie, and particular kinds of music.

Love is certainly complex. For example, what is the difference between loving someone and being *in love*? Is love a process or can it come instantly, such as in "love at first sight"? Many people speak about *making love*, and others about *falling in love*—an experience that some say happens by accident.

The whole matter is further complicated by those who say that there are many different kinds of love. The problem then becomes, how do we know which type of love a person is talking about? Two people who say "I love you" may have two quite different meanings in mind. A person romantically infatuated with another individual will probably be devastated if told that he or she is "loved as a friend." Because of all of this confusion about love we must ask the question: Is love really just "one big mess" or is it just that we don't understand it very well?

THE STUDY OF LOVE

There has been relatively little scientific research done on love. In the 1950s, psychologist Abraham Maslow criticized social scientists for neglecting the study of love. He argued that despite the importance of love, upon which marriage is built, none of the sociology or psychology textbooks deal with the topic.

Three reasons have been suggested as to why the study of love has been neglected (Berscheid and Walster, 1978). First, love was considered to belong to the field of romance, not of science. The view was held that in some mysterious way a person was attracted to his or her predestined beloved (Burgess and Wallin, 1953). Thus it was not considered even possible to study such a topic scientifically. The second reason research on love was neglected in the past was that "until fairly recently experimental research into romantic love was 'taboo.' " In the 1920s a University of Minnesota professor was fired for approving a questionnaire dealing with passionate love. In the early 1950s sociologist Nelson Foote received cynical and joking comments from his colleagues while preparing an article entitled "Love." Third, love was not studied because social scientists were simply not sure how to go about studying it (Berscheid and Walster, 1978).

By the 1970s love had become a more acceptable subject for study. The first government grant to study love was awarded to social psychologists Elaine Walster of the University of Wisconsin and Ellen Berscheid of the University of Minnesota. The grant, awarded by the National Science Foundation (NSF), was for $84,000 to continue work on passionate and companionate love. But Wisconsin's Senator William Proxmire was outraged that government funds would be spent for the study of love and gave the grant his famous Golden Fleece Award. The senator fired off the following press release:

> *I object to this not only because no one—not even the National Science Foundation—can argue that falling in love is a science; not only because I'm sure that even if they spend $84 million or $84 billion they wouldn't get an answer that anyone would believe.* I'm also against it because I don't want the answer.
>
> *I believe that 200 million other Americans want to leave some things in life a mystery, and right at the top of things we don't want to know is why a man falls in love with a woman and vice versa. (Walster and Walster, 1978, p. viii)*

After Senator Proxmire's objection to ''squandering'' the people's money, the NSF backed down from supporting further research on love. So while in the academic world it had become more acceptable to study love, politicians and religious leaders in the 1970s were still quite uncomfortable with the topic. In support of Proxmire's position a retired bishop said in the *Detroit News* that ''We already know why people fall in love'' (Walster and Walster, 1978, p. viii). Research on love to this day has remained largely unfunded.

One meaningful unfunded study was that of social psychologist Zick Rubin's research on liking and loving (1970). He conceptualized love as ''an attitude held by a person toward a particular other person involving predispositions to think, feel, and behave in certain ways toward the other person'' (p. 265). A condensed version of the love scale that Rubin developed is shown in Box 4.1. An individual's total score reveals how many different ways one person loves another person. When love feelings toward one's own sex were considered by Rubin, women loved

other women much more than men loved other men.

Aspects of Love

Most writers who use the word *love* don't bother to define specifically what it is they are talking about. An effort is made in this section clearly to conceptualize a model and definition of love. There appear to be four key aspects of love. These are attachment, emotion, thought, and behavior. These aspects are conceptually distinct but usually interrelated. The view of love presented in this chapter expands the definition cited by Zick Rubin above (1970).

LOVE AS ATTACHMENT. What do a person's love for his or her spouse, mother, friend, and dog have in common? Each object of love involves an attachment. Each may be so important to us that we may say that we ''love'' that person or animal. We love and become attached to others for a number of reasons. Being social animals, human beings do not want to be alone. Loneliness, or the fear of it, motivates most people to develop love attachments.

An attachment develops in all but a few marriages if the spouse is accessible and if the relationship offers at least minimal rewards. But most people are already attached in courtship. Attachment is supported in dating and marriage by mutual availability, as well as by the relative unavailability of others. Sociologist Robert Weiss found that no more than possibly 5 percent of the marriages he studied did not involve an attachment to a spouse (1975).

Attachments once developed have a tendency to persist. Attachments and other aspects of love often remain after a couple has separated or even divorced. Children will usually feel attachment even toward parents

BOX 4.1

A LOVE SCALE

A nine-item condensed version of Zick Rubin's original love scale is shown below. Put the name of the person that you love in the blank spaces and count up the total number of statements that you agree with as a measure of the intensity of your love. Compare your results with your partner. In addition, you may want to try to figure out what aspect of love—feeling, thought, or behavior—each statement is measuring.

1. I feel that I can confide in _____ about virtually everything.

2. I would do almost anything for _____ .

3. If I could never be with _____ I would feel miserable.

4. If I were lonely, my first thought would be to seek _____ out.

5. One of my primary concerns is _____ 's welfare.

6. I would forgive _____ for practically anything.

7. I feel responsible for _____ 's well being.

8. I would greatly enjoy being confided in by _____ .

9. It would be hard for me to get along without _____ .

SOURCE: *Z. Rubin, 1973, p. 216.*

who have abused them. Feelings of hate can even sometimes be interspersed with attached love. The loss of an attachment figure causes "separation anxiety" both in children and adults. Such anxieties provide testimony both to human dependencies and the power of love objects.

LOVE AS AN EMOTION. Love is most commonly defined as an emotion, or feeling. Emotions and feelings are used interchangeably here. Love is one of many emotions such as anger, happiness, fear, embarrassment, joy, grief, excitement, guilt, and jealousy. Most emotions have physiological responses connected with them. Fear, for example, can

cause the heart to race, the blood pressure to rise, and the adrenaline to flow.

Love is different from many other emotions in that it may or may not be accompanied by a physiological reaction. When one feels love for one's parents, bodily changes are not likely. Intense romantic love or infatuation, however, may involve both a feeling and a physical response. Thus it can be argued that in the emotional state of passionate love two conditions are necessary. "One will not experience passionate love unless physiologically aroused, but, given arousal, it is still not love unless the individual labels it love. If the situation is such that it is reasonable to attribute the aroused state to passionate love, then the individual will experience love" (Hendrick and Hendrick, 1983, p. 105).

However, some negative emotions, fear for example, produce most of the same physiological symptoms as passionate love. In addition, there is evidence that negative emotions, such as those resulting from being rejected by one's lover, can actually greatly increase one's feelings of love for that person. It is obvious that cognitive factors, such as those involved in labeling physiological arousal, are intertwined with emotions.

One of the problems with emphasizing the emotional dimension of love is that feelings seem to come and go, sometimes rather quickly. One of the reasons the divorce rate is so high in the United States is that many people see love as a feeling, a romantic, idealized feeling at that. When the heightened romantic feeling dies, as it usually does, some people indicate that they are no longer in love, that they made a mistake, and that they want to attempt to capture the romantic high again with another partner. Alexander Lowen (1972) argues that love as a feeling is not subject to one's willful control. Also, feelings, because of their "now" orientation, do not necessarily impose responsibilities or obligations for tomorrow. Indeed, when the feeling of love dies, it is often very difficult, if not impossible, to rekindle.

LOVE AS THOUGHTS. As mentioned, thoughts, or the cognitive aspects of love, are usually inextricably bound up with the emotional aspect. Besides experiencing feelings for another, one also thinks about the other person. Thus all feelings, including love, are guided by information processing. In our interaction with others we gain insight and information about our own feelings; we learn cognitively about our feelings. Humans perceive existing and potential rewards and costs and integrate them into thoughts about the potential for love with the people with whom they interact (Z. Rubin, 1973).

Zick Rubin (1973) argues that the processes of becoming committed in love relationships are to a large extent cognitive ones. But the thought of total commitment embraces the future as well as the present. The thoughts accompanying love involve more concern with the conscious meaningfulness of a broader spectrum of possible rewards (and costs) as well as the obligations involved with loving someone (Lowen, 1972).

One can still, however, be influenced by unreality in the form of cognitive fantasies—say, for example, that of a "perfect person" who is to be our "one and only." The anticipatory rewards in our thoughts may become clouded by not seeing another person accurately. It is not unusual to find conflict between what the "heart" and the "mind" say to do. For example, a young woman may really *feel* that she loves and needs a particular man, but her *thoughts* tell her that he really isn't good for her—"he's a bum," "he will never work," "he'll always be into drugs."

In no way do the authors mean to infer that emotions and feelings are nonrational and that thoughts and cognitive thinking are the only rational activities. Both feelings and thoughts are rational. They are real and represent "facts" to the individual experiencing them. There is nothing irrational about feeling the emotion of happiness on our wedding day or the emotion of fear when our lives are in danger. The all-too-common belief that emotions are irrational and cognitive activity is logical and rational only confuses the picture.

LOVE AS BEHAVIOR. We believe that the most important aspect of love is behavior. If love is not expressed in actions, it represents

"*Technically, I do love you.*"

Drawing by William Hamilton; © 1975. The New Yorker Magazine, Inc.

Liza Doolittle hurls forth her song to Fredie Hill:

> *Sing me no song, read me no rhyme,*
>   *don't waste my time, show me.*
> *Don't talk of June, don't talk of fall,*
>   *don't talk at all, show me.*
> *Don't talk of love lasting till time,*
>   *make me no undying vow. Show me now.*

Most people in love know that words can never truly express their deep feelings of love. The best way really to communicate love is to show it through verbal *and nonverbal* behavior (see Box 4.2). Actions do speak louder than words. But while behavior can show love, it is not the same as love. A specific behavior could be carried out for a variety of reasons, love being only one possible reason. Therefore, says Zick Rubin, "no single report or observation can be taken as a fully adequate assessment of an underlying attitude" (1973, p. 32). There are two ways in which behavior is involved in love—giving and receiving.

just empty words or feelings. People's behavior is the means by which they demonstrate their thoughts and emotions. Thus, again, emotions, cognitive activity, and behavior are all interconnected. One or another aspect may predominate in a particular individual, but usually all three are present, at least to some degree. Once more, each aspect of love has a strong influence in determining or changing the state of the other two aspects. Therefore, feelings and thoughts not only motivate us to exhibit positive behavior toward a person, but loving behavior in itself can also help determine another's feelings and thoughts toward us. Love as behavior is stressed in the musical *My Fair Lady* where

Love as giving. If there is one widely recognized aspect of loving behavior it is giving. To many people the word *love* is synonymous with giving behavior. Most religions of the world define love primarily as giving. The Bible focuses on two types of love—first, God as a giver of love and second, directives toward humans to give love to other humans. Love as a "feeling" is not emphasized in the Bible.

Love in religious books is often defined not only as giving but as *altruistic* giving. The Greek word *agape* is defined as "altruistic giving." It is putting other people before your own self-interests; it emphasizes sacrifice. While altruistic giving is fine as a theoretical

BOX 4.2

VERBAL AND NONVERBAL LOVE

Behaviors are the best measures of love. Behaviors can be either verbal or nonverbal, both of which can be indicators of underlying emotions and thoughts. Nonverbal symbols of love include such things as voice quality; the use of space, or how close you stand or sit to the other person; facial expressions; eye contact; body movements; and any other actions that are rewarding to the partner. There is scientific evidence supporting the connection of these nonverbal signals and love. For example, Zick Rubin found that "strong lovers"—those partners who have scored above the median on his love scale—carried out significantly more eye contact than "weak love" couples did. Sociologist Erving Goffman has noted that people purposefully try to avoid making eye contact with others with whom they want to minimize contact. Similarly, sociologist George Simmel called eye contact the purest and most direct reciprocity that exists anywhere (Z. Rubin, 1973).

Sociologist Herbert Otto suggests that an important aspect of nonverbal love behavior is the symbolic communication involved. He indicated that women are more responsive to symbolic love indicators than men are. Otto writes

> A woman's responses to a single red rose . . . [are] likely to differ qualitatively, on a feelings level, from a man's response. The woman seems more sensitive to the symbolic implications of communication and tends to ascribe more meaning to a symbolic gift. . . . Despite the eagerness with which such symbolic communication is received by the woman, only rarely will a man consistently and freely use the varied symbolic possibilities which are available to two people in love. This despite the fact that maximal use of such symbolic communication between lovers seems to greatly strengthen and foster the relationship. (1972, p. 68)

Since the beginning of time there have been both "sensitive" and "insensitive" people. Otto indicates that just as some people have sight or hearing impairments, "others have an impaired sensitivity to nonverbal communication which in turn has crippled their relationship to people" (p. 69). He argues that verbal skills represent only a fraction of human communication. One researcher found that communication is only 7 percent verbal (Mehrabian, 1971).

The function of verbal behavior is that it clarifies love feelings, thoughts, and other behavioral actions. Sometimes there is pressure from one person to induce the partner to verbalize "I love you," or one person asks the partner over and over again, "Do you love me?" The more insecure a person is, the

(Continued)

more he or she will seek such verbal reassurances. Of course, if statements of love are expressed too often, they begin to lose some value and significance. Periodic "I love you's" seem to supply the most meaningful positive reinforcements.

It is hard to overestimate the pressure that exists on an individual to reciprocate statements of "I love you." If someone says, "I love you" to any of us, it is very difficult not to say, "I love you, too." The reciprocity norm may force many people to make such a statement, even when it's not true. If, however, your partner responds with silence after you say, "I love you," it may be a cue that you have a problem on your hands.

---

or theological goal, there is little evidence of such behavior in day-to-day relationships. Moreover, the authors have seen many marriages end because one of the partners thought the other should love him or her in an altruistic way.

Love as receiving. Probably the most neglected aspect of loving behavior, in the social science literature as well as within religious groups, is the receiving aspect. No exchange of love can take place without the behavior that it exemplifies being accepted by the partners. While most of us expect rewarding behavior from those who love us, we will not accept such behavior if we do not see ourselves as worthy of it. Our concept of ourselves, our perceived self-worth, our self-esteem—all help to determine whether we are capable of receiving loving behavior. Non-acceptors of love, unfortunately, won't experience an emotionally close love relationship.

Love Defined

We see *love as an attitude,* a predisposition to feel, think, and behave in certain ways toward another person. Attitudes cannot be seen; they are invisible (Z. Rubin, 1973). For example, one could hold an attitude of liking, loving, hating, or indifference toward another human being.

Love feelings, thoughts, and behavior are all strongly influenced by the specific norms relating to love that exist in a particular society or subculture. Some societies are supportive of, and encourage, many different forms of love. Other societies strongly restrict the possibilities of certain types of love, romantic love being the best example (Goode, 1959).

Our overall definition of love, then, is as follows:

> *Love is an individual attitude involving an attachment to another person that includes strong positive emotions, mostly positive thoughts, and predispositions toward positive behavior or actions, all of which are strongly influenced by the specific norms relating to love that exist in a particular society or subculture.*

Love as viewed here is *a personal attitude* that is strongly influenced by personality factors. While two individuals may love each other, love does not have to be reciprocal for one person to experience it. Thus, there is no necessary relationship between John's love for Mary and Mary's love—or lack of love—for John. Love is just as real to a particular person who feels it, even when it is unrequited. Zick Rubin (1973) presents some evidence to support this point of view in that

Gift giving is one type of loving behavior.

the correlation of the scores on his love scale for 200 dating male and female couples is a modest .43. Thus a sizable discrepancy may exist between two persons in the extent to which they love each other. (See Box 4.3.)

WHY DO WE NEED LOVE?

All human beings are born with the need to be loved and with the urge to love. People indicate that the greatest source of personal happiness is love, throughout their lifetimes. Love greatly outranks money, status, or fame as a source of satisfaction (Lasswell and Lobsenz, 1980). Love, rather than just marriage itself, tends actually to increase happiness and reduce loneliness. The most lonely people of all are those who are married but who have

never experienced love with anyone (Rubenstein and Shaver, 1982).

Social psychologists Elaine Walster and G. William Walster (1978) submit that men and women alike have a desperate need for security, a yearning to be understood, and a desire to have someone to care for them when they need it. Loneliness is frightening and painful; it is related to anxiety, depression, and boredom. "The lonely yearn for love and, frequently, if their yearning goes on too long, it gives rise to hate" (p. 95). At the very least we can say that without love something very important is missing in making the human being into a complete whole. But, specifically, love affects each individual's quality of life and very survival. Anthropologist Ash-

(Text continued on page 109.)

BOX 4.3

TYPES OF LOVE

There is little question that there are various kinds of love. Love relating to a family member, a friend, a spouse, or a mistress is usually quite different in terms of feelings, thoughts, and behavioral content. In addition, the way each of us "loves" is influenced by our personalities. Of course, an individual may love different people in different ways, at any particular time in his or her life. To complicate the matter even further, the same individual may love the same person in different ways at different stages of the life cycle— relationships are dynamic, not static. One may also love a particular person in quite a different way than that person loves back. Remember that love is an individual attitude that influences how each of us feels, thinks, and acts toward another person; love is not a dyadic concept.

Below are six types of love analyzed primarily in terms of feelings, thoughts, and exchange behaviors. Individual love to a large degree is determined by the quality of exchange between two people. The exchanges involved in love relationships typically will have some different qualities than in other forms of human interaction. The six types of love are altruistic love, idealistic love, dependency love, familial love, friendship love, and total love (Kersten and Kersten, 1981).

ALTRUISTIC LOVE

Altruistic love is often projected as an ideal. It is perpetuated by religious groups and is noted by the word *agape,* meaning "a sacrificial type of love." To many people it represents an ultimate goal for human behavior. Such love is unconditional and places no demands on others. It is not only unselfish but it also suggests a "selflessness." "It can be defined as voluntarily rewarding another person or group of persons without any expected reward in return or any reduction of expected costs" (Kersten and Kersten, 1981, p. 104).

Altruistic love, then, involves no exchange. The rewards are one-way, to the receiver of the benefits. No reciprocal reward is expected by the giver, either extrinsically or intrinsically. While altruism exists theoretically as a kind of love, it would be unwise to expect to see much of it in practice. Individuals who are looking for someone to love them in an altruistic way are in for both "rude awakenings" and "extreme disappointment." This type of love emphasizes "behaviors" and puts much less emphasis on the "feeling" and "thought" dimensions.

IDEALISTIC LOVE

Love of the idealistic type generally involves a misreading of the partner, of one's self, and/or of the relationship. An accurate perception of the situation is lacking. Instead, love is based on false or naively optimistic views. Idealistic lovers are head-in-the-clouds people, who see the world through rose-colored glasses, people who have a high level of romance, passion, and other intense emotions involved in their love. Illusion, idealization of the partner, and infatuation are common. Despite what may be at times immense obstacles, these people feel that their love will win out. "Rescue fantasies" of "saving" another individual who has a host of personality problems are also common. Some idealists even believe that they can have multiple numbers of romantic lovers at the same time. These people fall in love with dreams or fantasies. Such fantasies, however, are unlikely to come true, since they are usually challenged by realities over time.

This kind of love is more common among young people, although adults can experience it also. Adolescents, for example, "often involve themselves in impossible, fantasized exchange relationships such as those with movie stars, rock musicians, or sports heroes. In such exchange fantasies, intrinsic rewards (or anticipatory extrinsic rewards) are often fantasized despite insurmountable evidence to the contrary" (Kersten and Kersten, 1981, pp. 104–105). The problem with this type of love is that it involves cognitive illusions combined with intense feelings. It's possible that it can even be experienced with minimal or no actual behavioral dimension at all, other than what is perceived in fantasy.

DEPENDENCY LOVE

Dependency lovers are people who need someone badly. They are individuals who have insecurities, who lack self-esteem and confidence, and are emotionally lonely. This type of love, like idealistic love, usually involves intense romantic feelings. There is considerable sensuality and desire for sexual involvement. A high level of stimulation and excitement is linked to passion and love. Love at first sight would not be uncommon among these needy people. These are love-prone individuals, who often are "in love with being in love"; they may move from one relationship to another rather quickly. But they have a craving to possess someone, to have their intense feelings reciprocated. This is an extrinsic type of love, of finding happiness through another, of being fulfilled by someone else.

Such individuals are frequently worried about not being accepted by others. "Anxiety, competition and intense possessiveness contribute to bringing about the very thing they fear the most— rejection and abandonment" (Kersten and Kersten, 1981, p. 105). They are often involved in "smother love" of the other person. These are aggressive lovers; they love hard, fast, and strong. Because of this they "usually forfeit any possibility of being the one with the 'least interest' in a relationship" (p. 105). Dependency lovers chase people, sometimes finding themselves in situations of unrequited love. Emotions rule dependency love.

FAMILIAL LOVE

Familial love relates to feelings, thoughts, and caring behavior toward the members of one's family. The exchange involved is the result of previous social interaction and is encouraged by societal or subcultural norms and values. The result is obligations, responsibilities, and investments, as well as attachments, developed over time. Individual choice or initiative is lacking

(Continued)

in the beginning of such love relationships in the sense that we do not "pick and choose our parents and parents cannot pick the children they want" (Kersten and Kersten, 1981, p. 105).

Even in families without much love, there is still a general belief held by most family members that they "should" love one another. Those who have not experienced much familial love often feel considerable deprivation, most intensely, for example, around holidays. "Children will usually return to their parents the love (or the hurt) that they experienced from them. Attempts to hurt parents are usually carried out through a process of negative exchange" (pp. 105–106).

FRIENDSHIP LOVE

Love of friends is usually relaxed and not filled with intense passion or emotions. An informal commitment is "just understood." Typically there is a fairly long history of mutual sharing, self-disclosure, warmth, and rapport. One can count on this other person to be there when needed. But the key ingredient is companionship.

Within male-female friendships sexual involvement usually does not occur, although the degree of closeness and type of exchange may vary. In-depth friendships are much more likely to involve members of the same sex, although love friendships among men are not as common. "Women generally would like more male friends but male attempts to include sexual activity usually hinder these possibilities. Some women have homosexual men as friends because they will not have to deal constantly with sexual harassment" (Kersten and Kersten, 1981, p. 106). In some marriages individuals will define their love mostly in terms of friendship, but typically friendship love is found outside of marriage. Usually feelings, thoughts, and behavior are all found to various degrees in friendship love.

TOTAL LOVE

Total love exists when an individual makes a voluntary, recognized, public pledge of commitment to another human being. The promise typically emphasizes fidelity, other elements of exclusivity, and a high degree of trust. Strong emotional gratification, thoughtful loyalty, and fair exchange and reciprocity are the rewards expected. There is a realistic awareness of responsibilities and obligations. Individuals will generally reveal most of their "inner selves" in total love; it involves the highest level of vulnerability. In so doing, the person hopes to be better understood and, consequently, have his or her personal goals, needs, and self-interests more completely satisfied. Extensive time and effort is put into total love. This love, like any love, may increase or decrease over time depending upon the quality of exchange. Generally total love is found in a male-female relationship, but it could include two persons of the same sex, as in some homosexual relationships. All three aspects of love—feelings, thoughts, and behavior—will be found in total love.

ley Montagu emphasizes that "the most important thing to realize about the nature of human nature is that the most significant ingredient in its structure is love" (1953, p. 22).

Sociobiologist Anthony Walsh in his book *Human Nature and Love* (1981) makes a strong case, with scientific evidence, that love is a human need. He stresses that he is *not* talking about romantic love, which someone falls in and out of. Walsh's view of love involves the need to give and receive affection and nurturance, "joyfully [to] acknowledge that we are our brother's keeper, that we not only respect and care for him, but take an active responsibility for his well being" (p. 96). Walsh believes that "beyond physical needs for sheer biological survival—oxygen, water and food—love is the most important need human beings have" (p. 97).

A need, says Walsh, is that which has to be fulfilled in order for the organism to function properly. To argue that something is a physical or emotional need, it must be demonstrated "that it is a causal condition of the organism's survival and well-being" (Branden, 1969, p. 19). Walsh believes that love can meet this demanding criterion.

Love and Health

Research shows that individuals lacking love have more trouble handling stress in their lives. Various scientists have found that the disruption of love ties is the greatest source of stress, that the most stress and illness are found among unloved individuals living alone, that problems in love relationships produce significant health changes, and that people who have someone who cares for them can more adequately resolve tension (Dodge and Martin, 1970; Levine and Scotch, 1970; Graham and Reeder, 1972). Walsh claims that the inescapable conclusion from the scientific literature is that

love deprivation is a major contributory factor in the onset of a variety of illnesses. It is not that the deprivation of love "causes" illness in the sense that it is analogous to an invading virus. It is rather a major stressor [love deprivation] which has the effect of generating biochemical changes. (1981, p. 101)

Exposure to prolonged stress eventually exhausts the body's hormonal defensive capacity. Certain diseases that are called "diseases of adaptation," such as hypertension, arthritis, and ulcers, are the result of extended stress. Walsh concludes that "I think it is fair to say that we can view love as a kind of immunological canopy that shields the bearer from, or helps him cope with, the manifold stressors that exist in modern society" (p. 101).

Love and Childhood Experiences

Childhood experiences, particularly the development of an attachment to a person taking care of us, appear to have a significant impact on our ability to love as adults. Sociologist Robert Weiss (1975) argues that the presence or accessibility of a specific other person appears necessary for security right from the beginning. Infants around the age of six to nine months appear content when they can see their mothers. But when the mothers are out of sight for some time, the infants become restless and disturbed. Montagu (1975) suggests that human beings learn to love in childhood by being loved themselves. He writes

There is now good evidence which leads us to believe that not only does a baby want to be loved, but also that it wants to love, that all its drives are oriented in the direction of receiving and giving love, and that if it

Childhood experiences have a significant impact on our ability to love as adults.

doesn't receive love it is unable to give it—as a child or as an adult. (p. 6)

There is reciprocal exchange between a mother and baby from the moment of birth on. Even if the baby's needs for food and shelter are taken care of, an infant will waste away and die unless he or she is also loved. Because this connection between loving nurturance and the baby's survival was not known in the first half of this century, a large percentage of infants under one year of age who entered hospitals, orphanages, and foundling institutions died (Montagu, 1975).

Children who have not been adequately loved, grow up to be persons who find it

extremely difficult to understand the meaning of love; they are awkward in their human relationships, "cold fish," they tend to be thoughtless and inconsiderate; they have little emotional depth; hence they are able to enter into all sorts of human relationships in a shallow way and drift from one marriage to another with the greatest emotional ease. They are "affectionless characters" who suffer from a hunger for affection. Awkward and ineffectual in their attempts to secure it, they often suffer rejection and end up by becoming more embittered than ever. (p. 14)

It is thus Montagu's view that childhood love is indispensable for healthy development; it is the chief stimulus to the development of social competence. "Mental health is the ability to love" (1975, p. 16).

As children grow older there is an increased capacity to tolerate separation from an attachment figure, if the person is still considered to be accessible (Weiss, 1975). In adolescence, attachment patterns change in fundamental ways. There is a slow withdrawal of attachment to the parents and a tendency to become attached to peers—a best friend, a heterosexual partner, or a peer group. Parents remain important in that they provide a secure base from which the adolescent can become somewhat more independent. In adolescence, with particular significant others, there begins to be "a convergence of attachment feelings and sexual strivings, so that the same person might be an object for both" (p. 41).

Love and Self-Esteem

One of the important outcomes of receiving love as a child is achieving a sense of self-esteem. A person will "love" differently according to his or her view of his or her own self-worth. Some degree of self-esteem is necessary before a person is willing to become vulnerable, or open to the risk of loving another. In other words, it is a prerequisite to love oneself before one can truly love others. Self-love is here equated with a positive self-concept.

Individuals with low self-esteem will either run away from love or actively seek it in a desperate sort of way; they may indeed be involved in "smother love" because of their great need to possess someone. "The creation of a positive or negative self-image begins in infancy" (Lasswell and Lobsenz, 1980, p. 28). If children are ignored, belittled, made fun of, verbally rejected, told that they are ugly or fat, continually compared negatively with a brother or sister, threatened that they may be abandoned, or told that no one will ever marry them, or if the parents indicated that they wished that their child had never been born—all such actions or comments help to produce low self-esteem. Those desperate for love when told by someone that "I like your jeans," may eagerly respond, "I love you too."

Social psychologists Carin Rubenstein and Phillip Shaver (1982) speak of two types of personalities—clingers and evaders—arising out of poor parent-child love relations. Children who are inadequately loved become what John Bowlby (1982) calls "anxiously attached"; "they cling, feel intensely anxious when separated from parents, and lack confidence in themselves and others. If rejection or abandonment goes too far, the child may become permanently detached and aloof, maintaining a self-protecting distance from everyone" (p. 43).

Rubenstein and Shaver argue that both clingers and evaders "suffer from an underlying lack of self-confidence and trust, and both are prone to chronic loneliness" (1982, p. 44). Clingers disclose too much to others and have a desperate need to attach themselves to someone. Evaders are to a large degree just the opposite. They try to present the appearance of not needing anybody; underneath they are very needy and lonely. They "defend themselves against the pain of rejection by refusing to open up to other people for fear that their deepest most real self will be rebuffed. They come across as cool, aloof, disinterested" (p. 44).

Because evaders rarely express their deepest needs to anyone, they are prone to self-administered anesthesia: solitary drinking or pill-popping, excessive television-viewing or eating.

The price of both self-protective strategies—clinging and evading—is extremely high. Paradoxically, both encourage rejec-

tion (just what the person fears most) and guarantee continued loneliness. (pp. 44–45)

A child wants, as do all human beings, to have approval and positive reinforcement. "The way each of us comes to feel about himself or herself reflects in large part the way other people respond to us" (Lasswell and Lobsenz, 1980, p. 29). Material things substituted for love do not create a positive self-image in a child. The result is often simply a "spoiled brat" with low self-esteem. A pattern of trying to find happiness through extrinsic "things" is often established in such a person.

Of course it's possible for parents to give children "too much love." "For instance, children who grow up with oversolicitous parents who go to extreme lengths to meet every emotional need may become overly dependent" (Lasswell and Lobsenz, 1980, p. 33). This type of person learns how to take love but not how to give it. He or she may marry someone who functions as a substitute mother or father, who will take care of the person. Parents who are too overprotective, who try to meet the child's every whim, who are focused on the child for reasons of their own personal happiness, do their child a great disservice. These children will not do well in adult "love" relationships because fair, reciprocal giving and receiving is unlikely.

Those who have a poor self-image do not see themselves as worthy of being loved. Therefore, as mentioned previously, they have trouble accepting love. They reason that "If even my parents didn't love me, how could someone else?" In fact, they say to themselves, "If someone says he or she loves me, there must be something wrong with this person—he or she must be crazy!" Such "nonaccepters" may have difficulty accepting anything positive (praise, admiration, com-

pliments, or material gifts) from someone else. These individuals also tend to feel that they have nothing to give in return. Their low self-esteem makes them better able to accept negative comments, such as criticism and put-downs.

Parents may use love conditionally as a reward or punishment. "Clearly the conditional withholding of love is a technique used frequently to establish authority or to control behavior" (Lasswell and Lobsenz, 1980, p. 31). Parents who have an extreme need to control their children's lives are more likely to withdraw their love when they are not pleased with particular behavior. They usually don't make it clear that it is the *behavior* they don't like; rather, they indicate that they don't like (or love) their child. Such children often end up trying to prove themselves, for example, getting all A's in school, in order to try to gain their parents' approval, acceptance, and affection. Some people spend a lifetime trying to obtain love from their parents when a pattern of conditional love has been established in the family.

Individuals who experience total rejection in childhood, or the total loss of a love object, have the most trouble in adult love relationships. If a child's parents die, if the parents put him or her up for adoption, if they simply abandoned or disowned the child, if one parent leaves the household, if the child has been institutionalized at an early age, or if he or she was shuttled from foster home to foster home—such a child often never has an attachment experience. He or she, therefore, often has trouble trusting others and frequently becomes rather bitter, hostile, and negative. His or her "love" relationships are usually filled with a lot of conflict, distrust, accusations, put-downs, and possibly even physical abuse.

A child cannot distinguish between "Particular people don't love me" and "I am inherently unlovable." "For this reason early experiences with rejection, abuse, neglect and lack of support can make a person both distrust others and dislike himself; it can make him simultaneously hostile and destructively self-critical. . . . Self-blame and hostility towards others appear to go hand in hand, these are both related to loneliness'' (Rubenstein and Shaver, 1982, p. 50).

Love and Behavioral Problems

Walsh argues that the deprivation of love significantly contributes to many kinds of behavioral problems. With child abuse, criminal behavior, and suicide, a lack of warm and loving involvement with other people is one of the contributing factors. Child abuse is much more likely if the parent had not been adequately loved. More specifically, a significant proportion of abusive parents were themselves abused as children. Walsh comments that it is meaningless for abusive parents to argue that they ''really do'' love their children. Verbal claims that are not demonstrated by actions are just empty words.

There is also a strong relationship between the deprivation of love and criminal behavior. Says Walsh (1981)

The more frequent and the more heinous the crimes, the less affectionate ties the criminal will have with other people. . . . Many [criminals] have a superficial charm with which they can manipulate others. . . . They are uninhibited, transient, sexual predators, unreliable, amoral, suffer little guilt, and are almost always heavily involved with drugs and/or alcohol. . . . The most frightening, senseless, and repugnant crimes are committed by the loveless psychopath. They may kill, rape, and mutilate nonchalantly, without remorse. . . . They walk in empty darkness, we walk in fear; and all for the want of love. (pp. 106–108)

The most common type of suicide described by sociologist Emile Durkheim is ''anomic suicide.'' It is a result of isolation, aloneness, and the lack of closeness with other individuals or the disruption of such ties. Suicide is much more frequent among the unmarried and divorced, among the lonely, and among those who lose a spouse through death or separation. Suicide, therefore, varies with the strength of love connections with others. ''Thus love ties one to life itself,'' says Walsh (1981, p. 108).

ROMANTIC LOVE

In the nineteenth century the concept of romantic love developed in America, and with it, sexuality became tied to both love and marriage. There was a unique attempt in the United States to combine romantic feelings with sexuality within the institution of marriage. The view was transmitted that ''Love is the ultimate justification for marriage; marriage alone justifies sex; sex and love are therefore the two basic hallmarks of the marital union and neither sex nor love are culturally acceptable outside of marriage'' (Crosby, 1976, pp. 62–63).

In romantic love today the picture has changed—and it is much more confused. There is still the norm that love is a prerequisite to marriage and that once married, sexual behavior should be confined to marriage. Sexual behavior, however, has gained an independence of its own before marriage. Sexual activity is no longer confined to marriage, and it is not even necessarily connected with love. Many people may say that it *should* be, but *real* behavior is often quite different. But there seems to be considerable agreement on the part of most people, particularly women, that sex is better with love.

Romantic love is viewed almost exclusively as a ''feeling.'' The cognitive and behavioral aspects are significantly diminished

BOX 4.4

THE ROMEO AND JULIET EFFECT

What happens when families bitterly oppose the romantic attraction a young couple may have? It appears to have the opposite results of what a parent may want. In reality, opposition seems to bring about a deepening of romantic feeling. Overt parental opposition and interference tend to result in an increased desire to hold on to the romantic partner. The more that the whole world appears to be opposed to the couple's relationship, apparently the more cohesively united the couple becomes. They develop a strong "in" group together—to fight the "out" group.

An interesting pattern often emerges, however, when the parents back off. Walster and Walster (1978) write:

> As soon as their parents became resigned to a relationship and began to interfere less, the lovers' interest in one another began to wane. When parents became concerned about a relationship and began to interfere more and more, the couples generally fell more deeply in love. Thus, parental interference is likely to boomerang. It tends to foster desire rather than divisiveness. (p. 86)

in importance. The feeling of romantic love is idealistic and tends to be artificially heightened. Ironically, feelings of romantic love can be heightened even further when opposition to the couple exists (see Box 4.4). If a young couple marries "with the expectation that the intense feeling (the chemistry, the electrifying, magnetic attraction) will continue, unabated and unchanged, disappointment and disillusionment are inevitable" (Crosby, 1976, p. 63). Sociologist John Crosby argues that Americans are naive in their belief that romance and sexuality are the key elements that will produce a successful and happy marriage. On the contrary, heightened romantic idealization is certainly a hindrance to intimacy. But romantic love continues to be a key factor in understanding "American mating patterns, marital expectations, and sexual customs."

The female has been idolized and idealized; young people are taught that love is the sole basis for marriage; love and marriage are described in terms that cannot possibly be realized. We are a people who have been socialized to fall in love with love. (1976, p. 65)

Is there a difference between romantic love and infatuation? Probably there is no difference at all at the time a person is experiencing them. There is one key distinction, however. "Lovers use the term 'romantic love' to describe loving relationships that are still in progress. They are more likely to use the term 'infatuation' to describe once-loving relationships that for a variety of reasons were terminated" (Walster and Walster, 1978, p. 53).

Thus it appears that it is only past loves that are labeled by many of us as "infatuation"; our current loves, however, are always "the real thing." "If the relationship flowers, we continue to believe that we are experiencing true love; if a relationship dies, we

The Romeo and Juliet effect occurs when parents disapprove of a couple's relationship.

conclude that we were merely infatuated'' (Walster and Walster, 1978, p. 53). Young people sometimes think that their parents can tell the difference between real love and infatuation. But, as Walster and Walster point out, when our parents and friends tell us that we are just infatuated and that it's not really true love, they are not actually focusing on our feelings.

> Actually they're telling us whether or not they approve of our relationship. If they approve of the relationship, they are likely to agree that this may well be love—only time will tell. If they don't approve, they are likely to insist that it's only infatua-

tion—here today, gone tomorrow. (1978, p. 53)

Myths and Realities About Romantic Love

For many Americans romantic love is the most important form of love. Given this fact, it is rather surprising to find a large number of myths surrounding this type of love. One myth is that ''Love conquers all.'' Love is by far the most common reason for marriage. But inasmuch as about half of all marriages are now ending in divorce, it appears that love does not conquer everything. People who try to live life based on romantic love usually don't live very long in such a state. Probably somewhat more realistic statements regarding romantic love—in contrast to "Love conquers all"—are *"Love is blind"* and *"All's fair in love and war."*

Another myth is that each of us has a *"one and only"* waiting for us somewhere. Women sometimes speak of their "knight in shining armor" or "prince charming;" that is, their predestined, true love. But the vast majority of people fall in love with more than one person in their lives. In fact, some people report being in love with two or more people at the same time. We also know that many people fall out of love with one person and in love with another. Despite these facts, there are still individuals who wholeheartedly believe in "the one and only" myth and are waiting for the man or woman of their dreams. Unfortunately, it doesn't make a lot of sense to sit around waiting for "Mr. Right" or "Ms. Right" to knock on your door.

In the 1970s there was a widely perpetuated myth that *"Love is never having to say you're sorry."* This view was compatible with the self-centered emphasis of the "me" generation. Quite the opposite, of course, is true: People who love with some sense of personal security are going to be able to admit mistakes and to say that they are sorry. But there are many people who do not have enough confidence and self-esteem—who do not want to give up personal control—to make such an admission.

A popular myth is the occurrence of *"love at first sight."* This belief is perpetuated in movies, songs, story books, and advertisements. We suggest, to the contrary, that the greater the "high" of romantic excitement in the beginning of a relationship, the *less* chance it has of lasting into a long-term commitment. Also, the greater the initial "high," the more quickly and the more dramatic the "fall." Certainly "first sight" love is likely to

be very much focused on physical attraction and idealized images. There are rare exceptions to this generalization, but they help to keep the myth alive.

Some people also see *"love as a miracle."* Such individuals tend to believe that "fate" is the key to "how we meet and who we fall in love with. . . . But actually, we ourselves have everything to do with what happens" (Marlin, 1984, p. 4). Therefore, it is argued that love just doesn't fall out of the sky; if we know how, we tend to make it happen. It should be expressed that "falling in love is an active rather than a passive pursuit" (Marlin, 1984, p. 4).

And then there is the love myth of the *"prince (or princess) and the pauper."* It's exciting and romantic to believe that extreme differences in social class are not barriers to love. Such stories are highly dramatized in romantic novels, but they are rare in real life. "What comes from the other side of the tracks is usually adolescent rebellion rather than lasting love" (Marlin, 1984, p. 5). Similar backgrounds are much more likely to be the basis of falling in love.

Another persistent myth is that *"Love will change people."* It seems to be particularly common for women to hold this view. In this situation an individual will usually choose a person who has problems, problems that are expected to disappear thanks to the "love" provided in marriage. Individuals who hold this myth will often pick partners who are drug addicts, alcoholics, or promiscuous; who have different values, goals, and priorities; or who are, in general, very exploitative. Of course, rarely does "love" change people; it may instead provide just what is needed to result in "no change."

The sweetest myth of all about love is *"They lived happily ever after."* In reality there is no guarantee of bliss once an individual finds love. Because there is so much emphasis on romantic love in American society, relationships are fragile. Feelings can come and go quickly. "The people who seem to run into the most problems are those who expect a mate to make them happy" (Marlin, 1984, p. 9).

Very pessimistic and negative individuals might even say that *"Love itself is a myth."* While there are many aspects or types of love that lend themselves more to perpetuating myths, it is the authors' belief that love *is* a reality. One's goal should not be to write love off but to understand better all of its many dimensions. If people follow this route, they will be less likely to be chasing after a fantasy or dream. We should realize that in a society that promotes romantic ideals and socializes people to "fall in love," it will be rewarding just to have the feeling of being in love, despite any and all obstacles. Romantic love is partly its own reward—while it lasts, that is.

When Romantic Love Ends

Romantic love, because it is so much focused on feelings, is very fragile, but seldom is the decision to end a love affair mutual. Only a small percentage of couples, about 10 percent, end a relationship jointly and mutually (Hill, Z. Rubin, and Peplau, 1976; Z. Rubin, 1969). Rarely is there a happy ending for both partners. Quite the contrary, there is frequently a lot of bitterness and anger at the end; many times there is a desire for revenge. One partner is often still emotionally attached to the other, even after it's "officially" over. One "may still thrill at the sight of the other; [he or she] may still feel comfortable only when with the other" (Weiss, 1975, p. 37). The loss of a romantic love attachment results in "separation distress" and usually painful loneliness. An attempt may sometimes be made, however, to hide anger and hurt behind a mask of indifference (Weiss, 1975).

Romantic love tends to be unstable because of extreme idealization. It is the hope of every individual that his or her current love will last forever; at least, that's the dream during the romantic stage. Walster and Walster (1978) point out that "although there's strong cultural support for the notion that a man and women *should* stay passionately in love forever, most of us have never heard of any couples who have" (p. 108).

It appears, according to the Walsters, that to a considerable extent no one really expects a passionate couple to remain that way. Romantic love seems to grow less exciting as time passes. For sure the intensity flickers, if indeed, it doesn't die. But romantic love need not always die; it can be redirected into another type of love. Walster and Walster say that it "can ripen into companionate love, the kind of affection we feel for those with whom our lives are deeply intertwined" (p. 124). Companionate love involves "shared understanding, emotions, and habits"—elements reflective of intimacy. Scientists interviewing dating couples, and then again when they were married, verified that romantic love decreased with time.

The researchers found that, at the beginning of a love affair, couples were romantically in love. As the relationships deepened, the "love" they expressed for one another began to sound less and less like passion—and more and more like friendship and companionate love. (p. 125)

Gender Differences in Romantic Love

Although love is a necessary condition to marriage in America, it is not usually a sufficient reason for it in itself. Most young people have other "pre-established ideals or requirements." In a computer dance study carried out by sociologists Robert Coombs and William Kenkel (1966), it was found that women were more particular than men. Women tested before the dance were much more concerned that their dates be of their own race and religion, intelligent, good dressers, ranking in campus status, and good dancers. The only factor that men were more concerned about than women was their partners' physical attractiveness.

When asked about their partners after the dance, men were "more satisfied with their dates on all criteria, felt more 'romantic attraction' toward them, and when asked to speculate about the chances that they and their date could have a happy marriage, were more optimistic" (Z. Rubin, 1973, p. 205). Even regarding physical attractiveness—an area where men had higher demands—the men reported that they were more satisfied in this regard than the women were. The conclusions of the study were that men are quicker to fall in love than women.

Other research has found the same results. One study showed that men were more strongly attracted to their fiancées at first meeting or shortly afterward than women were (Burgess and Wallin, 1953). In a well-known study of more than 1000 college students by William Kepart (1967), almost twice as many men as women said that they were "very easily attracted" to members of the other sex. Zick Rubin (1973) explains this consistent finding the following way:

> Since the woman rather than the man typically takes on the social and economic status of her spouse, she has more practical concerns to keep in mind in selecting a mate. In addition, the woman is often in a greater rush to get married than the man because her years of "marriageability" tend to be more limited. Thus, she cannot as easily afford to be strongly attracted to a date who

is not also a potentially eligible spouse. (p. 205)

Willard Waller, the father of family sociology in the 1930s and 1940s, was even more blunt about this sex difference. "A man, when he marries, chooses a companion and perhaps a helpmate, but a woman chooses a companion and at the same time a standard of living. It is necessary for a woman to be mercenary" (1938, p. 243).

A popular stereotype is that women are more romantic. "She is the starry-eyed and sentimental one, the one who reads the love magazines, and watches the soap operas, while he hides behind the sports section or the financial reports" (Z. Rubin, 1973, p. 205). But the scientific evidence seems to support the conviction that men are more romantic—are more likely to be swept off their feet—particularly in the beginning of a relationship. Zick Rubin (1973) found that men were significantly more likely to agree with the following romantic statements:

> "As long as they at least love one another, two people should have no difficulty getting along together in marriage."

> "A person should marry whomever he loves regardless of social position." (p. 206)

Marcia Lasswell in her study of various styles of loving also found women ranking lower on a romantic-love scale, a scale that mostly reflects emotions at the beginning of a love relationship. She believes that this again is a traditional response to the "good-provider role." But she argues that in these modern times "when women are more self-sufficient economically, pragmatic concerns for security may not be [as] important as they once were" (Lasswell and Lobsenz, 1980, p. 105). Nevertheless, recent studies still show that women "are not so apt to fall romantically in love as men." In addition, men are the ones who have the most trouble letting go.

> *Men tend to fall in love more quickly and to hold on longest when a relationship begins to crumble. It is usually the woman who takes the first steps toward ending an affair and the man who is most distressed when it does end. (After a disastrous love relationship, three times as many men as women commit suicide.) In their logical way, women seem more ready to accept the end of one love and to reorganize their lives. Men are not so easily resigned; they chew over the loss of love, wondering what they said or did wrong. (Lasswell and Lobsenz, 1980, p. 106)*

But Walster and Walster argue that there is some evidence to support the notion that women also are romantics in their own way and may be at different times in the relationship. When men and women were asked in a study to describe how they felt *when they were in love*, women, it turns out, were much more "romantic." Here women experienced the symptoms of love with more intensity than men—for example, "It felt like I was floating on a cloud," "I wanted to run, jump, and scream," "I have trouble concentrating," and "I feel giddy and carefree" (Kanin, Davidson, and Scheck, 1970). The evidence seems to suggest that while men fall in love more vigorously and cling more to love at the end, when the relationship has developed to its greatest intensity, possibily including mutual trust and commitment, "women experience the euphoria and the agony of love more intensely than do men" (Walster and Walster, 1978, p. 50).

Thus it is likely that women love harder in many ways once the relationship is established. Before the man is committed to a relationship the woman may play down or minimize her feelings (Murstein, 1980). But once commitment on both sides has been made, romantic love to women may reach its peak. This may be why symbols of love "remembering special occasions, special surprises, important dates, being given one rose" are so important to women.

When such romantic indicators of love on the part of the male are not forthcoming, this initiates a time period when many females begin to lose feelings of love. We have seen numerous cases of women in therapy who have fallen out of love, where the man was not even aware of his wife's state of mind. Women seem to have different expectations from men regarding the demonstration of love in marriage. Men often believe the marriage will take care of itself. Women, however, are expecting behavior that enhances intimacy, and when such actions are not forthcoming, and seem unlikely in the future, women, more often than men, emotionally fall out of love.

Controlling Romantic Love

A classic analysis of the functional significance of romantic love is found in William Goode's article "The Theoretical Importance of Love" (1959). He indicated that some writers see romantic love as functioning to attract people emotionally and to hold them together through the early period of marriage. This is a time of important adjustment for most couples, and romantic love helps them get through this tough period. Thus, romantic love is seen as serving a positive function both for society and for the individual couple. Other writers have seen romantic love as dysfunctional to the stability of marriage because of the idealistic expectations it promotes.

They view romantic love negatively as hurting both society and individuals.

Goode argues that Americans are socialized to fall in love before marriage. To some extent it's like a trick to cause people to marry so that there is emotional support and maintenance for the next generation. Romantic love also helps young people to break the close attachment between parent and child. Goode says that while romantic love is a universal possibility, it is rare in a host of societies. All societies, however, attempt to control or channel romantic love in some way. Love has potentially great disruptive effects on class stratification, lineage patterns, inheritance, power, and family honor. "Both mate choice and love, therefore, are too important to be left to children" (Goode, 1959, p. 150).

What are some ways used around the world to control love? Probably the best way to control it is to prevent it from appearing. The simplest way to accomplish this is to have "child marriages," marriages arranged either at birth or before puberty. Rarely do strong emotional attachments appear before puberty. A second way is to limit the class of eligible spouses. Usually marriages are allowed only within very narrow limits. Cross cousin marriages are common; for example, the father's sister's child marries the mother's brother's child (Goode, 1959).

A third method of restricting romantic love relationships is to keep young people isolated from potential partners. Social separation of the sexes is common. In this situation, parents generally arrange marriages for their children with little likelihood that passionate love will get in the way. A fourth pattern involves close supervision, such as by chaperones, to keep an eye on adolescents. There is usually a major concern with female chastity. Love is permitted before marriage but only between eligibles of the parent's choice. But romantic love is not encouraged,

except after engagement or marriage (Goode, 1959).

The final approach to controlling love is found in American society. Here romantic love is actually encouraged and love is considered to be a prerequisite to marriage. Choice is *formally* free. The process involves meeting and dating a number of individuals of the other sex and gradually, over time, narrowing the choice to one person. Controls are usually indirect.

In our society, parents threaten, cajole, wheedle, bribe, and persuade their children to "go with the right people," during both the early love play and later courtship phases. Primarily, they seek to control love relationships by influencing the informal social contacts of their children: moving to appropriate neighborhoods and schools, giving parties and helping to make out invitation lists, by making their children aware that certain individuals have ineligibility traits (race, religion, manners, tastes, clothing and so on). (Goode, 1959, pp. 153–154)

Another source of social control is an individual's own peer companions. Such friends often—whether asked or not—rate, evaluate, and criticize one's partner. In any event, no society, not even American society, allows for the entirely free choice of a love partner.

Love as Exploitation

The views of most radical feminists in the late 1960s and early 1970s were very negative toward love and marriage. Most feminists hold much more moderate views today. It is valuable, however, to reflect upon the hostility toward romantic love that some women held during the early stages of the modern feminist movement. The poem "There's a Me" indicates some typical feelings.

THERE'S A ME

Tell me not about your love
I know it well
I've felt it in your glance
Felt it from the lash of the whip
And worse
From out your tongue
Tell me not of your love
It is so fluid
It has drowned me
And mine
In its burning intensity
I have but few places left unscarred
The heat of your love has all but consumed my
brain
The security of your love has rendered me
fatherless
The gift of your love branded me bastard
The testimony of your love has imprisoned me
Your song of love has made me voiceless
I shall sing no more
I am no more
You have loved me into oblivion.

ALTHEA SCOTT

The radical feminists' view of love in the 1965–1975 era was "filled with anger, hostility, pain, hurt, grief," as the poem "There's a Me" expresses. Love was viewed as a means used by men to keep women in their place. "The result has kept women from achieving their potential, from gaining ego strength, from being fully functioning human beings" (Loring, in Otto, 1972, p. 74). Love is said to have "caused women to feel and be powerless." The anguish that the radical feminists felt was one of betrayal—"You loved me into oblivion."

It is argued that romantic love has put women on a false pedestal. As one woman noted in a comic strip, "Man places woman on a pedestal because we 'bug' them at eye level" (Loring, 1972, p. 75). Says Rosalind Loring, "Statues are static, not living, breath-

ing, feeling humans. The traditional words 'respect,' 'honor,' 'protect' and 'admire' have a hollow sound to those contemporary women who are also congruent with their situation" (p. 75).

Thus the anger, the frustration, and indeed the ambivalence that can be heard throughout the radical feminist literature, are based upon an inability to separate the effects of economic condition and political subordination from those due to romantic love. Love is experienced not only as a weapon, but also as a ruse, a technique, a method for concealing the true meaning of men's intentions regarding women. (pp. 75–76)

The attitudes of some feminists toward love and marriage have been particularly strong and negative. Militant feminist Ti-Grace Atkinson (1969) said, "Marriage means rape and life-long slavery. Love has to be destroyed." Germaine Greer in *The Female Eunuch* (1971) states that "Men have reduced heterosexual contact to sado-masochistic patterns by exploiting love and fantasies of romance." One of the founders of the radical feminist movement, Shulamith Firestone, in her book *The Dialectic of Sex* (1970) sees love as exploiting women. She argues that males are parasites "feeding on the emotional strength of women, without reciprocity" (p. 127).

Love is not altruistic, says Firestone. Love is rather the height of selfishness. "The self attempts to enrich itself through the absorption of another being" (p. 128). But it should not incorporate the other but rather be "an *exchange* of selves. Anything short of a mutual exchange will hurt one or the other party" (p. 128). Thus love between two equals is positive and blissful. This is seldom the case, however, says Firestone. "For every successful contemporary love experience . . . there are ten destructive love experiences . . . often resulting in the destruction of the individual'' (p. 129).

Firestone (1970) argues that romantic love becomes corrupted by *an unequal balance of power*. Without mutual vulnerability love turns destructive. In addition, the word *love* does not mean the same thing for men and women. Women, according to Firestone, are considered to be better at loving and more interested in ''relationships'' than ''sexual activity'' per se. Firestone indicates that men have difficulty loving. Women ''expect and accept an emotional invalidism in men that they would find intolerable in a woman'' (p. 135). The goal of men is to find an answer to the question, ''How do I get someone to love me without her demanding an equal commitment in return?'' (p. 137).

Firestone (1970) indicates that women have had to ''cling'' to men. In a society run by men, women are seen as inferior, and a woman who does not attach herself to a male is doomed. ''The continued *economic* dependence of women makes a situation of healthy love between equals impossible'' (pp. 138–139). She maintains that

> *Women without men are in the same situation as orphans: they are a helpless subclass lacking the protection of the powerful. . . . To participate in one's subjection by choosing one's master often gives the illusion of free choice; but in reality a woman is never free to choose love without external motivations. For her at the present time, the two things, love and status, must remain inextricably intertwined. (p. 139)*

Thus women are only able to love in exchange for security; they can't ''afford the luxury of spontaneous love.''

> *Men are right when they complain that women lack discrimination, that they seldom love a man for his individual traits*

but rather for what he has to offer (his class), that they are calculating, that they use sex to gain other ends, etc. For in fact women are in no position to love freely. If a woman is lucky enough to find ''a decent guy'' to love her and support her, she is doing well—and usually will be grateful enough to return his love. (p. 140)

After being married awhile, the woman, says Firestone, usually feels cheated. She now can see the reality of what she has caught. ''He may be a poor thing, but at least I've got a man of my own'' is typical of how she feels.

> *She has gotten not love and recognition, but possessorship and control. This is when she is transformed from Blushing Bride to Bitch, a change that, no matter how universal and predictable, still leaves the individual husband perplexed. (''You're not the girl I married.'') (p. 142)*

Firestone, writing at the end of the 1960s, argued that the situation of women really had not changed much from what it ever was in history. And in the previous 50 years, she says, the sexual revolution has proved to be of great value to men but has brought no improvements in the status of women. Women continue to be exploited—sexually and through romantic love. But women continue to need men because of economic and political dependence. One woman quoted in Firestone's book says, ''All men are selfish, brutal and inconsiderate—and I wish I could find one'' (1970, p. 145).

Love and Jealousy

Jealousy is an emotion that is often connected with love. Jealousy is defined as a fear of losing one's partner, whether real or imagined. Jealousy is often confused with the feeling of envy and it is important to distinguish the difference. "Envy stems from the desire to acquire something possessed by another, while jealousy is rooted in the fear of losing something already possessed" (Foster, 1972, p. 168). Jealousy, then, is concerned with the *maintenance* of a relationship (Clanton and Smith, 1977).

The big question about jealousy in the 1965–1975 era was whether it is an inborn part of human nature or whether it is learned. Family liberals, on the one hand, have taken the point of view that jealousy is not only learned but that it can also be unlearned. Mate swappers or swingers, members of communes, and participants in sexually open marriages typically see jealousy as learned. Family conservatives, on the other hand, see jealousy as inherent in human beings, just as it is in lower forms of animals. They point to research by social scientists, who find at least some degree of jealousy in all societies. Many cultures have norms against *showing* the emotion of jealousy (see Box 4.5), but even here the norms are often violated (Stephens, 1963; Reiss, 1986). It is important to distinguish between the *feeling* of jealousy and the *behavior* as a result of the feeling, the acting out of the feeling. Many people in American society who actually feel jealousy deny those feelings because they tend to see jealousy as more of a sign of individual weakness than as strength.

It certainly appears that jealousy is a normal emotion, normal in the sense that all human beings have the potential for feeling and showing it. There are individuals, however, who are pathologically jealous. This pattern shows up when people exhibit extreme behavior because of jealous feelings. Such behavior can be carried to the extent of so-called crimes of passion, including murder resulting from a love triangle. Evidence suggests that people with low self-esteem, insecurities, and less education are much more

likely to exhibit extreme jealous reactions. Also, people who have been unfaithful themselves tend to trust their partners less and exhibit much more jealousy. Very jealous people seem to be unhappy people and have unhappy marriages (Adams, 1980).

Jealousy is linked to love in a couple of ways. The prospect of losing a person or love object, or of no longer being able to take him or her for granted, will result in one's feeling even more need for that individual, hence one "loves" him or her more. Thus in one respect jealousy can increase feelings of love. One would not feel jealousy if one didn't care about or depend upon that other person, at least to some degree. Actually, verbalizing jealousy can often be beneficial to the maintenance of a relationship, rather than letting problems fester and grow in silent anger. "To hide these feelings and not talk about them is to hide that love which is often the stimulus for resolving conflicts in relationships" (Kersten and Kersten, 1981, p. 102). Those who are pathologically jealous, however, are, in reality, people who are desperate for love but who have trouble giving or receiving it.

Are there male and female differences regarding jealousy? Sociologists Gordon Clanton and Lynn Smith indicate that men are more likely to *deny* jealous feelings, as they are more likely to deny most feelings, except perhaps anger. Women are more likely than men to *acknowledge* jealous feelings. Clanton and Smith (1977) write the following about sex differences:

Men are more likely than women to express jealous feelings through rage and even violence. . . . Jealous men are more apt to focus on the outside sexual activity of the partner. . . . Jealous women are more likely to focus on the emotional involvement between her partner and the third party. Men are . . . more likely to blame

BOX 4.5

THE EYE OF THE BEHOLDER—A CROSS-CULTURAL LOOK AT JEALOUSY

People will most likely interpret a situation to be threatening when it involves the potential or actual loss of a spouse or mate to a real or imagined rival. Reactions in such a situation, whatever they may be, are typically labeled as jealousy. Ralph Hupka, of California State University, demonstrates that the interpretation of a particular event will not, however, be the same for all cultures. Claiming that "events have meaning only in the context of the culture" (1981, p. 325), Hupka goes on to argue that jealousy has cultural as well as human determinants.

To illustrate his point, Hupka presents the following fabricated situation, which takes place in a "primitive" society of approximately 100 members.

> On her return trip from the local watering well, a married woman is asked for a cup of water by a male resident of the village. Her husband, resting on the porch of their dwelling, observes his wife giving the man a cup of water. Subsequently, they approach the husband and the three of them enjoy a lively and friendly conversation into the late evening hour. Eventually the husband puts out the lamp, and the guest has sexual intercourse with the wife. The next morning the husband leaves the house early in order to catch fish for breakfast. Upon his return, he finds his wife having sex again with the guest. . . .

At what point in the vignette may one expect the husband to evaluate the interaction between his wife and the man as a threat to his well-being? It depends, of course, in which culture we place the husband. A husband of the Pawnee Indian tribe in the 19th century bewitched any man who dared to request a cup of water from his wife (Weltfish, 1965). An Ammassalik Eskimo husband, on the other hand, offered his wife to a guest by means of the culturally sanctioned game of "putting out the lamp." A good host was expected to turn out the lamp at night as an invitation for the guest to have sexual intercourse with the wife. The Ammassalik, however, became intensely jealous when his wife copulated with a guest in circumstances other than the lamp game or without a mutual agreement between two families to exchange mates, and it was not unusual for the husband to kill an interloper (Mirsky, 1937b).

The Toda of Southern India, who were primarily polyandrous at the turn of the century when Rivers (1906) observed them, would consider the sequence of events described in the vignette to be perfectly normal. That is to say, the husband would not have been upset to find his wife having sexual relations again in the morning if the man were her mokhthodvaiol. The Toda had the custom of mokhthoditi which allowed husbands and wives to take on lovers. When, for instance, a man wanted someone else's wife as a lover, he sought the consent of the wife and her husband or husbands. If consent was given by all, the men negotiated for the annual fee to be received by the husband(s). The woman then lived with the man just as if she were his real wife. Or, more commonly, the man visited the woman at the house of her husband(s) (Rivers, 1906). (1981, pp. 324–325)

Hupka (1981) believes that these illustrations show that "the culture of a society is a more potent variable than characteristics of the individual in predicting which event someone will evaluate as a threat" and thus react jealously (p. 325). Considering the diversified culture of the United States, however, where rules are not so clearly spelled out, individual characteristics, such as insecurity, may determine whether or not a man would experience jealousy when he observes his wife giving the man a cup of water.

the partner, or the third party, or "circumstances." Women . . . blame themselves. Similarly, a jealous man is more likely to display competitive *behavior toward the third party while a jealous woman is more likely to display* possessive *behavior. She clings to the partner rather than confronting the third party. (p. 11)*

Human beings are not just jealous of people. We have found in marital therapy that it is not uncommon for a wife to say that she is jealous of the time that her husband spends working long hours, of the television that monopolizes his time at home, of fishing or hunting trips that take him away from the house. In these instances the wife feels a loss of possible intimacy because the husband is too "busy" and because he separates his life from hers. Being a workaholic or playaholic can function as an escape from emotional closeness with a spouse.

DIFFERENCES BETWEEN LOVE AND INTIMACY

The words *love* and *intimacy* are thrown around with a casualness that can't help but lead to confusion. Probably the most distinguishing difference between love and intimacy is that love is conceptualized as an *individual* attitude and intimacy is *dyadic*. Love feelings can be felt alone even without an active, willing partner, whereas intimacy is always interactive. Also, not every love attachment, even mutual ones, involves intimacy. Intimacy requires interdependence or mutual dependence, while love only requires dependence, which may, but need not be, mutual.

Love can come on quickly, particularly the infatuation brand. People sometimes speak of "love at first sight" or "instant love." Intimacy, in contrast, will take considerable time to develop; there is no such thing as

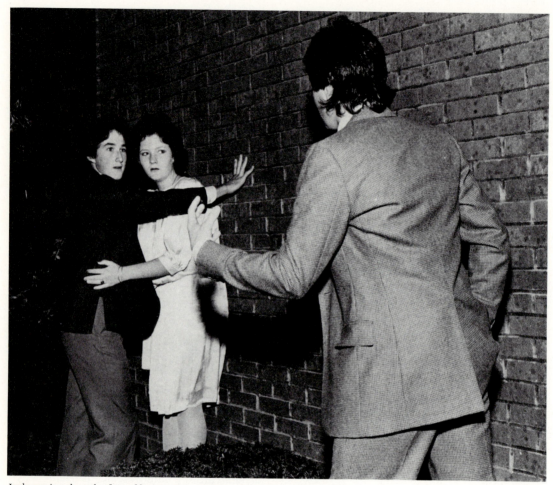

Jealousy involves the fear of losing one's partner.

"instant intimacy." Intimacy is a result of a long process. One problem with love, as most of us know, is that it can be fickle. It can be here today and gone tomorrow. So any commitments made while under the spell of love are subject to that emotional frame of reference. The receiver of such love can only count on a conditional security. Intimacy, however, is attained over time through proven commitment and trustworthiness. The end result

is much greater security than is typically found through "love."

It is particularly valuable to distinguish *romantic* love from intimacy. Romantic or passionate love usually involves, at least to some degree, the goal of sexuality. Intimate relationships do not necessarily include sexual activity; they may or they may not. Similarly, intimacy will not typically result in intense physiological reactions, such as heart palpitations, which are so often said to be found when romantic love strikes. While one can be romantically in love even with a fantasy or a dream, that is impossible with intimacy. With romantic love one could be "swept off one's feet" in a sort of uncontrollable way. Romantic love may be an "emotional roller-coaster," whereas intimacy is more relaxed, consciously controlled, and consistent. With romantic love there is often a "cognitive obsession" about the beloved that one would not find with intimacy.

It's certainly possible to love without experiencing intimacy. Love itself can be shown in a nonintimate way by nonintimate persons. But one cannot have emotional closeness without love, however it is defined. The opposite of love is individual apathy and indifference; the opposite of intimacy is the lack of dyadic contact or isolation. Of course, almost all of us will "love" many more people than we will be intimate with, a number that is of necessity small.

It's possible for love not to involve reciprocity. It may be mostly one-way, as in unrequited love. Intimacy always involves reciprocity, mostly the giving and receiving of *rewards*. Love can exist without much exchange at all, and even without commitment. In addition, feelings of "love" actually increase for many people upon being rejected. In contrast, rejection severely diminishes intimacy. Some so-called love is solely based on self-centered need, and the relationship may be highly exploitative. Dyadic intimacy, in contrast, is based on proven trust and commitment and is never exploitative.

Love comes early in some relationships. But over time love can grow so deep and so close that emotional intimacy is the end result. In American society, love is a prerequisite to marriage. It is the means used to induce people to marry. Intimacy isn't necessarily connected with marriage at all and is seldom even discussed. If real emotional closeness develops, it usually comes after marriage. But once developed, intimacy is more enduring and resilient; love will be broken more frequently. Also, love is much more easily taken for granted; one could never take intimacy for granted. Finally, it should be mentioned that love can linger on once a relationship has ended; intimacy will not.

CHAPTER REVIEW

1. Until recently there has been relatively little scientific research conducted on love. The mysterious nature of love has often discouraged social scientists from seriously pursuing its study. In fact, research on love was considered by some to be taboo; it was felt that the topic would be better left to philosophers and romanticists.

2. Love involves four key aspects—an attachment, feelings, thoughts, and behavior. It can be defined as an attitude toward another person that includes an attachment, strong positive emotions, mostly positive thoughts, and positive behavior or actions. The expression of love, in its various forms, is strongly influenced by the specific norms that exist in a particular society or subculture.

3. All human beings are born with the need to be loved and with the urge to love. Childhood experiences have a significant impact on one's ability to love as an adult. An important outcome of receiving love as a child is a sense of positive self-esteem. Research shows that individuals who lack love experience more stress and illness in their lives. In addition, the deprivation of love can con-

tribute to many kinds of behavioral problems—child abuse, criminal behavior, and suicide.

4. Romantic love involves intense feelings of attraction toward another person; it tends to be idealistic, illusionary, and artificially heightened. Romantic love continues to be a key factor in understanding mating patterns, marital expectations, and sexual attitudes and behavior in America.

5. Many myths about love exist, such as "Love conquers all," each of us has a "one and only," "love at first sight." A belief in these myths hinders an individual from having an accurate perception of love and may result in the person chasing after a fantasy or dream.

6. While a popular stereotype depicts women as more romantic than men, in reality, men tend to rank higher on romantic love than women, at the beginning of a relationship and at the end. Romantic love for women seems to reach its peak after a commitment to the relationship has been made.

7. The radical feminist view depicts romantic love as exploitation. Love, according to some feminist writers, is a means used by men to keep women in their place. The goal for men is to get a woman to love them without giving equal power and a full commitment in return.

8. Jealousy often accompanies the feeling of love. Jealousy involves the fear of losing someone you love. While jealousy for the most part is a normal emotion, there are some individuals who are jealous to an unhealthy degree.

9. It is important to distinguish between romantic love and intimacy. Love is conceptualized as an individual attitude; intimacy is always dyadic. Love can develop quickly; intimacy takes a considerable amount of time to develop. Intimacy does not necessarily involve sexual activity, whereas romantic love typically does.

5

Sexuality
and Intimacy

THE HISTORICAL ROOTS OF SEXUAL EXPRESSION

One of the more important historical factors affecting sexuality in America was the Victorian tradition, particularly as it affected the period 1865–1920. The major concern of the time was the control of sexual passion through the development of a strong will. For males this control was seen as a particularly difficult task because they were considered to be "naturally" lusty creatures (Mahoney, 1983).

Sexual desire was seen as intertwined with the body's energy system, which maintained health and life. But the amount of energy in one's body was considered to be limited; for example, "one was thought to have only so many orgasms, and when one used these up, one was thought to shrivel like a prune" (Mahoney, 1983, p. 9). The "loss" of one ounce of semen was said to equal the loss of 40 ounces of blood. Thus sexual activity was seen as contributing to physical deterioration. "This concern with using up a limited resource is clear in the Victorian term for ejaculation—'to spend,' [in] rather dramatic contrast to the present-day term 'to come,' which suggests that one has arrived at a desirable goal. Excessive sexual activity was thus seen as a real danger to life, limb, mind, and the very fabric of society" (p. 9). But what was "excessive"? While different frequencies of intercourse were recommended for married couples, 12 times a year was considered more than enough, or insanity would result (Mahoney, 1983).

But there was even more concern over masturbation than there was about sexual activity in marriage. A common view of a young male who masturbated is indicated below:

The frame is stunted and weak, the muscles underdeveloped, the eye is sunken and heavy, the complexion is sallow, pasty, or covered with spots of acne, the hands are damp and cold, and the skin moist. The boy shuns the society of others, creeps about alone. . . . He cannot look anyone in the face. . . . His intellect has become sluggish and enfeebled, and if his evil habits are persisted in, he may end in becoming a drivelling idiot. (Murstein, 1974, p. 252)

Extensive efforts were made to help lusty young males to keep from masturbating. A man named Sylvester Graham suggested a "calming" diet to diminish sexual desire, part of which would be his own "graham crackers." More severe suggestions included devices designed to inhibit erections during sleep (see Figure 5.1).

While males were thought "naturally" to have trouble controlling their sexuality, females were considered to be delicate, pure creatures who were basically passionless. As a physician, ironically named Dr. William Action, of the period noted:

. . . the majority of women (happily for society) are not very much troubled with sexual feelings of any kind. What men are habitually, women are only exceptionally . . . there can be no doubt that sexual feeling in the female is in the majority of cases in abeyance, and that it requires positive and considerable excitement to be aroused at all. . . . Love of home, of children, and of domestic duties are the only passions they [women] feel. (Murstein, 1974, pp. 253–254)

Female masturbation was viewed even more negatively than male masturbation, and the remedies were much more severe. The surgical removal of the clitoris, or clitoridectomy, was not uncommon. Such practices still exist in Africa and India today. The Victorian morality, emphasizing chastity and purity, had its greatest impact on the growing num-

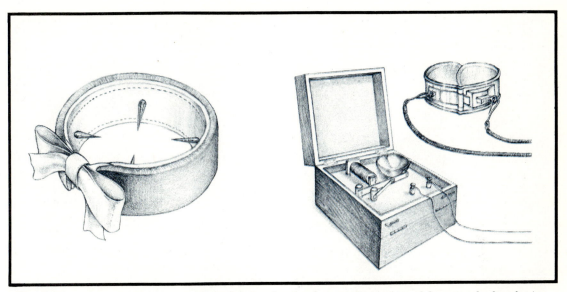

Figure 5.1 "These two devices were invented during the Victorian period to prevent adolescent males from having erections during their sleep. The device on the left, with its sharp points, is simple in both purpose and design. It was placed around the young male's penis when he went to bed. If he had an erection the results are obvious. The device on the right is more complicated. The box contained a small battery that supplied current through the two wires to the metal ring. This ring was split and was placed around the young male's penis when he went to bed. On the box was a spring steel bar that was held against the two poles as long as electrical current flowed through the two wires. If the male had an erection, the flow of current was broken by the metal ring expanding and breaking contact. This loss of electrical current resulted in a loss of magnetism in the two poles. As a result, the spring bar flew forward, struck the bell, and thus woke up his parents." (*Source:* Mahoney, 1983.)

ber of middle-class women. "A proper middle-class lady was not to dress in a revealing or provocative manner, she would not use vulgar language, and her mind was to remain free of any sensual thought" (Mahoney, 1983, p. 11).

After World War I, the 1920s and 1930s saw more sexuality, as a matter both for discussion and for experimentation. Sexual activity was no longer considered to be reserved for reproduction. The first sex-positive marriage manuals began to speak of sexual enjoyment as an end in itself; it was in these manuals that the female orgasm was "discovered" (Clanton, 1984). The so-called sexual revolution of the twentieth century began in the 1920s, but it received a big push from the scientific community with the publication of Alfred Kinsey's research on sexual behavior in 1948 and 1953. "His findings challenged existing notions of the prevalence and frequency of specific sexual behaviors. As a consequence, the public focused on sexuality as it had never done before" (Kilmann, 1984, p. 18).

The doors were now open for more scientific research. William Masters and Virginia Johnson (1966) began to study human sexual anatomy and physiology, as well as male and female sexual behavior. Many sexual myths were disproved. Also the 1960s saw the beginning of the women's liberation movement. As women became more vocal, they challenged with considerable energy traditional notions of female sexuality and the double standard. Another social movement

A proper Victorian lady was not to dress in a revealing or provocative manner and her mind was to be free of any sensual thoughts.

The so-called sexual revolution of the twentieth century began in the 1920s with increased sexual experimentation and dramatically different clothing styles for women.

in the late 1960s that contributed to the sexual revolution was gay liberation. As a result, while many people were made more tolerant of homosexuality, others were shocked at the open acceptance of what they called "sinful behavior" (Kilmann, 1984). (See Appendix B for a review of major research regarding sexuality.)

The 1965–1975 era was the high point (or low point, depending on one's values) of the twentieth-century sexual revolution. All types of sexual activity increased—premarital, marital, and postdivorce for both sexes— but most particularly for young women. Sexual acts once thought horrid, such as oral sex and various nontraditional positions of sex-

ual intercourse, were commonly practiced. Highly effective birth control allowed an "everything goes" attitude to prevail among many people (Kilmann, 1984).

In the 1980s liberal sexual *attitudes* continued to prevail. Family conservatives, however, represented a significant force regarding sexuality on many fronts—sexual education in the schools, abortion, birth-control availability for teenagers, opposition to homosexual rights and activities, and pornography. Other concerns that may have slowed liberal sexual *behavior* in the 1980s included fears about sexually transmitted diseases, particularly genital herpes and acquired immune deficiency syndrome (AIDS) (Kilmann, 1984).

BLOOM COUNTY   by Berke Breathed

(See Appendix C for a description of sexually transmitted diseases.)

SEXUAL DEVELOPMENT

Prenatal Sexuality

The rudiments of human sexuality begin to form even before birth. Evidence suggests that the fetus's skin, connected to the most important of all erotic senses (that of touch), is one of the first sensory systems to become functional. The fetus "is massaged with each movement of the mother as she carries on her daily activities. . . . [It] is active in the womb perhaps because activity reduces tension and increases pleasurable feelings" (Martinson, 1982, p. 3).

Fetuses with erections have now been photographed. Female infants experience vaginal lubrication soon after birth, and it is possible that this function exists before birth also. It seems clear "that the human sexual response system functions literally during the entire life span" (Calderone, 1983, p. 9). Of course, these very early "sexual" experiences are predominantly "reflexive"; the fetuses are unaware of what is happening.

Mother-Infant Interaction

Typically the mother-infant dyadic relationship is very close, involving as it does a sensuousness derived to a large degree from bodily contact. Infant-mother interaction involves the "ears, eyes, nose, hands, mouths, lips, tongue, breasts, and some genital contact when caring for the baby. Only extensive and prolonged genital contact is normally excluded from infant-mother interchange" (Martinson, 1982, p. 15).

Breast feeding, however, appears to be sensual to both the infant and the mother. Newborns seem definitely to prefer "sucking at the mother's breast to being bottle fed" (Martinson, 1982, p. 19). Mothers who enjoy breast feeding speak of the "tenderness and closeness" rendered by the act. Some nursing mothers describe the experience as sexually stimulating to the point of orgasm (Kinsey et al., 1953; Masters and Johnson, 1966). There is typically extensive touching and caressing by the mother during the breast-feeding process.

In American society we expect the interaction between a mother and infant to be emotionally close and sensual; "infants are

BOX 5.1

HUMAN SEXUALITY IN GLOBAL PERSPECTIVE

Cultures around the world vary greatly in the degree to which they accept human sexuality. It's possible to distinguish four types of cultures—repressive, restrictive, permissive, and supportive.

SEXUALLY REPRESSIVE CULTURES

Cultures that repress sexuality generally *deny* their sexuality. In fact, sexuality is viewed as extremely dangerous, and sexual inactivity is treated as a virtue. All forms of sexual acts are typically prohibited, except that which is required for procreation. Premarital chastity is required, and sexual ignorance among the young is a goal; certainly any sexual play between children is strongly prohibited. "Adolescent and adult sexuality . . . is associated with guilt, fear, and anger. . . . Sexually repressive cultures are common throughout Europe but are extremely rare on other continents. The traditional rural Irish community of Inis Beag (Messenger, 1971) provides one excellent example; the Cheyenne (Hoebel, 1960), buffalo hunters of the North American plains, is another" (Currier, 1981, p. 13).

SEXUALLY RESTRICTIVE CULTURES

Societies that would be included among sexually restrictive cultures are focused on the *limitation* of sexuality. "Sexual play in childhood is strongly discouraged. . . . Premarital chastity is required of at least one of the sexes, although some sexual license is generally granted to the other sex" (Currier, 1981, p. 13). Since one sex is required to remain celibate, there are few opportunities for heterosexual behavior in adolescence. "Sexual pleasure is typically valued more by the sex that was given more sexual freedom in early life. In general, these cultures are ambivalent about sex: They pursue it, but not without reservation. Sex tends to be feared, not so much in itself as for the problems it can cause. Sexually restrictive cultures are common throughout the world. Although they are a minority among primitive cultures, they are the dominant type among civilizations. The Mexican peasant village of Tepoztlán (Lewis, 1951) provides one example; the Dani (Heider, 1976), primitive agriculturalists of the New Guinea Highlands, provide another" (Currier, 1981, p. 13).

SEXUALLY PERMISSIVE CULTURES

Cultures that are sexually permissive tend to *tolerate* sexuality. Some formal prohibitions exist, but they are very loosely enforced. "Sexual play in childhood may be technically forbidden, but as long as it is kept out of sight adults maintain a public pretext that they do not know what is going on. Adolescents of both sexes are usually allowed considerable sexual latitude, and premarital sex is considered normal" (Currier, 1981, p. 13). Both sexes value sexual pleasure; sexuality is considered to be a natural and inevitable part of human life. "Sexually permissive cultures are found on every continent; they are rare in Europe, but they are common in the equatorial latitudes of Africa, Asia, and the Americas. The Semai (Dentan, 1968), aboriginal inhabitants of the Malay jungles, are an ideal example of this type" (Currier, 1981, p. 14).

SEXUALLY SUPPORTIVE CULTURES

Included among sexually supportive cultures are those that *encourage* sexuality, which is seen as necessary for human happiness. Early sexual experience is viewed as a valuable part of growing up. Such cultures provide *"both sexual information and sexual opportunity* to young people of all ages who are being encouraged, especially by the parental generation, to develop their sexual skills. . . . Special dwelling or meeting-places may be designated legitimate social arenas for juvenile and (especially) adolescent sexual activity" (Currier, 1981, p. 14). Homosexual activities may or may not be tolerated, but in any event, "sexual pleasure is both highly valued and positively demanded by both sexes. The lack of sexual gratification is considered intolerable, and it is sufficient grounds for terminating any sexual relationship, including marriage. . . . Sexually supportive cultures are common in equatorial Africa, Southern Asia, and (especially) Oceania. Old Polynesia, where this approach predominated, earned a well-deserved reputation among world travellers for the abundance of its sexual gratification. The Muria (Elwin, 1968) and the Trobrianders (Malinowski, 1929), inhabitants of a group of coral islands in the South Pacific, furnish classic examples of this type" (Currier, 1981, p. 14).

Cultures can change over time in their approach to sexuality. In American society the Victorian period was a sexually repressive time. In the first half of the present century, Americans changed from a repressive to a restrictive sexual culture. The 1965–1975 era was for many a period of sexual permissiveness. This permissiveness, however, has greatly contributed to the backlash by the family conservatives. The later 1980s saw a battle involving those who wanted to return to a period of at least sexual restrictiveness, those who were comfortable with permissiveness, and some liberals who said American culture should become sexually supportive.

---

supposed to be stimulated, cuddled, fondled, . . . by the mother from the moment of birth" (Martinson, 1982, p. 23). Such exchanges help the infant to develop emotional, intimate, and erotic potential. Insufficient physical, emotional, and sensual mother-infant contact may result in the later inability of the infant to form attachments and func-

tion in intimate relationships (Martinson, 1982).

While mother-infant exchanges are not intended to be sexual in and of themselves, some caregivers may experience guilt over the sensual interaction. Women who have found themselves to be sexually stimulated by the sucking process have often needlessly given up breast feeding because of "the fear that the experience may prove to be too sexually stimulating both for themselves and for the infant. Also, some mothers voluntarily reject the opportunity to nurse their newborns because of high levels of eroticism they had experienced during the nursing of a sibling of the baby" (Martinson, 1982, p. 23). Mothers typically do not fantasize erotically during the breast-feeding process, nor do they attribute erotic motives to the infant, even if the baby has erections (Martinson, 1982). In any event, however, mother-infant interaction is a highly sensual experience.

Infant Body Contact

Genital play, the touching of the genitals, is rather common in most boys by 6 or 7 months of age and for most girls by 10 or 11 months of age (Galenson and Riopke, 1974). It is important, however, to distinguish between *genital play* and *masturbation* in infancy. Most infants do not have either the motivation or the muscular coordination necessary for the rhythmic manipulation of the genitals with the hand. But many infants develop a rocking pattern, which can provide pleasurable genital sensations. Young female infants under 1 year of age may provide themselves pleasurable sensations just from pressing their thighs together (Martinson, 1982). Some infants under 1 year of age, however, have been observed in actual masturbation. Kinsey reports a few infants who did have the necessary hand and muscle coordination to stimulate themselves (1953).

Preschool Body Exploration

Among 2-year-olds and older there is an obvious awareness of the genitals, and masturbatory activity tends to increase with age. Although genital play "is often ignored in books on infant and child development, it has long been recognized as a near-universal phenomenon" (Martinson, 1982, pp. 31–32). "Masturbation appears to be a common experience in the development of normal . . . children. . . . It is recognized as a tension reliever, and is often observed among nursery-school children" (pp. 32–33). While boys do not ejaculate prior to puberty, all other mechanisms of sexual response exist from infancy on. Unfortunately, many children seem to suffer from considerable guilt over masturbation (Masters, Johnson, and Kolodny, 1982). Ten realistic facts about masturbation are shown in Box 5.2.

A study of the sexual behaviors of 400 young children in Norway was conducted through interviews with 60 kindergarten and preschool teachers (Gundersen, Melas, and Skar, 1981). The teachers indicated that the children were already very sexual by the age of 3; they showed their sexual feelings and curiosity through their sexual play. All the teachers had observed doctor/nurse/patient games. Also, "ninety-four percent of the preschool teachers interviewed stated that the children displayed a marked interest in their own genitals by studying them, fondling them, showing them to others, or so on" (p. 53). Eighty-five percent of the teachers indicated that the children masturbated in their schools. The researchers argue that "the masturbatory behavior in these cases seemed to have a soothing, sedative effect on the child" (p. 56).

In reality, scientific knowledge about childhood sexuality is greatly lacking; it has been called "the last frontier in sex research" (Money, 1976). "Attempts to interview children or administer questionnaires to them about their sexual attitudes and behavior have often been thwarted by community outrage about 'putting nasty ideas in children's minds' and accusations of undermining the moral fabric of our society. Except for some limited cross-cultural data from primitive so-

BOX 5.2

TEN FACTS ABOUT ADULT MASTURBATION

1. Masturbation is not confined to childhood and adolescence.
2. Masturbation is not necessarily a substitute for sex with a partner.
3. Masturbation can be shared.
4. There is no such thing as excessive masturbation.
5. Masturbation can be as physically sexually satisfying as intercourse.
6. Masturbation does not hinder the development of social relationships.
7. Masturbation is a good way to learn about one's own sexual feelings and responsiveness.
8. Masturbation does not lead to weakness, mental illness, or physical debilitation.
9. Males do not eventually run out of semen if they masturbate frequently.
10. Masturbation does not lead to homosexuality.

SOURCE: *Kelly, 1980, pp. 76–79.*

cieties in which childhood sex play is permitted and data from a few instances of direct observation, we are forced to rely on guesswork and inference in this important area'' (Masters, Johnson, and Kolodny, 1982). One recent survey of parents of 6- and 7-year-old children, however, found that 76 percent of the daughters and 83 percent of the sons had participated in some sort of sex play, with the majority of experiences involving play with siblings (Kolodny, 1980).

The Differential Treatment of Infants and Children

Mother-*infant* interaction has been seen as almost necessarily close, emotionally intimate, and highly sensual. Society accepts and encourages these interactions. But parents' attitudes and reactions begin to change when the youngster continues to act like a sexual creature, when genital play and masturbation are continued into childhood. Parents tend to become more restrictive of and negative toward *children* than *infants* in terms of sexuality. The parent-child relationship itself may become less emotionally close as the parents become disciplinary authority figures. In American society it is thought that the child must learn to become more independent during childhood and adolescence. It is often thought that habits of sensual parent-child interaction are to be left behind in infancy. There seems to be agreement in society that children should be "socialized away from body contact with self as well as with others" (Martinson, 1982, p. 43).

Children's touching patterns with parents

Preschool children often show their natural curiosity about the human body through body exploration and sexual play.

POEM

There is something I don't know
    that I am supposed to know.
I don't know what it is I don't know,
    and yet am supposed to know,
and I feel I look stupid
    if I seem both not to know it
        and not know what it is I don't know.
Therefore I pretend I know it.
    this is nerve-racking
    since I don't know what I must pretend to
    know.
Therefore I pretend to know everything.

I feel you know what I am supposed to know
but you can't tell me what it is
because you don't know that I don't know what
    it is.

You may know what I don't know, but not
        that I don't know it.
and I can't tell you. So you will have to tell me
    everything.

FROM R.D. LAING, *KNOTS*

---

gradually become more restricted. Mothers express an image of being asexual, sexually repressive, or even sexually punitive (Finkelhor, 1980b). Mothers are viewed by their children as holding more sexually repressive attitudes than fathers and they are more than twice as likely as fathers to punish their daughters for asking questions about sex, playing sex games, or masturbating. Fathers are often perceived as sexually "dangerous," especially for daughters (Martinson, 1982).

Parents tend to hold some gender-specific attitudes regarding affection and sexuality with their children. "For example, the kiss of the father on the neck of his daughter was not to be reciprocated. . . . [Also] 'too much' touching, especially among boys causes discomfort for many parents. . . . The male macho-image and the fear of homosexuality appear to inhibit sons in many families from openly-shared affection, especially with their fathers" (Martinson, 1952, p. 44).

Parents in American society do not typically reveal or admit their own adult sexuality to their children. Maybe this is why most children cannot really believe that their parents actually "do it." In front of their children most parents interact with each other more as associates or business partners rather than with extensive physical affection; they act like friends rather than like a close couple. In a 1978 study done in Cleveland, few of the parents ever had discussed any aspect of erotic activity with their children (Roberts,

Kline, and Gagnon, 1978). Two-thirds of the Cleveland mothers said that it was the child who usually brought up the subject of sexuality. "Hence, the level of conversation about sexuality in most homes would appear to depend upon the degree of sophistication and inquisitiveness of the child" (Martinson, 1982, pp. 45–46).

Puberty

Up until puberty the child secretes low levels of sex hormones. Then some unknown factor triggers the final development of the sexual and reproductive system. Puberty is a process, rather than an event, that begins between the ages of 8 and 13 in girls and 9 and 14 in boys. It may take several years to complete the process (Nass, Libby, and Fisher, 1984).

As part of this puberty process, sex hormones are produced in the female ovaries and the male testicles. These hormones act to prepare the body for reproduction by causing a number of physical changes. *Estrogen,* secreted by the ovaries, "feminizes" the body. The levels of estrogen are increased 10 times from what existed during childhood (Masters, Johnson, and Kolodny, 1982). Females also secrete small amounts of *testosterone* from their ovaries, but it is the estrogen that causes most of the secondary sex characteristics to develop. "These include enlargement of the breasts, uterus, and vagina; broadening of the hips; development of fat deposits on the breasts and buttocks; an increase in vaginal secretions; and the onset of menstruation" (Nass, Libby, and Fisher, 1984, p. 25).

The testosterone level in boys increases 10 to 20 times at puberty (Masters, Johnson, and Kolodny, 1982). Testosterone has a "masculinizing" effect on the body, creating male secondary sex characteristics. "These include changes in the hair distribution, body shape, and genital size; [and] maturation of the internal reproductive structures" (Nass, Libby, and Fisher, 1984, p. 25). Ejaculations are now possible, some of which might occur during sleep. In any event, after puberty both the male and female are ready, from a biological point of view, for sexual functioning as adults. See Figures 5.2 and 5.3, which show the male and female reproductive systems.

ADULT SEXUALITY

Sex as an Appetite

Sexuality involves erotic behavior, feelings, and thoughts. It is best understood as an appetite derived partly from biology but most of all from sociocultural learning. Thus, similarly to viewing an individual's desire or craving for food, it is possible to view sexuality also as an appetite. There is a biologically based urge for sexual release or physical pleasure seeking that exists, as has been indicated, possibly before birth but certainly from birth on. Sex is an appetite in a child that can be (1) totally denied; (2) discouraged, restricted, and punished; (3) ignored but tolerated (as if it didn't exist); or (4) encouraged and rewarded by parents or guardians. If the child's sexual appetite is dealt with positively, this attitude seems to strengthen later adult feelings about the legitimacy of sexual experience; it helps to create a healthy appetite.

For example, whether a parent evaluates a "playing doctor" experience in a child either negatively or positively can help to determine the child's comfortableness with his or her own sexuality. If a child's sexual appetite has been developed positively, he or she will grow up to find sexual activity pleasurable. If a person is deprived of positive sexual development, one of two outcomes is possible. First, the person may shy away from

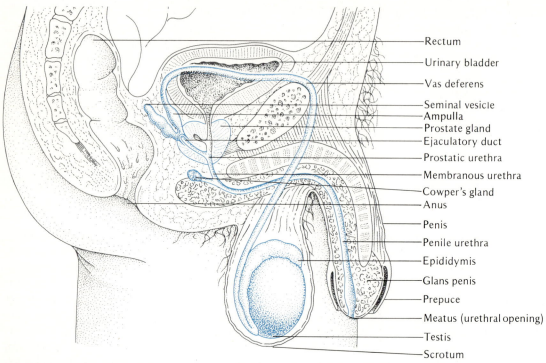

Figure 5.2   The male sexual and reproductive organs, side view. (*Source:* From Morton G. Harmatz and Melinda A. Novak, *Human Sexuality* [New York: Harper & Row, 1983], p. 80.)

sexual activity and have one or several sexual difficulties. Second, the person may feel greatly deprived and become a sexual addict with a gluttonous appetite, but he or she will have a very genitally oriented sexual focus.

Looking at sex as an appetite has several advantages. We can recognize that sexual appetites vary just as appetites do for food. One can have sex alone, just as we would not starve ourselves simply because someone refused to eat with us. Since we all may not be hungry at the same time, neither will we necessarily feel sexual at the same time. When eating together we do not all necessarily eat the same amounts or with the same gusto. Each of us satisfies his or her own appetite even though we may enjoy the meal together. There typically is not friction over who eats

what or how much (Crenshaw, 1983). Sex can be the same way. People should follow their own appetites regarding sexual activity. One should not feel forced "to go all the way" because someone else might say, "You led me on." Again, comparing sexuality with an appetite for food, Crenshaw argues, "Would you feel responsible for feeding him if he was hungry? . . . Would you feel compelled to eat for him (or even with him) because your cooking aroused his appetite, if you weren't hungry too?" (1983, p. 28).

The effects of hormones on sexual appetite have been studied extensively. Testosterone is the most important hormone affecting sexual functioning, in both men and women. While low levels of testosterone may cause a decrease in sexual desire, extremely

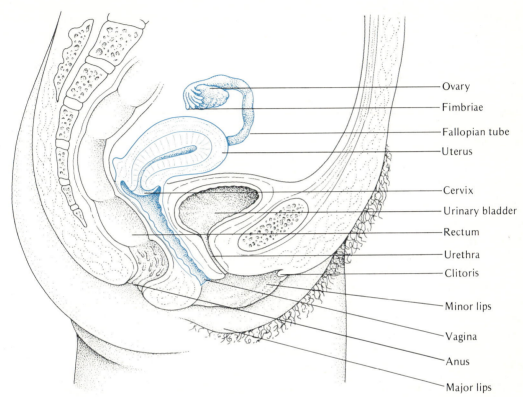

Ovary
Fimbriae
Fallopian tube
Uterus
Cervix
Urinary bladder
Rectum
Urethra
Clitoris
Minor lips
Vagina
Anus
Major lips

Figure 5.3 Internal sexual and reproductive organs of the female, side view. (*Source:* From Harmatz and Novak, 1983, p. 72.)

high testosterone levels may increase sexual interest. In men particularly, very low levels of testosterone may result in a difficulty in obtaining or maintaining an erection (Masters, Johnson, and Kolodny, 1982).

Estrogen, which also is present in both sexes, is more important to women from a sexual point of view. Estrogen produces vaginal lubrication and helps to maintain the condition and elasticity of the vaginal lining. Estrogen also helps to preserve the texture and functioning of the female breasts. Estrogen does not, however, seem to be an important factor in determining female sexual desire; the removal of the ovaries, for example, does not decrease the sexual appetite of

women. But in males too much estrogen can cause erection difficulties and enlargement of the breasts (Masters, Johnson, and Kolodny, 1982). A number of studies have shown that female sexual desire varies somewhat with the stage in the menstrual cycle. The two peaks of interest occur at ovulation (when both testosterone and estrogen reach their highest levels) and at premenstruation (when estrogen is dropping, while testosterone remains rather constant). Women, however, are most likely to masturbate around the time of menstruation (Nass, Libby, and Fisher, 1984).

It is important to note that the influence of hormones on sexual appetite is still somewhat unclear. Overall, social-cultural factors seem to be more important than hormone levels. Moreover, "some studies suggest that our hormone levels may even reflect our behavior patterns rather than vice versa. . . . Biology and social learning and activity are so closely intertwined that often it's hard to distinguish cause from effect" (Nass, Libby, and Fisher, 1984, p. 46).

Reflexive Arousal

There are two broad types of sexual turn-ons, both having significant biological interconnections. The most basic form of response, whether it involves arousal or actual orgasm, is a reflex (Francoeur, 1982). Similar in nature to the knee-jerk and sneeze reflexes, "certain stimuli can trigger sexual response reflexes automatically, without our being conscious of or in immediate control of the responses. Erogenous zones of the body and the sexual organs themselves react automatically to the stimulus of caressing touches" (Francoeur, 1982, p. 155).

For example, when the penis is touched or stroked, a message is sent through the nervous system to the erection center in the spinal cord. "This center then sends a message to the tiny valvelike channels leading from the arteries of the penis to the spaces in the penis' spongy tissues, telling them to relax. As a consequence, blood rushes into the chambers of the penis . . . the penis becomes distended and erect" (Offir, 1982, p. 98). This reflexive response is inborn, as is the pleasure it provides when the brain is later signaled through the sensory nerves about the erection. Similar processes regarding reflexive arousal exist for the female, producing vasocongestion, vaginal lubrication, and clitoral erection. Biology is obviously important in this reflexive sexuality. "Many men and women with injured spinal cords, for in-

stance, can experience reflex sexual arousal, but because nerve paths in the spinal cord that would normally carry messages about their reflexes up to the conscious centers of the brain are severed, these persons can become reflexively aroused and have no sensation of this" (Francoeur, 1982, p. 155).

There is also an orgasmic reflex. In men, for example, there are involuntary rhythmic contractions that take place when sexual arousal reaches a peak, which, in turn, trigger a reflexive release. It is important to distinguish between orgasm and ejaculation. While the two typically occur together, particularly in men, "orgasm refers to the release of muscle and nervous tensions following sufficient sexual arousal. Ejaculation refers to the release of seminal fluid" (Francoeur, 1982, p. 156). The complete sexual-response cycle is discussed in Box 5.3.

Psychic Arousal

Psychic arousal most typically involves erotic thoughts, which proceed from the brain down the neural pathways to the spinal cord and then to the genitals. Such arousal is affected by emotions, the senses, mood-modifying drugs, erotic materials, and fantasies.

EMOTIONS AND SEXUAL AROUSAL. Emotions have a great impact on the potential for sexual activity. Positive emotions and feelings encourage sexuality; negative emotions and feelings tend to inhibit the sexual appetite and actual sexual functioning. The emotions can include both feelings about oneself and feelings toward others. Examples of positive emotions that encourage sexuality include love, emotional closeness, happiness, warmth, trust, comfortableness, and acceptance. Examples of negative emotions that can inhibit sexuality—and even lead to sexual difficulties in functioning—include anxi-

(Text continued on page 148.)

BOX 5.3

THE SEXUAL-RESPONSE CYCLE

Based on their studies of 10,000 sessions of sexual activity, William Masters and Virginia Johnson (1966) have suggested four stages of sexual response: *excitement, plateau, orgasm,* and *resolution.* Regardless of how a person may be stimulated—by direct touch of the genitals, by the touching of other erogenous zones of the body, or as a result of erotic thoughts—the same general response pattern exists. Only the quickness of arousal and the intensity may vary somewhat.

The phases of sexual response are quite similar for both men and women. There are two basic underlying processes that occur throughout the sexual-response cycle—vasocongestion and myotonia. *Vasocongestion* relates to the process of the increased flow of blood to the pelvic region, the penis and vulva, resulting in the engorgement of tissues. *Myotonia* refers to the contraction of muscles in the genital area and other parts of the body. The four phases of sexual arousal are depicted in the accompanying diagram.

EXCITEMENT

The sexual-response cycle begins with the excitement phase and is most noted by vasocongestion. In men this results in the penis becoming erect, some increase in the size of the testes, and a drawing up of the testes closer to the body. Vasocongestion in women results in the almost immediate lubrication of the vaginal walls. Also, the upper two-thirds of the vagina expand in what is known as the "ballooning" effect, like an inflated balloon. In addition, the clitoris increases in size and becomes erect. The inner lips swell and open up, and the outer lips move apart. The breasts also swell and enlarge somewhat, and the nipples become erect. A *sex flush,* a reddish type of rash, may appear on the chest or breasts. Both the erect nipples and sex flush are more common in women. Both sexes, however, will have increases in the heart rate and blood pressure.

PLATEAU

In the plateau phase the responses of the excitement stage increase in intensity if stimulation continues. Vasocongestion reaches its highest level. The penis reaches an even greater degree of erection, the top (coronal ridge) swells, and there may be a reddish purple color in the glans. The testes increase about one-half their normal size and are pulled even higher and closer to the body. There may be a few drops of fluid from the Cowper's glands that appear at the opening of the penis. This functions as a small amount of lubrication for insertion of the penis; it is not ejaculate, but it may contain sperm.

In women the outer one-third of the vagina swells, and there is a change in color to bright red or a deep wine color. With this swelling, the vaginal opening is actually reduced in size, and this provides for a tighter gripping

(Continued)

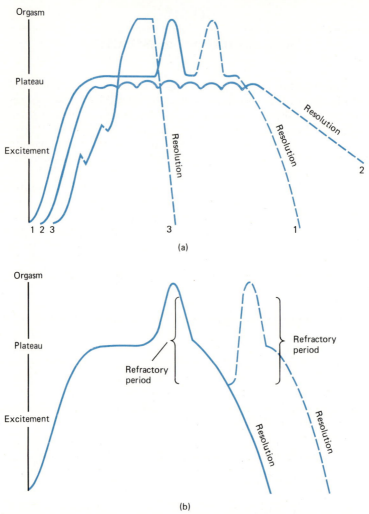

"a) Three representative variations of female sexual response. Pattern 1 shows multiple orgasm; pattern 2 shows arousal that reaches the plateau level without going on to orgasm (note that resolution occurs very slowly); and pattern 3 shows several brief drops in the excitement phase followed by an even more rapid resolution phase.

b) The most typical pattern of male sexual response. The dotted line shows one possible variation: a second orgasm and ejaculation occurring after the refractory period is over. Numerous other variations are possible, including patterns that would match 2 and 3 of the female response cycle." (*Source:* Masters and Johnson, 1966.)

of the penis. The shaft of the clitoris becomes shorter and disappears under the clitoral hood. The breasts experience further swelling, and the nipples become more erect. Both men and women experience increases in muscle tension, blood pressure, pulse rate, and breathing rate during this stage. The sex flush either becomes more pronounced, or it may first appear at this stage.

ORGASM

When vasocongestion and muscle tension reach their peak, there is a series of rhythmic contractions in the pelvic area accompanied by intense feelings of pleasure. In males this typically involves a two-stage process. The first stage is that of "ejaculatory inevitability," a sensation that ejaculation will begin soon and that it cannot be stopped. In the second stage, ejaculation takes place as a result of the rhythmic contractions of the muscles around the base of the penis. The breathing rate, pulse rate, and blood pressure all are at a peak. Muscles throughout the entire body contract, and the face may be distorted during orgasm.

Females experience a similar process of orgasm, a series of rhythmic muscular contractions of the vagina, uterus, and anus. The number of contractions can be the same as in most men—3 or 4—or there could be as many as 10 or 12 in a very intense orgasm. Involuntary muscle spasms throughout the body are common, just as in the male. Most studies suggest that the sensations of orgasm appear to be very similar in males and females, judging from written descriptions of orgasm (Vance and Wagner, 1976; Wiest, 1977).

RESOLUTION

After orgasm the body returns to an unaroused state. There is a relaxing of muscle tension and a release of blood from the engorged vessels. Resolution is a reversal of the process of buildup that took place during the excitement and plateau stages. The testicles return to their normal size and position, and the erection of the penis is quickly lost, most of it in less than a minute. While the male may move to an unstimulated, relaxed state rather quickly, the female may take much longer in achieving this state, as much as a half hour or even an hour. When completed, however, the clitoris returns to its normal color, size, and position; the sex flush disappears; and the nipples and breasts return to their normal size. Because the female can remain in an aroused situation for a long period of time, additional orgasms are possible. Men typically need a time of rest before more sexual stimulation may be possible, the *refractory period*. But in both men and women, blood pressure, pulse, and breathing rate quickly return to normal after orgasm.

AN ALTERNATIVE SEXUAL RESPONSE MODEL

Masters' and Johnson's model of the human sexual-response cycle has been criticized for dealing entirely with physiological processes and ignoring psychological subjective processes (Zilbergeld and Ellison, 1980). This is important because subjective feelings do not always match physiological response. For example, some individuals are very desirous of sexual activity, but they

(Continued)

are unable to achieve an erection or vaginal lubrication. Or they may have no sexual desire at all, even though the physiology works fine.

A five-stage alternative model of sexual response is offered by Zilbergeld and Ellison (1980) including (1) *interest,* (2) *arousal,* (3) *physiological readiness,* (4) *orgasm,* and (5) *satisfaction.* The first stage relates to how often a person wants to be involved in sexual activity—whether three times a day, or once a year, or somewhere in between. The second stage, arousal, is not a physiological measure but rather a purely subjective measure of how excited or turned on a person feels. Physiological readiness corresponds to Masters' and Johnson's excitement and plateau stages. Orgasm, according to Zilbergeld and Ellison, has both physiological and emotional components, the latter relating to the quality of closeness. And finally, satisfaction relates to how one evaluates or feels about the sexual experience. It is Zilbergeld and Ellison's basic point that a model including the subjective aspects of sexual functioning provides a better understanding of all aspects of sexuality, particularly when treating various types of sexual difficulties (see Chapter 9).

---

ety, embarrassment, sadness, boredom, anger, indifference, fear, guilt, and vulnerability. The impact of emotions on sexual arousal and particularly on sexual difficulties is considered in more detail in Chapter 9.

THE SENSES AND SEXUAL AROUSAL. The senses can actually create or reduce sexual desire.

Touch. Probably the most important sense connected with sexual pleasure is touch. Because touching is so commonly linked with sexual activity, "our society generally disapproves of touching outside of those relationships" (Nass, Libby, and Fisher, 1984, p. 59). Most often, people touch formally by "shaking hands."

Those with license to touch—barbers, tailors, hairdressers, doctors—do it impersonally so that their intentions will not be misconstrued. Touching by psychotherapists and sex therapists is usually carefully limited by professional guidelines. And caressing between adults and older children is

sometimes inhibited by incest taboos as well as fears of making homosexuals of the young. (Nass, Libby, and Fisher, 1984, p. 60)

There are parts of the body that are particularly sexually sensitive, such that the touching or stroking of them produces sexual arousal. While the genitals and breasts are obvious *erogenous zones,* the lips, neck, and thighs are also highly sensitive to touch. "But even some rather unlikely regions—such as the back, the ears, the stomach, and the feet—can also be quite erogenous" (Hyde, 1982, p. 197). However, the areas of the body that are turn-ons vary from one person to another.

Austrian sociologist and sexologist Ernest Borneman indicates that the "entire skin surface of the newly born is a single erogenous zone" (1983, p. 7). He refers to this "initial phase of infant sexuality as 'the cutaneous phase' . . . [and] the sexually mature person . . . is a cutaneously oriented person whose entire body surface is . . . sensitive" (pp. 7–8). Such people neither focus exclusively on the genitals nor are they obsessed by the need for orgasmic performance.

Sight. Another sense that plays a major role in terms of sexual arousal is sight. To most people, for example, physical attractiveness functions as a sexual turn-on. In the United States youth and beauty are considered attractive traits, and "gross fatness and bad complexions are thought to detract from sex appeal" (Nass, Libby, and Fisher, 1984, p. 54). There are no universal standards for physical beauty, however (Ford and Beach, 1951). It is women's appearance, more than men's, that is of more concern almost everywhere. But definitions of what is attractive in women varies greatly; a beautiful woman in some societies is plump as well as tall and powerfully built (Ford and Beach, 1951).

A partner's physical signs of being sexually aroused are often sexually stimulating to the viewer as well. This contagious element of sexuality exists with the "sex flush" of the aroused person, the outlines of a penis in tightly fitting pants, female nipples in clinging shirts, and the enlarged pupils of the eyes of a sexually aroused person. The actual revealing of body parts that have been previously kept covered is typically very exciting, at least at first. This seems to lessen as a sexual turn-on with continued full exposure, as newcomers to nudist camps or nude beaches can verify. The biggest turn-on may be to leave a little something to the visual imagination (Nass, Libby, and Fisher, 1984).

Sounds. Human beings can also become sexually aroused by sounds, including talk, instrumental music, and songs. But we tend to vary greatly as to what particularly turns us on as the result of our cultural conditioning. Some people find the lyrics of popular songs highly erotic, sometimes with subtle and not-so-subtle sexual meanings. Talking

about sexual activity is stimulating to many people, to some the "grosser" the better. For example, credit card telephone sex is a growing commercial activity. Other people are completely shut off by open and blatant sexual conversation. But sometimes sex is alluded to through the "clever use of puns, metaphors and double meanings" (Nass, Libby, and Fisher, 1984, p. 52). This is a way of sexual flirting without putting one's ego on the line with a more direct approach.

Direct come-ons using sexually explicit language excite some individuals; others prefer softer verbal invitations of the type "I want so much to make love to you." Sometimes there are differences between the genders such that what might be verbally arousing to a man is a turn-off for many women or vice versa. In general, men tend to be somewhat cruder in their sexual terminology than women, although this has changed over the years. Possibly even more important to some females is the negative reaction they have to "the unwanted connotation that something is being done *to* rather than *with* a woman" (Nass, Libby, and Fisher, 1984, pp. 57–58).

Smells and tastes. We can either be turned on or turned off by various smells and tastes. Many individuals go to great lengths to have what they think are seductive scents radiating from their bodies. Both "masculine" and "feminine" scents are believed to help produce sensual arousal. Some women even use flavored lipstick to try to make themselves "deliciously kissable" (Nass, Libby, and Fisher, 1984, p. 58). But to many people it's not so much the artificial smells and tastes that are important but natural body odors, ranging from the smell of clean skin to perspiration. The smell and taste of the sexual organs are particular turn-ons or turn-offs to some persons, primarily as a result of increased interest in oral-genital sex in the past 20 years (Nass, Libby, and Fisher, 1984).

Scientists have noted that lower forms of animals are influenced by substances called *pheromones*, from the greek *pherein* ("to transfer") and *hormones* ("to excite") (Offir, 1982).

> *Scientists who observe monkeys in the wild have noticed that in many species the male will sniff the female's genital area when sex is on his mind. Laboratory experiments show that a male rhesus monkey can tell by the odor of the female's vagina that she is at mid-cycle and is particularly receptive to his advances. . . . The chemicals to which the male responds are called copulins.*
>
> *Human females also produce copulins in the vagina. Perhaps that explains why, in some cultures, people think human genital secretions have aphrodisiac powers. (Offir, 1982, p. 107)*

Research on human pheromones is at an early stage, but it is unlikely that this factor is one of the key aspects of sexual arousal.

MOOD-MODIFYING DRUGS. Some people believe that mood-altering drugs such as alcohol and marijuana increase their sexual desire and enjoyment. Research has found, however, "that one of the chief ingredients in successful mood modifiers is our *expectation* that they will work. . . . In the short run some seem to create the desired effect; in the long run some may endanger our health" (Nass, Libby, and Fisher, 1984, p. 66).

Alcohol. The function of alcohol is such that it tends to depress the central nervous system; it ultimately hinders sexual arousal. It also lowers testosterone levels, which can reduce sexual appetite and arousal potential. Male orgasm, ejaculation, arousal, and overall pleasure are negatively affected by high levels of alcohol (Malatesta et al., 1979).

Alcohol does function to reduce sexual inhibitions; it seems to give people permission to do whatever they want. It allows them to let go, have something to blame for their actions, and also possibly reduces guilt. Some people say that they need to "loosen up a bit," and men still try to get women "high," since they seem to be less sexually inhibited this way (Nass, Libby, and Fisher, 1984).

The misconception that alcohol increases sexual abilities is widespread. One study (Briddell et al., 1978) "showed that merely *believing* we have consumed alcohol is more likely to enhance sexual arousal than actually having consumed it" (Nass, Libby, and Fisher, 1984, p. 67). Malatesta et al. (1982) found that female orgasmic reactions decreased both physiologically and behaviorally with greater alcohol consumption. "But women still *perceived* greater sexual enjoyment and became more sexually aroused after consuming alcohol" (Nass, Libby, and Fisher, 1984, p. 67).

> *It may be that women believe they are more satisfied with alcohol because they need alcohol more than men to overcome sexual inhibitions and guilt feelings. As with other drugs, alcohol is often used to compensate for sex-negative beliefs. (Nass, Libby, and Fisher, 1984, p. 67)*

Severe sexual difficulties can result from chronic alcoholic consumption. Damage to the nerve centers of the brain, spinal cord, and the genitals themselves can cause permanent erection difficulties in men. But studies show that heavy alcohol use diminishes sexual abilities in both genders. "Although the desire for sex may remain high, the ability to 'perform' decreases" (Nass, Libby, and Fisher, 1984, p. 67).

Marijuana. Users of marijuana often insist that it increases sexual pleasure. Women in particular are more likely to indicate that they have greater *desire* after smoking pot. But researcher Wayne Koff (1974) speculates that "marijuana's relaxing effect may be especially significant for women because it loosens their learned inhibitions against experiencing and expressing sexual desire" (Nass, Libby, and Fisher, 1984, p. 68).

The research shows, however, that marijuana use may actually diminish sexual enjoyment over time. Hollister (1975) and Chopra (1969) both report that marijuana in high amounts results not only in a lowered sexual drive but also in an inability actually to perform sexually. Marijuana, like alcohol, is a relaxant and depressant, and "as the pot user becomes more intoxicated, he or she may tend to withdraw into inner experiences or simply get sleepy and dizzy, lessening the sexual focus of the occasion" (Nass, Libby, and Fisher, 1984, p. 68). In addition, Hardin and Helen Jones (1977) found that the amount of testosterone and sperm may decrease in males (just as with alcohol), and pregnant women run the risk of having the fetus deprived of hormones during development (Nass, Libby, and Fisher, 1984).

EROTIC MATERIALS. Many people have their sexual appetites increased by seeing or hearing erotic materials in the form of movies, books, tapes, pictures, stories, or strip tease shows. Others, including most family conservatives, are offended, embarrassed, and angry about the existence of such materials, which they see as "obscene." Even many feminists now condemn what they call pornography. Family liberals, emphasizing free speech, support the rights of individuals and couples to view such erotica.

Gender differences in response to erotica. Popular opinion in the United States has always been that men are more sexual than women, and that men, therefore, would have more interest in and receive more enjoyment from erotica. Survey data collected since mid-century have confirmed this viewpoint. The two Kinsey studies provided strong evidence that men are more likely than women to be aroused by most forms of erotica (W. Fisher, 1983).

> *Specifically, of more than 6,000 people who were asked, men (77 percent) were far more likely than women (32 percent) to report that they had been aroused by photos, drawings, or movies that portrayed sexual activity. . . . Men were more likely than women were to prefer to have the lights on during sex, and men's public restrooms—compared to women's—were found to have more sexual graffiti. (W. Fisher, 1983, p. 265)*

Since Kinsey's research there has been a sexual explosion, particularly among women. There is much more permissiveness regarding sexuality. More recent studies, however, show that "men are still much more likely than women to report that they have been aroused by erotica" (W. Fisher, 1983, p. 266). *Survey* data continue to show broad differences between the two sexes.

But another form of research, *experimental studies*, offers a different perspective on gender differences regarding erotica. While survey research reports on people's experience with erotica *in the past*, experiments study people in the *present*. In experimental studies, individuals of both sexes are actually *shown* the same erotic materials—photographs, movies, or written passages—and male and female reactions are assessed and compared. In such experiments the participants then indicate their own degree of subjective sexual arousal, or their physiological arousal is determined more objectively by electronic monitoring equipment (W. Fisher, 1983).

The findings of the experiments were

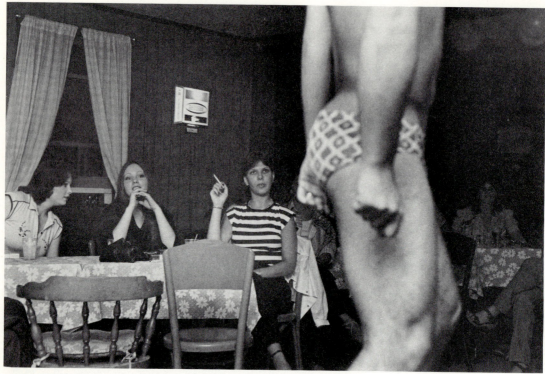

Most females' reactions to erotic dancers are similar to male reactions.

quite different from the survey research findings. In contrast to previous stereotypes, males and females were found to have very similar reactions to erotic materials, no matter whether subjective self-reports or physiological recording devices were used. Thus such studies tend to show that women are at least as physiologically turned on to erotica as men are (W. Fisher, 1983; Heiman, 1975; Mosher, 1973).

If women are indeed sexually aroused by erotica, why is it that they rarely purchase it or enjoy it more often? W. Fisher (1983) suggests three reasons. The first relates to the sexual socialization of females in childhood. Females have not been encouraged or taught to use erotica. Gender norms suggest that it

is OK for men but not for women. Boys are not only more likely to masturbate but to masturbate with the use of erotica.

The second reason for the male-female difference in the use of erotica may be found in the quality of erotica available for women. Most erotic materials are made specifically for men. The third reason offered by Fisher relates to the social acceptability of women being assertively sexual, to the extent of buying erotica. "It is still more socially undesirable for women to possess and enjoy erotica than it is for men to do so" (p. 276). Thus there is a fear of social disapproval for women. This disapproval may even prevent women from admitting that they are aroused by erotica in survey research. "North American culture has not traditionally given women the same permission to be fully sexual that it has given men" (p. 276).

Because girls and women learn to repress sexual interests to prove that they are "good girls," it makes sense that they will be more likely to have a positive response to erotica when an authority figure gives them the go-ahead. In an experiment, in contrast with a survey, the subjects' responsibility for seeing erotica belongs at least in part to the researcher who presented the erotic material. The fact that an authority figure was responsible for their exposure to erotica may facilitate "admission" of arousal by women in experiments. (pp. 276–277)

A fourth reason as to why women are not as atttracted to erotica may be added. While they can be physically sexually aroused by such materials, erotica may not represent their most desired turn-on. In American culture a preferred mental stimulus to sexual activity for many women may be emotional closeness, or intimacy. The physical body may "work" sexually as a result of viewing erotic materials, but that may not be the cognitive turn-on that many women *want, desire,* or *most prefer.* In other words, the stimulus that is most valued may be connected to the quality of a dyadic relationship.

FANTASY AND SEXUAL AROUSAL. From early adolescence it appears that most persons have sexual fantasies. While the majority of people accept their fantasies for what they are—fictional sexual play—some individuals suffer from considerable guilt. Contributing to their guilt is the view of some religious groups that a thought is the same as behavior. Thus thoughts are viewed as just as "sinful" and "immoral" as the act itself (Masters, Johnson, and Kolodny, 1982).

Fantasies can involve various contexts. Many are best described as old familiar sto-ries—from a book, a movie scene, or an actual experience. A particular script that is highly arousing can be played over and over again in one's mind. Other fantasies may be focused around the context of curiosity and creativity. Here there may be a desire to focus on something never previously experienced, something highly forbidden, or seemingly unattainable. "The fantasy does not necessarily mean that the person wants to actually participate in the fantasied behavior" (Masters, Johnson, and Kolodny, 1982, p. 246). Fantasies typically are formed around idealization—"blemishes, fatigue, and distractions disappear while passion mounts and the action is unencumbered by trivial details" (p. 247).

Fantasies can be either solitary experiences or shared. Probably most people keep their fantasies private, to themselves. Some therapists have suggested that shared fantasies between partners can help to bring the couple closer together. This let-it-all-hang-out point of view holds that people who keep their fantasies private are more likely to be sexually inhibited, or uptight. A word of caution should be stated about such oversimplified statements. There is certainly nothing immature about keeping one's sexual fantasies private. Partners are sometimes shocked by their spouse's fantasies, often they are misinterpreted, and there may be a misperception that the spouse wants to act out the fantasies. The fantasies themselves may make a partner feel very insecure or jealous. Also, highly charged fantasies sometimes fizzle out after they are shared. In reality, "there is no way of knowing beforehand if partners will benefit from sharing details of their sexual fantasies or if problems will result" (Masters, Johnson, and Kolodny, 1982, p. 247).

Functions of sexual fantasy. The most obvious purpose of fantasy is to begin or increase sexual arousal. "People with low levels of sexual desire typically have few sexual fantasies and will benefit from treatment that helps them form positive fantasies" (Masters, Johnson, and Kolodny, 1982, p. 250). Indeed, some individuals report that they cannot reach orgasm without fantasy.

Another function of fantasy is that it provides a safe protective atmosphere for letting sexual thoughts roam. Privacy makes sure no one will discover our fantasies. The fictional aspect of fantasy relieves us of accountability. Another safety factor is that we are in charge—in the director's role—of our fantasies. We can stop them whenever we want to if we become threatened or uncomfortable. "If you consider that most sexual fantasies involve situations, partners, and/or behavior that might be judged improper or illegal if they were real, the importance of safety as a backdrop for excitement becomes apparent" (Masters, Johnson, and Kolodny, 1982, p. 251).

Fantasies also function as a form of controlled rehearsal. It is a way of previewing an anticipated experience. We rehearse how to act and what to expect. This may be most common during adolescence or among people with limited sexual experience. Even though the act in reality may turn out differently from the fantasy, "a sense of comfort usually results from using fantasy as rehearsal" (Masters, Johnson, and Kolodny, 1982, p. 252).

Gender differences in sexual fantasies. In the past it was thought that men fantasized more often and more explicitly and that women's fantasies were "tamer" and more romantic. It is the impression of sex researchers Masters, Johnson, and Kolodny, however, that men and women are more similar than different when it comes to fantasizing patterns. "The idea that women do not have sex fantasies is now clearly recognized as outmoded" (Masters, Johnson, and Kolodny, 1982, p. 258). While Kinsey found in 1953 that 64 percent of the women interviewed masturbated with the use of erotic fantasies, recent data show this percentage to be 94 percent (Crépault et al., 1977). In addition, the sexual fantasies of women in recent years seem to be very explicit and sexually detailed (Masters, Johnson, and Kolodny, 1982). Perhaps male-female fantasy differences "were never quite as large as they were thought to be" (Masters, Johnson, and Kolodny, 1982, p. 258).

SEXUAL OPTIONS

Heterosexuality

By far the vast majority of people describe themselves as heterosexual; that is, they prefer a partner of the other gender rather than their own gender. We are interested in the changes that have taken place in the twentieth century in terms of heterosexual behavior and attitudes. Particularly in this chapter the focus is on premarital sexual practices, choices, and standards.

There were two periods of significant change in terms of sexual behavior in this century—during the 1920s and during the 1965–1975 era. A key source of research about the first half of the century comes from the work of Alfred Kinsey et al. (1948 and 1953). While most of the interviewing for this research was carried out in the 1940s, individuals born in four different decades were interviewed—before 1900, 1900–1909, 1910–1919, and 1920–1929. About 25 percent of the women born in the previous century were no longer virgins at the time of marriage. But about 50 percent of the women born in each of the first three decades of this century had premarital experience. Females born in the first decade (1900–1909) experienced peak available opportunities for pre-marital sex during or just before the 1920s. Thus it was in the so-called roaring twenties, or after World War I, that the first period of dramatic sexual change in this century occurred. There is also evidence from Kinsey's findings that show significant increases in petting to orgasm from the 1920s on. In addition, in this same time period, men began to have less intercourse with prostitutes than they did previously (Reiss, 1980).

The period from the 1920s up to 1965 included only moderate change regarding premarital sexual activity. The 1965–1975 era, however, became, once again, a time of rapid sexual change. National attitude surveys showed that "the percentage of adults who stated that premarital intercourse was 'always wrong' changed between 1963 and 1975 from approximately 80 percent to only 30 percent" (Reiss, 1980, p. 173).

But the biggest changes were in female sexuality. While Kinsey and his associates (1953) found that half of the women they interviewed had had premarital intercourse, two studies completed in the 1970s show much higher rates. Morton Hunt (1974) found that 81 percent of the married women under age 25 had experienced intercourse before marriage (see Table 5.1). Another study (Tavris and Sadd, 1977) found that 90 per-

cent of the women under the age of 25 had had premarital intercourse. There is little doubt that the 1965–1975 period saw a strong shift in both sexual attitudes and behavior (Wolfe, 1981; Zelnik and Kanter, 1980).

Since the Kinsey studies at mid-century, the following additional changes in premarital activity have occurred (Masters, Johnson, and Kolodny, 1982). First, few young males are initiated into sexual intercourse by prostitutes today. Second, oral-genital sex has increased dramatically. Fellatio (oral stimulation of the male genitals) has more than doubled in frequency. Cunnilingus (oral stimulation of the female genitals) has increased from 14 to 69 percent in comparison to mid-century (Hunt, 1974). Third, there is more sexual experimentation with intercourse positions, including anal intercourse. The fourth change involves the fact that women are having premarital intercourse with more partners than in the past. And fifth, the frequency of premarital intercourse has increased, particularly among women. Given these changes, it is not surprising to many people that we should also find the teenage pregnancy rate so high in the United States compared to other countries (see Box 5.4).

Sociologist Ira Reiss has conducted nu-

(Text continued on page 160.)

TABLE 5.1

PERCENTAGE OF MARRIED WOMEN WHO HAD EXPERIENCED PREMARITAL INTERCOURSE BY AGE

	18–24	25–34	35–44	45–54	55 and over
Males	95	92	86	89	84
Females	81	65	41	36	31

SOURCE: *Hunt, 1974, p. 150.*

BOX 5.4

TEENAGE PREGNANCY IN THE UNITED STATES

Why are teenage fertility and abortion rates so much higher in the United States than in other developed countries? What can be learned from the experience of countries with lower adolescent pregnancy rates that might be useful for reducing the number of unwanted teenage conceptions in the United States? A summary of the results of a comparative study of adolescent pregnancy and childbearing in developed countries—undertaken by the Alan Guttmacher Institute—sheds some light on these questions.

"The five countries selected for study—besides the United States—were Canada, England and Wales, France, the Netherlands and Sweden. The six countries represent a rather varied experience [in terms of the consequences of teenage sexuality]. At one extreme is the United States, which has the highest rates of teenage pregnancies, abortions, and births. At the other extreme stands the Netherlands, with very low levels on all three measures. Canada, France, and England and Wales are quite similar to one another . . . making up an intermediate group" (Jones et al., 1985, p. 55). "Sweden is notable for its low adolescent birthrates, although its teenage abortion rates are generally higher than those reported for any country except the United States. It is noteworthy that the United States is the only country where the incidence of teenage pregnancy has been increasing in recent years" (p. 55). Another important conclusion from the study is that "the reason that adolescent birthrates are lower in the five other countries than they are in the U.S. is *not* the more frequent use of abortion in those countries. Where the birthrate is lower, the abortion rate also tends to be lower" (p. 56). Therefore the explanation of differences among countries can focus on the determinants of pregnancy as the precursors of *both births and abortions.*

DATA AND FINDINGS: THE DETERMINANTS OF TEENAGE PREGNANCY

The Desire for Pregnancy.   Are the differences in birthrate due to the fact that more young women specifically choose to become pregnant in the United States? The number of marital births per 1000 teenagers is higher in the United States, and the proportion of teenagers who are married is at least twice as high in the United States as in the other countries. Yet the proportion of unintended pregnancies is larger in the United States and Canada than in England and Wales, France, and the Netherlands. "Even more striking is the fact that the abortion rate alone in the U.S. is about as high, or higher than the overall teenage pregnancy rate in any of the other countries" (Jones et al., 1984, p. 56). (See Figure 5.4.)

Exposure to the Risk of Pregnancy.   The study's findings show that "the differences in sexual activity among teenagers in the six countries do not appear to be nearly as great as the differences in pregnancy rates. . . . The

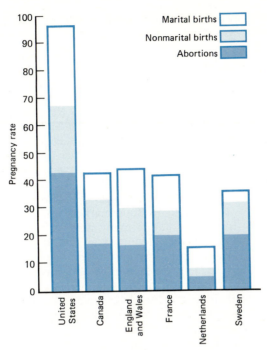

Figure 5.4 Percentage distribution of pregnancies, and pregnancy rates, by outcome, for women aged 15–19, 1980/1981. (*Source:* Jones et al., 1985.)

median age at first intercourse is very similar for the U.S., France, Great Britain and the Netherlands—something under age 18—and is about a year younger in Sweden, and may be about a year higher in Canada. . . . The examples of the Netherlands and Sweden make it clear that the postponement of first intercourse is not a prerequisite for the avoidance of early pregnancy" (Jones et al., 1985, p. 56).

Contraceptive Use. "It is likely that the U.S. has the lowest level of contraceptive practice among teenagers of all six countries. In particular, pill use appears to be less widespread among U.S. teenagers than among those in the other countries. This difference suggests that American adolescents use less effective contraceptives to avoid accidental pregnancy, even if they are using a birth control method" (Jones et al., 1985, p. 57). In each country except the United States "the medical profession accepts the pill as a highly appropriate, usually *the most* appropriate, method for adolescents. . . . In the U.S. there seems to be a good deal of ambivalence about pill use, both on the part of the medical profession and among potential users. In the U.S. [but not in all of the other countries] medical protocol requires that a pelvic exam be performed before the pill can be prescribed, a procedure some young

(Continued)

people find daunting" (p. 58). This requirement, whether justified or not, undoubtedly influences method selection among young women.

Access to Contraceptive Services. "Teenagers are much less likely to get free or very low-cost contraceptive services in the U.S. than in the other countries" (Jones et al., 1985, p. 54). "Contraceptive services appear to be most accessible to teenagers in England and Wales, the Netherlands and Sweden" (p. 57). All six countries have clinic systems. The Netherlands and Sweden, however, have clinics especially designed for young people. A drawback of the U.S. system is that it was developed as a service for the poor and is often avoided by teenagers who consider clinics as places where only welfare clients go.

"Condoms are widely available in England and Wales, the Netherlands and Sweden. They are . . . sold in supermarkets and other shops and in vending machines. In France and in many parts of Canada and the U.S., condoms are less freely available" (Jones et al., 1985, p. 57).

"Confidentiality was found to be an important issue in every country" (Jones et al., 1985, p. 57). Even in the Netherlands and Sweden, where attitudes toward sex are very open, the researchers were told "that young people wish to keep their personal sex lives private. The need for confidential services is probably best met in Sweden, where doctors are *specifically forbidden* [italics added] to inform parents about an adolescent's request for contraceptive services. . . . In Canada and the U.S., many individual doctors insist on parental consent before they will provide contraceptives to minors" (pp. 57–58).

Access to Abortion Services. Abortion services are most accessible in the Netherlands and Sweden. In Sweden, Great Britain, and France there is no charge for abortion; and in Canada women usually pay only a small portion of the cost. "In the Netherlands the cost of an abortion is borne by the patient but is not high. . . . Most U.S. women must pay for the abortion procedure themselves. For a second-trimester abortion, in particular, the cost may be substantial" (Jones et al., 1985, p. 58).

Sex Education. Sweden has the distinction of being the first country in the world to have established an official sex education curriculum in its schools. The curriculum, which is compulsory and extends to all grade levels, gives special attention to contraception and the discussion of human and sexual relationships. Perhaps most important, there is a close, carefully established link in Sweden between the schools and contraceptive clinic services for adolescents. None of the other countries comes close to the Swedish model.

"In Canada, England and Wales, and the United States, school sex education is a community option. It is essentially up to the local authorities— school principals or individual teachers—to determine how much is taught and at what age" (Jones et al., 1985, p. 58). "In Sweden sex education is completely accepted by the vast majority of parents, most of whom themselves had sex education while they were in school. . . . In the U.S. . . . many of the school districts that provide sex education give parents the option of excusing their children from such courses'' (p. 58).

Government and Public Attitudes Toward Teenage Pregnancy. In the four European countries, ''The government, as the main provider of preventive and basic health services, perceives its responsibility in the area of adolescent pregnancy to be the provision of contraceptive services to sexually active teenagers. . . . Teenage childbearing is viewed, in general, to be undesirable, and broad agreement exists that teenagers require help in avoiding pregnancies and births. . . . In France, the Netherlands and Sweden, the decision to develop contraceptive services for teenagers was strongly linked to the desire to minimize abortions among young people. . . . One reason for the more successful experience of the European countries may be that public attention was generally not directly focused on the *morality* of early sexual activity but, rather, was directed at a search for solutions to prevent increased teenage pregnancy and childbearing. . . . In the United States, in contrast, some powerful public figures reflect the view that the availability of contraceptive services acts as an incitement to premarital sexual activity and claim, therefore, that such services actually cause an increase in abortions'' (Jones et al., 1985, pp. 58–59).

''There seems to be more tolerance of teenage sexual activity in the European countries than there is in most of the United States and in parts of Canada. . . . In the U.S., sex tends to be treated as a special topic, and there is much ambivalence: Sex is romantic but also sinful and dirty; it is flaunted but also something to be hidden. This is less true in several European countries, where matter-of-fact attitudes seem to be more prevalent'' (Jones et al., 1985, p. 59).

Religious Factors. ''While the association between sexual conservatism and religiosity is not automatic, in the case of the United States the relationship appears to be relatively close. . . . Fundamentalist groups in America are prominent and highly vocal. Such groups often hold extremely conservative views on sexual behavior, of a sort rarely encountered in most of Western Europe. Furthermore, both the nature and the intensity of religious feeling in the U.S. serve to inject an emotional quality into public debate dealing with adolescent sexual behavior that seems to be generally lacking in the other countries'' (Jones et al., 1985, p. 59).

Social and Economic Factors. ''The final difference between the U.S. and the other countries that may be relevant to teenage pregnancy concerns the overall extent and nature of poverty. Poverty to the degree that exists in the U.S. is essentially unknown in Europe. Regardless of which way the political winds are blowing, Western European governments are committed to the philosophy of the welfare state'' (Jones et al., 1985, p. 60). The contrast between those who are better off and those who are less well off is much greater in the United States than in the Netherlands, Sweden, England and Wales, and France. In every country the description of the kind of young woman who would be most likely to bear a child was ''adolescents who

(Continued)

have been deprived emotionally as well as economically, and who unrealistically seek gratification and fulfillment in a child of their own" (p. 60). In the United States this explanation tends to apply to a much larger proportion of people growing up in a culture of poverty.

Summary. "In sum, increasing the legitimacy and availability of contraception and sex education is likely to result in declining teenage pregnancy rates. . . . Regarding their exposure to messages about sex, American teenagers seem to have inherited the worst of all possible worlds: Movies, music, radio and TV tell them that sex is romantic, exciting, titillating; premarital sex and cohabitation are visible ways of life among the adults they see and hear about; their own parents or their parents' friends are likely to be divorced or separated but involved in sexual relationships. Yet, at the same time, young people get the message good girls should say no. Almost nothing that they see or hear about sex informs them about contraception or the importance of avoiding pregnancy" (Jones et al., 1985, p. 61).

merous studies relating to premarital sexual activity and attitudes. He has attempted to analyze changes taking place by conceptualizing several premarital standards in the United States. He identified four such standards:

1. *Abstinence:* Premarital intercourse is considered wrong for both men and women, regardless of circumstances.

2. *Double standard:* Premarital intercourse is more acceptable for men than for women.

3. *Permissiveness with affection:* Premarital intercourse is considered right for both men and women when a stable relationship with love or strong affection is present.

4. *Permissiveness without affection:* Premarital intercourse is considered right for both men and women if they are so inclined, regardless of the amount of stability or affection present (1980, p. 177; also see 1960).

Abstinence before marriage has been the ideal norm in the Western world since the advent of Christianity. In history, however, the vast majority of males in most societies have had sexual intercourse before marriage. The real question was who their partners should be. "In some societies the partners for males were prostitutes and lower-class women; in others it was the girl next door, and in some, all of these. . . . So throughout the past 2000 years while abstinence was our *formal* standard the double standard was our *informal* standard" (Reiss, 1980, p. 177).

Until 1965 the public norm was abstinence along with acceptance of the double standard. As a result of changes in the 1965–1975 era, it appears that "permissiveness with affection" has become the dominant standard. While there is still evidence of the existence of a double standard, the gap between men and women has narrowed considerably (Reiss, 1980). Family liberals would like to see the double standard done away with completely; family conservatives would like to see a return to more restrictive sexual patterns, particularly for women. In any event, there does not appear to be rampant promiscuity in American society today. Only a small minority in the 1980s holds to the view of "permissiveness without affection." In the 1980s there has also been a greater public awareness about sexually transmitted diseases (see Box 5.5).

Religion still has a significant impact on premarital sex. The *Redbook* survey of married women found the following data:

RELIGIOSITY	PERCENT HAVING PREMARITAL SEX
Strongly religious	61
Fairly religious	78
Mildly religious	86
Not religious	89

SOURCE: *Tavris and Sadd, 1977, p. 65.*

The stronger people's religious feeling is, the less likely they are to have premarital sex. But even the majority of the strongly religious women are likely to have sex before marriage.

Premarital sexual behavior differs somewhat between blacks and whites. In general, there appears to be more approval of premarital sex among blacks. In addition, black men are more accepting of premarital activity than black women; however, the difference is not as large as that between white men and white women. But black women, like white women, are more likely than black men (or white men) to attach other relationship factors such as affection and love to premarital sexual activity (Staples, 1972). In general, both race and class differences regarding premarital sex tend to be declining during the latter third of the twentieth century. While Kinsey found large differences between social classes on premarital sexuality at mid-century, Hunt's more recent study has shown these to have largely diminished.

But just because sexual intercourse takes place before marriage does not necessarily mean that contraception is being used or that it is used effectively. In a study of almost 2500 college students it was found that nearly 50 percent of them did not use contraception. While condoms, withdrawal, and the rhythm method were mentioned by those who did use birth control, "prayer was the method most often used to prevent conception," especially during their high school years (J. Segal, 1984, p. 143). Studies show that young people know about birth control methods and know that contraception is available. But research by Melvin Zelnick and John Kanter (1980) involving a national sample of teenagers "shows that they are having more sex with *less effective* contraception protection and *more* pregnancies" (Nass, Libby, and Fisher, 1984). The advantages and disadvantages of the various methods of birth control are shown in Box 5.6 on pages 164 and 165.

The question is commonly raised, particularly by family conservatives, about the long-term effects of having experienced premarital intercourse. Does sex before marriage improve or reduce the chances of having a successful marriage? Kinsey found that those who had intercourse before marriage were more likely than virgins to have extramarital sex in their marriages. A number of studies in the 1960s found similar results (Reiss, 1966; Shope and Broderick, 1967). One study by Athanasiou and Sarkin (1974) "found that people with *extensive* premarital sexual experience tend to have numerous extramarital affairs and also noted that the more premarital coital partners a person had, the greater the tendency to have less happy marriages" (italics added) (Masters, Johnson, and Kolodny, 1982, p. 298).

The *Redbook* study also found more ex-

BOX 5.5

FIVE WAYS TO PREVENT SEXUALLY TRANSMITTED DISEASES

Some practical guidelines can be offered to help minimize the chances of contracting a sexually transmitted disease (STD) or spreading it once you've caught it.

1. *Be informed.* Knowing about the symptoms of STDs can help protect you against exposing yourself to the risk of infection from a partner and help you know when to seek treatment.

2. *Be observant.* Knowledge alone is not enough. Looking is the best way of discovering if you or your partner has a genital discharge, sore, rash, or other sign of sexual infection. (This can't be done with the lights out or in the moonlit backseat of a car.) If you see a suspicious sore or blister, don't be a hero about it; refrain from sexual contact and insist that your partner be examined. While "looking" may seem clinical and crass, you don't have to announce why you're looking, and often a good close look can be obtained in the sexual preliminaries (getting undressed, giving your partner a massage). A step beyond looking is commonly used by prostitutes (and doctors) to check for gonorrhea and nonspecific urethritis (NSU) in men. The penis is gently but firmly "milked" from its base to its head to see if any discharge is present; the "exam" is sometimes called a "short-arm inspection."

3. *Be honest.* If you have (or think you may have) an STD, tell your partner (or partners). This can avoid spreading the infection and will alert your partner to watch for her or his own symptoms, or to be examined or tested. Similarly, if you are worried about your partner's status, don't hesitate to ask. It's foolish to jeopardize your health to protect someone else's feelings.

4. *Be cautious.* Use of a condom will significantly lower the chances of getting or spreading STDs. Using an intravaginal chemical contraceptive (foams, jellies, creams) reduces the woman's risk of getting gonorrhea. Urinating soon after sexual activity helps flush invading organisms out of the urethra and so limits risks to a small degree. *If you think you've been exposed, promptly consult your doctor for advice.* If you *know* that you've been exposed, also abstain from sexual activity until your tests show everything is OK.

5. *Be promptly tested and treated.* A quick diagnosis and an effective course of treatment will help you prevent some of the serious complications of STDs. Treatment can be obtained from your private doctor, hospital clinics, or public health service clinics. After treatment, you must be rechecked to be certain that the disease has been eradicated.

SOURCE: *Adapted from Masters, Johnson, and Kolodny, 1982, p. 422.*

tramarital sex among women who had had sex before marriage. But on further analysis it turns out "that it was not premarital sex per se that was related to extramarital affairs, but the age at which premarital sex first occurred" (Tavris and Sadd, 1977, p. 86). It was primarily women who had had intercourse by the age of 15 who were much "more likely to have had extramarital affairs, and more extramarital lovers, than the women who had their first sexual experience in their late teens" (p. 86). Both the age of first intercourse and the number of different partners a person may have had are probably better predictors of extramarital affairs than just having had intercourse before marriage.

Homosexuality

Homosexuality has always existed in history. It has been seen as highly desirable behavior, as in ancient Greece, and as disgusting and immoral behavior by many family conservatives in American society. Until rather recently (1974) it has been viewed as a form of mental illness by the American Psychiatric Association. The modern homosexual-rights movement began in the late 1960s and attempted to stop discrimination against individuals based on their sexual preference. Most homosexuals prefer the term *gay* as designating a more positive view of their sexual preference or activity.

Homosexuals are people who are attracted sexually to their own gender, either in terms of thoughts or fantasies or in terms of actual behavior. Kinsey, however, has suggested that neither homosexuality nor, for that matter, heterosexuality is an all-or-none proposition. Taking into account both subjective preferences and thoughts and fantasies, as well as actual sexual activities, Kinsey developed the seven-point continuum shown in Figure 5.5 on page 166. Thus heterosexuality,

bisexuality, and homosexuality all exist along a continuum, and our sexual orientation in reality is typically a lot more complicated than just being either "homosexual" or "heterosexual," as most people see themselves.

Masters and Johnson offer further evidence that homosexuality and heterosexuality are best not treated as all-or-nothing orientations. In a study of the content of sexual fantasies it was found that "the most common fantasies of heterosexuals and homosexuals are remarkably similar. Homosexuals frequently fantasize about heterosexual situations, and heterosexuals commonly fantasize about homosexual encounters" (Masters, Johnson, and Kolodny, 1982, p. 252). (See Table 5.2 on page 166.)

It is difficult to know or determine specifically the incidence of homosexuality. Kinsey's data showed that 37 percent of males had a homosexual experience to orgasm. Only about 10 percent, however, were considered to be exclusively homosexual (number 6 on Kinsey's continuum). About 19 percent of all females had experienced sexual activity with someone of the same sex, but only 3 percent were exclusively homosexual. Recent studies have shown similar levels of homosexual activity.

A significant number of people have what is referred to as "homophobia," an extreme intolerance and fear of homosexuals. These individuals see homosexuals as "sick." Persons who cherish traditional family life around a heterosexual marriage may see homosexuality as "wrong" and "counterproductive" (Nass, Libby, and Fisher, 1984). Many such people want to "convert" homosexuals to heterosexuality.

THEORIES OF HOMOSEXUALITY. No one is really sure about the causes of homosexuality just as no one is sure of the "causes" of heterosexuality (Masters, Johnson, and Ko-

BOX 5.6

COMPARISON OF BIRTH CONTROL METHODS

Method	How it works	Description
Withdrawal	Penis is withdrawn from vagina before ejaculation.	—
Rhythm	Couple has intercourse only during a woman's "safe" days (when she is not fertile).	—
The Pill	Introduces estrogen and progestin into the body—giving false signals about hormone levels and thus preventing the release of eggs from the ovaries.	Small dispenser package that contains either 21 or 28 pills.
IUD	Prevents or interferes with initial stages of pregnancy.	A flexible plastic device placed in the uterus by a physician. A nylon thread hangs down from the uterus through the cervix and into the vagina. This enables the woman to check her IUD to be sure it is in place.
Diaphragm	Blocks sperm from moving into the uterus and reaching the egg.	Small rubber dome that fits inside the vagina, up against the cervix.
Condom	Acts as a barrier, preventing sperm from entering the vagina.	Thin piece of latex rubber or animal skin. Comes rolled up and, when unrolled, fits over the shaft of the man's erect penis.
Cervical Cap	Blocks sperm from moving into the uterus and reaching the egg.	Small, rubber, cuplike device that fits snugly over the cervix and is held in place by suction.
Spermicidal Agents—Vaginal Foam or Cream	Slows and kills sperm.	Comes in the form of cream, foam, jelly, or capsules.
Morning-after Pill	Large dose of synthetic estrogen sends a hormonal message to pituitary gland that woman is already pregnant.	25-mg pill taken twice a day for five days after unprotected intercourse.
Tubal Ligation	Prevents the egg from being fertilized by blocking the fallopian tubes.	Tubes are burned, cut, or clipped shut. Out-patient surgery is required.
Vasectomy	Prevents male from releasing sperm by severing sperm ducts.	Minor out-patient surgery; pieces of vasa deferentia are removed and ends tied off.

Effectiveness	Advantages	Disadvantages
Poor	1. Causes no health problems. 2. Better than nothing if no contraception is available.	1. Sperm, contained in the drops of fluid that come out of the penis before ejaculation, can fertilize an egg. 2. Requires great control.
Moderate	1. Causes no health problems. 2. Little religious objection.	1. Sometimes it is difficult to predict "safe" days. 2. Requires long periods of abstention from sexual intercourse.
High	1. Easy method to use. 2. Does not interfere with process of sexual activity. 3. Regularizes menstrual cycles and causes lighter flows. 4. Can relieve premenstrual tension.	1. May cause serious health problems such as strokes or blood clotting if user smokes. 2. May cause weight gain.
High	1. Protection is provided if IUD is in place. 2. Does not interfere with sexual intercourse.	1. Can increase the possibility of pelvic inflammatory disease. 2. Can cause heavy menstrual bleeding, cramping, and pain. 3. Spontaneous expulsion can happen for some.
High—if used with spermicidal agent.	1. Does not cause health problems. 2. Useful for women who want to have intercourse during their menstrual period.	1. Must be inserted for each session of intercourse. 2. Must be fitted by a doctor. 3. Taste of spermicide may be offensive during oral sex.
Moderate—if used only by itself High—if used with spermicidal agent	1. Easy to use. 2. Offers protection from STDs. 3. Causes no health problems. 4. No prescription needed.	1. May detract from pleasure. 2. Can break.
High—if used with spermicidal agent	1. Can be left in place longer than a diaphragm. 2. Is small and cannot be easily felt during intercourse.	1. Limited availability in the United States. 2. Harder to insert and remove than the diaphragm.
High—if used with condoms, cervical cap, or diaphragm	1. Kills sperm. 2. Inhibits transmission of gonorrhea, trichomoniasis, and possibly other STDs. 3. Provides extra lubrication for intercourse. 4. No doctor's prescription required.	1. May cause irritation in male or female. 2. Unpleasant taste during oral sex. 3. Must be used before each sexual session. 4. Considered messy by some couples.
Unknown	1. Prevents pregnancy after unprotected intercourse.	1. User may experience extreme nausea and vomiting. 2. Future children may be harmed; (e.g., genital abnormalities, infertility, and cancer in women).
High	1. Does not interfere with sexual activity.	1. Difficult to reverse.
High	1. Does not interfere with sexual activity.	1. Difficult to reverse.

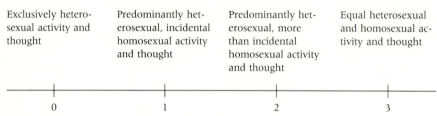

Figure 5.5   Continuum of Sexual Orientations. (*Source:* Adapted from Kinsey, Pomeroy, and Matin, 1948.)

lodny, 1982). Biologically oriented theorists believe that homosexuals have no choice in their sexual preference and that some innate predisposition determines their sexual orientation. The search by scientists for biological factors causing homosexuality centers primarily on hormonal theories. Some findings have noted that gay males have lower levels of testosterone than heterosexual men. Other researchers have discovered higher levels of estrogen in gay men. Also, higher testosterone levels in homosexual women have been demonstrated. Further research, however, has failed to replicate these findings, and there are exceedingly complex methodological issues involved in these studies (Masters,

TABLE 5.2

COMPARATIVE CONTENT OF FANTASY MATERIAL BY FREQUENCY OF OCCURRENCE

Heterosexual males
1. Replacement of established partner
2. Forced sexual encounter with female
3. Observation of sexual activity
4. Homosexual encounters
5. Group sex experiences

Homosexual males
1. Imagery of male sexual anatomy
2. Forced sexual encounters with males
3. Heterosexual encounters with females
4. Idyllic encounters with unknown men
5. Group sex experiences

Heterosexual females
1. Replacement of established partner
2. Forced sexual encounter with male
3. Observation of sexual activity
4. Idyllic encounters with unknown men
5. Lesbian encounters

Homosexual females
1. Forced sexual encounters
2. Idyllic encounter with established partner
3. Heterosexual encounters
4. Recall of past sexual experience
5. Sadistic imagery

SOURCE: *Masters and Johnson, 1979.*

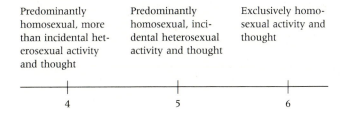

Predominantly homosexual, more than incidental heterosexual activity and thought	Predominantly homosexual, incidental heterosexual activity and thought	Exclusively homosexual activity and thought
4	5	6

Johnson, and Kolodny, 1982). Additional research does not support the biological-hormonal perspective. Writes Masters,

> *For example, treating adult homosexuals with sex hormones does not alter their sexual orientation in any way. . . . And conflicting reports on the sex hormone status of adult homosexuals leave many questions unanswered. Most notably, there may possibly be many "types" of homosexuality (and heterosexuality) which—until discovered—will confound attempts at pinpointing the biological influences on sexual orientation. (Masters, Johnson, and Kolodny, 1982, p. 320)*

There remains strong interest in hormonal theories of homosexuality, but it now seems apparent that no simple cause-effect relationship exists. If there is a connection, it is very complicated. But the possibility remains "that prenatal hormones may influence brain development in ways that could predispose individuals to certain adult patterns of sexual behavior" (Masters, Johnson, and Kolodny, 1982, p. 320).

Social-cultural theories argue that something in the environment has contributed to homosexuality, particularly in terms of parent-child relations. But the evidence shows that homosexuals can come from families with distant or hostile mothers and fathers or overly close mothers and fathers (Marmor, 1980). In addition, "many homosexuals come from perfectly well adjusted family backgrounds. . . . The present evidence simply does not show that homosexuality only or usually results from improper parenting" (Masters, Johnson, and Kolodny, 1982, p. 321).

Behavioral theories suggest that homosexuality is learned by conditioning "associated with the positive or negative reinforcement of early sexual behavior. . . . Thus, the early sexual experiences of a person may steer them [sic] toward homosexual behavior by pleasurable, gratifying same-sex encounters, or by unpleasant, dissatisfying, or frightening heterosexual experience" (Masters, Johnson, and Kolodny, 1982, p. 321).

In the end, however, there is no clear agreement about the "causes" of homosexuality or heterosexuality. Bell, Weinberg, and Hammersmith (1981) tested almost every possible social cause for homosexuality and could not find support for any of them. They therefore concluded that there must be a biological basis to homosexuality, but they did not measure any biological factors. Masters, Johnson, and Kolodny believe that in the final analysis several theories of homosexuality "may be correct and may account for a cer-

In the last 20 years many homosexuals have joined subcultural groups for emotional support.

tain percentage of homosexuals in our society'' (1982, p. 322).

PATTERNS OF SEXUALITY. Homosexuals, like heterosexuals, may involve themselves in a variety of sexual encounters. Some sex may take place as part of deeply committed intimate relationships. Other sex may be very impersonal, of the instant-gratification variety. Gay males tend to be more sexually active than lesbians or heterosexual men and women. Bell and Weinberg found that more than three-quarters of white male homosexuals and about one-half of black homosex-

uals had more than 100 homosexual partners over a lifetime. Twenty-eight percent of the white and 19 percent of the black homosexual males had more than 1000 partners. Only 2 percent of the white lesbians and 4 percent of the black lesbians had 100 partners or more. Seventy-nine percent of white gay males and 51 percent of black gay males had strangers for more than half of their partners (Bell and Weinberg, 1978).

But homosexuals also enter into long-term, committed relationships, although these relationships are less visible to the general public. Philip Blumstein and Pepper

Schwartz in their research for *American Couples* (1983) included married, cohabiting, gay male, and lesbian couples—12,000 questionnaires in all, plus 300 interviews. Thus for the first time a comparison was made between heterosexual and homosexual couples.

In the beginning of relationships gay men have sex more often than any other type of couple.

But after ten years, they have sex together far less frequently than married couples.

To understand gay men's sex lives we must realize that as a group they are much less monogamous than other couples. Although interest in sex with their partners declines, interest in sex in general remains high. Sex with other men balances the declining sex with the partner. (Blumstein and Schwartz, 1983, p. 195)

Lesbians have sex far less frequently than any of the four types of couples—"a lower sexual frequency at every stage of a relationship, at every point in their lives" (Blumstein and Schwartz, 1983, p. 197). But it is important to note that Blumstein and Schwartz's questionnaires referred only to genital sexuality. What was found through the in-depth interviews was that lesbians most wanted nongenital physical contact—touching, hugging, and cuddling—probably more than any of the other couples. But even more important, "they are much more likely to consider these activities as ends to themselves, rather than as foreplay leading to genital sex" (p. 197). We would expect such relationships to have a very high degree of emotional closeness.

Gay men are the least possessive and jealous of all the four types of couples. They can most easily separate sex from love. As mentioned previously, it is common for gay men to have sex without an emotional relationship. Both partners expect such sex to have very little, if any, emotional content. "When a gay man understands casual sex for himself, he understands it for his partner" (Blumstein and Schwartz, 1983, p. 258). Lesbians differ greatly from homosexual males in that they have difficulty with casual sex. Since they feel that they should be less bound by traditional female sexual values, however, they tend not to be as possessive as wives. But like women generally, most lesbians could not separate sex from love.

Bisexuality

Bisexuality involves being erotically aroused by both sexes or engaging in sexual activity with both sexes. While actually including a number of subtypes of behavior, exhibited in various ways, bisexuals as a group are often simply referred to as "AC/DC" or as "switch hitters." Bisexuality appears to be quite complex, and there has been relatively little research on the subject. One reason for the lack of scientific study is the fact that in American culture people tend to see sexual behavior in all-or-nothing terms; for example, most people tend to see one homosexual act as enough to qualify that person for the label of homosexual personality. In reality, if we want to use Kinsey's homosexual-heterosexual continuum for data, we find many more people classified as bisexual (between categories 2 and 4) than as exclusively homosexual.

MacDonald (1982) has categorized bisexuals into four subgroups. One subgroup is *transitory,* meaning that members experiment with bisexuality but return finally to their preferred sexual choice. A second subgroup is *transitional,* meaning that persons finally switch from one preference to another, usually from heterosexuality to homosexuality. Members of a third subgroup practice *homosexual denial* in that to avoid the stigma of being called homosexual they insist that they are turned on by both sexes. And the fourth bisexual subgroup is made up of *enduring bisexuals,* who continue consistently to show interest in both sexes. Masters and Johnson (1979) refer to this last subgroup as *ambisexual.* They define these people as never being in a committed sexual relationship with either sex and as having frequent sexual contact with both sexes.

While a few bisexuals say that they have always been sexually aroused and attracted to both men and women, most seem to have started their bisexual careers later in life. Blumstein and Schwartz (1977) argue that there are three types of circumstances conducive to developing bisexuality. A common type of experience, especially for women, involves sexual activity arising out of "an intense emotional attachment with a person of the gender they had never before eroticized" (p. 42). An example might be closeness developed between college roommates. Bisexual behavior could also begin with multiperson recreational sex—a ménage à trois or group sexual activity. What starts in a very nonthreatening way involving experimentation with a focus on physical feeling can turn into the acceptance of such behavior on a regular basis.

The third circumstance for moving into bisexual behavior is ideological commitment.

> *For example, some people came to a bisexual identification (occasionally without any corresponding behavior) because of adherence to a belief in humanistic libertarianism. They felt that everyone should be free and able to love everyone in a perfect erotic utopia. For them, love meant sex, which was seen as a means of communication and "becoming human." Encounter groups or group massages often progressed to a sexual stage. (Blumstein and Schwartz, 1977, p. 42)*

Another type of ideological commitment relates to the women's movement, in which women are encouraged to become closer to one another in all ways. "Sometimes these women instigated sexual encounters for ideological rather than erotic reasons, but soon developed erotic responses and became more generally physically attracted to other women" (Blumstein and Schwartz, 1977, p. 43).

Many people become bisexual or act in bisexual ways on a temporary basis. Both men and women in prison may be involved in homosexual activities but return to a totally heterosexual way of life when released from correctional institutions. Such sexual activity is defined as "situational." So-called rest-room sex among men surprisingly involves mostly males who are married and who see themselves as heterosexual (Humphreys, 1975). Literally speaking, such men, if judged by their activities, are bisexual.

Men and women differ in the ease with which they are able to incorporate homosexual activity into their heterosexual lives. Men tend to find initial experiences more traumatic, and they are more likely than women to think of themselves as homosexual based on a single experience. Women more often see such activities as a natural extension of affectionate behavior. Men worry about their masculinity, thinking that they may never again be able to function with a woman. Such men sometimes deny the reality of their homosexual acts by engaging in impersonal sex in public rest rooms. Bisexual men typically have their first homosexual experience with a stranger, whereas with women it is typically a close friend with whom the woman has a strong emotional attachment. The plasticity of human sexuality is certainly demonstrated by accounts of bisexuality (Blumstein and Schwartz, 1977).

INTIMATE SEXUALITY

Certainly one can have sex without intimacy. It is also possible to have intimacy with or without sexual activity. Not all so-called good sex is found in intimate relationships. There is no solid evidence to prove that sex is "better" with intimacy *for any particular individual.* "Good sex," like beauty, to a considerable degree is in the eyes of the beholder. As Masters, Johnson, and Kolodny state

> *Under certain circumstances and for some people, impersonal sex may be enjoyable in its own right. Others are offended or distressed by impersonal sex and could never consider participating in a group sex scene or having sex with a stranger or prostitute.* (1982, p. 237)

It is true that many people enjoy sex most when it is combined with emotional closeness. It is also true that sex may help to create intimacy itself. But sometimes sex functions as a substitute for the intimacy that people desire, but do not know how to achieve. In addition, there are individuals who use sex as part of a whole process of avoiding emotional closeness.

It is literally possible for any person to have sexual relations with almost anyone else. One can be sexual with a stranger, an acquaintance, a proximity friend, a selected friend, a significant other, or an intimate other. In each situation the biological sexual response may not vary much, and certain typical physiological changes will take place in each individual. But the emotional dimensions of sexuality will vary greatly depending upon an individual's desire for or fear of emotional closeness.

Sex therapist Helen Singer Kaplan (1979) takes the view that in general, sexual experiences will be better if the two partners know each other intimately. Sexual activity with emotional closeness also involves less risk, fewer misunderstandings, and less chance of exploitation. Kaplan believes that people are probably more afraid of intimacy than they are of sexual activity. Certainly not everyone who is capable of sexual relations is also capable of intimacy. Some people feel more comfortable with impersonal sex, in order to avoid the pain of possibly being rejected or exploited while emotionally open. Rather than accept the risks of vulnerability or their hunger for intimacy, these "people compromise with a 'safely' impersonal version of sex" (Nass, Libby, and Fisher, 1984, p. 114).

> *Often, people with initmacy problems . . . can allow themselves to feel and act sexually free with someone they can't have or whom they regard as unimportant emotionally, but they can't work up much erotic interest in someone if there is potential for closeness.* (Botwin, 1985, p. 152)

It is also not uncommon to see relationships where the sexual activity starts out good. But when the couple begins to draw closer together toward a greater commitment, then sometimes the sexual interest dies. This could happen when they start living together, when they become engaged, or even after they marry. Sometimes problems of closeness and commitment surface for a married couple with a pregnancy or the birth of a child. Shutting off sexually is a method of withdrawal and creating distance. It is protection against threatening intimacy. A person who regularly dates married people may also be indicating a fear of intimacy (Botwin, 1985).

A major difference between sex and intimacy involves the question of timing. Sexual activity often develops rather quickly in a relationship, but as has been noted, intimacy takes a long time to develop. There can indeed be "instant sex," but again, there is no such thing as "instant intimacy." Does having sexual relations early in a relationship spoil the chances of having intimacy develop? The authors doubt very much whether sexual activity is a key variable in determining whether emotional closeness could develop. In one research study it was found that how quickly a couple had sexual intercourse in a relationship was not at all related to how long the relationship lasted or the quality of the relationship. The researchers state: "We found no evidence that early sex necessarily short-circuits the development of lasting commitments, nor that sexual abstinence or moderation consistently increases or decreases the development of a lasting relationship" (Peplau, Rubin, and Hill, 1977, p. 103). But Nass, Libby, and Fisher write

What is probably important is the meaning *individuals attach to intercourse. If they see it as a vehicle for emotional intimacy, then they'll probably think they are emotionally more intimate once they've started intercourse. If they see intercourse as debasing if love has not developed, having intercourse ahead of schedule may damage their relationship. (1984, p. 127)*

Sexual activity can be carried out alone (as in masturbation), in a dyad, in a threesome, or in a larger group. Intimacy, in contrast, is always dyadic. But intimate couples may participate in a wide variety of sexual practices; particular sexual activities have little, if anything, to do with intimacy. Heterosexuals, homosexuals, and bisexuals all may or may not be involved in emotionally close relationships. The bottom line is that as humans we can be aroused by many individuals and by various erotic stimulants, but we can be intimate with only a few people. And sexual activity itself can be very nonintimate—that is, without any significant emotional

meaning. In countries such as Japan, for example, it is typical for husbands and wives to engage in very nonemotional sexual activity (see Box 5.7).

It is possible to define *intimate sex.* It involves sex in an ongoing relationship, typically monogamous, where there is a strong sense of commitment. There will be extensive trust, empathy, interdependence, sensitive self-disclosure, warmth, and abundant touching carried out for its own sake. While this emotional closeness may not provide a better-quality orgasm, the emotional dimension of sexuality will be very positive. In this relationship of equal power the initiation of the sexual activity is shared between the partners.

It is in terms of the emotional dimension that intimacy primarily contributes to high-quality sexuality. But sex therapist Helen Singer Kaplan argues that the emotional dimension will even have an impact on physical functioning. Overall sexual experiences are more pleasurable if your partner knows you intimately; when he or she is open and vulnerable, when you trust him or her not to reject or disappoint you, but to care about your feelings and to take pleasure in your pleasure. "Sex becomes less risky, the reflexes are more likely to work and abandonment is easier if you can be yourself and can discard your defenses in the bedroom" (Kaplan, 1979, p. 183).

High-quality sex seems to be partly based on personal self-disclosure. The *Redbook* survey of more than 100,000 women found that the ability to talk about one's sexuality with one's partner was highly correlated with sexual satisfaction (Tavris and Sadd, 1977). Men tend to talk less to their partners about sex than women would like.

Doing it is the only thing that matters, and aside from the "I'm going to do it to you" and "Do it to me harder and faster" rou-

BOX 5.7

SEXUALITY AND INTIMACY IN JAPAN

Japanese men and women are raised in a culture that emphasizes the *family group*, industriousness, and the maintenance of social order. Anything that could be a threat to these values, such as seeking *individual* sexual happiness through marriage, is strictly controlled by the norms held by the Japanese people. Sexuality is not seen as an evil, however. In Japan there are two types of sexual activity—"sex for pleasure" and "sex for reproduction." The husband-wife dyad emphasizes the latter, and men go outside the marriage for "fun" and "sex," using geisha girls, prostitutes, and frequenting bars and clubs.

Although this culture seems sexually open, "Japanese men display signs of sexual repression, as do Japanese women" (Coleman, 1983, p. 167). When men gather at bars to drink, they joke extensively about sexuality, suggesting anxiety about the topic. Also, "There are sanctions against displaying undue interest or preoccupation in sexual matters; the man who initiates discussion of sexual topics runs the risk of being stigmatized as . . . 'shiftless' " (p. 168). In Japanese baths where men bathe together, their "embarrassment and anxiety over sexuality are intense enough to cause a dislike of complete nudity . . . [with] most men taking care to keep their genitals hidden from the view of fellow males [by using towels]" (p. 168).

Sexual indifference is praised by men. "Sexual identity receives more reinforcement from another source, the productive career. Men's occupations have an intimate symbolic link with male sexuality and role identification" (Coleman, 1983, p. 168). Mothers prod their sons to be industrious, to have a successful career; and they instill in the sons negative thoughts about women. This is done because sexuality is viewed as a distraction to a successful career. Sexuality, as a human need, is recognized but kept "in its place." That place is not in the home, with a wife, but it is considered to be a part of "after-hours leisure."

The public expression of any affection is taboo; whatever feelings a couple may have for each other are kept away from the eyes of others. A male "college student expressed his revulsion at public scenes of affection by saying, 'It's as shameless as dogs mating in the middle of the street' " (Coleman, 1983, p. 170). Thus, sexual attitudes are in a state of conflict; sexuality is viewed as private, titillating entertainment for men, while an open interest in touching and affection is looked down upon.

The men "assert that their own sex drives are stronger than women's and that they always enjoy sex" (Coleman, 1983, p. 171). However, a wife whose sexual demands can not be met is known as a "praying mantis wife" and is considered a hazard to her husband. In marriage, women are "encouraged to resign themselves to their husbands' extramarital affairs by consoling themselves with the impersonal, contractual aspects of their legal and social states as wives" (p. 176). If the wife does enjoy sex with her

(Continued)

husband, she is thought to be competing against the professionals. She is "taught to thank her husband after sexual intercourse" (p. 176). Japanese men want their wives to be passive, naive, modest, and shy. They do not require that the wife be a virgin upon marrying; however, she must be "pure in spirit" (p. 172). A woman who has dated more than several men is not desirable.

This encouraged naiveté leaves the woman uncomfortable with her sexuality. Because of embarrassment, Japanese women rarely go to a gynecologist or obstetrician. They also have an aversion to touching their vaginas or placing anything in them, so the diaphragm and intrauterine device (IUD) are rarely used. The birth-control pill also tends not to be used widely. The belief is held that a woman asking her partner, or anyone else, about these types of birth control is too experienced and is thought to be "messing around." This leaves the rhythm method and condoms as the only methods of birth control, abortion being accepted as a type of birth control of "last resort." The condoms are a problem also, for both men and women are bashful about buying them at the drugstore. To alleviate this problem "home sales companies recruit women who appear older and have children themselves" (Coleman, 1983, p. 158) to sell condoms door-to-door. This method is very effective, for it saves the woman a trip to the gynecologist or obstetrician and social embarrassment.

Young wives try to have frequent sex with their husbands until their decided-on quota of children has been reached. Their sexuality is used for reproduction, not for pleasure. If not competing with geisha girls and prostitutes, the Japanese wife is certainly competing with her husband's job. "The workplace makes a claim on his time and energy that can distract substantially from his participation in a full marital sex life" (Coleman, 1983, p. 177). Since Japanese men derive their sexual identities mainly from their jobs, the wife comes second, or even third if the geisha is a factor.

Wives must deal with these circumstances as best they can; most put their energy into their children. "Japanese social scientists have conjectured that the vicarious success of the 'education mama' in her children's accomplishments offers her a psychological consolation for a lack of communication with her husband" (Coleman, 1983, p. 178). "Sexually frustrated wives channel their interests in their sons' success" (p. 178) and this starts the cycle once again—the sons striving to please their mothers in the work world and disregarding their wives, love, and intimacy.

The parent-child ties are strong; children often sleep between their parents until age 4 and on all public outings the children walk or sit between their parents. This separation of the husband and wife by the children leaves parents little private space for emotional or sexual closeness. Thus, the wife uses intimacy with her children as a substitute for intimacy with her husband, and he substitutes work for intimacy with his wife. The Japanese pattern does not emphasize the importance of close, dyadic relationships between a husband and wife. The notion of sexuality as a form of communication between the spouses is alien for both Japanese men and women.

tine, what could there possibly be to say? The superstuds . . . never feel fear or concern or tenderness or warmth, they never have problems, they never need to stop or rest. So where can a boy or man turn for an example of emotional sexual communication? No place at all. (Zilbergeld, 1978, p. 38)

Many men tend to hide their "feeling under a mask of aggressive sexuality, cool confidence or stony silence" (Zilbergeld, 1978, p. 39). Talking is the medium for intimacy, but many people have sexual relations in silence. Just as nakedness is a form of physical self-disclosure, verbally sharing sexual needs and desires helps to bring intimacy to sexuality. In this process it is possible for open sexual interaction to contribute to emotional closeness. Therefore, the authors claim that intimacy not only improves the quality of sexuality, but positive sexual disclosure and communication can contribute to a greater sense of emotional closeness.

CHAPTER REVIEW

1. The relationship between the mother and infant can be potentially emotionally close and sensual. As children grow older, however, parents in American society tend to become less permissive, less touch-oriented, more restrictive, and more negative in terms of the child's sexuality.

2. It's possible to view sex as an appetite. Sexual appetites tend to vary among people. The sexual appetite can be influenced by biology, but most significantly it is influenced by cultural factors.

3. Sexual response occurs on two levels—reflexive and psychic. Certain stimuli can trig-ger sexual response reflexes automatically without the person being in control of the response. Psychic arousal involves erotic thoughts, which cause the brain to send messages down the neural pathways to the spinal cord and then to the genitals. Psychic arousal can be influenced by emotions, the senses, mood-modifying drugs, erotic materials, and fantasies.

4. Meaningful changes in premarital sexual activity have occurred during this century, starting with the 1920s. During the 1965–1975 era the most significant changes in attitudes and behavior regarding premarital sexual activity took place, including a greater acceptance of premarital intercourse. Females changed much more than males. Having premarital intercourse in itself does not seem to have a significant impact on a marriage. But a greater number of premarital partners and a younger age at which intercourse first occurred are correlated with more extramarital sex.

5. Sexual orientations can be conceptualized on a continuum ranging from exclusively heterosexual thought and activity to exclusively homosexual thought and activity. There is no agreement on any specific causal factors for either homosexuality, heterosexuality, or bisexuality. All three sexual preferences may or may not involve intimate relationships.

6. Sexual activity certainly does not always involve intimacy, although most people appear to enjoy sex more when it is combined with emotional closeness. While sexual activity can develop rather quickly in a relationship, it will take a long time to realize intimacy.

Developing Close Relationships

CHAPTER

6

The Tendency
to Couple

There appears to be a natural tendency for human beings to pair off. The desire for the security found with an attachment is a major objective. In America "coupling" for a man and woman is facilitated by "falling in love." "Love" then is the basic motivating force in the search for a significant other and is the reason for marriage in the United States. Most people desire to marry—to find a significant other.

While intimacy is not typically an expressed goal of the coupling process, most partners want it, or at least some degree of closeness. Intimacy develops slowly, however, and for the majority of couples it will not be achieved until many years into the relationship or marriage, if indeed it is achieved at all. Young people, in particular, often seem not to be mentally aware of either the concept of emotional closeness or who is or who is not capable of supplying it. This problem is further complicated by the fact that most couples experience an "illusionary intimacy" during the courtship process.

COURTSHIP AS SOCIAL EXCHANGE

The process of searching for a "significant other" in our lives can be best analyzed from an exchange-theory perspective. People, choosing for themselves, naturally seek the most rewarding and least costly situation. All of us try to obtain the best deal possible on a prospective mate; certainly we try to obtain what we think we deserve.

Exchange and Bargaining for Mates in History

Bargaining implies a certain objective awareness of the reward-exchanging process. It suggests knowledge of an individual's own social worth, of options available, and of

what he or she was able to demand in the past. It also implies an awareness of other people's marketability in interpersonal relationships. Sociologist Michael McCall has specified three broad types of courtship patterns—the *traditional,* the *intermediary,* and the *contemporary*—each specifying quite different types of courtship bargains (McCall, 1966).

THE TRADITIONAL PATTERN. The traditional model of mate selection involved bargaining between kin groups or the parents of the young individuals. The terms of exchange were set in a similar way to the way prices are set in stores today.

> *Goods are marked with a price, and the buyer can either pay the price or he must shop elsewhere. . . . The kin group decided in which market they would shop, on the basis of the prices charged there and the quality of the merchandise. That is, they decided who the eligibles were, knowing full well the prices they would have to pay and the kind of mate they would be getting. (McCall, 1966, p. 194)*

The only matter bargained over was marriage. There was no bargaining about the conditions of courtship because there was no courtship. The bargain resulted in an "arranged marriage." Marriages typically were arranged when both kin groups were concerned about protecting family economic interests, "both in the exchange of goods that accompanies the marriage and in the effect of marriage on the dispersal or concentration of inherited property, wealth, and resources" (Zelditch, 1964, pp. 686–687). Bride prices, bride labor, and dowries were often involved in the economic arrangements—such practices go back to biblical times.

This pattern of arranged marriages has rarely existed as a form of mate selection in

America, although it is still found in many places of the world, including India, Japan, Africa, and many Muslim societies. Marriage in the United States has seldom been a kinship affair. Family systems did not have a lot of power in early America because of the emphasis in this country, right from the beginning, on the "freedom of the individual to make his own decisions" (McCall, 1966, p. 194). A modern society which still uses arranged marriages—as well as matchmakers—is Japan (see Box 6.1).

THE INTERMEDIARY PATTERN. In the intermediary pattern both the kin group and the young couple were involved in the mate-selection process. This pattern predominated throughout American history, up until quite recently. It was dominated by "love" and "falling in love." But certain preconditions typically had to be met before one allowed oneself to fall in love. In other words, love was guided and directed by rather stringent concerns of social class, income, education, religion, and race (Berger, 1963).

It is to this intermediary pattern that the term *courtship* most properly applies. There were a number of bargains struck. First of all, there was bargaining over eligibility, decided to a significant degree by the social and economic position of one's parents. A person tried to marry equally or slightly higher than the present family station in life. But also important was an individual's own educational level and occupation. One could actually raise one's marketability level by "hard work," by advancing one's education, or "even by a display of great personal charm." Not everyone was eligible to be accepted as a suitor for a particular woman, but to a meaningful degree even eligibility could be bargained about (McCall, 1966).

With the first bargain completed, "Suitors began to bargain over the conditions of association in the courtship process" (McCall, 1966, p. 195). Since a woman might have several suitors and a young man might court several women, individuals bargained against the competition for position, time, and special occasions. Slowly the field of suitors was narrowed by dropping those offering the least favorable bargains. The ultimate goal of everybody was to find his or her "one true love," the person that was meant for him or her. "In large part, 'being meant for one another' came down to complementarity of personality and needs" (p. 196). Under this intermediary pattern both the man and woman were selected for their potential abilities to carry out certain expected roles—the male as a good provider and the female as the keeper of the home and nurturer of the children. The complementary role pattern was emphasized for practical survival reasons.

The two individuals finally turned inward toward each other at the stage of engagement, after the couple had already progressed through "keeping company." But even before engagement, many couples had what was known as a "private understanding," a sort of transitional stage in which both individuals had quite clearly decided to focus only on the other person. With engagement the couple was ready to form "a permanent contract of exchange. This contract was a bargain to end any further cross-sex bargaining" (McCall, 1966, p. 196). The great length of the whole courtship process was purposely intended so that the partners would be "sure that they were meant for each other, because there could be no turning back (divorce) after marriage" (p. 196).

The parents of both parties participated in the bargaining process. Aside from determining their son's or daughter's place in the stratification system, they were also involved at other stages of the process. For example, "This courtship pattern dictated that the

BOX 6.1

MATCHMAKERS—JAPANESE STYLE

Before World War II Japanese boys and girls grew up completely segregated from each other in school and at play; young people enjoyed few opportunities for premarital contact. "Since marriage was of immense importance to the family, the choice of partner could never be left to immature youth but had to be primarily the responsibility of parents. Families avoided direct dealings with each other, lest one family risk the grave insult of rejection. To avoid such embarrassment, a go-between, a matchmaker, the *nakodo*, conducted the arrangements." (Murstein, 1974, p. 490). Today about two-thirds of all marriages in Japan are arranged, although matchmakers are involved in some way in most all marriages, including so-called love marriages.

"The role of matchmaker is highly regarded. . . . Many *nakodo* are friends or relatives of the family and act in that capacity only when requested to do so. Others are semiprofessionals: they have arranged hundreds of marriages and receive a proportion of the marriage expenses as a 'present,' or fee" (Murstein, 1974, p. 490).

The process usually begins with a social visit to the *nakodo* by the girl's mother. If the *nakodo* impresses her, the mother casually mentions that she has a daughter of marriageable age, and the *nakodo* decides whether or not to commit himself to the case. If he does, he might resort to his stock of photos of eligible men. "Since the woman's physical appearance was important to a man, he might arrange to have the mother go for a walk with the daughter at a prearranged time, so that the prospective groom could unobtrusively view the candidate" (Murstein, 1974, p. 490).

If physical appearance is no problem, the preferred next step is to call in another *nakodo* to represent the man's family and for each *nakodo* to investigate the qualifications of both sides in more detail. The objective criterion to consider is the family's socioeconomic position, including its lineage. Also important is the health of the potential spouse and the possibility of genetic taint. Is there a history of fertility and especially of healthy sons? Are any ancestors "outcasts"? Are there indications of intelligence and domestic ability for the woman? Does she have a diploma for the tea ceremony and flower arrangement? Is she suitably docile? Regarding the man, a primary consideration is his ability to provide financially for the family, his integrity, his willingness to work hard, and his reliability.

If all the qualities are acceptable, a formal introduction, *miai*, is held, with the potential couple, their parents, the *nakodo*(s), and, sometimes, representatives of the family in attendance. The main participants, who are on trial, are often extremely stiff and forced in their interaction. The *miai* is a public recognition that a marriage *could* be in the offing. Nevertheless, the official social character of the *miai* permits "either party to break off negotiations. A socially acceptable reason, such as incompatible horoscopes, might be offered without loss of face" (Murstein, 1974, p. 491). Assuming that the *nakodo*'s interrogations of the neighbors and the employer of the young man reveal no hidden defects, that the *miai* is successful, and that the monetary negotiations between the parents are concluded satisfactorily, the wedding could proceed.

Sometimes, however, despite the earnest attempts of parents to arrange a marriage, a boy and a girl might meet and "fall in love" without benefit of a *miai*. The behavior of the parents, if the relationship cannot be broken off, is exactly the opposite of that in the United States. In America, love is the primary acceptable criterion for marriage and if an individual "marries without being in love (a marriage of 'convenience'), he finds it necessary to avoid embarrassment by feigning love. In Japan, however, in order to avoid embarrassment the couple is often forced to contact the *nakodo* and subject themselves to the *miai* in order to go through the semblance of an arranged marriage" (Murstein, 1974, p. 491).

As urbanization and industrialization have accelerated since World War II, "The role of the *nakodo* is increasingly being played by a man's business supervisor. The transition is made easier by the fact that Japanese industrial concerns are among the most paternalistic in the world, with each employee enjoying life 'tenure' " (Murstein, 1974, p. 495).

The function of the *miai* has changed considerably in recent years to provide a variety of services. "At one time a positive arrangement at or prior to the *miai* meant that the marriage would take place in a short time, but today the *miai* is not quite as binding. A considerable number of persons participate in more than one *miai*, and it is now perceived as the beginning of a new phase in the relationship—dating. Indeed, marriage bureaus, private and public, now interview prospective marriage applicants, recording their income, health, likes and dislikes, and the kind of partner desired, and then arrange a *miai*. The *miai's* present-day function is to pair off marriageable persons while permitting them to date each other sufficiently so that they can determine if they are really compatible" (Murstein, 1974, p. 495).

"It may be concluded, therefore, that the *nakodo* has weathered the changes in marriage ideology by modifying his role to permit freer interaction between a couple. While a good many couples date without benefit of a *miai*, the continued existence of this institution probably signifies that the present industrial age has failed to provide the opportunity for young people to meet potential marriage partners in a socially approved manner" (Murstein, 1974, p. 495). There is still an absence of social organizations and youth clubs. "Greater dating contacts are rapidly being achieved by coeducation in the public schools, and future contact between the sexes will be more spontaneous" (p. 495).

But "apparently, gains in greater role flexibility and role status by Japanese women have not yet led to greater emotional closeness between husband and wife, as in the United States. The study by Blood, in which he compared 'love-match' couples with 'arranged marriage' mates, enables us to determine whether the presumably greater interaction of the former resulted in more marital satisfaction. The result, in the case of couples married nine years or more, showed that *miai* husbands were the happiest of the lot, followed by the 'love-match' wives and 'love-match' husbands, respectively,

(Continued)

while the *miai* wives were least satisfied. Apparently, therefore, for men the emotional interaction at the cost of giving up the traditional privileges associated with the 'arranged marriage' is not as satisfactory as the retention of the traditional masculine role. For women, for whom emotional closeness is often more meaningful than for men, the love match offers many more rewards than the more stultifying traditional match" (Murstein, 1974, p. 498).

young man ask the girl's father and then, with his consent, propose marriage to the girl" (McCall, 1966, p. 196). Thus the young man was forced to bargain with the young woman's parents, and the father was likely to ask the famous question, "Young man, are you able to support my daughter in the manner to which she has become accustomed?" "The role of the boy's parents was also largely economic; if they disapproved of the young woman of his choice, they might cut him off from a share of an inheritance" (p. 196).

THE CONTEMPORARY PATTERN.   The intermediary system began gradually to break down beginning in the 1920s, and by the 1960s the contemporary pattern was firmly entrenched. In this pattern the parents have lost most of their power as mate-selection agents. Now the two young people make a joint decision on their own and announce to their parents that they are going to be married. The trend throughout the world is now toward free choice in marriage, although in many countries this change is quite slow (Murstein, 1980).

In the contemporary pattern, theoretically "Every person with whom the individual comes in contact is eligible as a possible mate, regardless of marital status, religion, ethnicity, or social class" (McCall, 1966, p. 197). Of course this view stresses "everyone a person comes *in contact with*"; thus in real-

ity, not everyone is a possible mate. Hence one's social position would certainly limit the types of people one would come in contact with. Another change under the contemporary pattern is a diminishing of the belief in the one-and-only philosophy. If a person can be married more than once or have a series of deep involvements, it's not realistic to search for the one person meant for each person.

In the contemporary pattern the sole area of bargaining has to do with "commitment to the relationship . . . but an individual is expected to become committed *each* time he [or she] becomes involved" (McCall, 1966, p. 197). The search is less for a complementary partner in terms of roles than it is for early exclusiveness, sexuality, and quality of interaction. The emphasis is more upon similarity of values and interests and compatibility of personalities—all of which help to increase the possibilities for emotional closeness. Thus a couple is "turned inward" from the very beginning. But because this pattern is based upon the goal of personal happiness, rather than duty-directed roles, "Each person is free to leave any involvement (including marriage) at any time" (p. 197).

Thus involvements today, even marriage commitments, function as "restrictive trade agreements" rather than necessarily as lifelong contracts (McCall, 1966). Two persons may agree to exchange exclusively with each

Parents have lost some power in the contemporary pattern of courtship. They can still express opinions about potential partners, however, and can influence their children indirectly.

other, but only until the exchange seems unfair to one of the partners, until one sees more potential rewards as coming from some other person, or until, as is common, one simply falls out of love.

Dating in the Twentieth Century

Beginning in the 1920s, dating was "the most significant new mechanism of mate selection in many centuries" (Hunt, 1959, p. 356).

In place of the church meeting . . . and the chaperoned evenings in the family parlor, modern youth met at parties, made dates on the telephone, and went off alone in cars to spend their evenings at movies, juke joints, and on back roads. (p. 356)

Dating allowed a person to see and talk to someone without making a commitment—"compared to the Victorian entrapment known as 'keeping company'" (p. 357).

Young people now had a potentially long period of time to experiment with relationships with the other sex and to develop social skills. Most individuals ended up trying out a series of tentative choices before finally selecting one. Mothers under this new system actually began to push their young children into heterosexual situations with planned parties and dances. Then later, teenagers took over themselves. "In backseats . . . and bull sessions, boys and girls would try to piece together some knowledge of what it meant to be a male or a female. By the late teens most of them had been through a crush or two" (p. 357). More serious attachment resulted in "going steady." While parents were wary of this practice, most youths picked someone from their own social class or religious group, people with similar backgrounds to their own (Hunt, 1959).

Some social scientists were initially very negative about dating. Sociologist Willard Waller in 1937 spoke of a "rating and dating complex" among college students, described as a competitive game in which the primary goal was prestige and a high rating by obtaining dates with the most desirable people. "Sexual success" was also a goal; the male tried to go as far as he could, and the female tried to give as little as possible—but still enough to maintain his interest. Waller (1938) also saw the dating process as involving extensive idealization. He reported

An interaction of idealizations takes place which carries the couple farther from contact with reality. . . . As the love relationship develops, A idealizes B, replacing the actual B to a considerable extent with a creature of his own imagination. . . . Because of his idealization of B, he displays to her only a limited segment of himself; he puts his best foot forward . . . in her presence he tries to be the sort of person who would be a fit companion for the sort of

person he thinks she is; all of this facilitates the idealization of A by B, and B in turn governs her behavior in such a way as to give A a false impression. (pp. 187–188)

Anthropologist Margaret Mead also criticized dating, saying,

Dating is not courtship, but a loveless contest designed to give the adolescent a feeling of success and popularity, neither of which he has much other way to gain in our culture until later in life. . . . The entire system works to the distinct disadvantage of marriage. (Mead quoted in Hunt, 1959, p. 358)

But other social scientists saw dating as a positive behavioral pattern. They considered it not only as "fun" but as "an educational process gradually leading from playful heterosexual behavior to companionship and love capable of initiating a marriage" (Hunt, 1959, p. 358). Dating, it was argued, allowed young people to get to know the personalities, values, and goals of others, "a need which hardly existed in the stable small town life of earlier centuries, when every young man was known, or known about, by nearly every young girl he was likely to court" (p. 359).

Of course to select another human being and to ask him or her for a date is to treat that person as someone special; it certainly is an indication of preference. To proceed with such an action involves taking a personal risk, specifically possible rejection. An effort is being made to start a different kind of relationship with the person. But what a date really "means" varies according to one's stage of life.

The script for a "date" between two college students who meet during their senior year in college will differ from the script for a

"date" of two fourteen-year-olds—even though both couples may be going to a school dance or a local movie. A "date" between two divorced people in their thirties who meet in a singles bar will have a still different script. This variation suggests some of the limitations on the word date. *Because it has been used to apply to so many different social encounters between people it has lost some of its precision. At the same time since "date" does mean that a particular selection has been made to see whether a further relationship might ensue, it does cover many of the contacts between men and women outside of marriage through the life cycle.* (Gagnon and Greenblat, 1978, pp. 122–123)

Dating, however, has changed over the past half century. For one thing, it appears to start at an earlier age. Since the 1960s some young people are beginning to date at the ages of 12 to 14. There has also been a shift from dating a number of people at the same time to more exclusive dating, either going steady continually with one person, often for years, or having a sequence of dating relationships that lasts a shorter period of time. In the 1930s through the 1950s the recommended pattern was to date many people on a relatively casual basis, a sort of social promiscuousness. The dates were supposed to have relatively low levels of sexual or emotional closeness. This pattern is far less common today and, in fact, appears very difficult to be accomplished (Gagnon and Greenblat, 1978).

A more recent trend is for young people to pair off into exclusive couples rather quickly after they have begun dating. Ironically such a pairing was previously seen (before the 1960s) as an indication that the individuals were personally insecure and thus in need of a steady relationship. "This interpretation seems to have been largely the result of the fact that parents did not want young people to 'go steady'" (Gagnon and Greenblat, 1978, p. 127). In reality, it is not typically people with personality problems who form exclusive units; it is, instead, those who are the "most interpersonally competent" and secure (Burchinal, 1964). It appears then that exclusivity is the preferred pattern, not one "resorted to in order to cope with anxiety or inability." But parental fears about exclusive pairing are valid in that such relationships do result in higher levels of attachment and sexual activity (Gagnon and Greenblat, 1978).

Even though exclusive dating is the preferred pattern for most young people, many individuals find it difficult to begin or to maintain such a relationship. A substantial number of young adults do not have partners, and a lot of young people feel as though they are failures at dating, are uncomfortable on dates, or do not find dating a pleasurable experience. Even so, most of those who don't have a partner would like to date more frequently. But it appears that dating itself may be a somewhat difficult game to play, and therefore having an exclusive partner eases some of this burden of being involved in the dating rat race (Gagnon and Greenblat, 1978). James Skipper and Gilbert Nass (1966) have indicated four motives for dating.

1. *Fun*—Dating is pursued because of enjoyable recreational activities which are shared together.
2. *Learning about the other sex*—Dating provides an opportunity for young people to get to know members of the other sex who may have been socialized differently.
3. *Gaining status*—Dating can be an opportunity to gain prestige or experience social mobility in status.

BOX 6.2

IS DATING DYING?

The traditional stereotypic "date" has declined, but it certainly is not dead. The date "in which the male picked up the female at her house at an arranged time, wined and dined her at his expense, and returned her to her residence at an arranged time" is certainly declining (Murstein, 1980, p. 780). Particularly in high schools and colleges, dating per se has decreased in the 1970s and the 1980s. There are a lot more group activities, which sometimes result in the young people forming pairs and sometimes not. "Dutch treating" is much more common. In addition, there seems to be less protocol as to what is appropriate male-female behavior (Murstein, 1980).

> Off campus in the noncollege or postcollege crowd, dating still exists. The search for partners has led to computer matchups, video tape selections in which the prospective partner is chosen from his/her video interview, singles' clubs, singles' bars, and through an increasingly used vehicle, the newspaper or magazine advertisement. The satisfaction with such gambits is largely unknown. (Murstein, 1980, p. 780)

4. *Serious partner selection*—Dating is a means of association with the other sex for the purpose of finding a person to marry. (pp. 412–413)

There can also be varying motives for dating at different stages of the life cycle, although any of the above motivations could occur at any age level. Dating in the 1980s, however, does reflect some changes from previous periods (see Box 6.2).

Dating takes somewhat different patterns among the upper, middle, and lower classes. Among the upper class it is much more controlled and supervised by adults, at least among teenagers. Parents make an effort to influence the people with whom their children interact by organizing dances and parties. In addition, by sending children to private schools, upper-class parents are encouraging them to meet and date other children from upper-class families (Saxton, 1986). "Going steady" is often discouraged, since the parents want their children to date a wide variety of partners. While it is more difficult for parents to supervise their children's contacts when they go off to college, the influence of the family's social class still persists. It is likely that the upper-class students may gravitate to upper-class organizations and cultural and social activities.

Middle-class parents are not likely to supervise and control their children's dating quite as much as upper-class parents. Their influence, however, is felt through their supervision of school, church, and family functions (Saxton, 1986). Instead of just going out on dates, it is more common for middle-class teens and young adults casually to "hang around" in one another's homes (Saxton, 1986). When they do go out, the activities center often around sports—basketball

Dating services often serve as modern matchmakers.

games, football games, roller skating, skiing, or bowling. "Hanging around" shopping malls, a school, or a park and going to movies or dances are other typical middle-class activities.

Dating patterns among the lower classes are somewhat different yet. Supervision and control by parents appear to be less than in either upper-class or middle-class families. Parents are often too much preoccupied with money problems and earning a living to be keeping a watchful eye on their children's dating activities. Also, a small and crowded family dwelling makes entertaining teenage friends difficult. Therefore, dating takes place most of the time in commercial establishments, rather than in the home (Saxton, 1986). "Going steady" usually begins in the mid-teens and often includes sexual inter-

course. If a pregnancy occurs, there is pressure on the young couple to marry, according to Lillian Rubin (1976). In Rubin's study of working-class couples, 44 percent of the couples she interviewed married because the woman became pregnant.

It is rare for lower-class boys to date outside of their social class. A girl, however, may date "up," especially if she is physically attractive. To be accepted seriously by a middle-class family, however, she must have other qualities, such as middle-class language, manners, dress, and attitudes (Saxton, 1986).

Brinkmanship in Courtship

In his classic work on courtship, "Excursus on Love," sociologist Peter Blau (1964) indicates that there needs to be "brinkmanship" on the part of both parties, that is, skill in avoiding dangerous situations that may harm a relationship or cause its breakup. Initially there may be a considerable amount of "flirting." Flirting involves the expression of attraction in a semiserious fashion that is designed to obtain some reaction from the other in advance of taking some serious action oneself. "The joking and ambiguous commitments implied by flirting can be laughed off if they fail to evoke a responsive cord [sic] or made firm if they do" (p. 77). The conduct of the flirtatious persons implies that although they are not ready to make outright unambiguous statements of affection, their hope is that further association may lead to significant rewards (Blau, 1964).

The person who is less deeply involved in a relationship has an advantageous position, "since the other's greater concern with continuing the relationship makes him or her dependent and gives the less involved individual power" (Blau, 1964, p. 78). This is *"the principle of least interest"*—the person with the least interest in the relationship has the most power. The power of least interest could even be used to exploit another individual, as in the case of a man who might sexually exploit a woman who is in love with him or in the case of a woman who might exploit a man's romantic interest in her for economic gain. "Hence, the lover who does not express unconditional affection early gains advantages in the established interpersonal relationship. Indeed, the more restrained lover also seems to have a better chance of inspiring another's love for himself or herself" (p. 78). Any partner can test the principle of least interest and the degree of the other person's dependence on the relationship by the simple means of temporary withdrawal or asking for space (Blau, 1964).

Everybody expects to obtain rewards from a "love" relationship. If the rewards come too easily and too quickly, however, their value may be depreciated. Blau refers to this situation as "the dilemma of love"—a person is under pressure to give evidence of love to a partner, but if he or she "does so too readily" the value of his or her affection will suffer. In addition, the value of the other person depends to a significant degree on his or her popularity with the other sex. For example, a man's attractiveness to a woman "depends in part on evidence that others find her attractive too" (1964, p. 79). Furthermore, a woman (or man) who is in great demand "is not likely to make firm commitments quickly, because she has so many attractive alternatives to weigh before she does" (p. 79).

If a woman has the reputation of readily engaging in sexual affairs, the value of this expression of her affection greatly declines, largely because her sexual favors entail less commitment to, and ego support for, a man than those of a woman who very rarely bestows them. (p. 80)

The more deeply emotionally involved a partner is, the more likely he or she is to exhibit jealousy. Showing this emotion "constitutes an explicit demand for a more exclusive commitment on the part of the other, and it frequently provides the final stimulus for the less involved lover to withdraw from the relationship" (Blau, 1964, p. 82). Thus the growth of love is often suppressed and smothered by too much affectionate pressure; love involves feelings, thoughts, and behaviors that cannot be commanded (Blau, 1964). It is important that commitments made by the two partners develop at roughly the same pace "for a love relationship to develop into a lasting mutual attachment. If one lover is considerably more involved than the other, his greater commitment invites exploitation or provokes feelings of entrapment, both of which obliterate love'' (p. 84).

The giving of rewards, or the showing of love, often *appears* to be unselfish or altruistic. But, says Blau, this so-called selfless devotion is motivated by self-interest in trying to encourage and maintain the other's love. ''Even a mother's devotion to her children is rarely entirely devoid of the desire to maintain their attachment to her'' (1964, p. 76). It's obvious that most individuals derive pleasure from rewarding those that they love and that they sometimes appear to make great sacrifices. Such a pattern of giving can indeed become intrinsically gratifying to many. Blau quotes Aristotle in saying, ''Benefactors seem to love those whom they benefit more than those who have received benefits love those who have conferred them'' (p. 78). Thus, it is entirely possible for the giver to derive more rewards from the giving than the receiver derives from the rewards given.

While Blau indicates that we are attracted to individuals who play hard to get, research has not totally supported this contention. Instead Elaine Walster et al. (1973) found that a woman who is *in general* hard to get but who is *easy* to get for a particular person is most desired over a generally hard-to-get or a generally easy-to-get date. ''Apparently, the high prestige value of the woman plus the low cost in terms of the potential humiliation of rejection were a winning combination'' (Murstein, 1980, p. 780).

What's Exchanged in the Marriage Market?

We become interested in people who provide us with rewards or who reduce costs for us. To some degree, rewards and costs are relative; they are in the eyes of the beholder and associated with individual needs. But to a significant extent, there is consensus as to what makes a partner rewarding. On the one hand, most of us would evaluate a person's behavior toward us in a positive way if the person is friendly, warm, kind, honest, sincere, and has a sense of humor. On the other hand, if the individual is aloof, thoughtless, selfish, bad mannered, or dishonest, we would see such behavior as costly to us. ''In short, we are *pulled* to people who reward us and *repulsed* by people who punish us'' (Berscheid and Walster, 1978, p. 23).

RECIPROCITY OF LIKING. Evidence suggests that most of the time if we perceive, or are told, that another person likes us, we will tend to like that person in return. Thus, as social psychologists Ellen Berscheid and Elaine Walster point out, ''As a consequence of our discovery that another likes us, we may become attracted to him or her'' (1978, p. 40). Liking and loving, however, are not *always* reciprocated. One thing that seems to matter more than anything else is whether individuals believe that they deserve to be liked or loved. As has been noted previously, people who do not see themselves as worthy of accepting love will not even be able to accept praise and compliments from others. Thus people possessing high self-esteem are very open to praise; people of low self-esteem expect, and can accept, criticism more than compliments. Therefore, ''We should like those who like us, only if we like ourselves; if we dislike ourselves, we should dislike those whose feelings about us are positive, and thus inconsistent with our own'' (Berscheid and Walster, 1978, p. 48).

Similarly, if someone else tells us that we are what we ourselves know we *are not,* the other person will ''lose points.'' It is important that compliments be sincere and accurate. Telling someone who obviously has a big, ugly nose that his nose is beautiful is not going to work. An evaluator gains some le-

BOX 6.3

NEVER GO OUT WITH ANYONE WHO . . .

Never go out with anyone who says he loves you more than his wife or girl friend.

Never go out with anyone who cannot *not* have sex.

Never go out with anyone who tells you that she is not a good person. She probably knows what she is talking about.

Never go out with anyone about whom all your friends say, "Well if you like him, you must see something in him. How would *I* know?"

Never go out with anyone who says he likes everybody.

Never go out with anyone who won't help you with your housework but who thinks you should wash the dishes when you're at his place.

Never go out with anyone who thinks that women have it pretty darn good, and doesn't see the need for the women's movement.

Never go out with anyone who has no direction in life.

Never go out with anyone whom you feel you must save.

Never go out with anyone who believes that it's your problem if you're angry that he's sleeping with other women.

Never go out with anyone who will absolutely not wear jeans.

Never go out with anyone who always brings you a present.

Never go out with anyone who can't understand why you want to pay your own way when he has less money than you do.

Never go out with anyone who initiates physical contact and then accuses you of trying to seduce him.

Never go out with anyone who is totally normal and healthy and can never act even a little bit crazy.

Never go out with anyone who feels insecure because you are independent, honest, and self-confident.

Never go out with anyone who does not appreciate the qualities that you value in yourself.

Never go out with anyone who thinks that she has needs but that you don't.

Never go out with anyone who thinks you're shallow and no fun because you don't care to discuss your "pain" with her on the second date.

Never go out with anyone who barely knows you and says he wants to give you a baby.

Never go out with anyone who can give (criticism, love, whatever) but can't accept it.

SOURCE: *Adapted from Sheva Zucker as quoted in Novak, 1983.*

gitimacy simply by being perceived as being accurate. But one doesn't have to tell the other person about his big nose; he already knows about it and it would be insulting anyway, even though accurate. It is better to find something to flatter the person about. Flattery is best, however, when people are praised not for "virtues they *know* they possess, but for those they *hope* they possess" (Berscheid and Walster, 1978, p. 55).

PHYSICAL ATTRACTIVENESS. Researchers did not begin to study physical attractiveness until the mid-1960s. This neglect was in large part due to the emphasis in the social sciences upon environmental determinants of behavior; physical attractiveness is largely a biological variable (Aronson, 1969; Berscheid and Walster, 1974). Most of the research that has been done on attractiveness concerns heterosexual attraction.

Is what is beautiful, good? People tend to believe that very attractive individuals "have it made." A common view is that beautiful people are assumed to be more intelligent, successful, happier, and so on. Dion, Berscheid, and Walster (1972) conducted a study in which males and females viewed photographs of attractive, average, and unattractive individuals. The participants were asked to rate each individual they viewed on many different characteristics. The outcome was that physically attractive persons were judged as having more socially desirable personalities, greater occupational success, and greater marital happiness than were the less attractive persons (Hendrick and Hendrick, 1983). The results supported the stereotype that what is beautiful is good.

Other social scientists have found that there is *a radiating effect from a beautiful woman* to a man whom she dates or who associates with her (Sigall and Landy, 1973). What appears to happen is that the desirable

qualities of a very attractive woman transfer to the male in terms of the perceptions of other people.

> *Thus not only is beauty good, but it may rub off on the lucky member of the opposite sex who happens to be associated with the beautiful person. The strong preference for association with attractive others is therefore very understandable. Beauty is treated by our society as a valuable commodity. (Hendrick and Hendrick, 1983, p. 51)*

Other studies show similar results. Landy and Sigall (1974) had individuals rate the quality of an essay as well as the writer's ability. A photograph of the writer, which varied in attractiveness level, was clipped to each essay.

> *The results showed that more attractive persons received more favorable ratings on their essays, and these ratings were independent of the actual quality of the essay, which had been experimentally varied. It appears that beauty can bias judgment of the quality of the beautiful person's work in a positive direction. (Hendrick and Hendrick, 1983, p. 51)*

The "radiating effect," however, seems to have some different effects on males and females. If an ugly man is married to a beautiful woman, he is perceived as "really having something going for himself." He tends to be evaluated as having very high income or high professional and occupational success (Bar-Tal and Saxe, 1976). The radiating effect is most powerful when transferred from females to males, but it tends to be quite weak when transferred from males to females. Overall the physical-beauty stereotype—in terms of impact on success or happiness—is much stronger for females than for males.

Body image and physical appearance. Which gender sees itself as more physically attractive? More than 60,000 *Psychology Today* readers completed a questionnaire in which they evaluated their own degrees of satisfaction or dissatisfaction with 24 body parts and characteristics. The results showed that women disliked their bodies more than men disliked theirs. On 20 of the body parts in the questionnaire women not only showed more dissatisfaction than men, but the degree of dissatisfaction was much greater. The top four areas with at least some level of dissatisfaction for females were the abdomen (50 percent), hips (49 percent), weight (48 percent), and buttocks (43 percent). These features are primarily related to mid-torso areas of the body. The top four areas of dissatisfaction for males were the abdomen (36 percent), weight (35 percent), teeth (28 percent), and muscle tone (25 percent) (Berscheid, Walster, and Bohrnstedt, 1973). In another study, females were almost twice as likely as males to see themselves as unattractive (Kersten and Kersten, 1981).

But are males actually better looking? The answer to this question is probably no.

The wide differences between the two sexes are more likely the result of women judging themselves very harshly. Right or wrong, good or bad, physical attractiveness remains a primary power base for women—much more so than for men. In advertisements, television, and movies, for example, women are looked at and judged to a large degree on the basis of their beauty, and to a much lesser degree on other qualities. It is for this reason that women spend so much more money than men on cosmetics and clothes in attempts to improve their appearance. (Kersten and Kersten, 1981, p. 79)

The matching hypothesis.   One important question about relationships that researchers have investigated is the "matching hypothesis,"—the idea that persons tend to pair off with someone equal to their own desirability level, including physical beauty. Thus very attractive individuals would tend to pair off with each other, average with average, and unattractive with unattractive. In a landmark study by Walster et al. (1966) an effort was made to test the matching hypothesis. A "computer dance" was organized for approximately 750 male and female college students. The couples were randomly paired, and individuals were privately evaluated on attractiveness when they signed up for the dance (Hendrick and Hendrick, 1983).

The researchers hypothesized that pairs who by chance were of the same social desirability level would be more satisfied and attracted to each other than pairs of unequal social desirability. On the night of the dance the couples danced and talked a couple of hours. Then males and females were separated during an intermission and asked to complete a questionnaire assessing their date. Results showed that the only variable determining how much a subject liked his or her date, wanted to see the date again, and how often the man asked the woman for future dates was the physical attractiveness of the date. (Hendrick and Hendrick, 1983, p. 48)

Thus, the findings of this study did not support the matching hypothesis, since a date was liked primarily on the basis of his or her attractiveness, regardless of one's own attractiveness. Berscheid et al. (1971) some years later suggested a reason the matching hypothesis failed, namely because the dates had been assigned and there were no risks of rejection for anyone in asking for a date. The staged dance then is unlike the real world of courtship, where one's ego is on the line in asking for, or accepting, a date. It is when people run the risk of possible rejection that they seem to be more likely "to play it safe and approach only others who are at about the same level of attractiveness" (Hendrick and Hendrick, 1983, p. 48).

In two later studies done by Berscheid and her colleagues they asked men to *choose* a dating partner from pictures and also told them that there was the possibility of being rejected; they couldn't guarantee the date.

> *The results of both experiments found support for the matching principle. . . . It was clear that highly attractive men and women* did *tend to choose more attractive dates than did less attractive individuals. (Berscheid and Walster, 1978, p. 185)*

Another study that offered support for the contention that men and women of equal levels of attractiveness tend to pair off together was done by Silverman in 1971. In this research, male and female teams of observers and evaluators went to places where dating couples might go—social events, movie theater lobbies, or bars—and watched college-age dating couples. Using rating scales, the evaluators found that the two partners were extremely similar to each other in terms of physical attractiveness.

The observers also evaluated how physically affectionate the couples were—did they touch each other, hold hands, stand really close to each other. The hypothesis being tested was that "couples more similar in attractiveness would be happier with each other, and this would be reflected in their degree of physical intimacy" (Berscheid and Walster, 1978, p. 187). Silverman found that he was right.

> *Sixty percent of the couples who were highly similar in physical attractiveness were engaged in intimate physical contact of some kind. Only 46 percent of the moderately similar couples and 22 percent of those in*

> *the lowest similarity group did so. (Berscheid and Walster, 1978, p. 187)*

Thus there is strong evidence suggesting that people of similar levels of physical attractiveness tend to pair off together. But is beauty the only trait upon which couples can be matched? There is evidence that the small number of individuals who are much less attractive than their partners, and therefore unmatched in terms of physical attractiveness with those partners, actually provide some other benefits to their partners, a sort of *compensatory exchange.* Thus if a physically unattractive, middle-aged, wealthy physician proposed marriage to a very beautiful young woman, "He would probably be trading his prestige and power for her physical attractiveness and youth" (Murstein, Goyette, and Cerreto, 1974, pp. 3–4). In reality, however, the matching principle is still validated; only other variables besides attractiveness have been added.

Considerable evidence has been found to support the idea of compensatory exchange. Berscheid and Walster have argued "that if a person is vastly 'superior' to her partner in one sphere—say physical attractiveness—she will be able to attract and keep a partner who has more to contribute in other spheres" (1978, p. 188).

> *The authors found that the more attractive a person is compared to his or her partner, the richer, the more loving, and the more self-sacrificing his or her partner was likely to be. It appears, then, that the asset of beauty can be used to attract a beautiful partner, or it can be used to attract a partner who possesses quite different assets. (Berscheid and Walster, 1978, p. 189)*

Research evaluating relationships has also shown that the more equitable a relationship between a man and a woman, the

Compensatory exchange occurs when a man uses his money and power to win a physically attractive, youthful woman.

more likely it is to be currently intact, the more the partners expect the relationship to remain intact in the future, and the longer such a relationship does, in fact, last.

> Men or women who felt they were getting far *less* than they deserved from their relationship (and who have every reason to wish that something better will come along) were naturally quite pessimistic about the future of their relationship. So were those men and women who knew that they were getting far *more* than they deserved from the relationship, and had every reason to hope *the relationship would last. They, too, had to admit that their relationship probably would not last. (Berscheid and Walster, 1978, p. 190)

In summary, the following conclusions can be made. First, individuals *prefer* to date or marry partners who are as desirable as possible, particularly in terms of physical attractiveness. In actuality, however, most people end up choosing a partner who is approximately equal to their own "social worth," if not their own physical attractiveness. In the final analysis, then, "romantic choices appear to be a delicate compromise between our desire to capture an ideal partner and one's realization that we must eventually settle for what we can get" (Berscheid and Walster, 1978, p. 191).

THEORIES OF RELATIONSHIP DEVELOPMENT

Proximity

Sheer proximity (also referred to as *propinquity*) has an important impact on the development of friendships and on the selection of a marriage partner. Research shows that "The closer two individuals are located geographically, the more likely it is that they will be attracted to each other" (Berscheid and Walster, 1978, p. 29). Numerous studies have shown that "Students tend to develop stronger friendships with those students who share their classes or their dormitory or apartment building, or who sit near them" (p. 29). One researcher found that the proximity of seating in a classroom was a better predictor of friendship than such other variables as age, marital status, religion, or ethnic background (M. Segal, 1974).

In terms of spouse selection many studies have shown that "The closer eligible men and women live, the more likely they are to meet and to marry" (Berscheid and Walster, 1978, p. 31). One study done by Clark (1952) discovered that more than 50 percent of the individuals who married in Columbus, Ohio,

lived within 16 blocks of each other when they had their first date. In 1958 Katz and Hill reviewed 14 studies that all showed that most people date and finally marry individuals who live near them.

But there are other areas besides geography in which proximity functions, including work, play, and religious groups. People may actually be brought into more contact within these other groups than they are in their residential communities. In all likelihood, nonresidential proximity is probably more important today than in the past because of the general decline in a sense of a community, because of better transportation, and because of more female participation in the world of work and recreation.

Similarity

The idea that we like people similar to ourselves (also referred to as *homogamy*) or that "likes marry likes" is not new. For example, extensive research has been done supporting the idea that the sharing of similar attitudes and values with another person stimulates attraction. When someone else holds the same values and opinions that we do, we tend to believe even more that our views are the correct ones, since other people hold to the same position. We are therefore given social validation. In addition, similarity of attitude is more likely to lead to positive exchange and dissimilarity of attitude to negative exchange or withdrawal.

It can also be argued that if others are similar to us, we can more likely assume that they will like us, "and it is *this*—the anticipation of being liked—that makes us like them" (Berscheid and Walster, 1978, p. 68). But even attraction itself can lead to *perceived* similarity, and such similarity tends to be largely rewarding and can contribute to affection. Of course, similarities count the most when they are related to important issues (Berscheid and Walster, 1978). In summary,

> There is little doubt that similarity of attitude produces esteem with great consistency. When we meet others who hold attitudes similar to our own, we like them. When the others also discover our attitudes are similar to theirs, *and how much we like* them, *their liking for us may be expected to increase. Knowledge that* they *like* us bolsters, in turn, our esteem for them. In this way, . . . "attraction breeds attraction." (Berscheid and Walster, 1978, p. 71)

In a classic study carried out by Ernest Burgess and Paul Wallin (1943) 1000 engaged couples were found to be similar on almost every characteristic they studied.

> Similarity was found with respect to (1) family background, including place lived in childhood, educational level, nativity, income, and social status of parents; (2) religious affiliation; (3) types of family relationships, including happiness of parents' marriage, attitude toward the father when a child, and sex of siblings; (4) social participation, including the tendency to be a lone wolf rather than socially gregarious, leisure time preference ("stay at home" vs. "on the go"), drinking habits, smoking habits, number of friends of the same sex, as well as opposite sex, and so on. (Berscheid and Walster, 1978, p. 86)

Burgess and Wallin thus present impressive evidence that likes tend to marry in terms of *social characteristics,* that homogamy is a common pattern in dating and mating. But, say Berscheid and Walster, the accepted view that we tend to choose a spouse from a wide range of candidates is probably wrong.

> The "ecology" of mate selection is such that we are preprogrammed to meet and marry those like ourselves. Very few of us ever have an opportunity to meet, interact with, become attracted to, and marry, a person markedly dissimilar from ourselves. . . . Society's "sorting process"—which exerts its influence on the nursery school we first attend, to the neighborhoods in which we live, and which continues throughout our lives—seems to operate principally on the dimension of similarity. (Berscheid and Walster, 1978, p. 87)

Complementary Needs

A popular belief is that "opposites attract." Sociologist Robert Winch (1958) was one of the first researchers to argue this point of view, a theory of complementary needs. He indicated that both sexes are attracted to friends and lovers who provide them with maximum need gratification and that they prefer partners whose needs are complementary to their own. A couple's needs and personalities may be complementary, for example, when one spouse has the need to dominate and control while the other spouse has the need to please the partner.

How much available evidence supports this theory? There is some, but not a lot. Winch's own study of 25 married couples has been criticized on methodological grounds. He hypothesized that people look for friends and mates as complementary partners, that is, as complementary *personalities* separate from social characteristics. Winch's study included batteries of personality tests, clinical interviews, and a subjective determination of the partners' personality needs. Winch claims to have found evidence that individuals choose from a "field of eligibles" a person who is complementary in personality rather than similar (Winch, 1958).

One other study has given support to the idea that individuals search for a complementary personality. Kerckhoff and Davis (1962) developed and tested what has come to be known as a *filter model* of mate selection. The first filter relates to homogamy, or *similarity of social characteristics*. The second filter involves *value consensus;* that is, people who have more common values move more easily and faster toward a commitment than those who have conflicting values. The third and final filter is *personality complementarity*. The first two filters operate early in a relationship, whereas complementarity is most important after the relationship is well underway. It was found that couples who had complementary personalities moved faster toward marriage than those couples who did not. Other studies have failed to support either Winch's or Kerckhoff's and Davis's findings.

Even though there is not a lot of scientific support for a theory of personality needs, social scientists seem reluctant to write off completely the complementarity idea. George Levinger (1964) contributes significant insight into this issue by suggesting that one person's needs may be satisfied by another person of similar personality and another person's needs by a dissimilar personality. For example, a shy individual who wants to meet many people might desire an outgoing partner, whereas a shy person who does not want to meet people may want a recluse for a partner.

Parent's Personality

Another theory of mate selection—one that typically is ignored in marriage and family textbooks—assumes that young people tend to pair off and marry someone with a personality like one of their parents. Burgess and Wallin (1953) found that the most common pattern was one where one's beloved "resembles the parent of the opposite sex." A second pattern was "reversed"—where the primary influence is the parent of the same sex. A

third and frequent pattern involved a combination of the personalities of both parents. A fourth pattern, less common, was one in which an individual is attracted to someone who is the direct opposite of a parent. Finally, if an individual's relationship in childhood was not particularly meaningful or close with either parent, "There may be a surrogate image of a grandparent, an older brother or sister, an uncle or an aunt, or a friendly and admired adult outside the family" (Burgess and Wallin, 1953, p. 197). In this instance the substitute parent functions in the same way as the real parent in terms of a model for mate selection. More research is obviously needed in the area of parental personality.

It's possible to understand better and integrate all of the theories of mate selection by applying exchange theory. All people want to obtain the best bargain possible, consistent with what they think they deserve. The proximity or physical closeness of people increases their chances of developing a friendship or finding a potential mate. The geographical or social closeness of particular individuals reduces costs in terms of time and money. Proximity also results in a greater opportunity for interaction, which in turn can lead to greater liking.

Similar social characteristics and value consensus increase the possibilities for more extensive positive exchange. Interactions are likely to be rewarding because the individuals have more in common and each is likely to support the other's convictions. Thus the similarity of social characteristics and values allows for the ease of exchange, which tends to be rewarding in itself.

Depending upon one's own personality, the similarity or complementarity of a partner's personality will be rewarding or costly. The ultimate goal is a compatible personality "fit." All people want their needs met in a relationship in which they feel comfortable. Some people are comfortable in close relationships with "personality similarity"; others are comfortable interacting with personalities complementary to their own. Either way, similarity or complementarity of personalities, it is the ease of exchange that is important. Choosing a person who has a similar personality to one's parents can also make for comfortableness. In the final analysis, all of the theories of relationship development seem to provide a meaningful contribution to understanding mate selection.

THE COUPLING PROCESS

It's possible to describe the process that relationships go through as they move from first glimpse to marital commitment (Reiss, 1960; Kersten and Kersten, 1981). Relationships can, however, become stalled at any of the four stages discussed below and not move further. The coupling process includes (1) initial attraction, (2) investigatory exchange, (3) trust development and attachment, and (4) committed reciprocity.

Initial Attraction

Relationships start with some kind of attraction to another individual. One perceives the potential balance of rewards and costs associated with the other person. The motives of both parties are self-interested, and the hope is that the other individual has qualities one can share or benefit from. Each person has probably already sampled the market and has knowledge as to what is generally available. An individual is also typically aware of his or her own bargaining value. Thus any initial contact will more than likely be with a person whom one thinks one might deserve. At minimum the person chosen is evaluated as the best available possibility at the moment. One

factor at first meeting is the proximity of the other person. Those standing or sitting closer are more available to strike up a conversation.

During this initial stage, people look for any one of a variety of clues, in behavior or body language, or ask others for information. Does the person act as if he or she is alone and available or does the person seem somehow connected with a person of the other sex? Does she move her body with the music so as to give a clue that she is interested in dancing? Has there been extended eye contact, a big indicator of interest? What can we learn from studying his or her face, mannerisms, or clothing? It's possible to gain meaningful clues about an individual's personality simply from observation. Is she wearing a lot of makeup that might represent some sort of insecurity? Does he seem shy, or is he the extroverted life of the party? Is he drinking a lot or smoking cigarettes, which we might detest? But the basic question is whether he or she reflects those traits that we ourselves are looking for; does the person fit our preconceived conception or fantasy of what we desire?

It would not be possible to list all of the many items that might attract any one person. But any list would certainly include traits such as the following: level of physical attractiveness, potential as a good provider, intelligence, social status, manner of dress, wealth, a sense of humor, warmth, height, age, marital status, friendliness, and so on. Not all of these traits can be specifically determined across a room, but you can gain a good idea on enough of them to lead you into the next stage if you so desire.

Investigatory Exchange

Now the inquiry becomes more focused and direct. It's launched with the first discussion or the first date and may continue for a significant period of time. Exploration of the other person begins immediately with the opening conversation. The goal in this stage is to find out as much as one can about the other individual. Almost always from the start, people look for similarity or for things that they both might have in common. Early questions in the conversation have to do with the particular setting they find themselves in, their hometown, what their major is in college, do they know so-and-so, and their favorite music, sport, or classes. There is also a major effort to find out the degree of value consensus. It is generally very rewarding for both to discover things that they have in common; more relaxed interaction and the building up of rapport are the results. Discovery about the other person depends to a significant degree on one's own level of self-disclosure.

This discovery period is often a fun-filled, exciting, and enjoyable time in a relationship. Some couples, once they get started talking, often converse half the night or for many hours every night for a week or more. But all of the questions, discussions, and self-disclosures serve an important purpose—the investigation into another human being. Out of this investigatory exchange each person makes a decision whether to continue or to break off the relationship. This decision will be determined by the rewards and costs that are being exchanged, as well as by the perceived estimates of future anticipatory rewards and costs. Thus if one or both persons find that they lack things in common or that there is too much existing or potential conflict or that they just don't feel comfortable with each other, then the relationship may end at this stage, as a great number of relationships do.

Each partner, and increasingly the relationship itself, is in a constant state of evaluation during this stage. Comparisons can't help but be made with people from the past or with other people known at present. Comparison levels of alternatives will be made, judging whether more rewards are possible from some other relationships (Thibaut and Kelley, 1959). Proximity will become a negative factor if the partners are separated by significant time and distance. Personalities now come under more scrutiny than in the first stage. Is there real potential here? Could we be compatible together? Do we seem to make a good "fit"?

While this stage can last as much as a year or longer, there are some dangers. People in the early stages of relationships often are on their best behavior and do not reveal their real selves for fear of rejection. In addition, there are people who purposely misrepresent themselves in order to exploit others. Furthermore, it is in this stage where the potential for infatuation is the greatest. Individuals, particularly needy ones, often see what they want to see and hear only what they want to hear. A real awareness of differences often escapes early interactions. Each person may be trying to create the best impression by maintaining an air of politeness and avoiding conflict. Obviously, a marriage at this stage stands a good chance of being a disaster. It takes considerable time for people really to know each other.

Trust Development and Attachment

As the interaction proceeds and more personal information is revealed, there is somewhat less likelihood of a false presentation of self. Personality factors become increasingly important as the relationship continues. The questions asked are now more specific. Can I get along with this person on a day-to-day basis? Can he or she really meet my needs? Is this individual too controlling, too insecure, or too smothering? Is this the type of person who will be there when I really need him or her? It is to be hoped that a somewhat more realistic appraisal is possible at this stage.

If the partner turns out to be a predictable and trustworthy individual, then a greater degree of emotional investment and exclusivity can result. As the degree of trust grows, security grows. Greater openness and sharing, a deeper level of exchange, now typically exist. Self-disclosure is at a higher level in terms of vulnerability and dependence. With increased investment there is further hope for greater immediate and future rewards through better understanding and a broader sense of voluntary reciprocity.

But there are still cautions that need to be taken into account. Many human beings lack the ability to reveal their real selves, even though they may want to; they may not even know themselves. Those who are not aware of their real selves may disclose false impressions, but not necessarily as a manipulation. Others know their feelings but don't know how to communicate them accurately. Still others will not admit weaknesses in order to avoid becoming truly vulnerable for fear of rejection.

In any event, by this time and in this stage, an attachment to another human being typically has been made. It feels good and provides security to have someone to call our partner. We feel emotionally lonely if that person is away for an extended period of time, we look forward to seeing and hearing from that person, and we would be ''greatly hurt'' if the relationship broke up; we would experience separation anxiety for at least some period of time. Hence, the partners are now emotionally attached. It becomes more and more difficult to think of the relationship ending, and it becomes harder and harder to get out of it without a great deal of pain. At

this point alternative competing relationships are no longer desired or considered a possibility.

Committed Reciprocity

The couple is now motivated to make the ultimate dyadic commitment, that of marriage. The partners are ready for what they perceive as lifetime permanence. The degree of interdependence is so high that the partners do not want to be without each other. Thus two people now say that they love each other so much that they are willing to take vows tying the two of them together for life. The commitment itself is a reward. Commitment is a compliment to the chosen person, and it provides individual security and, it is to be hoped, relationship security.

At this point each partner is prepared to put all of his or her eggs in one basket. There is a willingness to give up alternatives and settle down. A final decision on exclusivity has been reached. The relationship is ready to be publicly legitimized by *institutionalization*. Now there are not only expectations within the couple but also from family, friends, and the society as a whole. A legal contract will be signed detailing promises and defining reciprocal obligations and responsibilities. Individuals proceed with this step of institutionalization of committed reciprocity with the goal of maximizing happiness and minimizing human loneliness.

IS THERE A MAN SHORTAGE?

William Novak in his book *The Great American Man Shortage* (1983) interviewed close to 200 single women in major cities around the country. They were middle-class professionals and business people, mostly between the ages of 30 and 45. By and large they were economically successful women. They talked about what they perceived as a man shortage. States one of Novak's respondents

For the men I know, it's like a candy store out there. There's always something more alluring in the next jar. Today it's licorice, tomorrow it's a fireball, and after that, who knows? There's almost too much there to enjoy. There's no incentive for men to make a commitment, or even to treat a woman well, because there's always somebody else waiting to go out with them. But most of my women friends stay home every night. We can't understand what's happened to all the men. (1983, p. 21)

Is the man shortage real? Novak cites a number of reasons to explain why many women have trouble finding a man. The actual numbers in 1980 indicated that there were roughly 6.5 million more women than men in this country, about a 6 percent surplus. But a surplus of women has not always existed in American history. Up until World War II, men always outnumbered women in this country. The sex ratio—the number of men per 100 women—was 108 in 1910, by 1950 it was 99, in 1960 it was 97, in 1970 it was 95, and it was 94 in 1980.

Two major factors caused this shift. First, there is no longer a large number of male immigrants coming to this country. When immigration was common, the husband usually came first to look for work; among the young and unmarried it has always been far more acceptable for men to leave their families and venture out into the world. Second, the death rate of mothers at childbirth has declined. "As both immigration and childbirth deaths have fallen off, women gradually have come to outnumber men" (Novak, 1983, p. 23).

This pattern now exists despite the fact that there are typically 105 males born for every 100 females. Also, females seem to be the stronger sex when it comes to health and

length of life. There are more miscarriages of males, more males die at birth, and 25 percent more male babies than female babies die during the first year of life. At every age level throughout life, death rates are higher for males. To add to this problem, men are much more resistant to carrying out preventative health care or to visiting a doctor. Furthermore, "A man can expect to live only to seventy and a half years, while a woman can look forward to living until she is over seventy-eight years old. So it is not surprising that in 1980, among Americans over sixty-five, there were 13.6 million women and only 9.5 million men. This is where the man shortage is more severe" (Novak, 1983, p. 23).

When one considers just single people, of whom there are more than ever before, the 1980 census estimates that there are 30 million unmarried women compared to 21.5 million unmarried men. An important factor related to the man shortage is divorce and remarriage. There is a much higher rate of remarriage for men, and they remarry more quickly after a divorce. Most significant, however, is the fact that both divorced and widowed men marry women much younger than themselves.

The most informative figures of all are the 1980 totals combining the single, divorced, separated, and widowed. The following figures demonstrate that the surplus of women increases with age.

Age	Number of Women/100 Men (Single, Divorced, Separated, and Widowed)
30–34	102
35–39	128
40–44	135
45–54	147
55–64	208

Thus in the 55–64 age category there are

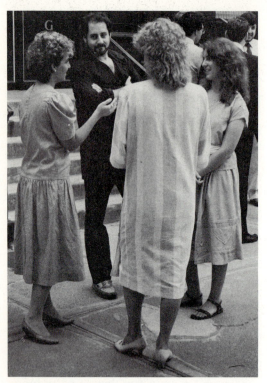

Most singles' organizations have a surplus of women.

more than twice as many unmarried women as men. But by and large, "The man shortage begins to get serious as women pass the age of thirty-five" (Novak, 1983, p. 25).

An obvious solution for women of any age faced with a shortage of men is to date and marry younger men. Although this is an increasing possibility, there are still strong social taboos against this practice. Women who choose younger men are often seen as immoral and primarily seeking "erotic pleasure." In actuality, an older woman and a younger man are often better matched sexually than are couples where the man is older. "Many women in their forties and fifties find that men their own age are lethargic and tired whereas the women feel more alive and stimulated" (Novak, 1983, p. 29). Some women

believe that younger men are "less afraid to show their feelings." Nevertheless, society still frowns somewhat on younger men-older women relationships; this disapproval is despite the fact that husbands typically die seven to eight years before their wives. Women could, however, become much more assertive in making connections with men—both younger and older (see Box 6.4).

And there is more bad news for women: There is the biological clock factor. If women are going to bear children, generally they have to accomplish this task by a certain age. Beyond the middle 30s there are increasing medical risks, and at some point women are no longer able to conceive at all. The biological clock represents another aspect of the double standard of aging. Males can father children at almost any age until they die; there is no male equivalent to menopause. Once again, women are the losers, says Novak; "There is not only a man shortage, but a time shortage as well" (1983, p. 33).

And then there is the gay factor. A lot of women casually express the complaint that "all the good men are married or gay." Are there actually more gay men than gay women in the population at large? The evidence suggests that gay men significantly outnumber lesbians. According to Paul Gebhard of Indiana University's Institute for Sex Research, male homosexuals outnumber lesbians three to one. And among never-married single adult men, "about a quarter of them are predominately homosexual, compared to only six percent of never-married women" (Novak, 1983, p. 38).

Another factor related to male homosexuality is that in the past a large number of gay men would marry and hide their sexual preference. "Today, with much freer cultural norms, these same men don't always marry in the first place, and thus are unavailable as potential husbands" (Novak, 1983, p. 39).

BOX 6.4

WHY YOU SHOULD CALL MEN—AT LEAST OCCASIONALLY

While women are now considerably more assertive in approaching men than they used to be, in the overwhelming majority of cases it is still the man who makes the first move. It is the man who picks up the telephone, who nervously calls the woman, who initiates the social contact. Most women, it seems, would rather be manning the phone than phoning the man. . . .

Although most men are rarely or never asked out by women, many of them believe that *other* men are being called daily. . . . Women are reluctant to call men because they're afraid of appearing foolish or needy or aggressive. Above all, they're terrified of rejection. . . . Most men are flattered and thrilled when women call them, and the most frequent complaint heard from single men on this topic was that women are far too reluctant to assume any responsibility for the dating process. . . .

It's certainly true . . . that for women to call men is to break with many years of tradition. But as the men point out, women seem eager to break with tradition in virtually every other aspect of life. Why should this one be different? . . .

There are a number of reasons for you to call men—at least occasionally. A man you've been introduced to may not have fully noticed you. He may assume that you're not interested in him. He may not realize that the two of you might be good together, whereas you may have a hunch that something nice could develop. If you're like most women, you probably believe that women are generally more intuitively aware than men about what would constitute a successful match. If that's the case, shouldn't you be *acting* on that greater awareness?

There are other reasons, too, to call men. Most men are automatically interested in any woman who shows an interest in them. In addition, if he's the kind of man who is threatened or resentful that you're calling, then he's probably not right for you anyway. It's better to learn that now rather than to wonder forever if you should have called.

Women who call men have more dates—and more possibilities for love—than women who don't. They also have the self-confidence that comes from knowing that they are taking an active role in their own social lives. They no longer feel like passive bystanders, waiting to be noticed, and they're less likely to be depressed or to feel that life is passing them by. . . .

Rejection *is* painful, but it won't kill you, and it's not one of the more intense pains of life. Women who call men understand that being rejected by somebody they barely know is no reason to be overly upset. . . . Because you're probably afraid of rejection, you may be tempted to call only those men who are most likely to say yes, rather than the man you actually want to go out with. Resist that temptation. If you're going to call, call somebody whose positive response will make you glad that you took the risk.

If the prospect of making a telephone call is simply too frightening, there

(Continued)

are other ways to contact a man. You can always write him a note, or send a card, or even a specific invitation. You can buy two theater tickets and send him one. For some women, contacting a man through the mail seems easier because if he says no, it's easier to take through the mail (or through the lack of a response) than is a refusal over the telephone. On the other hand, he may *not* say no, and you have to determine whether *that's* what really frightens you.

SOURCE: *Adapted and quoted from Novak, 1983.*

Such men are also removed from the dating process.

Coming out as a homosexual is certainly an effective way to remove oneself from the tense and difficult dating process, and these days the gay community appears to offer a strong sense of companionship, solidarity, and identity that is in sharp contrast to the socially isolated lives of many unattached heterosexual men. (Novak, 1983, p. 39)

A final factor that affects the man shortage is the fact that women traditionally have tended to "marry up" in terms of income, education, and status. This pattern is commonly known as the "marriage gradient" (Bernard, 1972, pp. 33–34). As Figure 6.1 shows, if people pair off according to the marriage gradient then

The men at the bottom have nobody to marry, for there are no women left who are in a position to look up to them. The women at the top share a similar fate in reverse, as there are very few men above them. The result, Bernard observes, is that the never-married men in society are often the bottom of the barrel, while the never-married women are the cream of the crop. (Novak, 1983, p. 41)

There really are few available men for women at the top. As *Savvy,* the magazine for exec-
utive women, has stated, "The female elite have become the demographic losers. . . . They've priced themselves out of the market" (February, 1980, p. 47).

A related factor is that men who are professionally successful tend to marry fairly early; women who are successful tend to marry late or not at all. In American society for a young man on his way up in the corporate world, marriage is usually advantageous. But for women, marriage and children often restrict careers. "The standard pattern is that the women with the most education and income are the least likely to be married. If they are married, they are less likely to remain married than other women, or than their male counterparts" (Novak, 1983, p. 42).

ILLUSIONARY INTIMACY

Probably to most people marriage itself is the ultimate relationship achievement. But with about half of all marriages in the United States ending in divorce, something must be wrong. How can so many couples who are deliriously happy at the time of their weddings become so confused, angry, and desperate, often just a year or two into their marriages? Is society playing a dirty trick on most young people by having marital choice dominated by romantic love?

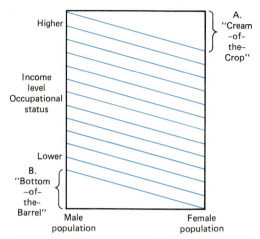

Figure 6.1 The marriage gradient. (*Source:* Bernard, 1982, p. 33; Jorgensen, 1986, p. 223.)

But still most couples whom we see in marital therapy forthrightly say that "their communication was good in the past," that "it was really an exciting relationship," that "they used to have lots of fun together," or that "they were a close couple." They may say that this is the way the relationship was *before* they were married or that the relationship was good for a year or two or more into the marriage. We suggest that what most people, particularly young individuals, perceive of as emotional closeness before or just after marriage is not really intimacy at all. Rather what they have experienced can best be described as "illusionary intimacy." It is true that much of what is felt in courtship and early marriage resembles intimacy. Fun, positive exchanges, self-disclosure, exclusivity, and equality all exist. There is also, however, much that is imaginary and idealized. The French phrase *folie à deux,* or the folly of the couple, best describes what the partners are experiencing.

Illusionary intimacy may be defined as a feeling of closeness perpetuated by romanticism and unrealistic perceptions of the part-

ner and the relationship. Indicated below are nine factors that help to produce the state of illusionary intimacy and lead to its decline.

1. *The superficialness of courtship and surface self-disclosure* help to create illusionary intimacy. The concern here is that throughout the dating period individuals are usually on their best behavior; they put their best foot forward. Since we want the other person to like us, we often say the things we know that he or she wants to hear. Total leveling with a person is more unlikely than likely. The goal is primarily to please the other and "capture" the marital "prize." Real intimacy is typically not a goal. Add to this the excitement of the time, of finding one's lifetime partner. Emotions are often at a fever pitch. *Any* self-disclosure from this potential lifetime partner seems like a lot, even though there may be little depth to it. Negative emotions are avoided if possible. The result is that the partners end up with an idealized view of each other and of the relationship. One might really only know the outer shell of his or her partner and not the core of what that person stands for or desires. The bottom line is an illusion fueled by each person's fantasy, an illusion lacking realistic perception. It is certainly easy to understand why premarital counseling is so seldom sought out and is so difficult to do, if indeed a couple does seek it.

It is argued by Philip Marcus (1977) that women are more likely than men to feel as though they have made a mistake in choosing a marriage partner. "The male possesses better predictors of his future wife's behavior than the female has about her husband" (p. 26). In courtship and in the early period of marriage the male is often more expressive than he will be in the following years. His attentiveness and what appears as emotional sensitivity all flatter the female (Marcus, 1977). This *earlier expressiveness,* still limited though it may be, *contributes to illusionary intimacy.*

2. Illusionary intimacy also exists partly as a result of *the confusion between love and intimacy.* Love is often perceived of as being the same as "intimacy." To love someone, as has previously been pointed out, relates to *individual* needs, and love itself can be defined as meaning almost anything. Some types of love are particularly conducive to fantasy and illusion but not to intimacy. In addition, as has been seen, two people may love each other in different ways and for different reasons. In any event, there is a general feeling in American society that love conquers all, that nothing else is needed for a happy marriage. But after marriage, even love (however it is defined) is often taken for granted; it is neglected rather than nurtured.

3. There is also usually *confusion between emotional closeness and sexuality,* or physical closeness. Romantic passion, sexual openness, or multiple orgasms may have nothing necessarily to do with emotional closeness. An engaged woman may feel that since she and her partner are involved sexually, they must be a close couple. Sexual behavior for most married couples involves a relatively small amount of time per week compared to other types of interaction.

4. Under illusionary intimacy there is *an equality between the genders that often doesn't last.* After marriage many couples return to a pattern of traditional roles. For men, success at their work becomes the major priority; they focus on the instrumental good-provider role. In addition, men sometimes treat their new spouses as possessions. They often feel that now that they have "a wife," the marriage will take care of itself; significant further investment is not needed. In addition, once both partners are "in love" or actually married, there appears to be less concern about giving and receiving fairly. Ironically, "love"

appears at times to release people from the need to exchange in an equitable way. It is reasoned that since both are "in love," there is no longer any reason to keep tabs on who gives what, or who is contributing what, compared to the other person. The result may be that the relationship becomes unfair, resentment begins to rise, and the marriage begins to go downhill in terms of quality.

As the male gets more and more into "his work," the wife often feels more and more distance developing between him and her. "The female finds it relatively difficult to help with male job anxieties when she is removed from the specific circumstances" (Marcus, 1977, p. 28). The masculine image often prevents the male from sharing his work with his wife. The couple grows farther apart, and the female becomes disillusioned at an increasing rate. Because of illusionary intimacy the female has no reliable method to determine whether a man actually has the abilities and securities to function in a really intimate relationship (Marcus, 1977).

5. *Marriage itself is generally not seen very accurately* under illusionary intimacy. At first there appears to be a lived-happily-ever-after attitude. But in reality, people often know little about what it takes to build a good marriage. Sociologist Jessie Bernard has written about a "shock theory of marriage," where the young couple after the wedding, particularly the woman, experiences "the end of romantic fantasy," "disenchantment," and "the exposing of the myth of the strong and protective husband." The woman typically goes from being catered to in courtship to being the caterer to in marriage (1972, p. 41).

Typically, marriage is viewed by both the male and the female as an end in itself rather than as the beginning of a building process toward emotional closeness. Simply put, the similarity of social characteristics and the fun times together found in courtship are not enough to sustain the relationship over time. Interactive factors that made the relationship exciting previously often disappear. Many couples complain that the relationship is no longer as much fun as it once was. Shared enjoyable quality time, play, humor, and companionship all may diminish as the partners quickly become "an old married couple." The activities shared together, which previously helped to create the illusionary intimacy, often stop. In American society, just as romantic love induces a move toward marriage, the decline of romantic love encourages divorce. Most of those who divorce tend to do so relatively early in their marriages.

The peak period for divorce is two to five years after the marriage, a statistic that has not changed much. Given the time required to make the decision to divorce, separate, file, and wait for a final decree, this peak period reflects evidence of serious marital problems very early in the relationship for most couples who eventually divorce. (Spanier, 1986, pp. 87–88)

6. Another reason that early illusionary intimacy tends to be short lived is that *people largely do not understand the concept of real intimacy,* let alone how to achieve it. Part of the explanation for this is the immaturity of the partners; the glamorized romance perpetuated in movies, magazines, and on television; and the fact that emotional intimacy is simply not talked about very much. Thus when the romantic fantasy dies, as it practically always does, the response of many individuals is "I made a mistake," "I picked the wrong person," "I don't love him or her anymore," and "I'll find somebody new to love and try to get that 'romantic high' back again." Many people believe that illusionary intimacy is the real thing; particularly women seem to be misled by it. But even when disillusionment sets in, people usually cannot pinpoint ex-

actly what went wrong. All they know at this point is that the marriage is not working out the way they thought it would.

7. Illusionary intimacy is helped by the fact that in many instances people *don't get to know their partner's actual personality* until after marriage. For example, behavior in courtship that was interpreted as "cocky confidence" may be seen after marriage as masking very low self-esteem. An underlying fear of vulnerability may not be evident until after the marital commitment has been made. Men may hide their personal dependence more than previously because they believe that husbands should project strength and independence, really to take on the role of the man of the household. Admitting dependence, more than ever before, is viewed as a sign of weakness, which could possibly lead to rejection. Also, women who were attracted to men who appeared to be "in control" of their lives before marriage may find such men to be smothering and suffocating in their attempts to control after marriage. Male shyness that was seen as "cute" by the female during courtship is seen after marriage as the inability to be close to anyone.

In addition, many people never understand the meaning of the marital commitment until after the ceremony. The impact of one's loss of freedom is often belated. Also, touching behavior typically decreases after marriage for men. Touch was used before marriage often as a means to initiate sexual activity. Now that sexual activity is readily available, the preliminaries are often passed over and the focus is on sexual intercourse itself. It's almost impossible to hide one's real personality in a marriage; a person's degree of sensitive disclosure, self-esteem, trustworthiness, and empathy are going to be known over time. In a lot of instances newfound realities do not match the perceptions experienced under illusionary intimacy.

8. The exposing of real personalities often *increases the level of conflict,* and this is a major reason for the decline of illusionary intimacy. What was previously swept under the rug to avoid dealing with conflicts is now more likely to land on the table. Usually conflict-resolution skills leave much to be desired, and the typical couple has not had a lot of practice and experience in this area, partially as a result of previous avoidance of conflict. Conflict often occurs as "Persons first reveal to each other certain feelings, doubts, disappointments, expectations, ideals, and assessments they have made about the relationship" (Braiker and Kelly, 1979). As a result of interpersonal conflict, a couple may make changes in the relationship. They may attempt to redefine the relationship or to raise questions, such as whether they were meant for each other, what could be done to make them a closer couple, should they lower their expectations, or should they call it quits?

9. Finally, certain *situational problems may become more evident* when illusionary intimacy fades. There may be in-law problems that were not seen previously, or a partner may be exceedingly close to the members of his or her family and spend so much time with them that it interferes with the marriage. One partner may express an honest negative evaluation of the other partner's family, which, even though true, is deeply resented and may never be forgotten. Long work hours, dual-career marriages, or the two spouses working different shifts can lead to little time together as well as to resentment.

There may be privacy problems connected with housing. Different wake-sleep cycles that were not noticed before may hinder closeness and cause anger. Other needs may now take precedence—job responsibilities or the demands of children. All of these factors may diminish any remnants of illusionary intimacy. In the final analysis,

emotional closeness evolves from significant investments that the two partners make over a long period of time. The couple needs a history together after a marital commitment has been finalized before intimacy is possible. As David Mace has said, a wedding is not a marriage (Mace, 1982)!

CHAPTER REVIEW

1. Coupling involves a process of searching for a partner who offers the most rewards at the least costs. Bargaining and exchange are evident in all courtship processes, including the traditional, intermediary, and contemporary patterns.

2. During the 1920s dating became a new mechanism for mate selection. It allowed individuals to experiment with relationships with the other sex and to develop social skills. Dating continues today as a major activity in mate selection, although it starts at an earlier age and tends to involve more exclusivity than dating before the 1960s.

3. Brinkmanship in courtship involves the skill of avoiding dangerous situations that may harm a relationship or cause its breakup. It includes, among other things, flirting, the principle of least interest, and the avoidance of showing smothering affection.

4. People want to obtain the best bargain possible in a mate, consistent with what they think they deserve. Most individuals, however, tend to pair off with someone equal to their own level of physical attractiveness.

5. Several theories attempt to explain the process of mate selection. The theory of proximity states that the physical closeness of people increases the chance of developing a friendship or finding a potential mate. Similar social characteristics and value consensus have also been attributed to relationship de-

velopment. In addition, similar or complementary personalities can facilitate a relationship, usually depending upon one's own personality. Choosing a partner who has a personality similar to that of one's parents is also a common pattern in mate selection.

6. As a relationship develops, partners go through a process of coupling before marriage. The stages of this process include (1) initial attraction, (2) investigatory exchange, (3) trust development and attachment, and (4) committed reciprocity.

7. A problem voiced by many women is a "man shortage." Demographically women do outnumber men; and as women grow older, the men become fewer. One solution is for women to date and marry younger men, but there continue to be some social taboos limiting these practices.

8. The phenomenon of illusionary intimacy can help explain why partners feel so close in the early stages of a relationship but do not really become intimate until years later. Nine reasons for illusionary intimacy and its decline are presented in the chapter.

7

The Marriage Commitment

Marriage may be the butt of many jokes, the topic of comedians' monologues, and a subject of ridicule in various cartoons. But despite all the bad press, this institution has never lost its popularity. Consider the following:

Ninety-five percent of all Americans eventually marry.

Seventy-five percent of all divorced persons remarry.

The greater acceptance of nonmarital cohabitation has not diminished the frequency of marriage.

A majority of Americans hold marriage to be a more central value than either work or leisure pursuits.

The marriage rate climbed during the last half of the 1970s and has remained at a sustained high level in the first two-thirds of the 1980s.

Thus a marriage partner today is still defined as "the *most significant other* in adult life" (Berger and Berger, 1983). Such an emphasis on marriage, however, appears to be a mixed blessing. Unusually high expectations for marriage are likely to lead to disillusion and disenchantment. In fact, the high divorce rate itself may be partly a result of excessively high hopes for marriage rather than an indication that people are turned off to marriage. "In other words, divorce is mainly a backhanded compliment to the ideal of modern marriage, as well as a testimony to its difficulties" (Berger and Berger, 1983, p. 166). Hence, the jokes, the cartoons, and the negative comments about marriage may be the result of people's disappointments that marriage has not delivered all that was expected. Nonetheless, high expectations continue to persist among newlyweds and re-newlyweds.

Marriage stands out today as theoretically one of the few social relationships that pro-vides some stability to individuals in our rather segmented American society. People's lives are more stable, reliable, and anxiety free when their relationships with significant others are enduring and dependable. It is the fragmented nature of our society that causes the great emotional need for marriage. Brigitte and Peter Berger write:

Suffice it to say that, under these conditions, it is a vital necessity for the individual's sanity and emotional well-being that there be some relationships that are stable, reliable, and unfragmented—that is, relationships intended to be lifelong, whose basic presuppositions do not change, and which confirm all aspects of the individual's identity. . . . One might say that if such a relationship did not exist, it would have to be invented. . . . The profound need it is designed to meet . . . goes far in explaining why it continues to be aspired to even by those who have been disappointed in their experiences of marriage. (1983, p. 166)

Long-term trends regarding marriage rates reveal the following. The marriage rate was quite steady during the first four decades of this century except for a brief upturn at the end of World War I and some decline during the depression of the 1930s. After World War II, the postwar marriage boom, which meant a substantial widespread increase in marriage rates, helped produce the baby boom. The rates remained high through the 1950s and 1960s and then fell sharply again in the later 1960s and early 1970s. The last half of the 1970s saw them climbing, and in the 1980s they have begun to stabilize at levels very similar to those of the first few decades of the century (Thornton and Freedman, 1983).

The current high marriage rate cannot be totally attributed to first marriages; an increasing percentage of legal unions is remarriages. Table 7.1 shows that about 55 percent

TABLE 7.1

PERCENT DISTRIBUTION OF MARRIAGES BY MARRIAGE ORDER OF BOTH BRIDE AND GROOM: 1970–1981[a]

MARRIAGE ORDER OF BOTH BRIDE AND GROOM

Year	All marriages	First marriage of bride and groom	First marriage of bride, remarriage of groom	Remarriage of bride, first marriage of groom	Remarriage of bride and groom
			Percent		
1981	100.0	54.7	11.8	10.1	23.4
1980	100.0	56.2	11.3	9.8	22.7
1979	100.0	56.4	11.2	9.5	22.9
1978	100.0	57.1	11.1	9.3	22.5
1977	100.0	57.5	10.8	9.0	22.6
1976	100.0	58.5	10.7	8.8	22.0
1975	100.0	60.1	9.9	8.6	21.3
1974	100.0	62.9	9.2	8.1	19.8
1973	100.0	64.6	8.7	7.9	18.9
1972	100.0	66.7	8.2	7.4	17.6
1971	100.0	67.7	8.0	7.3	17.0
1970	100.0	68.6	7.6	7.3	16.5

[a] Based on sample data. Beginning in 1977, figures exclude data for Iowa. Computed from totals excluding marriage order not stated.

SOURCE: Monthly Vital Statistics Report, *Vol. 32, No. 11, February 29, 1984, p. 9.*

of all marriages conducted in 1981 were first marriages of both the bride and the groom, and 45 percent were remarriages of one or both partners. These proportions have changed from the previous decade. In 1970, 69 percent of all marriages were first marriages, and 31 percent were remarriages (U.S. Department of Health and Human Services, 1984, p. 9).

The age at first marriage has increased meaningfully since 1970. The median age for women is 23.3 years and for men 25.5 years (U.S. Bureau of the Census, 1985). Blacks tend to marry at a later age than do whites, a pattern observed since 1960 (Blackwell, 1985). "In 1980, 79 percent of all black 20–24-year-old males were never married in contrast to 69 percent of the white males in the same age cohort" (Blackwell, 1985, p. 85). The percentage of never-married 20–24-year-old black females was 69 in 1980, and of white females of the same age cohort it was 50. The increasing number of blacks delaying marriage may be attributed to those blacks who postpone marriage to attend college "as well as those who postpone it because of uncertain job prospects, military service . . . or other reasons" (Blackwell, 1985, p. 85).

Although marriage remains a popular institution, among both the never-married and the divorced, people's attitudes toward it have shifted over the past decades. Individuals today seem more aware of the burdens and restrictions that marriage imposes rather than focusing only on the opportunities it offers. Respondents in two national random surveys conducted in 1957 (Gurin, Veroff, and Feld, 1960) and 1976 (Veroff, Douvan, and Kulka, 1981) were asked, "How is a man's (woman's) life changed by being married?" In 1957, irrespective of marital status, more than 40 percent gave answers indicating a positive view of marriage as enlarging the individual and opening new opportunities, and about 20 percent responded negatively. In 1976 less than a third of all respondents (29 percent) offered a positive view of marriage, and almost as many (26 percent) revealed a distinctly negative view of the changes that marriage brings. Unlike the 1957 respondents, the people in 1976 were more realistic and more likely to say that "marriage both enlarges *and* restricts life." Sociologist David Mace (1983) offers some realism about marriages by reviewing some marital myths (see Box 7.1).

Doubt about the stability and viability of marriage was raised during what has been called the "decade of crisis"—during the 1965–1975 period. Marriage was in serious trouble during this time according to sociologist Jessie Bernard (1982). It was a time of antiestablishment protest movements of many kinds—civil-rights, antiwar, consumers, students—and of socioeconomic events such as recessions, oil crises, and public scandals. The whole structure of American society was shaken. Marriage, as a part of society,

was not spared. While marriage rates and fertility rates declined, divorce rates doubled. By the mid-1970s, for the first time in American history, the number of marriages dissolved by divorce exceeded the number terminated by death. Alarm spread as the "imminent demise of marriage" became a possibility (Bernard, 1981). In the 1980s, however, there is no longer a fear that marriage is dead. Statistical trends seemed to have stabilized. Also, negative attitudes toward marriage have been countered by the strong "pro-family" movement with its wide ramifications.

THE MARITAL COMMITMENT

Young couples living together may question what difference a piece of paper—that is, the marriage license—makes to a relationship. The piece of paper makes no difference per se; it's the commitment that it represents that makes the difference (Bernard, 1982). The key characteristic that distinguishes marriage from most other relationships is the public commitment that the two individuals make.

Humans make all kinds of commitments. For example, when we take a new job, we are pledging or promising to fulfill the responsibilities of that role. If we don't provide certain services, we can be fired. Commitment in marriage, however, involves more than promising to fulfill some contractual obligations. Most partners are committing themselves to more than perfunctory services or a ritualistic exchange. They are making an *emotional commitment*. Typically they are committing themselves to a search for meaningful personal happiness through the relationship. Ideally their lives are shared, needs are expressed, conflicts are resolved, and emotional support is provided.

Intimacy, of course, will not occur without some assurance of commitment. We are not likely to reveal our innermost thoughts

BOX 7.1

TEN MYTHS ABOUT MARRIAGE

To illustrate the widespread confusion in our thinking, here are ten commonly accepted misconceptions about marriage:

1. *Marriages are made in heaven.* This is the romantic illusion that just because two people are attracted to each other and go through a wedding ceremony, some special dispensation spares them the toil and effort that are normally necessary for success in most other human undertakings. All couples awaken from this rosy but deceptive dream sooner or later.

2. *A wedding is a marriage.* We often use the words *wedding* and *marriage* interchangeably, talking about "getting married" when we should say "getting wedded." A wedding is only the *beginning* of the task of achieving a marriage. In the U.S. today, about two and a half million men and women annually report to a court of law that they have had a wedding but have failed to achieve a marriage, and now they want their agreement canceled.

3. *Married couples must accept what happens to them "for better or for worse."* These words imply that some impersonal fate decides the issues for them. Not at all. Whether their marriage turns out to be for better or worse than the average is decided by what the couple themselves make of the resources they bring to each other.

4. *Couples must be "compatible" for a marriage to succeed.* There is some truth in this. But the idea, first started by Plato, that the "right" partners fit each other like pieces of a jigsaw puzzle, is nonsense. Every marriage must involve a long process of mutual adaptation which may take most of a lifetime.

5. *Don't expect behavior changes in your marriage partner.* It is true that putting pressure on your spouse to change will be ineffective. But partners who *work together* can achieve remarkable changes. It is known that even very old people can change their behavior if they are effectively motivated and suitably rewarded.

6. *Happily married couples never disagree.* All couples have disagreements. Happy couples are those who have developed the skills necessary to resolve their differences amicably, while couples who avoid and suppress disagreements are not happy.

7. *Couples who stay together must be happily married.* The view that "stable" marriages are necessarily successful is now unacceptable. Many couples who don't divorce might have more and better reasons for doing so than many who do split up.

8. *Don't unload your personal problems on your spouse—keep them to yourself.* If marriage partners can't seek sympathy and support from

(Continued)

each other in the ups and downs of life, who can they turn to? A loving, caring relationship involves everything that concerns the couple.

9. *Married couples should never discuss their marital difficulties with other couples.* We call this the "intermarital taboo," and it deprives couples of all kinds of mutual support and help they could otherwise be giving each other.

10. *You don't need marriage counseling until you are in really serious trouble.* By that time it may be too late, because alienation has undermined the couple's motivation to work at the relationship. The counselor can do most for those who seek help early.

SOURCE: *Mace, 1983.*

---

to people who can't make a promise that they will "stick around" and that they will be there when we need them. Marital partners are promising or pledging to behave in certain ways for emotional reasons—because they care about the other person. It is this sense of caring, and the demonstration of the caring, that serves as the foundation of marital commitment.

But what exactly do we mean by commitment in marriage? How does it specifically differ from commitments in other relationships? Under what conditions does a commitment evolve?

The Meaning of Commitment

COMMITMENT AS A PROCESS. The making of a commitment is not a particular event. It's a process, a sequence of actions that sustains the relationship over time. In other words, simply making a pledge or promise to maintain a relationship does not always result in the person remaining in it. Thus commitment is not *one* explicit act but a series of events or acts in which each person repeatedly makes clear his or her intention to continue the relationship (Hinde, 1979).

What are the clues or signs that a com-

mitment is developing? The process of commitment involves actions "in which one person changes his or her behavior to suit the other's desires" (Kelley, 1983, p. 301). The two attempt to coordinate their lives so that they "mesh with each other's." They "work out understandings about what activities they do (or do not do) with each other and about what they should or should not do with outsiders" (p. 301).

Hence, a scenario unfolds: Jane arranges her work schedule so that she can play racketball with John. Aware of Jane's love for music, John buys tickets for a local concert series so he and Jane can attend. Jane decides to live in the same city as John so that she can be closer to him. John quits dating other women and dates Jane exclusively. Jane no longer advertises in the personal ads for a man, and so it goes on. Each person attempts to coordinate his or her life-style so it will mesh with the other.

During the commitment process each person is becoming more willingly dependent on the other and is revealing this dependence in his or her behavior. What results is "an understanding between the two that each is attached to the other, that each regards the attachment as stable, and that each fully accepts the long-term implications of such attachment" (Kelley, 1983, p. 301).

In essence, they are striking a bargain in which each agrees that "I'll stick with you if you'll stick with me" (Kelley, 1983). Of course, this process of commitment does not always proceed in a symmetrical or an entirely equal manner. At times one person may be more committed than the other, resulting in either a renegotiation of the relationship or its dissolution.

Even after a formal commitment is made, it may vary during the course of a marriage. A couple's commitment after ten years of marriage may not be at the same level as at the time of marriage. For example, on the one hand, a number of "destabilizing forces" may be experienced during the course of the marriage, which may cause the couple to question or reevaluate the degree of their commitment.

On the other hand, many people actually have a rather weak commitment at the time of marriage, but the commitment increases over time. Commitment can be viewed as an individual capacity that may grow over the course of marriage. "People committed at or near their own capacity at the onset of marriage may grow both in capacity for commitment and in commitment itself as they acquire experience in marital and other relations, and as they free themselves from youthful idealism, insecurity and self-deception" (Rosenblatt, 1977, pp. 74–75). Although both partners may not have the same level of commitment, generally there are pressures that tend to push couples toward a symmetrical commitment. A similar level of commitment is the ideal in marriage. However, "there appear to be many marital relationships with asymmetrical commitment" (p. 75). In some societies, for example, women may seem more committed to marriage than men. Often in such situations women do not have access to potential alternative relationships, or men are scarcer than women, or women rely more on men for life's necessities.

PERMANENCE. When individuals say that they are committed to something, they usually mean that they are "likely to stick with it and see it through to its finish" (Kelley, 1983, p. 287). There is an expectation of *duration* or *perseverance.* In marriage this means that "through thick and thin," "for better and for worse," partners are expected to stay in that relationship. Unlike most other commitments that we make to people, the marital commitment is intended to be lifelong. Research studies suggest that almost all people who marry do intend to stay married for a lifetime (Lasswell and Lasswell, 1973). In fact, the concept of permanence is one characteristic of marriage that appears to be universal (Stephens, 1963). In no society is marriage supposed to be a temporary arrangement; it's certainly not a short-term contract.

It is this duration or permanence that also differentiates married couples from cohabitors. Cohabitation does not involve a lifelong commitment; most cohabitating couples either marry or end their relationships in a relatively short time. In fact, the sociologists Philip Blumstein and Pepper Schwartz (1983) in their study of 12,000 American couples were unable to find many unmarried couples who had lived together for as many as ten years. With no expectation for permanence a couple cannot plan for the future. As a way of life cohabitation tends to be unstable and transitory.

The permanence of the marital commitment provides for security in the relationship. A commitment that is not permanent is not a guarantee of security at all. Jessie Bernard (1982) stresses that regarding marriage, "For centuries, stability was considered almost the only component of the commitment that absolutely had to be insisted upon. 'Till death do us part' was the indisputable rule" (p. 94).

In one respect the till-death-do-us-part permanence of marriage seems to be much more of a commitment today than in the past. Shorter life expectancies 100 years ago meant that marriages did not last nearly as long as they do today. "A vow to remain together until death parted them was not so hard for brides and grooms to take when death was not so far off. Childbirth, for instance, exacted an enormous toll among women" (Bernard, 1982, p. 98). In colonial times a man might go through several wives in his lifetime. The serial monogamous marriages that we see today are more the result of divorce. One hundred years ago they were the result of high death rates.

COMMITMENT AS THOUGHTS AND BEHAVIORS. Commitment involves both thoughts about the relationship and behaviors with the partner. Many thoughts and behaviors seem to occur almost simultaneously. By engaging in certain behaviors, such as saying "I love you," by participating in sexual activity, or by giving up dating other people, partners come to decide that they are "committed." Engaging in such overt behaviors tends to encourage and promote internal thoughts about being committed to the relationship (Kelley, 1983). The reverse is also true with thoughts leading to behavioral patterns demonstrating commitment.

Thus, as Jane spends most of her spare time with John and engages in sexual activity with him, she thinks, "I must be committed to John." Once she thinks that she is committed she will continue to behave accordingly unless commitment is something she doesn't want. By doing things together, the partners begin to define themselves as a couple and to refer to themselves as "we" and to their activities and possessions as "ours." In addition, other people in their social environment define them as a couple and, in turn, encourage them to function as a couple.

Types of Commitment in Marriage

THE LEGAL COMMITMENT. One of the most binding commitments in marriage is the legal commitment. Marriage law spells out certain reciprocal rights and obligations between spouses and any children. Unknown to most brides and grooms when they marry is the fact that they are actually agreeing to a specific, formal marriage contract dictated by the state in which they are married. It is usually only when the marriage is breaking up that the partners, upon consulting their respective lawyers, discover their real obligations and to what extent their freedom to decide their own fate is restricted by the terms of the state-dictated marriage contract (Weitzman, 1981).

Until recently the legal contract that governed the couple's relationship was based on traditional expectations of the family. The obligations and responsibilities outlined in this contract included the following:

1. The husband is the head of the household.
2. The husband is responsible for support.
3. The wife is responsible for domestic services.
4. The wife is responsible for child care, the husband for child support.

The courts said that the husband had a duty to provide the family with food, clothing, and shelter; the wife had a duty to render services in maintaining the home and to care for the children with resources furnished by the husband. The duties were complementary. The purpose of the state-imposed obligations was "to preserve the traditional family."

This traditional marriage contract has been criticized by Lenore Weitzman (1981). The contract is said to discriminate on the basis of gender by assigning one set of rights and obligations to husbands and another to wives. Also, the law imposes a single family form on everyone, ignoring many of the families in present-day American society.

However, in response to the dramatic changes in family patterns in American society in the past two decades, marriage laws have also changed.

> The U.S. Supreme Court has ruled that laws obligating spouses to support one another must be sex-neutral. . . . All of the states have, in one way or another, changed their laws to make sex-based roles in marriage obsolete, although these changes do not prevent couples who wish to play the traditional marital roles from doing so. (American Bar Association, 1983, p. 7)

Some couples, however, feel it is necessary to put their expectations and obligations for their marriage in writing (see Box 7.2).

INSTITUTIONAL VS. VOLUNTARY COMMITMENTS.

When analyzing marital commitment, it is helpful to distinguish between two types of pledges or goals in the relationship. First, a commitment can be made to the *relationship*, that is, to its continuation no matter what happens. Second, a commitment can be made to *individual happiness* in the relationship, a commitment that lasts only as long as personal happiness is found in the current relationship or more potential satisfaction is not perceived of as coming from an alternative relationship.

Blumstein and Schwartz make this distinction between commitments by labeling two types of marriages *institutional* and *vol-*

untary. The "institutional" couples feel that "their marriage may become unfulfilling, but they have entered an unbreakable covenant and therefore they will persevere" (1983, p. 104). This is a commitment to the relationship—to the institution of marriage—and helps to explain those marriages that are unhappy but stable.

In contrast, the "voluntary" couples believe that "while the institution may be important, it is not as important as how the partners feel about each other" (Blumstein and Schwartz, 1983, p. 104). These couples feel that marriage must justify itself on a continual basis. "They believe that when a marriage has ceased to fulfill the partners' emotional needs, its continuation should be reevaluated" (p. 104).

Bernard warns that this second type of commitment may be difficult to interpret. In the commitment "to fulfill emotional needs" or to "provide a climate that stimulates and invites individual growing," how would one know when or if it was being violated (1982, p. 93)? It appears that the typical individual uses a simple measure as to whether he or she wants to stay in the marriage any longer; the measure is whether or not a person still loves his or her partner. It appears, in American society at least, that individuals can "fall out of love" just as they can "fall in love."

In their comparison of institutional couples with voluntary couples, Blumstein and Schwartz found, for example, that when married people have institutional attitudes toward their relationship they are more likely to want to pool their money. The researchers concluded, "Only couples who are committed to the institution of marriage, not simply to each other, feel safe enough to be able to trust their resources to one another" (1983, p. 105). It's obvious that differing thoughts or attitudes about commitment in marriage can result in different behaviors.

BOX 7.2

GETTING IT IN WRITING: PRENUPTIAL AGREEMENTS

"Now that both husband and wife are likely to have money and property that they wish to protect, and as divorce has become statistically more likely, people are increasingly using prenuptial contracts" (American Bar Association, 1983, p. 9). Such a contract is an agreement entered into by two parties before marriage. The courts are now more likely to uphold prenuptial agreements than in the past. The American Bar Association expects that such contracts will become "more widely used as the rules are made clearer and their functions become better known" (ABA, 1983, p. 9).

In *Law and Marriage: Your Legal Guide,* the Bar Association spells out the advantages and disadvantages of prenuptial agreements. The advantages are summarized as follows:

1. Anticipating areas of possible disagreement and settling them in advance can improve a couple's communication.
2. Special inheritance provisions can be made in cases where either or both of the parties have children from a prior marriage.
3. "Potentially, a prenuptial agreement can make a divorce less traumatic for all concerned by smoothing the negotiations surrounding the divorce settlement" and child custody arrangements (ABA, 1983, p. 10).

The disadvantages are as follows:

1. In the event of a divorce, "a typical prenuptial agreement may do a disservice to one of the parties" since the judge may have awarded one partner a better settlement than he or she would have been likely to work out for himself or herself in a prenuptial agreement.
2. Some people consider the agreements "unromantic" and "inconsistent with the trust that two people who are about to be married should feel for one another" (ABA, 1983, p. 10).
3. It "does not provide complete assurance that its provisions will be carried out" (ABA, 1983, p. 10).

Generally, prenuptial agreements are "most useful in prearranging financial matters" (ABA, 1983, p. 11). Some typical financial, as well as nonfinancial, examples are as follows:

A couple with children from previous marriages makes a contract agreeing that each will receive only a limited inheritance if the other dies, the rest of the estate going to the deceased's children.

A couple, each of whom has a separate income and property, signs an agreement that property and income will be kept separate. The contract also provides for how the couple will share the expenses of caring for children and maintaining a home. (Note: This latter provision is one of those which would not be legally enforceable during a marriage.)

Couples agree in advance that if their marriage ends in divorce, they will make a preestablished financial settlement and handle child custody in a preestablished manner. (Note: The agreed-upon financial settlement is subject to court approval, and the child custody agreement is not binding on the court.)

Couples may use prenuptial agreements to create a moral, though not a legal, commitment to divide household chores and child care chores in a preestablished manner.

Couples may use prenuptial agreements as a way to facilitate communication (for example, they might agree to full disclosure of their sex lives), or negotiate the solutions to potential disputes (one might agree not to squeeze toothpaste tubes in the middle) in advance of marriage. Such contractual provisions are not legally enforceable, but they do carry moral weight. (ABA, 1983, p. 11)

"A prenuptial contract not negotiated by two lawyers is not likely to hold up in court" (ABA, 1983, p. 13). Prenuptial contracts, in reality, only rarely appear with first marriages.

Commitment in a marriage, however, need not be focused on only one of the two types of commitment to the exclusion of the other. One can be committed to both—to one's own and one's partner's emotional well-being and to the continuation of the relationship as well. In an ideal intimate relationship these two objectives—individual happiness and satisfaction and commitment to the permanence of the relationship—are intertwined. Therefore, marital couples may want to strive for a combination of the "institutional" and "voluntary" commitments. To some individuals, the idea of a "renewable marriage" has appeared attractive (see Box 7.3).

Commitment-Building Mechanisms

MORE REWARDS THAN COSTS. If the rewards outweigh the costs of a relationship, an individual is more likely to stay with his or her spouse. But partners in an intimate relationship will not be constantly monitoring rewards and costs. If the costs temporarily outweigh the rewards, this does not mean the commitment will end. An intimate relationship is built on a history of positive exchange and an accumulation of past rewards, a situation that helps the partners to expect rewards in the future. Also, as a result of the history of positive interaction, the partners can experience "secondary reward value" through mentally reliving past rewarding and happy events (Kelley, 1983, p. 298). The process of reflecting on past satisfactions may help partners further to commit themselves to the marriage. Thus, past rewards are not lost, and such satisfactions themselves increase the likelihood of future rewards. In addition, the anticipation of future rewards is a reward itself, and this helps to propel the marriage forward.

BOX 7.3

RENEWABLE MARRIAGE: A LIMITED COMMITMENT

With the divorce rate so high, some people have questioned commitment in marriage, especially the permanence aspect of marriage. "Renewable marriages" look like an attractive alternative. This type of marriage requires a commitment of only a limited duration—for three, five, or ten years. Partners would promise to maintain the marriage for at least this limited period of time. At the end of the period they decide if they want to recommit themselves to it (Bernard, 1982). A far-out idea? Not to some. The legislature in Maryland in 1971 introduced a bill to institutionalize such limited-commitment marriages.

The rationale of such nonpermanent commitment is that it keeps both partners on their good behavior and prevents them from falling into a taken-for-granted status of neglect (Bernard, 1982). A 28-year-old woman lawyer in a renewable marriage to a 35-year-old, previously divorced man describes its benefits this way:

> We work together, we live together, it's a beautiful one life. The agreement helps. Nobody feels tied down. When we meet someone who's attractive and good looking, we don't say to ourselves. "Oh, I'm, tied down." We can relax. Only a fool would sign a contract for life. (Bernard, 1982, p. 96)

The dissolution of a marriage with a renewable contract is not, however, any easier. "There is always heartache in the breakdown of a human relationship as intense as that of marriage. Neither a change in the law nor brave-new-world resolutions can change that fact. Divorce or non-renewal, call it what you like, it will be as painful in the future under one name as under any other" (Bernard, 1982, p. 98).

A PUBLIC ANNOUNCEMENT OR CEREMONY. In most societies, marriage begins with substantial publicity and some type of ceremony, ranging from the private and simple to elaborate and extravagant. This ceremony announces to one's "society"—particularly to relatives, friends, and neighbors—the commitment that the bride and groom are making. Generally speaking, one can appraise the commitment to and value of marriage *for the society* by the amount of effort put into the ceremony. Ceremonies are more substantial in terms of expenditure, attendance, and duration where marriages have bigger implications in terms of property and alliance (Rosenblatt, 1977).

Even widely differing cultures share many common elements of the marriage ceremony. In all of them the focus is on the bride and groom pledging themselves to the marital state. A statement commonly is made before an official to the effect that the man and woman accept the statutes and duties of husband and wife under the law of the land.

A public announcement and a ceremony are part of a marriage commitment.

Wedding customs function everywhere to impress upon the couple the importance of the step they are taking; the ceremonies help to distinguish the relationship as one of high commitment (Rosenblatt, 1977). Despite some current "modern" attitudes about marriage, most ceremonies are based on very traditional views.

The wedding ceremony is one commitment-building mechanism absent from the state of nonmarital cohabitation. In other words, when two people choose to live together without marital vows, there is no public ceremony to legitimize the arrangement. Cohabitors may hope that they can somehow create a bond or commitment that does not need any public announcement in order for the relationship to be "durable and satisfying" (Blumstein and Schwartz, 1983). But relationships are public as well as private. "It is difficult to create an institution without

support from society and this society still recognizes only marriage as an institution" (p. 321). Living together continues not to be a fully sanctioned activity.

Thus whether we like it or not, society's reactions do play an important role in supporting commitment in close relationships. "For example, parents may not want to acknowledge a cohabitor's partner as a family member. Even if they want to be welcoming, they may be unsure of what to expect of such a person; they may not know how to act toward him or her" (Blumstein and Schwartz, 1983, p. 321). Do they act toward a cohabitor like another member of the family? What are their expectations for this individual? How do they introduce the cohabitor?

As minor as a marriage ceremony may seem to some people, the ceremony, along with other rules and roles of marriage, has a significant effect on the commitment two people make. Of course, a marriage ceremony in itself does not guarantee a long-lasting commitment, but it aids in the building of a commitment. Other pressures from people may help to maintain the commitment, such as a couple's children, extended-family members, and friends. When children leave home or when a couple moves far away from relatives and friends, perhaps even when they go away on a vacation, the relationship may be weakened by the loss of such social supports.

IRRETRIEVABLE INVESTMENTS. Besides the continuing rewards and benefits that individuals may receive from an ongoing marriage and that, in turn, influence a person's commitment, we must also consider what people put into their relationships. Certain investments—time, money, personal self-disclosures, emotional support, and so on—cannot be retrieved if the relationship breaks up (Kelley, 1983). These instrumental and expressive types of "irretrievable investments" (M. P. Johnson, 1978) often function to keep people in a relationship. Leaving may be more painful and difficult if the partner has made many sacrifices and put extensive effort into the relationship as opposed to not investing much. "If we find that we have put a great deal of effort into an activity, we are likely to feel that it must be worth pursuing" (Aronson, 1961, p. 300).

Utopian communes use the commitment-building mechanism of "irretrievable investments" to promote commitment to the community (Kanter, 1968). Signing over one's property to the community in order to join it and not being reimbursed for one's work for the community if and when one wants to leave are a couple of such mechanisms. Successful communes—that is, those of long duration—were more likely to imple-

ment such rules than were unsuccessful communes. Clearly, this evidence shows that "investment promotes membership stability" (Kelley, 1983).

One of the reasons cohabitors do not pool their resources is because these investments can not be easily retrieved (Blumstein and Schwartz, 1983). Buying a car, furniture, or other things together makes it difficult to retrieve one's investments when breaking up. And there is no law to protect one's share. Therefore, to play it safe, in the event that the relationship does not last, these couples buy things separately.

> *Cohabiting couples shy away from pooling if they doubt the durability of the relationship. Keeping their money separate makes it easier for the relationship to be impermanent. Since the majority of cohabitors do not favor pooling, these facts say important things about pooling and commitment. When couples begin to pool their finances, it usually means they see a future for themselves. (Blumstein and Schwartz, 1983, p. 106)*

AVAILABILITY OF ALTERNATIVE RELATIONSHIPS. One factor that enhances the continuation of a marriage is the reduction of possible alternative partners. One way alternatives are reduced comes simply from the mere fact of publicly announcing a marriage. The announcement discourages persons who might have been available as partners from competing, and such people are more likely to look elsewhere for associations. Needless to say, an announcement won't discourage everybody, but it will most people.

Alternatives may also be reduced by breaking off interactions with persons who might otherwise constitute alternative partners. Contacts with previous friends of the other sex are avoided, and singles' hangouts are no longer frequented. Such actions are not only signs of a person being committed to someone but also function to help maintain a long-term commitment. In trying to convince oneself that the current partner is the better one, one may downgrade other potential partners' attractiveness, elaborate on their negative qualities, and compare them unfavorably with the current partner (Kelley, 1983).

A similar practice of downgrading alternatives has been observed within communes (Kanter, 1968). Members of these communities usually describe outsiders in negative terms and often separate themselves from them. They try to reduce contact with alternative life-styles that may appear more attractive to the people living in the commune. Some communes go as far as requiring members to give up interactions with their spouses and families as part of an effort to engage them into the community.

One way of determining that people have reached the point of commitment is when they no longer consider alternate partners; that is, they no longer are looking for possible alternatives, no longer sizing others up and down, and no longer comparing others to the current partners. Eliminating or reducing alternatives says that the person is confident that the existing partner will provide him or her with a satisfying relationship in the long run. Attention is focused on the current partner, and any alternatives are put out of mind.

One reason for the lack of potential alternative spouses for married people relates to the investments put into the relationship and the history spent together. No other person can easily replace the current spouse. "In a long-term relation, one shares with one's spouse many memories that no other person could provide, and one's pattern of living might be so tied to one's spouse's patterns that no other person could provide the same

level of comfort" (Rosenblatt, 1977, p. 79). The more intimate the relationship, the more difficult it will be to replace the spouse who is part of such an interdependence.

Certain situations, however, may encourage the possibility of looking at alternatives (Leik and Leik, 1977). For example, when involved in a social network with many people, there's the possibility that alternative relationships will come to the person's attention. "Unless the couple is wholly isolated from other contacts, there is always the chance that an outside relation will create a challenge to their current one" (Kelley, 1983, p. 306).

TYPES OF MARRIAGES

"Theirs is a contemporary marriage." "They have a traditional marriage." "Their marriage is like a fairy tale." "I don't think they have much of a marriage at all." We often use labels like these to describe the marriages of our friends, relatives, or neighbors. In marriage counseling a therapist may also try to conceptualize a couple's marriage. In any event, as the partners interact over the course of their marriage, it is common for certain characteristic patterns of interaction to emerge.

Since each partner brings into the marriage his or her individual personality, expectations for the marriage, values, and reward systems, the varieties and assortment of marriages might seem to be endless. But if the analysis is limited to several characteristics, it is possible to arrive at a typology of a limited number of marriage types.

The typology of marriages discussed below is based primarily on the following five important factors:

Power. How is the power distributed? Is the power one-sided or equally balanced? Does one person make the major decisions or are both partners involved in decision making?

Conflict handling. Is conflict recognized, dealt with, resolved, or swept under the rug? How much conflict exists in the relationship? Are conflicts settled primarily by the person with more power?

Intimacy. Is there intimate interaction consisting of mutually sensitive self-disclosure, empathy, touching, shared activities? What barriers to intimacy exist?

Rewards. What type of personal rewards are the spouses seeking? What do the partners find rewarding about being married?

Commitment. Are the partners committed more to the institution of marriage or to their personal well-being and happiness? What are some of the commitment-building mechanisms in the marriage?

As with any typology developed by social scientists, the marriages described here are "ideal types," that is, prototypes. What are found in the world are "real types." Hence, many marriages may fit most of the characteristics of one type but not *all* the characteristics. Also, since marriage is not static but changing over months or years, a couple's marriage may be classified as one type at one time and another type at a later time. In addition, at any given time a particular marriage may have traits of more than one of the six marriage types.

The value of such a typology is that it helps couples to recognize the kind of marriage they have. In addition, they become aware of other types of marriages and may see a kind of marriage that they would like to have. They also gain knowledge about the marriages of their parents, siblings, and friends. Most important is the understanding of their current interactions in their own marriage and where they are headed. Such an

awareness can help a couple to determine if they want to continue with the same marital pattern or to change to a different type of marital interaction. Two other marriage typologies, in addition to the one discussed below, were developed by John Cuber and Peggy Harroff (1965) and William Lederer and Don Jackson (1968).

The Traditional Marriage

The most characteristic aspects of a traditional marriage are male dominance and female subordination. The husband's role is clearly superior to the wife's; hence, the husband's power is greater. When decisions are made, he has the last word. Major decisions—such as place of residence, his job, how they budget their money—are usually made unilaterally by him. Minor decisions—food to buy, clothes the children wear—are usually made by her. Conflict tends to be minimal because the husband's role as the final decision maker is accepted by both partners.

Many of the working-class couples studied by Lillian Rubin (1976) exemplified this type of power arrangement regarding decision making. A 36-year-old plumbing foreman from her study responds,

Yeah, I make the major decisions as far as financial things, as far as any important things are concerned, I guess. I don't think she minds, though. She agrees with me that I'm used to making decisions and she's not, and that I know more about making decisions and have more experience in that type of thing. (pp. 107–108)

Another husband responds to the question, "How are decisions made in the family?" with the following:

They're mutual, you know, fifty-fifty. She asks me whether we can buy some furni-

The most salient features of the traditional marriage are male dominance and female subordination.

ture, let's say. If I say okay, she goes out and looks around. When she picks out something she likes, she asks me to go look at it. If I approve of it, she buys it. If not, she looks some more. (p. 111)

The husband plays the good-provider role; he's the breadwinner and the *main* supplier for physical needs. The wife plays primarily an "expressive" role—that of nurturer, child caregiver, and homemaker. She may also work outside of the home to bring in a supplemental income to the family.

The unequal distribution of power and the rigid roles hinder the possibility of reciprocal intimate interaction between the husband and wife. Typically the wife gives emotional support but does not receive it in return. She discloses her most private feelings and listens empathetically to her husband, but he doesn't reciprocate with his own self-disclosure and empathy.

Why isn't there more mutual interaction? First, it is seen as the wife's role to provide emotional support; it's her job and she's believed to be better equipped to handle the "feeling" aspects of the marriage. Second, if the husband were honestly to reveal his deep and private feelings, which may include feelings of weakness, vulnerabilities, and fears, he might jeopardize his superior position in the marriage. This position of authority and power allows the husband to act as the more autonomous and independent partner while the wife has relatively little freedom or independence.

A wife in a traditional marriage responds:

I guess what it boils down to is that the man does the harder physical work, but the woman does the harder emotional work. I mean, he has to get up every morning and go to work; I don't. It's true, I work three days a week; but it's different. The family doesn't depend on my working; it does on his. But when it comes down to the emotional work in the family, that's mine, all mine. In the long run, I guess that's harder because it never ends; the worries are always there—whether it's about the kids, or our families, or how we're getting along, even about money. He makes most of it, but it's never enough. And I have to worry how to pay the bills. (L. Rubin, 1976, p. 106)

A husband expresses his difficulty with emotions:

I'm pretty tight-lipped about most things most of the time, especially personal things. I don't express what I think or feel. She keeps trying to get me to, but, you know, it's hard. Sometimes I'm not even sure what she wants me to be telling her. And when she gets all upset and emotional, I don't know what to say or what to do.

Sometimes she gets to nagging me about what I'm thinking or feeling, and I tell her, "Nothing," and she gets mad. But I swear, it's true; I'm not thinking about anything. . . .

Yakketty-yakkers, that's what girls are. Well, I don't know; guys talk, too. But, you know, there's a difference, isn't there? Guys talk about things and girls talk about feelings. (L. Rubin, 1976, pp. 124–125)

What could partners in a traditional marriage find rewarding? For the husband, control, power, and the emotional support he receives from his wife are the rewards of such an arrangement. He has a wife who submits to his commands and who will stand by him, giving him the emotional nurturance he needs. The wife has someone to depend on for economic support. In addition, she may receive intrinsic rewards from supporting her husband emotionally, serving as his helpmate and ego booster. Women who believe that this is their job, their duty, also feel a sense of internal satisfaction in fulfilling this role faithfully. Both have a sense of security regarding the marriage, as each partner provides a vital complementary role that rewards the other person or the family.

Consider the rewards of the traditional marriage for this husband:

I like being married now. I don't even feel tied down anymore. I'm out all day and, if I want to have a drink with the boys after work, I just call her up and tell her I'll be home later. When I get home, there's a meal—she's a real good cook—and I can just relax and take it easy. The kids— they're the apples of my eyes—they're taken care of; she brings them up right, keeps them clean, teaches them respect. I can't ask for any more. It's a good life. [Thirty-eight-year-old plumber, father of three, married seventeen years] (L. Rubin, 1976, p. 95)

And the rewards for the wife:

He's a steady worker; he doesn't drink; he doesn't hit me. That's a lot more than my mother had, and she didn't sit around complaining and feeling sorry for herself, so I sure haven't got the right. [Thirty-three-year-old housewife, mother of three, married thirteen years] (L. Rubin, 1976, p. 93)

The traditional marriage, however, often provides more rewards for men than women, as suggested by Jessie Bernard (1982) (see Box 7.4).

BOX 7.4

HIS AND HER MARRIAGES

HIS

In every marital union, states Jessie Bernard in *The Future of Marriage* (1982), there are two marriages, his and hers. And despite all the complaints and denigrating remarks men have been lodging against marriage for centuries, his is better than hers.

Research comparing the married man to the never-married man shows that marriage is good for him. If married, he is mentally healthier, has less emotional distress, and is less likely to commit suicide. He is generally happier and less likely to commit a crime and has more earning power than the never-married man.

If the married man loses his wife through divorce or death, he tends to marry again; in fact, his rate of remarriage is higher than for a never-married single man. "Half of all divorced white men who remarry do so within three years after divorce" (Bernard, 1982, p. 18). It appears that the man who has known marriage cannot live without it.

Does marriage really make men happier, healthier, and more successful? Or are they merely "better prospects"—women chose to marry these men because they possessed these positive characteristics in the first place? To minimize this possible selectivity factor, research has been conducted to compare married men to the widowed—both groups of men who once chose marriage or were chosen by someone. Men who are deprived of marriage by the death of their spouses are miserable. "They show more than expected frequencies of psychological distress, and their death rate is high" (Bernard, 1982, p. 19). Five years after bereavement their survival rate is lower than that of married or remarried men, and "Death resulted twice as often among widowed men as among widowed women" (p. 19).

These and other studies comparing married and unmarried men in similar occupations convinced Bernard that "The weight of the evidence explaining differences by marital status seems [to her] to be overwhelmingly on the side of the beneficent effects which marriage has on men rather than on the initial superiority of the married men" (1982, p. 21).

The married man lives longer as well as reporting greater happiness. One study showed that "Almost twice as many married as never-married men reported themselves as very happy, and conversely, more than twice as many never-married as married men reported themselves as not too happy" (Bernard, 1982, p. 21).

HERS

Bernard claims that the wife's marriage is quite different from the husband's and also much worse. The wife is more likely than the husband to report

(Continued)

marital frustration and dissatisfaction, negative feelings, marital problems, that the marriage is unhappy, that she has considered separation or divorce, that she has regretted the marriage, that she has sought marriage counseling.

Bernard cites various studies that compare the married woman's mental health to the married man's. More married women than married men have felt they were about to have a nervous breakdown, have experienced psychological and physical anxiety, reported feelings of inadequacy in their marriages, showed more phobic reactions, depression, and passivity; "and blame themselves for their own lack of general adjustment" (1982, p. 29).

To rule out the notion that these differences are merely gender differences, studies that compare the mental health of single women to married women are also cited. Again the married women show more signs of poor mental health: depression, passivity, phobic symptoms, insomnia, nervousness, nightmares, and headaches. These conditions show up less frequently among unmarried women.

Enormous gender differences do show up when comparing the unmarried men to the unmarried women. These differences, however, are quite the opposite of those found when comparing married men and women. "Now it is the women who show up well and the men poorly" (Bernard, 1982, p. 31). The studies show that compared to single men, single women report greater happiness and show less psychological distress, less depression, and less neurotic and antisocial tendencies. They are also "more educated, have higher average incomes, and are in higher occupations" than single men (p. 34). Thus in terms of the best mental health, single women come first, followed by married men, then single men; married women have the poorest mental health.

Bernard is convinced that traditional marriages literally make women sick. Wives often become more submissive and conservative after marriage. Women who are able to take care of themselves before marriage become helpless after many years of marriage. Wives conform more to their husbands' expectations and make more of the adjustments called for in a marriage than husbands do. "The husband upon marriage maintains his old life routines, with no thought or expectation of changing them to suit his wife's wishes" (1982, p. 40).

It is not marriage per se that makes women unhealthy, but being a housewife does. The status of a housewife is degrading, says Bernard. Her work is not as important as his. Housework provides no room for growth nor for intellectual or social stimulation. The housewife is expected to cater to her husband's needs. It is no wonder, then, that a comparison of housewives to women working outside the home shows working women to be psychologically healthier. "Far fewer than expected of the working women and more than expected of the housewives, for example, had actually had a nervous breakdown" (1982, p. 47).

Seemingly perplexed, Bernard asks, "Why in the face of all the evidence do more married than unmarried women report themselves as happy?" Being married conforms to society's expectations. Therefore, a woman who conforms to these expectations may reason, "Since I am married, I must be happy.'' The wife may also confuse happiness with marital adjustment. She may have resigned herself to her marriage and accepted her lot in life. She may, Bernard thinks, blur the distinction between such acceptance and happiness.

The Extrinsic Marriage

The partners in an extrinsic marriage are primarily focused on things and activities outside the marriage. They look for happiness in the accumulation of material things—nice homes, expensive clothes, and ''toys'' such as boats, sports cars, jacuzzis, and snowmobiles. They may be impulsive spenders, sometimes finding themselves in debt or caught in the credit-card trap. To keep up with their extravagant tastes and life-styles, usually both partners work—some to the point of being committed more to their career than to their spouse.

Besides material things, these couples may be involved in many activities with groups of people. They may socialize extensively, and they seem to need continual reinforcement and approval from others. In some instances there are problems with drug and alcohol use or extramarital sex. These activities are carried out in an attempt to add excitement to their lives and marriages. The rewards that come from being married are primarily externally focused; the partner is someone with whom to party and to purchase material possessions.

Power is usually quite evenly distributed in this type of marriage; neither partner exerts a lot of control over the other. They may function as quite independent individuals. Conflict is limited, since most of the couple's desires are met outside of the marriage, not by or through each other. When conflict does occur, it is likely to be a situation where one partner's planned activity interferes with the other's. Conflict may also arise if only one partner has an extrinsic orientation. Conflict then develops as each spouse pressures the other into living a different life-style.

This type of marriage is not likely to involve much emotional closeness. The couple does not take the time that would be necessary to develop intimacy. They are always ''running,'' always ''on the go.'' Most of their energy and effort is put into material success and having a good time.

Robert Blood and Donald Wolfe (1960) found in their study of marriages that couples who are extremely involved in joint membership in organizations tended to have very little overall quality companionship. The researchers suggest that these over-organized couples escape into the outside world to avoid boredom with each other. Their focus on the external world prevents their having quality time alone with each other. The couple's lack of emotional closeness in the marriage is also reflected in their interactions with their children, if they have any. Being unwilling or unavailable to provide the children with time and emotional support, they give to them in the only way they know how to give, that is, materially.

An extrinsic marriage in certain respects resembles the ''open marriage'' proposed by Nena and George O'Neill in the early 1970s.

Dissatisfied with the traditional type of marriage, these authors proposed a relationship in which the partners allow each other total freedom to pursue outside interests. The rationale was that these outside activities would bring more excitement and happiness into the marriage. Some of the basic components of an open marriage include independence, personal growth, individual freedom, flexible roles, and open companionship (O'Neill and O'Neill, 1972).

The Empty-Shell Marriage

An empty-shell marriage lacks fun and emotional closeness; the partners tend to have few common interests that they share. The marriage could have been initiated for a variety of reasons, but long-term intimacy was not one of them. When marrying, the couple were likely to be young and in a romantic fog; both conditions clouded their perceptions of their mate. The romantic love of courtship may have persisted into the early years of the marriage, but the test of time unquestionably killed it.

The interaction between these partners is very superficial, consisting primarily of small talk and forced conversation. Whatever activities they may share they share out of a sense of duty rather than because they enjoy each other's company. There is little or no sharing of real feelings, such as their hopes and dreams for the future. The couple merely exists together, like roommates or "ships passing in the night." Power and conflict are not issues; the marriage is simply an arrangement of convenience, of accommodation, and of resignation. If they have children, the children may be the only thing they have in common. Any family activities are usually conducted for the children's sake. William Goode (1961) has captured the prisonlike mood of empty-shell marriages: "The atmo-

sphere is without laughter or fun, and a sullen gloom pervades the household. Members do not discuss their problems or experiences with each other, and communication is kept to a minimum" (p. 441).

What possible rewards are forthcoming from such marriages? Mainly practical reasons are given for the continuation of this type of relationship—"We are staying together for the kids," "It's too late to find someone else," "It's a comfortable life-style with no demands," "We're in business together and I don't want to give it up," "My religion is opposed to divorce." So these couples stay together mostly to avoid the costs of leaving. The commitment they have in their marriages is an "institutional" commitment rather than one seeking personal satisfaction. Finally, there is an important reward in experiencing the mere presence of another human being. While these people can live with emotional isolation, they may not be able to live with social isolation.

A 45-year-old wife who has resigned herself to an empty-shell marriage says the following:

"I'm just tolerating the situation at home now. We talk but it's just polite conversation—chit-chat—nothing real meaningful. There's no tension around us—we pretty much go our own way. At least we're not getting in each other's hair. . . . I don't think either one of us wants a divorce. It's too late to start my life over again. Besides I just can't face up to breaking my wedding vows."

Her husband says:

"The excitement and romance has been out of our marriage for a long time. I'm not attracted to her even on a sexual basis. . . . But she and the kids need me. I'm just staying because it's my duty and obligation

but I would rather be somewhere else.'' (authors' counseling files)

The Pseudo-Intimate Marriage

The pseudo-intimate marriage consists of two very insecure and weak partners. Their commitment is so strong that they seem to be merged into one person instead of having their own separate identities. Togetherness, to them, is the name of the game. The couple maintains an image of a "couple front," the belief that a husband and wife should almost always appear together as a couple at social functions, leisure-time activities, and other areas of daily life. To appear without one's partner would not look good to these couples. To observers on the outside, these marriages may look very good, happy, and intimate.

But are these couples really intimate? The idea of the "couple front" is "quite antithetical to genuine intimacy and emotional closeness" (Crosby, 1985). Pseudo-intimate relationships, in reality, are built on some idealized views of a "good" marriage, perhaps an image projected by the media in the 1950s. In this instance the couple confuses closeness with togetherness. Crosby explains,

> Togetherness may be nothing but a cover for lack of closeness. Many couples who enjoy a healthy sense of closeness do not necessarily appear to have a great deal of togetherness. . . . When others achieve authentic closeness there is, by definition, no pseudomutuality and no need to carry out a charade of togetherness à la the couple front. (p. 93)

To achieve what they conceive of as an ideal marriage, these partners try always to be on their best behavior. Thus, any discontent, anger, or negative feelings about the other person or the relationship are sup-pressed. Potential conflict is swept under the rug. "Disagreements and conflict are explained away, downplayed, or denied. In short, there is self-deception on the part of each mate whereby each tries to convince himself or herself that, 'Yes, we are a really compatible couple'" (Crosby, 1985, p. 93). It is a marriage in which honest self-disclosure is lacking, in which the partners are hiding behind masks for fear that if their true selves were revealed, they would be rejected. About the only real feelings that are disclosed relate to their neediness and dependence on each other. This need keeps the couple together as each partner thinks, "This person really needs me."

Power is not a major issue for these couples; neither partner seeks it. Each partner gives in and is accommodating to the other. Decision making is often difficult for them since nobody wants to take control. Each is just trying to do what he or she thinks is best for the other. The primary reward each person receives is the satisfaction of pleasing the other.

Another reason for maintaining a facade of a marriage is for the happiness of the children. Such couples don't want the children to see their parents exchange cross words. The couple is concerned with projecting an idyllic image for the children. It is important to note, however, that the couple's "front" is not just for the sake of others; it is also for the sake of the couple. The "couple front" becomes part of their own self-deception (Crosby, 1985).

Sometimes the individuals in this kind of relationship are intensely involved together in a particular public cause or causes. Or the wife could be involved to a great extent in her husband's career. Or they could be "professional parents," who devote their lives totally to their children. Both the husband and wife are seen as working together and investing a great deal of energy in their common causes. As Lederer and Jackson (1968) point out, however, "Couples who rely on causes for their togetherness have no time for intimate talk or occasional chit-chat," but "in the eyes of their peers, the marriage may appear quite sound" (p. 149).

Thus these marriages are not easily observable, and in addition, they are not commonly seen by marriage counselors. In public, as mentioned, the partners may appear as an intimate couple. It is only by knowing them behind the scenes that one can really determine whether this is an intimate relationship or a couple putting on a facade.

The marriage of the "total woman" proposed by Marabel Morgan (1973) can be described as pseudo intimate, as well as traditional. This marriage is characterized by the wife totally adapting herself to her husband and pleasing him. Genuine feelings on the part of the wife are not encouraged or expressed, just those feelings that are positive toward the husband. No matter what her spouse does or how he behaves, the "total woman" is to accept him. Morgan writes,

> I finally realized that my man's home is his castle, or at least it should be. He should feel free in the privacy of his own castle, free to do what he wants, even if that means draping his clothes on the furniture, drawing pictures on the walls, or eating pizza for forty-seven straight days. (p. 52)

The "total woman" attempts continually to build her husband's ego by showering compliments and admiration, even if she has to be dishonest in doing so. In addition, the woman is closely bound to her husband's identity and career. "Behind every great man is a great woman, loving him and meeting his needs" (p. 66). Thus, the woman achieves her selfhood through his success.

Morgan suggests that by trying to keep the marriage passionate, by pleasing the husband at all costs, and by not airing complaints and disagreements, the marriage will be "intimate." This type of relationship, however, is based on submission, deception, and minimal reciprocity—all barriers to an emotionally close relationship. The "total woman's" goal is to maintain an image of togetherness, unfortunately at the expense of genuine intimacy.

The Negative-Exchange Marriage

As strange as it may sound, some marital couples thrive on almost constant conflict and fighting; they actually find negative exchange rewarding. Such interaction allows individuals to express anger and bitterness that has built up inside them over the years. Continual faultfinding and nitpicking prevail in this kind of marriage. Minor concerns quickly become major ones, and then verbal abuse rages uncontrollably. It may even turn into physical abuse. In their own family backgrounds such individuals may never have known or seen much positive exchange.

When conflicts arise between the partners, each usually takes a noncompromising position. Each defends his or her own point of view; neither one is willing to yield power or control. The same issues may come up over and over again, but the arguments offer few new insights or solutions. The spouses do not know how to stop such confrontations and begin to collaborate on solutions to problems. Each is more concerned about "winning" and "blaming" than in dealing effectively with the issues at hand.

Obviously, intimacy cannot flourish in an atmosphere of negative exchange. Self-disclosure here consists of mainly negative feelings, usually expressed to hurt the partner. Trust, a basic ingredient of intimacy, is typically lacking. Any closeness that may exist occurs during moments of "making up," of-

Some married couples find negative exchange rewarding.

ten through sexual activity. These are short-lived experiences, but perhaps they help to sustain the relationship.

Such a marriage sometimes involves a series of breakups, separations, and reconciliations. Commitment is tenuous since threats to leave the relationship are common. The end result is usually a situation in which ''they can't live with each other, but they can't live without each other.''

The interaction within the negative-exchange marriage is similar to what George Bach and Peter Wyden (1968) referred to as the ''Virginia Woolf'' style. Based on the play and film *Who's Afraid of Virginia Woolf?*, this style of negative interaction primarily involves wild, low-blow fighting with ''chronic-redundant insult exchanges.'' These ''hostility rituals'' are the only ways some couples know to ''express their disappointment, anger, and frustration with their life together, a togetherness they do NOT want to destroy'' (1968, p. 334).

There are rewards for the individuals in this type of marriage. Negative exchange is a way to express frustration, anger, and resentments. Revenge in itself can be a reward. In addition, the negative interaction focuses the blame or responsibility away from oneself and onto the other person. In this way an individual does not take responsibility for his or her own behavior or for problems in the marriage. Lederer and Jackson (1968) describe similar benefits of this type of marriage.

> They [the couple] . . . may recognize that they have a miserable marriage, but usually they are unwilling or unable to do anything about it. Often they need or desire the combat which their marriage provides. Frequently they . . . are angry people who are not prone to introspection or self-accusation. . . . [They] find a degree of comfort in being hostile to each other, for the situation enables each to shift the responsibility for his unhappiness on the other. In fact, it is sometimes for this advantage that people are drawn to each other in the first place. Another major attraction of this mutual hostility is that it prevents personal change by keeping the participant's attention focused away from himself. (pp. 141–142)

Finally, negative exchange may add excitement to a couple's rather boring and dull relationship. Fighting may be the only common interest or activity that they have.

The Intimate Marriage

The intimate marriage is one that consists of mainly those factors—the personal, interpersonal, and situational—that were discussed as part of the model of intimacy development in Chapter 2. This is a marriage in which both partners have a secure sense of themselves—positive self-concepts, confidence, and the ability to trust. They seek their relationship not out of personal weakness, desperation, or inadequacy but out of strength—the ability to love and to be loved by another person.

Both partners put time, energy, and effort into building emotional closeness. They work hard at sensitive self-disclosure, companionship, resolving conflicts, and maintaining a balance of power. They share common interests and values.

In addition, they share similar priorities and don't allow other matters, such as individual work and leisure activities, to interfere with or negate the importance of their marriage. The partners, unlike the pseudo-intimate couple, have a clear, distinct sense of their individual identities—their interests, likes, and dislikes. And they are not afraid to share these with their partner; they are two strong individuals who do not fear vulnerability in a relationship.

Commitment is strong in an intimate marriage. The focus is on security in the relationship (that is, mutual emotional closeness in the marriage) *and* to each individual's personal well-being and happiness. Exclusivity and the expectation of permanence are additional components of this commitment.

Conflict is faced head on. Each partner is willing to communicate his or her real positions. But each also is flexible in compromising with the other or collaborating on a solution. Rigid gender roles are not likely to be adhered to. The marriage is viewed as an equal partnership, with each spouse helping wherever and whenever it is needed.

DUAL-INCOME MARRIAGES

The Interconnection of Marriage and Work

One consequence of industrialization was the separation of work from the home, creating a public sphere of work and a private, domestic sphere. Despite this physical separation of the home from the income-producing workplace, there is still in modern society a close interdependence between work and family. A family's life-style is certainly influenced by the pay, hours, and other demands of work on its members.

The influence, however, is not totally one-way with only the workplace affecting marriage and family behaviors. The family also exerts an influence on the workplace. During the early stages of industrialization the family regulated the labor-force participation of women and children according to economic need and the family's stage in its life cycle (Voydanoff, 1984). Today some corporations are responding to the family in various ways, such as providing child-care services, employing the spouse of an existing worker, developing flextime, and reducing the number of transfers to different cities.

The Protestant work ethic perpetuated in American society encourages individuals to pursue their work as though they have no commitments other than work (Kanter, 1977). This work ethic is especially applicable to what is meant by a career to the middle and upper classes. Many Americans have an all-consuming attitude toward a career. A career often symbolizes "one's major contribution to life" and represents a lifelong focus, incorporating the notions of progress, advancement, and social contribution (Tropman, 1983). A career is often a "single-minded" activity, and those serious about their life's work frequently subordinate the rest of their activities to their work (Holmstrom, 1972). It is common for those who are unwilling or unable to focus on their careers to this extent to experience sanctions against them at the workplace. Expectations are set by corporations, for example, such that the career is often pursued at the expense of family obligations.

The demands of a career and the assumptions of the work ethic give "fathers an *incentive* to stay away from their families" (Pogrebin, 1983, p. 123). A man can always justify his lack of involvement in parenting and familial responsibilities by attributing it to the demands of his job or jobs. For the most part, this attitude has been acceptable for the man but not for the woman. The all-encompassing notion of a career discourages mothers from pursuing careers that would interfere with their family responsibilities. When either spouse has an all-consuming attitude toward a profession, research shows that there tends to be lower marital satisfaction (Bailyn, 1970). Tension in the marital relationship may occur when either partner cannot fulfill family obligations because of being so highly involved in a job. Changes in the workplace, however, could alleviate some of these conflicts between work and family roles (see Box 7.5).

The most significant trend in the world of work that has influenced the family in the past couple of decades has been the rise in the participation of women in the labor force. Two-paycheck couples today outnumber the "traditional" couple of a breadwinner father and a homemaker mother. This trend has brought the number of working wives to two-thirds of all wives in the United States in 1981 (*Ann Arbor News,* 1984). This number increased from 50 percent of all wives in 1970 and 40 percent in 1960. Many working wives are employed only part time, but still about 50 percent have full-time, year-round jobs.

What started out as a movement "to help out" with additional expenses at home—to save for the down payment on a house, to buy clothes for the children, or to meet the rising expenses of college—has turned into a permanent life-style and expectation. Until the 1970s, most working women regarded themselves either as temporary or exceptional. They were always planning to settle

BOX 7.5

TOWARD A BETTER BALANCE OF WORK AND FAMILY ROLES

How can work roles and family roles be more smoothly coordinated? To eliminate tension between these roles there needs to be more flexibility in the workplace. Listed below are several suggestions:

1. Incorporate Flextime at Work.   Flextime allows a worker to start and finish work at his or her own time discretion, provided a fixed number of work hours per week are completed (Sullivan, 1981). It has been highly successful in increasing worker productivity and work satisfaction and in decreasing tardiness. But its benefits for family life are still questionable.

The families most helped by a flextime program are those with the fewest work-family conflicts, namely those without children (Sullivan, 1981). Flextime does not make a measurable difference in job-family stress for employed adults with the most family-related obligations, namely, single mothers and two employed parents. Therefore, it is necessary to look further than flextime for ways to help such families.

2. Develop New Alternatives to the Traditional Career Path.   The traditional career path usually requires earning a college degree and then working through many phases of the organizational structure while under constant and stringent evaluation. Promotion and advancements demand a dedication to the job involving extensive productivity, commitment, time, and energy. Little time for family togetherness—or for the consideration of the development of the other spouse's career—is left as one climbs the ladder to the top.

Alternative models to the traditional career path have been suggested. The apprenticeship model involves "fairly long periods of continued learning and training during the early phase of career development and operates at a slower pace than the traditional career success mode. Commitment to the job and involvement in the corporation increases with time on the job and age of employee" (Sullivan, 1981, p. 317).

3. Establish Permanent Part-Time Employment with Fringe Benefits Similar to Full-Time Employment.   Part-time employment allows spouses to have more time to devote to family responsibilities while still working. This arrangement should not be considered as only the wife's option but also the husband's.

4. Offer the Option of Job Sharing.   Job sharing involves two persons holding one full-time job together and arranging work schedules most suitable to both (Sullivan, 1981). By sharing one position, two workers can increase their flexibility, switching time slots or covering for each other in emergencies with no loss of pay or efficiency. Job sharers tend to be more productive because they are working fewer hours at their top energy level. Such a program, however, costs employers more since they must pay benefits such as unemployment compensation to two persons instead of one. But for employers "During busy periods, the company can ask job sharers to work full time temporarily and save the cost of hiring and training new workers" (English, 1985, p. 76). Job sharing is more of an option for married employees since many single parents cannot exist on partial income and benefits (Pogrebin, 1983).

down to the life of a full-time homemaker (Bird, 1979).

But since the early 1970s, more and more women seem to be pursuing "high-commitment careers." And these women are not taking several years off to stay home and rear their children. One result of the wife's pursuit of a career is more pressure on the husband to take on a more equal role at home. This role includes the need to be more flexible and at times to rearrange his own schedule to fit in with his wife's.

Wives working outside the home is not a new pattern for some groups. For example, it has been traditionally common among black couples for women to work. This is not only true for working-class black families but also among middle-class black families (Willie, 1985).

Consequences of Dual-Income Marriages

CONSEQUENCES FOR WOMEN. Research has substantiated the positive impact of work on women's sense of well-being. For example, Baruch, Barnett, and Rivers (1983) conclude from their research:

In the past, a woman's love life, her age, and whether she was or was not a mother were considered more central to her life

than her work. Our study shows that these aren't very useful in predicting a woman's sense of pride and power—her Mastery, in our terms. But the relationship between paid work and Mastery, particularly among women in high-prestige occupations, shows just how vital a role work plays. (p. 103)

Other studies have revealed similar findings, namely that for many women "merely assuming the role of paid worker contributes to a sense of resourcefulness that compensates for problems experienced on the job" (Veroff, Douvan, and Kulka, 1981).

Working outside of the home does, however, affect a wife's family role. Intrusion of the work role on the family role seems to be greater for women since their family role is still considered by many to be their primary role in life. "It is still true that *a woman's work molds itself to her family while a man's family molds itself to his work*" (Pogrebin, 1983, p. 124). Some of the consequences of a dual-career marriage for women include (1) role overload, (2) role cycling, and (3) internal conflicts.

Role overload. Perhaps the most obvious problem for working wives is the multiple responsibilities of work and family roles. Even though women have expanded their involvement in the work world, dramatic changes by men to include more family re-

One of the most significant social trends in recent years has been the increased participation of women in the workforce.

sponsibilities still remain to be seen. When women go to work, they receive relatively little, if any, extra help from their husbands with household chores. Time budget studies reveal that on the average there is *no* variation in husbands' mean time in household chores, regardless of their wives' employment status (Pleck, 1985). Husbands' family time does increase slightly when their wives are employed and have a child under 2 years old.

How does this compare with the time working wives put into household responsibilities? While the husbands are contributing about 10 hours per week, the wives—who are also holding down full-time jobs outside the home—are clocking about 25 hours per week (Wakin, 1983). Another study found that "even *unemployed husbands* did much less housework than wives who worked 40-hour

weeks'' (emphasis added) (Blumstein and Schwartz, 1983, p. 145). The researchers conclude that the idea of shared responsibility of household chores is largely a myth (Blumstein and Schwartz, 1983). Although some husbands outwardly claim that men *should do* more housework, they inwardly resent doing it and blame women for shirking what is "their responsibility." One husband expresses his feelings in the following way:

To be honest, I find I resent doing housework. That bothers me because I thought I was beyond that kind of hang-up. But I guess the stereotyped ideas about "man's work" and "woman's work" are so ingrained that what we think doesn't always jibe with what we feel. So I hear myself saying, "Damn it, it's my wife's job to get

For Better or For Worse   by Lynn Johnston

dinner ready!'' (Lasswell and Lobsenz, 1983, p. 100)

How do working wives cope with responsibilities of both work and family? One way in which they manage is by doing less housework than nonemployed wives. In addition, they juggle their roles by learning to tolerate more dirt, cutting down on their sleep, eliminating leisure activities, or by hiring outside help.

Role cycling.   One problem of the dual-career couple is that of trying to coordinate their individual career cycles with the cycle of their family. Decisions need to be handled regarding when and where to move for the best career opportunities, whose career should take precedence in a move, and when to have children, if they are desired. To add further to the stress is the inflexibility of the work world, which requires a fixed sequence of climbing the career ladder and discourages time spent away from the profession.

Internal conflicts.   Internal conflicts may also exist, particularly for working women who have a family. These conflicts do not stem solely from the time demands of two different roles but from the contradictory values underlying these demands (Coser and Rokoff, 1974). One contradiction is that the professional woman is supposed to give her job the same priority that a man would, but at the same time she is expected to give priority to her family. A ''cultural mandate'' states that women's priorities belong to the family and that they should expect men to be the providers of economic means and of prestige.

When career and family life are presented as mutually exclusive alternatives for women, then a conflict will ensue when they try to pursue both. ''The American family appears as a 'greedy institution' which demands total allegience of women'' (Coser and Rokoff, 1974, p. 498). It is not so much that women shouldn't work but that they are not expected to be committed to their work. If they were committed the way men are, they would tend to undermine the cultural mandate, causing disruption in the family system. For example, when the children are sick, it is the mother, more often than the father, who stays home from work.

CONSEQUENCES FOR MEN.   Just as work roles influence women's family roles, so do they affect men's roles in marriage and the

The increase in women working outside the home has put more pressure on men to take on an equal role at home.

family. It is socially legitimate for men, however, to place a higher priority on their jobs than it is for women. But what has been the impact on men when more wives work outside the home? The consequences of a dual-career marriage on men can be seen in terms of (1) the husband's self-esteem, (2) less emotional support from the wife, (3) a sharing of the family financial support, and (4) a lack of social supports.

Self-esteem. Can a connection be made between wives' employment and the emotional well-being of husbands? Does a wife's employment have psychologically damaging consequences for a husband, or does it tend to increase his self-esteem? Being married to a woman with a busy schedule, an income

of her own, outside friendships, and commitments to nonfamily members might seem to produce feelings of insecurity in a husband (Moore and Sawhill, 1984). A review and analysis of studies examining these two variables—the wife's work and the husband's well-being—reveal "no evidence to support the hypothesis that husbands whose wives work report more distress than husbands whose wives do not. . . . The simple correlations between wives' employment and husbands' self-reported well-being, personal competence, and health satisfaction were small and nonsignificant" (Fendrich, 1984, pp. 877–878).

Income, however, plays a significant role in the relationship between a wife's employment and a husband's self-esteem. The higher the wife's income, the higher is the husband's self-esteem, up to a point. Husbands report high self-esteem when their wives are bringing in a respectable income. But when the employed wife's income exceeds his income, husbands are more likely to feel psychological distress; the husband perceives his own role as family breadwinner to be of lesser importance (Fendrich, 1984). So a husband may feel better about his wife working if she brings in a respectable income, but he becomes somewhat threatened if she actually earns more than he does (Z. Rubin, 1984).

The type of job a wife holds may also impinge upon her husband's well-being and how he views her income. Apparently it is more threatening to his self-esteem when both he and his wife have typical male occupations than when the wife holds a typical female job. "Job-segregation is an 'ego protector for men.' It's okay . . . for your wife to have a . . . higher-status job, as long as she's a nurse or a teacher—because that's what women are *supposed* to be" (Dana Hiller, quoted in Rubenstein, 1982, p. 38). Among working-class couples, where men in particular value their breadwinner role, husbands are likely to feel more threatened and inadequate when their wives begin to make meaningful incomes. The husband may then interpret the wife's employment as a sign of his own failure as a provider and ultimately as a man (Z. Rubin, 1984). "Many men and women still feel keenly that it's his job to support the family, hers to stay home and care for it. For her to take a job outside the house would be, for such a family, tantamount to a public acknowledgement of his failure" (L. Rubin, cited in Z. Rubin, 1984, p. 204).

A wife's employment may also challenge the working-class husband's authority as the head of the household. The loss of complete economic control may be especially devastating to those husbands who have little authority in their lives except for their homes. Daniel Yankelovich (cited in Pleck, 1977) suggests that those men whose jobs are not inherently satisfying find pride in their hard work and in the sacrifices they make in providing for their families' needs. In such a situation a working wife becomes threatening and she can diminish a major source of the husband's identity (Pleck, 1977).

Less emotional support from wife. When a wife holds outside employment, the husband may experience at least some loss of her emotional support. This is suggested by a study that found that husbands whose wives were employed were less satisfied with their wives as confidantes than those whose wives were full-time housewives (Greenglass, 1982). Their own work loads and pressures may prevent employed wives from providing the same level of emotional support to their husbands that full-time housewives do. "Not only is the employed wife less likely to cater to her husband's needs in this respect, but she may even turn to her husband for support and encouragement in *her* employment role" (Greenglass, 1982, p. 157). Some husbands, particularly those holding to traditional gender roles, may resent this switch in roles; they may feel that it's not their role to be the "emotional supporter." In addition, many men may not know how to give the emotional support the working wife needs.

Sharing the financial support. A working wife shares the breadwinning role, and the family benefits from a second income. The husband may find relief in not having to carry the total financial burden himself. He may discover that his wife's income gives him the security to refuse overtime or other demands from an employer that intrude on his family life (Moore and Sawhill, 1984). Additional income in itself, however, is not the key to good financial planning (see Appendix D).

Many men may welcome both the opportunity to share the burden of family support with their wives and the chance to spend more time with their families. It appears, however, as though men are not taking advantage of the opportunities to carry out more activities with their families. They are not increasingly turning down overtime, refusing travel, or rejecting transfers because of the work commitments of their wives.

A recent study found that more wives wanted to work than husbands wanted to let them. "Husbands were more likely to believe it was unnecessary, because they felt it was the man's duty to provide for the household" (Blumstein and Schwartz, 1983, p. 4). Although changes have been made, wives' employment, particularly in high-commitment careers, is still not totally accepted by many husbands.

Lack of social supports.   There is a lack of general societal support for those husbands who *do* want to take on more family responsibilities as their wives take on work roles. These men may be reluctant to carry out what others see as "feminine," or unacceptable, roles.

A man who engages in behavior deviant from traditional expectations can expect comment—not only from family, friends, and acquaintances—but from anyone observing it. One father, for example, reported on the response of neighborhood women to his frequent presence on the community playground as the afternoon caretaker for his son: "I heard one woman whisper to another, 'That poor little boy, his mother must be dead—it's always his father who brings him here'." (Lein, 1979, p. 491)

Such comments discourage men from publicly taking on the traditional feminine role of caring for and nurturing young children. In addition, men's peer groups sometimes explicitly ridicule or ostracize their members for involvement in "women's responsibilities." "Men may downgrade the efforts of other men to contribute to homemaking and pressure them to spend more time and effort on the job or in the peer group" (Lein, 1979, p. 492). Men need support and encouragement from their friends, relatives, and the workplace if they are to initiate and maintain a family orientation. The importance of this orientation was revealed in one study in which marital satisfaction was high in dual-earner marriages if the husband was "family-oriented" but markedly low if the husband was "work-oriented" (Voydanoff, 1984).

CONSEQUENCES FOR THE MARRIAGE.   The dual-income couple presents new challenges but also new opportunities for intimacy as well. To facilitate emotional closeness each partner needs to be quite sensitive and responsive to the work-related stresses felt by the other. In a study of dual-income couples, in 75 percent of those marriages described as "low quality," husbands consistently underestimated their wives' stress levels. In contrast, "high-quality" couples had similar perceptions of the importance of careers and of the wife's stress level. Almost every husband in a high-quality marriage appeared particularly sensitive to the wife's experiences of stress, either estimating the amount accurately or overestimating it.

Communication between dual-income partners may at times be strained. After communicating all day at work, they may arrive home suffering from "interpersonal overload." In addition, they may be highly verbal but discuss issues more on a cognitive, analytical level, giving less attention to feelings. This type of communicating may be functional in the work setting but inhibiting in a close relationship. A major difference between those dual-income couples with a high-quality marriage and those with a low-quality marriage is the extent to which husbands *listen* and are *sensitive* to their wives' work-related problems, activities, and achievements (Thomas, Abbrecht, and White, 1984). The researchers conclude that the most critical issue for working couples may be their ability to communicate intimately, as opposed to concern over the division of household chores, which often receives much wider popular attention.

Several studies report few outside social relationships among dual-income couples. Two-career marriages are more likely to have a narrow circle of friends, loose kinship ties, and a lack of social activities. This is especially characteristic of dual-career couples in a low-quality marriage. Those in a high-quality marriage were "able to maintain an adequately satisfying social life despite the time constraints of their busy lifestyles" (Thomas, Abbrecht, and White, 1984, p. 518).

Finally, the dual-career couple needs to cope with time pressures. "A serious career requires an expenditure of a great deal of time" (Holmstrom, 1972, p. 87). When both partners undertake professions, time for the relationship becomes a scarce resource. Besides the absolute amount of time available, the scheduling of time may also be a challenge. Work schedules may conflict with family responsibilities. In some professions, one has a great deal of control over his or her work schedule and thus great flexibility. In other occupations there is no control and one must succumb to the dictates of the job. Some partners who are highly committed to their careers may resort to a commuter marriage in order to maximize their career satisfactions (see Box 7.6).

Holmstrom (1972) found in her study of two-career families that women, in particular, carefully organize their use of time. "They budgeted time almost like one might budget money and were very conscious of how they allocated time and effort" (p. 89). There was a general tendency for the professional woman to follow a routine. Likewise, most of the men in these marriages followed a routine too. The men, however, seldom reported that they consciously thought of certain hours as reserved for their families.

The husband's acceptance and approval of his wife's employment influence marital quality. The more husbands approved of their wives' employment, the higher the marital quality (Thomas, Abbrecht, and White, 1984). The majority of husbands in dual-career marriages are initially very supportive of their wives' career goals. In many instances, however, this level of support diminishes over the years. Researchers found that for wives in happy marriages the support had often increased, while in unhappy marriages it decreased or was a mixture of support and sabotage (Thomas, Abbrecht, and White, 1984). Intimacy is most likely to be enhanced when the dual-career partners perceive themselves as having equal support for each other's work.

CHAPTER REVIEW

1. Despite high divorce rates and more pessimistic attitudes surrounding its durability, marriage continues to remain a very popular institution in the United States. But people today seem more realistic about both the restrictions and opportunities that marriage can provide than individuals of a generation ago.

BOX 7.6

COMMUTER MARRIAGES: A VIABLE ALTERNATIVE?

Married partners who live apart are not a totally new phenomenon. Merchant marines, construction workers, politicians, members of the military, professional athletes, and entertainers, for example, all require regular periods of separation. Traveling salesmen and many business executives regularly leave their families for their work. And it's not unusual in many societies to find men migrating to work in a distant country with the hope of eventually bringing their families to join them.

Naomi Gerstel and Harriet Gross (1984) have conducted some in-depth studies of commuter marriages. They found that these partners prefer to live in the same city, but due to the lack of jobs for both partners, they resort to working in different geographic locations and spending a majority of their time in separate residences. These partners are quite dedicated to their individual careers. The arrangement does not greatly increase their incomes, since the commuting costs—transportation, long-distance telephone calls, and housing costs—are so high. In fact, the commuting may actually result in a net financial loss. So the reward is primarily the personal satisfaction provided by increasing career involvement. Work is important to *both* spouses, and they are willing to live in separate residences to maximize their career satisfactions (Gerstel and Gross, 1984).

The commuter marriage produces both losses and gains for an intimate relationship. First, some of the losses. Commuter couples complain that there is less opportunity "to engage in informal conversations and to share daily experiences regularly" (Gerstel and Gross, 1984, p. 54). Although this daily talk may not be the most intense and personal communication, they do experience daily conversation as a serious loss. One commuter wife describes this type of daily communication:

> The relaxed conversation while you're cooking dinner. Or the reading something to him I come across in the newspaper while we're both sitting in the living room. That's gone and I find I really miss it. (Gerstel and Gross, 1984, p. 54)

Many commuter couples complain that telephone conversations do not totally compensate for the lack of daily face-to-face interactions. Telephone calls are often described as awkward—consisting of summaries of the day, no long silences, and constant talking. The relaxation of casual conversations in the shared home is lost.

The sharing of leisure time together is another loss for commuter couples. Since they have such limited time together, they have to plan in advance how to spend it. Impulsive, unplanned recreation is not feasible. The intimacy between a couple suffers from this decreased companionship.

Besides reduced companionship with each other, commuter couples also experience the loss of outside friendships. Since they are apart so much of the time, they choose to spend time with each other as much, and as intensely, as possible. No longer is there a lot of time to socialize with others when they're together, and it's difficult to make new friends that are couples and maintain them when apart—it's as though they are temporarily single. Thus, it can be concluded that the physical separation of the spouses limits their personal relationships with others (Gerstel and Gross, 1984).

Commuter couples talk about a type of "stranger effect" in their relationship. Partners often feel a sense of emotional distance and awkwardness when they reunite. They talk of feeling "weird" and "strange" yet wanting to be close when they initially meet again.

> "I've noticed with my husband now, there's a period of strangeness. It takes several days for that to break down and for us to begin chattering in detail—to really feel comfortable."
>
> "It's usually sort of strange. There's a 'What do we talk about first'—a distance. It's weird." (Respondents in Gerstel and Gross, 1984, p. 67)

Despite the disadvantages of a commuter marriage, there are several aspects of this arrangement that might actually promote intimacy. First, "some commuters speak of greater 'appreciation,' 'rediscovery,' or 'less boredom' in their marital relationship" when they're together (Gerstel and Gross, 1984, p. 74). They talk of not taking each other for granted. Also, there is an excitement around the anticipation of being together again. A woman states:

> "It's really kind of exciting to be separated from him, because when we do have contact, it's just the biggest thrill in the world. And we don't get bored. We really appreciate each other more. I think we've always had a good relationship, but, like the saying goes, we did kind of take each other for granted."

A husband remarks:

> "I think our marriage has, in some ways, been strengthened by the outside new experiences we can bring back to each other. I bring home interesting things and she has a lot to tell me about what happens during her week." (Gerstel and Gross, 1984, pp. 74–75)

Second, these couples report fewer trivial conflicts with the commuter arrangement. Petty and minor things that bothered them before "fall by the wayside." Thus the couples are less disturbed by minor infractions and they argue less often. Anger seems not to build up, and they are able to focus on the more pleasant aspects of their marriages.

Third, living apart provides commuter husbands and wives with new

(Continued)

and positive feelings about themselves. Most expressed a fear, before commuting, of being alone. However, after commuting for a while, they discovered they can be "alone but not lonely." They found a "desire for private space." For women commuters, in particular, they found a renewed sense of self-hood—partly because for women, "Commuting allows full participation in the professional world" (Gerstel and Gross, 1984, p. 121).

Husbands tended to evaluate commuting differently from their wives; husbands were typically more negative. This difference holds up no matter what the specific conditions of commuting—whether the wife is traveling or the husband. Overall, the arrangement seems to be a boost to the wives' sense of self-esteem and autonomy, while the husbands found themselves quite lonely. It appears that men benefit more from the traditional marriage arrangement. When apart, the domestic tasks tend to be redistributed and more equalized. "Consequently, a woman's professional work output increases when she is living in a separate home, while her husband's is less likely to do so" (Gerstel and Gross, 1984, p. 132). Strain seems to be less on those couples who had been married for a long time and those who had frequent visits. It was more difficult for couples recently married to maintain this type of arrangement.

Gerstel and Gross (1984) concluded from their studies that there is a certain paradox within commuter marriages.

> On the one hand, daily companionship, security, and comfort are desired and, in their absence, missed. On the other hand, the daily presence of the partner contributes to less enthusiasm, less appreciation, and, possibly, boredom between spouses. By living apart, couples rediscover each other at the cost of daily intimacies. (p. 78)

2. Perhaps the most distinguishing feature of marriage, in contrast to most other close relationships, is the commitment involved. Commitment develops over time; it's a series of events that makes clear each person's intention to continue the relationship. Furthermore, there are different types of commitments, for example, institutional and voluntary. Factors that keep people in the marriage commitment include irretrievable investments and the lack of available alternative relationships.

3. It is possible to distinguish different types of marriages based on such factors as power, conflict resolution, intimacy, rewards, and commitment. The marriages outlined in this chapter include the traditional, extrinsic, empty-shell, pseudo-intimate, negative-exchange, and intimate marriages.

4. As women increase their participation in the work force, spouses are facing more challenges in terms of juggling work and family roles. Some of the particular challenges for women include dealing with role overload, role cycling, and internal conflicts. The employment of the wife seems to affect a hus-

band's self-esteem, to reduce the amount of emotional support to the husband, and to assist the husband in the financial support of the family. There is a lack of societal support for husbands to increase their family respon- sibilities. For a high-quality and intimate marriage, both spouses need to be sensitive and responsive to each other's work-related stresses.

8

Intimate
Communication

In a survey of more than 500 family therapists, ''communicating'' was chosen as the most important trait of a healthy family (Curran, 1983). Other scientific studies indicate a positive relationship between marital adjustment and a couple's capacity to communicate (Feldman, 1961; Locke, 1951). Likewise, distressed marriages have generally been found to be deficient in good communication skills (Gottman et al., 1976).

Contrary to common belief, it is *not the lack of communication per se* that is really the problem in troubled marriages but *what* is said and *how* it is said. There could be an extensive amount of actual communication between partners, but it may be primarily negative and destructive. Thus while couples could be presenting ''honest'' self-disclosures and ''open'' communication supposedly to resolve conflict and build closeness, in fact they could be affronting their partners with insults, chronic nagging, and put-downs.

One study of married couples revealed that the most important item distinguishing good and poor communication between partners was the question: Does your spouse have a tendency to say things which would be better left unsaid? (Bienvenu, 1970). Although the amount of communication is important, being selective in what is said appears to be more important. That is, some feelings and attitudes are, apparently, destructive when communicated and are better left unsaid. In other words, quality communication is much more important than sheer quantity; the content is more important than the amount (Barnes, 1985).

Communication is intrinsically tied to the ability to resolve conflicts and to make decisions. Indeed, it is during times of conflict and disagreement that partners need to communicate their needs clearly and to listen closely to the other person. Failure to communicate effectively during these times re-

sults in further misunderstandings, which only intensify the conflict.

The close involvement of two people will inevitably give rise to some conflict. In fact, it is usually in family relationships—where contact is frequent and continual—that more occasions exist for conflict to occur. Goals, expectations, or needs are not always going to be compatible, or the same, for two people.

Although conflict is thus inherent in intimate relationships, in no way does it need to be a destructive force. ''Healthy'' families have the ability to resolve conflicts that arise. One writer asks and answers a basic question: ''Why have we neglected to teach families the important art of reconciling? . . . Because we have pretended that good families don't fight'' (Curran, 1983, p. 53). Facing conflict head on and resolving it promote harmony and closeness in the family. A process of conflict resolution that emphasizes the understanding and respect of each person's needs can actually bring the people closer together.

PRINCIPLES OF COMMUNICATION

Content and Relationship Communications

There are two aspects to communication—*content* and *relationship* (Watzlawick, Beavin, and Jackson, 1967). Content is ''what-is-communicated''; it involves the information itself. Relationship communication tells us how the communicating persons are related—for example, as parent to child, teacher to students, employer to employee (Stewart, 1973). Consider the following examples:

> ''Please stand up,'' ''All rise,'' and ''Git up, dammit!'' have almost identical content, but their relationship aspects are significantly different. . . . So far as the re-

SALLY FORTH   by Greg Howard

> **Hilary:** HOW COME YOU AND DAD NEVER FIGHT?
>
> **Mom:** WE DO NOW AND THEN, HILARY, BUT WE MAKE AN EFFORT NOT TO FIGHT IN FRONT OF YOU
>
> **Hilary:** WHAT ARE YOU TRYING TO DO, GIVE ME A DISTORTED VIEW OF MARRIAGE?

SALLY FORTH by Greg Howard. © 1983 by Field Enterprises, Inc., by permission of North America Syndicate, Inc.

lationship aspect is concerned, ''Please stand up'' suggests that the relationship between speaker and listener(s) is characterized by equality and mutual respect. ''All rise'' sounds like it belongs in a courtroom where the bailiff is pretty clearly saying, ''You are inferior to the judge; show your respect by standing.'' And you wouldn't seriously say, ''Git up, dammit!'' to someone unless you considered yourself pretty superior to him, or at least wanted to define yourself that way. (Stewart, 1973, pp. 20–21)

So communication involves more than just communicating words; it can define the nature of the relationship itself. At times each person's notions regarding the nature of the relationship may differ. For example, if a husband views the marital relationship as one in which he is superior to his wife, his demands will be resented by a wife who views marriage as a relationship between two equals.

Communication in an Intimate Relationship

How does communication in an intimate relationship differ from communication in more impersonal relationships? What is it about an emotionally close relationship that makes the communication different from that in other types of relationships? In several ways, communication within an affectionate relationship will be unique. The following interactive and situational factors of intimacy will influence the type of communication: (1) the depth of self-disclosures, (2) the balance of power, (3) the degree of exclusivity, (4) the length of the relationship, and (5) the degree of value consensus.

In an intimate relationship the partners expect to communicate to each other their most personal feelings. Great importance is attached to understanding each person's needs. It is often in-depth self-disclosure that greatly enables an emotionally close relationship to develop in the first place. Nonintimate relationships, in contrast, do not typically have as a goal very personal knowledge or the understanding of a person's feelings. Communications between a sales clerk and a customer, an employee and an employer, a teacher and a student do not require an intimate sharing and understanding of feelings.

Intimacy is most likely to occur between two people who hold roughly the same amount of power. A balance of power between two close partners infers that the communication probably will be truly reciprocal. That is, communication is mutual; if one wants to express some complaints, the other has the right to express some also. In a work relationship, however, when the boss complains about something one has done or not done, one is not likely to reciprocate with a complaint about the boss. Thus an unequal balance of power makes reciprocal disclosures less appropriate.

The exclusivity of the intimate dyad means that much of the communication will often be shared only between the partners. In other words, what they share will not be common knowledge. This makes the communication private and more special to each partner. Nicknames, private jokes, and a personal language are examples of communication between intimate partners that may exclude others.

The expectation that the relationship is going to continue for an indefinite period of time also affects what is communicated. If we experience aggravations with acquaintances, we may ignore or tolerate them because our contact with these people is quite limited and of short duration. However, if pet peeves in a marriage, a relationship of expected long duration, are not communicated, they may build up and affect the couple's future interaction.

Similar world views, beliefs, values, and priorities held by intimate partners enhance the development of good communication. An empathy and understanding of what one is communicating is aided by the fact that each person sees the world, and people in the world, from similar points of view. When world views differ widely, human understanding will be difficult to achieve. An eternal optimist and a pessimistic partner will likely have more difficulty understanding and communicating with each other than if they were two optimists or two pessimists. Finally,

an individual may be apprehensive about sharing personal views that he or she knows differ sharply from those held by a listener.

A Model of Communication

Exactly what do we mean by communication? Communication is an exchange of information. Whether it be verbal or nonverbal, it's still communication so long as it carries a message. The message may be intended or unintended, distorted or clear, but as soon as a message gets through on any level, it is communication. Ironically, one can communicate with another person without knowing that one has communicated anything. For example, if you are whistling a light and merry tune while cooking dinner, you may be communicating to your spouse that you are happy.

Since our actions and behaviors are continually conveying messages to those around us, it is impossible *not* to communicate. Even silence is a message. Nonresponse is a response, meaning any one of a number of things—the person is bored, disagrees with what was said, is worried about something, or is angry at the partner (Strong, 1983). Silence is open to numerous interpretations, and none of them may correspond with what the silent person is actually feeling or thinking.

Why does communication break down? Why is it that communication that is intended to be positive is sometimes interpreted as negative? Why are the things that we say sometimes misunderstood? The process of communication involves several steps, and at any one of these steps a problem can occur. One way of viewing the process of communication is with the following model:[*]

* This model is adapted from Adler and Towne (1984).

Communication begins with a particular idea we would like to share with another person. The idea may not already be in words in the initial stage. It may rather be more like a mental image, consisting of unverbalized feelings (anger, excitement, sadness); intentions (wants, needs, and desires); or even mental pictures (such as how you want a job to look when it is finished). So the first thing to do is to put those images into words that others can understand. This is the process of *encoding*. To begin communicating with

someone else, "We need to organize our thoughts, feelings, and personal meaning about our world in a way that makes sense in our listener's world" (Strong, 1983, p. 18).

Once an idea has been encoded, the next step is to send it. This is the *message* phase of the communication model. The message can be sent through a number of different *channels*, such as writing, speaking, touching, or gesturing.

When one's message reaches another person, much of the same process described

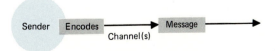

earlier occurs in reverse. The receiver must make some sense out of what has been sent

by *decoding* the message back into feelings, intentions, or thoughts that mean something to him or her.

While some types of communication—newspaper, radio, or television, for example—flow in a one-way manner, that is not an accurate representation of interpersonal communication. It ignores the fact that receivers *react* to messages. Receivers are continually giving some response to the sender's message. This *feedback* can again be verbal or nonverbal. A yawn from a friend as we give a blow-by-blow description of our weekend is feedback. Likewise a laugh as we tell a joke and a question meant to clarify our remarks are forms of feedback.

Feedback serves several purposes. It can help the listener receive a more updated and accurate image about what the speaker is saying (Strong, 1983). It also helps the original speaker to know if the listener understands what he or she is saying. Third, it helps the original speaker identify and understand his or her own feelings. Thus, feedback leads to greater clarity in communication. It allows us to pinpoint areas of disagreement and to understand better our ideas and reasoning that lead us to different conclusions.

By adding the element of feedback to the model, communication becomes a symbolic interactive process. A sender formulates and

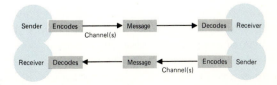

transmits a message to a receiver, who, in turn, formulates and sends a response.

The end product of this process of communication, one hopes, is shared meanings; that is, the messages sent are the same as the messages received. From experience all of us know that this is not always true; a suggestion we make may be taken as criticism, a question may be misunderstood, a friendly joke is taken as an insult.

A number of factors can cause misunderstandings. Each person is bringing to the situation at least somewhat differing life orientations. Understanding is hindered when backgrounds consist of cultural differences, different languages, different experiences. These differences cause us to see situations in a unique way. A hug and a kiss between two men in one country may communicate a friendly greeting, while in another country they may be met with disgust and inferences of homosexuality.

It is through shared symbols, knowledge, and experiences that we are more effectively able to communicate. Because of the greater common interests, goals, and values of intimates, one would expect that misunderstandings during the process of communication would occur less frequently.

If the message sent by one person matches the message received by the other, can we always call the communication good or constructive? To be sure, effective communication is not always synonymous with constructive communication. If a husband stomps off to the bedroom, slams the door, and then puts his fist through a wall, he is communicating his anger very effectively to his wife. But such messages are usually not constructive or helpful in dealing with conflict. So a person may indeed be able to put his or her message across, but the result may be negative and potentially harmful to the relationship. The goal is communication that is *effective* but also *constructive* in resolving

conflict and in developing emotional closeness between partners.

DESTRUCTIVE COMMUNICATION: BARRIERS TO INTIMACY

Double Messages

It has been noted that there are different channels through which a person can communicate. Double messages occur when two different modes of communicating are sending different messages at the same time. For example, a feeling can be communicated in a nonverbal manner that contradicts a spoken message. The speaker's tone of voice, body language, gestures, facial expressions, or posture might be saying the opposite of the spoken word. Verbally a wife may tell her husband, "It's OK with me if you go out with the boys tonight." But her nonverbal behavior (long face, pouting, sighing with her eyes rolling upward) is saying, "I'm displeased with you spending another night with the boys." The husband receiving the incongruent messages may be eager to respond to the verbal message but would do better to respond to the nonverbal message by asking his wife if she is displeased.

Many communication theorists contend that nonverbal communication is more powerful than verbal communication. Studies have shown that when a listener perceives an inconsistency between verbal and nonverbal messages, the unspoken one carries more weight (Adler and Towne, 1984). Albert Mehrabian, a renowned researcher of nonverbal communication, asserts, "touching, positions (distance, forward leans, or eye contact), postures, gestures, as well as facial and vocal expressions, can all outweigh words and determine the feelings conveyed by a message" (1971, p. 45).

Contradictions between behavior and

Nonverbal gestures can convey feelings as much as words.

words can cause considerable interpersonal strife, irritation, and confusion. If the words of a spouse say, "I love you," and then there are actions that say, "I don't care about your feelings and wishes," this contradiction will indeed be puzzling to the other spouse. An individual receiving a double message does not know which aspect of the communication the other person really means or which message to respond to. Communication needs to be clear, concise, and unambiguous.

Putting the Other on the Defensive

Certain communications tend to elicit defensiveness from the listener. This can occur when the speaker assumes a superior attitude or is taking the position of "prosecutor, judge, and jury." The speaker may regard himself or herself as more intelligent and more knowledgeable about a topic or life in general. Or perhaps he or she is trying to hide feelings of inadequacy or insecurity. In any event, such people rarely consider themselves to be "wrong."

When a person is put on the defensive, he or she becomes so focused on the message about his or her supposed inferiority that it's highly unlikely that any other messages will get through (Strong, 1983). That person will also more likely resist what the speaker wants him or her to do. The primary concern of the receiver will be to defend his or her position. A superior, know-it-all attitude will only serve to diminish further self-disclosure on the part of the other person. It is difficult to open up to, or be receptive to, a person who does not give one equal respect. Some communications that evoke defensive behavior include evaluation, deception, a superior attitude, and dogmatism (Gibb, 1973).

"Why" questions, in particular, put people on the defensive. Although we have reasons for behaving the way we do, we are not always aware of them. So when people continually ask us "Why?" we feel pressure to search for a reason in order to defend our actions. Sometimes "why" comes across in an accusatory tone—"Why did you ignore me at the party?" Immediately the person is on the defensive, and while he or she is trying to come up with reasons or excuses for the behavior, he or she largely ignores the feelings of anger the person is really trying to express. Thus, arousing defensiveness interferes with communication, making it difficult—and sometimes impossible—for people to convey ideas clearly and to move effectively toward the solution of a problem (Gibb, 1973).

Overgeneralizations and Absolute Statements

To stress one's feelings or to put a point across, people will often exaggerate by using "strong," colorful words. The goal is not to give an accurate or an objective account but to make a point, to make a certain impact on the listener. There's a time and place for this type of exaggeration—in literature or humor, for example. But in interpersonal communication overgeneralizations can be destructive.

Overgeneralizations occur when people make statements that are too broad and inclusive. For example, "You just can't think straight. You're too emotional. That's just the way all women are," or "I can't think of one good thing to say about our marriage."

The use of the words *always, never,* or *all*

the time is a specific way of making absolute statements: "You *always* leave your clothes lying on the floor" or "You *never* take me to the movies." Absolute comments can be especially destructive when accusations are being made (Wahlroos, 1983). Seldom is anything 100 percent in terms of human behavior. While criticisms can be potentially valuable to intimate partners, they must reflect an accurate picture of the partner and must be sincere and respectful. If the criticism is exaggerated and distorted, however, the listener will more likely be resentful and angry and less likely to work on improving the relationship. Also, a person who frequently exaggerates will not be trusted and believed. He or she may not be taken seriously by others. (See Table 8.1.)

Mind Reading

A large percentage of the misunderstandings in communication result when marriage partners "read each other's minds." When partners are mind reading, they are making assumptions about what the other person is thinking or feeling and then responding only to these assumptions. The problem is that very often these assumptions are wrong, and they do not even resemble what the other person really is thinking or feeling.

In an intimate relationship, partners tend to be aware of the preferences and dislikes of each other. But no matter how well one knows one's partner and how close one is to the other, one cannot be sure of everything. Feelings and thoughts change—people are not static.

For real intimates, the process of eliciting information about a partner's feelings never ends because their relationship is forever evolving. One spouse or both may read

TABLE 8.1

DESTRUCTIVE AND CONSTRUCTIVE COMMUNICATION GUIDELINES

Destructive	Constructive
Double messages	Positive communication
Putting the other on the defensive	Turning the other cheek
Overgeneralizations and absolute statements	Leveling
Mind reading	Tactfulness
Put-downs	Verification feedback
Lecturing	Touching
Sarcasm	
Gunnysacking	
Annoying modes of delivery	
Faultfinding	

a stimulating new book; or make new friends; or take an eye-opening adult education course. . . . All such events can set off changes in a partner's feelings, and the wise spouse will try to keep up to date on developments. (Bach and Wyden, 1968, p. 86)

Perhaps it is because we think we know our partners so well that we don't have to check everything out with them. Or perhaps we want to have our own way so badly that we just assume it's OK with the other person. In either situation, the failure to test assumptions can result in misunderstandings and conflicts. Comments such as, "Well, I didn't think you would mind" or "How was I to know that you would object?" are made after assumptions have been made.

In some instances it appears that individuals *expect* their partners to have an ability to read their minds. In counseling situations when individuals are asked to state what they would like their partner to do for them, they sometimes resist. "He should know what I want. I shouldn't have to tell him." But even

in intimate relationships partners must indicate their needs and *share* the responsibility for making these wishes and preferences clearly known (Wahlroos, 1983).

An extreme form of mind reading occurs when a person thinks that he or she knows more about the thoughts and feelings of other people than these people know about themselves. So confident are these individuals of their ability to know the other person's thoughts, feelings, and intentions that it is not unusual for them to correct the other's statements about their own convictions. Sometimes mind readers go to the extent of simply denying another person's stated feelings. Mind reading to this degree inhibits constructive communication or any effective conflict resolution (Saxton, 1986).

Any time a person assumes that his or her perception of an ambiguous or nonverbal message is correct without checking it out verbally, he or she is also mind reading. "I know you were thinking about your old boyfriend and comparing me to him. It makes me angry and I don't want to talk about it!" Such mind reading thus allows misunderstandings to persist without being cleared up. Consider the following scenario:

> A husband comes home from work, briefly greets his wife, and lies down on the couch. As the wife prepares dinner she is wondering what is wrong. She starts imagining that he is angry at her for something, perhaps a discussion they had the night before. Or perhaps it is the spaghetti she is fixing for dinner. Her anger builds as she thinks about what a picky eater he is and if he made more money, they could afford better meals, etc. During dinner she gives him the ''cold shoulder,'' which causes him to keep his distance. Finally, she asks him what he was mad about when he came home. He explains he was tired and wanted to catch some sleep before dinner and wasn't angry about anything. All her worry and anger were based on false assumptions!

Put-Downs

Put-downs are part and parcel of "dirty fighting." They include blaming, attacking, and criticizing with the intent to hurt, to punish, or to seek revenge. This kind of communication encourages negative exchange—the continual giving and receiving of attacks and hurts. For example, a husband calls his wife a terrible cook, and she returns the insult by telling him that he is a lousy lover. Regular occurrences of negative exchange raise the level of anger, annihilate intimacy, and can cause the partners to avoid each other. They also prevent the movement toward the resolution of any conflicts, since both partners will resist listening to the other person's viewpoints at this stage.

Anger is a normal and healthy emotion, which should be expressed. But it can be verbalized without the use of unfair put-downs, attacks, and blaming. It is possible "to stay reasonable when you are angry" (Wahlroos, 1983, p. 96). Much of the work

in marital and relationship counseling involves helping people face up to their anger and learn to handle it as sensibly and appropriately as possible, without letting it get out of hand in terms of behavior so as to be destructive to the relationship. (See Box 8.1.)

Put-downs often begin with the word *you*. "You" statements usually provoke a hostile or defensive response from the other person. For example, *''You are never on time''* or *''You are always telling me what to do''* are typical "you" statements that can bring about protective and angry responses.

In addition, put-downs often involve labeling a person in a negative way as a totality. Instead of focusing on the particular behaviors of a person, the individual is placed into a category. For example, a spouse exclaims, "You're such a bore!" as opposed to saying "I wish you wouldn't talk so much about yourself but let others into the conversation." Labeling dehumanizes another person because he or she is not being viewed as a unique individual but only as part of a particular stereotype or category—in the above instance, as a "bore." Needless to say, when such labels are verbalized, the other person is often put in a defensive mood. Negative exchange can erupt as the individual defends himself or herself by trying to disprove the label. But unfortunately, the original issue or concern that started the whole interaction is lost sight of.

A continuous exchange of put-downs can lead to hitting below the belt. George Bach and Peter Wyden (1968) contend that everyone has a "belt line," a point above which blows can be absorbed and are tolerated or considered fair. Blows below this line are intolerable and unfair. Belt lines will vary according to individuals. Some wear them up around their ears and cry "foul" at every attempted blow, while others can tolerate

(Text continued on page 266.)

BOX 8.1

TAKING THE HEAT OUT OF CONFLICT: THE MYTHS AND REALITIES OF ANGER

As Ann opens the mail she finds an overdrawn check. She's furious as she realizes that Joe forgot to record his checks and now they've overdrawn their bank account. Perhaps this shouldn't bother her, but it's the sixth time he's done it, and after a long talk last week he promised he wouldn't do it again. Furious and steaming with rage, when he comes home tonight, Ann should:

1. let it all out—tell him exactly how she feels.
2. go talk to a friend and then discuss it with Joe later.
3. keep the anger stifled and try to talk to him in a calm, logical manner.
4. wait until her anger has cooled down and then discuss the problem with him.

Does your choice among Ann's options coincide with any of the following myths about anger?

MYTH 1: VENTING YOUR ANGER HELPS GET RID OF IT.

Contrary to common belief and to the philosophy of encounter groups, "letting it all hang out" does *not* lessen anger. According to Carol Tavris, a researcher specializing in the study of anger, instead of lessening their anger, people who are prone to vent their rage grow angrier. Murray Straus, a sociologist in the field of family violence, finds that couples who yell at each other do not thereafter feel less angry, but more angry. His studies found verbal aggression and physical aggression to be highly correlated. It is a small step from bitter accusations to slaps. Ventilation by yelling does not reduce anger. "Telling someone we hate him supposedly will purge pent-up aggressive inclinations and will 'clear the air' . . . Frequently, however, when we tell someone off, we stimulate ourselves to continued or even stronger aggression" (Berkowitz, in Tavris, 1982a, p. 32).

But don't people feel better in other ways once the anger is out? Studies show that many people indicate that their self-esteem drops after they have let themselves express anger. They report feeling depressed for several days. In addition, there are the negative and hurt feelings that are felt by the recipients of the rage. "Any emotional arousal will simmer down if you just wait long enough, although some people, particularly hypertensives, must wait longer than others" (Tavris, 1982a, p. 27). The traditional advice for anger control—count to ten—has some validity (Tavris, 1982a).

MYTH 2: TALKING OUT ANGER GETS RID OF IT, OR AT LEAST MAKES YOU FEEL LESS ANGRY.

Talking to a friend about your anger makes you feel better. Right? Not according to what the research shows. Talking out anger doesn't reduce it;

(Continued)

it rehearses it. If you are upset with your spouse and go off for a few drinks with a friend to talk things over, you may just, in further talking about it, decide that you are really furious after all, maybe even more furious than before. You're not getting rid of your anger, merely practicing it. Reciting your grievances adds fuel to your emotional fire.

Does this mean we should keep quiet when we are angry? Not necessarily. Tavris suggests, "The point is to understand what happens when you *do* decide to express anger, and to realize how our perceptions about the causes of anger can be affected just by talking about them and deciding on an interpretation. . . . Discussing your anger can lead to practical solutions, but it can also become obsessive, useless wheel spinning" (1982b, pp. 134–135).

MYTH 3: SUPPRESSED ANGER IS LIKELY TO HAVE NEGATIVE MEDICAL CONSEQUENCES.

Again the contemporary ventilationist view stresses that "It is always important to express anger so that it won't clog your arteries or your friendships" (Tavris, 1982b, p. 121). The assumption is that stifled anger can lead to negative medical consequences. But this is a naive approach, overlooking the social context and the consequences of anger. "If your expressed rage causes another person to shoot you, it won't matter that you die with very healthy arteries" (p. 121).

Contradictory findings about anger and heart disease exist. The problem is that many variables play a role in determining any connection between anger and physical consequences. Researchers in these studies need to ask their subjects what they were angry about. For example, anger experienced by a white, middle-class, "Type A" man may be quite different from that of a black, working-class man coping with chronic poverty, discrimination, and periodic unemployment. "Anger appears to be a symptom instead of a cause of the basic problem. What matters more is the reason that people feel angry, and whether they feel that they can do anything about it" (Tavris, 1982a, p. 29). If you feel you have *control* over people or the events making you angry, then the experience of anger may not be as depressing as it is for those who feel they have no control. Having supportive friends and family may also help you deal with the cause of the anger.

LEARNING HOW TO HANDLE ANGER

Anger is not an uncontrollable emotion; we have responsibility for how we act on our anger. Here are some suggestions:

1. Keep quiet about momentary irritations, and distract yourself with pleasant activity until your fury simmers down. This procedure does not mean total silence. Each of us needs to find his or her own compromise among "talking too much," "expressing every little thing that irritates us," and "not talking at all." "As the catharsis

studies convincingly show, sometimes the best thing you can do about anger is nothing at all. Let it go, and half the time it will turn out to be an unimportant, momentary shudder, quickly forgotten. The other half of the time, keeping quiet gives you time to cool down and decide whether the matter is worth discussing or not" (Tavris, 1982b, p. 223).

Know what you're angry about and what the outside circumstances are. Discriminate between the sources of anger that you can do something about and those you cannot. Decide between taking responsibility for your own actions and failures and attributing blame elsewhere for events beyond your control.

Be civil when expressing your anger. Calm, nonaggressive reporting of your anger (using I-statements) is the "kindest, most civilized, and usually most effective way to express anger; but even this mature method depends on its context" (Tavris, 1982a, p. 34). Results of studies on anger support good, old-fashioned, motherly advice: If you can't say something nice about a person, don't say anything at all, at least if you want your anger to dissipate and your associations to remain congenial. But if you want to stay angry, if you want to *use* your anger, keep talking (Tavris, 1982b, pp. 134–135).

Don't let anger get out of hand during conflict; "Nip it in the bud." If you feel anger mounting, disengage immediately from the argument. You might say to yourself, "I'm starting to feel angry," or "This is becoming a fight," and *stop.* You can agree to return to the discussion when both of you are feeling more calm—a couple of hours later or the next day—and continue to discuss the issues.

Those people with a quick temper should learn how to reduce tension. Techniques of yoga or meditation, for example, help to relax the heart rate, slow breathing patterns, and calm distracting, worrying, or infuriating thoughts.

Learn how to think differently about your anger. Anger can be maintained or exacerbated by thought statements we make to ourselves when we are provoked—"Just who does he think he is to treat me like that?" "What a vile and thoughtless woman she is!" Anger can be controlled by reinterpreting a supposed provocation: "Maybe he's having a rough day," "She must be a very unhappy person if she would do such a thing." Empathizing with the provoker's behavior and trying to find justification for it help to slow down the anger response.

In the final analysis, people need to take responsibility for their anger and their actions. Anger can be controlled. Getting angry without taking other people's feelings into account may ruin a relationship. "Once anger becomes a force [with which] to berate the nearest scapegoat instead of to change a bad situation, it loses its credibility and its power. It feeds only on itself. And it sure as sunrise makes for a grumpy life" (Tavris, 1982b, p. 226).

blows quite easily and wear the belt below their waists. High-belters feel smug and self-righteous when they complain about low blows, to the point of feeling justified in fighting back viciously in "self-defense" (1968, p. 82). Although people vary on how much they will tolerate, there are limits of tolerance in everybody. It is at these points that partners feel that they can make no concessions and will no longer negotiate, at least for the time being.

Lecturing

Although usually well-meaning, some people feel compelled to jump in with a lecture when asked for particular information or their feelings about something. They carry on a monologue without allowing the other person to get in a word edgewise. What appears to be a great deal of self-disclosure is usually merely a way to control the conversation. Often these people feel insecure and fearful of criticism by another. So as long as they can dominate the conversation, they prevent others from saying things they don't want to hear, and they can avoid threatening issues.

When a person is lecturing, he or she often proceeds from one topic to another with no interruptions or breaks of time. It becomes virtually impossible to interrupt such people since they run their sentences together, taking breaths in the middle of a sentence (Saxton, 1986). They are so preoccupied with their own talk that they often ignore messages from others and may even change the topic of discussion if they can.

The lecturing form of communication is also counterproductive when attempting to resolve conflict. The lecturing person may appear to be working on a problem, but he or she is not listening to the other's point of view. He or she simply persists with his or her own position as forcefully as possible,

using numerous examples and illustrations (Saxton, 1986). Such people seem to think that if they talk enough, the other person will see their point of view, their side of the issue, and agree with them.

Even making simple decisions is hindered by lecturing. Because lecturing doesn't allow input from others, many facts about a topic of discussion or an issue remain unknown. Hence, decisions are made prematurely or without adequate information. The other person who had tried to converse with a lecturer may give up at some point in time and resign himself or herself to never really being heard.

Another barrier to constructive communication, which often accompanies lecturing, is interrupting when someone else is speaking. Whether it is finishing another person's sentence, cutting in to "get your two cents in," or changing the topic altogether, this habit can become quite aggravating and annoying.

> WIFE: One thing I like about Carol . . .
> HUSBAND: Her sense of humor?
> WIFE: No, what I was trying to say . . .
> HUSBAND: Oh. I know, you like the fact that you're both teachers. I wonder what grade she'll be teaching this year.

By this time, the interrupter has shifted the topic. The wife's original thought was never finally expressed, has now been lost, and certainly was never understood by her husband.

Sarcasm

A good sense of humor is an important element in a close relationship. Humor can be used to release tension and anxieties, and it can help a couple through an adverse situation. "A sign of loving intimacy between two people is the ability to laugh at each other's mistakes and weaknesses without ridicule or mocking and without either one losing face'' (Wahlroos, 1983, p. 220).

Unfortunately, however, humor can also be used as a "vicious weapon" in interpersonal communication. Sarcasm occurs when a somewhat humorous statement is made, usually reflecting the opposite of what is actually said and usually meant to hurt. Underneath the communication is typically hostility, bitterness, or cynicism. For example, "Sure, you're always perfect. You never do anything wrong." Ridicule, mockery, and flippancy are similar destructive uses of humor.

Humor needs to be used with tact and sensitivity to another person's feelings and needs at the moment. Timing is extremely important (Wahlroos, 1983). Joking, for example, when a person is trying to have a serious discussion, can be quite aggravating; it shows an insensitivity to the other person's feelings. It may also be a way of avoiding a potential conflict or a threatening issue.

Teasing is an example of how joking can be taken too far. Although teasing may be good-natured and above the belt for the most part, it can also get out of hand and be used to vent hostilities. In an attempt to remedy the situation when a negative chord is struck, the teaser often replies, "I was just kidding—can't you take a joke?" Usually this response is not enough to repair the damage already done. The "I was just kidding" excuse is an attempt on the speaker's part to avoid being accused of giving direct criticism or complaints.

Gunnysacking

Gunnysacking occurs when unresolved marital complaints are kept in an imaginary bag or gunnysack for an extended length of time and then are brought out when a person thinks it's advantageous to use them. Very little constructive problem solving and good communication is possible when unresolved complaints from the past continue to enter into the present discussion. It may be a minor problem that triggers a discussion, but it often becomes major as unresolved grievances and grudges from the past are unleashed.

When unloading past grievances from the sack, partners will often disagree with each other's interpretation of past events. An argument often ensues about who is right regarding the details of past behavior. Besides being irrelevant to the present issue, the exact truth of what happened in the past cannot be retrieved, and it becomes more and more distorted over time.

WIFE: You were really cold to my parents when they were visiting us last summer.

HUSBAND: I wasn't cold—I was as nice as I could be with them.

WIFE: Well, you didn't want to take them sightseeing.

HUSBAND: They didn't want to go sightseeing . . . *etc.*

What is most constructive is the partners communicating what they want or feel *now* regarding the other's behavior and forgetting about the past as much as possible, and throwing away the gunnysack.

Annoying Modes of Delivery

The vocal properties and speech mannerisms of communication in part determine how our messages will be received. Have you ever grown impatient and stopped listening when a person talks very slowly? Or have you started to fall asleep as someone drones on in a monotone? Or have you ever felt lost as a person rambles along in his speech as though he were going to a fire? Or has someone spoken so softly that you have had to strain to hear him—or so loudly that you felt intimidated by her?

The following list contains many ways in which the delivery of messages affects the listening and comprehension of what is being said: fast talk, slow talk, overtalk, undertalk, loud talk, quiet talk, singsong speech, monotone speech, and stuttering. "In addition, there is affective talk, as in expressing too much emotional vocal behavior (e.g., crying, whining, screaming), considering the content of what is said, and unaffective talk, as in expressing too little emotion vocally, given the content of what is said" (Thomas, 1977, p. 39). A desirable delivery consists of speaking at an adequate rate, for an appropriate length of time, and at an appropriate volume, reflective of the emotional content of the words.

Faultfinding

It is not uncommon for the daily life of a family or marriage to be mired in detailed discussions of seemingly minor, repetitive actions. The nit-picking and faultfinding that may be involved in judging these actions exist because people do not distinguish between what is important and what is not important. Sometimes such people cannot find anything that falls into the unimportant category.

Constructive criticism—that is, pointing out significant ways to improve another's behavior—can be a meaningful part of developing a close relationship. But it is a waste of time to complain continually about trivial matters. Criticism must be discriminate, taking into account the fact that nobody is perfect and that there are many matters that are so unimportant that they should be ignored. Indiscriminate criticism, or faultfinding, usually leads to very destructive consequences in human interactions (Wahlroos, 1983).

Faultfinding typically results in the recipient turning the speaker off completely or storing up resentment. She may think, "Here he goes again with his constant picking and criticizing—can't he ever get off my back?" Faultfinding is certainly an ineffective way of changing the behavior of others. In fact, the "others" involved will only try to avoid the faultfinder or completely ignore what he or she has to say. Faultfinding only creates resentment, hurts other people's feelings, often provokes the other person into the opposite behavior from what the speaker desires, and ensures that he or she will not "be heard" at some time in the future when the speaker really wants and needs to be (Wahlroos, 1983). When a person is sparing in criticisms, he or she will create a more harmonious atmosphere and have a better chance of being heard and understood when something important comes up.

CONSTRUCTIVE COMMUNICATION IN INTIMATE RELATIONSHIPS

Positive Communication

When communicating positively, one is showing respect to the other person, providing support for his or her self-esteem, or self-worth, and building his or her self-confidence. Praise, compliments, and manners are all involved in positive communication. The idea is not to say only positive things—to overwhelm the person with admiration—but to keep in mind the proportion between positive comments and negative comments. In addition, when negative comments are made, they need not be put-downs or in any way belittle the person's character or self-esteem.

Research on marital happiness indicates that high rates of negative communications have the most harmful impact on marital satisfaction (Margolin, 1981). The more that negative and displeasing communications outweigh positive ones, the more likely it is that couples will say they are unhappy. Thus for happy couples, positive exchange tends to exceed negative exchange.

For most people it seems easier to see the negative aspects of another person's behavior. We usually notice the person's mistakes, inappropriate actions, and failings. Good behavior is taken for granted and overlooked, perhaps because "it's expected." But adults, as well as children, need rewards and positive reinforcement for their "good" behaviors.

"But how can I praise the person if he does nothing right?" The authors hear this comment in counseling a lot, usually from a very negative person talking about his or her child. The point is that you need to look for positive aspects of an individual's behavior. Certainly particular behavior may not be "perfect," but it may be better than the day or week before. In fact, the person's *past* performance can be used as a yardstick. Recognition and praise can be based on *improvements* from past behavior (Wahlroos, 1983). Hence, this approach does not require a person to be false about another's behavior. Overall, it is much easier to see positive behavior when one is trying to focus on positive, rather than negative, actions.

Turning the Other Cheek

When one is insulted, provoked, or put down, there is a tendency to retaliate with insults and put-downs about the other person. There is a fear of letting the person "walk all over you" or in some way take advantage of you. But retaliating with negative comments will only lead to negative exchange, a continuing reciprocal exchange of punishments. When a person says something that is considered insulting, provoking, or unfair, it's

an invitation to argue. But it's advantageous to decline the invitation. One can do so by reacting in a reasonable, concerned, and tactful manner (Wahlroos, 1983). For example, if you feel insulted by another person, you may tell that person, calmly and with sincere concern, that you may have done something to hurt him or her but you're sorry and you want to correct it. Try to continue the conversation without retaliating, without stooping to the other person's destructive and unfair techniques.

Responding in a "reasonable, sincere, and constructive" way does not in any way invite the other person to "walk all over" you. If the other person is using poor or destructive communication techniques, it doesn't give you the right to use them also; instead use a constructive technique when replying. The examples on p. 270 depict how invitations to fight can be accepted or declined (Wahlroos, 1983, pp. 78–79).

Turning the other cheek also should involve an honest assessment of your own behavior in order to determine to what degree you may have contributed to the other person's dissatisfaction.

Leveling

Leveling involves getting matters "on the table." It means expressing one's feelings, wants, and desires openly and honestly, without putting the other person down or on the defensive (Gottman et al., 1976). There are different ways to level—"You're a rotten driver," "You're going to get us killed," or "When I am in the car with you and you drive so fast, I feel scared" (Gottman et al., 1976, p. 30). The most constructive and effective way to level is by using I-statements. "When you do X in situation Y I feel Z" (p. 37). For example, "When you criticize me (X) in front of our friends (Y), I feel hurt (Z)."

ACCEPTING OR DECLINING TO FIGHT

INVITATION	ACCEPTED FIGHT	DECLINED FIGHT
Wife to Husband:		
"I wish you could at least learn not to throw your clothes on the floor!"	"Who are you to talk? Just look at the mess you constantly have in the kitchen!"	"You are right; it is a bad habit of mine and I'll make a conscious effort to work on it."
Husband to Wife:		
"I have changed my mind; we are not going to the mountains on our vacation."	"What kind of damned dictator are you anyway? I am through slaving for you, hear? I'll have the divorce papers served on you right in your office and then you'll see who calls the tune around here!"	"I want to talk to you about what kind of marriage we want. I do not want the kind of marriage where one tells the other one what to do without discussing it first."
Parent to Child:		
"You always forget to turn off the light in the bathroom."	"That's not true; I almost always remember. It is you who always picks on me whatever I do."	"I'm sorry, I do forget too often and I'll work on that. But I also feel that you pick on me too often and I'd like you to stop doing that."

I-statements also imply that the person is taking responsibility for his or her own feelings. Instead of saying, *"You* make me angry," it's better to say, *"I'm* angry." By describing their own feelings, their own situations, and their own interpretations, partners can better understand each other and there will be less mind reading. Statements that begin with "I think," "I feel," "I believe," "In my opinion," or "My perception is" are very helpful in transmitting clearly a speaker's ideas and feelings so that the listener can understand them accurately (Strong, 1983).

Leveling begins a process of communication that allows partners to resolve conflicts in a productive way and in a way that can bring the couple closer together (Gottman et al., 1976). Openly expressing one's feelings, wants, and desires enables the other person to deal with them directly (Saxton, 1986). One is then clear in communicating where one stands and what one wants.

A close and trusting relationship requires partners to be open and honest about their feelings, to "level" with their partner, and to bring up significant problems, concerns, and worries. You have probably heard suggestions like this before—and they may seem trite—but nevertheless they still deserve emphasis. Those who are not open and honest—who evade fights and bottle up feelings—are only doing harm to themselves and the relationship. Merely accommodating or going along with a partner often creates an inner resentment and a feeling of powerlessness. There may be a limit, however, to the amount of honesty that is beneficial for the relationship (see Box 8.2).

Tactfulness

Along with leveling must come tactfulness. Tactfulness includes "being sincere and open in communication while at the same time showing respect for the other person's feelings and taking care not to hurt him [or her] unnecessarily" (Wahlroos, 1983, p. 170). It requires an awareness of, sensitivity to, and empathy for the feelings of others, sensing the right time and place to bring up subjects for discussion. It also involves not taking advantage of another person's feelings—contrary to many encounter-type groups. "Encounter-type approaches have tended to view tactfulness as an obstacle to or a shield against intimacy. The fact is, however, that true intimacy can never develop where tactfulness is absent" (p. 171). What is being discussed here is the manner in which feelings are expressed, not a hiding of the feelings themselves.

Sometimes people will use tactfulness as an excuse when they are really trying to avoid honest self-disclosure. Too often a statement like—"It would upset him, so I won't tell him how I feel"—is a cop-out. This type of statement is most likely to be made when a person wants to avoid facing anxiety-producing issues, rather than really protecting another person from being "hurt."

The statement itself implies distrust of the partner, or at least a lack of confidence in the partner's ability to handle sincere communication. It also implies pessimism with regard to the relationship ever developing into one of intimacy and trust, since intimacy and trust are dependent upon openness and sincerity of communication. (Wahlroos, 1983, p. 85)

Verification Feedback

Listening must be active in order to be effective. Giving feedback is a way an individual shows that he or she has been listening actively to what has been said. Verification feedback is checking on whether the speaker's feelings, opinions, or needs have been correctly understood. One can begin feedback statements with, "Let me see if I understood you correctly," "You mean that . . .," "As I understand it, you feel . . .," "What I hear you saying is . . .," "I think I hear you indicating that . . ." Basically the listener is trying to restate in his or her own words the message he or she thought the speaker had just sent—without adding anything new (Adler and Towne, 1984). It is better to paraphrase than to repeat back verbatim what was said.

Verifying what a person has said implies an obvious interest in what that person is saying and lets the speaker know he or she has been listened to. In this way it helps in building a close relationship. "Being actively listened to can be an enormously rewarding

BOX 8.2

CAN THERE BE TOO MUCH HONESTY?

A key sensitivity in relationships is sensing "when frankness may hurt rather than help." Those who self-disclose too bluntly may be honest, but they may also be insensitive, idealistic, and immature. Once more, "Asking a partner to 'tell all' may indicate a need to control that person by finding out everything about him or her" (Lasswell and Lobsenz, 1983, p. 94). In addition, it must be remembered that whatever we say can be used against us. For example, telling too much about your past sexual experiences or about your fantasies may cause other people not to trust you.

> One man kept asking his fiancée to tell him about all the sexual experiences she had before they met. The woman was reluctant; she had had an active sex life and feared the man would be upset at hearing about it. Finally she yielded to his insistence—and the man was furiously jealous. He continued to suspect her every time she had to work late or go out of town on business. Ultimately, his constant suspicion and their arguments about it led to their breakup. (p. 94)

It's a good idea before pressing for total frankness to ask yourself, "Do I *really* want to hear this? Will total frankness help our relationship?" Several sociological studies have revealed that "Couples said the biggest difference between good and bad communication was whether a partner tended to say things that would be better left unsaid" (Lasswell and Lobsenz, 1983, p. 95). It really isn't wise to tell your partner that he has a big nose, that her rear end is the size of a blimp, or that her breasts are too small. Perhaps "appropriate honesty" is the pattern to seek; that is, "sharing whatever information seems likely to reduce tensions and increase satisfactions while keeping mum about whatever seems likely to be needlessly damaging" (p. 95). Lasswell and Lobsenz offer the following three guidelines for "appropriate honesty":

1. Before you volunteer information or respond to a question, ask yourself, "Is what I am about to say really true? Is it necessary that the other person know it? Will there be a more appropriate time and place to make this statement?"
2. Be as sure as you can about the other person's emotional capacity to handle a frank answer or comment. In general, someone unwilling to level with you is unlikely to want you to respond frankly to him or her.
3. Be sensitive to the other person's values, and talk about matters you know are important to him or her with particular gentleness and tact. (pp. 95–96)

Active listeners convey to speakers that the message is understood.

experience and builds bridges between con-flicted people'' (Saxton, 1986, p. 351). It pro-motes a sense of understanding. When we believe we are understood we are more likely to want to become closer to and to create an affectionate bond with that person (Scoresby, 1977).

Verification feedback also attempts to bring about a clear message, a message that is received by a person in the way it was meant to be received. Communication based on verified feedback is obviously more accu-rate than communication based on assump-tions. As previously mentioned, getting feed-back also helps *the speaker* to obtain a clearer image of his or her own feelings and thoughts. One of the goals of listening is to let the speaker know what his or her world looks like from the outside from the eyes and ears of another, from the listener's perspec-tive. This feedback helps both listener and speaker develop new ideas about how they relate to each other and to their environment.

Touching

Constructive communication can also involve physical touching. "We have learned the art of communication when we realize that it is not all a matter of words. . . . The most prim-itive mode of establishing contact with another person is to touch him—to hold his hand, or to hug him'' (Jourard, 1971, p. 88). At times there may not be words to express our feelings. Or perhaps one may want to punctuate his or her feelings with nonverbal gestures. Either way, intimate partners will be expected to express their feelings for each other with many physical gestures: stroking, caressing, holding, hugging, squeezing, and kissing (Saxton, 1986). Nonverbal gestures can also convey active listening to another individual. A touch, a smile, a nod, continued eye contact, or leaning forward can all acknowledge the speaker's feelings.

We cannot underestimate the power and impact that touching has on communication. ''Nonverbal understanding is at least as important as verbal. It can be a way of releasing our real selves when our limited words won't do it'' (Jourard, 1971, p. 89). Frequently this is the type of communication sought by partners in an emotionally close relationship. But it's not always achieved. In fact, as mentioned previously, a common complaint among

Constructive communication can also involve touching.

TOUCH ME

Touch me—in secret places no one has reached before, in silent places where words only interfere, in sad places where only whispering makes sense.

Touch me—in the morning when night still clings, at midday when confusion crowds upon me, at twilight as I begin again to know who I am, in the evening when I see you and I hear you—best of all.

Touch me—like a child who will never have enough love for I am a woman who wants to be lost in your arms, a woman who has known enough pain to love, a mother who is strong enough to give.

Touch me—in crowds when a single look says everything, in solitude when it's too dark to even look, in absence when I reach for you through time and miles.

Touch me—when I ask, when I'm afraid to ask.

Touch me—with your lips, your hands, your words, your presence in the room.

Touch me—gently for I am fragile, firmly for I am strong—often, for I am alone.

ANONYMOUS

wives in marriage counseling is the lack of touching by their husbands. For most of these women the poem ''Touch Me'' strongly expresses this need. Dating couples typically engage in many types of touching communications, although often they are forgotten when the couple is married. Once married, many couples only engage in physical touching when they are involved in sexual intercourse.

To assess the quality of communication among couples and family members, David Olson and his colleagues have developed communication scales. (See Box 8.3.)

Nonverbal communication is evident in many ways.

RESOLVING CONFLICTS IN INTIMATE RELATIONSHIPS

Is Conflict Normal?

If a couple never experiences any conflict, does that mean that they are blissfully happy? If two partners disagree and argue, will that diminish the possibilities of intimacy in their relationship? Perhaps because of romantic notions about marital bliss and happiness, to many people the presence of conflict seems to mean that love is gone or is dying (Scoresby, 1977). But if partners define the goal of a marital relationship as a "life without quarrels," they will be reaching for a fantasy. "Perfect agreement on everything, like perfect intimacy, is to be found only in romantic novels and heaven" (Tavris, 1982b, p. 214). Believing that "harmony is normal and conflict is abnormal," many young couples are dismayed and disillusioned when first confronted with a conflict in their marriages. Conflict is one of the key factors resulting in the end of illusionary intimacy.

In any relationship that endures over time, conflict will be a normal state of affairs. In a large national study, 32 percent of the persons describing their marriages as "very happy" reported they had conflict in getting along with each other (Gurin, Veroff, and Feld, 1960). When conflict is frequent, however, marital satisfaction will be less. Based on diaries of conflicts and arguments in one study, distressed couples reported an average of 3.4 conflicts over a five-day period. Happily married couples reported, on the average, one conflict during a five-day period (Birchler, Weiss, and Vincent, 1975).

Conflict is particularly inevitable in close relationships. This perhaps seems like a paradox; the person to whom you are close will also be one with whom you'll experience conflict. Perhaps a definition of conflict will help clarify this issue. Conflict is an event that occurs between two mutually dependent persons who perceive some incompatible goals or scarcity of rewards (Wilmot and Wilmot, 1978). The very fact that an intimate relationship involves two interdependent persons makes some conflict inevitable.

Thus, if a couple were not close and dependent on each other, conflict would be more easily *avoided*, and hence, less conflict would occur. This does not mean that intimate partners are destined to be constantly at odds. But given that human beings are self-interested and reward-seeking creatures, it seems obvious that at times self-interests will conflict. "Even in the closest of friendships negative affect is nestled in with the positive, since no relationship can be totally gratifying. Conflict we shall always have with us" (Raush et al., 1974, p. 30).

On the one hand, the desire for an intimate relationship and the commitment involved in such a pairing motivates the couple to deal with conflict appropriately so as to ensure that the relationship will continue. On the other hand, in relationships that are tem-

BOX 8.3

HOW DOES YOUR COMMUNICATION RATE?

THE FAMILY COMMUNICATION SCALE

Good communication involves more than just talking to one another. It requires openness, understanding and trust. With good communication, family members are better able to support each other; yet individual growth is encouraged. Without good communication, members tend to drift apart.

Cover up the answers of the persons before you and try to be as honest as you can. Next to each statement below, insert the number of the response that best describes the way you feel about the statement.

RESPONSE CHOICES

1	2	3	4	5
Definitely false	Usually false	Neither true nor false	Usually true	Definitely true

FAMILY MEMBERS
A   B   FAMILY MEMBERS
                                         C   D

1. I can discuss my beliefs with my parent(s)/child(ren) without feeling restrained or embarassed.

2. My parent(s)/child(ren) are always good listeners.

3. My parent(s)/child(ren) can tell how I'm feeling without asking.

4. I am very satisfied with how my parent(s)/child(ren) and I talk together.

5. If I were in trouble, I could tell my parent(s)/child(ren).

6. I openly show affection to my parent(s)/child(ren).

7. When I ask questions, I get honest answers from my parent(s)/child(ren).

8. My parent(s)/child(ren) try to understand my point of view.

9. I find it easy to discuss problems with my parent(s)/child(ren).

10. It is very easy for me to express all my true feelings to my parent(s)/child(ren).

SCORING

Add up the total number of points for each column to find the total score for each person.

A   B   C   D

NOTE: Parents should use the scores below in the column on the left. Children should use the scores on the right.

NOW FIND THE RATING FOR YOUR TOTAL SCORES	YOUR SCORE PARENT'S SCORES	CHILD'S SCORES	
	43 or more	40 or more	HIGH
	37–42	35–39	ABOVE AVE
	31–36	29–34	BELOW AVE
	30 or less	28 or less	LOW

INTERPRETING YOUR WELLNESS PROFILE

The guide below will tell you how to interpret your Wellness Profile more specifically.

FAMILY AND COUPLE COMMUNICATION

HIGH	You feel understood and are able to share your feelings with other family members.
ABOVE AVERAGE	You feel generally understood and can share most of your feelings with the family.
BELOW AVERAGE	You are not comfortable sharing many of your feelings with the family.
LOW	You do not feel the family understands you, and you rarely share your feelings with the others.

THE COUPLE COMMUNICATION SCALE

Being able to share intimate thoughts and feelings is essential in a good relationship. This scale will show whether you and your partner see things the same way and measure the quality of your communication.

Next to each statement below, insert the number of the response that best describes the way you feel about the statement. Remember: Keep the first partner's answers covered while the second partner is completing the scale.

RESPONSE CHOICES

1 Definitely false	2 Usually false	3 Neither true nor false	4 Usually true	5 Definitely true

PARTNER A		PARTNER B
	1. It is very easy for me to express all my true feelings to my partner.	
	2. When we are having a problem, my partner often gives me the silent treatment.	
	3. My partner sometimes makes comments that put me down.	
	4. Sometimes I am afraid to ask my partner for what I want.	
	5. I wish my partner were more willing to share his/her feelings with me.	
	6. Sometimes I have trouble believing everything my partner tells me.	
	7. Often I do not tell my partner what I am feeling because he/she should already know.	
	8. I am very satisfied with how my partner and I talk with each other.	
	9. I don't always share negative feelings I have about my partner because I'm afraid he/she will get angry.	
	10. My partner is always a good listener.	

SCORING

A.		Add your choices for items 1, 8 and 10—insert the total on line A		A.
B.	+42	Add 42	+42	B.
C.		Subtotal—add lines A and B		C.
D.		Add your choices for items 2, 3, 4, 5, 6, 7 and 9—insert the total on line D		D.
E.		Subtract line D from line C to find your FINAL SCORE	FINAL SCORE	E.

NOW FIND THE RATING FOR YOUR FINAL SCORES	YOUR SCORE 40 or more 35–39 30–34 29 or less	HIGH ABOVE AVERAGE BELOW AVERAGE LOW

SOURCES: *Copyright © by D. H. Olson, D. G. Fournier, J. M. Druckman; Copyright © by H. L. Barnes and D. H. Olson*

porary or superficial, conflict can often be avoided or "swept under the rug," and attempts are not made to make changes.

Conflict is neither "good" nor "bad" in itself. Contrary to common belief, many positive outcomes can result from conflict. At the very least, conflict allows for the stating of needs and the possibility of meeting these needs through conflict resolution. If needs go unstated, it is possible of course that overt conflict may be avoided, at least for a while. Unstated needs, however, have a discouraging way of remaining unmet. This creates the potential for even greater conflicts, and very often it results in significant resentment, bitterness, and possible breakdown of the relationship.

During the early phases of a relationship, conflict is less likely. The interaction at the time consists almost totally of superficial information (Altman and Taylor, 1973). In fact, a person is usually on his or her best behavior while maintaining an air of politeness and avoidance of conflict. Awareness of any discrepancies between expectations for the other person and actual behavior usually does not occur at this time.

As the interaction moves beyond a presentation of a "false self" and beyond superficial topics, such as one's favorite music or recreational interests, into more personal topics and into deeper aspects of both personalities, conflicting interests are made known (Braiker and Kelly, 1979). Conflict often occurs as persons reveal to each other certain feelings of doubt and disappointment about the relationship as well as their expectations and ideals. For example, feelings of being smothered, which are typically hidden early in the relationship, later may be expressed by one person when the partners begin to level with each other. At the point of uncovering different preferences and expectations for the relationship, the couple can either work out the conflict and perhaps redefine the relationship or decide to dissolve it, breaking off interaction completely.

When is conflict destructive? Conflict can become destructive when the couple is lacking appropriate ways of handling it. If one or both partners are very rigid and cannot tolerate change, the intensity of the conflict could actually tear the relationship apart. If both partners are flexible, needless wear and tear on the relationship can be avoided. Flexibility makes it possible to adapt to changing life situations while at the same time maintaining stability in the relationship (Lasswell and Lobsenz, 1983).

Destructive conflict tends to feed on itself; it expands and escalates so that it often becomes independent of the initial problem. This pattern is sometimes referred to as a "kitchen sink fight" because "the kitchen plumbing is about all that isn't thrown as a weapon in such a battle" (Bach and Wyden, 1968, p. 18). Consider the following "kitchen sink" fight:

HE: Why were you late?

SHE: I tried my best.

HE: Yeah? You and who else? Your mother is never on time either.

SHE: That's got nothing to do with it.

HE: The hell it doesn't. You're just as sloppy as she is.

SHE: (getting louder): You don't say! Who's picking whose dirty underwear off the floor every morning?

HE: (sarcastic but controlled): I happen to go to work. What have *you* got to do all day?

SHE: (shouting): I'm trying to get along on the money you don't make, that's what.

HE: (turning away from her): Why should I knock myself out for . . .

(1968, p. 18)

Destructive conflict tends increasingly to rely on threats, coercion, and deception—tactics that are likely to be reciprocated.

Researchers Harriet Braiker and Harold Kelley (1979) conclude that positive outcomes from conflict may occur when (1) conflict is infrequent and not intense, (2) there is a history of positive exchange between the partners, and (3) the couple has superior conflict-coping capabilities.

Power in Interpersonal Conflict

Power is closely tied to interpersonal conflict. Often in a problem situation each of the partners is attempting to exert at least some power to change the other person's mind or in some way to change the relationship in order to achieve his or her own goals. If partners have a vested interest in the continuation of a relationship, each person will try to ensure that his or her needs are being met by the other person and at the same time try to make sure that the other individual has enough rewards to stay in the relationship also.

A common notion regarding power is that it is negative. Especially in close relationships individuals may not want to acknowledge that power plays a significant role. A motto such as "power corrupts" infers that only evil results from its use. Asserting influence and power in a conflict, however, is not necessarily bad. Power is usually necessary to move a conflict along to some constructive resolution.

If people have no influence over each other, they cannot participate in conflict together, since their communication would have no impact on the situation. With no influence, persons are not in a conflict at all, but are simply in a mutual monologue. Influence, therefore, is necessary. . . . Power is central to the study of conflict and can be used for productive or destructive ends, but it is always present. (Wilmot and Wilmot, 1978, p. 47)

A dictionary definition of power is "the ability to control" or "to influence someone" or "to produce an effect on something or someone else." Another definition of power is the "capability of having one's way and achieving one's goals—even though others may resist" (Scanzoni and Scanzoni, 1981, p. 439). But actually to understand power in an interpersonal relationship is not quite so simple. Power needs to be defined in the context of a relationship. In other words, in a relationship one may have power over somebody because one has resources that the other person values—economic success, warmth and tenderness, or other resources. But, if the other person does not value the types of things one offers, then one would have no power over that person. Hence, power is relative to a particular social relationship and also is a product of that relationship. It is not a fixed amount of something that we carry around with us.

Measuring power in close relationships is a complex task. The more powerful partner in a relationship is usually the one who has the most *resources*—skills, information, income, physical attractiveness. In general, the person who has, or is believed to have, the most resources makes the most *decisions* (Lasswell and Lobsenz, 1983). Although an individual may have plenty of resources, it's possible not to be aware of them and, hence, not to utilize the power that exists. Thus assessing power in a relationship involves more than just adding up each person's resources or the number of decisions each makes.

What appears objectively from the outside may not truly reflect who holds the power. For instance, the partner who appears to "run the show in the relationship" is not necessarily the one with the most power (Wilmot and Wilmot, 1978). An outgoing, lively husband may seem to have more power, yet he may be extremely dependent upon his wife for emotional support, guidance, and other resources. A considerable amount of power is subjective, behind-the-scenes power. The actual interaction and communication patterns between spouses would need to be closely observed before an assessment could be made about who has more power. In addition, a number of questions would need to be asked to determine the power distribution.

One question would be: "Who accommodates the most?" The "Mr. Nice Guy," the "pleaser," who is always giving in to the other person, certainly seems to exert little power. This individual may receive rewards from continually trying to please his or her partner. But imprisoned by his or her "niceness," he or she exerts little power to change, influence, or confront the partner (Wilmot and Wilmot, 1978). If a person is regularly apologizing, smoothing things over, and avoiding upsetting others, that person is usually operating from a low power position.

A second question that needs to be asked in determining power is: "Who makes the decisions?" Robert Blood and Donald Wolfe in their study of marriage in the 1960s measured power by who made the final decision in each of eight areas: (1) husband's job, (2) car to buy, (3) whether to buy life insurance, (4) where to go on a vacation, (5) what house or apartment to take, (6) whether the wife should work or quit work, (7) what doctor to have when someone is sick, (8) how much money the family can afford to spend per week on food. All of these decisions in Blood's and Wolfe's study were given equal weight, even though not all decisions have the same degree of importance in the life of the family. How much food to buy may be a frequent decision to make but in terms of importance, what job the husband should take will have a greater impact upon the family—in terms of income, social status, residence, and family time. Thus, power in family relationships may not be solely determined

by the number of areas of decision making.

In any event, the more powerful partner may not be the one who makes the most decisions but rather the one "who *decides* who should make the decisions." Or to take this a step further to illustrate the complexity of the question of decisions and power, is the person who gets his or her way the one who has the power, or is the person who makes the decision as to who gets what the one who has the power, or does the person who makes the decision as to who shall make the decision as to who gets what, have the real power (Lasswell and Lobsenz, 1983)?

As male and female roles change and overlap with each other, areas of decision making are changing also. No longer is it automatically assumed that men are the experts in making decisions regarding mechanical things—cars and home repairs, for example—and women about decorating the home and child care (Lasswell and Lobsenz, 1983). It is to be hoped that as the roles change, couples will be more flexible to "decide for themselves who is better equipped to make which decisions" (p. 55). In addition, since gender-role changes have vastly increased the resources of women, the power between the partners has been further equalized. No longer is it totally left up to the man or assumed that he will have a final say for the couple. While this equalization may involve more discussion on decisions, and possibly more conflict, there is also a greater chance for intimacy to develop between the partners. It is easier to feel close to somebody who respects your opinion and ability to make sound decisions.

A third question that needs to be answered in determining power is: Who is less interested in the relationship? If one partner is less motivated in maintaining the relationship, that position can be a source of power for him or her. The person who is making more of an effort to please the partner, who is constantly working at maintaining the relationship, has less power. Willard Waller and Reuben Hill (1951) applied this concept of the "principle of least interest" to the partner who is less invested in the relationship for satisfying his or her needs and hence has power to induce the other to do just about anything.

A fourth question is: Who has more resources outside the marriage? The greater one's sources of rewards, the more power he or she will hold. A husband, for example, may exercise a great deal of power over his wife when she is dependent on him for providing for her total economic, social, and emotional needs while she is a full-time homemaker with small children and is isolated in a house in the country. But when she learns how to drive, gets a well-paying job, and has several good friends, her husband's relative power decreases.

Partners have a better chance of resolving conflict in a positive way if there is an equal balance of power. An imbalance of power in which one partner dominates may make conflict resolution simple—whatever he or she says goes. But resentment, frustration, and hopelessness usually grow in a powerless individual. If low-power persons are continually subjected to dominance and their goals and needs minimized or dismissed, they may resort to extreme means to exert some power over the other person. Often violence erupts. It is the powerless person who is sometimes likely to turn to the extreme last resort—aggression and violence. Hence, it may not be power, but powerlessness, that corrupts (May, 1972).

Styles of Handling Conflict

Individuals and couples have various approaches for dealing with conflict. In order to help couples make changes in this area, it is valuable first to understand their current approach to conflict resolution. A typology of five styles of handling conflict has been developed by Kenneth Thomas and Ralph Kilmann (cited in Wilmot and Wilmot, 1978). The model is based on two partially competing goals—*a concern for self* and *a concern for the other* (see Figure 8.1).

Every conflict has degrees of cooperation and competition. If one's style of handling conflict is *competitive*, it is characterized as involving aggressiveness and a low degree of cooperation, focusing on the pursuit of one's own concerns at the expense of another's. The person with a competitive style attempts to gain power by direct confrontation, by "winning" the argument without adjusting to the other's objectives and desires. "His or her goals are accomplished at the expense of others" (Wilmot and Wilmot, 1978, p. 29). Tactics involving put-downs, berating, and other oppressive techniques are often used with this style. A negative-exchange marriage generally involves such a competitive style used by both partners.

Avoidance, as the name implies, is the style of conflict in which the partners avoid pursuing both their own concerns and those

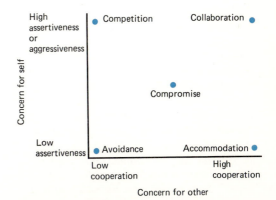

Figure 8.1 Styles of Handling Conflict. (*Source:* Wilmot and Wilmot, 1978, p. 19.)

of the other person. "It is a way of dealing with conflict by trying not to recognize its existence or your part in its creation" (Wilmot and Wilmot, 1978, p. 31). It is characterized by being nonassertive, passive, and low in cooperation. Either one or both parties can be avoiding. This could be a common style of handling conflict in both pseudo-intimate and traditional marriages. Avoidance may be used at times when an issue simply does not seem that important or when there is a fear of the ramifications of overt conflict in the relationship. Tactics such as changing the subject or withdrawal are used to sidestep issues.

When patterns of avoidance are characteristic of both partners, the possibilities of change within the relationship are minimal (Raush et al., 1974). The avoidance of conflict, however, does not necessarily mean that the marriage is unstable or that it does not offer some rewards. But such avoidance does seem to inhibit the growth and development of the relationship. Harold Raush et al. (1974) observed a "static quality of the interchange" where avoidance predominates as a mode for dealing with interpersonal conflict.

"Fight evading," however, can still lead to disaster. Consider the following case:

Mr. Jacobson rarely said much. Peacefully, he went along with whatever his wife wanted to do. . . . Shortly after their younger child went off to college, Mr. Jacobson packed his clothes while his wife was out shopping and left home without leaving a note. It took Mrs. Jacobson some time to discover through her husband's lawyer that he meant to leave for good. As usual, he just hadn't felt like arguing about it. His wife was incredulous and then horrified. Their many friends were flabbergasted. None would have believed that this marriage could break up. (Bach and Wyden, 1968, p. 23)

Accommodation occurs when an individual neglects his or her own needs in order to satisfy the concerns of the partner. It is a nonassertive but cooperative style of handling conflict. The accommodating person easily gives in to another's point of view without pushing his or her own point of view. The individual may later say he or she did not agree, but "a decision had to be reached." The price for reaching such a decision was the nonfulfillment or ignoring of the person's own needs and desires. Unfortunately, resentment can build over time from continuous use of the accommodating style. In the empty-shell marriage and in the traditional marriage on the part of the wife, accommodation is a common style of handling conflict.

Compromise is based on the point of view that each partner cannot have his or her own way and one has to be satisfied with just "part of the pie." Compromising means each person will have to give in a little. This style addresses the conflict more directly than the avoiding style, but it does not explore the issues and each person's needs in as much depth as does the collaborative style.

For example, a couple going on a vacation disagrees on the amount of money to take along. He says that they should take $1000 in traveler's checks, while she thinks $500 would be enough. They compromise and take $750. "The problem with the compromise style is that persons sometimes give in too easily and fail to seek a solution that would more adequately meet each parties' wants" (Wilmot and Wilmot, 1978, p. 31). Did the husband thoroughly explain the reason why he thought they needed $1000 in traveler's checks? Did he tell his wife that he was planning to pay bills with the checks because their credit cards were over their limit? Did he tell her that the traveler's checks were good anywhere but that some places don't accept credit cards? Did he tell her about his plans to buy an expensive fishing rod while on vacation? The "giving in" of the compromise style can become so habitual that it becomes a goal in itself. Alternatives for problem solving then are largely ignored.

The *collaboration* style of handling conflict emerges when high assertiveness aimed at reaching one's own goals is paired with a high concern for the other person. It sounds almost contradictory, but it really isn't. Collaboration occurs when two people work creatively to find new solutions that will maximize goals for both. It differs from compromise, which involves looking for some middle ground that partially satisfies both parties. Collaboration means that one person asserts individual goals while being concerned with the goals of the other person also. For example, a couple may use this style as they resolve a conflict over where to spend their vacation. The husband wants to spend it at a cabin on a lake where he can fish. The wife wants to vacation at her parents' home because they belong to a country club and the children could go swimming in the pool and she could play tennis. They collaborate and in the end decide to go to a lake resort in Wisconsin, which has all the facilities they would need to satisfy both individuals' goals.

To conclude, the goal of conflict resolution in an intimate relationship is a situation of *maximum joint profit*. That is, the partners are providing benefits to each other (at cost to each individually), but in return they are receiving certain rewards.

> *The situation is comparable to that in which a single buyer of a certain commodity and a single seller of that commodity enter into bargaining. Maximum profit for each is the goal. Such a situation appeals to the mutual interests of the participants, and would seem to call for harmonious cooperation between them.* (Siegel and Fouraker, 1960)

If the two opposing factors—cooperation and competition—can be made to work together in the conflict-resolving process, it becomes possible for the two parties to arrive at a solution that is in their *mutual* interest. Each partner, *and the relationship* as a whole, will benefit (Scanzoni and Scanzoni, 1983).

Resolving Conflict to Build Intimacy

The difference between successful and unsuccessful relationships is not whether conflict exists but how well the partners manage to deal with it. If a process of resolving conflict involves the sharing of feelings and needs, taking each other's wishes and values into consideration, and attempting to understand each other's position, then conflict resolution can actually help bring a couple closer together.

Constructive communication is part-and-parcel of positive conflict resolution. If the partners feel that they have not had the opportunity to express themselves and have not been listened to, they are not going to be open to suggestions from the other person. Therefore, during the process of resolving conflict, each person needs to practice constructive listening and speaking skills. Ironically, though, it is usually during conflict—when tempers are flaring and anger is raging—that the rules of constructive communication are completely ignored. Conflict can only be made worse by ineffective and destructive communication.

The following model illustrates an approach toward resolving conflict while at the same time building intimacy.

1. *Defining the conflict and one's needs relating to it.* The first step in resolving conflict is to recognize a conflict situation and to decide to deal with it. One specific issue needs to be singled out. In this way, the conflict takes a specific focus around a stated problem. In addition, specificity helps to prevent the conflict from escalating and moving on into other topics.

In moving toward a clearer definition of the conflict, it is necessary for each person individually to list his or her separate needs—before even considering solutions. For example, if the spouses disagree about the way in which their money is handled, they may each be asserting different needs. The husband may feel his need is to save money, while the wife's need is to have some input in making money decisions. The goal then is to focus on meeting their respective needs—in this situation, for example, finding ways to save money and involving the wife in making financial decisions.

2. *Providing feedback to each other.* Once the partners understand the relationship between their own needs and the conflict, this information itself can be shared with each other. An appropriate time to discuss their needs—a time when neither is hungry, tired, or in a hurry—should be chosen. The focus of this step is solely on understanding each other's point of view and feelings. There's a tendency for couples to start talking about solutions long before their needs and goals are clearly defined and understood. If the needs are not clearly stated, short-sighted and inadequate solutions can result, as with the proverbial sisters who quarreled over an orange. After arguing over the orange, they finally decided to divide it in half. The first sister took her half, ate the fruit, and threw away the peel. The other sister threw away the fruit and used the peel from her half in baking a cake (Fisher and Ury, 1981). Obviously, making suggestions for alternatives and deciding on one were premature at this stage.

This second step requires the basic listening and speaking skills previously discussed. Listening needs to convey empathy, acceptance, and verification feedback. Speaking skills should include I-statements, asking questions, and no put-downs or interruptions. If the partners feel that their feelings have been ignored, minimized, or negated, that their needs haven't been heard, or that they've been put down, they are not likely to be open to suggestions from the other person (Strong, 1983). Likewise, when each partner knows the feelings, thoughts, and expectations of the other, each can better adjust his or her own reactions and behavior toward the other (Raush et al., 1974). When an unresolved conflict persists and frustrates a relationship, "It is often because not *all* opinions, needs, and feelings pertinent to the conflict have been perceived accurately by one or both parties" (Guerney, 1977, p. 16).

3. *Seeking alternatives.* Once needs and feelings are clearly expressed and understood, the couple can begin the process of generating alternatives. Brainstorming, that is, producing as many ideas as possible to solve the problem, is the most effective way to start this process. The key ground rule of brainstorming is to "postpone all criticism and evaluation of ideas" (Fisher and Ury, 1981). The couple simply generates options without pausing to consider whether they are good or bad, realistic or unrealistic. The ground rule of no criticism or evaluation, it is hoped, removes inhibitions and stimulates many creative ideas. Hence, while brainstorming, people need not fear looking foolish, since wild ideas are explicitly encouraged (Fisher and Ury, 1981).

4. *Choosing the best alternative(s).* The next step is to discuss and evaluate the possible solutions and arrive at an agreement that is acceptable to both parties. The no-criticism rule of brainstorming is now relaxed in order to weed out the least promising suggestions. The most promising options should be selected and then discussed further. The couple should analyze together whether each option fulfills the needs of both parties or how a particular alternative could be made better.

5. *Implementing and evaluating selected alternatives.* "Good decisions are useful only to

the extent that they are implemented" (Strong, 1983, p. 280). In order to implement an alternative, the couple sets down in detail the steps that need to be taken (Lasswell and Lobsenz, 1983). After deciding which alternative(s) to implement, they set an evaluation time. They decide on giving the alternative a certain amount of time at the end of which they can evaluate its effectiveness. If the alternative fails, they can choose another from their list of options.

WHEN MARRIAGE OR FAMILY COUNSELING IS NEEDED

Not all couples or families are able to resolve their conflicts or communicate constructively by themselves. Some will need the assistance of a third party, namely a marriage and family therapist. But when is counseling really necessary?

Marriage counseling is usually needed when negative exchange outweighs positive exchange. In this situation, communication is often incessantly hostile. We know that conflict is inevitable in a marriage. But when the interaction is primarily conflictual with very little positive interaction occurring, marital therapy may be necessary to help the couple break out of the negative-exchange cycle and begin to build a repertoire of more positive interactions.

For the most part, routine differences or decisions do not warrant the help of a professional counselor. When a couple, however, has attempted repeatedly to resolve the same problem to no avail, and recurrent tensions or frustrations keep emerging, a third party may be needed. A conflict that has been unresolved for a long time may harden into a "rigid confrontation"—in which neither partner feels able or willing to retreat from his or her inflexible position (Lasswell and Lobsenz, 1976).

Perhaps the couple have not explored various creative alternatives, and they each persist with their own solutions. For example, a wife may insist that the only way to improve the marriage is for her workaholic husband to work less. Her husband insists that the marriage will improve if she would quit nagging him. A cycle of negative exchange continues as the wife interprets the husband's workaholism as rejection and nags him about it, and he tries to avoid the nagging by spending more time at work, further distancing himself from her. Marriage therapists are trained to open channels of communication and help couples generate alternative solutions to their problems.

Another cue that professional help is needed is when at least one of the partners has an individual problem inhibiting the couple from developing a close relationship. Such problems include severe depression, feelings of low self-esteem and insecurity, and alcoholism or other drug addiction. The model of intimacy development presented in Chapter 2 depicts several personality traits basic to the development of intimacy. When there are problems in these areas, individual counseling may be needed along with marital therapy.

Finally, in marriages with an extreme imbalance of power, the powerless partner is often dissatisfied with the situation and may need the help of a professional in order to help restore or create a more equal balance of power. Needless to say, it is often the controlling, more powerful partner who will be threatened by counseling. He or she will be the one who stands to lose some power in the marriage. If that person, however, can be convinced that there is the likelihood of a more emotionally close relationship developing if the power is more equal, he or she may opt for less power and a more intimate marriage. A spouse unable to give up some control sometimes ends up with no marriage.

Are some marriages beyond repair? In-

BOX 8.4

ENRICHING MARRIAGES: A CLOSE ENCOUNTER
OF A NEW KIND

Over the past couple of decades numerous marriage-improvement programs have sprung up. Their basic purpose is enriching marriages. Since they serve a preventative function as opposed to a remedial or therapeutic one, couples with serious marital problems are either screened out or discouraged from attending. Many of these programs are sponsored by religious groups and community-service agencies. There are several common elements in each of the orientations such as a group setting, an emphasis on education, and experiential learning. They differ, however, in such areas as the structure of the approach, the training of the leaders, and the theoretical basis. Several approaches teach specific intimacy-related skills such as mutual self-disclosure, empathic responding, and conflict resolution. A few of the most popular programs are described below.

MARRIAGE-IMPROVEMENT PROGRAMS

Association of Couples for Marriage Enrichment (ACME). This marriage enrichment program is organized for those people whose marriages are fairly good and who wish to make them even more satisfying. The meetings focus on assisting couples in enhancing communication skills, on broadening and deepening their emotional and sexual lives, and on reinforcing and fostering existing marital strengths. One of the goals of this program is to develop and maintain an effective support system for couples. David and Vera Mace started the Association of Couples for Marriage Enrichment (ACME) in 1961 with weekend retreats for Quakers.

ACME still offers weekend retreats as preventative programs. A few couples serve as facilitators rather than as leaders of the group discussions. The weekend tends to have no structured agenda but deals with topics that the participants bring up. Such weekends are viewed as one-shot experiences, meant only to serve as the beginning of improvement in a couple's relationship. In addition, ACME offers ongoing growth groups and couples' communication courses. Topics discussed in these meetings may include intimacy, communication, friendships, and gender roles.

Marriage Encounter. One of the most popular programs is Marriage Encounter. It was originated by the Roman Catholic Church in Spain and spread to the United States. It is designed usually for weekend retreats under the auspices of the Roman Catholic Church or other religious organizations. More than a million couples have participated in encounter weekends, with the number increasing at the rate of perhaps 100,000 a year.

Most Marriage Encounter weekends follow a similar format. Couples numbering from 10 to 25 meet together from Friday night to Sunday afternoon at some suitable retreat. Two or three previously experienced couples and a priest or a clergyman lead the group in an exploration of the meaning of their lives and of their marriages. Following brief comments by the leaders, the husband and wife are taught the tool of "dialogue," which encourages open communication on sensitive marital issues. The procedure involves each partner writing individual responses and reflections into a notebook, touching on their feelings about numerous topics. Then time is provided for couples to meet alone to hold a private dialogue about what they have written in an effort to understand each other more deeply.

In contrast to ACME, most of the dialogue in Marriage Encounter occurs between the partners, and there is very little group interaction. Couples are urged to join various follow-up support programs after the weekend is over. They are also encouraged to commit themselves to daily practice of ten and ten: ten minutes of writing and ten minutes of dialogue.

Relationship Enhancement (RE). The Relationship Enhancement (RE) program teaches couples communication skills; the goal is for the individuals to develop a greater capacity to understand themselves and each other. Developed by Bernard Guerney (1977), the program uses small groups, with at least three couples per group and two co-leaders. The group participants learn self-disclosure and empathic listening skills. Leaders demonstrate and model the skills for the couples. Homework assignments are given, and positive reinforcements are administered by the leaders. RE leaders go through at least 80 hours of training, and many have a professional background in the social sciences. While these groups meet for various lengths of time, the programs typically last about ten weeks.

A great deal of research has been conducted by Guerney and his students to establish a scientific basis for this model of marital improvement. Relationship Enhancement couples have demonstrated significant positive changes in communication skills, marital adjustment, empathic ability, and mutual trust.

Couples Communication Program (CCP). The training approach of this program teaches skills in awareness, disclosure, and problem solving. A five-minute videotape of the couple's interaction process assesses their communication patterns. Major skills emphasized include "awareness" (understanding rules of interaction) and particular "communication patterns" (changing past rules and interaction styles). The couple is taught a new mode of communication, which is accepting, open, responsive, understanding, caring, and cooperative (Miller, Nunnally, and Wackman, 1976). This is probably the most thoroughly researched program in communication training. Many studies offer support for this program to improve communication skills.

DO THESE PROGRAMS HELP TO INCREASE INTIMACY?

Strengths.

1. It appears that these types of programs can help to prevent a marriage from becoming a boring, empty shell. They can breathe new life into a relationship that isn't torn by great conflict but simply needs more closeness and intimacy.
2. Some of these programs teach interpersonal behaviors to individuals. Couples often have difficulty achieving emotional closeness because one or both partners simply lack the skills to empathize, to listen, or to resolve conflicts. The educational focus of these programs helps teach these skills.
3. The formats of the programs encourage men to express feelings more freely. Thus, they discourage traditional gender stereotypes that promote the "strong, silent" image for males.

(Continued)

4. Studies testing the outcomes of these programs testify to some immediate positive effects on communication behavior and satisfaction with the relationship.

Weaknesses.

1. The long-term effects of these programs have not been substantiated. A single weekend encounter group might lead to a "marital high" that cannot possibly be maintained when the couple returns to everyday life.
2. The group approach may discourage some individuals, especially the men, from attending or participating owing to their fear of self-disclosure in front of a group. Since the privacy of the couple is an important component of intimacy, it is questionable how much self-disclosure can be encouraged in a group setting. Some of the programs can adapt their procedures to working with individual dyads.
3. Most of these programs provide a simplistic approach to improving marriages by focusing on only one or two particular skill(s). William Doherty and Brian Walker (1982) discovered a number of marriage encounter casualties in their research because the couples were taught to self-disclose with no attention to other skills, such as problem solving. More self-disclosure and the expression of feelings actually led to more conflict, which they were not able to resolve. More careful screening of couples and the teaching of more than one skill could help prevent some of these casualties.
4. The same approach is used for everyone in these programs, regardless of different types of marriages, particular problems, skill deficits, or personalities involved.

---

deed there are some relationships that probably cannot be helped by a marriage counselor. Unfortunately, once a marriage has reached the stage where at least one partner is emotionally divorced, it cannot be easily saved—if indeed it can be saved at all. John Gottman (1982), who has conducted extensive research on marital interaction, states, "Americans have an idea that anything can be fixed. When it comes to relationships however, they may not always be so easily 'fixed.' The patterns of interaction are very repetitive, very stereotyped in unhappy relationships. Once anger has turned to bitterness, it's very hard to change it" (p. 43). Marriage therapists are not magicians or miracle workers. And unfortunately many couples wait too long before they seek help.

What professionals are the best marriage counselors? Marriage counseling may be offered by different types of professionals; they may be psychologists, psychiatrists, sociologists, social workers, and clergy. But not all these professionals are necessarily trained in marital therapy. The best approach to finding a marriage counselor is to find a professional who is licensed by the American Association for Marriage and Family Therapy. Some states, also, regulate the use of the title "marriage counselor," but many do not. In the latter states anybody can assume the title and the practice—and the consumer must beware.

Unfortunately, many professionals practicing marriage therapy do not have any specialized education in this type of counseling. For example, psychologists make up the majority of marriage counselors, but a survey of approved Ph.D. programs in clinical psychology revealed that only 7 percent offered a course in marital therapy (Prochaska and Prochaska, 1978). A psychiatrist may not be the best choice either. Psychiatrists also do not typically receive specific training in dealing with couples who are in therapy together. The end result is that many of these professionals meet with the partners individually, trying to enhance individual functioning (or "growth") at the expense of the relationship. *Conjoint marital therapy,* in which the counselor sees the husband and wife together, has several advantages.

> *To begin with, it may be the first thing the couple have done together for a long time. Spouses unable to talk to each other out of fear or anger can vent their feelings under the emotional protection of a counselor's presence. Nor do they have to worry that one partner is privately telling lies or secrets about the other, or that the counselor is taking sides. Everything that's said is out in the open. Another advantage is that the counselor can see the couple interacting, which is more useful than merely hearing a possibly distorted version of something that has happened between them. He or she can correct their misunderstandings—the "my wife never" and "my husband always" charges—on the spot. The therapist can observe the progress they are making and call it to their attention. (Lasswell and Lobsenz, 1976, p. 271)*

In addition, when problems involve several family members, counseling with the entire family together may be necessary. Sometimes a couple can receive enough help from a marriage-enrichment type program and do not need marital therapy (see Box 8.4).

CHAPTER REVIEW

1. In intimate relationships what is said—and how it is said—may be more important than the sheer amount of communication. Communication in close relationships differs from that in other relationships in respect to the depth of self-disclosure, the equal balance of power, the degree of exclusivity, the consensus of values, and the expected length of the relationship.

2. Communication occurs when a sender encodes a message, sends it—via one or more channels—and then it is decoded by the receiver. Many opportunities, however, exist within communication processes for misunderstandings to occur.

3. It's important in marriage that communication not only be effective, that is, clearly understood, but it should also promote a feeling of closeness and well-being. Destructive types of communication such as put-downs, lecturing, and sarcasm are barriers to intimacy. While others—"turning the other cheek," leveling, tactfulness, and touching to name a few—help to build intimacy.

4. At least some conflict is inevitable in any close relationship. But whether it has a devastating impact on the dyad or whether it helps to promote closeness depends upon how the partners go about resolving conflicts. If the partners can collaborate and compromise rather than compete with each other, a more satisfactory resolution is likely to occur. If approaches to conflict resolution involve listening to each other's wants and feelings—as well as the use of constructive communication—the process can actually bring the partners closer together.

Most sexual activity takes place in marriages. But marital sexual pleasure has not always been an accepted goal. Husbands and wives have not always been normatively free to seek maximum satisfaction from their sexual activities. Western societies in particular have tended to restrict sexual enjoyment among married couples. Early Christianity viewed sex as an evil—in fact, the more it was enjoyed the more sinful it was considered to be. "The same church that had made marriage a holy act thus characterized the essential sexual part of it as an unholy . . . lapse from purity" (Hunt, 1974, p. 176).

Through the centuries there have been periods of greater or lesser tolerance for sexuality. The latter part of the nineteenth century stands out as one of the most restrictive times of all. There developed an extremely negative view of marital passion. While men were allowed to "make use" of their wives, women were silent, passive, unresponding, and usually unseen receptacles; "quick sex" and sex in the dark were the rule. The woman did her "conjugal duty," and the man "took his pleasure." Thus, for the vast majority of lower-class and middle-class wives, intercourse was "only tolerable at best, and a substantial majority regarded it as revolting, messy, vulgar, animalistic, shameful and degrading" (Hunt, 1974, p. 177).

Beginning after World War I, the acceptance of sexual enjoyment—even by women—was under way. Marital intercourse very slowly came to be viewed "as a positive and healthy activity rather than a shameful . . . indulgence" (Hunt, 1974, p. 177). The most dramatic sexual revelation, however, came at midcentury with the research of Alfred Kinsey. The results of his studies provided evidence that sexual liberation was indeed under way; for example, the percentage of women achieving orgasm through intercourse was climbing among younger married women in comparison to older married women.

> At almost every age, in almost every stage of marriage and in nearly every detail—the degree of nudity during intercourse, the kinds of foreplay used, the use of positional variation—the differences between the older and the younger generation, though not large, were consistently in the direction of greater freedom, pleasure and mutuality. The beginnings of sexual egalitarianism and the legitimation of pleasure were changing marital sex as nothing else had in nearly two millennia. (Hunt, 1974, p. 178)

CHANGES SINCE MIDCENTURY

Has the quality, quantity, and variety of sexual activity in marriage changed much since midcentury, when Kinsey carried out his classic studies? Are there remnants of the conservative Victorian tradition still reflected in marital sex? By and large it appears that since Kinsey's time the liberating forces have become even more powerful. Morton Hunt found in his 1970s studies that modern marriages involved higher frequencies of sexual intercourse than at midcentury, particularly among younger individuals (see Table 9.1).

For every age category the median frequency of intercourse per week had increased substantially. Probably, says Hunt, marital intercourse is now more likely "to represent the desires of both partners rather than of the husband alone" (1974, p. 191), as was typical in the past. Indeed Hunt found that only about one in ten of the married females "reported finding marital sex either neutral or unpleasant . . . and . . . even within this small minority, only a quarter said they would prefer less frequent intercourse with

TABLE 9.1

COMBINED MALE AND FEMALE MEDIAN FREQUENCIES OF SEXUAL INTERCOURSE PER WEEK IN KINSEY'S AND HUNT'S RESEARCH

KINSEY'S RESEARCH		HUNT'S RESEARCH	
Age	Median	Age	Median
16–25	2.45	18–24	3.25
26–35	1.95	25–34	2.55
36–45	1.40	35–44	2.00
46–55	.85	45–54	1.00
56–60	.50	55 and over	1.00

SOURCE: *Hunt, p. 191.*

the spouse'' (p. 192). Certainly the women in Hunt's sample appear to have many fewer inhibitions and to find marital intercourse more rewarding than in Kinsey's days.

Hunt also found that married couples were spending much more time in what is commonly referred to as ''foreplay'' in comparison to Kinsey's couples. Particularly there was a substantial increase among people of lower educational levels, among whom previously foreplay had been minimal. The younger marrieds carried out the most extended foreplay of all the couples.

But, writes Hunt, ''The most dramatic changes are those that have occurred in the formerly all-but-unmentionable oral-genital acts (which, incidently, are still classified as punishable 'crimes against nature' in the statutes of most of our states)'' (1974, p. 197). As Table 9.2 shows, both fellatio and cunnilingus (oral-genital sex) have become rather common sexual practices. Among younger college-educated people in Hunt's study, more than 80 percent of the males and fe-

males under 35 practiced oral sex. Once more, among males and females under 25, of all educational levels, more than 90 percent practiced both fellatio and cunnilingus.

Hunt also found modern marrieds using a greater variety of positions for sexual intercourse than Kinsey found at midcentury. ''The female-above position is now used, at least occasionally, by nearly three quarters of all married couples, as compared with about a third of all married couples in Kinsey's time'' (1974, p. 202). Twice as many used the on-the-side position as in the past. The rear-entry vaginal position was used by only about 10 percent in Kinsey's sample, but by 40 percent in Hunt's. Young people in the 1970s seemed to feel that almost any imaginable position was acceptable as long as both partners found it exciting. Nearly 25 percent of the couples under age 25 at least experimented with anal intercourse, despite sanitary hazards. Most said, however, that this position was used rarely.

Kinsey had estimated that about three-

TABLE 9.2

ORAL-GENITAL SEXUAL ACTIVITY AMONG MARRIED COUPLES

Educational level completed	PERCENT OF MARRIAGES IN WHICH FELLATIO WAS USED		PERCENT OF MARRIAGES IN WHICH CUNNILINGUS WAS USED	
	Kinsey's research	Hunt's research	Kinsey's research	Hunt's research
High school males	15	54	15	56
High school females	46	52	50	58
College males	43	61	45	66
College females	52	72	58	72

SOURCE: *Hunt, 1974, p. 198.*

quarters of all males reached orgasm within two minutes or less after the beginning of intercourse. Hunt found, in contrast, that the goal of married couples in the 1970s was to prolong the act for the sake of both partners. Hunt's figures, based on both married males and females, were around ten minutes of intercourse before ejaculation, five times longer than Kinsey's estimates. Young couples spent an even longer time at coitus, despite the popular view that the young "highly charged" male has trouble controlling himself (Hunt, 1974).

Modern married women were also more likely to be orgasmic in the 1970s than at midcentury. Says Hunt, "According to our survey data, there is no doubt that today more wives are having orgasm in nearly all of their marital intercourse, and fewer are having it rarely or never, than was true in Kinsey's time" (1974, p. 207). Hunt found that half of the wives were experiencing or-

gasms even in the first year of marriage. "Somewhat surprisingly, the degree of religious devoutness had little or no relation to orgasm regularity" (p. 211). Hunt believes the increase in the rate of female orgasm was due to "experience, continuing education, and the growth of intimacy and trust" (p. 213).

Intimacy and Marital Sex

Hunt asked his respondents how pleasurable their sexual relationship had been in the past year. He also asked each of them how "close" a couple they were in their marriage—a subjective measure of intimacy. Hunt found sexual pleasure and emotional intimacy to be strongly linked. (See Table 9.3.) Specifically he found the following:

A large majority of married men and married women for whom marital sex had been

TABLE 9.3

PERCENTAGE EXPERIENCING SEXUAL PLEASURE BY DEGREE OF MARITAL CLOSENESS

Married males	CLOSENESS IN MARITAL RELATIONSHIP		
Marital sex life in past year	Very close	Fairly close	Not too close or very distant
Very pleasurable	79	45	12
Mostly pleasurable	20	50	47
Neither pleasurable nor nonpleasurable	1	2	17
Mostly or very nonpleasurable	—	3	24
	100%	100%	100%

Married females	CLOSENESS IN MARITAL RELATIONSHIP		
Marital sex life in past year	Very close	Fairly close	Not too close or very distant
Very pleasurable	70	30	10
Mostly pleasurable	26	58	28
Neither pleasurable nor nonpleasurable	1	8	45
Mostly or very nonpleasurable	3	4	17
	100%	100%	100%

SOURCE: *Hunt, 1974, p. 231*

very pleasurable in the past year rated their marriages as very close.

Of those men and women for whom marital sex in the past year had been either lacking in pleasure or actually displeasing, virtually none rated their marriages as being very close and only a few as being fairly close. (Hunt, 1974, p. 230)

Hunt thinks that there is little doubt about the existence of a cause-and-effect relationship between sexual pleasure and emo-tional closeness in marriage. He sees the two phenomena as reciprocal—each being both cause and effect of the other. Thus, an emotionally close marriage is more likely to involve a higher quality of marital sex than a distant one (1974). Even for the wife to be orgasmic, the *Redbook* survey found that "Apparently some women need the security and intimacy of marriage to relax sufficiently to enjoy sex fully" (Tavris and Sadd, 1977, p. 110). But the strongest specific indicator of both marital and sexual satisfaction among the women in the *Redbook* sample was their ability to express their own sexual feelings to their husbands.

> *The more they talk, the better they rate their sex lives, their marriages, and their overall happiness. In fact, communicating about their sexual feelings is just as important as acting on them. The women who never express their sexual feelings, and even those who do so only occasionally, are not the ones for whom everything is so perfect they have nothing to say. They seem to be the women who are suffering in silence.* (Tavris and Sadd, 1977, p. 151)

Marital Sex in the 1980s

What is the nature of sexual activity among married couples in the 1980s? Philip Blum-stein and Pepper Schwartz (1983) found that heterosexual married women want extensive nongenital touching and not just a focus on intercourse. They see snuggling and holding as part of the total sexual experience. "While males want fondling to conclude with intercourse, many women would be just as happy to continue touching and holding for more extensive periods—sometimes never escalating to genital sexuality" (1983, p. 198). Women are often misunderstood when they initiate touching and cuddling just for the sake of being close. The husband tends to misperceive that she wants sexual intercourse (Blumstein and Schwartz, 1983). (See Box 9.2.)

Husbands in the 1980s still hold the balance of power in the bedroom; they "have traditionally been the sexual aggressors and

BOX 9.1

FIFTEEN WAYS TO MAKE SEX GOOD (AND KEEP IT THAT WAY)

1. Make time for sex.
2. Communicate about sex to your partner.
3. Give positive feedback.
4. Never fake orgasms.
5. Tune in to your own sexuality.
6. Discuss ahead of time the possibility of sexual refusals and how you will handle them.
7. Create privacy.
8. Guard against falling into rigid or boring routines.
9. Make use of fantasies and other aids to enhance interest and excitement.
10. Take responsibility for your own pleasure.
11. Learn that you turn yourself off.
12. Don't expect sex to be great all the time.
13. Don't turn sex into hard work.
14. Remember that the foundation of good sex in a committed relationship is trust in and respect for your partner.
15. Don't let a problem go on too long before attending to it.

SOURCE: *Adapted from Botwin, 1985.*

Some couples are comfortable hugging and kissing in the presence of their children—others are not.

women have traditionally waited for men to approach them'' (Blumstein and Schwartz, 1983, p. 206). While it might be expected that men and women are moving away from narrow definitions of what each ''must always do,'' the evidence suggests that at least some of the old ideas are still alive. Thus even in the 1980s the initiation of sexual activity is much more likely to be the husband's right and responsibility. ''To this day, men take this prescription very seriously. And they also feel guilty when they do not fulfill their duty to

initiate sex'' (Blumstein and Schwartz, 1983, pp. 209–210).

Many wives are aware of their husbands' insecurities regarding initiating sex. They also know that at times they must reinforce their husband's need to be in control. In addition, ''men and women who hold traditional values about sex are more likely to reject any positions that require the woman to be more physically active or more in control than the man'' (Blumstein and Schwartz, 1983, p. 228). Thus in relationships where women

BOX 9.2

TOUCHING AS AN END IN ITSELF

Ann Landers conducted a survey among women in 1985, asking, "Would you be content to be held close and treated tenderly, and forget about 'the act'?" Readers were asked to write in with a simple yes or no response, together with an indication of whether the woman was over or under age 40. The response was intense and voluminous; many women sent in four- and five-page letters. Landers said, "I guess I touched a hot button."

Landers was surprised by the outcome of the more than 90,000 responses. A very large number of women answered yes—64,000, or 72 percent—and 40 percent of these were women under 40. "I'd expect that some women 50 to 70 had had enough sex," observed Landers. "But in this so-called enlightened age, with liberated womanhood—that's pretty startling" (*Time*, January 28, 1985).

What does Landers say about this dramatic emphasis on touching not leading to intercourse? The survey "means that a tremendous number of women out there are not enjoying sex. . . . [many] are so dissatisfied with their sex lives that they [would] just as soon not be bothered with it" (*Newsweek*, January 28, 1985).

This survey raises valid questions about intimate and sexual relationships in America today, even with its methodological limitations. In their work, William Masters and Virginia Johnson have found that many people have problems with touching; the origin of this problem stems from childhood and continues into adult relationships. "The lesson is taught early in life and remains deeply ingrained. 'Don't touch!' is a childhood litany" (1975, p. 245).

"In time some young men and women gradually find at least partial answers to their questions [about sex and touching]. But even for the more fortunate among them success is usually flawed by their continuing inability to grasp the true function of the act of touching. They still think of it exclusively as a means to an end: touching for the purpose of having intercourse" (Masters and Johnson, 1975, p. 251).

"Once a sexual relationship has been established, most young couples use touch as little more than a wordless way to communicate a willingness, a wish, or a demand to make love. It is functional; beyond that, it seems of limited value and is regarded, especially by men, as a waste of time and effort, an unnecessary postponement of intercourse" (Masters and Johnson, 1975, p. 251).

For other couples, however, who also consider touching to be just a means to the same end, it happens to be a means they enjoy almost as much as the end itself. "They have advanced past the adolescent notion of touch-as-trigger to the more sophisticated notion of touching-as-technique. . . . Thus, in the name of sexual liberation, men and women are taught not how to touch another human being but how to manipulate another body" (Masters and Johnson, 1975, p. 252).

"*Touch is an end in itself.* . . . It bridges the physical separateness from which no human being is spared, literally establishing a sense of solidarity between two individuals. . . . In reaching out spontaneously to communicate with touch as well as with words, a husband and wife reaffirm their trust in each other and renew their commitment. They draw on this emotional reservoir when one turns to the other with physical desire. Because their touching has a continuity, because it is part of an intimate dialogue that does not begin and end in bed, they feel secure. . . . Where no such security exists, two individuals in a sexual encounter may touch physically but remain out of touch emotionally" (Masters and Johnson, 1975, pp. 253–254).

SOURCES: Time, *January 28, 1985;* Newsweek, *January 28, 1985; Masters and Johnson, 1975.*

have less power the couple's position of intercourse is more likely to be the missionary position (the man on top, the woman on her back). But Blumstein and Schwartz indicate that for many couples,

The woman sometimes assumes the "male" position. This happens more in couples where the man does not completely dominate the relationship and where the partners share power more equally. In these couples, the man does not always feel compelled to be in control, and his partner feels freer to try another position if she wants to. (1983, p. 229)

Most men in Blumstein's and Schwartz's study expected that their wives should find the males' genitals appealing and attractive. The majority want their spouses to perform fellatio (oral sex) on them, and if the wives resist or are squeamish, the men are often displeased. "While many women may enjoy fellatio, others see it as a form of submissiveness, even degradation" (1983, pp. 233–234). A woman, however, may be more willing to perform fellatio when it is not demanded. Other wives in Blumstein's and Schwartz's study were not at all reserved about oral sex. These women think of oral sex in egalitarian terms and do not connect

it with any feelings of dominance or submission. A few women said that "They enjoy it because their partners enjoy it so much, thereby making them feel sexually powerful. They believe that men expect sexual intercourse but appreciate oral sex" (p. 236).

Marital Sex and Social Class

As mentioned previously, there tends to be a greater separation of roles in lower-class marriages than among middle- or upper-class couples. Often this rigid pattern influences the quality of sexuality. As part of his attempt to maintain a dominant position in the marriage, the lower-class husband is more likely than the middle-class husband to view sexual activity as primarily for his enjoyment and not for hers. The attitude found by sociologist Lee Rainwater (1971) was that "Sex is a man's pleasure and a woman's duty." He found that in situations of rigid roles, 80 percent of the white husbands and 75 percent of the black husbands enjoyed sex more than their wives (Rainwater, 1965). (See Table 9.4.)

The differences in marital sex among the social classes can also be partly explained by the attitudes of the couples regarding the purpose of sex. Both the husband and wife in

TABLE 9.4

DEGREE OF ROLE SEGREGATION AND COMPARATIVE ENJOYMENT OF SEXUAL RELATIONS AMONG LOWER-CLASS HUSBANDS AND WIVES

	Husband enjoys more	Equal enjoyment or wife enjoys more
Whites		
Intermediate segregation	38%	62%
Highly segregated	80%	20%
Blacks		
Intermediate segregation	33%	67%
Highly segregated	75%	25%

SOURCE: *Rainwater, Lee, 1965, p. 69.*

highly segregated-role marriages view marital sex as primarily physical and as a form of relief of tension. In those marriages with less role segregation both the husband and wife are more likely to view sex as a means for expressing and increasing emotional closeness. (See Table 9.5.) Sexual relations with the purpose of achieving emotional closeness are likely to involve more consideration of the partner's sexual pleasure, as well as one's own.

In terms of actual sexual behavior, lower-class males use less varied sexual techniques and less foreplay than men in higher classes (DeLora, Warren, and Ellison, 1981). With this finding—coupled with the deemphasis of the wife's enjoyment of sexual activity—it is not surprising to find that lower-class women are less likely to experience orgasm in marital sex than women in the middle and upper classes (Rainwater, 1965).

More recently, studies have revealed some changes occurring among lower-class couples, in both sexes. Lillian Rubin (1976) found that many working-class husbands desire some specific sexual activities but that their wives are reluctant to engage in certain practices. For example, many men pressure their wives to perform oral sex on them. But working-class husbands are beginning to express a concern that their wives experience orgasm. It appears, however, that this concern is more a matter of her orgasm reflecting his ability to be a "good lover." This accomplishment appears to be more of a boost to the man's own ego than a genuine interest in the wife's sexual enjoyment.

It appears that in the lower class, on the one hand, sexuality may be the one area where a man can allow himself the expression of deep feelings, the one place where he can experience the depth of his emotional side. His wife, on the other hand, is closely connected with her feeling side in all areas, and she keeps asking for something she can understand and that she is comfortable with—a demonstration of his feelings in non-sexual ways. Lillian Rubin suggests that in

TABLE 9.5

ATTITUDES TOWARD THE FUNCTION OF MARITAL SEXUAL RELATIONS, BY SOCIAL CLASS

FUNCTION	MIDDLE CLASS	LOWER CLASS	
		Intermediate role segregation	High role segregation
Husbands			
Emotional closeness and exchange	75%	52%	16%
Psychophysiological pleasure and relief only	25%	48%	84%
Wives			
Emotional closeness and exchange	89%	73%	32%
Psychophysiological pleasure and relief only	11%	27%	68%

SOURCE: *Rainwater, 1969, p. 135.*

the lower class a man's "ever-present sexual readiness is not simply an expression of urgent sexual needs but also a complex compensatory response to a socialization process that *constricts the development of the emotional side of his personality in all but sexual expression*" (1976, pp. 147–148).

Rubin concludes that marital sex among working-class couples is moving toward greater similarity to that of middle-class and upper-class couples. Certain situational factors, however, continue to contribute to the lesser degree of sexual enjoyment among lower-class couples. Larger families and longer working hours can hinder a couple's attempt to achieve a satisfying sexual relationship. Despite these obstacles, it appears that some lower-class couples are changing to more permissive attitudes about sex in marriage.

SEXUAL DIFFICULTIES AND SEX THERAPY

Sexologists William Masters and Virginia Johnson have estimated that 50 percent of all married couples have sexual dysfunctions at some time in their marriages. These result from a variety of specific sexual problems that individuals can experience. Males may experience problems with achieving or maintaining erections, they may ejaculate too quickly, or they may have difficulty ejaculating at all. Females may have difficulties becoming orgasmic, or they may be nonorgasmic in particular situations or in particular ways. Women may also sometimes suffer from vaginismus—the involuntary tightening of the muscles surrounding the entrance to the vagina—or from painful intercourse. Both sexes may experience low sexual desire.

In the treatment of sexual problems the goal is to create an atmosphere for the couple in which the normal processes of desire, arousal, and orgasm can occur unhindered by anxiety. It is assumed that sex is a natural function and that if the process isn't working smoothly there must be some obstacle. It is the sex therapist's job to help eliminate any blocks to sexual responsiveness. "There are many different kinds of blocks, and uncovering precisely which ones are operating in any particular situation often calls for sophisticated detective work on the part of the therapists and their clients" (Tiefer, 1979, p. 97). The therapist attempts to explain and demonstrate, through clients' sexual behaviors, how anxiety operates to diminish sexual response. "Usually the therapist will insist that couples avoid intercourse altogether for several weeks in order to remove the demanding expectations from the situation and allow for nonanxious habits to develop" (Tiefer, 1979, p. 102).

It is the sex therapists' assumption that each person is responsible for his or her own sexual satisfaction. In contrast, a considerable number of people in the general population hold to the view that it is their partner who provides them with sexual enjoyment. For example, men particularly tend to take on the responsibility for "giving" an orgasm to their spouses (Tiefer, 1979).

One objective of sexual therapy is to have the individual or couple experience one successful sexual act "as a result of improved technique, understanding, trust and communication. Once the goal (firm erection, presence of pleasure, orgasm) is attained, the individual or couple is encouraged to identify

the factors that contributed to the success, and incorporate them into future lovemaking" (Tiefer, 1979, p. 100).

Another objective of therapy is to provide accurate knowledge and to correct sexual misinformation. Even in this day and age many problems result from the lack of understanding of the sexual response cycle and from unique individual differences. Education is probably one of the most important factors involved in alleviating sexual problems. Examples of such information include the role of the clitoris in female sexual arousal, the insignificance of penis size in sexual intercourse, and correct facts about the aging process and its impact on male and female sexuality (Tiefer, 1979).

It is common for people to have considerable concern over what is considered "normal." This applies to the frequency of intercourse or masturbation, positions of intercourse, types of fantasies, and male and female sexual differences. Typically in marital sex, the guilt and fear that are connected with particular sexual practices cause more harm than the practices themselves. Just educating people about the commonness of certain sexual activities, and any necessary precautions that need to be taken, usually has a positive impact (Tiefer, 1979).

One of the key functions of the sex therapist is to give people permission to experiment with various aspects of their sexuality. Many activities that parents had previously tried to discourage (talking about sex, sexual fantasizing, masturbating) are reintroduced during sexual therapy with the therapist communicating a different message. Sometimes increased comfort with experimentation allows "a person to cure him or herself in a short period of time" (Tiefer, 1979, p. 101). Permission is also given for people to focus on themselves, on their own sexual self-interests.

Most sex therapists give couples "homework" assignments, which are carried out between the meetings with the therapist. Typically one of the first assignments involves having each partner take turns caressing the body of the other, omitting the genitals. The purpose of this exercise is to diminish the pressure of sexual performance and therefore to diminish anxiety. The couple is encouraged to communicate with each other about what they like or do not like about the various caresses and to what extent, if any, the activity is arousing. The caresses give each person a chance to identify what parts of the body are most pleasurable and sensitive, both to himself or herself and to the partner.

Sometimes couples do not complete assignments. The discussion and analysis of these situations with the therapist will usually reveal how one or both partners avoid sexual communication, how they avoid giving or receiving pleasure, and how they produce sexual anxiety in themselves and each other. These so-called failure sessions are actually very illuminating to the therapist, since they reveal how the couples maintain their sexual difficulties. Thus "resistances" in complying to various assignments provide active insight for discussion into the sexual problems of the couple (Tiefer, 1979).

Quick Ejaculation

Probably the most common male sexual difficulty is premature, rapid, or quick ejaculation. It is found more often among younger

In sex therapy, homework assignments involving body caresses diminish the pressure of sexual performance anxiety.

males but can exist in men of all ages—some suffer from it all their lives. This condition has been defined in a variety of ways. Typically the time between the insertion of the penis in the vagina and ejaculation is the crucial factor. Some writers define this in "minutes" or even in the number of "thrusts." Masters and Johnson (1970), however, indicate that quick ejaculation exists when the husband reaches orgasm more than 50 percent of the time before the wife. The problem with this definition is that the time it takes for a woman to reach orgasm is highly variable; in fact, she may not be orgasmic at all through intercourse.

Sex therapist Helen Singer Kaplan (1974) sees the crucial aspect of quick ejaculation as *"the absence of voluntary control* over the ejaculatory reflex . . . whether it occurs before the female reaches orgasm or not. . . . Conversely, ejaculatory control may be said to be established when the man can tolerate the high levels of excitement which characterize the plateau stage of the sexual response cycle without ejaculating reflexly" (pp. 290–291). This view of voluntary control is criticized by sex therapist Joseph LoPiccolo. He sees orgasm as a semivoluntary control response similar to the sneeze. The average number of minutes in intercourse before ejaculation is 4 to 7 (LoPiccolo, 1986).

Both the husband and wife are negatively affected by quick ejaculation. Even though the husband may help the wife achieve orgasm by stimulating her clitorally, "The fact remains that premature ejaculations curtail the wife's sensuous enjoyment, and certainly the husband's pleasure is heightened and intensified if he can prolong the periods of intense excitement prior to orgasm" (Kaplan, 1974, p. 292).

Despite its potential ill effects, reactions to quick ejaculation vary. "Some premature ejaculators seem unaware of the fact that the condition hampers their potential sexual pleasure, and may consider their rapid functioning normal and even desirable" (Kaplan, 1974, p. 292). Kinsey himself viewed quick ejaculation positively; he "considered speed in biological function a sign of excellence" (Kaplan, 1974, p. 292).

But there are many men who are very unhappy and distressed over what they see as a serious sexual problem; significant numbers are "desperate" to do something about their situation. They try all sorts of things, such as thinking about something else, possibly about someone they dislike immensely; inflicting pain on themselves, perhaps by biting their lips; buying some drugstore anesthetic ointments to deaden the penis; wearing two condoms to decrease sensations; drinking alcohol; taking prescription drugs for relaxation; or masturbating to orgasm just prior to attempted intercourse. Not surprisingly, says Kaplan, "None of these methods has proven effective in fostering ejaculatory control. . . . they do not improve control once intense erotic arousal is achieved" (1974, p. 296).

Men sometimes become so concerned about their quick ejaculation that they are ready to adopt any "common-sense" suggestion. They may feel sexually inadequate and guilty because they can't give their partner more pleasure. At times they withdraw and try to avoid sexual contact all together. Other times, because of their extreme anxiety, they bring about additional problems, such as erection difficulties. An angry and frustrated wife may add to the man's sense of urgency and despair (Kaplan, 1974).

Erection Difficulties

One of the great fears of men is that they will no longer be able to achieve an erection. Difficulty with erections, or impotence as it is widely referred to, is one of the most humiliating and devastating of sexual conditions. There are two forms of erection difficulties—*primary* and *secondary impotence.* Primary erection difficulties relate to men who have never had successful sexual intercourse, even though they may have good erections while masturbating or while sleeping. Secondary erection difficulties, which are much more common, relate to people who have functioned well in the past but are not able to at present. The possibilities for successful treatment are much better for secondary erection problems than for the primary type.

The cause of erection problems may be either physical or psychological or some degree of both factors. What happens is that the vascular reflex mechanism fails to pump sufficient blood into the penis to render it firm and erect (Kaplan, 1974). A man can *feel* aroused and sexually excited, but the penis may not become erect. Some men can't achieve erections even in foreplay; others can obtain erections with manual manipulation or oral sex but lose their erections quickly upon insertion into the vagina. Others still can have erections alone by themselves, such as in masturbation, but cannot achieve even a partial erection with any partner. Or a person may be impotent with his wife but not

Sexual difficulties can produce much frustration and distress for couples.

with his mistress, or vice versa. Every individual suffering from erection difficulties should have a complete physical examination and laboratory tests before starting sex therapy (Kaplan, 1974).

> *Impotence may be due to a wide variety of physical factors. Among the most prevalent are stress and fatigue, early undiagnosed diabetes, low androgen level, non-specific debilitating illness, hepatic problems, and the use and abuse of narcotics, alcohol, estrogenic and parasympatholytic medication. (Kaplan, 1974, p. 258)*

But erection difficulties are most often the result of psychological factors, the most common of which is "performance anxiety." Behind such anxiety is often a relationship problem or the clashing of personalities. Writes Kaplan, "Dyadic factors often play a crucial role in the genesis of impotence. Destructive interactions between a couple can indeed produce the classic picture of the 'castrating' woman and her victim, the impotent man" (1974, pp. 260–261). Since one of the goals of therapy is to modify destructive interactions, it is important that the partner be involved in therapy with the impotent individual (Kaplan, 1974). Often couples undertake marital therapy before, or along with, sexual therapy. A male should resist getting a surgical penile implant as much as possible until all other possibilities regarding the relationship have been explored.

During the past 25 years there has been an increase in sexual expectations and a demand for high-quality sexual abilities, both of which can result in performance pressure on the male. But "Sex must develop freely and spontaneously to be successful; the negative emotions engendered by coercion and expectation can easily impair the sexual response of the sensitive individual. . . . [sexual arousal] cannot be commanded or produced

at will. On the contrary, commands or demands tend to impair the sexual reflexes" (Kaplan, 1974, p. 262).

The most successful approach to erection difficulties involves focusing on immediate causal factors. "Particularly prominent among these factors are the fear of sexual failure, the pressure of sexual demands, and the man's inability, for a variety of reasons, e.g., guilt, conflict, etc., to abandon himself to his sexual feelings. The fear of failure, with possible attendant fears of abandonment by the partner, is regarded by many workers in this field as a powerful castrator" (Kaplan, 1974, pp. 261–262). Therefore, an effort is made to create a nondemanding atmosphere in the treatment of erection difficulties. The goal is to diminish anxiety-producing pressure on the male. It is important that he stop evaluating his performance, that he concentrate only on the erotic sensations he may be feeling, and that his wife experience orgasm in other ways than through sexual intercourse. "Self-observation, obsessive thoughts, overconcern for his partner, and excessive preoccupation with the quality of his performance may all impair the patient's ability to function well" (Kaplan, 1974, p. 263). A self-help approach to both quick ejaculation and erection difficulties is found in Bernie Zilbergeld's book *Male Sexuality* (1978).

Orgasmic Difficulties

One common sexual problem found among women is the lack of orgasm. Orgasmic difficulties can be of the *primary* type, meaning that the female has never experienced orgasm, or they can be of the *secondary* type, where the problem exists now but the person was orgasmic in the past. In addition, the problem may be *absolute* or *situational*. If it is defined as absolute, it means that the woman is unable to achieve orgasm either clitorally

© Earl W. Engleman.

or through intercourse under any circumstances. If it is a situational orgasmic difficulty, then the person is able to reach a climax but only under particular conditions (Kaplan, 1974).

Situational and secondary orgasmic difficulties are more common than the absolute and primary conditions. Typically in the former cases the woman cannot reach an orgasm under conditions that make her even slightly anxious. Thus, she may be able to reach a climax with masturbation when she is by herself but not when a partner is present. Or she may have been able to achieve orgasm with a previous partner but is unable to do so with her current partner. Other women can reach a climax only through very long periods of intercourse and are not orgasmic through clitoral stimulation at all. Such women often put tremendous pressure

on their husbands, sometimes leading to cases of impotence (Kaplan, 1974).

Of course, all women are capable of experiencing orgasms, assuming they are not suffering from rare neurological, endocrinological, or gynecological diseases. But it does not seem to bother some women that they are nonorgasmic, and they indicate that they greatly enjoy other aspects of sexuality. Many of these women fake orgasms during intercourse for the sake of their husbands, who are often greatly concerned about providing their wives with orgasms. There is the possibility, however, for nonorgasmic women to become progressively disinterested in sex, particularly those women who become discouraged because of frequent failures at attempted orgasm (Kaplan, 1974). It should be noted that extensive controversy continues to surround the female orgasm (see Box 9.3).

BOX 9.3

THE CONTROVERSY OVER THE FEMALE ORGASM

Throughout the twentieth century there has been extensive controversy over the female orgasm. Freud indicated that there were two distinct types of female orgasm—a vaginal orgasm and a clitoral orgasm. He saw the clitoral orgasm as immature, part of an infantile stage of sexual development. The vaginal orgasm, by contrast, was considered to be the mature orgasm of the adult female. If women were unable to achieve vaginal orgasm, even if they could achieve clitoral orgasm, they were thought to be in need of psychoanalysis to solve their "problem" (Kilmann, 1984).

With Masters's and Johnson's work (1966) the idea of two orgasms was strongly challenged. Their laboratory research showed only one type of female orgasm. They had observed that no matter what type of stimulation takes place—clitoral or vaginal—the clitoris is always the focal point of sexual sensations, and there are always contractions of the vaginal muscles. The action provided by intercourse produces clitoral stimulation.

Many women, however, have continued to claim that an orgasm as the result of only clitoral stimulation, such as through masturbation, results in different sensations than an orgasm produced by intercourse (Fisher, 1973). Josephine and Irving Singer (1972) have gone even further by suggesting that there are three different kinds of orgasm. One type, called the *vulval orgasm,* results from either clitoral stimulation or intercourse and is characterized by involuntary, rhythmic contractions in the genital area. This orgasm involves the pudendal nerve, which extends from the spinal cord to most of the muscles in and around the outer third of the vagina and around the clitoris.

A second distinct type of orgasm, called the *uterine orgasm,* "is characterized by breathing changes: tension in the diaphragm, which lies above the abdomen; a few strangling gasps, leading to involuntary breath holding because of a strong contraction in the muscle at the back of the throat; and then explosive exhalation" (Nass, Libby, and Fisher, 1984, p. 39). This type of orgasm involves the pelvic nerve, which extends from the spinal cord to only "about one-third of the muscles in the outer third of the vagina, the bladder, and the uterus and cervix. Probably, those women who have orgasm by deep vagina penetration are highly sensitive in the pelvic nerve pathway. Thus, pressure against the cervix, uterus, and inner part of the vagina is sexually stimulating" (Mahoney, 1983, p. 131). This second type of orgasm would be achieved only with intercourse.

The third kind of orgasm identified by the Singers is the *blended orgasm,* which is a mixture of the first two. "It occurs during intercourse and is characterized by both interrupted breathing and a sensation of contractions in the vagina. These contractions may be experienced subjectively as 'deeper' than those of the 'vulval' orgasm" (Nass, Libby, and Fisher, 1984, p. 39). The blended orgasm may involve both the pudendal and the pelvic nerves.

Recent intriguing research by John Perry and Beverly Whipple (1981) suggests that the stimulation of the *Grafenberg spot* may trigger uterine orgasms. The Grafenberg spot is a very erotically sensitive area located on the anterior wall of the vagina. The sensitivity of the Grafenberg spot seems "to differ as much from that of other areas of the vagina as the clitoris differs in sensitivity from areas surrounding it" (Nass, Libby, and Fisher, 1984, p. 40).

> When doctors can locate and press on the spot, women who've never been contacted in this area before at first interpret the sensation as a need to urinate. The spot lies close to the bladder, and the sensations may be confused because women are not accustomed to making fine spatial distinctions in this part of their body. They may be frightened by the feeling until they recognize that it's not a urinary sensation but, rather, a pleasurable sexual sensation. (Nass, Libby, and Fisher, 1984, p. 40)

The sensations of the Grafenberg spot can result in the expulsion of fluid from the urethra with orgasm. This fluid, according to Perry and Whipple, is not urine but rather is a prostatic secretion. This concept of "female ejaculation" has been highly debated in the 1980s. Knowledge about female ejaculation remains rather limited.

Many women have *multiple orgasms*. Kinsey (1953) was the first to suggest that women could have more than one orgasm in each sexual session. In his interviews with women, about 13 percent told him that they could reach additional orgasms soon after an initial one. Most people in the scientific community could not accept this idea of women having more orgasmic potential than men. Then Masters and Johnson were able to document through scientific measurements the fact that some women indeed were multiply orgasmic. Women do not experience a similar refraction period as men do. While Kaplan (1974) found that 32 percent of the women in her studies were multiply orgasmic, Masters and Johnson believe that any woman can be if she wants to be, given appropriate stimulation. Multiple orgasms are more likely to result from hand, oral, or vibrator stimulation; few men have the endurance to provide for continuous orgasms through intercourse. Some women have achieved as many as 50 orgasms in one "sitting" with the use of a vibrator. Many women, however, are completely satisfied with only one orgasm and do not seek more.

Obviously the 1965–1975 era brought additional performance pressures in terms of sexuality. Besides multiple orgasms many couples adopted the goal of *mutual orgasms*—both partners having orgasms simultaneously. To some degree this development tended to turn sex into work rather than play. Moreover, it has been suggested that there is a major disadvantage in couples' seeking orgasms at the same time since concentration on one's own orgasm tends to limit the possibility of being aware of and sharing in the partner's pleasure. "For some people, to enjoy the beloved's orgasm is as deep and intimate a pleasure as the sharing of responses that are timed in perfect unison" (Singer, 1974, p. 149).

Women are nonorgasmic for a variety of reasons. A female may lack commitment to a relationship, have fear of possibly being abandoned, may not be assertive enough in stating her needs, may have considerable guilt about her sexuality, or may have a lot of hostility toward her spouse. Any or all of these factors could result in the establishment of "over-control" of the orgasmic reflex. It is common for nonorgasmic women to have a "fear of losing control over feeling and behavior," and therefore they "hold back" the orgasmic reflex. The nature of the female orgasm is that it is easily subject to inhibition (Kaplan, 1974).

After several repetitions of this voluntary inhibition of the orgastic reflex, the inhibition seems to become automatic and can no longer be controlled voluntarily so that after a while the woman who has learned to inhibit her orgasm cannot climax even if she is calm, in love, properly stimulated, and otherwise responsive. (Kaplan, 1974, p. 384)

One of the key techniques used in therapy with nonorgasmic women is masturbation. This activity is typically carried out alone without one's partner, since the presence of an "audience" can in itself inhibit many women, at least at first. For some women there is considerable anxiety about self-stimulation; they may have been taught in childhood that masturbation is "wrong" and "shameful." The woman is reassured that masturbation is a very common activity among both sexes (Kaplan, 1974).

Many sexual therapists believe that improving the muscle tone of the pubococcygeal (PC) muscle also helps in producing orgasm. This is a large muscle surrounding the vagina, which contracts during orgasm. A series of exercises was developed by Dr. Arnold Kegal, which have become popularly known as the "Kegal exercises." A good description of these exercises—as well as a self-help approach to orgasmic difficulties—is found in Lonnie Barbach's book *For Yourself: The Fulfillment of Female Sexuality* (1975).

A common concern of women is failure to experience orgasm during intercourse. "There are millions of women who are sexually responsive, and often multiply orgasic, but who cannot have an orgasm during intercourse unless they receive simultaneous clitoral stimulation. Most of these women enjoy intercourse and the pleasure of reaching orgasm with the penis contained in the vagina, but coitus in itself is not sufficiently stimulating to enable them to reach a climax" (Kaplan, 1974, pp. 397–398). To compound this problem "Many men have a paranoid reaction to their wife's failure to reach orgasm during intercourse. They either feel rejected or inadequate or attempt to defend against such feelings by convincing themselves that their wife is 'sick' or 'frigid' " (Kaplan, 1974, p. 398).

The fact of the matter is that many women seem to need more intense stimulation to orgasm than can be produced by intercourse. Such sexual patterns appear to be not only very common, but also normal and certainly not "sick." "It is possible for partners who either 'take turns' having orgasm or use special techniques to provide clitoral stimulation during coitus to . . . have a gloriously rich and fulfilling sex life, provided neither feels that this is an inferior mode of sexual expression" (Kaplan, 1974, p. 399). In fact, a pattern of mutual masturbation is often found in couples with high levels of emotional closeness.

Low Sexual Desire

Low sexual desire (LSD) has been said to be the most prevalent of all sexual difficulties, accounting for 40 percent of the problems of those seeking help (Lief, 1977). It is also the most rapidly increasing sexual problem. Men and women suffering from this problem have abnormally low sexual appetites. Moreover, their sexual experiences—if they have any—are generally not satisfying. Any pleasure tends to be fleeting, and it is localized in the genitals. Such people describe their sexual experiences as "similar to eating a meal when one is not really hungry." Normally arousing situations are reported by these individuals as involving "an absence of feeling or even negative sensations or irritation, tension, anger, anxiety and/or disgust" (Kaplan, 1979, p. 62). Many people with LSD avoid sex altogether. Others participate without desire for such reasons as to avoid hurting the partner or to reassure themselves that they are capable of sex. "But sometimes if sex is attempted in such a low desire state, the genital reflexes may not function well, and a secondary performance anxiety may develop" (Kaplan, 1979, p. 62). Busy dual-career couples often can't even find time for sex, if indeed they have the desire (see Box 9.4).

Primary LSD involves a lifelong history of asexuality and is quite rare. *Secondary LSD* is much more common and involves the loss of sexual desire after more or less normal sexual functioning. This condition may be the result of a variety of physical factors and also arises from relationship problems in marriage, "the birth of children, a traumatic rejection or object loss, anger at or disillusionment with a partner, or nonsexually related stress such as a job loss or an accident" (Kaplan, 1979, p. 63).

Obviously physical health and emotional mood both affect sexual appetite. Being "in love" tends to increase desire; in fact, love appears to be one of the better aphrodisiacs known to human beings. But poor health and stress tend to reduce desire, even though love is present (Kaplan, 1979).

Not all controlled desire or asexuality is abnormal. Some people have sexual appetites that fall on the low side of what would be considered a normal pattern. Sometimes this can lead to problems in the marriage when the partners have divergent sexual needs. However, "A couple can learn to accommodate with sensitivity and love to an imbalance in sexual appetite, as loving couples do with imbalance in other spheres of life" (Kaplan, 1979, p. 68).

Sexual desire tends to be kept in balance by both inhibiting and activating mechanisms. When the activating centers of the brain predominate, there will be an increase in sexual desire; when inhibiting forces predominate, sexual desire will be decreased. Negative emotions function to help serve individual survival; they motivate people to avoid danger. Thus fear and anger will win out over sexual desire (Kaplan, 1979).

It makes good sense for the activity of a man's sex circuits to become inhibited so that he does not stop to seduce his mate while he is under attack from a saber-toothed tiger. But this adaptive mechanism can go awry if the "dangers" are not accurately perceived. If an individual reacts to fantasy dangers, if he reacts with alarm to fears that have no basis in reality, his sex drive will become inhibited just as sure as if there was a real tiger in his bed. (Kaplan, 1979, p. 79)

Psychological factors tend to be more common than biological factors in causing LSD. The culprit appears to be negative thoughts. When people make themselves fearful, angry, or distracted, they tap into the natural biological inhibitory mechanisms, which suppress sexual desire when it is appropriate and in the person's best interest. In other words, sexual desire is normally low when the individual is in danger or in an

BOX 9.4

JOBS SAP COUPLES' CRAVING FOR SEX

She gets home at 6:30 P.M. He gets home at 7:30. Both have had hard days at the office. They're tired. A quick dinner goes into the microwave. They eat, put the kids to bed, watch TV for an hour, crawl in bed, and go to sleep.

Sound familiar? It does to sex therapists, who say they hear the story time and again from two-career couples.

The missing ingredient: sex.

"Sheer exhaustion is the biggest problem affecting people's sex lives today," says New York therapist Shirley Sussman [sic]. "With both people working, there is little time for intimacy. Most come home feeling 'I'm beat, just leave me alone.' "

A "study of 218 couples who sought sex therapy found that working women were more likely to lose sexual desire because of stress and fatigue than men or women who didn't work," says researcher Constance Avery-Clark of the Masters and Johnson Institute. "It's the woman's life that has changed. She's now working and taking care of kids. He's helping more but she is still doing most of it. And she's tired," says Avery-Clark. Half the couples in the study are dual-career pairs; in the other half, only the man works.

But men get tired and burned out, too. "It's not just that the men want more sex" and women are too tired, says Oakland, Calif., therapist Bernie Zilbergeld. "In many of the couples I see today, the woman is the one who wants more sex."

But "working couples are beginning to cope," says Sussman.

Therapists recommend that two-career couples:

1. Make dates. Arrange to spend time alone.
2. Schedule sex. Don't expect spontaneity. Late at night is not the best time.
3. Take the pressure off. Allow your partner time to relax and to switch gears.
4. See sex as an opportunity to have fun, recharge your batteries.

SOURCE: USA Today, *May 8, 1985, p. 10.*

emergency (Kaplan, 1979). More specifically, it is common for a person with LSD to

focus his/her attention selectively on one of the partner's unattractive physical features—his pot belly, her unkempt hair, her fat thighs, the odor of his breath, or his

genitals, etc.—in the service of shutting down the sex centers. Or the memory of the partner's unacceptable behavior or past injustices may be employed. . . . Other persons use negative thoughts about themselves to "protect" them from feeling sexy: "I am too fat"; "My breasts are too small or too large to be attractive''; ''I am too old''; ''I will come too soon''; ''It will take too long to come''; ''I will not be able to have an erection'' . . . [And] work, children and money are commonly used ''turn offs.'' (Kaplan, 1979, pp. 83–84)

Typically people are not aware of the active role that they play in creating their own low sexual desire. Ironically individuals with LSD generally see themselves as victims. "They usually have no insight into the fact that they are actively evoking negative images or permitting them to intrude. They do not recognize that they have a choice, that they do not have to do this, that they have control over the focus of their attention" (Kaplan, 1979, p. 85). LSD people "tend to report that they 'don't feel anything' or they feel uncomfortable, i.e., tense, bored and angry, in response to sexual stimulation, and they feel relief when they manage to avoid sex" (Kaplan, 1979, p. 85).

One major source of LSD is the fear of intimacy. Kaplan believes that people in American culture are even more afraid of intimacy than of sexuality. "Such persons may have good sex in the early stages of a relationship . . . but experience a loss of sexual interest after they reach a certain level of closeness with and commitment to a partner" (Kaplan, 1979, p. 88). A high level of commitment and a dependence on another person may be too threatening to an individual who wants to retain his or her own freedom and independence.

Anger is another common cause of LSD. Kaplan indicates that it is not possible to experience sexual desire toward someone with whom you are angry.

If you are angry at someone, if you want to hurt him, then it is difficult to give in to sexual desire and to be close. You don't

''want'' to feel desire for this person. . . . An angry partner resists giving and receiving pleasure. Partners engaged in power struggles don't want to be close and intimate. A distrustful partner does not want to make himself vulnerable. (Kaplan, 1979, pp. 90–91)

An angry couple will have to "make up" before they can be close sexually; "Anger must be resolved, at least in part, before desire and erotic feelings can be expected to emerge" (Kaplan, 1979, p. 92)

Other Sexual Difficulties

NONEJACULATION. A small number of males are unable to ejaculate; this condition is sometimes referred to as "retarded ejaculation" or "ejaculatory incompetence." The individual can get and maintain erections, but there is inhibition of the ejaculation reflex. In mild cases this condition is confined to specific anxiety-provoking situations or to a particular woman. Cases coming to the attention of therapists are typically more severe; for example, where an individual has never been able to ejaculate during intercourse. Usually this person can ejaculate manually or with oral stimulation. The causes of this problem could be physical but typically are psychological in nature (Kaplan, 1974).

VAGINISMUS. The condition of vaginismus involves the muscles surrounding the vagina. When penetration is attempted, the vagina closes tightly as a result of an involuntary muscle spasm. Women suffering from vaginismus tend to have a great fear of intercourse, and they experience pain when attempts are made, which reinforces their fears. These women can be sexually responsive and experience clitoral orgasms; it may be only intercourse that they fear.

PAINFUL INTERCOURSE. Dyspareunia, or painful intercourse, is a female complaint that is commonly the result of inadequate lubrication, often because of failure to become sexually aroused. Another cause is infection, which can cause burning, itching, and aching in the vagina. Sometimes there is pain around the clitoris because of material (smegma) collected under the foreskin of the clitoris. There can also be deep pain in the pelvis from tears in the vagina walls or in the ligaments supporting the uterus. It is important to note that it is not uncommon for women to say they are experiencing pain as a way of avoiding intercourse.

The Fear of Intimacy and Sexual Difficulties

All activities for most people, including sexual experiences, are more pleasurable and enjoyable when they can be shared with an intimate partner. When each partner is open and vulnerable, when each trusts the other that he or she won't be rejected, when partners care about the other's feelings and take pleasure in their pleasure, there will be a greater closeness between them. The result is that "Sex becomes less risky, the reflexes are more likely to work and abandonment is easier if you can be yourself and can discard your defenses in the bedroom" (Kaplan, 1979, p. 183).

Of course, intimacy problems will typically negatively affect a married couple's sexuality. If there are mild problems with closeness, they often are helped by the sexual-therapy process itself, including the pleasuring exercises and the sharing of the erotic aspects of the relationship. Thus a couple can actually become emotionally closer by focusing on and improving the sexual aspects of their relationship. The more difficulties there are with emotional closeness, however, the more it will be necessary—at least to some degree—to resolve the marital problems first before a couple can even start to enjoy a sexual relationship. This will involve both a focus on the personalities of the partners and on the interaction processes in the relationship (Kaplan, 1979).

Unfortunately, fears of intimacy are usually not consciously apparent; there is less awareness than there is of anxieties about sexual performance. Ironically, people with intimacy problems often indicate that they are lonely and that they want to be close to someone. The source of such problems is typically found in childhood experiences, much earlier than concerns about sexual performance (Kaplan, 1979).

It should be stressed, finally, that sexual therapy is not simply the teaching of sexual mechanics. Typically the procedures used involve intense emotional experiences, which have significant ramifications on the relationship itself. The quality of marital interaction often improves with sexual therapy itself. Both partners learn to be more open and to communicate at a deeper level. "In the process, they often develop a growing intimacy and mutual trust which extends beyond their sexual interactions" (Kaplan, 1974, p. 410).

EXTRAMARITAL SEX

The vast majority of Americans, about 80 to 90 percent, indicate that they are opposed to extramarital sex. But what they *say* and what they *do* often appear to be two different matters. Already back in midcentury Kinsey (1948 and 1953) found that by the age of 40, 51 percent of the men and 26 percent of the women had experienced extramarital sex at least once. Recent research suggests that the rate hasn't changed that much for men, but that women are catching up to men in terms of extramarital activities. The double standard has not totally disappeared, but differences in male and female behavior are not very large anymore, either.

Motivations for Extramarital Sex

The following are five of the more common reasons for having extramarital sex:

1. *Excitement and adventure.* This is more likely to be given as a reason by a man; this motivation emphasizes sexual variety as the "spice of life." Sex is viewed as a form of recreational activity, a way to release built-up tension, or as a form of escape. Sometimes there is sexual satisfaction in the marriage, but more than likely the individual is looking for reassurance of his or her own desirability level through having other partners.

2. *Seeking emotional closeness.* This reason is more likely to be given by a female; typically the person is emotionally isolated or lonely. Often the individual is unhappy in the marriage. The relationship may involve an empty-shell marriage, or it may be filled with a lot of negative exchange. The person having extramarital sex is seeking closeness through an outside partner basically because intimacy is lacking in the marriage.

3. *Curiosity.* Individuals who use this reason typically married at a very early age or felt as though they missed out on a lot, sexually and otherwise. The person may have had only limited sexual experience before getting married and has great curiosity about what sex would be like with another individual. Such people may also be curious about their own abilities to attract another person.

4. *Revenge.* Sometimes people have extramarital sex as a way to hurt their marriage partner. It can be a way of "getting back" or "getting even" for something that the partner has done to hurt him or her, although the injury may not necessarily have been sexual. Enjoyment may come not so much from the sexual activity itself but from letting the partner find out about it and from the resulting hurt that the partner may experience.

5. *Partner agreed to it.* Here the spouse actually gives permission for extramarital activity. Sometimes one partner specifically tells the other to "seek sex elsewhere." This consensual extramarital sex could also be part of an open marriage or could involve swinging, or mate swapping.

Extramarital Intimacy

In her book *The Extramarital Connection* (1982) sociologist Lynn Atwater reports on her in-depth interviews with 50 married women who were having, or recently had, extramarital relationships. Forty percent of the women had experienced only one extramarital relationship. Traditional romantic factors played a minor role—"Only four women had described themselves as being 'in love' at the time of first involvement, and most of the other women did *not* fall in love as time went by. . . . In response to questions concerning their emotional feelings, about two-thirds of the women said they 'liked' or were 'friends' with their extramarital partners" (p. 58). The women's descriptions of the feeling that they held for their extramarital partners was one of "affection," but it was not the same as "romantic love." Some indicated that the English language did not have words to describe their feelings accurately. But the general public has words to describe extramarital affection, and it is usually always negative and involves sexual terms.

Only one woman described her relationship in purely sexual terms. Most said that there were intellectual, social, and emotional factors that led them to their relationships. But particularly this "extramarital intimacy helped to fill a painful void in their lives" (p. 60).

SECRET MEETINGS

Ellie and Marvin
Have been having secret meetings twice a week
For the past six months
But have thus far failed to consummate their
    passion
Because
While both of them agree
That marital infidelity is not only unrealistic but
    irrelevant,
He has developed sharp shooting pains
In his chest, and she's got impetigo, and
He's got pink eye.
Ellie and Marvin
Drive forty miles to sneaky luncheonettes
In separate cars
But have thus far done no more than heavy
    necking
Because
She's developed colitis, and
He has developed these throbbing pains in his
    back, and
She has started biting her nails, and
He's smoking again.
Ellie and Marvin
Yearn to have some love in the afternoon at a
    Motor Hotel
But have thus far only had a lot of
Coffee
Because
He is convinced that his phone is being tapped,
    and
She is convinced that a man in a trench coat is
    following her, and
He says what if the Motor Hotel catches fire, and
She says what if she talks in her sleep some night,
    and
She thinks her husband is acting suspiciously
    hostile, and
He thinks his wife is acting suspiciously nice, and
He keeps cutting his face with his double-edged
    razor, and
She keeps closing her hand in the door of her car,
    so
While both of them agree that guilt is not only
    neurotic but also obsolete

They've also agreed
To give up
Secret meetings.

JUDITH VIORST

Women, in talking about the kind of in-
volvement they had, are saying they enjoy
the pleasures of relating interpersonally to
a variety of people. They are reflecting con-
temporary attitudes which emphasize add-
ing greater personal contact and intimacy
to our private lives as an antidote to the
increasing isolation and impersonality of
American life. (Atwater, 1982, pp. 60–61)

Atwater argues that it is the affluence of
modern society that allows for the freedom
and luxury to focus on needs for personal
intimacy. Few of us totally concentrate on
requirements for survival; rather we have become more focused on

the nonphysical aspects of living that make
life more pleasurable and rewarding. This
psychic satisfaction is dependent on the
quality of our relationships with others. We
learn about others by interacting with
them, and at the same time we learn about
ourselves through the social reflection we get
from others. These twin pleasures, relating
to others and learning about the self
through outside relationships, were the
dominant meanings of extramarital inti-
macy to these women. (p. 61)

Thus these extramarital relationships had
many more social meanings than sexual
ones. Two women said:

I guess essentially what I get is the compan-
ionship, the closeness and the ability to com-
municate with a male.

The feeling of being treated as an equal; poems from him, all kinds of communication. (p. 61)

Such responses focus on the *mutuality* of communicating and caring. "Only one-quarter of the women talked about the dimensions of sex, variety and thrills that one might more typically expect from extramarital activity" (p. 62). Thus sex itself was mentioned quite rarely in describing a relationship that is thought by the general population to be primarily sexual.

At first glance, it could be said that nothing is new in this pattern of social meanings, since women are expected to be more interested in the social rather than the sexual aspects of relationships. . . . Females are said to be "expressive specialists," to be interested in nurturance and emotional support of others, to enjoy communicating words and feelings to people. (Atwater, 1982, p. 63)

But if a closer look is taken at the women's reasons for these extramarital relationships, it must be noted that the "women emphasized the mutuality of the expressiveness, or in some cases the getting instead of giving of emotional support, which *is* a significant variation of the usual female role" (p. 63).

These women are not throwing away their traditional interest in expressiveness, but they do want to reshape and modernize it. They no longer wish to be part of the emotional "blood bank" system that we have set up between the sexes, in which women are consistently donors and men consistently withdrawers. (Atwater, 1982, p. 63)

Apparently these women were not getting the emotionality and expressiveness they needed from their husbands. All but one wife said that communication was the area of least satisfaction in their marriage. Since the majority of wives are now working outside the home and sharing the economic burden of the family, more and more women are raising their expectations of men regarding expressiveness. As mentioned, even lower-class wives are now looking for more expressiveness from their husbands (L. Rubin, 1976).

Atwater makes a strong case for attempting to destroy "the traditional female monopoly on emotionality." She argues that both sexes would "benefit by making expressive competence a unisexual trait" (p. 65).

Spouses who prefer a monogamous marriage would have an improved probability of keeping it that way, for accumulated research on extramarital behavior suggests that "the greater the discrepancy between the personal and relational satisfaction a person desires and receives from marriage, the more likely is extramarital involvement." In other words, the more closely we meet our spouses' expectations, the less likely they are to seek outside relationships. (Atwater, 1982, p. 65)

Thus extramarital involvement represents an opportunity for women

to obtain the expressive equality they are looking for in their relationships with men. These women are social innovators. If they do not find what they want and need in a conventional male-female relationship, they improvise and form new relationships, in this case extramarital ones. . . . Their actions are a rejection of traditional feminine passivity, of women waiting for things to happen, and a substitution of activity and initiative, to take charge of the shaping of one's own life. (Atwater, 1982, p. 66)

These women see few options for themselves.

> If we examine the set of socially acceptable
> alternatives, we see that there are none for
> women and men who wish to enjoy friendly
> intimacy with each other. Such pairings are
> always assumed to include sexual expres-
> sion, so there is a strong inclination . . . to
> succumb to the self-fulfilling prophecy of this
> assumption. It is characteristic of our cul-
> ture to eroticize the problems of intimacy.
> We direct nearly all our needs for human
> warmth to sexual interaction, neglecting the
> possibilities of friendship. It is necessary to
> recognize the complex intimacy needs of in-
> dividuals today, so that we can begin to
> enlarge social scripts. (Atwater, 1982,
> p. 66)

One of the factors that has made it possible for these women to achieve expressive
equality with men is that "they vigorously
believe in male-female equality." Another
factor is that unlike marital relationships, extramarital relationships are completely voluntary. Atwater argues that traditional marriages still prove to be resistant to equal
partnerships.

What aspects of expressive communication did women find so rewarding in their
extramarital relationships? They were things
not met in the marriage:

> We talked about what happened during our
> day. . . . and he listened. Which was neat.
>
> We talked a lot about problems. . . . It's
> just hearing response that I like. That was
> fun. My husband doesn't say too much.
>
> My husband never hit me with a pillow in
> his whole life. I mean that kind of fun—
> and I have missed thirty years of fun.
>
> I think talking sometimes is much more
> consuming than sexuality because you have
> much more time to do it, in a much freer

> atmosphere and for me that's so paramount
> that I can't imagine being without it.
> (p. 68)

All of the women said that the communication in their extramarital relationships was
quite different from that found in their marriage. They needed "playfulness, small talk,
sensitivity, or just to be listened to. . . . All
knew what it was they lacked or wanted"
(p. 69).

How did the men provide this extramarital expressiveness? Who were these men
who were so competent at intimacy? Were
these emotional con artists who were being
temporarily sensitive to obtain the sex they
wanted? Atwater doubts that these were deceptive men. These were not "one-night
stands" where one would expect to find more
exploitation. Writes Atwater, "It is implausi-
ble, I feel, that women, as expressive 'specialists,' would generally be incapable of de-
tecting male insincerity, especially given the
test of time" (p. 70). In addition, about a third
of the men were single and young, early thirties or younger. These men may be less likely
to hold traditional traits of masculinity.

What about the older married men who
were part of these extramarital affairs. Were
they the inexpressive husbands of other
women? (See Box 9.5.) A number of the men
"were in helping professions that required
high skill levels of communication" (p. 70).
But there is also another possible factor. Men
may be *situationally expressive* extramaritally,
even though they are inexpressive in their
marriages. "It may well be that the force of
institutionalized marital roles and the burden
of husbandly responsibility serve to inhibit
expressiveness in marriage" (p. 70).

> The absence of economic responsibility in the
> extramarital situation may provide men
> with the necessary freedom to allow their

*expressiveness to emerge. Traditional mo-
nogamous marriage may not be the best
vehicle for contemporary males to nurture
and maintain expressiveness, especially if
they are subject to demands for maximum
performance in the instrumental or wage-
earning area. (Atwater, 1982, p. 71)*

Most of the women who had extramarital relationships were not overwhelmed by
guilt. While they regretted the deception involved, they saw it as unavoidable. No one
person ended a relationship out of guilt. The
rewards received from adding more intimacy
to their lives far outweighed the costs involved. Such may not be the case, however,
if their husbands find out about their extramarital activity.

Swinging

Swinging—also known as mate swapping,
comarital sex, and group sex—is simultaneously shared extramarital sex, or adultery, on
the part of the husband and wife. It is estimated that approximately 2 percent of all
married couples participate in this practice.

Probably the best study of the backgrounds and personalities of swingers was
done by Brian Gilmartin (1978). In this study
a group of 100 suburban, middle-class couples who were engaged in swinging were
compared with a group of 100 conventional,
nonswinging couples from the same immediate neighborhoods where the swingers
lived. Both questionnaires and extensive
three-hour interviews were used. The swingers were all married, and 82 percent had children. Typically it was the husbands who first
initiated and convinced the wives to try
swinging.

Swingers are said to have the ability completely to compartmentalize sex as a form of
recreational activity and to see it as quite different from the emotionally intimate aspects

of a marriage. Sex is not viewed as the "cement of marriage" or the "be-all and end-
all" of marriage. "To the American swinger
psychological and emotional bonds tend to
be viewed as the real cement of a marriage"
(Gilmartin, 1978, p. 58). Mate swappers simply do not see sexual monogamy as natural
or desirable. They are concerned with emotional faithfulness, not sexual fidelity.
"Swingers do not perceive their recreational
interest in sex as being in any way competitive with marriage and family life" (p. 64).

Do the family backgrounds of swingers
differ from those of nonswingers? Gilmartin
found that swingers were more than twice as
likely to have experienced unhappy and less
emotionally satisfying relationships with their
parents than did nonswingers. The parents of
swingers tended to be either much too strict
or authoritarian, *or* they showed a "couldn't
care less" type of permissiveness.

*The authoritarian parent imposes his
wishes arbitrarily and without considering
the feelings of the child. The highly permissive parent is usually so uncomfortable
about communicating with children that he
just lets his children do whatever they want.
(Gilmartin, 1978, p. 84)*

The result is a child or teenager who lacks
feelings that he or she is loved, trusted, and
accepted.

In addition, swingers, compared to nonswingers, were more than three times as
likely to have had their parents divorce. Even
among the swingers' parents who did not
divorce, the level of marital satisfaction was
unusually low in comparison to that of the
nonswingers' parents. Having been products
of unhappy marriages, swingers were "much
more open to the exploration of different
types and styles of marriage and family alternatives" (pp. 97–98). At the very least their

BOX 9.5

MARRIED MEN AND THEIR MISTRESSES

An affair between a married man and his mistress involves an exchange of trust and confidences. But is it an intimate relationship? Is it a relationship in which both persons share equally, give and receive fairly, and disclose themselves reciprocally?

Most affairs are concealed by necessity. Secrets are a matter of course; confidentiality is the code name. For the married man, taking a risk with a mistress demands trust. "The longer the affair goes on, the more and more trust builds. After all, the mistress holds her married man's secret, his infidelity, in her palm. She protects that secret as she protects all the others" (Sands, 1981, p. 179).

Apparently these married men share their feelings about almost everything—their jobs, their children, their wives, their goals. Verbal communication is the basis of many affairs, and the men do most of the talking. Thus married men can and do talk, and if your own husband isn't talking to you, that doesn't necessarily mean he is incapable of verbal self-disclosure. Each and every mistress has heard privileged information and family secrets and seen the sensitive vulnerability of the married man. In fact, it is these very confidences that hook the mistress. Hearing secrets can be spellbinding. "Being treated like a confidante is a flattering role. Being trusted and being needed can be addictive. Married men need to talk, and mistresses find that they need to listen" (Sands, 1981, p. 180).

"It is hard to turn your back on someone who is unveiling himself so intimately. . . . The married man's ability to communicate verbally so intimately is at the very heart of his potent appeal. He means it when he tells her she is his best friend and number one confidante. However, the confidential relationship is often a one-way street. Mistresses do tell some secrets, but rarely all. For instance, many mistresses can't let on how badly they want their man to divorce. This is their ultimate secret. Or how much pain jealousy brings them. Mistresses more often put on a happy face and choose conversational topics that are going to please, free, or interest *him*. His problems take precedence. Therefore the married man is not the mistress' best friend or prime confidant. . . . How can he be a best friend when he is rarely there in an emergency or when you need him most? Yet she holds on to this illusion that her married man is her best friend. . . . The married man often stops talking when the mistress starts asking the wrong questions. Hence, too many mistresses know this instinctively and don't ask. The friendships in affairs are therefore imbalanced" (Sands, 1981, pp. 180–182).

"It is still true that men hold a double standard with regard to women. You may be familiar with the double-standard terminology with regard to sex. You may not be familiar with it with regard to confidences. But there are some men who feel that verbal intimacy is not for wives; it is for mistresses. This breed is the masked man who divulges his secrets only to the stranger. . . . This type of man does not see marriage as a confidential relationship'' (Sands, 1981, p. 187). If you are a woman, how you react to the statement "My wife doesn't understand me" can tell you if you are confidante material or not. "Mistresses rarely dismiss it immediately, even if it is a cliché. Clichés attain that status for a reason—that is something we tend to forget" (Sands, 1981, p. 188).

"Men need to communicate and they do. They are spies looking for a warm retreat. They are double agents whose loyalties are an impenetrable maze. Married men often live by odd codes which mistresses and wives both try to decipher. Affairs tend to bring out the depths in most married men. Mistresses seemingly have an added talent for truth-getting although it is a talent that is not in their own best interests. . . . The insides of the married man can't always be seen from the outside. Sometimes it takes an outsider like the mistress to get an inside view" (Sands, 1981, p. 188).

---

parents' marriages served as a poor advertisement of the conventional marital style (Gilmartin, 1978).

In their current relationships with parents and kin, swingers interacted with their relatives only one-third as much as nonswingers. "Only about one-seventh of the swingers felt that they could really 'let their hair down' with their close relatives. . . . On the basis of these findings, it seems that emotional dependency which normally prevails between children and their parents never became firmly established in the families of orientation of most swinging husbands and wives" (p. 106).

By not experiencing closeness with their families, these children were forced to find their own resources for satisfying deep socialemotional needs. The result was that "friends" were used as replacements for family ties. More than 80 percent of the swingers visited with friends once or more per week, compared to only about one-third of the nonswingers.

Most of their ''closest'' or ''best friends'' were (at the time of the interview) fellow swingers. . . . Their fellow swingers had become a kind of quasi-kin group—a

functional equivalent of what for most Americans would be a group of very close relatives. (Gilmartin, 1978, p. 115)

Thus close swinging friends acting as quasi-kin seem to find "much of the in-group intimacy that conventional people usually find through close and frequent interaction with relatives. . . . Most swingers feel a bond, and in some cases a very strong bond (particularly among long-time swingers)" (pp. 115–116). Swinging families may spend entire weekends together. Couples may freely contact each other and stay overnight when vacationing around the country.

Swingers are much more likely to be family liberals. About three times as many nonswingers labeled themselves as being part of the "silent majority," which has not been very silent at all in the 1980s. Swingers compared to nonswingers are much less likely to be involved in organized religion. In addition, in contrast to nonswingers, they tend to be much more concerned about individual rights, to be more opposed to the censorship of pornography, to favor the legalizing of marijuana, to favor the woman's liberation movement, to favor legalized abortion, and to practice nudity or frequent nudist club activities. Swingers were also more likely to have been previously divorced, to have begun having sexual intercourse at an earlier age, and to have had more premarital sexual partners.

Most swingers try to convince themselves that jealousy is a learned emotion and therefore can be unlearned. But there is always the possibility that a husband or wife may find other partners superior to their own spouse—both sexually and in other ways. "But for them to admit this would be to end the swinging and therefore the only way this diversion can continue is if both partners reassure each other that they are, of course, the 'best' " (Masters and Johnson, 1975, p. 177).

Masters and Johnson see great difficulties in dealing with the emotion of jealousy in swinging. Real feelings, jealousy included, typically go underground.

Once the insecure partner has been persuaded or cajoled into participating in swinging, so that nominal jealousy is no longer reasonable, true feelings can no longer be expressed and so they simmer, building pressure to a point where it must ultimately explode. This does not augur well for the future of the marriage; it is safe to say that under these circumstances the dissolution of the marriage would not be unexpected. (Masters and Johnson, 1975, p. 177)

Most studies that have been done on swingers have focused primarily on those individuals currently involved in swinging (Bartell, 1971; Rubenstein and Margolis, 1971; Smith and Smith, 1970; and Gilmartin, 1978). Such studies have sometimes given optimistic views on the value of swinging to a marriage. The failures of swinging, the swinging dropouts, have rarely been studied.

One exception is a study of swinging dropouts by Denfield (1974). Denfield sent questionnaires to marriage counselors and asked them if they had dropouts from swinging in their counseling practice. The counselors had seen a total of 1175 such couples. The counselors were asked to give the reasons that the former swingers had dropped out. The results, in order of frequency, were (1) jealousy, (2) guilt, (3) threat to the marriage, (4) development of outside emotional attachments, (5) boredom and loss of interest, (6) disappointment ("did not live up to expectations"), (7) divorce or separation, (8) wife's inability to "take it," and (9) fear of discovery.

Those therapists who were counseling individuals who were currently in swinging found a similar list of problems; jealousy, guilt, and threat to the marriage led the current swingers' lists also. Active swingers also had a fear of venereal disease. In both groups, swingers and dropouts, wives were more hesitant and more bothered by swinging. Many wives agreed to swinging to save their marriages. Wives were much more likely than husbands to initiate the withdrawal from swinging.

CHAPTER REVIEW

1. Since Kinsey's studies at midcentury, marital sex now includes more time spent in foreplay, experimentation with a variety of positions for sexual intercourse, and more oral sexual activities. In addition, the wife is much more likely to be orgasmic than in the past.

2. Research in the 1980s has found that wives want more extensive nongenital touching and not just a focus on intercourse. Husbands, however, still hold the balance of power in sexual relations and generally are the initiators of sex. Among lower-class couples the view is more often held that sex is primarily for the husband's pleasure; it is the wife's "duty."

3. It has been estimated that as many as 50 percent of all married couples experience some type of sexual dysfunction. The most common problems include quick ejaculation, erection difficulties, orgasmic difficulties, and low sexual desire.

4. A major goal in the treatment of sexual difficulties is to create an atmosphere for the couple in which the normal processes of desire, arousal, and orgasm can occur unhindered by anxiety. Improving the quality of sexual activity for a couple can also result in the development of a greater degree of emotional closeness.

5. Although the majority of Americans disapprove of extramarital sex, studies indicate that approximately one-half of the married men and somewhat fewer married women have engaged in extramarital sex at least once. Motivations for extramarital sex include excitement and adventure, emotional closeness, curiosity, revenge, and partners' encouragement.

6. Extramarital sex can be shared simultaneously by marital partners in the activity of swinging. Swingers contend that they can compartmentalize sex as a form of recreational activity and separate it from emotional involvement. The backgrounds of swingers reveal a lack of closeness in their families of origin.

10

Parent
and Child
Relationships

A generation ago for most couples the decision to have children was not really considered to be a deliberate choice. Having children was almost synonymous with being married. Childless couples were not only considered strange and immoral but also were pitied by those around them. In today's society, however, parenthood is no longer a role that automatically comes with marriage. Due to improved contraceptives, societal acceptance and encouragement of their use, legal abortions, and the promotion of family planning, parenthood is now much more of a personal choice among married couples than ever before.

Findings from a national survey show that attitudes toward parenting between the 1950s and 1970s have changed. Veroff, Douvan, and Kulka (1981) found that respondents in 1976, in comparison to respondents in 1957, were less positive toward parenthood and children. These individuals expressed a stronger sense of the difficulties of parenting and of the loss of freedom than were expressed a generation earlier. The researchers concluded that Americans in the 1970s were no longer overly invested in the role of parenting as they were in the 1950s. In addition, these researchers found changes in attitudes toward voluntary childlessness; there was certainly greater acceptance of this alternative in the 1970s. Childless couples were no longer strongly morally condemned as being selfish.

A more active and deliberate choice in parenthood will, it is hoped, eliminate many unwanted births. Certainly, the more voluntary the birth of a child is, the more positive the couple should be toward parenting. While parenthood is becoming a more conscious choice, social pressures to have children still exist for many men and women (Thompson, 1980). A cross-sectional sample

of voluntarily childless women in the United States amounted to only 4 percent of all currently and ever-married women (Mosher and Bachrach, 1982). They are not only a rare but also a distinctive group in regard to a number of socioeconomic characteristics, including high levels of education, high occupational status, and marriage at a relatively late age (Mosher and Bachrach, 1982).

REASONS FOR BECOMING PARENTS

Whether or not to have children, how many to have, and when to have them are becoming increasingly important issues for women in the last decades of the twentieth century. Part of the indecision is due to the increased numbers of women assuming careers; combining a career with motherhood is a delicate juggling act. The tendency of contemporary women to achieve educational and career goals before having children has contributed to making late motherhood a growing pattern. Sometimes those who planned to have children "later" never do. Infertility may be one reason, or another possible factor is known as "drift"—"The longer a couple waits, the more likely they are to become involved in other ego- and energy-involving activities and the less likely they are to give up a comfortable lifestyle for the unknowns of parenthood" (Burgwyn, 1981, p. 24).

There is so much ambivalence regarding the question of having children that one California therapist holds decision-making workshops for indecisive couples. Her workshops include role playing by the couple pretending they are going to have a child. Also, the couple tests their parenting potential by borrowing a child during a full work week (Burgwyn, 1981). The actual effectiveness of these experiential techniques may be questionable, but this kind of workshop testifies to the difficulty that at least some people have with making this decision.

Why specifically do people choose to have children? With the growing recognition of the difficulties of raising children—not to mention the growing costs, reaching close to $100,000 per child (including college)—the reasons for having children may be changing also. The following are some of the most frequently cited reasons for choosing parenthood.

Meeting Needs for Intimacy

In recent years the reasons most frequently given for having children tend to focus on love and affection (Hoffman, Thornton, and Mannis, 1978). Having children in order to obtain affection and closeness may be related to the coldness and impersonality of modern society. People who feel lost in the bureaucratic maze of the workplace, isolated and lonely by geographical mobility, and lacking in a sense of community tend to look to the special role of the nuclear family as a source of human closeness.

In many families, children may provide more emotional closeness to a parent than a spouse can provide, especially for the wife. Among lower-class families, in particular, wives often claim that their children are a major source of affection (Rainwater, 1960; Komarovsky, 1967). The segregated roles of husbands and wives in these families contribute to lower marital satisfaction, which in turn results in children becoming objects of emotional closeness. For these women, "Children come to represent an avenue of compensation for their husbands' lack of affection" (Rainwater, 1960, p. 87).

Unmarried mothers, in particular, may value a child as a source of affection. Some young girls, feeling deprived of emotional closeness during their own childhood, believe that a child will give them the intimacy with another human being that they so desire. "A little baby will love me and cuddle me," thinks a teenage mother. Perhaps it was a desire for intimacy in the first place that resulted in the pregnancy. Unwed mothers may have been trying to substitute sexual contact for the closeness that was lacking in their families. In any event, expecting a baby or child to provide affection and to fill an emotional void results in many young parents becoming disillusioned by the reality that a baby takes much more than he or she gives.

The idea of children providing emotional closeness is not as often expressed by men. "Men are more likely to say that having an influence, forming the character of the child, is a major pleasure of parenthood" (Veroff, Douvan, and Kulka, 1981, p. 219).

Fun and Stimulation

Another frequent reason for having children is the fun and stimulation in watching children grow. This is a particularly common reason among women who work outside the home (Hoffman, Thornton, and Mannis, 1978). Children add an element of excitement and unpredictability—"Something new is always happening," "There's never a dull moment." Observing them grow, develop, and change is a special experience cherished by many parents.

Playing with their children gives parents a chance to experience and to relive their own childhoods. It allows them to engage in a type of fun that they may not have had enough of in their own youth. Play activities allow people to experience a sense of closeness as they "let their hair down" and reveal themselves in a spontaneous and genuine way.

Establishing Adult Status

Especially with the first pregnancy, many people feel they are on the verge of adulthood. Parenthood may help establish a person as a mature, adult member of society. In the Hoffman, Thornton, and Mannis study, the majority of respondents felt that becoming a parent was an "initiation into adulthood."

For women, in particular, motherhood has traditionally been defined as a major role in adult life. Up until fairly recently, few acceptable alternative roles were available, especially for lower-class, uneducated women. From an early age, girls viewed motherhood as part of their identity as women and found the idea of being an adult female without children difficult to comprehend. Still today, having children gives many women a sense of fulfillment in their lives and, hence, exists as a goal for most women.

An Extension of Oneself

Children provide adults with ties to the future and in some sense a degree of "immortality." Many people feel the need to "carry on the family name" or to continue a sense of themselves beyond their own lifetimes. Having children is a way of reproducing oneself and of "having one's characteristics reflected in another who will live longer" (Hoffman and Hoffman, 1973, p. 48). This reason for having children is expressed more by men than by women (Hoffman and Hoffman, 1973). Children usually carry on the man's name.

Moral and Religious Reasons

Childbearing is viewed by some people as a moral act and as an obligation that must be fulfilled. Raising children is closely tied to the values of hard work and adult responsibility. Even today people occasionally refer to a childfree couple as selfish and irresponsible, as though they were not fulfilling certain moral obligations.

Religious beliefs have also been cited as a reason for having children. The Judeo-Christian tradition often views children "as blessings from heaven and barrenness as a curse, sometimes as a punishment for some particular misdeed" (Pohlman, 1969, p. 45). So the desire to have a child, or even a large family, could stem from the need to appear morally and spiritually right in the eyes of others and in the eyes of God.

Economic Value

In nonindustrial societies, although not so much in modern urban life, children can be an economic advantage to parents. Especially in the rural areas of developing countries, children are valued as economic assets. Farming in many developing countries demands seasonal labor rather than steady labor. Finding workers who can be hired and fired depending on the seasons is difficult. The marginal farmer cannot afford to pay for labor that is not needed, and laborers cannot live in an area where there is no income for long periods. One's own children, however, can help with farm work even when they are very young. Children in such situations may well be viewed as economic necessities (Hoffman and Hoffman, 1973).

Another way in which children can be of economic value is when they are seen as a form of social security for the parents' old age. In many countries there are no governmental programs to provide adequately for the elderly, and therefore parents are forced to turn to their own children. Although the economic costs of raising small children may be quite high, these are tolerated for the expected benefits later in life.

THE TRANSITION TO PARENTHOOD

The transition to parenthood differs quite dramatically from taking on other roles, such as becoming a spouse or a full-time worker. There is a sense of inevitability, "no turning back," with becoming a parent. Indeed, parenthood is for life; and there may be a feeling of panic as this realization hits home.

> As another father-to-be said, it was the first time in his life that there was no turning back. If he didn't like college classes, he could cut them. If he didn't like a job, he could quit. If his marriage didn't work out, he could get divorced. But he could never undo the conception. He would always be a father to this child, about to be born. (Galinsky, 1981, pp. 45–46)

Lack of Preparation

Although secure and socially healthy children are largely the result of quality parenting, American society provides little formal training in preparing parents to raise children. This lack of training for such an important role has led some people to propose a license for parenting—just as we issue licenses to drive a car (see Box 10.1). The concern is that there is no guarantee that the individuals having children have been taught the necessary skills for child care and child rearing.

Of course one's own family may be used as an example of child rearing. But this certainly is not always a positive example to emulate. American schools tend to teach what they consider to be of primary importance in society—subjects such as English,

Pregnancy can be an opportunity for the couple to anticipate the necessary adjustments they need to make for parenthood.

science, or mathematics. They almost totally neglect those subjects most relevant to successful family life—interpersonal skills, child care, parenting, and sexual behavior. Thus if a child's own home was deficient in training in these areas, the child as an adult is left with no positive preparation for a major segment of his or her adult life (Rossi, 1968).

Just as people sometimes idealize marriage, they can also conjure up romantic and illusionary views of parenthood. Typical idealizations depict children as appealing little "bundles of joy" and parenthood as basically fun (LeMasters and DeFrain, 1983). These images are perpetuated by the media, which portray only the excitement of a birth

BOX 10.1

"LICENSING PARENTS: A NEW AGE OF CHILD REARING?"

People who work extensively with families have long been aware of the fact that many parents are deficient in basic child-rearing skills. Most parents have little knowledge of general nutrition, developmental psychology, or the legal rights of children. In fact, to become a parent requires no training or experience at all; no license is required. American society typically deals with problems in parenting by aiming its programs—juvenile training facilities, correctional institutions, psychiatric hospitals, for example—toward the maladjusted young adult, an after-the-fact approach.

Jerry Bergman (1978) proposes that we treat these problems before the fact, by requiring that couples pass some sort of licensing examination *before* they can become parents.

> The present system of letting people produce children and rear them until the parents are proven incapable is no more sensible than letting a doctor practice for a while to see if he can cure anyone. When he mistakes a spleen for an appendix, he can no longer practice. Unfortunately, in the case of children, the damage done is often just as irreparable. Presently society cannot declare parents incompetent until the damage is clear and obvious. Only by identifying bad parents before they become so can irreversible damage be avoided. And this means looking at a couple before they become parents. By the time it shows up in the child, it is often too late. (1978, p. 298)

Bergman speculates that the main benefit of licensing parents is "that it will teach parents just how serious is the business of raising children by forcing them to think about the problems they will likely confront as parents" (p. 299). While Bergman admits that such a procedure will not be without its flaws, he believes that

> the tragedies caused by neglect, ignorance, and inability will not be eliminated, but they will indoubtedly be reduced. Even a small reduction would probably justify a licensing program, for even a small reduction, once achieved, would allow us to restructure future programs in an attempt to guarantee good parents for everyone. (1978, p. 299)

and a fun-filled, problem-free, and humorous side of parenting. These idealized descriptions hardly prepare people for the realities of being a parent (see Box 10.2).

An Abrupt Transition

Parenthood is a role for which there is no gradual transition. There is typically no period during which couples try out and develop their skills at parenting. At least during the engagement period preceding marriage, an individual has opportunities to develop relationship skills and to make adjustments that ease the transition to marriage. The engaged couple usually has spent numerous hours discussing their individual needs, values, goals, and life expectations. There is extensive planning and it is hoped that the engaged couple has developed compatible interactions and an interdependence in advance of the marriage itself (Rossi, 1968).

Pregnancy can be a time during which the couple anticipates the necessary adjustments for parenthood. The parents-to-be think about what kind of parents they want to be. Often they will reflect on their own experiences as children and form images of the way they would have liked their parents to have treated them. Some will attempt to emulate their parents, while others may pick alternative models, sometimes even opposite patterns (Galinsky, 1981). Consider this response of one father-to-be.

> I intend to take some time off from work after the baby's born. I'm going to take as much time as I can get from my boss—at least an afternoon and a part of a morning a week and say, "Dock me if you want to. I don't care, I'm going to spend time with my baby." I would like not to be as distant and as frightened and as squeamish of intimacy as I think my father is. (Galinsky, 1981, p. 15)

Other thoughts of the partners during pregnancy may be in terms of the couple's relationship as it is affected by the baby. Preparing for a change in the relationship is of considerable importance. The couple needs to communicate responsibilities and expectations of each other. For example, if the wife envisions her husband changing diapers and feeding the baby, and the husband doesn't

envision this, she may be quite disillusioned with, and resentful of, his behavior after the baby arrives. Couples who do not talk to each other about their expectations are more likely to have a rough time after the child is born.

The Effect of Children on Marriage

The birth of a child usually has a tremendous impact on the marital relationship. Statistics on marital happiness show that in general, the level of happiness decreases at the point of the birth of the first child (Russell, 1974; Ryder, 1973). It does not return to nearly as high a level until the last child leaves the home. In a recent study of more than 250 families, it was discovered that "Having babies doesn't turn good marriages into bad ones or bad marriages into good ones. . . . The best marriages seemed to stay the best after the arrival of the baby, and the worst marriages stayed the worst" (Belsky, 1985, p. 1B).

How does a child impinge on a couple's relationship? First, parents find they must compete with the child for time with their spouse. Especially during the early years, the infant is so dependent on others that its needs will demand an inordinate amount of time and attention. Therefore, the demands of an infant may frequently take precedence over the couple's relationship needs. Time for personal contact and social activities will suddenly be given a lesser priority.

Another change for the marital relationship is that there is a shift from a dyad to a triad or to three dyads. There are no longer two people in the family but three. The typical intimate bond or attachment between the mother and child can be threatening to the father. He now feels he must share his wife with someone else. The wife also may feel that the father is intruding on the emotional closeness she is experiencing with her infant.

BOX 10.2

MYTHS OF PARENTHOOD

Rearing Children Is Fun.   . . . The truth is—as every parent knows—that rearing children is probably the hardest, and most thankless, job in the world. No intelligent father or mother would deny that it is exciting as well as interesting, but to call it fun is a serious error. The idea of something being fun implies that you can take it or leave it, whereas parents do not have this choice. Fathers and mothers must stay with the child and keep trying, whether it is fun, or whether they are enjoying it or not. . . .

Children Are Sweet and Cute.   When young people see small children they are apt to remark: "Your children are so cute!" It is true, of course, that small children are cute (at times), but this hardly exhausts the subject—or the adjectives parents use to describe their children when they are not being cute. Think back on the other adjectives you have heard used commonly to describe children, some endearing, some impairing. . . .

Children Will Turn Out Well If They Have "Good" Parents.   Logically, this should be so, and one would certainly like to believe that it is so. For that matter, it probably is usually a correct statement—but not always. Almost everyone knows of at least one nice family with a black sheep in the fold. It seems to be a rare family, indeed, that has not had some tragic experience with at least one child (assuming the family consists of several children).

It would be comforting to think that parents can guarantee happiness and success (the twin gods of our civilization), but the sad truth is that they cannot. Children are so complex and so different, and our society is so complicated, that fathers and mothers simply do not have the quality control one finds in industrial production. Parents with skill and ability, of course, probably have a better batting average than those of us with more modest talents—but even the good parents do not bat a thousand. . . .

Today's Parents Are Not as Good as Those of Yesterday.   It is impossible to prove or disprove this sort of belief, of course, but it does seem to be prevalent. The truth is . . . that standards applied to parents today have been raised, and it is also true that the laboratory in which parents have to operate (the modern world) has become infinitely more complex. All this tends to create the impression that parents as a group have deteriorated since the good old days of the 18th and 19th century. . . .

Childless Couples Are Frustrated and Unhappy.   This may have been true in the 19th century or the early decades of the 20th century when fertility was more or less a cultural neurosis—but if it was true then, it is certainly not true now. Actually, the very early studies of marital satisfaction by Ernest Burgess and Leonard Cottrell, also by Burgess and Paul Wallin, failed to support this belief: some of the highest scores on the marital satisfaction scales used in these studies were made by childless couples. . . . •

Parents Are Adults. This bit of folklore might depend on the definition of the word adult, but the fact is that more than 22 percent of teenage girls in the United States bear a child before their 20th birthday.

One teenage mother said to us: "My husband and I are just kids. We're growing up with the baby." This experiment may turn out well, but it frightens most child-development specialists. . . .

Parenthood Receives Top Priority in Our Society. This is a choice bit of folklore. Ask any employee if the company gives priority to his role as a parent when they need a person in another branch in a different city. As a matter of fact, parenthood in American society has always had to defer to military and industrial needs, to say nothing about other community needs. Millions of fathers and mothers have to sandwich their parental role into niches between their other roles in society. . . .

Love Is Enough to Guarantee Good Parental Performance. Bruno Bettelheim, one of the authorities on child rearing, says that love is not enough. His main point is that love has to be guided by knowledge and insight and also tempered with self-control on the part of the parent.

It is quite possible, however, that the reverse proposition is true: that no amount of scientific or professional knowledge about child development will do parents (or their children) any good unless it is mixed with love for the child and acceptance of the parental role. . . .

The One-Parent Family Is Pathogenic. No one would deny that it is helpful to have both a father and a mother in the home when children are growing up—this assumes, however, that the two parents are compatible and share the same philosophy of child rearing. In view of the rate of marital failure in our society, this statement is a large assumption.

But has it been proven that children cannot grow up properly in a one-parent family? In a careful review of hundreds of studies of children, Kadushin reached this conclusion: 'The association between single-parent familyhood and psychosocial pathology is neither strong nor invariable.' Kadushin's main finding was that our society is not properly organized for the one-parent family—our social institutions were designed for the two-parent family system. . . .

Parenthood Ends When Children Leave Home. It doesn't, of course. The out-of-sight, out-of-mind phenomenon does tend to help though; if you don't *know* that the kids are out late at a rock concert and that they're probably drinking or stoned, you can probably sleep better. Getting the young adults out of the nest certainly helps in this regard. But they still usually keep coming back: for money, to have their clothes washed, for advice and consolation, and so on. Parents are still giving more, and children are still receiving more for a long time after the nest empties.

SOURCE: *LeMasters and DeFrain, 1983, pp. 22–34.*

When she is breast-feeding her five-week-old son, Dawn says, "It is just the two of us and I feel very circular about it, like there's a little wall around both of us. Nat [her husband] always touches the baby's head while I'm feeding him. I insist that it is bothering the baby. It doesn't really affect the baby at all. The baby's just sucking away like crazy. But I don't want any intrusion into that little wall. Of course, after I've breast-fed, I say, 'Sorry—I know you want to be part of this wonderful thing that both of us are going through and next time I'll let you pat his head.' And the next time comes around and I still can't stand it. It's a feeling that I never thought I'd have. I thought I'd be very loving and giving about this baby, and I'm really really not." (Galinsky, 1981, p. 85)

Another stress that affects marital closeness is the lack of privacy. As children grow older and become more mobile, the privacy that the couple once experienced before parenthood diminishes. The couple cannot talk as openly and disclose themselves as freely in front of the children.

The impact of children on the partners' emotional closeness has been cited by some couples as the reason they remain childfree. Many of these couples recognize the stress that children can have on an intimate relationship. Often couples without children seem closer and more involved with their mates as friends. They are also more dependent on each other and have more time to spend together (Burgwyn, 1981). With children, such closeness is obviously more difficult to maintain.

SOCIAL DEVELOPMENT OF CHILDREN

Infancy

THE NATURE OF HUMAN BEINGS. What is the nature of infants at birth? With what mo-

tivations are they born? A long historical debate has been carried on among social scientists, philosophers, and theologians as to whether human beings are "good" or "bad" by nature. Early writers of child-care manuals often took a negative view of human nature, characterizing human infants as selfish and pleasure-seeking creatures. Total infant depravity was the view taken by many early American writers. Books stressed "beating the devil out of a child." Parental responsibility and discipline were highly emphasized because of the conception of the child as essentially willful, self-centered, and sinful. Early Puritan and other Christian writings stressed that "Children must not have their every whim and impulse gratified, for otherwise they will never develop that sense of humility without which human happiness is impossible" (Blustein, 1982, p. 54).

Other social scientists and philosophers have taken a much more optimistic view, stating that the newborn infant is good by nature. It is the evil found in society that prevents individuals from behaving as they should. It is said that if the right combination of social conditions can be found and put into practice, individuals could live as almost "perfect" creatures. Most utopian writers and many communal societies have taken this position. This humanistic perspective stresses the idea that within each person there is the capacity for goodness, but it is inhibited by societal rules, norms, and expectations.

A third position emphasized by many sociologists, anthropologists, and behaviorist psychologists is the "blank slate" approach. The infant is seen as neither good nor bad at birth; the child is a blank slate, waiting to be written upon. Whatever a person becomes in life is totally the result of environmental influences. Biological influences are usually excluded or minimized in this point of view.

The "blank slate" view has been criticized as being an oversocialized view of human beings. That is, social scientists have placed too much emphasis on the socialization process, on culture, in determining human behavior (Wrong, 1961). Human beings are said to be much more than a "blank slate" at birth, a "blob" to be determined by society and taught to play roles and behave in particular ways. Humans are more than "hollowed-out, empty beings filled with substance only by society" (Montagu, 1983, p. xxxvi).

Whether one wants to describe the nature of infants as "good," "evil," or "neutral," there is general agreement that the infant is primarily concerned with self. He or she has no regard for the well-being of others. The infant does not, and cannot, to any significant degree, consider the needs of other human beings.

Infants are not purposefully selfish and self-interested. Their total dependence at birth requires self-centeredness for survival. This condition is determined not by choice but by biological necessity. Infants are totally dependent on others to provide them with food, water, a change of diapers, comfort, and protection. And their one means of communicating these needs is crying.

Fortunately, as most children grow older, they do not remain totally *self-centered*. They will, however, remain *self-interested*. Self-interest is not an undesirable trait; it is a neutral description of what motivates human beings. Acts carried out in our own self-interest can result in *either* positive or negative effects on others. Indeed, a primary goal in the socialization of children involves teaching them that it is in their own self-interest to be good and kind to other individuals.

Humans vary, however, in their degree of self-centeredness, which is considered to be a negative trait. As adults, our degree of self-centeredness varies depending on the quantity and quality of nurturing we received in early childhood and on the positive and neg-

ative reinforcements we receive throughout life (Kersten and Kersten, 1981).

THE INFANT'S REPERTOIRE OF SOCIAL BEHAVIOR.   Recent research reveals that babies are more attuned to the world around them than was originally suspected. "They see more, hear more, understand more and they are genetically prewired to make friends with any adult who cares for them" (Friedrich, 1983). Within a few weeks, they can recognize the sound of their mothers' voices.

An infant is biologically programmed with certain perceptual and motor abilities that lead it and enable it to engage in social interaction. Through a limited repertoire of a series of reflexes, such as visual responsiveness, fleeting smiles, hand grasps, and other body movements, a newborn exchanges reactions with the caregiver. These reflexes play a critical role in bringing forth nurturing responses from the caregiver.

Social scientists are beginning to study more closely the effects infants can have on the people in their environment. No longer do they confine their studies only to the influence of the caregiver on the infant.

It should also be considered that an individual who starts an interaction by that very fact is exercising control over the other. The other has to react on the initiator's behavioral "home ground," so to speak. Thus, when we realize that an infant or young child starts approximately 50% of the interactions (Bell, 1971), we must consider that a substantial degree of control is exerted thereby over the parent, even if it is not exerted in any other way. In this respect there is a type of balance in the relationship, which fits neither the notion of the parents socializing the young in a unidirectional fashion, or the opposite, that the young socialize adults so that they become parents. (R. Q. Bell, 1974, p. 14)

Although the infant's behavior is largely reflexive, it can be quite effective in eliciting particular behaviors from its parents. "It [the baby] has a set of behaviors which are highly effective in bringing about support, protection, and maintenance of optimal states" (R. Q. Bell, 1974, p. 14).

The infant's gaze, for example, is one behavior that has an important impact on the caregiver. Within minutes of birth, most alert newborns can follow with their eyes and head any objects passed across their visual field (Stern, 1977). It also appears, from the very beginning, that the infant finds the human face fascinating, and the caregiver's face in particular attracts the infant the most. Throughout the first few months the infant's gaze develops further. By gazing into the caregiver's face the infant is able to attract his or her attention and elicit some response. Thus, an infant's behaviors can invite or discourage the caregiver to interact.

TEMPERAMENT. The interaction between the caregiver and the infant is strongly colored by the temperament of the infant. Ask any mother of two or more children if each of them demonstrated different temperaments at birth, and she will almost certainly agree. In the late 1960s a group of researchers—Stella Chess, Alexander Thomas, and Herbert Birch—began to analyze and describe some differences in temperament in children. The term *temperament* refers to the style of an individual child's behavior, the "how" (manner) of that behavior rather than the "what" (content) or "why" (motivation). These researchers (1965) grouped the temperaments of the children they observed into three major categories—easy babies, slow-to-warm-up babies, and difficult babies.

Easy babies are described as being in a predominantly positive mood, highly regular in their biological functions, readily adapta-

ble, less intense in their reactions, and usually agreeable in approaching new situations (Chess, Thomas, and Birch, 1965). These are infants who have regular and predictable sleeping and feeding schedules, who smile at strangers, who can accept unfamiliar foods, and who can adapt to changes in their routines. The easy child is likely to evoke favorable responses in those around him or her and thus will tend to experience the world as warm, pleasant, and accepting.

Difficult babies are irregular in their biological functions, have predominantly negative responses to new situations, are slow to adapt to change, and are moody (Chess, Thomas, and Birch, 1965). In contrast to easy children, these infants have an unpredictable sleeping and feeding schedule; initially reject new foods or toys; require long periods of adjustment to altered routines, and are more likely to fuss than express pleasure. Violent tantrums are often their response to frustration.

The temperament of *slow-to-warm-up* babies falls in between those of the easy and the difficult children. These infants will initially react to new situations with a combination of negative, though mildly intense, responses. But they will gradually adapt after repeated contact with the situation. Slow-to-warm-up children cannot be pushed into facing a new situation. Pressure to do so will only intensify the child's tendency to withdraw, and a negative interaction may ensue.

Given the different temperaments of infants, what is of utmost importance is the match between the temperament of the infant and that of the caregiver. A "live-wire" baby and a slow, passive parent, for example, will have more difficulty adjusting to each other than will an active baby and an active parent (Galinsky, 1981). Likewise, an active and intense parent may find a passive, slow-to-warm-up baby difficult to adjust to. There

Infants begin to develop the capacity for intimacy and interpersonal behavior with their attachments to their mothers. Infants can also provide a degree of intimacy for their attachment figures.

needs to be a "goodness of fit" between the temperament of the adult and that of the child. For example, a difficult child requires a caregiver who has the patience and tolerance to handle his or her special demands. And a slow-to-warm-up child will resist insistent pressure and demands from a caregiver, but will respond to patient encouragement.

Thus intimate interaction with a caregiver will vary in part according to the infant's temperament. For example, an easy baby will be more likely to cuddle than the other two types, hence fostering close contact between the caregiver and the infant. In comparing 16 babies of high cuddliness with 16 babies of low cuddliness, researchers found differences in the mother's handling of the infant to be significantly influenced by the infant's cuddliness (Will, 1978).

Certain infants are sociable almost from birth, smiling frequently and obviously enjoying cuddles and caresses, which encourages family members to respond warmly to them. In contrast, some infants seem un-

comfortable with physical closeness. Being cuddly with them is less rewarding for family members, who learn not to be too affectionate; with experience, these children become even less socially oriented. For both kinds of children, temperament and experience reinforce each other, unless family members deliberately encourage the unsociable child to be sociable. (Rubenstein and Shaver, 1982, p. 55)

Temperament can, therefore, encourage or discourage various responses from caregivers. Positive responses from caregivers, in turn, encourage the child further to develop certain characteristics or behaviors.

An extreme example of the effects of a child's temperament on the caregiver's behavior can be seen in some cases of child abuse. In some studies of battered children, parents saw the *child* as the cause of the problem. In fact, the parents thought they were being abused by the child. This could easily be interpreted as a parent attempting to defend or excuse his or her abusive behavior. It is quite common, however, to find that other children in the family of an abused child are not abused.

Constant fussing, strange and highly irritating crying, or other exasperating behaviors, were often reported for the one child subject to abuse in the family. Some children were abused in successive foster homes in which they were placed after the initial abuse. . . . The deviance in the child was at least as substantial a factor in explaining the incidents as was deviance in the parent, and the stressful circumstances under which they lived. (R. Q. Bell, 1974, pp. 5–6)

ATTACHMENT—THE FIRST CLOSE RELATIONSHIP. Up to this point, we've mainly discussed interactions between an infant and his or her caregiver, who is usually the mother.

As the infant and the mother interact, what forms, it is hoped, is the infant's first close relationship. Many people believe that the capacity for intimacy and other interpersonal behavior begins with this attachment to the mother—or other primary caregiver. An attachment is a strong affectional tie that an infant forms with another person, binding them together and enduring over time (Ainsworth, 1973). It is this attachment figure to whom the infant clings when upset, runs to following separation, and relies upon as a source of security so as to be able to move about the environment and freely explore (Belsky, Lerner, and Spanier, 1984). Through the attachment relationship the infant learns to trust in the reliability of his or her environment and to develop a basic and general sense of trust in the world.

Near the end of the first year, certain behaviors of the infant indicate whether an attachment relationship has been formed. More specifically, some time around the ninth month the infant manifests *stranger anxiety.* This reaction varies from mild apprehension to extreme distress at the approach or presence of a stranger. Shortly after the appearance of stranger anxiety, most infants show a *separation reaction* when the primary caregiver leaves their presence, and they show a *reunion reaction* when she or he returns (Stern, 1977). The separation anxiety is usually one of distress, varying in intensity depending on the individual infant. When the infant is reunited with the caregiver, the reaction is one of joy and affectionate behavior.

What type of caregiving behavior enables an attachment to form? To begin with, it is not merely the quantity of time spent with the infant that determines the quality of an attachment. It is the caregiver's degree of sensitivity in responding to the infant's signals that is most important. The caregiver's ability to read the infant's cues and respond appro-

A separation reaction is one indication that an infant has formed an attachment relationship.

priately to its needs is significant. It is the *consistent* nurturance and sensitivity of the caregivers that promote a basic trust of the world in the infant.

More specifically, in studies of mothers whose infants had formed secure attachments, the mothers were found to demonstrate particular caregiving behaviors during the infants' first year. They were more responsive to infant crying, held their infants more tenderly and carefully, displayed greater consideration of infant behavior when initiating and terminating breast-feeding, and were more responsive to infant emotional expressions during face-to-face encounters (Ainsworth et al., 1973). Again the infants' behaviors also play a role in the formation of the attachment. Smiling and vocalization are responses that maintain the caregiver in the social interaction and ultimately promote and maintain attachment (R. Q. Bell, 1974).

While parents or parental substitutes are potentially the most common attachment figures, siblings or other children can also serve such a function for infants (Bank and Kahn, 1982). (See Box 10.3.) If a sibling attachment occurs, however, it is usually "incomplete, unsatisfactory, and of an anxious nature." Siblings can serve as "auxiliary attachment figures," especially when the attachment to the mother is not secure. An older brother or sister who is chosen by the parents to be the preferred baby-sitter, can be a constant object to which an infant can turn for reassurance, security, and a warm embrace. However, if the "sibling caretaker has mixed feelings about being put in such a role, the infant may become anxious and forever tentative in its

BOX 10.3

A CASE OF GROUP ATTACHMENT

The potential for attachments to be formed between children of similar ages is illustrated by a case study of six German-Jewish children, who were victims of the Hitler regime (Freud and Dann, 1976). These children, all unrelated, were orphaned soon after birth and spent their first few years of life together. Since there were no consistent adult caregivers, the children became closely attached to one another. After the war the children were sent to a British nursery. The caregivers at the nursery observed an extreme closeness and emotional dependence on one another. Anything that was given to one child was shared by all six. They showed separation anxiety when they were separated from one another, even for short periods of time. The ties of the children to adults at the nursery never reached the strength of the ties among the six children.

responses toward its sibling who does not provide adequate nurturance'' (Bank and Kahn, 1982, p. 29). A sibling attachment may be so strong, however, that a baby can suffer serious depression when separated from that sibling. Consider the following case, originally reported by Ruth Meyendorf (1971):

The nineteen-month-old girl had been placed in her aunt's home, accompanied by her five-year-old brother and three-year-old sister, because her mother had suddenly been hospitalized. There was no remarkable reaction to that separation. However, after one week the girl was moved to another relative's home, but this time without *her siblings. Within the next week, the child had become stuporous, had lost her power of speech, refused food, was withdrawn and agitated, and resisted the affections of anyone, including the mother and father when she was reunited with them. She looked as if she were dying, and would sit listlessly, sometimes calling out her siblings' names. Only after her brother and sister were returned to her, did she seem emotionally responsive, begin to look alive, regain her* speech and usual demeanor, and once more become physically active. (Bank and Kahn, 1982, p. 29)

The quality of an infant's first attachment relationship appears to have a strong impact on social functioning beyond infancy. In one study, those infants classified as having an early secure attachment displayed the most interpersonal and personal competence with peers at age three and a half (Waters, Wippman, and Stroufe, 1979). Infants with secure attachments were observed to be more self-directed in their activity, more curious, more sought out by other children, less withdrawn, more likely to be leaders, and more sympathetic to the distress of peers than age mates judged insecure as infants.

Almost nonexistent is research evidence connecting infant attachment behavior with social behavior as an adult. We can only speculate that these warm and intimate interactions found in an infant-parent relationship involving an attachment contribute to future abilities as an adult to be warm and intimate

Siblings can also serve as attachment figures.

in interpersonal relationships. The importance of the effect of a secure attachment on healthy social development can be seen, however, when an infant is deprived of one. The potential effects of such a deprivation can result in emotional disturbance, physical sickness, or retardation, and under extreme conditions, deprivation can be fatal.

Dr. René Spitz during the 1940s revealed the debilitating effects that the lack of an affectionate dyadic relationship can have on an infant. Children who were institutionalized in foundling homes and who did not receive sufficient tactile stimulation, nurturance, and care failed on all developmental tasks as op-

posed to institutionalized children who were loved and nurtured by their own mothers. The foundling homes studied by Spitz had extremely high mortality rates with one home having 37 percent of the children dying during a two-year observation period. Spitz concluded that death is but an extreme consequence of the general physical and psychological decline that affects children who are completely starved of emotional interchange. ''They die from the privation of love, just as if they had been deprived of food and died of hunger—for what they indeed die of is an unsatisfied hunger for love'' (Montagu and Matson, 1979, p. 116). Apparently, if development is to proceed normally, an adequate emotional attachment must occur some time during the first year of life.

Other social scientists have carried on similar research on nurturant deprivation. John Bowlby (1963) has documented the extensive physical, emotional, and intellectual damage that can result from a young child's separation from his or her parents, especially from the mother, for extended periods of time. James Robertson (1958) studied similar pejorative effects on children who were hospitalized and separated from their mothers. The findings of many other investigators, both on humans and on various lower animals, abundantly testify to the critical importance of a secure attachment early in life.

Childhood

BEYOND EARLY ATTACHMENT. During the preschool years (2 to 4 years old) the child begins to spend more time interacting with other children than exclusively with his or her parents. The child still uses the attachment figure, however, as a secure base from which he or she can explore the world. The child slowly becomes more competent in social exchange, although only a limited understanding of interpersonal relationships and friendship exists. A friend, for example, may be defined as "someone who lives near them, whose toys they like to play with, or who happens to be with them at the moment" (Gurian and Formanek, 1983, p. 26).

During this period, play provides the young child with opportunities to rehearse adult roles and relationships. While dressing up in their parents' clothes and speaking and acting like them, children attempt to imitate their parents and role play their relationships. Children act out certain situations in the home such as family discussions, mealtimes,

and fights. They play different roles, and as they grow older the stories become more precise and complicated. In general, play provides a laboratory in which children experiment with language, communication, leadership, and interpersonal relationships. Through play, children try out social skills, make friends with new children, learn to share, and deal with rejection.

CHANGES IN THE CHILD-PARENT RELATIONSHIP. During childhood (2 to 12 years of age) the close affectional bonds once characteristic of the parent-infant relationship are replaced to a considerable degree by an emphasis on disciplining and training the child. This period marks a transition during which the child makes the passage from baby to teenager, from being fully reliant on parents for all his or her needs to being quite independent from parents in many ways. The parent is more and more involved in training the child to be increasingly self-reliant. Emphasis shifts from a strong emotional closeness in infant-parent interaction involving fondling, cuddling, and caressing to that of teaching the child to be a responsible individual. More demands are placed on the child with age, and close supervision is usually applied.

During this period, the child spends less time solely with the mother (or primary caregiver) and more time interacting with the family as a whole. Although the family may interact as a group, it will most likely not be as physically and emotionally close as was the dyadic interaction between the mother and infant. Hence, the family interaction is not characterized by the same type of closeness and intimacy that once defined the mother-infant exchange. A majority of family activities involve recreation, visiting friends and other families, and chores around the home. A parent may still treat the child in a warm and nurturant way, but he or she will not typically be as permissive as in the parent-infant relationship (Martinson, 1981).

LEARNING SOCIAL SKILLS. Childhood is also a period during which the young person sharpens his or her social skills through interactions with siblings and other children. Becoming less reliant on the security of the family, children form ties with their peers. "Friendships provide a training ground for trying out different ways of relating to others" (Gurian and Formanek, 1983, p. 10). By interacting, children learn how to do whatever needs to be done according to the "rules of the game."

Typically, self-centeredness gradually gives way to the social pressure to work and play with others in cooperation. Empathy, too, is further developed. When children get into conflicts with peers, they can begin to understand the others' positions and learn to accommodate to others' views. Children begin to realize that if they are really going to get what they want (for example, a turn at bat), they will have to cooperate with others.

Playing with children of various ages may encourage the learning of a wide range of social skills. By interacting with an older child, a youngster can have someone to emulate and to depend on. In interactions with younger children, they can learn to give help and provide support.

Siblings can also influence a child's social skills. Those children growing up with a sibling of the other sex are found to be more socially competent in male-female interactions (Rubenstein and Shaver, 1982). In addition, an older sibling can hasten a child's social competence. In fact, the effects of siblings can carry over to the child's capacity to be intimate as an adult. Floyd Martinson surmises, "The degree to which men develop intimate and meaningful relationships with women also appears to depend upon having a female sibling in the household. Sisters as peers, rather than mothers, appear to be the facilitators of male awareness and sensitivity to the female world" (1981, p. 30).

Adolescence

TRANSITION FROM CHILD TO ADULT. Adolescence marks the transition from childhood to adulthood. It is a time period when the young person further separates from his or her parents. But even though adolescents are distancing themselves from parents and trying to be less dependent on them, they are still powerfully affected by parental attitudes and comments. "Financially and legally, if not emotionally, adolescents still depend on their parents for basic survival necessities. . . ." (Csikszentmihalyi and Larson, 1984).

In the process of loosening ties to the family, adolescents look to their peer group for support, approval, and security. They need others of the same age to help them define who they are. Peers serve as models, mirrors, and helpers. Dyads, cliques, or groupings in particular further help individual teenagers establish their selfhoods. That is, by conforming to the group they feel more confident in their own identities.

Compared to the family, friends have everything going for them, at least from the point of view of the adolescent. Teenagers cannot choose their families, but they are free to select their friends. If conflicts arise, the relationship can be ended. . . . Friends do not have to fight over chores, or the bathroom, or other issues that come up in sharing a household.

. . . they [friends] have enough in common to share and validate each other's reality. Family members usually live in a different world, exposed to different expe-

While loosening family ties, young people begin to look to their peer groups for support, approval, and security.

riences. Friends share the teenager's skills in basketball, music, or art; they know the songs of the same rock stars and are going through similar problems with teachers, parents, or boyfriends. (Csikszentmihalyi and Larson, 1984, p. 156)

What appears to be a rebellion from or a rejection of parents may actually be just a stronger pull to be accepted by the peer group. Adolescence is an important developmental stage in which friends, rather than parents, serve the primary educating role. Parents often mistake the primary role of friends in their adolescents' lives for rebellion.

But it is not "flight *from* parents as much as a powerful pull to the peer arena. In fact, it is home that provides a haven from the stress of the peer group rather than the other way around" (Seltzer, 1981). Hence, home is where the adolescent can experience security and the "ultimate friendship" in order to deal with life outside.

An extreme self-consciousness is often typical of adolescents. It can be seen in their concern with clothing and continual attention to their appearance. As adolescents begin to reflect on their own thoughts and feelings, they imagine how others think and feel about them. This occurs to the extent that they tend to believe that everyone can—and wants to—see their thoughts. Because their thoughts have suddenly become evident to them, they assume that they are also evident to everyone else.

THE CAPACITY TO BE INTIMATE. Adolescents are constantly concerned about conforming to group standards and being accepted by their peers. This anxiety about receiving approval from others prevents them from relaxing and makes intimate relationships more difficult to achieve (Rubenstein and Shaver, 1982). Peer relationships may offer adolescents an opportunity to be emotionally close, but often they are so concerned with conformity and acceptance that they will not want to risk disclosing personal feelings for fear of rejection. It is not until adolescents have developed confidence and security in themselves that they can risk the revelation of their deepest feelings and thoughts.

In general, the skills to relate intimately with a person of the other sex have not fully developed in adolescence. The teenager still appears somewhat awkward with emotional relationships. Several reasons account for this awkwardness. First, teenagers lack experience in intimate interaction with the other sex. Second, young people lack power or feel that they lack power. They may feel they do not have much to give to another person. Finally, adolescents may have difficulties with an intimate relationship because they are quite idealistic about relationships; often lacking is a realism that comes from experience in dealing with human beings (Kersten and Kersten, 1981).

Despite this awkwardness, during adolescence there is a shift from same-sex groups to opposite-sex dyads (see Figure 10.1). But relationships with the other sex are often superficial or described as "pseudo-attached." Ironically, an adolescent may be "going with" someone but doesn't really know or care much about that person. An 18-year-old remarks, "I had a boyfriend during those years, but I didn't like him much. . . . I needed someone to take me places, and he seemed

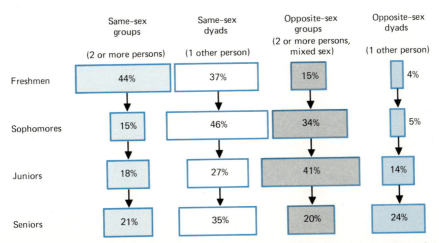

Figure 10.1 The shift from same-sex to opposite-sex friends. The diagram shows the percentage of time with friends that students in each grade spent with different types of friends. (*Source*: Csikszentmihaly and Larson, 1984, p. 160.)

willing, but we never really talked much about anything. I felt a lot closer to my dog than I did to him" (Rubenstein and Shaver, 1982, p. 75).

Since the skills to develop heterosexual intimacy are in short supply to adolescents, there is a tendency for them to value popularity over a few close friendships. Teenagers are not constantly searching for an emotional relationship; rather they appear more preoccupied with becoming a cheerleader or a star jock. "This is unfortunate," Rubenstein and Shaver point out, "because popularity is, by definition, in short supply, while friendship, mutual self-disclosure, and emotional support are potentially available to everyone" (p. 78). Teenagers become frustrated in their attempts to attain popularity. And those who do attain it are disappointed to find it is not all it was cracked up to be.

TEENAGE FRIENDSHIPS. In a classic study of 3500 adolescents, Elizabeth Douvan and Joseph Adelson (1966) analyzed the friendship patterns of teenagers and found different patterns for males and females. As girls proceed through adolescence, their friendships become closer and involve greater emotional investment. For 11- to 13-year-old girls, friendship was based on mutual activity rather than intimacy; they were busy and cooperative in activities but not necessarily close. There appeared to be more emotional commitment and closeness to their families than their friends.

For somewhat older girls, 14- to 16-year-olds, friendships were more emotional and intimate. "They want a friend they can confide in, someone who can offer emotional support and understanding" (Douvan and Adelson, 1966, p. 188). These girls stressed security, trust, and loyalty in these friendships. At these ages, girls may spend more spare time with friends than with family.

The 17- and 18-year-old girls were "calmer" about their relationships with girlfriends and more secure about their boyfriends. As girls' self-esteem increased so did their capacity for intimacy. In fact, the researchers found intimate relationships were closely related to girls' self-esteem and confidence, to a greater degree than for boys. With higher self-esteem and confidence, teenage girls could approach their relationships with less anxiety about conformity and acceptance, and thus they were more willing to disclose their true feelings. Although girls will form groups with their peers, they are also likely to have at least one or two friends to whom they're especially close.

Boys' friendships throughout adolescence are generally quite nonintimate. Teenage boys of all ages are "less sophisticated about friendship and less eager for intimacy than girls of the same age" (Douvan and Adelson, 1966, p. 195). Boys' friendships consistently revolve around activities. They want friends mostly for cooperation and assistance, and they are less interested than girls in emotional closeness. Their socialization has typically stressed activity and achievement, and there is little focus on cultivating traits such as sensitivity, warmth, and empathy. Unlike girls, they probably lack a friend with whom they are especially close.

CURRENT ISSUES IN PARENTING

Styles of Child Rearing

The dependence upon "experts" to tell us how to raise our children is not a new phenomenon. Since the late 1700s, books and manuals have been written about child care. The difference between then and now is primarily the focus of these books. A sole concern with the moral and physical well-being of children has been largely replaced by focusing attention on their social and emotional well-being.

Changes in child-rearing practices are primarily the result of specific cultural and societal changes. The high infant mortality rate during the 1700s and 1800s caused parents to be preoccupied with the physical health of the infant. During the 1700s, one-half of the babies born died before they reached 5 years of age, most dying before their first birthdays (Hardyment, 1983).

With this expectation of early death, the moral upbringing of the child became extremely important. The prospect of heaven or hell was a major source of motivation in parents' attempts to "form the minds" of their children (Newson and Newson, 1976). They wanted to ensure that the child would be "saved" at least spiritually, if not physically.

Particular child-rearing styles depend on the cultural norms and attitudes of the larger society. The purpose of child-rearing practices is to socialize children so they can later fulfill adult roles in society. Since cultural expectations can vary from society to society, so will the styles of child rearing vary. (See Box 10.4.)

Within American society today child-rearing practices differ somewhat among socioeconomic classes. Again these differences reflect an overall purpose to prepare children for later adult roles. In her study on working class families, Lillian Rubin (1976) found that early childhood training in these families tends to focus on "respect, orderliness, cleanliness—in a word, discipline" (p. 128).

Professional, middle-class families, by contrast, are more likely to emphasize creativity, spontaneity, and innovation as important values in raising children. Why the class difference? Rubin attributes it to the larger social context in which these families live. Namely, to succeed in jobs typical of the lower classes, creativity, innovation, and initiative are considered by superiors a hindrance. Working-class parents are preparing and training their children for jobs that require obedience and respect, similar to their own jobs. Professional, middle-class parents assume that their children are also destined to do work like theirs, work that requires innovation, initiative, flexibility, creativity, and sensitivity to others.

Various child-rearing techniques, ranging from common sense to the absurd, have come and gone in American society. But still there exist anxiety and confusion about the "correct" or "right" way to raise children. Parents' personal philosophies and child-rearing practices may depend on which "expert" or "parenting guru" they choose to follow. The multiplicity of approaches and theories of child rearing have at times caused more anxiety than relief, traditionally to mothers. Baruch, Barnett, and Rivers (1983) explain:

> Child-rearing "experts" have placed a burden of guilt on women by giving the impression that specific techniques of child rearing make the difference in how children turn out. Child rearing has too often been presented as an exact science, and mothers worry that if they aren't up on the latest theory or technique, their children are bound to suffer. (p. 86)

But how *does* a parent's approach to child rearing affect a child? Attempts to answer this question begin by trying to classify parenting into different styles. One notable classification identifies three types of parents: authoritarian, permissive, and authoritative (Baumrind, 1971). Diane Baumrind based her categories on the degree of control that parents try to maintain over their children.

The *authoritarian* parent, on the one hand, values obedience as a virtue. Punitive, forceful, disciplinary measures are used when

BOX 10.4

CHILD REARING—JAPANESE AND AMERICAN STYLES

Child-rearing approaches are based on particular assumptions about the innate nature of human beings. The Japanese, for example, believe that the infant is a willful, asocial creature. The child will move away from people unless the mother can "tame" him and "deflect his natural instincts" (Kagan, 1976). The Japanese mother usually soothes and quiets her infant, suppressing the excitement that the American mother tries to arouse (Kagan, 1976). The relationship between mother and child in Japan is intensely close. So close, in fact, that a common and accepted practice is co-sleeping—the child and the mother sleeping together for as long as 10 years—a practice frowned upon by most middle-class Americans. In both verbal and nonverbal ways, the Japanese mother conveys to the child a deep, warm feeling that the child is the most important thing in the world to her. The mother-child relationship in Japan focuses on forming a dependence in the child, which fosters compliance and obedience (Garfinkel, 1983, p. 56).

While the Japanese encourage dependent behavior, Americans discourage it. A popular American conception of the infant is that he or she is inherently helpless and that it is up to the caregivers to teach the child to become independent. Therefore, in the United States, in contrast to Japan, there is more pressure for children to separate from their parents and to think independently.

The ultimate purpose of any child-rearing orientation is to produce certain types of adult personalities who will "fit in" with the particular society. The Japanese mother stresses to her child the most pervasive values of Japanese society: "the work ethic, selflessness, and group endeavor." The whole philosophy of child rearing in Japan aims at a strong group orientation, which is part and parcel of the Japanese culture. Harmonious human relations is a basic value orientation in Japan, as is a strong sense of reciprocal obligation, responsibility, and dependence.

Unlike the Japanese, parents in the United States attempt to instill in their children a sense of individualism. Independence and self-reliance are often overemphasized at the expense of cooperation and harmonious human relationships. Whereas the Japanese stress obedience and the authority of parents, modern American parents try to be "friends" to their children (Newson and Newson, 1976).

the child's actions or beliefs conflict with what the parents think they should be. Such parents believe strongly in respect for authority and emphasize the maintenance of order and the traditional social structure.

The *permissive* parent, on the other hand, is not active in shaping or altering a child's behavior. The child is largely left to govern and control his or her own activities. The parent tries to act in a nonpunitive and accepting manner. The adult merely offers himself or herself as a "resource" to be used as the child wishes. Moreover, the parent does not encourage the child to obey any particular social standards of behavior.

Baumrind's third type of parent, the *authoritative,* appears to be the most nurturant, offers a high degree of positive reinforcement, and infrequently uses punishment. Although these parents are quite responsive to their children's demands for attention, they are by no means indulgent. They are ready to direct and control their children's activities, but they are at the same time sensitive to their children's thoughts, feelings, and unique developmental capabilities. They do not insist on obedience for its own sake, although guidelines and rules tend to be enforced in a consistent manner. It is common for such a parent to share with the child the reasoning behind parental actions.

Regarding the effects of these parenting styles on the child's social development, Baumrind found that certain patterns evolve. Children of authoritarian parents were found to be "less cheerful and more moody" than others, as well as apprehensive, unhappy, easily annoyed, and vulnerable to stress. And they tended not to be socially competent. Baumrind observed that children of permissive parents tended to be impulsive and aggressive. The permissive parent does not give enough support or control to the young child, who has very little control over his or her own behavior. These were children seemingly out of control, who had difficulty inhibiting their desires. Their mood was more cheerful, however, than that of the children of authoritarian parents. Lastly, the children of authoritative parents appeared to be the most socially competent. These children tended to display high levels of self-reliance, self-control, cheerfulness, and friendly relations with peers.

But what about the long-term effects of various parental styles? One longitudinal study begun in the 1950s attempted to answer this question. A group of researchers charted 150 separate child-rearing techniques used by approximately 400 mothers of kindergarten children. In the 1970s another researcher and his colleagues interviewed the now grown children and gave them a battery of personality tests (McClelland et al., 1978). They found that specific techniques used by parents didn't seem to make much difference in how the children turned out. The researchers concluded, however, that the most important ingredient in the parent-child relationship was how the parent *felt* about the child. "When parents loved the children, and expressed that love so that the children were aware of it, the children grew up to achieve the highest levels of maturity. The only specific practice that seemed to harm the children was parental rigidity" (Baruch, Barnett, and Rivers, 1983, p. 87).

Thus, a close relationship between the parent and child seems to be a crucial factor influencing the child's social and emotional health. It appears that specific techniques do not make a significant difference, except for extreme practices. Rather the nature of the parent-child relationship plays the strongest role in predicting the positive development of children.

Mothers Working Outside the Home

The percentage of women working outside the home has steadily increased during the past 30 years (see Figure 10.2). This is one of the most important revolutions of the twentieth century. Nearly 65 percent of women with children age 6 to 17 were working in 1980. Close to 50 percent with children under age 6 were working.

Numerous studies have concluded that

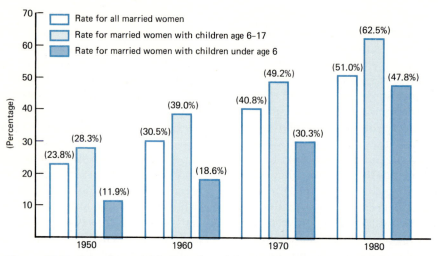

Figure 10.2 Labor force participation of married women and married women with children, 1950–1980. (*Source*: U.S. Dept. of Labor.)

working has a positive impact on a woman's sense of well-being (Baruch, Barnett, and Rivers, 1983; Veroff, Douvan, and Kulka, 1981). Working outside the home can enhance self-esteem and a sense of competence, particularly if a woman wants to work. But when a mother goes to work, what are the effects on her children? Will children be better off or possibly harmed by their mothers' working? How does a mother juggle her time among work, husband, and children? These are questions continually asked in discussions among mothers and heard repeatedly in counseling sessions with overstressed parents. The answers are not simple and straightforward but involve a complexity of variables. Indicated below are some positive and negative aspects of maternal employment on children.

ELIMINATING RIGID GENDER ROLES.
Growing up as the child of a working mother allows for the development of broader ideas of what men and women can do. Living with a mother who has a career conveys to a daughter the possibility that she herself may want to pursue one and that she is not re-

stricted to one role, that of housewife and homemaker. Girls today are learning that women, too, have career goals, are capable of financial independence, and can be contributing members of society outside the home. Knowing this, a daughter can exercise a choice among working, raising a family, or both.

Boys with working mothers can also gain from the experience. When they reach adulthood, these boys may have learned to relate to females in the workplace in a more unbiased, equal, and accepting way than men of past generations. In addition, the firsthand experience of having a working mother may also influence any meaningful heterosexual relationship boys might have later (Long and Long, 1983). Like the daughter, the boy will view women as having a choice and will not automatically assume that they will become full-time homemakers.

MORE INDEPENDENCE AND RESPONSIBILITY FOR CHILDREN. A household with no full-time homemaker usually means that children are entrusted with more household chores and with responsibilities to care for them-

"Hurried children" may be encouraged to dress like scaled-down versions of adults.

the working women in one sample felt that they didn't have enough time for their children (Bodin and Mitelman, 1983). Women with younger children in particular felt the need to spend more time with them.

Children of working mothers are also cognizant of the lack of time with parents. An often-cited problem mentioned by latch-key children (children who come home to an empty house) is that they feel their parents are uninterested, or unavailable, at best. In the absence of their parents, these children will often confide in and share their life experiences with friends in the neighborhood or in school. Parents often feel as though they've "missed out" when their children are reluctant to repeat what they've already shared at length with a friend (Long and Long, 1983).

Time constraints force working mothers to establish priorities. If a working mother has only two hours in the evening, she may need to decide whether to spend that time preparing her family a gourmet dinner or helping her child with homework and reading him or her a bedtime story. Time spent in parent-child interaction may be chosen over time spent on domestic tasks.

selves. One research study on children of working mothers found that these children usually are more independent and responsible than children of nonworking mothers (D. Gold, 1983). These additional responsibilities may foster a sense of competence and trustworthiness. In addition, the children view themselves as important and as contributing members of the family. At the same time, parents need to be sensitive to the amount of responsibilities placed on children. Demanding that they take on adult obligations and burdens too early may "hurry" the children to the point that they feel they missed out on childhood. (See Box 10.5.)

SCARCITY OF TIME WITH PARENTS. The lack of time is a concern most frequently cited by both parents and children. Fifty percent of

Research demonstrates that women who choose to pursue a career and strive to maintain a close relationship with their children must make personal sacrifices. They sleep less and have less time for the pursuit of personal interests. Time is spent with children on the weekends to compensate for the lack of time during the week and evening outings are limited. But these sacrifices are necessary when both parents work in order to help the children feel they are a wanted part of the family rather than a liability. (Long and Long, 1983, p. 161)

INADEQUATE CHILD CARE. A frequently encountered obstacle for many working mothers is finding adequate child care. The need

BOX 10.5

THE HURRIED CHILD

It was a party like any other: ice cream and cake, a donkey poster and twelve haphazard tails, and a door prize for everyone including Toby, the birthday girl's little brother who couldn't do anything but smear icing.

"Ooh," sighed seven-year-old Melissa as she opened her first present. It was Calvin Klein jeans. "Aah," she gasped as the second box revealed a bright new top from Gloria Vanderbilt. There were Christian Dior undies from grandma—a satiny little chemise and matching bloomer bottoms—and mother herself had fallen for a marvelous party outfit from Yves St. Laurent. Melissa's best friend gave her an Izod sports shirt, complete with alligator emblem. Added to that a couple of books were, indeed, very nice and predictable—except for the fancy doll one guest's eccentric mother insisted on bringing. (From S. Ferraro, "Hotsy Totsy," *American Way,* April 1981, p. 61, quoted in Elkind, 1981, p. 8)

The child as a mini–fashion plate is just one example of the way children today are expected to be scaled-down versions of adults. According to David Elkind, author of *The Hurried Child* (1981), childhood is no longer seen as a special stage of life but as an anteroom to life, a room from which children are encouraged, expected, and pressured to flee. Children are hurried into adulthood, quickly adopting the outward appearance of adults, while remaining children inside.

Parents, schools, and the media all contribute to the increasingly popular, though medieval, image of the child as a miniature adult. Academic pressures are felt at an earlier age than ever before. Reading and math, once reserved for older children, are often subjects for kindergarteners. Books and movies expose children to complex information that leaves them knowing much more than they can understand. On television programs and in advertisements, intellectually or sexually advanced children are the norm. Television's "Webster" and Jordache jeans commercials provide just two examples among the many video versions of the hurried child. The message children are receiving is that the precocious child is the valued child. To be average in today's fast-paced, cope-without-cracking society is tantamount to being a loser.

"Today's child," Elkind states, "has become the unwilling, unintended victim of overwhelming stress—the stress born of rapid bewildering social change and constantly rising expectations" (p. 3). Parents, too, suffer from the stress of competing demands, role changes, and uncertainties over which they exert little control. To escape from the added stress of child rearing, parents hurry their children into adulthood and sometimes expect them to fill roles that provide adult support and partnership.

Changing attitudes that encourage women to have careers outside the home have unfortunately left some nonworking mothers feeling like less than adequate persons. Sometimes these mothers can bolster their sagging self-esteem by having a precocious son or daughter as a status symbol. In addition, if both parents work, children are burdened with adult responsibilities that could interfere with healthy emotional development. Moreover, the child of a working single parent is not only given extra household responsibilities but sometimes serves as a confidant or therapist to the parent. Consider the following example.

> Janet is ten years old but has many adult responsibilities. In addition to taking care of her clothes and room, she must prepare breakfast for herself and her younger sister and make sure that they get off to school on time. (Her mother leaves for work an hour before Janet needs to get to school.) When she gets home, she has to do some housecleaning, defrost some meat for dinner, and make sure her sister is all right. When her mother gets home Janet listens patiently to her mother's description of the "creeps" at work who never leave her alone and who are always making cracks or passes. After Janet helps prepare dinner, her mother says, "Honey, will you do the dishes? I'm just too tired," and Janet barely has time to do some homework. (Elkind, 1981, p. 149)

The consequences of such expectations for children may seem benign on the surface. How many of us have noted, with amazement, how mature for their age our little relatives are? Unfortunately, this adult facade can interfere with our understanding of the child underneath. It can also interfere with children's understanding of themselves. "The task of self-discovery is more difficult when children are presented with the problems and difficulties of others before they have had a chance to find meaning in their own lives" (p. 83).

The lack of self-understanding is further reinforced when the hurried child has neither the opportunity nor the resources to form intimate friendships. Rather, friends may be others with whom one shares his or her adult facade. Experimentation with sexual behavior, drugs, and alcohol may not only enhance one's status in his or her peer group, it may also fill the void behind the mask and provide an escape from stress.

Parents should consider whether their expectations are reasonable for their children's developmental levels. If parents believe they are hurrying their children, they may want either to cut back their demands or increase their supports. Elkind recommends responding to the child's feelings rather than intellect, giving the child more opportunities for pure play and fantasy rather than expecting only work and responsibility.

In her book, *Children Without Childhood* (1983), Marie Winn suggests that "An understanding that early childhood is not the only important stage of childhood, that the middle years are equally important, may lead parents to compromise their career and social ambitions and devote more time and attention, more care and supervision, to their post-toddler children, capable and unchildlike though they may seem" (p. 209). While society may seem bent on hurrying its children, parents can take crucial steps to slow down the pace.

for good-quality day-care facilities is greater than the available services. It is estimated that day-care spaces are available for only one out of seven children who have to be cared for. Most parents use a variety of informal arrangements: exchanges with friends, neighbors, and relatives; paid baby-sitters; or leaving the child to take care of herself or himself. In spite of the various types of child care, it is estimated that one-fourth of all child-care users would change their arrangements if options were available to them. At least half of these parents would change from an informal arrangement to a day-care center (Rowe, 1978).

During World War II the federal government established child-care centers in order to help women move into the workplace. The action serves to underline what seems to be universal in many industrial societies; child-care facilities are provided and have high priority when women's labor is needed; otherwise they are a low-priority item (Bardwick, 1979).

The long-term effects of day-care centers on children have been of major interest to many parents and social scientists during recent years. The effect of day care depends to a large degree on the extent to which the

setting resembles the child's experience at home. In other words, a day-care center where one particular adult is assigned a particular child allows for a possible close, one-to-one relationship to be established between the child and the caregiver. What may harm children most is a multiplicity of caregivers. When all the children are the wards of all the staff, there is less opportunity for the development of a one-to-one relationship. It is unlikely that multiple caregivers will really get to know each child, nor will they see or understand each child's emotional needs and anxieties.

For those working mothers with school-age children, the problem becomes finding someone to watch their children before and after school. Owing to the lack of availability of this type of care, children are frequently left to themselves. If properly arranged, this is a viable alternative. But for many children this responsibility is too overwhelming and results in many fears and anxieties. Programs such as "Phone-A-Friend," a telephone hotline for latchkey children, have been developed to alleviate some of the loneliness and fears.

In sum, no general conclusion can be made that maternal employment is "good"

cathy®   **by Cathy Guisewite**

In day-care centers, one adult is often assigned to a large number of children. Unfortunately, this does not allow a one-to-one relationship to be established between the child and the caregiver.

or "bad"; there are advantages and disadvantages in certain circumstances. The impact of a mother's work on family life will depend on several factors. The first is the way the mother, father, and society in general *feel* about the way the mother's working will affect the child. If the parent feels guilty, stressed, and in conflict about meeting family needs versus career needs, working may become an unpleasant experience. Many women feel that a career is still not legitimized by society as a whole and that they should be staying at home with their young children. Constant guilt about their work and the lack of care for their children may hinder their concentration at work and their subsequent work performance. "If the woman feels guilty, if a husband thinks he has somehow failed to provide adequate support, if a child feels that all the other kids' mothers are staying home and only he is being shuttled off to caregivers, then these attitudes can make a mother's working an unhappy experience all around" (M. Long, 1983, p. 5).

The second factor is the quality of the child care acquired for the preschooler or for the child before and after school. Warm and nurturing caregivers who provide consistent care and on whom the child can depend will help to foster the positive emotional and social development of the child.

The third factor is the nature of the parent-child interaction. The *quality* of time needs to be attended to closely since the quantity is so sparse. A close and trusting relationship between parent and child becomes especially critical in dealing with the situation in which both parents work. Limited time together and the stresses of working make close family ties difficult to maintain.

> *Parents must make sure they [the children] feel both loved and wanted. Convincing children of this when they're feeling rejected isn't easy. Consistency is critical. If parents want to maintain intimacy with their children, it is important that they work regularly to develop a close and open relationship, taking the time to listen to both daily happenings and problems. . . .*
>
> *Dependability is another way of communicating concern. A parent who says, "I'll be home at 5:30," but doesn't come home until 7:00, is likely to be misinterpreted as a sign of not caring about the child. Too often parents hear confirmation of this when their children say things like, "Your work is more important to you than I am," or "If you cared about me you'd come home from work sooner." (Long and Long, 1983, p. 172)*

Fatherhood: A Neglected Role?

A slow but gradual trend for fathers to become more involved in parenting has been developing. Nearly 80 percent of all husbands are now present with their wives during childbirth, compared with only 27 percent a decade ago (Gallup survey of 645 women in *USA Today,* n.d., 1985). With more and more women working outside the home and returning to work earlier after the birth of a child, pressure is being put on men to participate in child care. In divorces more fathers are seeking custody of their children and are somewhat more successful in obtaining it than in the past. In 1979, approximately 10 percent of divorced fathers had custody of their children in the United States (Parke, 1981).

However, the degree to which fathers are spending time with their children in two-parent families appears still to be minimal. Time studies have revealed some astounding statistics in this area. Depending on the particular study, the average amount of time a father interacts with his baby ranges from 38 seconds a day (Rebelsky and Hanks, 1974) to as much as 15 minutes a day (Parke and Sawin, 1977). "Other fathers studied have averaged 26 minutes a day interacting with a child under age five, and 16 minutes with children between the ages of six and seventeen" (Pogrebin, 1983, p. 201). Some argue that the sheer *quantity* of time is less important than the *quality* of interaction (Parke, 1981). But even 15 minutes—let alone 38 seconds—of interaction with an infant is hardly enough time to change a diaper or rock the baby to sleep! Indeed *both* quantity and quality of time are needed for parenting.

Could the role of mother be easily replaced by the father? Is the interaction between mother and child qualitatively similar to that of father and child? Research shows that soon after birth, mothers and fathers may show a similar amount of interest in their infants. Parke and O'Leary (1976) observed fathers with their babies in the mother's hospital room. The fathers showed a wide variety of parenting behaviors—touching, holding, kissing, exploring, and imitating the infant. Fathers appeared as fascinated with their babies as were mothers.

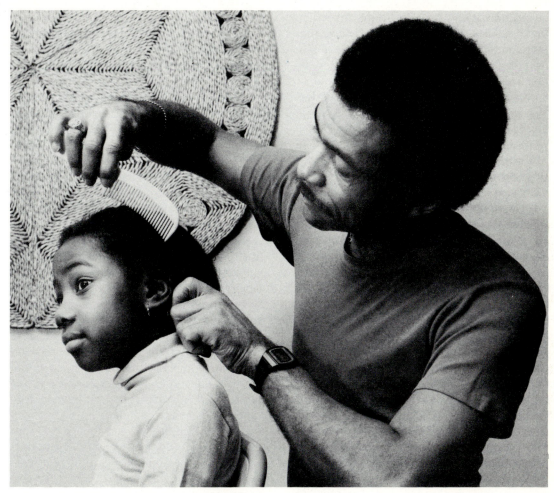

Fathers are gradually becoming more involved in parenting.

Although both mothers and fathers seem equally interested in their infants, there are some differences in the way the two sexes interact with infants and children. When the infant vocalizes, the father is more likely to respond by talking to the baby, while mothers are more likely to react with touching it (Parke, 1981). Fathers are more likely to be found playing with their infants, while mothers spend more time in physical care such as feeding and bathing. Even in families where

the couple hold egalitarian views this traditional division of roles occurs (Parke, 1981). Fathers seem to contribute to their infants' development primarily through play.

A father's involvement in parenting can be influenced by the mother's attitudes. If a father is going to be extensively involved and take responsibility for his children, the mother needs to be willing to share these responsibilities and to encourage her husband to become involved. Some women may resist giving up some "turf" in an area in which they feel they are the experts or believe that the fathers for the most part lack the ability to care for their children. Research reveals that men married to women who hold to traditional gender roles are found to be less involved in child-care activities than those married to more "liberal" or "androgynous" women (G. Russell, 1978).

Research on "solo fathering" also reveals differences between men and women. In one such study conducted in England, Hipgrave (1981) found the problems of solo parenting to differ for the two sexes. The men felt somewhat inadequate in providing intimate emotional support to their children, particularly to their daughters. In contrast, "solo mothers" reported anxiety regarding their inability to maintain the past standard of living and a breakdown of disciplinary control, particularly where sons were concerned. Discipline problems were not considered a concern by the "solo fathers," who appeared to follow stricter rules and who were more consistent in disciplining their children.

Studies of families in which the fathers have the primary child-care responsibility— while the wives work or attend school—also provide knowledge about the role of fathers. These fathers engage in more "cognitive stimulation" with both sons and daughters in comparison to the traditional families studied (Radin, 1982). They engaged in more direct teaching efforts, and the children of these fathers scored higher on verbal intelligence than did the children in traditional families. The majority of these fathers report personal costs of this arrangement in terms of impeded careers. The wives express the loss of close involvement with their children (Radin, 1982).

Fathers also appear to enjoy interacting with their children more when they're older than when they're tiny infants. Why this re-luctance and discomfort in dealing with infants? Alice Rossi (1984) stresses that fathers experience a loss of control when infants cry constantly or in other ways are clamoring for attention. Infant care also involves a high degree of physical and emotional intimacy, which may be somewhat awkward for the male. Feeling he is in an area where he has little expertise, he may feel more comfortable staying at a distance from the infant. Women's "greater empathy, affiliation, sensitivity to nonverbal cues and social skills" and men's greater emphasis on "skill mastery, autonomy and cognitive achievement" obviously show up in their styles of parenting (Rossi, 1984).

How can fathers learn the behaviors necessary for relating more intimately with infants? How does society go about changing the role of parenting for men? In those families where fathers are trying to become more involved in parenting, obstacles seem to stand in their way. "Prior socialization no doubt presents difficulties to contemporary young adults who attempt co-parenting and solo fathering. They are negotiating new turf with few cultural guidelines and little social support" (Rossi, 1984, p. 8).

Several attempts are being made to encourage more involvement of fathers in parenting. Sweden is one country in particular that has introduced policies, such as parental-leave provisions, to foster father involvement. The underlying purpose of these policies is to help women achieve equality at work, an achievement that requires men to become more active at home.

The provisions of the parent-leave plan are designed to offer handsome benefits to either mothers *or fathers* who choose to stay home with their children. The plan provides the parents of any newborn with up to nine months of paid leave, divided between them in any way they choose. For example, either parent may take the entire nine months of leave; one may take three months, the other six; or they may both work half time for nine months. The Parental Insurance Fund, which is supported by tax revenues, pays parents 90 percent of their regular salaries. During the last three months, however, the payment is reduced. This is a major deterrent for fathers, since the last three months are often the most popular time for fathers to take leave. In spite of this attempt at egalitarianism, relatively few Swedish men have taken advantage of the legal provisions encouraging paternity leave.

> *When the Parental Insurance Plan was introduced in 1974, the Social Democratic government of Olof Palme launched an advertising campaign portraying men taking care of their children. The goal was to encourage fathers to share the responsibilities of parenthood with their wives. Despite an intensive campaign, however, fathers were slow to respond. The proportion of eligible fathers taking at least one month of paid leave has increased slowly over the years, but now seems to have stabilized at 5 percent; about 2 percent of those eligible take two months or more. (Lamb, 1982, p. 74)*

Several reasons account for this lack of participation. One reason is the employee's concern about retribution by his employer. Legal policies guarantee that employees must be reemployed in their former jobs at their former salaries, but this guarantee hasn't totally reduced their fears. In addition, some male employees claim their wives have less prestigious jobs and can more easily be replaced than they. Other families may still simply believe that mothers *should* take care of young children while the fathers assume the breadwinning role.

What effects did the paternal leave have on the fathers' involvement with their chil-

dren? One research study concluded that parental leaves "did not produce changes in the characteristic maternal and paternal styles observed in many previous studies" (Lamb, 1982). In addition, they found that increased paternal involvement and decreased maternal involvement did not lead to preferences for fathers over mothers. Clear preferences for mothers were found regardless of variations in relative maternal and paternal involvement.

Two American companies, the Ford Foundation and Bank Street College of Education, are following the Swedish example by offering paid paternity leave. So far there have been few takers. Nearly 10 percent of the major American corporations offer *unpaid* paternity leave, but few men have taken advantage of this costly option. It is apparent that changes will need to occur before many fathers give serious consideration to paternity leaves. More equalization of men's and women's jobs and more concern with the role of fathering are two such attitudinal changes to be made.

CHAPTER REVIEW

1. Although social pressures to have children are not as great as in previous generations, most couples still choose to have them. The greater freedom to choose to be parents, however, makes the decision more difficult. Parenthood restrictions on personal freedom and career demands must be weighed against the personal fulfillment couples receive from parenting—the intimacy, fun, and excitement, among other benefits.

2. Unfortunately, modern society often does not adequately prepare couples for the reality of parenthood. Little is done actually to teach couples about child development and child rearing; no classes are required. Unlike many

other roles, the transition to parenthood is quite abrupt. Also, it is not a role one can easily give up, and it can be quite a strain on the marital relationship.

3. The capacity to relate to others and the ability to be an intimate person stem partly from early relationships with caregivers. While early dyadic attachments are significant to an infant, as he or she develops, the focus shifts in childhood from relationships only within the family to include those in the social world outside the family as well. Adolescents become more and more attracted to their peers, with whom they further develop the capacity for dyadic intimacy with same-sex friends and, ultimately, with the other sex.

4. The style of child rearing adopted by parents reflects the type of adult roles that are encouraged in the particular culture. Rather than specific techniques in child rearing, however, what is most important is the feeling that the parents have toward the child, in particular, whether the parents love the child and *express* that love so that the child is aware of it.

5. As mothers are now more commonly found working outside the home, questions have been raised regarding the impact of their work on children. Certainly this trend has imposed limits on the amount of time mothers have to spend with their children, and the lack and inadequacy of child care has added to this burden. But the *quality* of parent-child time spent together is still more important than simply the quantity of time.

6. Although the role of the father has gained more importance in recent years, it appears that the amount of time men are willing to devote to this role is still quite minimal.

CHAPTER

11

Close Relationships in the Middle and Later Years

Many marriage and family textbooks tend to say relatively little about close relationships after a couple has completed the period of early parenting. Often neglected are the exchanges between middle-aged parents and their teenage children, relationships between older parents and their adult children, and the marriage itself among the elderly (Troll, Miller, and Atchley, 1979). Figure 11.1 illustrates that more than half of the family life cycle is spent in middle age and old age. A couple of developments have inspired social researchers to take a closer look at family life beyond the first decade or so of marriage.

First, an extended life expectancy has resulted in a longer period of time in marriage

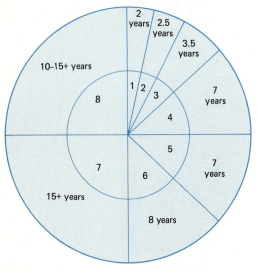

1. Married couples prior to the arrival of children
2. Families bearing children (oldest child 2.5 or less)
3. Families with preschool children (oldest child 6 or less)
4. Families with schoolchildren (oldest child 13 years or less)
5. Families with children in their teens (oldest 13 to 20 years)
6. Families in launching-of-children stage (first child gone to last child leaving)
7. Parents in middle age (post-child rearing; empty nest to retirement)
8. Parents in old age (retirement to death of both spouses)

Figure 11.1 Eight stages of the family life cycle. (*Sources*: Williamson, Munley, and Evans, 1980, p. 97; Duvall, 1971, p. 121.)

after the children leave home, after retiring from the job, and during the stage of grandparenting. Second, the notion of an individual's personality and self-concept as being stable and unchanging throughout life is currently being challenged. Evidence from numerous resources—self-reports, longitudinal studies, observational data, and objective descriptions by friends—substantiate that people do indeed change in adulthood. "The evidence shows and most agree that the individual as he moves through the adult years becomes transformed in appearance, social or life patterns, interests, relationships, and also with regard to inner qualities, for example, ways of experiencing and expressing emotions and motivations and preoccupations" (Brim, 1976, p. 3). To some extent the person is becoming *different* while still remaining the *same* in certain other respects (Brim, 1976).

To assume that marriage in the middle and later years is merely an extension of marriage from the early years ignores the fact that these stages of life are unique and that they often involve lengthy time periods with special needs and concerns. Thus, when we look more closely at midlife and the later years in the family, we see distinct reasons why these segments of existence should be examined apart from the rest.

CHANGES IN MIDDLE AGE

Midlife is a distinct period in the life cycle that might best be defined in terms of attitude and behavior changes rather than chronological age. It has been referred to as a stage of "rebirth," a time when many aspects of life are nearing an end and new opportunities and challenges are facing the person (Joan Robertson, 1978). Another writer defines midlife as "the time to start pleasing ourselves" (LeShan, 1975, p. 304). Lillian Rubin takes a similar perspective when she refers to midlife as a period "when perhaps for the first time in her adult life, a woman can attend to her own needs, her own desires, her own development as a separate and autonomous being" (1979, p. 7).

Marriage partners at midlife differ in some important ways from the earlier years of their marriage. The changes during midlife, however, will generally be different for husbands and wives and for various social classes. In particular, we are interested in the impact of midlife changes on an individual's capacity for emotional closeness.

Midlife Changes for Men

Adults may undergo some changes in attitudes and behaviors as they interact with a progression of life events. The changes largely result from social or biological events that require the person to "reaccommodate"—for example, early retirement, the "empty nest," or physical changes (Haan, 1981). Numerous researchers have found that at least some value and behavior changes occur beween 40 and 50 years of age. Donald Levinson et al. (1978) called this period the "mid-life transition" and found it to be a time when many men make changes in their work and family roles. Note that Levinson chose the word *transition* as opposed to the popular term *midlife crisis*. Even though some men may experience this stage of life as a crisis, it is not typical of most. The majority of social researchers studying this time span seem to agree—changes occur, but they are for the most part not unexpected and do not warrant the "crisis" label.

There is a tendency for men to "mellow out" during the middle years, showing less aggressiveness and less concern for power (Brim, 1976; Gutmann, 1974; Lowenthal et al., 1976; Neugarten, 1968). During the early adult years, many upper-class and middle-class men expend their energies on their work, focusing on the material support of their families. But in the middle years these men are more likely to turn inward toward the family for increased emotional support, nurturance, and intimacy. There often is an increase in family activity and a tendency toward gentleness, ease of social interaction, and self-satisfaction. Men move from a concentration on "mastery" in the instrumental world toward more interpersonal commitment (Lowenthal et al., 1976).

What factors account for these changes in men as they go from being aggressive and controlling to being more tender and intimate? First, there are biological changes taking place throughout life. The intense sexual drive experienced by men during their teens, 20s, and 30s gradually declines. From about the age of 30 on there is a gradual decrease in the secretion of androgens, particularly testosterone, for the male (Brim, 1976). A man is by no means totally lacking in youthful desires—in "lustful passions," in the capacity for anger, assertiveness, and ambition. "But he suffers less from the tyranny of these drives" (Levinson et al., 1978, p. 25).

Also at midlife a typical man suffers some loss of his youthful vitality. Although he is not experiencing severe bodily decline, nor is he likely to be on the threshold of death, he may feel somewhat threatened by the physical changes (Levinson et al., 1978). Along with this bodily decline is the growing awareness of death, the "realization that one's life span is finite and one's options limited" (Livson, 1981). Gaining a sense of mortality and an awareness that he is no longer as invincible and as self-sufficient as he once thought, he may turn to developing closer relations with his family.

Midlife is also marked by an occupational reevaluation. According to Levinson, as a

In the middle years, men often turn their attention toward the intimate environment of the family and provide more emotional support and nurturance.

man enters the "midlife transition," he is likely to review his progress and ask, "What have I done? Where am I now? Of what value is my life to society, to other persons, and especially to myself?" (Levinson et al., 1978, p. 30). The middle-class man takes a look at how far he has gone and perhaps realizes now that he is unlikely to fulfill all of his occupational goals, for example, to make it to the top. "He must deal with the disparity between what he is and what he has dreamed of becoming" (Levinson et al., 1978, p. 30).

There appear to be two predominate ways in which middle-class and upper-class men look at their work. Either they will be satisfied with their goal attainments and therefore can relax and turn their energies to families and interpersonal relationships, or they can resign themselves to the fact that they probably won't go any farther and look for meaning and rewards in other areas, namely the interpersonal arena. Those who cannot come to grips with the discrepancy between where they are and where they want to be may feel that midlife is more of a crisis. But those men who are less dominated by the ambitions, passions, grandeur, and illusions of youth can become more deeply attached to others (Levinson et al., 1978).

Hence, the reduction in energies and drives for work and sexuality allows men to develop another way to enrich their lives, namely through emotionally close relationships.

The quality of his love relationships may well improve as he develops a greater capacity for intimacy and integrates more fully the tender, "feminine" aspects of his self. He has the possibility of becoming a more responsive friend to men as well as women. He can be a more facilitating parent to his adolescent and young adult offspring as he recognizes that they are no longer children and that he is no longer the youthful controlling father. He can become a more caring son to his aging parents (for whom he increasingly assumes parental responsibilities), and a more compassionate authority and teacher to young adults. (Levinson et al., 1978, p. 25)

Midlife Changes for Women

Certain changes also occur for women as they pass from early adulthood toward later adulthood. Like men, certain physical changes, such as menopause, play a role in this transition for women. Changes in physical appearance are also experienced and often are more negative for women than for men. Women tend to perceive themselves as becoming less attractive, "while men of the same age even seem to gain in attractiveness" (Troll, Miller, and Atchley, 1979).

A decrease in physical attractiveness is not a small matter in a society where a woman's looks have traditionally been one of her most highly valued commodities in all social classes (L. Rubin, 1979). In Lillian Rubin's (1979) study of women at midlife a preoccupation with appearance was quite prevalent. Most of her respondents, including those who were quite beautiful, expressed dissatisfaction with their looks. In fact, she found

the most attractive women to have the most trouble with aging, peering worriedly at every wrinkle and speaking anxiously of every bulge.

A behavioral change of middle-aged women frequently found in the research is the display of increased assertiveness and control. According to one author, females during midlife become "more aggressive and managerial" (Zube, 1982). In a study of the experiences of young women and middle-aged females, "Young adult women saw intimacy as being very salient in their present self-perceptions though they anticipated it would be less so in middle age, while middle-aged women recalled being more concerned with intimacy in young adulthood than they saw themselves in the present" (Ryff, 1983, p. 9). David Gutmann (1974) in his cross-cultural studies also found that even in patriarchal societies, women tended to become more aggressive during midlife, less emotional, and more domineering. They were somewhat less interested in interpersonal relations and became more instrumental-oriented (Gutmann, 1974).

Other changes occur during the middle years. Generally for a middle-class woman there emerges a new sense of a "self." Taking care of the home and family may no longer provide the necessary satisfaction for her life. After years of continual care and concern of others the midlife woman embarks on a life course that concentrates more on herself. Ironically, at the same time that the husband is turning his attention more toward the family and close relationships, the wife is beginning to "branch out" and add new roles to that of wife and mother.

Although middle-aged and middle-class women devote more of their energies to jobs and activities outside of the family, they still very much define themselves in terms of their

Women frequently display an increased assertiveness and control in middle age.

interpersonal relationships. This finding puzzled Lillian Rubin during her study of married midlife women. She continued to search for just one woman who defined her self-concept in terms of her work role. Even women in powerful and prestigious positions defined themselves according to their family roles, such as wife or mother. "Not one said, 'I'm a teacher,' 'I'm a secretary,' 'I'm a psychologist,' 'I'm a seamstress,' 'I'm a personnel manager,' 'I'm a lawyer.' Few included the words *competent* or *capable* in their definition of self" (1979, p. 55).

In trying to understand a woman's conception of herself, a distinction between *being* and *doing* is helpful. "*Being* is internal, *doing* external; *doing* is work, *being* identity" (1979,

p. 57). This is illustrated by an attorney interviewed by Rubin:

> *I don't really know why I didn't say anything about my work. It's certainly very important to me; I love what I do. I think maybe it has something to do with how I see myself as a whole person. [With a bright smile of sudden understanding] Yes, that's it. Being a lawyer is what I* do; *you asked me what I* am. *(1979, pp. 57–58)*

In contrast, a man's view of himself is typically defined by his work. This is illustrated by an unemployed male who struggled to find words to describe who he is: "You see, right now I can't really describe myself because I'm in a very big transition period. I'm unemployed" (1979, p. 59).

Explanations of Midlife Changes

In general, researchers agree that some changes in feelings and behavior do occur during middle adulthood. The reasons for these changes, however, are less clear, although various explanations have been given. Orville Brim (1976) notes that two extreme interpretations exist: At one extreme are physiological theories that stress the importance of hormonal shifts, and at the other extreme is a cultural orientation, which views personality change as a product of lifelong socialization experiences.

The sociocultural perspective suggests that certain social norms and behavior that may have been very strong during youth and young adulthood seem to play a lesser role in middle adulthood. For example, in order to adapt and survive, as people grow older it may be necessary for the two sexes not to behave according to traditional "feminine" and "masculine" behavior patterns. Thus, greater aggressiveness and dominance in women may be important traits for single or widowed females in old age. Survival becomes more important for them than following traditional cultural prescriptions of what males and females should be like. Sinnot (1977) concludes that satisfaction and survival in later ages is related to adopting sex roles which combine both "masculine" and "feminine" traits.

Gutmann (1974) links the attitude and behavioral changes in midlife to changes in parenting roles, not to the middle years of life per se. He indicates that historically in the early child-rearing stage of the family it was necessary for each parent to provide for particular needs of the child, the mother providing the emotional and the father providing for the physical needs. It was this task of meeting the needs of young children that intensified the gender differences between men and women.

As parents enter middle age, however, and as their children take responsibility for their own security, the need for distinct gender roles decreases. "The general consequence of this period of mid-life relaxation is that both sexes can afford the luxury of living out the potentials and pleasures that they had to relinquish early on, in service of their particular parental task" (Gutmann, 1974, p. 181). For men, the emotional expression, the tenderness, and the nurturance that were previously repressed in the service of the good-provider role can now be directly expressed. Likewise, women can become more controlling, independent, and instrumental and express more "masculine" traits during this period of life. Men and women thus become more similar.

What about hormonal changes; can they account for these midlife behaviors and feelings? Sociologist Alice Rossi (1984) argues that researchers analyzing the midlife changes have left out biology as a possible explanation. She states that these same changes in gender role with age were found in four very different societies, "But the researchers have not proposed any biosocial or biopsychological mechanism through which this transformation takes place" (p. 9). It's indeed possible that part of the explanation is endocrinological. Over time the wife loses more and more of her estrogenic hormones, resulting in an overall higher proportion of testosterone. As mentioned, the husband, on the other hand, is producing less testosterone as he grows older.

The research on midlife changes leaves many questions unanswered. Social scientists have yet to make comparable studies on women without children and/or women who are employed throughout their adult lives. Likewise, research is lacking on midlife changes for men who are not fathers or who have never married. In other words, are the above noted changes limited to individuals involved in family life and related to the life cycle of the family, or do all individuals experience them? Certainly more research is needed.

Midlife Changes and the Marital Relationship

If middle-class males and females develop in seemingly opposing directions during midlife—with males becoming more "intimacy-oriented" and females more aggressive and "career-oriented"—what are the implications for marriage? Do these changes create a potential for conflict? What happens to the balance of power, especially if the wife is gaining major rewards outside of the marriage for the first time?

On the one hand, if the wife begins to participate in the work force during the postparental stage, the husband must adapt to the competition in the breadwinner role. Also, the wife's excitement and involvement in a career may occur simultaneously with the husband's doubts and ambivalence about his own career. This timing could create further distance between the spouses (McKenry, 1984). In addition, the time and energy a midlife woman is investing in her own outside work may conflict with the emotional needs and desires of her husband (McKenry, 1984). Some researchers have found that many women complain of their husbands' dependence during this period of life (Lowenthal et al., 1976).

On the other hand, men's increased interest in intimacy may cause greater closeness

to develop between the husband and wife. The husband, no longer preoccupied with his achievements at the workplace and having a more relaxed sex drive, can pursue a relationship with his wife characterized by emotional fulfillment for both partners. Changes in assertiveness that the wife is making may result in pressure on the husband to be more responsive to her needs and to provide her with emotional support as she pursues her outside activities.

Also, as the midlife woman searches for greater meaning and more confidence in her own life, she may help create a more equal balance of power in her marriage. A higher self-esteem will certainly allow her to relate to her husband on a more equal basis. The potential for intimacy is the greatest when both partners respect each other as equals. Of course, not all couples will experience these emotional and behavioral changes or greater marital intimacy. Those partners, for example, who have always lacked individual prerequisites to intimacy or who had incompatible personalities as a couple from the beginning of their marriages, probably will continue to have problems during the middle years of marriage also.

EMPTYING THE NEST

Life with Teenagers

If coming to terms with midlife transitions does not provide enough of a challenge for couples, surely living with teenagers does. These are not easy years for parents. In research on marital happiness across the life cycle, a recurrent theme is the disruptive influence of teenage children on the marriage. Marital satisfaction tends to reach its lowest point in the entire marriage when the children are adolescents, and it tends to rise after the children leave home (Rollins and Cannon, 1974) (see Figure 11.2). In comparison, samples of childfree couples do not show similar low levels of marital satisfaction at midlife (Troll, Miller, and Atchley, 1979). Teenagers' struggles with physical and emotional maturity, their search for a secure self-concept, and conflict between closeness with and distance toward their parents all are stressful to the parents.

One particular stress on the parent-child relationship is the teenager's increase in power. Obtaining a driver's license, working part-time jobs, and earning money are all ways adolescents have of gaining more power. Also the more the adolescent is involved in a peer group, the more available are nonparental social rewards and the less valuable are parental rewards. Hence, with less reliance on parents for rewards, it is less likely that parental dictates will be followed, at least not without a struggle (Richer, 1968).

The price of getting teenagers to comply with parental wishes goes up during adolescence. Of course those parents, such as lower-class parents, who cannot meet the price of compliance watch helplessly as their sons and daughters "do their own thing." Hence, parents feel hopelessly frustrated over their own lessening control, as they see their son with a pierced ear, smoking cigarettes, or attending rock concerts and their daughter dating someone they don't approve of, tinting her hair green, and wearing "punk rock" clothes.

In addition, the growing freedom and separation of teenagers stirs up fears in parents. No longer are parents able to protect their children, sheltering them from dangers that lurk outside the home.

When the phone rings while a teenager is out, parents talk about having an instantaneous crackle of fear, like lightning: Something has happened. Part of this fear comes from their own memories. They may remember themselves or their friends taking dangerous risks as a teenager: driving a hundred miles per hour, riding on a motorcycle over the snow-slippery streets without a crash helmet, taking crazy dares, and

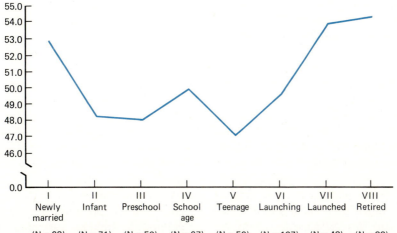

Figure 11.2 Marital satisfaction at each stage of an eight-stage family life cycle measured by the Locke-Wallace Scale. (*Source*: Adapted from Rollins and Cannon, 1974, p. 275.)

then remaining silent or lying to their parents about these adventures. (Galinsky, 1981, p. 277)

Youthful idealism and optimism only add to the parents' concern over their children's danger or to their worry that they might get into trouble. So stressful is this period for parents that some have banded together to form support groups (see Box 11.1).

Parents are often in their midlife transition at the same time that their children are going through adolescence. Sons and daughters who are in their late teens or early twenties bring parents to the realization that they are middle-aged and that their children view them as old. Coming to terms with the approaching later years of life may be strained by seeing a young son or daughter embarking on his or her own life. The vitality and energy that the parent once had is now seen in the son or daughter. Middle-aged fathers may begin to envy their youthful sons in terms of their strength, their energy, and their different opportunities for living (Levinson et al., 1978). The middle-aged woman may be sensitive to her declining physical attractiveness when she sees her teenage daughter with her beautiful figure, skin, and hair at the peak of her youth.

The issues that adolescents are dealing with—sexuality, interpersonal relationships, the search for self-esteem—quite ironically are similar to the conflicts that the middle-aged parent is going through. Some parents push their teenagers into popularity and encourage interpersonal relationships to relive vicariously their own lives through their children's lives. Other parents become jealous and resentful when their teenagers are maturing and want increased contact with the other sex, an expanding social life, or adult sexual experiences. Some aging parents may even attempt to stay young by dressing and

behaving like their adolescents—only causing further embarrassment for, and distance from, their teenagers (Rice, 1978).

The results of an appraisal of one's own life—one's aspirations and accomplishments—which occurs during midlife, also have an impact on the relationship with teenagers. When the appraisal leads to regrets and disappointments, expectations for the children's achievements may become even more important. The parent may hope that the adolescent son or daughter does not repeat the same "mistakes."

A positive midlife transition for parents is also correlated with the smooth passage of adolescents out of the home. A study of 30 families in therapy because of a troubled adolescent revealed this connection. In nearly all of the families, the teenagers' problems were found to be linked to a crisis in the lives of their middle-aged fathers. "Just as the adolescent was facing the need to separate from the family and establish an independent identity, the father was undergoing deep doubts about the meaning of his own life course. The child's open options in love and work seemed to lead these fathers to regret the choices they had made in their own lives" (Goleman, 1980, p. 59). A parent who has a strong sense of self-worth can allow a child to seek a life direction of his or her own. But those fathers who are threatened by their children's steps toward independence often respond only with criticism of the child or with a total disengagement (Goleman, 1980).

Not only is a midlife parent's relationship with his or her child changing but the middle-aged couple's relationships with their own parents are changing. Elderly parents may become more dependent on their own adult children for help because of health problems, loneliness, changes in economic conditions, and, in general, a reduced capacity to respond to the demands of their environment. Parents

BOX 11.1

TOUGHLOVE

Toughlove is a program for parents who are troubled by their teenagers' antisocial or uncooperative behavior. If their sons or daughters are breaking the law, abusing drugs, skipping school, or consistently ignoring their parents' rules, Toughlove's message to parents is this: Don't blame yourself for your child's unacceptable, rotten, selfish behavior. Your children are responsible for their actions and must accept the consequences. You must set clear rules—clear penalties if the rules are broken—even if that means asking your child to move out.

A parent or community support group is fundamental to the Toughlove approach. Sharing their problems with one another, the parents of troubled youngsters can "learn to look at their problem differently and gradually change their responses to their children's behavior" (York, York, and Wachtel, 1982, p. 15). Viewing these problem behaviors as a social dilemma, Toughlove also seeks the cooperation of community resources such as schools, the legal system, and human-service agencies and professionals.

Attempts at identifying the "hidden motivation and psychological reasons" behind a young person's failure to cooperate are seen as unproductive. "That is not to say that therapists, rehabilitation centers, and counseling programs are useless. But without a clear focus on the real responsibility for problem behavior, by getting distracted in blaming parents or other 'causes,' we are largely wasting our resources. . . . Our cultural dilemma needs a cultural solution" (York, York, and Wachtel, 1982, p. 12).

The founders of the national Toughlove movement, Phyllis York, David York, and Ted Wachtel, have summarized their philosophy in what they call the Ten Beliefs to serve as a kind of "Ten Commandments for troubled parents." These are as follows:

1. Family problems have roots and supports in the culture.
2. Parents are people too.
3. Parents' material and emotional resources are limited.
4. Parents and kids are not equal.
5. Blaming keeps people helpless.
6. Kids' behavior affects parents. Parents' behavior affects kids.
7. Taking a stand precipitates a crisis.
8. From controlled crisis comes positive change.
9. Families need to give and get support in their own community in order to change.
10. The essence of family life is cooperation, not togetherness. (1982, p. 23)

Toughlove is seen by some as a welcome practical way to deal with an impossible situation. Its critics, however, decry the Toughlove approach as one that fuels already existing anger and further separates children from their parents. They say it provides a superficial remedy for a current crisis rather than a permanent solution to a long-standing family problem.

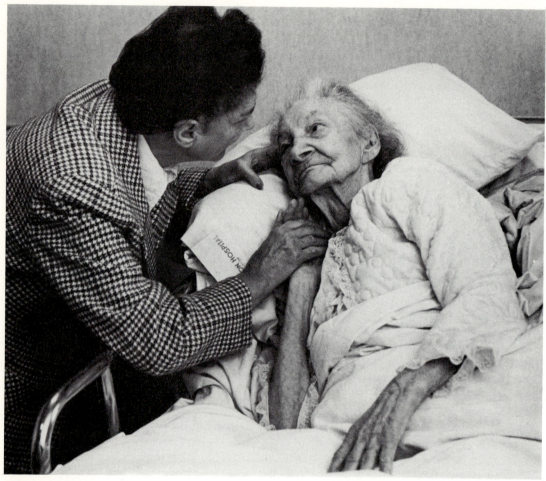

Parents at midlife are caught in generational cross fire—they often must be, in effect, parents to their aging parents as well as parents to their own children.

at midlife are caught in a "generational cross fire"; as well as being parents to their own children, they often must be, in effect, parents to their aging or dying parents as well (Scarf, 1982). This can be especially stressful if the elderly parent suffers from a serious illness, such as Alzheimer's disease (see Box 11.2).

Anticipating the Departure

Unlike some sudden transitions during family life, a child's final departure from home has usually been anticipated for some time. Short-term departures have more than likely been experienced by the parents throughout the years of child rearing—children may have gone to camp, on school field trips, or to college. In fact, some young people leave home in a very gradual process. They may live at home the first year or two of college, then move into a dormitory on a nearby campus, and then live at home for a short time after graduation. So there's no set or predetermined way of leaving home, but typically

BOX 11.2

LIVING WITH ALZHEIMER'S DISEASE

There are perhaps few diseases that take as heavy an emotional toll on families as Alzheimer's disease. And with an increased life expectancy, more people are developing age-related diseases such as Alzheimer's. Up to 6 percent of people over 65 have Alzheimer's disease, and by the age of 80 the incidence reaches about 20 percent (Butler, 1984). Alzheimer's disease is a gradual, irreversible deterioration of nerve cells in the brain, which leaves the victim confused and disoriented. Family members stand by frustrated as there is no hope for the patient's mental capacities to grow better, only worse.

With the progression of the disease, the person can no longer live alone. This means that either family members become primary caregivers or the patient is put in an institution. Behavior problems of the Alzheimer victim often include short-term memory loss, wandering, sleep disturbances, losing and hiding things, repeating a question, repetitious actions, urinary incontinence, and clinging to or persistently following the caregiver, to name a few (Mace and Rabins, 1981).

So disabling is this disease that patients need to be watched virtually 24 hours a day. If Alzheimer's victims, for example, wander off from their residence, they may not be able to find their way back or even be able to tell another person where they live and who they are. An irony about this disease is that to an outsider the patient can appear quite "normal"; social courtesies are still in the person's behavioral repertoire.

Caring for the patient can put a tremendous burden on family members. Conflicts sometimes emerge as family members disagree on the type of care needed and who should provide it. Role reversals in the family occur as a son or daughter takes on the role of a parent to their parent, who is now totally dependent on the offspring. Sometimes particular family members will not help at all because they have not accepted the reality of the impaired person's illness. Therefore, the burden of care may fall on only one person.

The care of an Alzheimer's victim is a drain on the caregiver—emotionally, physically, and financially. A married couple caring for an Alzheimer's parent may find stress and tension added to their relationship. Emotional reactions of the caregiver can cover a spectrum of feelings—anger, helplessness, embarrassment, guilt, grief, depression (Mace and Rabins, 1981). A helpful book for families of patients with Alzheimer's disease is aptly entitled *The 36-Hour Day*.

---

it is not an abrupt departure. In addition, for parents, "emptying the nest" can span a long period of time, beginning when the oldest child leaves and ending when the youngest leaves.

Thus, parents have opportunities to prepare for postparental life, and most take advantage of these opportunities. This "anticipatory socialization" helps to ease the transition to the "empty nest." The young adults' attendance at college or service in the military gives parents the chance to practice living without children for extended periods of time, even though the children may return home. While such absences do not prepare the couple fully for the "empty nest," they provide some indication of things to come.

Parents often have a preconceived idea of the "right age" for their children to move away from home. Departure could be expected after high school, after finding employment, when going to college, or at the time of marriage. In fact, the *timing* of the departure has been found to be a more significant issue than its actual occurrence. If a child does not become "successfully independent" when it is expected, the situation becomes more troublesome for the parents (Harkins, 1978).

Lillian Rubin (1979) also found timing to be an important factor in the way midlife women responded to the departure of their children. She found leaving home to be somewhat more problematic for working-class mothers than for middle-class mothers.

> *Almost from birth, most middle-class parents know when the big break will come—at eighteen, when the child leaves for college. There's plenty of warning, plenty of time to get ready. But in working-class families, college attendance is not taken for granted . . . and children are expected to live at home until they marry. . . . Since the age of marriage is not clearly fixed, that means the time of departure is also indefinite—for both parents and children, somewhat like living with an indeterminate sentence rather than a firm release date that's agreed upon and understood by all. That difference alone—the unpredictability of the departure date—makes preparation for separation more difficult in working-class families. (L. Rubin, 1979, p. 19)*

Consequences for Mothers

It's a common belief that when children leave home, mothers experience something called an "empty-nest syndrome," characterized by depression, sadness, and despair. "Indeed, the very words *empty nest* conjure up a vision of a lonely, depressed woman clinging pathetically and inappropriately to a lost past— a woman who has lived for and through her children" (L. Rubin, 1979, p. 14). The most recent research—conducted on the general population—has revealed evidence contradicting the "empty-nest syndrome." Even though there will be individual differences to the reaction of children leaving, very few modern women, married or divorced, suffer the classical symptoms that warrant calling it a "syndrome."

Rubin (1979) found in her study of midlife women that almost all the women responded to the departure of their children, whether actual or impending, with a sense of relief. The women, in general, were glad to be freed of the responsibilities of mothering. The following epitomizes this relief:

> *When the youngest one was ready to move out of the house, I was right there helping him pack. We love having the children live in the area, and we love seeing them and the grandchildren, but I don't need for any of them to live in this house ever again. I've had as much as I ever need or want of being tied down with children. (1979, p. 16)*

Other research has produced similar findings. In an analysis of several studies, Norval Glenn (1975) found that women on the average showed a greater happiness or enjoyment of life in the postparental category. Irwin Deutscher (1973) discovered that the majority of middle-aged women viewed this postparental phase of the family cycle as a time of new freedoms—"freedom from the economic responsibilities of children; freedom to be mobile (geographically); freedom from housework and other chores" (p. 516). There's also a sense of accomplishment, of a job well done, when the children leave home.

Relief, enjoyment, and a sense of freedom are not the only feelings experienced by mothers. Most women feel some sadness that accompanies such a loss. Rubin (1979), however, found a wide variation in the duration of this latter feeling—"some speaking of days, some weeks, much more seldom, months." The intensity of such sadness, however, rarely reached the depths of devastation or depression.

Those women who do experience some feelings of distress while launching their children are typically mothers who have "put all of their eggs in one basket." That is, their children have been the primary purpose and interest of their lives. When the children leave, instead of pursuing other interests, these women often try to continue to prolong their mothering role. A study of middle-aged wives in San Francisco (Lowenthal et al., 1976) found that those women "who had prolonged their motherhood role as a primary focal point in their lives tended to have more troubles than those who turned to other interests." Until the mother becomes interested in something else—going back to school, to work, into community volunteering, whatever—she often has difficulty with the children's departure.

Consequences for Fathers

Although the primary focus of the empty nest has been on its consequences for mothers, fathers also experience some costs when children leave home. In fact, some authors contend, "It may be fathers more often than mothers who are pained by the children's imminent or actual departure" (L. Rubin, 1979, p. 31). Why would fathers feel more distress?

Since a mother is more likely than the

"*Well, now that the children have all grown up,
I guess I'll pull up a chair.*"

Drawing by Claude; © 1974. The New Yorker Magazine, Inc.

father to have built a close relationship with her children, the father may feel as though he has missed out on the possibility of such a relationship. In addition, the relationship with the mother will be more likely to continue even after the children have left home. But a father who was too busy pursuing economic security for the family to take time with his children while they were growing up may feel that they are gone now without his having a chance really to get to know them. Thus, the "empty nest" can elicit feelings of resentment and disappointment with oneself as the father looks back on missed opportunities to build a relationship with his children.

Consequences for the Marriage

How does an empty nest affect the marriage itself? Will the marriage be strengthened when the stress of children is removed? Or will it be weakened when the shared interest of children is gone? Research findings on marriage in the middle and later years is still quite lacking, and the conclusions from existing research are often contradictory. For example, some popular reports claim that marriages are more likely to break up when the children leave home. Other studies suggest a "second-honeymoon" phenomenon when the husband and wife are alone again. The variety of findings led to the conclusion that the "diversity of marital style in later years is even greater than in earlier years" (Troll, Miller, and Atchley, 1979, p. 40).

With the departure of the children, the spouses must shift their focus from a "mutual concern with child care to a mutual concern with their own relationship" (Tamir, 1982). Two things can happen as a result of this change. First, the shift can solidify the relationship, creating a closeness and intimacy that were hampered when the children were

around. Second, the shift can arouse interpersonal tension, since spouses no longer have their children as a means to divert attention from themselves. Questionnaire results from a study by Brecher and the editors of Consumer Reports Books (1984) found evidence to support the first result. A majority of respondents found that the "empty nest" had a positive impact on their marriages. In fact, respondents described what might be called an "empty-nest honeymoon." A 56-year-old wife married for 34 years responded:

> Now that the children are grown and gone, we are delighted to be a "single couple" once again and have been on a honeymoon ever since we have been alone. We find that our shared experiences have made us closer, wiser, and funnier. Our little understandings, communicated by a lifted eyebrow during some cocktail party; the little words that are a private joke within the family and the ability to sit down and talk about feelings have all come with age. We like being able to make love in the afternoon, if we wish, or to wait a few days longer than usual if one or another of us is not in the mood. It is a LOVELY time of life. (1984, p. 58)

One advantage for couples during the postparental period is increased privacy. Many of Brecher's respondents described "the great relief they felt when their last child left home and they could at long last have sex in their own bed without restraint or fear that the children might 'hear noises'" (1984, p. 18). Intimate behaviors—in-depth self-disclosure, touching, gestures of affection, family secrets—that couples felt had to be kept hidden from their children, can now be openly considered when the children are gone.

But even with this increased opportunity for intimacy, some women still felt that their

When children leave the nest there is the potential for couples to experience a second honeymoon.

husbands could not provide them totally with the emotional support they needed. Lipman and Longino (1983) found that in terms of the *most important family members,* golden-wedding wives ranked their husbands first, their children next, their siblings third, and their friends last in order of importance to them. In terms of *emotional support,* in particular, however, children and women friends were chosen over husbands as providing emotional support for wives throughout their lives. "Husbands, and men in general, have tended to specialize instead in doing things for their families, like being good providers and keeping the house in good repair. When their wives have a problem, they are more likely to express their concern by asking what they can *do* to help" (p. 11). Although men may change to be more interested in the intimate aspect of marriage during the middle

and later years, the lack of intimacy skills and the expectation of providing instrumental services may still persist.

While a greater intimacy seems to characterize most empty-nest marriages, some couples grow farther apart at this stage. This is more likely to occur when a shared interest in the children has been the only bond for the spouses. For example, the empty-shell marriage—in which the partners have resigned themselves to stay together for the sake of the children—will experience difficulties when it comes to the empty-nest stage. Indeed this is a common reason for marriages at this stage to dissolve. "Many couples try to mask growing differences during the child-rearing years under an appearance of cordiality" (Williamson, Munley, and Evans, 1980, p. 99). When the children leave, however, the masks, which may project pseudo-intimacy, are no longer needed and can be removed.

GRANDPARENTHOOD

Being a grandparent is no longer a state that exists only in old age. In American culture the most common age of becoming a grandparent is around 49 to 51 years for women and 51 to 53 years for men. And with a longer life expectancy, about 79 years for women and 71 years for men, most people can expect to spend a long time in this role, getting to know their grandchildren and even their great-grandchildren quite well. Grandmothers, in particular, are likely to see their grandchildren develop from infants well into their adult years (Troll, 1983).

Children born today—compared with those born at the turn of this century—are more likely to have all four grandparents living. Under 1900 mortality conditions, only one-fourth of the children would have all their grandparents alive at birth, whereas by 1976 this figure increased to almost two-thirds. The probability of three or more grandparents being alive when the child is age 15 has increased from 17 percent to 55 percent. The increased presence of grandparents suggests that they may play a more significant role in the lives of children than in years past (Uhlenberg, 1983).

Since one can be a grandparent at as early as 30 years of age and as late as 100, it is difficult to make generalizations about the relationship between grandparents and grandchildren. The respective ages of the two generations will make a significant difference. For example, are we talking about a 90-year-old grandmother and her 40-year-old granddaughter or a 50-year-old grandmother with her newborn grandson? Certainly older grandchildren will be seen as providing quite different rewards or services to grandparents than younger grandchildren. Some grandparents will be vigorous, youthful adults; others will be feeble and badly in need of help (Troll, 1983). Some will enjoy the fun and stimulation of grandchildren; others may prefer a quiet and peaceful visit with them. So the style of grandparenting is often closely connected to the grandparent's age and stage of life.

Exactly what significance does grandparenting have for adults? What rewards may be forthcoming from such a relationship? Unlike parenting, one cannot specifically choose to be a grandparent, but people usually desire to be one. A study conducted by Neugarten and Weinstein (1973) revealed the types of benefits accrued from grandparenthood. Their data came from interviews with 70 middle-class families.

Like parents, grandparents view their grandchildren as an extension of themselves. Grandparenthood seems to be primarily a source of *biological renewal*—"It's through my grandchildren that I feel young again." In addition, grandchildren provide a *biological continuity* with the future—"It's through these children that I see my life going on into the future" or "It's carrying on the family line" (Neugarten and Weinstein, 1973).

For some, grandparenthood involves primarily an *emotional self-fulfillment*. Grandfathers, in particular, may find this significant, since with their own children they probably played primarily an instrumental role. Grandfatherhood can be a "second chance" for those fathers who missed getting emotionally close to their own children.

As one man put it, "I can be, and I can do for my grandchildren things I could never do for my own kids. I was too busy with my business to enjoy my kids, but my grandchildren are different. Now I have the time to be with them.'' (Neugarten and Weinstein, 1973, p. 507)

Grandparenting can also provide a rewarding new role of *teacher* or *resource person.* Thus, grandparents can contribute to the grandchild's welfare, either by financial aid or by offering advice from their own life experience.

However, almost one-third of the grandparents in Neugarten and Weinstein's sample—27 percent of the grandmothers and 29 percent of the grandfathers—reported feeling quite *remote* from their grandchildren and acknowledged that grandparenthood had *little effect* on their own lives. This feeling occurs despite the fact that they lived geographically near at least one set of grandchildren. They also appeared apologetic about expressing these feelings. Some grandfathers expressed a degree of discomfort with very young grandchildren, remarking that when the children grow older, they will feel different. A grandfather expressed the following about his 3-year-old grandson:

''Well, I don't know what to do with a three-year-old. I can bounce him up and down on my knee and play Ride the Horsey with him for a couple of minutes, but that's about all. But when he gets to be six, I can take him to the ball game and play catch with him and things like that.'' (Dodson, 1981, p. 4)

The characteristics of the grandparent role vary with cultural expectations and family structure. In early rural America the grandparent was likely to own the family homestead and was revered and respected by sons and daughters, their spouses, and his grandchildren—all of whom usually lived nearby (Boyd, 1978). Today in America, along with many other industrialized societies, grandparents are less often viewed as authority figures, to be revered by other family members. The role of grandparent in contemporary society has shifted somewhat to that of a more permissive, indulgent older adult, a ''friendly equal'' to grandchildren. At times, the grandparent may become ''an ally'' of the grandchild ''against parental misunderstanding, non-acceptance, and authority'' (Boyd, 1978, p. 366).

There appear to be some racial differences in grandparenting. A comparison of black and white young adults found greater contact with grandparents among the black respondents than among the white (Hays and Mindel, 1973). Thus the pattern of interaction among the generations is often different between black families and white families.

Martin and Martin's (1978) study of the black extended family revealed that the dominant family figure is often an elderly woman who has outlived her husband. These important persons act as communication centers for the family: They direct family celebrations, help socialize the children, define what constitutes deviant behavior, and help arbitrate family conflicts. This role of elderly women in strengthening families' capabilities to meet crises and difficulties is striking, for their efforts are directed to enhancing the welfare of others, not primarily to insuring their own welfare. (Streib and Beck, 180, p. 948)

James Blackwell's (1985) study also found that black grandparents, more often than not a grandmother, often provide residential accommodations and upkeep for children who do not reside with their parents, on either a temporary or a permanent basis. This pattern among black families is in sharp contrast to the situation of family interaction where the help flows *to* the elderly, not *from* the elderly to other generations. (See Box 11.3.)

RETIREMENT

Attitudes Toward Work

The status of being a retiree has become an expectation for most Americans today. Retirement as a final and separate phase of an individual's work span, however, was virtually unknown during preindustrial times. Most people worked the land until they died or became physically incapacitated. Some may have stopped working the fields prior to infirmity, but still they in no way saw themselves as "retired" (Williamson, Munley, and Evans, 1980).

Industrialization changed this, giving work a special time and a special place. Time was set aside specifically for work and specifically for leisure. Retirement, therefore, became a separate stage in a person's life. But has society really accepted and legitimized this role completely? Is it a valued role in society? Adjusting to retirement depends largely on the attitudes that society in general holds toward work and on the attitudes of the individual regarding his or her own work.

Remnants of the Protestant work ethic still exist in modern American society. Although work may not be equated with moral righteousness as in years past, it is still given a high priority. A strong emphasis on productive activity, especially paid activity, exists. Work provides people with meaning to life, and it continues to be a primary measure of personal worth and success.

Those individuals who have approached their jobs with an all-consuming fervor find retirement difficult to handle. Research shows that particularly very work-oriented

men, who devote little time to interpersonal relationships, have low morales upon retirement (Lowenthal and Robinson, 1976). However, men who did not adhere to a strict, good-provider role and who placed a high value on interpersonal relations throughout their lives did not experience a serious decline in self-esteem at retirement.

Adjustment to retirement in part depends on an individual's particular experience with work. Some people, such as lower-class workers, may look forward to retirement as a welcome relief from a boring and unfulfilling job. In contrast, others see retirement as interrupting a very fulfilling career. The majority of retirees lie between these two extremes.

Most men and women who are still working look at retirement with negative feelings, or with mixed feelings at best. After retirement, however, there is often a marked change toward only positive feelings toward retirement (Brecher et al., 1984). "We found that retirement is for many husbands and wives a mere bugaboo—distressing in anticipation but enjoyable after it occurs" (Brecher et al., 1984, p. 62).

Anticipatory Socialization for Retirement

As with many roles—spouse, parent, worker—it helps to go through some socialization for the role before actually taking it on. The anticipatory socialization for the role of a retiree occurs in various formal and informal ways. One way in which an individual can prepare for retirement is by enlarging his or her interests while still working. By acquiring new hobbies and activities, the retiree will have something to look forward to and to pursue upon retirement.

In a more formal sort of socialization, how-to-retire classes are offered by some cor-

(Text continued on page 386.)

BOX 11.3

"GRAM"

The following is an account of a young woman's visit to a nursing home to see her grandmother, who had recently had a stroke. While only a very small minority, about 5 percent of the elderly, live in nursing homes, families often must make some tough decisions about the care of an elderly parent or other relative. A common issue among families relates to the extent and nature of their obligation for the care of their elderly parents—for example, how much do they owe them and what type of care would be in the older person's best interests. For instance, in the story below, Debbie and her parents experience guilt about having to place Gram in a nursing home. They sense that perhaps they should be doing more and are negligent and selfish regarding Gram. The norm of reciprocity—"you help me and I'll help you"—applies to the interactions between generations in families. Hence, family members may question whether or not they are doing enough for their parents in comparison to what their parents may have done for them in the past.

Notice in this story the way the family communicates with Gram. Debbie's parents hold a conversation *about* Gram, yet Gram herself is in the room. Their communication conveys the message that Gram is not there or does not exist. This behavior could be interpreted as psychological abuse. As you read the case, ask yourself, how would *you* feel if you were Gram?

> I was used to thinking about Gram as a strong, active, fiercely independent woman, with white hair combed neatly back into a nape bun, moving briskly about her house in a homemade apron. Gram cooked and baked and put up preserves from the berries in her garden. She let no one help her with the housework, yet the house always looked as if she had just gone over it with her ancient carpet sweeper, no matter when we popped in for a visit. And she still had time to fix huge family dinners for as many as could squeeze into her dining room.
>
> My father pulled into a half-empty parking lot beside the sprawling red brick building. A huge plate glass window reflected the neatly clipped lawn, brown and dead now. "Wilmot Nursing Home" proclaimed a big black and gold sign. . . . We had unconsciously lowered our voices, as if we were entering a hospital or a funeral home or some other place where old age and death continually hover.
>
> Dad helped open the glass doors for us. I peered down the wide corridor, feeling uncomfortable. My father steered me forward and to the right. "Look, Deb, the recreation room."
>
> The smell of the place was so strong that I stepped back, trying to fight it off. It was a sickish sweetish conglomeration of aging flesh, urine, pine disinfectant, and the lingering perfume of visitors who had left long ago. I wanted to run. I longed for the fresh air outside and gripped my father's arm. "The smell," I

(Continued)

whispered fiercely. He nodded, his nostrils drawn up. "I know. We've been coming here for months, and I still feel sick whenever that stink hits me."...

I wanted to whisper that I'd wait for them in the car, but Dad turned to me and said, "C'mon, Debbie." Then Mom said gaily to Gram, "Mom, Debbie came to see you today. Look, here she is," and I had no choice but to enter the room.

It was small, pale green and dim, even with the yellow and green curtains pushed all the way to the sides of the window. Flanking two neatly made beds with dark green institutional covers were two formica topped night tables. My father was standing by the closet door, and Mom was seated on the bed nearest the window, next to a small dark figure.

"Hi, Gram," I said softly.

Gram turned to me slowly and my stomach contracted. Her face was thin and pinched and covered with wrinkles. Her eyes, always bright and alert, were dulled. She looked wasted, shrunken. Her hands lay motionless in her lap, as neatly as if someone had arranged them. She stared at me and I stood in the doorway, unable to move.

"That's Debbie, Mom, my big girl," my mother said. A bright artificial smile seemed to paralyze the lower half of her face. "She's been away at school, you know. She's almost nineteen now. Hasn't she grown up?"

My father reached out and touched my stiff shoulder. "Go give Gram a kiss, Debbie," he prompted. I moved toward Gram and planted a kiss on her withered cheek. Around her hung an unfamiliar papery dry smell, and wisps of yellowed hair strayed from her bun. She kept staring at me. There was no recognition in her eyes.

"You know Debbie, Mom." my mother urged. She motioned for me to sit on the other side of Gram and leaned across her to tell me, "Well, at least she knows you're one of hers. Just talk nicely to her and smile and kiss her, and she'll be satisfied. We really can't expect anything more." I was shocked. How could we discuss Gram so casually when Gram was sitting right between us?

My mother patted Gram's hand and leaned over to open the drawer of Gram's night table. "Well, Mom," she said brightly, "and where did you put your dirty things this week? Let's see— ah yes, here's a bunch of them, right in with the clean ones. You know, dear," she said, extracting a few pairs of soiled pink cotton bloomers from the drawer and dropping them on the floor, "I wish you wouldn't mix the dirty things with the clean ones." An unmistakable odor came from the discarded clothes and I bit my lip. Gram used to be so meticulous that she would wash her hands even before she gardened.

"Well, that's the last of it, I think," Mom said, tossing a soiled lacy slip into the pile. "And next week I'll bring them back to you, Mom, all nice and fresh." Gram was watching carefully as Mom gathered the dirty clothes into a plastic laundry bag. "Look how she's watching me, Debbie," my mother said. "They steal things left and right here. Look at her. She wants to make sure I'm not a crook." Gram gazed at my mother as if she hadn't heard what Mom had just said. I wanted to grab her and squeeze her tight until she protested, like she used to do, that I'd break her bones if I kept her in such a bear hug. But only her polite smile, I was sure, would answer me. I was a stranger to her, and my Gram was a stranger to me.

We faced each other, I smiled at Gram experimentally and her polite smile popped back at me. "I like college," I blurted.

Gram nodded. "What a big girl you are," she said in the tone she used when I was seven or eight.

I swallowed. "It's very far away, you know. It's about 400 miles away." She was still nodding. "I live in a dormitory with lots of other girls."

"Momma lets you go so far away from home."

I was stymied. "Well, I go to school there. Mom knows. It's all right." "Oh." She was nodding again, uncomprehendingly. Her eyes were mild, passive.

"I have tons of work," I plunged on, "especially in chem— chemistry, I mean. And I'm taking French, too. Next term I'll be taking lit—I mean, a literature course." I stopped. She was still watching me, but her eyes were cloudy again. "What a big girl you are."

I started again, slowly. She kept her eyes on me. I talked on about my roommate and professors and the boys I was dating. She never stopped me. She just sat, her wrinkled hands clasped in her lap, nodding and smiling until my throat became so constricted I stammered to a halt.

"And I missed you, Gram," I said. I threw my arms around her and hugged her fiercely. Slowly her hands came up from her lap and her arms went around me.

"We'll be back next week," my mother promised, and then she looked at me. I nodded. "And Debbie will come too," she added. "Oh look, the elevator is here already. Goodbye, Mom," she called. As the doors closed, Gram raised her hand and tentatively waved goodbye.

We hurried past the big recreation room. I peeped in again. The visitors had departed. Only the old people and the attendants were left. Somebody had switched on the television, but nobody was watching. We stepped out into the cold.

With the typical winter perfidy, the sun had disappeared be-

(Continued)

hind a bank of mottled gray clouds and the air was knife sharp. I inhaled deeply, relieved that the stench of the Home was out of my nostrils, and ran ahead to the car. I had a peculiar sense of freedom, of being let out of a cage, and I felt painfully sorry for all the poor old people whom we had left behind.

In the car, my mother turned to me. The brittle smile was gone from her face and she looked exhausted. "Well Deb, what did you think?" I looked at the street. "It's awful," I said flatly. "It's horrible and ugly and smelly and I can't understand," my voice rose, "how you can let Gram be so miserable!" My mother turned her head slightly so I couldn't look directly into her eyes. My father glanced away from the icy street long enough to give Mom a look of compassion.

"We know, Deb," he said mildly. "We know. But there's really nothing else to do."

SOURCE: *Saul, 1984.*

---

porations and communities. These preretirement programs often help familiarize workers with pensions and benefit levels they can expect. They can also explore issues such as mental and physical health, leisure activities, housing, and the legal aspects of retirement. Studies indicate a fairly high payoff to those who participate. Comprehensive preretirement programs, which cover most all aspects of retirement, are still quite rare, however (Williamson, Munley, and Evans, 1980, p. 155).

Financial planning at the preretirement stage is a crucial part of the anticipatory socialization. A retiree may have planned many activities and interests for retirement, but unless he or she has the finances to pursue them, the planning will be useless. It is not enough to save money for the basic necessities of living, such as rent, clothing, and food. Enough money should be saved to cover those hobbies, travel plans, and any large catastrophic event—such as a fire, long illness,

or accident—that may occur. Those retirees on limited incomes express the most negative feelings about retirement (Brecher et al., 1984). Obviously middle age, not old age, is the time when financial planning for the future should be of major concern. It is in middle age that one can really implement future plans (Peterson, 1973). This action is crucial if one expects to have a full and active retirement.

But regardless of the financial planning and other preparations that one makes for retirement, the sudden drop of status is seemingly unavoidable. The self-concept of most individuals, especially of men, has been defined by their role in the workplace. Perhaps the loss of status partially explains the increased need for recognition, or "social approval," at the time of retirement. "Having given up the prime method for gaining approval in our society—working—the retired person covets acceptance. For instance, individuals who had taken up a new interest, such as painting, want to see their works admired'' (Peterson, 1973, p. 526).

The retiree may begin to look more to the spouse for support of his or her self-concept. ''If work was the arena in which this older person received primary reinforcement of self, the family becomes the arena for support after retirement. In some cases, the marital partner may be the only person available to provide reinforcement'' (Ade-Ridder and Brubaker, 1983, pp. 27–28). So the value of rewards from the family begin to magnify as the work reinforcements dwindle.

We must remember that retirement not only means the loss of one's job but also the loss of the interpersonal relationships that were linked to the job (R. R. Bell, 1981). The daily interaction with proximity friends at work ends upon retirement. The shared work-related experiences no longer serve to bring the same people together. Certain special selected friendships rarely continue after retirement unless the friends share other interests. So the retirees will need to build new friendships outside of the work setting.

Retirement Among Blacks

Retirement may be experienced quite differently by blacks and whites. Research shows that feelings of well-being in blacks seem to increase with retirement (Gibson, 1983). This may be a surprising fact, given that retired blacks are worse off than retired whites in income, education, and incidence of widowhood. To be old is one disadvantage in American society, but to be both old and black has been dubbed a ''double jeopardy.''

The increase in well-being for retired blacks can be explained in a couple of ways. First, owing to the unfavorable lifetime employment experiences of today's older blacks, retirement may be viewed as a relief from a punishing work life. Second, postretirement incomes from Social Security and Supplemental Security Income payments, although no more adequate than their salaries were, are often steadier and more reliable. Black women, in particular, have often experienced lifetime work patterns that were unsteady (Gibson, 1983).

Throughout the postretirement years elderly blacks show a ''buoyancy.'' It may be the very disadvantages that many blacks have faced throughout their lifetimes that makes growing old more of a transition than a crisis. Blacks have learned to cope with discrimination and lower incomes by reaching out to a wide variety of people for support. Thus, older blacks are found to use an informal support network, friends and multiple family members, much more extensively than older whites. There is a pattern of collective support and ties with the extended family among blacks, which has continued even as blacks have obtained upward mobility (McAdoo, 1978).

Elderly whites, in contrast, are more likely to limit seeking help to spouses or a single family member (Gibson, 1982). Thus when blacks reach retirement, they are likely to have a network of ''helpers'' already in place, thereby easing the transition of blacks into old age. An additional factor that helps black women ease into retirement is the fact that older black women are often held in high esteem within the black family, and they are still needed, usually to take care of young children.

The Retirement Marriage

HOUSEHOLD TASKS. When spouses retire, do they begin to share household jobs and responsibilities, ignoring traditional gender roles? Do men, in particular, begin cleaning the house more, cooking the meals, and carrying out other chores that were previously the sole responsibility of the wife? In general, a majority of both men and women *expect* the husband upon retirement to share in household activities (Lipman, 1961; Kerckhoff, 1964). Wives specifically are more likely than husbands to advocate the sharing of tasks. Couples in the middle and upper occupational groups are found to be more likely than those in the lower groups to support such norms (Dobson, 1983).

While the expectations regarding household tasks are for less differentiation by gender, in reality that isn't what occurs. Retired husbands may increase their household activity, but it is very unlikely for it to be in an area that was traditionally women's work (Ballweg, 1967). The husband's increased activity is largely confined to more ''masculine'' tasks, such as yard work, home repairs, and taking out the garbage. Women continue to do most of the housework and cooking. The partners may attempt more task sharing right after retirement, but usually after a brief time period, they return to their earlier division of labor (Keating-Groen, 1977). In the end, there appears to be very little redistribution of activities, if any at all. In most cases the allocation of household responsibilities in later life resembles that in the preretirement years.

MARITAL INTIMACY. The marital relationship takes on a new emphasis during the retirement period. Both spouses tend to look forward to more companionship, shared activities, and intimacy. "Companionship, love, and being able to express true feelings are reported to be among the most satisfying aspects of marriage in later years" (Zube, 1982, p. 152). Of course, the overall personality compatibility of the spouses becomes very

important, since they are now spending much more time together as a couple.

Overall retirement seems to have little effect on marital happiness for either wives or husbands. Brecher et al. (1984) found no significant differences between employed and retired couples. Research on marital happiness, however, needs to be cautiously interpreted, since marital satisfaction is often not clearly defined, and social pressure exists to report a happy marriage. In Brecher's study, for example, most of the people agreed to having a happy marriage anyway; 86 percent of the employed and 88 percent of the retired stated that their marriages were happy. So any differences found between these high reports of marital happiness are insignificant. Other studies (Rollins and Feldman, 1970; Gurin, Veroff, and Feld, 1960; Burr, 1970) have found that marital satisfaction goes up during the retirement period. But again the change between the stages—preretirement and retirement—is minimal. In fact the reported levels of marital happiness in all of the stages of the life cycle are relatively high. These results suggest that the value of self-reported happiness research appears very questionable.

In looking at marital happiness across the life cycle, Lillian Troll makes a distinction between attraction and attachment. "Attraction is high in the beginning of a new relationship, but attachment is low. Over the years, attraction wanes as novelty wanes, but attachment increases" (Troll, Miller, and Atchley, 1979, p. 60). If marital satisfaction is primarily measured as attraction, we would expect to find a steady decrease over time, with perhaps a temporary rise when children leave because their departure creates a novel situation for the husband and wife. One study (Reedy, 1977) found that "Couples married a short time said that love was very important; those married many years said that loyalty was more important'' (Troll, Miller, and Atchley, 1979, p. 60).

SEXUALITY IN THE LATER YEARS. If a couple has had a satisfactory sexual relationship through years of marriage, the chances are that they will be able to continue to experience mutually rewarding sexual activity in their retirement years also. The physiological changes that occur with aging need not hinder sexual enjoyment. In fact, ''Free from the worries which beset younger couples—child rearing, work aspirations, and the like—older couples in good health have greater time to devote to sexual activity'' (Williamson, Munley, and Evans, 1980, p. 56). Thus there is an enormous potential for satisfying sexual activity in the later years of marriage.

Sexual interest typically continues to be a vital part of the lives of older adults. Many of the 4246 men and women in Brecher's study on sexuality and aging are testimony to the fact that sexual interaction need not end in the later years:

For example, a 74-year-old husband writes, ''It's amazing how much sex satisfaction can be had with a very understanding mate, especially after age 60.''

A wife, aged 60, writes: ''When I look back on the sexual aspects of my own 36-year-marriage, I see a picture of gradual growth in sexual pleasures—beginning with a warm husband and a somewhat frigid wife! And, at the age of 60, I feel there may still be new wonders to discover with my spouse.''

A husband, aged 65 and married for thirty-nine years, comments: ''I was surprised that our sex life kept on being enjoyable. I thought when I was younger that by my age (65) it would all be over. [Sex is] less intense and less frequent [now], but very enjoyable and satisfying.'' (respondents in Brecher et al., 1984, p. 84)

As the couple ages, some changes in sexual functioning will occur. As men age, they may notice some of the following changes: (1) It takes longer and more direct stimulation to get an erection; (2) the erection is less firm; (3) the amount of semen is reduced and the intensity of ejaculation is lessened; (4) there is less physical need to ejaculate; (5) the loss of an erection during sex occurs more frequently; and (6) a longer ''refractory period'' is needed (that is, the time it takes to have another erection after an orgasm) (Masters, Johnson, and Kolodny, 1982; Brecher et al., 1984). For the most part, these changes have to do with a decline in the supply of blood to various organs, such as the penis, which naturally occurs as people age (Brecher et al., 1984).

As a woman ages, she too will experience changes: (1) It takes longer to produce vaginal lubrication; (2) the volume of lubrication is less; (3) there is a thinning and loss of elasticity in the vagina; and (4) the orgasmic experience is shortened (Masters, Johnson, and Kolodny, 1982; Brecher et al., 1984). In the female a decline in blood supply to the genital region results in taking a longer time to produce sexual arousal and vaginal lubrication (Brecher et al., 1984). Knowledge that these changes in sexual functioning are to be anticipated during the later years helps to reduce fears of performance anxiety. Uninformed men and women can become concerned or even frightened by any change in their established sexual response patterns. Anxiety about performance can in itself then result in a withdrawal from sexual activity. Older people should also be made aware by their doctors of the effect of medications on their sexual functioning.

In general, physical changes in sexual functioning do not lessen the interest and desire for sexual activity for a majority of older adults. In Brecher's study, the majority of men and women age 50 and older indicated a strong or moderate interest in their sexuality. Although the interest declined with each decade, it was still only a minority who expressed a weak interest or no sexual desire at all. In reality, the physiological changes may actually bring some benefits to sexual activity. Since it takes longer to attain an erection and to ejaculate, more time is likely to be spent in touching, caressing, and kissing. Premature ejaculation, a common concern of young men, is no longer a worry for older men. For women, having gone through menopause alleviates any concern regarding an unwanted pregnancy. They, too, can experience the additional pleasure of prolonged tactile stimulation. According to Masters and Johnson (1973), there are only two factors necessary for the continuation of effective sexual functioning throughout life; first, a reasonably good state of general health and second, an interested and interesting partner.

The fact that older people have sexual needs is slowly gaining acceptance in American society. Nursing homes are now required by federal standards to provide for privacy when a spouse visits a resident and to allow married couples to share a room, unless sound medical reasons prohibit it (Williamson, Munley, and Evans, 1980). "Petting rooms" in nursing homes have been suggested as an aid for the expression of sexual closeness among residents (Williamson, Munley, and Evans, 1980). Ironically, it is usually the sons and daughters of the residents who are the most negative about such arrangements, to the point of removing their parents from such homes. Many adult children are embarrassed about the sexuality of their elderly parents, and unfortunately many attempt to inhibit its expression (Masters, Johnson, and Kolodny, 1982). Certainly, aging does not necessarily mean a deterioration of sexual functioning, or other types of functioning for that matter (see Box 11.4).

WIDOWHOOD

I have been in love with the same woman for 53 years, and we have never cheated or been untrue to each other. We have complete trust in each other. The only trouble with a relationship like this is, when one of us passes on, it's going to be catastrophic for the one left behind. (80-year-old husband quoted in Brecher et al., 1984, p. 31)

As relationships have a beginning and middle, so must they eventually end. Although this is usually anticipated to some extent, the timing and the degree of suddenness will influence the way an individual copes with the loss and the new status of widowhood. The unexpected death of a spouse is associated with more severe grief reactions and the slower completion of the grief process than with more lingering fatal illnesses (Balkwell, 1981). For example, because women in general outlive their husbands, men do not expect to survive their wives and are often emotionally unprepared to deal with their wives' deaths.

The Grief Process

The adjustment to widowhood depends to a certain degree on the completion of the various stages of the mourning process. Carolyn Balkwell (1981) has outlined four stages of this process. The initial stage is a state of *shock* in which the "newly widowed person feels numb and may refuse to believe that the spouse is dead" (p. 120). Generally lasting from one day to two months, the widowed person may at times be restless and active and at other times be in a "numbed stupor."

The second stage of grief begins with a *rise in the level of emotion*. Feelings may include an intense longing for the dead person, anger, and guilt. This period occurs somewhere between the first month and the first

BOX 11.4

AGING WITH STYLE

Until recently it was thought that if people lived long enough they would become senile. New research in the field of gerontology, however, has disproved this assumption. The decline in intellectual functioning is much less than previously reported and is usually caused by disease, not by the aging process (Butler, 1984). In fact, there is increasing evidence that intellectual growth can continue through the later years.

What seems to be crucial in determining the decline or improvement of intellectual capacities of older people is the quality of life. Depression and the loss of mental abilities, conditions typically linked to aging, possibly have more to do with life-style. The elderly who keep learning, who exercise, and who remain socially active are much less likely to be depressed and less likely to experience a deterioration of mental capacities.

Certain mental tasks may, in fact, become easier with age. The psychologist Raymond Cattell has divided intelligence into two types: *crystalline* and *fluid.* Crystalline intelligence continues to grow with increasing information and experience in problem solving. It has to do with judgment and insight and improves with the passage of time. Fluid intelligence involves abstract relationships such as mathematics, physics, and other sciences and may stabilize or decline with age. Based on this distinction regarding intelligence, the fields that require qualities of wisdom, judgment, experience, and insight into human beings—such as philosophy, history, painting, and writing—may prosper with age.

The belief that if one lives long enough, he or she will become senile is a myth. Senility is a disease, not part of the normal aging process. Those elderly people who continue to exercise their mental capabilities find minor decline, if any, in their intellectual function. Social involvement, for example, is a major factor in maintaining or improving mental capacities. A study of aging conducted by Warner Schaie revealed that ''Elderly people who lived with their families and were actively engaged with life actually showed an increase in mental abilities over a 14-year-period, while those who lived on their own and were withdrawn from life had a decline. The greatest decline was among widowed housewives who had never had a career of their own and led restricted lives'' (Goleman, 1984).

The study also found that people in midlife who had more flexible personalities and were able to see life from differing points of view performed at higher intellectual levels in old age. In addition, declines in such ability as spatial orientation can be reversed in the elderly with simple tutoring. ''The use-it-or-lose-it principle applies not only to the maintenance of muscular flexibility, but to the maintenance of a high level of intellectual performance as well'' (Schaie quoted in Goleman, 1984). Thus how one adapts and behaves during the later years comes down to personal and psychological factors more than chronological age. ''People who are actively involved in life will seem younger than people who are emotionally and physically sedentary'' (Butler, 1984).

(Continued)

According to Goleman, the following three suggestions will help people maintain their mental capabilities through old age:

Stay socially involved. Old people who withdraw from social life experience the most deterioration.

Be mentally active. People who continue their intellectual interests actually tend to increase their verbal intelligence through old age.

Have a flexible personality. Those people most able to tolerate ambiguity and enjoy new experiences in middle age maintain their mental alertness best through old age.

---

year of widowhood. The "widowed person may behave in a hostile manner toward family and friends and may disengage from social relationships as loneliness for the companionship of the spouse is experienced" (Balkwell, 1981, p. 120).

The next stage is described as an *exploratory* phase in which new roles are tried out. Although usually able and competent, the widowed person may find himself or herself engaging in actions and behaviors with seemingly no purpose. He or she may make unwise decisions. Increased dependence on others and depression are also frequent characteristics of this stage of grief. During the last stage of the grieving process, the "wounds of being widowed start to heal." Either there is an *acceptance of one's status* or a *re-engagement* with new roles and relationships.

This model of the grief experience should not be interpreted to mean that bereaved persons automatically move from shock through depression to recovery. Indeed some people never recover from the loss of their spouses. Others periodically experience pangs of grief and longing for the loved one, long after they have successfully begun to resolve their grief. "Human beings do not just bury their dead and then 'get on with it.' Appropriate modification of an internal world after it has been disrupted by the loss of a loved one takes

time" (Williamson, Munley, and Evans, 1980, p. 350).

Besides time, however, there are a number of other factors that influence the degree to which the widowed person recovers. Some of these factors include the following:

1. the quality of the marital relationship before the loss
2. the mourner's mental image of the deceased—idealized, negative, or ambivalent
3. the personality of the widowed person, that is, tolerance of frustration, self-esteem, capacity to adapt
4. the physical health and age of the mourner
5. other significant losses
6. the social and cultural environment of the mourner at the time of and following bereavement
7. the degree of forewarning of the spouse's death (Williamson, Munley, and Evans, 1980).

During the time immediately following the death of a spouse, the widowed individual is usually provided with support from friends and relatives. But what happens months and years later? Are these people still rallying around the widow or widower or has she or he been forgotten? Unfortunately, too many times the latter occurs.

Loneliness

One of the major tasks in widowhood is overcoming loneliness. Two kinds of loneliness are experienced—emotional and social (Weiss, 1973). An *emotional* loneliness, or isolation, occurs when the person is missing an attachment figure, a significant or intimate other. Since an emotional attachment is characteristic of most marriages, the loss of a spouse will be an emotional loss.

To alleviate emotional isolation the widowed person will be trying to replace the lost partner with another person with whom he or she can be close. This perhaps explains why even though an elderly widowed individual may have numerous social contacts with relatives, friends, and acquaintances, she or he still complains of loneliness. What she or he seeks is a relationship of an emotional nature with someone of a similar age, background, and status, a relationship in which there is a reciprocal exchange of empathy, understanding, touch, and self-disclosure.

The presence of a confidant is an important factor in adjusting to widowhood. Such a close relationship serves as a buffer against the traumatic loss. In a two-year study of 280 elderly persons, Lowenthal and Haven (1968) found that widowed individuals who had a confidant reported higher morale than individuals who were married but lacked a confidant. Thus emotional closeness with others and a relationship of mutuality are "vital factors" in the well-being of older adults, not just marriage.

Widowhood can also produce a *social* loneliness. Since the widow or widower now functions as a single individual instead of as part of a couple, she or he will have a more difficult time fitting into a former social network of couples. Both the widowed person's discomfort and the discomfort of the married friends may result in a mutual withdrawal. "Most of the friendships will be permitted to fade, and although one or two may be maintained the widow is apt to find herself marginal to her former social network" (Weiss, 1973, p. 96). So social isolation is experienced when the widowed person longs for the style of social life and social activities formerly carried out with the spouse. The company parties and picnics, neighborhood barbecues, church gatherings, and other events are often not engaged in after the spouse dies. So losing a spouse can result in another loss, the social group to which two persons formerly belonged.

Of course, people will approach widowhood in their own individual ways. Not all will experience the same degree of loneliness. In fact, some spouses who were quite independent and self-reliant before widowhood may not find widowhood particularly stressful. There appears, however, to be a distinct difference between the experience of the widower and the widow.

THE WIDOWER.   The major loss the widower must face is the loss of the emotional support his wife provided. Men typically tend to "put all their eggs in one basket" when it comes to their emotional needs; it is usually only the wife to whom the husband turns. As was mentioned previously, men are more dependent emotionally on their wives than they care to admit. Studies of self-disclosure, for example, testify to the fact that the wife serves as the primary confidante, with little depth of self-disclosure occurring with other people. Therefore, the death of a spouse can have a greater negative impact on the emotional well-being of men as compared to that of women.

In addition to the end of emotional closeness that comes with the loss of his wife, the widower often feels inadequate in making new social contacts to reduce social isolation. Most men have relied on their wives to initiate and maintain social contacts and activities. Wives typically provide the links with family and friends, and social life in general.

> One of the major consequences of a wife's death was that the man saw less of his children. He acknowledged it was the mother who held the family together. ''My daughters used to come round often when my wife was alive, but I don't see so much of them now. But they like to know I'm comfortable and being looked after.'' Widowers in fact saw less of their children, particularly of their sons, than married men and married or widowed women, as judged by average frequency of contact. (Weiss, 1973, pp. 184–185)

Other factors also make it difficult for men to cope with widowhood. Since widowers are fewer than widows, there are fewer organizations or social groups solely made up of widowed men and specifically catering to their needs. ''Because widowers who have not remarried are not very common in the community until after age seventy-five, their common status does not solidify them into groups'' (Troll, Miller, and Atchley, 1979, p. 76). Also, losing a spouse often occurs during the time of retirement, an event that has further isolated the man from his former friends.

The loneliness and grief that result from the loss of a major source of companionship or intimacy can take a severe toll on the widower's health. ''Most people seem to recognize the medical reality of a broken heart. Many of us have watched couples who have lived together die 'coincidentally' within a few months'' (Lynch, 1977, p. 56).

But compared to widows, widowers' death rates are much higher. White widowers have a death rate 78 percent higher than their married counterparts. Among white females, the widowed death rates are 30 percent higher than for the married females. Among nonwhite males the widowers had the highest death rates, being 89 percent above the married levels; the death rate for nonwhite widows was 65 percent above the rate for nonwhite married females. In summary, the greatest increases in death rates among the widowed occurred for white and nonwhite males, with cardiovascular disease in all cases being the leading cause of death (Lynch, 1977).

Compared to men with living spouses, elderly widowed males are also dramatically more likely to commit suicide (R. R. Bell, 1981). This greater suicide rate is dramatic evidence of the problems that men have in coping with widowed life. The reason for the high suicide rate is ''not just because they had lost a significant [partner] . . . but also because they were isolated in many other ways—from kin, friends, neighbors, and formal organizations'' (R. R. Bell, 1981, p. 194). Involvement in other social groups is a key to preventing suicides among widowers and in giving some meaning to life. Bell contends that in general the high suicide rates among the widowers result from the loss of most of their roles—losses of marital and occupational roles—as well as the loss of interaction with friends and kin. Without these roles one could lose a sense of meaning to life. The highest suicide rates among the elderly are found at the lower-class levels.

THE WIDOW.   One of the most disrupting aspects of losing a husband is the loss of identity for the woman. This is especially true when a wife is almost totally dependent on her hus-

Females usually have close friends on whom they can rely when their husbands die.

band for her self-concept—that is, her major or sole role in life was that of a wife, whose identity was "so and so's wife."

> *Being a widow changes the basis of self-identity for those women for whom the role of wife and mother is central. . . . In answering the question, "Who am I?" such women would usually have put* wife of *at the top of their list, but many find it harder to do the same with* widow of. *They have also lost the person who supported their self-definition. (Troll, Miller, and Atchley, 1979, p. 72)*

Although wives may depend less on their husbands for emotional support—less than men do on them—there is still the loss of companionship around the house. There is also the constraint on social relationships with former couple friends, as was found with the widowers. Widows, however, are more likely than widowers to join clubs and organizations. There are also many more widowed women available with whom they can form friendships.

Remarriage for the woman who becomes widowed in her later years is often not an option. "Among women over 50, widowhood usually is a permanent status, although not necessarily a role they prefer. Only 5% who become widowed after age 55 ever remarry. This is in sharp contrast to widowers, most of whom remarry if they are under 70" (R. R. Bell, 1981, p. 195). Widowers have a better chance at remarriage since the widows greatly outnumber widowers. Also men are more likely to marry younger women, with far greater social approval to do so.

As in the early years of life, people in the later years continue to desire emotional closeness. "No matter what our age, we each need intimacy . . . —at least one other person with whom we can share both pleasure and pain" (Porcino, 1982). Just as infants and children who are never held or touched suffer emotionally, it is also true of older people.

CHAPTER REVIEW

1. Significant changes in individuals and family relationships occur during the middle and later years. Some of the changes in family interaction result from a personal midlife transition—when males are reappraising their life's work and turning more attention to their familial roles and when women are gaining more interest in the world outside the family. Several explanations account for these transitions; some stress physiological causes, such as hormonal shifts, while others stress a cultural perspective, a process of lifelong socialization experiences.

2. Launching children, or emptying the nest, is another event faced by couples in the middle and later years. The departure of children, however, is usually anticipated and typically occurs in a gradual process. On the one hand, contrary to common belief, the empty nest is usually a blessing to mothers, not a so-called syndrome. On the other hand, fathers often feel a sense of deprivation. Overall, the children's departure may produce a positive impact on the marriage and an increase in the level of intimacy. Without the "kids" around, couples may find it easier to engage in personal, intimate behaviors. Other couples may only grow further apart as they soon discover that the only shared interest and bond between them was the children.

3. Being a grandparent is a more frequent occurrence today than ever before in history. It is a somewhat "roleless role," however, in that there are no clear prescriptions as to how grandparents are supposed to behave. Grandchildren can provide numerous rewards such as a source of biological renewal, biological continuity, emotional self-fulfillment, and a chance for the grandparent to be a teacher or resource person.

4. Retirement is yet another stage in the family life cycle. The way individuals adjust to retirement depends on their attitudes toward work, their preparation for retirement, and particular ethnic and social class influences. Spouses during the retirement years tend to look more to each other for companionship. While the attraction between spouses may not be as high as in earlier years, attachment and loyalty are highly valued during this period.

5. Widowhood or widowerhood concludes the family life cycle. After coping with the initial grief process, there is the loneliness to deal with, both emotional and social. Women, in general, are likely to have at least one confidant besides their husbands and several significant other friends. These relationships aid them in adjusting to widowhood. Widowers, in contrast, are likely to have "put all their eggs in one basket"—namely the wife. Coping with loneliness is much more difficult for them.

Relationship and Commitment Options

Since the 1965–1975 period, it has become more acceptable to seek closeness in alternative ways to marriage and the nuclear family—or not to seek closeness at all. Homosexual relationships, although still viewed negatively by a large percentage of the population, have come out in the open to a greater degree than ever before in the history of the United States. Communal groups, which were popular in the third quarter of the nineteenth century, again multiplied in the 1965–1975 decade. Living together without marriage was another alternative that became increasingly public. Finally, remaining unmarried became a much more acceptable option. In this chapter these various alternative relationship and commitment options will be reviewed, and the degree of intimacy that these alternatives might provide will be analyzed.

SINGLEHOOD AS AN ALTERNATIVE LIFE-STYLE

An alternative to marriage that has appeared to increase in popularity in the past 25 years is the single life. With more people delaying marriage, combined with a high divorce rate, it seems as though the percentage of single adults has increased significantly. Being single is not, however, a new life-style that has only recently emerged. "Young Americans are returning to levels of singlehood that have been characteristic throughout the history of this country—but which were interrupted by a few decades of unusually high marriage rates and low ages at marriage" (Kain, 1984, p. 4). What *has* changed is the general attitude toward being single.

Singleness is increasingly recognized as a legitimate life-style. Remaining single is viewed less negatively and marriage is not necessarily always considered to be the best choice for every individual (Thornton and

Freedman, 1985). In comparing attitudes between the 1950s and 1970s, Veroff, Douvan, and Kulka (1981) noted an increased tolerance of people who reject marriage as a way of life. In the 1950s more than half of all respondents (53 percent) conveyed negative attitudes toward a nonmarrying person, indicating that such an individual was either "sick or immoral, too selfish or too neurotic to marry." In the 1970s only about one-third (34 percent) responded with such hostility to the idea of not marrying.

Typifying the negative stereotype of singles during the 1950s is a *Newsweek* article from 1956, which referred to people who didn't want to get married as having "marriage phobias" and needing psychiatric help. This article described the plight of singles and reported on 20 cases with happy endings: "With psychotherapy, all 20 lost their complexes and married" (Kidd, 1977). Another study, the 1980 Study of American Families, revealed that most young people would be bothered at "least a little" by the failure to marry, but relatively few respondents said that they would be "greatly" bothered by such an outcome (Thornton and Freedman, 1985).

This change of attitude toward singleness can be understood by looking at the privileges that were historically bestowed on married people but were denied to those who remained single (Thornton and Freedman, 1985). In colonial times, only by marrying did an individual become a fully adult member of society (Demos, 1970). Unmarried people usually lived with a family, either with their own parents or in the homes of others where they worked as servants. Regardless of age, unmarried persons remained dependent upon the families with whom they lived.

This living arrangement gradually changed as unmarried persons became more economically independent during the nine-

Today many single men carry out traditionally female tasks.

teenth and early twentieth centuries. They were able to earn wages for labor outside the family, and some moved into boarding houses. These boarding houses still played a family-type role for singles. Thus, despite some changes, "Even in the first decades of the 20th century, most young people continued to live with their own families or as servants or boarders with other families, and they rarely achieved full economic independence" (Thornton and Freedman, 1985, p. 33).

Another benefit the unmarried person did not have was access to a regular sexual partner, given the moral climate of the time.

Ineffective methods of birth control and disease also added to the risk of engaging in sexual activity outside of marriage.

What has occurred in recent years is that "Single persons now have access to many of the benefits traditionally reserved for married couples" (Thornton and Freedman, 1985, p. 33). The majority of single men and women are employed, most have achieved economic independence from their families, and most live apart from their parents (Thornton and Freedman, 1985). Marriage appears to be no longer essential in order to find emotional support, sexual activity, and companionship (Stein, 1975). People can choose to try to cultivate closeness through friendships rather than through a spouse and children.

Today the single life-style offers many benefits, according to the results of one study. These include "self-reliance," "complete independence," "privacy," "freedom of movement, choice, and of lifestyle" (Barkas, 1980, pp. 24–25). Another study found similar "pulls" toward being single to include "freedom, enjoyment, opportunities to meet people and develop friendships, economic independence, more and better sexual experiences, and personal development" (Stein, 1975, p. 494). But as with any lifestyle, there are trade-offs. Singles mention the following costs of the single life-style: "lack of someone to share with," "trouble lining up a date," "no one to care for me when I'm sick," "loneliness," "I tend to feel neglected," "sexual dissatisfaction," and "I hate eating alone" (Barkas, 1980, p. 26). Common ideas about single adults and their life-styles have been dispelled by recent research (see Box 12.1).

The Single State: Temporary or Permanent?

Do persons actually choose the single life-style as a permanent state? Or is it viewed by most as a transitional period until one gets married? Being single does not always involve a choice. "Some persons choose not to marry, and others are not chosen for marriage" (R. R. Bell, 1981, p. 116). Most singles, however, plan to marry; approximately 75 percent of single men and women speak positively of marrying and would actually prefer to be married (Simenauer and Carroll, 1982). One-fourth of the singles in Simenauer's and Carroll's research spoke disparagingly about marriage and intended to stay unmarried. Most of those in this category were divorced.

Other studies (Barkas, 1980) concur with the desire of most singles to marry. For a vast majority of singles, then, singleness is a "tran-

sitional" state, "a holding pattern," not a destination. These singles may accept the single life-style for the time being, but they are continually looking for someone to marry.

But some men and women do choose singleness as a permanent state. These singles are not searching to find a marriage partner but are seemingly content to remain unattached. Perhaps a bad experience with a previously committed relationship has discouraged them from pursuing another. Or perhaps other things such as a career or their freedom have been placed in a higher priority in their lives. Those who are willing to choose this form of single life-style indicate that they can find satisfaction in their "friends, work, hobbies, outside interests, and romantic liaisons" (Barkas, 1980, p. 43).

Ironically, often the never-married men and women who accept their singleness and feel good about themselves soon leave the single state (Barkas, 1980). In other words, those who do well in the single state—who can accept it, who feel secure with themselves, and who have high self-esteem—are attractive to other people, and hence they are more likely to end up finding a marital partner.

According to social psychologists Walster and Walster (1978), one quality that makes a person most appealing to the other sex is the ability to relax. Being comfortable about one's singleness could certainly project an image of self-confidence and aid in achieving a relaxed atmosphere. People will perceive the single person as having no urgency to need someone else. "The happy single enjoys life, and seeks someone to enjoy it with, while the unhappy single wants someone to *make* him or her happy" (Barkas, 1980, p. 135). There isn't the tendency to cling to others out of desperation when the individual is relaxed about being single.

There is also a group of unmarried men and women who wish that singleness would

BOX 12.1

SOME MYTHS ABOUT SINGLES

Cargan and Melko (1982) in their survey of 151 singles and 250 married persons attempted to sort out the myths of being single from the realities. The following are a few of the myths they dispelled when analyzing their data.

Singles are tied to mother's apron strings.   You see a bachelor, who should be married by now, and he tells you he is going to visit his mother over the holidays. And you think, "Uh, huh, that's the problem. Hasn't been able to let go of those strings."

It is even worse if the single person is living with a parent, particularly a mother. A man becomes a figure of ridicule. A woman is perceived as an old maid who might have flourished if she could have gotten away from her possessive mom.

But even if they aren't living "at home" . . . you wonder if an attractive man or woman has failed to find a partner because of unresolved relationships with a parent. And "failed to find," . . . of course, presumes that a search was attempted. The data from this study do not support this image. There is little difference between never marrieds and marrieds in their perceptions of relations and their parents. They do not differ in their perceptions of warmth or openness, nor are they much different about parental conflict. . . .

Singles are selfish.   The stereotype is that singles do not get married . . . because they are too centered on themselves. Having only themselves to think of, they become egocentric, and being egocentric, they remain single. . . .

To be fair, another image also exists, that of the single who, not having family to give to, is loving toward larger groups of people: children, minorities, old people, nations, humankind. Jesus was a single and Buddha left his family because it would distract him from a greater work. . . .

But the selfish single does not emerge from the examination of the data mentioned here. In some areas the single appears to be more selfish, in some more selfless. . . .

[Singles] prove to be greater contributors to community service. Of those contributing two or more hours to community service weekly, the ranking among our four aggregates was as follows:

never married	20 percent
divorced	18 percent
remarried	13 percent
married once	9 percent

(Continued)

Singles are rich.   Singles ought to be richer than marrieds. They have no spouses and children to support; they can live in condominiums or bachelor pads. The Internal Revenue Service takes this image into consideration in taxing them. The supermarket does too, in setting its bargains for large family sizes.

. . . It turned out that over 20 percent of the married placed their incomes above $20,000 a year. Under 10 percent of the singles said they were making that much. Of the divorced, only 6 percent reached that figure. . . .

Many are young, at the bottom of the economic ladder. Others are divorced, trying to support children and two households. On the whole, the marrieds are better off economically than singles.

Singles are increasing in numbers.   This is literally true in America, if we are considering numbers. But usually we aren't counting numbers; we are considering that within a group of a certain size we notice more singles than there used to be, or else we mean that the number is rapidly growing. Either way, it is clear that this is not so. . . .

We [Cargan and Melko] have seen from our demographic study that the percentage of singles was over 40 percent from 1900 through 1940, but had dipped to 32 percent by 1960, rising back toward 40 percent by 1980. . . . Our demographic survey, however, has given us good reason to believe that the growth of singles in the 1960's and 1970's was largely a function of the baby boom of the forties and fifties, and that even if the percentage of divorced population continues to increase, it is not likely to compensate for the decrease in the percentage of young adults. . . .

There are more singles than ever. But the percentage of singles is lower today than it was at any time before World War II and today's percentage appears to have peaked and to be approaching decline. It could be that even in numbers singles will be declining by the late eighties or early nineties.

There is something wrong with singles.   We [Cargan and Melko] have already concluded that singles are not particularly tied to parents' apron strings, nor especially selfish when compared to marrieds. What else can be wrong? We had, in our historical review, detected a note of defensiveness or apology on the part of the singles themselves. But this defensiveness was in response to a social expectation, not the result of any inherent problem within the singles themselves. And in the 1970's it appeared they were losing interest in defenses. . . .

But by measures of happiness or loneliness, singles may not be as well off as marrieds. However, there is nothing wrong with being lonely or sad some of the time, or more often than your neighbor. By measures of freedom, singles may be better off than married, but that does not make it wrong to marry. A married person may sometimes or often wish for freedom from the responsibilities of marriage but on the balance may consider it better to remain married. So may a single consider it better on the balance to remain single, even if loneliness is a price to be paid.

be transitional but unfortunately have found it to be permanent. "These 'unwilling' singles are disgruntled and outspoken against singleness" (Barkas, 1980, p. 43). Barkas makes the following observation about these singles: "These are the ones who implore, 'Where are the decent men?' or 'Why can't I find a woman?' . . . These never-marrieds are naive and almost childlike in their unwillingness to settle for anyone less than the 'perfect' spouse" (p. 43).

The Single Who Fears Intimacy

Whether or not being single was originally a choice, a reason some persons remain single is their fear of intimacy. It is uncertain as to how prevalent this fear is. But research indicates that a common complaint among singles is that a permanent relationship requires relinquishing individual freedom, independence, and self-reliance. Stein (1975) found such attitudes among the singles he interviewed. "Most respondents concluded that the security and interdependence of marriage inhibits independence, experimentation, and learning. They rejected what they saw as a stalemated, boring situation" (p. 494). Barkas (1980) maintains that the "battle" the single person needs to conquer is not merely loneliness but also "togetherness." Such a single person needs to overcome the fear that being close to someone else is the equivalent of losing one's sense of autonomy and individuality.

In recent years single women have been more frequently expressing a fear of intimacy (see Box 12.2). Many women have witnessed their mothers relinquishing their own self-fulfillment to achieve an image of an idyllic family reminiscent of the 1950s. It's no surprise then that marriage is threatening to some women today and to their view of themselves as self-sufficient people. The majority of unattached singles of both genders that Barkas (1980) interviewed expressed a fear of "choking intimacy." He states,

> To them, commitment meant being in a relationship that demanded loss of freedom. Those who feared intimacy consistently picked 'the wrong' partners. . . . They concerned themselves with finding the 'perfect' partner next time, rather than striving for autonomy and interdependence within the relationship this time. (pp. 181–182)

Thus, instead of dealing with this fear of intimacy within a relationship, this type of single person continues to jump from one short-term relationship to another, fleeing whenever one partner becomes "too serious." Reasons such as "He (or she) is not the right one" are often merely excuses to hide one's own apprehension about emotional closeness.

Self-reliance and intimacy are not mutually exclusive. In fact, intimacy is more likely to be achieved by two individuals, each

BOX 12.2

THE NEW FEAR OF INTIMACY

The fear of intimacy was once exclusively a male problem. But according to journalist Megan Marshall, women have now borrowed it from men. Marshall bases her conclusions on intensive interviews that she conducted with 40 single, professional women. Many of these women, born during the baby boom of the 1950s, bought "lock, stock and barrel" the notion of independence, freedom, and self-sufficiency that permeated American culture during the 1965–1975 era. Such movements as feminism, self-fulfillment, and sexual liberation taught women to be assertive and independent. Other single, professional women became their role models. The role their mothers played—the "1950s Mom," the passive, helpless housewife, the "wageless slave"—was evaluated by this generation as one of "failure."

Determined not to repeat their mothers' mistakes, many women of this generation devoted their energies exclusively to the development of a career. "The vision of a mother inseparable from her family was replaced by a working woman attached to no one; a dream of giving was replaced by a dream of doing; a life defined by connections to others was replaced by a life of solitary self-exploration" (Marshall, 1984, p. 29). These women believed that the search for self was the primary goal of a woman's life, one that she must pursue alone. "If woman's total devotion to husband and children had kept her from developing her own potential, ran the popular ideology, our solution would be to cut off family ties and grow free" (p. 20). In no way were these women going to define themselves only as so-and-so's wife or mother.

The fear of a life of self-annihilation in marriage and motherhood and the desire to be successful prompted these women to pursue their careers with great intensity and dedication. There was often a struggle to gain a place and acceptance in the work setting. A woman had to stifle her emotions because to be emotional might be interpreted as a weakness, a lack of control. To prove herself capable she had to conform her dress and actions to those of a man's world.

Dressing in subdued clothing, working overtime, traveling frequently, and even moving to another city when employers demanded it were all ways to outperform her male colleagues. Quite often the challenge of competing with men, rather than the career itself, became the major reward. "Relationships with anyone outside work became handicaps: throughout the 1970s, singleness was the price most women paid for success" (pp. 53–54). An intimate relationship was viewed as a threat to all she had worked for. "We dreamed of becoming the tough professional who had none of the crippling personal commitments to husband and children that most women made in their early twenties" (p. 33). Marshall found that when relationships got serious these women would run. They feared that intimacy would take away their newfound freedom and independence.

"The first time a man asked me to marry him," one thirty-year-old woman boasted, "I immediately applied to journalism school and left town." Whether it was by moving away, dating unsuitable men, maintaining impossibly high standards for lovers, or a dozen other diversions, women were becoming experts at rejection and avoidance. (p. 41)

A crisis of female identity emerges in the "independent" woman when she realizes that what she has in reality isn't what she wants. It becomes a conflict because she feels she must choose between two mutually exclusive choices—commitment to a career or commitment to a relationship. Love and work are viewed as opposing each other. If she falls in love, she is compromising her feminist ideals, and her "newfound self" will be lost.

Marshall argues that women can have careers and still participate in intimate relationships. One can be strong, and also caring. It is not necessary to reject love, commitment, and nurturance in order to be competent. Also, the professional woman may not realize that by avoiding emotional closeness with a man she may be shutting out a relationship that might provide her with support through the difficult years of climbing the career ladder. The new challenge then for women is "to learn to reconcile their anger at past injustices and their need to prove themselves with the rhythms of human life and love" (p. 218). Marshall concludes:

> Marriage will never be the panacea that our mothers were taught it would be in the 1950s. Marriages will continue to end in divorce for all the old reasons, and for the new ones stemming from our current devotion to the single life. Yet we must now prove that our new selfhood runs deeper than simple competence in the material world. We must permit ourselves to believe in the long-term love that a good marriage protects, and to discover that love teaches us as much about ourselves as does solitude. For the human self does not exist in isolation. We must find others to care for, and who will care for us, making ourselves full members of a community with far greater boundaries than the professional world. Only then will we have discovered ourselves as women. (p. 222)

with his or her own positive self-image, and less likely by those who simply take on the identity of the other person because of their own low self-esteem. What many single persons do not realize is that one can sustain his or her individuality and still be close to another. The answer to the extremes of separateness and choking intimacy is a "healthy emotional interdependence" (Olds, 1978). Hence, the unattached single who fears relationships needs help "in learning how to establish, develop, and maintain a fulfilling interdependence with someone else" (Barkas, 1980, p. 179).

"Friends as Family"

Living singly does not necessarily mean one's life will be void of close relationships. Since some singles remain unmarried over a long period of time, possibly their whole lifetimes, they need to adopt a life-style that can satisfy at least some of their social and emotional needs. Thus friendship is typically very important to the single person. It "may serve in some ways as an alternative to marriage—in meeting both individual and social needs" (R. R. Bell, 1981, p. 115).

One key to a quality life-style for the single person is contact with people. An elaborate network of friends, activities, and romantic relationships supports the contented single individual. Stein's interviews with singles revealed such findings.

> The greatest need single people feel, in their departure from traditional family structure, is for substitute networks of human relationships. . . . While individuals may be driven into singlehood through a negative reaction to marriage, they cannot sustain it for long without validation from people they respect. . . . This context of friendly relationships, as reported by our respondents differs from the family environment in being more open, more subject to change, and based more on a sense of choice and free exchange than on an accident of birth, blood ties, conventionality, and reciprocal role-obligations. (1975, p. 501)

Making close friends and building a stable support network are not always easy tasks. In recent years there has been an increase in the "loneliness business," designed to provide social opportunities for singles (Gordon, 1976). Dating services, singles' bars, fitness clubs, singles' apartment complexes, religious singles' organizations, and the like all capitalized on the singles' search for friends and romantic partners.

Singles tend to develop personal relationships almost exclusively with other singles. "Couples in America are very reluctant to have single men or women as close friends. The unattached party is almost always considered a threat to one of the partners in the marriage" (Gordon, 1976, p. 75). Unfortunately, the network of single friends dwindles as its members marry.

The diaries kept by singles in one study indicated that people who live alone actually spend very little time alone (Rodin, 1985). Time by oneself was always broken up by telephone calls from others who lived alone. If feeling lonely, the informants would telephone friends to talk or to arrange to meet them at a health club, to go shopping, to go to a movie, to play racketball, or to enjoy other recreational activities. In addition, networks of social support are formed to assist for special purposes, such as moving and house painting. These "cooperative labor groups" exchange routine domestic services also. (See Box 12.3.)

While a friendship between two singles can be close, when the search for a mate is of paramount interest to either friend, problems can develop. "The friend is important when there isn't someone of the opposite sex around. But when the possibility of a date arises, out goes the friend" (Gordon, 1976, p. 75). For some friends, the "cement" holding them together is a common search for love. Discussing how to find a mate and going out and looking for one together consumes a great deal of their time with each other. Once a mate is found, there is no longer this common tie between the friends. Success at finding a mate often leads to the "destruction of the friendship" (Gordon, 1976).

For many singles, relying on one's family for aid or support becomes less appealing over time; turning to friends becomes more acceptable and appropriate for them (R. R.

As singleness has increasingly become a legitimate life-style, various social activities for singles have become popular.

Bell, 1981). In many instances, friends function as the single person's "family." It's not a family built around kinship or marriage but around "real preference, shared interests and genuine affection" (Edwards and Hoover, 1974).

If our relatives are not, do not wish to be, or for whatever reasons cannot be our friends then by some complex alchemy we must transform our friends into our relatives. If blood and roots don't do the job, then we must look to water and branches. (Howard, 1978, p. 262)

Through interviews Karen Lindsey (1981) tried to determine what classified certain friends as "family." Two major criteria were expressed over and over again. The first is that "the friend is someone accessible in emergencies." This "family" friend would loan you money in a pinch, supervise your children for the night you will be in the hospital, or help you meet a deadline by typing an important report. The second criterion is history. "Friends become family when you've not only known each other for some time, but have been involved in important parts of each other's lives" (p. 114). A history with certain friends gives a sense of stability in the midst of change in our lives.

Some singles form cooperative types of living arrangements, where several singles live in the same dwelling. This provides a sense of belonging as a group and has been

BOX 12.3

LIVING ALONE DOESN'T MEAN YOU'RE LONELY

Single people who live alone are not always lonely. The typical view of the single person is that he or she is waiting to be married or remarried. This implies that being single, per se, is a negative emotional state characterized by loneliness. The fallacy of this implication is based on the belief that the terms *loneliness* and *aloneness* are synonymous.

Judy Rollins (1983) distinguished these two terms and defined them as follows:

> *Loneliness*—A condition wherein a single person who lives alone experiences a sense of restlessness and discontent, feels a strong need to change his or her lifestyle and views the single lifestyle as a negative condition.
>
> *Aloneness*—A condition wherein a single person who lives alone has a general sense of well-being, values his or her lifestyle, and has no urgent desire to change this lifestyle. (p. 29)

Rollins's research reveals that many of her single subjects who live alone are happy and content. From these subjects, Rollins was able to discover positive aspects of aloneness that distinguish it from the negative emotional state of loneliness. Singles who live alone have greater flexibility to be creative in their residences. Their homes can sometimes be a welcome haven "from the 'noise' of colleagues, friends and family. . . . Developing leisure-time activities for singles is far more open. . . . They have more time to pursue these activities and can choose friends who enjoy the same activities" (n.d., p. 15).

Research by Alwin, Converse, and Martin (1983) also reveals that those who live alone are likely to make more friendly contacts with others outside the home than those who do not. It is to be hoped that studies such as these will prevent people from making the erroneous assumption that single people who live alone are automatically lonely.

referred to as an opportunity for "having the cake of commitment while eating its crumbs of relative freedom" (M. Adams, 1981, p. 225). Thus such a household can give the single a sense of security with the feeling of some independence and freedom. It must be stressed that this type of group living is not necessarily accepted by everyone and is, in fact, quite rare. The greatest appeal seems to be to younger singles. For older single people the separate single dwelling is still the most common living arrangement (M. Adams, 1981).

In sum, being single is becoming a more acceptable and viable life-style. But a difficulty in studying the single way of life is that one is not looking at a homogeneous group. There are many varieties of being single and many reasons for them. What can be concluded is that most singles don't want to remain permanently single. Those who choose to do so often do so out of a rejection of traditional marriage or because of a fear that an intimate relationship will rob them of their own self-fulfillment. Those resigned to the single state and accepting of it look for intimacy through close friendships and for social support through a larger network of friends.

LIVING TOGETHER

Most people want to develop a close and enduring relationship with another human being. But marriage may not be the only avenue by which this may be pursued. Couples may seek the benefits of an intimate relationship without necessarily taking marital vows.

Approximately 1.8 million couples are choosing the option of living together without being married to each other (Spanier, 1983). This is about 4 percent of all couples. Statistics on living together, however, are not always totally accurate. Since the Bureau of the Census asks no questions regarding the nature of the personal relationship in these living arrangements, the data may include a variety of situations even such as a male college student who rents a room in the home of an elderly woman. Nevertheless, the majority of the unmarried-couple households reported in the latest census contained partners in the same age group (Bureau of the Census, 1983).

Nonmarital cohabitation is clearly not a single entity but comes in a variety of forms. Cohabiting relationships differ in the amount of time that partners spend together, the nature of the living arrangement, and also in the partners' degree of commitment (Macklin, 1983). For example, some arrangements for living together appear quite casual and temporary. Some are situations of convenience for short periods of time, such as while attending college. On university campuses living in the same apartment is often a result of a drifting process—couples gradually sleeping together more and more frequently. It may not be the result of a mutually discussed decision. Cohabitation can also exist as a form of preparation for marriage, a form of "trial marriage" to see if the couple should proceed with a legal marriage. But probably more than anything else today, living together functions as a stage in the courtship process.

In addition, cohabitation can be viewed as a substitute for, or an alternative to, marriage. Couples living together for this reason may be making "an ideological statement" rejecting the institution of marriage (Blumstein and Schwartz, 1983). These cohabitors "may love one another and plan a life together but they do not want the law or tradition to define the structure of their relationship. Their ambition, if their relationship is successful, is to have a lifetime of cohabitation" (Blumstein and Schwartz, 1983, p. 85).

Many "ideological" cohabitors were previously married and "turned sour" on the institution of marriage at that time or during the divorce process. Possibly while going through the divorce proceedings they learned the consequences of owning things in common. Also, divorced women who have sacrificed their careers or missed out on education may be determined never again to put themselves in the marital situation. "Some see cohabitation as the only way to have a relationship and still preserve their own interests" (Blumstein and Schwartz, 1983, p. 86).

Cohabitors who ultimately marry are different in some respects from those who make cohabitation a lifetime commitment. As might be expected, the cohabitors who end up getting married are a more conservative group of people. They have more traditional ideas about the roles of men and women, want to spend more time with each other, are more possessive, and are more likely to pool their resources earlier in the relationship (Blumstein and Schwartz, 1983).

Interdependence of Cohabitors

One of the hallmarks of an intimate relationship is a significant amount of interdependence between the partners. This interdependence underlies a "we-ness" and a togetherness. It implies a trust in each other and a pooling of resources. Blumstein and Schwartz (1983) found a tendency for cohabitors to "hold interdependence at arm's length." For example, cohabiting couples typically avoid owning things jointly. "They feel it is safer to keep separate ownership clear so that, should the relationship break up, they know who owns what" (p. 84).

Cohabitors are also less likely to pool their money than married couples. It is interesting that women are more opposed to pooling the money than the men. Apparently, women want to hold on to some degree of autonomy by keeping their money separate. Financial separateness also indicates some doubts about the durability of the relationship. Those cohabitors who have lived together for a long time are more likely to share their money (Blumstein and Schwartz, 1983).

The Gender Roles of Cohabitors

Cohabitors appear to be more liberal than married couples regarding male and female roles. For example, "Many more cohabitors than married couples think both partners should work" (Blumstein and Schwartz, 1983, p. 125). Although it's not surprising that cohabitors have more liberal attitudes, the real question is how these attitudes are reflected in behavior in the relationship. And if intimacy is best achieved in relationships in which the partners treat each other as equals, would the potential for emotional closeness be greater for cohabitors than for married couples?

Cohabiting women, in particular, feel strongly about equality for men and women. By cohabiting—as opposed to getting married—women are taking a stand on being financially responsible for themselves and not dependent on a marriage. Most cohabiting women want an equal sharing of the economic role, especially older cohabiting women. The result of this economic partnership for women is a higher self-esteem and a feeling that they can support themselves. Many female cohabitors were previously married, and they felt that their careers suffered during their marriages and they weren't going to let that happen again (Blumstein and Schwartz, 1983).

Likewise male cohabitors, in general, do not want to shoulder the total financial burden of the relationship. Those who intended to marry their female partners, however, were more willing to take on more of the good-provider role. Blumstein and Schwartz stress that males who prefer that their female partners not work are ill-suited for cohabitation. The cohabiting woman wants to work and will resist any attempts on the male's part to stop her.

Since cohabitors hold egalitarian standards regarding work in general, one would expect that their attitudes toward housework would be egalitarian also. The research shows that the *attitude* is egalitarian, but the *behavior* does not necessarily match the attitude. Blumstein and Schwartz found that while cohabiting women do less housework than working wives, cohabiting men do not do any more housework than married men. Female cohabitors who earn less or work less than their male partners tend to make up for this discrepancy by doing more housework. It is the woman's way of providing her fair share. But since women, in general, earn less money in American society, they will more often carry the greater burden of the housework. Blumstein and Schwartz (1983) conclude, "Men assured us they shared housework and were indispensable at home. However, when the men and women filled out their questionnaires independently, the number of hours the men reported was much less than that of their female partners" (p. 148). The avoidance of housework by cohabiting men is the cause of many arguments between cohabiting partners. The more he is involved with housework, the more peaceful the relationship and the more satisfied she appears about the whole situation (Blumstein and Schwartz, 1983).

The Potential for the Development of Intimacy

Both advantages and disadvantages for the development of intimacy coexist with the cohabitation arrangement. First, as previously mentioned, cohabiting partners appear more conscientious about equality; they're less likely to rely on traditional gender roles. This aids in building mutual respect, satisfaction with the relationship, and greater closeness.

A primary disadvantage of living together involves the lack of interdependence and commitment. Legal commitment tends to promote a feeling of security and trust, an atmosphere in which partners can fully disclose their feelings and allow themselves to be vulnerable. The more interdependent the partners are, the bigger stake they have in the relationship and the more they will invest in it. Thus when conflicts arise in a marriage,

there may be a greater effort to work them out so that the relationship can continue harmoniously. Without full commitment the relationship can be more easily dissolved.

Cohabitation, unlike marriage, is not an *institution*, with standard practices that help interaction to proceed smoothly. An attempt to make living together an institution, durable and satisfying, without the government's participation and based solely on the partners' love for each other is difficult. As an institution, cohabitation lacks structure and acceptance from the rest of society (Blumstein and Schwartz, 1983). (See Box 12.4.)

The treatment of cohabitors by other members of society also lacks agreed-upon norms. For example, even if the parents approve of a young couple's living arrangement, there is some awkwardness in terms of how to act toward one's son's or daughter's partner. Do they include the "live-in" as a family member? What do the parents call the person—boyfriend, girlfriend, significant other, lover? Even the Census Bureau has difficulty, labeling its new category POSSLQ ("persons of the opposite sex sharing living quarters") (Kain, 1984).

Living Together as Preparation for Marriage

Some couples enter cohabitation as a "trial marriage" to see what it's like living with each other on a daily basis. As soon as they have learned enough about each other, they either marry or break up, depending upon what they have learned. On the surface it would seem that living together would help couples to be more realistic about selecting a mate and about the decision to marry. Also, one would think that the transition to marriage would not be as difficult an adjustment for couples who have lived together. These

BOX 12.4

LIVING WITHOUT THE TIES THAT BIND

The irony of the life-style that guarantees privacy and simplicity is that it also can breed nagging legal complications and frustrations dealing with life, property, child care, separation, and death. Legally, live-in lovers are no closer than total strangers. . . .

Specifically, here are some of the major problems unmarried partners encounter due to their lack of legal status:

Personal finance. Attorneys advise maintaining separate bank accounts, inventories of property and belongings, credit accounts, and expenditure records. Each person is 100 percent liable for debts incurred under joint names, and bank assets kept in a joint account can be seized by creditors owed debts by either person.

Property rights and obligations. In leasing an apartment or buying a house together, unmarried couples must follow the normal business transaction procedures, ranging from a joint purchase agreement to terms of payment and ways to split the proceeds from its sale. Many couples now sign joint purchase forms for furniture and appliances as well.

Health care and medical decisions. Critical medical decisions can be delegated to the unmarried partner only with a medical power of attorney.

Insurance. Job-related fringe benefits are extended only to married spouses and children unless—in the case of life insurance, profit sharing or savings plans—the unmarried partner is designated in writing as the beneficiary.

Inheritance. When a husband or wife dies without a will, the assets go to the surviving spouse and children. In case of an unmarried person dying without a will, his or her live-in partner would not inherit. The deceased person's legal next of kin—parents, brothers or sisters, etc.— have first claim.

Child custody and financial protection. Custody disputes involving unmarried couples are handled by the Circuit Court and the Friend of the Court, as are all post-divorce proceedings. To protect the child's rights to future claims to property and inheritance, both unmarried parents must acknowledge in writing the paternity of the child. . . .

There is an increasing demand for legal help in preparing contracts, agreements, wills, and other legal papers for unmarried couples seeking protection in case of an emergency, breakup, or death. The most common document is called a Living Together Agreement (or LTA, for short) that clearly spells out the couple's expectations and promises.

SOURCE: *Adapted from "Unwed: Living Without the Ties that Bind," 1984,* Ann Arbor News, *December 9, p. G1.*

assumptions were made when several researchers investigated the question: Does premarital cohabitation lead to better marital adjustment when compared to those couples who did not cohabitate before marriage?

Roy Watson (1983) studied the effects of cohabitation and of noncohabitation during the first year or two of marriage. It was expected that previously cohabiting couples would obtain higher scores of "marital adjustment." Contrary to this expectation, however, noncohabiting respondents were found to have significantly higher adjustment and satisfaction scores.

A couple of explanations could account for these differences. First, the noncohabiting spouses may still be experiencing a "honeymoon stage" of their relationship (Watson, 1983). Often conflicts and disagreements have been concealed or avoided so the relationship has progressed fairly smoothly. Thus the noncohabiting couples may still be experiencing the "illusionary intimacy" characteristic of courtship and/or early marriage. Romantic idealization and unrealistic perceptions of the relationship are often held by the couple during the early phase of marriage. And although the partners may *feel* emotionally close and happy with each other, they have frequently yet *to see* the "real" behavior and personality of their spouse. Cohabitors, in contrast, are more likely to have moved beyond this early stage of the relationship because of their longer experience of shared living.

A second possible explanation of lower marital adjustment scores for couples who have lived together is that marriage carries a different meaning for cohabitors and noncohabitors. For noncohabitors, marriage may be a "liberating" experience whereby new possibilities, such as establishing a common household, are now open to the couple and "celebrated" (Watson, 1983). Cohabitors

have already established a common residence, have defined their roles to each other, and perhaps have defended their action before their parents. "To them, the aspect of marriage which is emphasized is not the freedom it brings but the assumption of new responsibilities" (Watson, 1983, p. 146).

DeMaris and Leslie (1984) also looked at the relationship between cohabitation and subsequent marital quality among 309 recently married couples. They expected that cohabitors would rank higher on both communication and dyadic satisfaction. This hypothesis was based on the belief that "Cohabitation should serve as a more effective screening device than does traditional courtship for weeding out poorly adjusted couples" (1984, p. 78). In addition, "Cohabitors would be expected to have faced and adjusted to many of the problems traditionally encountered in the first few years of marriage by noncohabitors: becoming accustomed to divergent living and housekeeping habits, deciding on how to share household chores, agreeing on frequency of sexual activity, and so forth" (p. 78). However, "Compared with noncohabitors, cohabitors scored significantly lower in both perceived quality of marital communication and marital satisfaction" (p. 83).

DeMaris and Leslie recognized that the very factors that led couples to live together in the first place (such as more liberal attitudes and a greater tendency toward independence and assertiveness on the part of females) could be playing a role in determining the degree of marital satisfaction. So they controlled for such factors as sex-role traditionalism, church attendance, and other sociocultural differences between cohabitors and noncohabitors. Even when these variables were controlled, having cohabited before marriage was still associated with slightly lower satisfaction for husbands and wives. In addition, the length of cohabitation had nothing to do with the degree of marital satisfaction.

DeMaris and Leslie (1984) concluded that the difference in marital satisfaction between these two groups is not "alarmingly large," but the results run counter to common-sense expectations regarding the advantages of living together before marriage. It appears that living together does not screen out less compatible couples, and that cohabitation appears to attract couples who from the outset are somewhat less likely to report high satisfaction once they are married. Perhaps those who cohabit are the least likely to conform to traditional marriage conventions and, therefore, are the most likely to be dissatisfied with their marriages (1984). Also, because these studies use subjective reports of marital satisfaction, the noncohabiting couples, who are more traditional, may feel social pressure to report happier marriages.

These researchers still contend that other variables may be playing a role in the discrepancy between the marital happiness of cohabitors and noncohabitors. At least it does not appear that merely cohabitation per se is the key variable. If it were, we would expect marital satisfaction to be lower the longer the couple has cohabited prior to marriage. No such relationship, however, was found.

To this date, there has been relatively little study of any differences between the personality traits of cohabitors and noncohabitors. But in one study Kersten and Kersten (1981) found that cohabitors, as opposed to noncohabiting individuals, rated lower in trusting others, lower in their own trustwor-

Most homosexual couples want some durability and permanence in at least one relationship.

thiness, higher in negative reinforcements received in childhood, higher in drug use, higher in self-centeredness, lower in self-esteem, and in general were poorer social exchangers. Given these negative personality traits, it would not be surprising to find these individuals experiencing a somewhat lower level of satisfaction in their marriages.

In sum, although living together before marriage is no longer an uncommon phase of courtship, cohabitation appears to have no particular advantage over more traditional practices in guaranteeing couple compatibility in marriage (DeMaris and Leslie, 1984). Future studies need to use more objective measures, such as actual communication patterns, the depth and frequency of self-disclosures, and conflict resolution skills.

HOMOSEXUAL COUPLES

Studying the relationships of homosexual couples helps us to gain a better understanding of the impact that gender has on the development of close relationships. In Chapter 3 we looked at the way gender affects what males and females seek in a relationship and at differences in the behavior of men and women. But what happens in relationships when both partners are of the same gender? Does the common gender encourage a bond and greater emotional closeness between the partners? Or does having two people of the same sex living together magnify certain traits that hinder intimacy? More specifically, do such partners tend to take on particular roles; for example, one that of a traditional male and the other that of a traditional female?

Until recently same-sex relationships have not been given the scholarly attention that heterosexual relationships have received. In part this imbalance stems from the tendency for society not to accept homosexual pairs as legitimate. Two gay persons often are not publicly acknowledged as a real couple. Nor are they typically extended the same commonplace courtesies offered to spouses. For example, a homosexual partner is seldom invited to an office party or to a retirement banquet (Blumstein and Schwartz, 1983).

Another reason for the lack of knowledge regarding same-sex couples relates to common misconceptions about the homosexual life-style. There is a general view that most same-gender relationships are very short-lived, do not involve commitment, and should not be taken seriously. Gay males especially are stereotyped as promiscuous and as not interested in establishing a relationship with only one other person (Blumstein and Schwartz, 1983). Also, gay couples are not given societal support to stay together as married couples are. But most homosexual couples do want some durability and permanence in at least one relationship. This goal has been even more common since the discovery of AIDS.

The Interdependence and Commitment of Homosexual Couples

The way homosexual couples combine their resources provides a clue about the level of commitment between partners and the amount of interdependence in the relationship. Like cohabiting heterosexual couples, same-sex couples are also reluctant to pool their resources. Blumstein and Schwartz (1983) found that neither gay men nor lesbians pool their incomes until they are convinced of the durability of the relationship.

But determining when the relationship is stable and enduring is not an easy task. Unlike married partners, lesbian and gay male couples do not have a "symbolic demarcation" such as a wedding or marital vows symbolizing their commitment to a permanent relationship. There is no "institutional understanding" that moving in together is a lifetime commitment. "So these couples can remain tentative about the relationship for a longer time.... The issue of permanence is something many same-sex couples discuss and negotiate over a period of time" (Blumstein and Schwartz, 1983, p. 105).

In a study of 156 male couples, McWhirter and Mattison (1984) found a merging of money and possessions to occur during a stage of relationship development taking place between 11 and 20 years. These authors emphasize that the combining of resources is a process; proving a commitment and building trust appear to take many years. It is especially difficult for men because they are trained to pay careful attention to money. "It represents power and a sense of self" (1984, p. 104).

So it becomes a "proud accomplishment" of male couples when they develop a sense of "our" money and "our" possessions. It is an "important new symbol of what they want, hope, and expect to be a permanent relationship" (McWhirter and Mattison, 1984, p. 105). According to McWhirter and Mattison, this combining of money is the single most identifiable activity signifying ongoing commitment. Early in the relationship men dared to say, "I love you." But it is not until many years later that "they put their money where their love is. It represents the surrender of each partner's last major symbol of independence" (p. 105).

Equality Among Same-Sex Couples

Since gender cannot be used as a variable that sets the partners apart in homosexual relationships, one might expect that equality could be more easily achieved. That is not true, however, for gay males; in fact, it is very difficult for them to achieve equality in their relationships. Instead of gender, a person's

salary is used as a source of power in male gay relationships. When there is a disparity in incomes between two male homosexual partners, the one with more money is usually the more powerful person in the relationship (Blumstein and Schwartz, 1983). This same pattern, of course, occurs also in marriage, where a husband's higher income gives him power. But along with the husband's power is the responsibility to support his wife and family. "Often both husband and wife take pleasure in his ability to support them, whereas gay men are usually uncomfortable being the provider or being provided for. Each man thinks he should be able to pull his own weight, but if one greatly surpasses the other, he may feel entitled to be dominant, leaving the other feeling inadequate" (Blumstein and Schwartz, 1983, p. 110).

On the one hand, men have a long tradition of using their earning power as a standard of their worth in their relationships. Women, on the other hand, are not as accustomed to judging their own worth by how much money they make. Gay females apparently do not judge their partners by such standards either. Thus among lesbians, unlike gay men, money does not establish the balance of power in the relationship (Blumstein and Schwartz, 1983).

Lesbians are aware of the power money can exert in a relationship, and therefore they make a conscious effort to keep their relationships free from such a form of control or domination. They try to keep money matters equitable and in balance, trying to avoid the good-provider role that exists in heterosexual relationships (Blumstein and Schwartz, 1983).

The assignment of household responsibilities also reveals how much equality exists in the relationship. Since homosexual couples cannot divide household responsibilities according to gender, they consider other things such as available time, their work schedules, abilities, and preferences. The process of resolving who does what is often one of "trial and error" as well as trying to minimize the number of tasks each hates doing. McWhirter and Mattison found that during the early stages of the relationship gay males often do household tasks together; shopping, laundry, or paying bills are all done jointly. But later in the relationship, since there are typically no set "husband" and "wife" roles, they each assume tasks they feel competent with.

It is interesting to note that lesbians, on the average, do slightly *less* housework than gay men (Blumstein and Schwartz, 1983). "This may be because some of them are rejecting a role that has been symbolic of women's low status. Lesbians are especially careful to devise an equitable organization of household duties" (Blumstein and Schwartz, 1983, p. 149). Just as gay men try to avoid the traditional provider role, lesbians want to avoid putting a partner in the traditional homemaker role.

For married couples, decisions based on traditional gender roles may be simple and easy to make, but they are likely to be more unfair and inequitable. "For heterosexual couples, *gender provides a shortcut* and avoids the decision-making process" (Blumstein and Schwartz, 1983, p. 324). The disadvantages to this arrangement are that it inhibits change, discourages innovation and *choice* regarding roles and tasks, and assumes the man is the dominant partner. Same-sex couples have perhaps a greater opportunity to develop an equality in their relationships, but it may take more time and effort to accomplish this.

Companionship Among Same-Sex Couples

While for the most part lesbian partners are eager to succeed in their careers and to invest considerable time in their work, they also express a desire for more time with their partners; lesbian couples appear to be more relationship centered than male couples. Male homosexuals do not seek additional time together. Gay men can be compared to husbands who are absorbed in their careers, who desire a lot of personal freedom, and who do little to adapt their lives to spend a lot of time with a partner. But unlike husbands, a gay man is in a relationship with someone who feels the same way he does. There is no female partner (or wife) who is complaining because she wants more time for companionship. As gay men grow older, however, they tend, like husbands, to settle down and "develop a greater appreciation for companionship" (Blumstein and Schwartz, 1983, p. 179).

In general, same-sex couples spend more time together sharing leisure activities than do heterosexual couples. Such companionship can help a couple build a closer relationship. Heterosexual men and women are more likely to engage in separate leisure activities. When heterosexual partners spend time on hobbies or attending social events (for example, hunting, fishing, jogging, club meetings), they are more often alone or with their own friends. In contrast, "Same-sex couples are more likely to include their partners in leisure activities. Very often they share hobbies, belong to the same clubs, go to sports events, and socialize with friends together" (Blumstein and Schwartz, 1983, p. 180).

Same-sex partners have experienced a lifetime of similar experiences simply because they're the same gender. This fact alone helps to make communication easier and helps facilitate a feeling of commonality, which may be much more difficult to achieve with someone of the other sex. For gay persons the need for friendship and the need for romantic love can both be met in one person, while heterosexuals lead more segmented lives in their leisure time. As a result, heterosexual partners "who do not see each other during work time or spend a lot of playtime together may discover that much of their interaction is concerned with the mundane—and not very enjoyable—details of life" (Blumstein and Schwartz, 1983, p. 183).

Development of Intimacy Among Same-Sex Couples

Companionship and equality are aspects of homosexual relationships that encourage closeness. But several roadblocks still remain to the development of intimacy among same-sex couples. Perhaps their biggest problem is the unacceptability of their life-styles to a large segment of society. Since homosexual relationships are not formal institutions, they do not have a legal contract or marital vows to support them. No formal ceremony confirms the commitment the two partners make to each other. Rather, commitment must be demonstrated on a daily basis by each partner's behavior.

In addition, sometimes it's years before family and friends recognize these couples as couples, if they ever do. Although social pressure alone is generally not enough to keep couples together—as evidenced by the current high divorce rate—it still helps to encourage a long-lasting commitment and permanence in a relationship. Those social factors that exert pressure on a heterosexual couple to stay together are virtually absent from the homosexual relationship.

Because men tend to be less relationship oriented than women, one would expect that male couples would have more difficulty in attaining intimacy than female couples. The fact that American culture socializes men to be nonintimate, at least to some degree, presents a serious obstacle to the development of committed gay male relationships (Reece,

1979). Barriers to intimacy include competition, the withholding of dependence, and the lack of emotional expressiveness.

These obstacles exist for men in both heterosexual and gay relationships, although they may be magnified among homosexual couples. For example, while males may feel a need to compete and to be dominant in a marriage, such actions may not produce as many conflicts as they would in a gay relationship, where *both* partners are aggressively competing (Reece, 1979). Hence, how can two men who are taught to be competitive, to win, and to be number one work out an emotionally close relationship with each other? An intimate relationship requires the ability to be vulnerable, to let weaknesses and real feelings be known by the other. For many gay men that is too great a risk.

McWhirter and Mattison (1984), however, present a different opinion. They contend that for most gay men there has been some variation in their gender-role socialization while growing up. "Childhood traits, such as high sensitivity, willingness to compromise, and lack of competitiveness, earned them [the gay males] the label 'sissy.' However, these very same traits that made the boys feel different and wrong are now the highly valued building blocks for finding compatibility and developing complementarity in the relationships" (p. 49). If these authors are correct, gay males will follow a less traditional masculine role and display more androgynous behavior, that is, having traits of both genders. Further research needs to be conducted to look specifically at the gay males' ability to be intimate compared to heterosexual males.

Since women are more likely than men to be adept at relating intimately, the potential for an intimate relationship between lesbian partners is greater than between gay male partners. Lesbians are not going to be faced with the same barriers of competition, the inability to be vulnerable, or inexpressiveness that plague many male relationships. Female homosexuals want the best of both worlds—a close, intimate relationship and a challenging career. "Lesbians want an intense home life, but they also want a strong, ambitious . . . partner" (Blumstein and Schwartz, 1983, p. 328).

Among female couples there is a "strong emphasis on being able to take care of oneself" (Blumstein and Schwartz, 1983, p. 328). Neither partner wants to be in a position of extreme dependence on the other, which may have been the situation in a previous marriage. If they are able to balance this autonomy with the interdependence of a relationship, they can attain a truly intimate life-style. Blumstein and Schwartz conclude,

> The lesbians are trying to carve out a new female role. This is an exceptionally difficult challenge and it is a testimony to their persistence that so many of their relationships do thrive. We think that one reason some are successful is because lesbians still retain women's desire for closeness and nurturance. Most are still relationship-centered and are willing to put time and effort into working out their problems and being attentive to their partner's emotional needs. (p. 329)

Unlike gay males, lesbian couples probably experience more acceptance of their relationship by other people. Female friendships, which can be some of the most intimate of human relationships, are widely accepted. In fact, many lesbian couples are considered just that, two friends living together. Most people do not immediately assume that the two women are homosexual. The acceptance of the relationship by family and friends may encourage the women to stay together.

Like the gay males, lesbians may also be more androgynous in their behavior, displaying both masculine and feminine traits. In fact, the rigid assignment of roles, such as "butch" and "femme," at one time present in the lesbian community have changed just as gender roles among heterosexual couples have changed (Blumstein and Schwartz, 1983). Traditionally the "butch" woman was expected to perform male tasks and be the greater financial provider for the couple. The feminine counterpart was the "femme," who projected a more feminine demeanor and style of behavior. While gay men did not use such terms, there also was a tendency for one partner to be more masculine and the other more feminine.

> Role playing, however, is no longer in vogue. While many gay and lesbian couples had already rejected role playing on ideological grounds, the women's movement and the reevaluation of sex roles in our society affected lesbians and gay men just as they affected heterosexuals. (Blumstein and Schwartz, 1983, p. 45)

THE COMMUNE: AN ALTERNATIVE FAMILY

Dissatisfied with traditional forms of the family and/or society as a whole, some people throughout history have ventured forth to establish alternative utopian family groups. Rosabeth Kanter (1974) found that communal groups have one of three major purposes: (1) "a desire to live according to religious and spiritual values, rejecting the sinfulness of the established order"; (2) "a desire to reform society by curing its economic and political ills, rejecting the injustice and inhumanity of the establishment"; or (3) "a desire to promote the psychosocial growth of the individual by putting him into closer touch with his fellows, rejecting the isolation and alienation of the surrounding society" (p. 541). While many nineteenth-century communes had strong religious underpinnings, more recent communities have tended to be primarily an escape from a largely anonymous and impersonal culture. "In the midst of an advanced technological society seen as isolating, meaningless, fragmented and machinelike, today's utopians wish to recreate a shared life together" (Kanter, 1972, p. 311).

Perhaps one of the best-known and successful communes in history was the Oneida Community (1848–1881), formed in upstate New York. Founded by John Humphrey Noyes, this community was based on an extreme form of Christianity known as Perfectionism. The teachings of this group asserted that perfection could be expressed in an actual community, in the form of the kingdom of heaven on earth. Two central ideas were predominant in this commune: *self-perfection*, that is, the "improvement of one's spiritual state, one's character, and one's intellect," and *communalism*, which entailed "sharing everything with the Community" (Carden, 1971). The Oneida Community isolated itself from the surrounding society and implemented practices such as "economic communism, communal living, 'complex marriage' or free love, communal child-rearing, and government by mutual criticism" (Kanter, 1974). In 1879 special state legislation against Oneida was passed, and Noyes fled into Canada to avoid arrest. The loss of its charismatic leader led to the ultimate disbanding of the community.

The Israeli kibbutz is a form of commune that continues to exist today. It practices the common ownership of property, communally organized production, communal dining, and communal child care. The first kibbutz was founded in 1909 on the banks of the River Jordan near the Sea of Galilee. Today kibbutzim number about 250—including 100,000 members (kibbutzniks)—less than 3 percent of the total Jewish population of Israel (Queen, Habenstein, and Quadagno, 1985).

A typical commune in America today may consist of two or three couples pooling their resources to buy an old house in a city or in a rural area. Many of these communes attempt to create their own version of an extended family, and they are trying to follow an intense and meaningful group-based way of life (Kanter, 1972). These groups are not typically based on a religious or political ideology; rather the participating individuals feel that a group situation allows for more opportunities to fulfill their social and emotional needs. Members feel that living within a single marital dyad limits a person's potential. Enlarging the relationships to a three- or more-person group increases the possibility of finding mutual interests. The multiple relationships of communal living may provide "several of the kinds of interaction a person needs or enjoys, ranging from support to instruction to nurturing, and from social to intellectual challenge" (Ramey, 1978, pp. 356–357).

Are commune members able to form closeness in their families? Is there, after all, such a thing as "group intimacy"? Or does there even exist a need for intimacy among individuals raised with so many people from birth? The discussion that follows will look at some answers to these questions and also at the ways in which communes build commitment to the group and try to create a viable, alternative family system. The Oneida Community and the kibbutz will be used extensively as examples.

Minimizing Dyadic Intimacy

By various means, communes typically seek to discourage exclusive attachments or bonds between two people. The fear is that an attachment to another person weakens commitment to the group as a whole. Thus in order to survive as a community, policies and practices are enforced that discourage members from developing close, dyadic relationships. "Exclusive two-person bonds within a larger group, particularly sexual attachments, represent competition for members' emotional energy and loyalty" (Kanter, 1973, p. 86).

To control two-person intimacy, communes institute practices of either "free love," in which "every member was expected to have . . . sexual relations with all others, or . . . celibacy, in which no member could have sexual relations with any other" (Kanter, 1973, p. 87). Both practices attempt to minimize private dyadic ties and to emphasize the cohesiveness of the total group. Also, minimizing intimacy meant that people were freed from nuclear-family obligations and were more available for community work (Kanter, 1973).

Kanter found in dividing the "successful" nineteenth-century communes from the "unsuccessful," that all but one of the successful groups practiced either celibacy or free love at some time in their history. Most of these successful communes preferred celibacy. The moral tone of the time and the need for effective birth control appeared to contribute to the choice of celibacy over free love.

The members of the Oneida Community, however, did practice a form of free love called "complex marriage." Noyes, the leader, started this practice himself.

In May, 1846, he found himself attracted to a member of the Community, Mary E. Cragin; she returned his feelings. At the same time, Mrs. Cragin's husband George and Noyes's wife admitted their growing affection for each other. After a careful discussion the four agreed they shared the conviction that it was God's will for them to exchange sexual partners—and they did so.

Two more couples soon joined them in the practice of complex marriage. . . . They agreed to an absolute community of property, including people as well as material possessions. (Carden, 1971, p. 21)

Personal reasons aside, a primary purpose for the practice of complex marriage, according to Noyes, was that a monogamous relationship prevented individuals from loving their neighbors. The intimate dyad was viewed as a threat to group cohesiveness and solidarity. "Two people should not 'worship and idolize each other. . . . The heart should be free to love all the true and worthy,' and there should be no form of 'selfish love' " (Carden, 1971, p. 49).

The practices of both free love and celibacy tended to be "highly controlled in the successful communities and subject to a large number of rules" (Kanter, 1973). The free love of the Oneida Community was controlled by its leaders. In the early years of the commune a man could approach any woman for a sexual encounter and spend the entire night with her. The problem with this approach was that people "fell in love." In later years more restrictions were imposed by the leadership, and sexual meetings were limited to a couple of hours. Such limitation of time helped to prevent long private conversations that might lead to "exclusive love." If couples did fall in love, they were highly criticized for their "exclusive" or "special" attachments. If a unique attachment persisted, one of the offending pair was sent to a branch community until he or she had overcome this "worldly impulse" (Carden, 1971).

The Shakers, a community founded in the eighteenth century, tried to separate men and women as much as possible while living a life of celibacy. Rules separating the sexes were carefully enforced by the elders. Not only sexual activity but *any* kind of physical contact was prohibited between the sexes.

*Men and women (''brothers and sisters'')
slept in different rooms on different sides of
the house. They ate at different tables in
the common dining room. They were not
permitted to pass one another on the stairs,
and—as if this were not enough—many of
the dwellings included separate doorways.
Even the halls were made purposely wide
so that the sexes would not brush by one
another. Needless to say, all physical contact
was prohibited, including shaking hands,
touching, and ''sisters mending or setting
buttons on the brethren's clothes while they
have them on.'' (Kephart, 1982, p. 216)*

Shaker men and women were prohibited
from being alone together without a third
adult present. Whenever possible, all contact
between the sexes took place in groups. A
''union meeting'' was held three or four times
a week to bring men and women together for
conversation (Kanter, 1972; Kephart, 1982).
A half-dozen or so women would sit in a row
facing an equal number of men. The two
rows were a few feet apart, permitting the
woman to converse freely with the man opposite her.

*The pairs were presumably matched (by the
elders) on the basis of age and interests. The
ensuing conversation might relate to aspects
of Shaker economy, theology, or similar topics. Although the talks were required to be
on an impersonal basis, the participants
employed levity, humor, and other techniques used by people everywhere. Occasionally the get-together developed into a
songfest. The principle of the union meeting, however, was to encourage a positive
relationship between the sexes rather than
the strictly negative one that might arise
from forced segregation. (Kephart, 1982,
p. 217)*

Thus the interaction between the sexes was
kept superficial and impersonal, preventing a
more intimate relationship from developing.

Exclusive relationships of *any* kind were
prohibited by the Shakers. The leaders would
rotate the members of work groups in order
to limit the possibilities of strong private relationships forming between individuals of
the same sex (Kanter, 1972). But overall,
much of what the Shakers lacked in terms of
dyadic intimacy was replaced by a community feeling of social support.

Not all communes go to such extremes
as free love or celibacy to control close relations. The kibbutz, for example, uses a more
moderate approach. Although marriage exists
on the kibbutz, the married couple is often
encouraged to play down their relationship.
According to kibbutz philosophy, the primary
focus of individual energies should be on the
larger community and the growth and development of a ''new society of agricultural so-
cialists'' (Queen, Habenstein, and Quadagno,
1985).

Marriage is also minimized in other ways
on the kibbutz. The terms *marriage, husband,*
and *wife* have been abandoned. A man and
woman do not get ''married''; but rather they
become a ''pair'' *(zug)*. A woman or man does
not acquire a ''husband,'' or ''wife''; he or
she acquires a ''companion'' (Queen, Habenstein, and Quadagno, 1985). When a man
and woman decide to become a ''couple,''
they petition to share a room. No elaborate
ceremony or vows take place at this time. A
formal marriage ceremony according to the
laws of the state usually occurs around the
time of the birth of the first child. Under state
law, children born out of wedlock have no
legal rights (Queen, Habenstein, and Quadagno, 1985). ''In the kibbutz, husband and
wife remain first and foremost part of the
group. So even in the marital relationship this
makes for a more outward relatedness to the
kibbutz than toward each other'' (Bettelheim,
1970, p. 274). Another innovative arrangement to control close relationships in a com-

mune can be seen in a modern commune called Kerista Village. (See Box 12.5.)

Loosening the Parent-Child Bonds

Not only are intimate adult dyads threatening to communes, but also close ties between parents and children can compete with communal commitment. Kanter (1973) found that "In a higher proportion of successful than unsuccessful nineteenth century communities families did not share a dwelling unit (rooms, apartment, or house), and children were separated from parents, sometimes to be raised in a separate children's residence by community members assigned to that function" (p. 90). In the Oneida Community, for instance, if a woman appeared too much attached to her child, "exhibiting too much exclusive 'mother spirit,' she might be subjected to criticism and denied visiting privileges for two weeks" (Kanter, 1973, p. 90).

Exclusive attachment between parent and child is also discouraged on the kibbutz. For the most part, all child-rearing functions—discipline, education, child-care activities—are left up to the commune. Specific practices to discourage mother-child intimacy are enforced soon after the birth of a child. The newborn enters the infants' house four days after birth. This speed is so that separation won't be as difficult as if it occurred later, after an attachment has been formed. During the first six months of life, the infant stays in the nursery, and the mother visits during the day and both parents might visit after working hours (Queen, Habenstein, and Quadagno, 1985). The mother may spend an amount of time with her baby equivalent to that of other nonkibbutz mothers. The main difference is that the baby sleeps in the infants' house at night.

At six months, the *metapelet* (nurse-house mother) becomes the primary caregiver, and contacts between the baby and mother are limited to a couple of hours a day. How does this limited contact affect the mother-infant relationship? Rabin and Beit-Hallahmi's research (1982) shows that there isn't less of an attachment between the mother and infant but that for most children the mother and the *metapelet* became interchangeable attachment figures. Nevertheless, interviews with young adults reared on a kibbutz and adult children from a moshav (a noncommunal agricultural settlement in Israel) revealed some differences in attachment. Compared with the adult children from the moshav, the kibbutz children showed a lower level of attachment to the mothers. No significant differences in ratings of attachment appeared for the fathers (Rabin and Beit-Hallahmi, 1982).

A visiting time for parents and children to come together occurs for approximately two hours, late afternoon or early evening, every day. All activities are child oriented, and no other activity takes place. The father is also typically actively involved in this exchange with his children (Gerson, 1966). The goal is for parents and children to have only good times together so that no hostility is created in the child toward his or her parents.

As Bettelheim (1970) states, "For two hours the parents and all their children are what we would call a family" (p. 128). Can this be enough time for a closeness between parent and child to develop? It's doubtful. They have not spent enough time for an exchange of emotions, *both* negative and positive, in a full give and take. Bettelheim compares this arrangement to a typical American family.

It is not that our middle-class mothers spend more time with their children but that the timing of emotional giving is not preset by the clock. It is exactly the unscheduled sit-

BOX 12.5

THE KERISTA VILLAGE: AN ALTERNATIVE LIFE-STYLE OF "POLYFIDELITY"

A most fascinating attempt at controlling sexual exclusivity and dyadic intimacy has taken place during the last ten years at Kerista Village, an equali-
tarian, nonmonogamous utopian community in San Francisco. Kerista Village involves nine women, six men, and two children. This group of people
got together because they strongly believe in communal living and share a
commitment to a utopian ideology to make the world a better place to live.

The commune claims to be a "polyfidelitous family." *Polyfidelity,* a word
coined and defined by one of the group's leaders, is a "group of best friends,
highly compatible, who live together as a family unit, with [heterosexual
relations] . . . occurring equally between all members, . . . no sexual involvement outside the group, an intention of lifetime involvement, and the intention to raise children together with multiple parenting" (Pines and Aronson,
1981, p. 374).

Family members do not become sexually involved with one another
until they have made a mutual commitment to "a current intention of a
lifetime involvement" and an intention to be totally faithful to one another.
In this way, a polyfidelitous family resembles a traditional marriage. But it
differs from a traditional family in "its basic assumption that one can have
many primary relationships simultaneously" (p. 374). "All 15 members of
the family report that they feel a high degree of love and tenderness for each
other. Each of the 6 men in Kerista Village claims to be equally 'in love' with
each of the 9 women, and vice versa" (p. 374).

The family members have an interesting way to manage sexual relationships within the family. Such relationships occur according to a balanced,
rotating sleeping pattern. Schedules are set up regarding who sleeps together
each night. Whether or not to have sexual intercourse is left up to the two
partners sleeping together that evening.

Interactions among Kerista Village members are like a "round-the-clock,
ongoing encounter session" (p. 374). Members are encouraged to be very
direct and honest and to express verbally their thoughts, feelings, fantasies,
fears, and observations.

Instead of discouraging dyadic intimacy from forming, the members view
all one-to-one relationships as "unique and [they] are given equal importance." The ideal of "nonpreferentiality" is that each one-to-one bond is so
strong that no member sees the strength of any other relationships as a threat
to the uniqueness of her or his intimacy bonds. What the Keristans are trying
to do is "extend the limits of a twosome to include 15 people" (p. 377).
Since less resources of time and emotional involvement are invested in each
individual partner, the loss of that partner is likely to be less traumatic than
when all the resources are invested in one person.

The Keristans offer an example of how intimacy is controlled in a communal life-style. Their style of "free love" is not quite as liberal as in the
Oneida Community. In fact, the Keristans are quite conservative in some of

their sexual attitudes. Not many people today require a lifetime commitment before they become involved sexually as the Keristans do. "The Keristans do not practice open marriage. They are totally faithful to their partners—only in their particular case that means being faithful to six, nine, and eventually perhaps 12 partners" (p. 387).

The Kerista Village has a majority of highly articulate and intelligent women. Unlike many communes where the power structure is predominantly male, female members exert much power in the Kerista Village. Their influence can partly explain the emphasis on such things as open expression of feelings, total self-disclosure, and multiple parenting.

---

ting with one's child through the night, when he is sick or afraid and needs it most—and not on the next afternoon—that makes for replenished emotions and allows the child to freely expend them on others. (p. 157)

Developing a Group Identity

Children on communes are typically raised in groups of peers. The peer group replaces the family as the major socializing agent, providing the child with support, security, and a sense of continuity. Just as the infants on the kibbutz are sent off to join other infants in the infants' house, in the Oneida Community soon after weaning, mothers sent their infants to the children's house, a wing of the adult residence. The children remained with this peer group, "day in and day out," throughout childhood and adolescence. With the children, as within the community as a whole, "the emphasis was on group activity and love for all, rather than on selfishness or exclusive love" (Kanter, 1973, p. 13).

The practice of "mutual criticism" was one of the Oneida Community's major forms of social control and ways of ensuring conformity to the group (Kanter, 1973). Children were taught that reporting one another's misbehavior was a virtue. They were told that it was desirable that "sinners" be corrected as soon as possible. Undoubtedly, this practice had a stifling effect on the members, discouraging them from disclosing honest feelings or showing individual behaviors for which they might be criticized.

On the kibbutz the development of a group identity begins at an early age. Cooperation and respect for the rights of other members of the group are stressed. There develops a "group conscience." Any deviation from proper behavior or neglect of duty comes to the attention of the rest of the group. At meetings of the group the offender is confronted by other members and is in some way disciplined. This accountability to the group serves as a deterrent to deviant behavior. It is too threatening to go against the group because "this is where their emotional security resides. Without the peer group they are lost" (Bettelheim, 1970, p. 233). (See Box 12.6.)

Communal Child Rearing and the Capacity for Intimacy

What kind of adults result from being raised on a commune? Are they less self-centered, more attuned to the needs of others, and more cooperative? Do they have the capacity to be emotionally close to another person? Most communes do not last long enough for these questions to be studied. Researchers, however, have been able to investigate quite thoroughly the adult personalities of those raised on a kibbutz.

In communal living, the development of a group identity begins at an early age. Children are separated from their parents and spend most of their time with their peer group.

Growing up with such a strong group identity, kibbutz young adults often openly try to discourage dyads from forming. A twosome immediately becomes the center of opposition; it is seen as "something alien, as an effort to escape from the group" (Bettelheim, 1970, p. 254). Many schemes and plots are used by the larger group to try to break up dyads. Frustrated with attempts to form close and intimate friendships, young adults will resign themselves to a group life devoid of true intimacy (Bettelheim, 1970).

The collective group identity also hinders a kibbutznik from developing the capacity to be intimate. Among the kibbutzniks there is very little individual experience, only a group experience. In their willingness to give their lives to their peer group, the children forfeit personal feelings for group feelings. Emotional experiences are experienced as a group. They will speak of an experience "we all had together," rather than "an experience *I* had" (Bettelheim, 1970). "It is almost as if the high value placed on the collective emotional experience makes the deeply private one—the experience that belongs to oneself or to a twosome—seem kind of indecent" (Bettelheim, 1970, p. 277).

BOX 12.6

DANGEROUS ALTERNATIVE FAMILIES

The communal living arrangements discussed in this chapter have been relatively positive ones, in the sense that none of them has been particularly harmful or damaging to the members. Karen Lindsey (1981) suggests that there is an ugly, negative side to some types of alternative families. Seeking desperately for a semblance of belonging and recognition, some people fall victim to exploitative groups. They will gravitate to groups with a charismatic leader who has visions of creating a utopian community. "Dominant members can prey on the needs of the weaker members (whether that weakness is economic, physical, or emotional) for nurturance, companionship, or security, and thus destroy the people who turn to them" (Lindsey, 1981, p. 248).

Many pimps convey a family imagery to the prostitutes who work for them in order to insure their loyalty and obedience. A contract may actually be set up, such as the following: "You are reading this because you have passed one of the requirements to become a member of the illustrious family of _____ . . . . anyone or anything opposing my will must be and will be destroyed" (p. 252). The pimp sets himself up as the patriarchal father-husband figure, who has absolute control of the woman's life and demands her total obedience to his will. Hookers sometimes become "sisters" to each other.

Cults are another form of negative alternative family. "These groups are usually structured as surrogate families: their members are all 'brothers and sisters,' who act as devoted children of a single parent figure—be it a guru, a self-appointed messianic figure, or the leader of a self-styled religion" (Zeitlin, 1980, quoted in Lindsey, 1981). To enlist loyalty to this new "family," often members are encouraged to break all ties with their biological families. "The 'family' created by such cults is an isolated emotional unit and, as a result, becomes more restrictive, more oppressive, than the original family" (p. 254).

Most cults are led by men and are run like exaggerated forms of the patriarchal family. Both male and female members are expected "to renounce any independent thought or action, and to follow their leader in blind obedience" (p. 254). In 1978 the mass suicides of Jonestown, Guyana, testified to the extent to which this blind obedience to a father figure can actually kill people.

Another example of a negative family was the little band of men and women in California who followed Charles Manson during the 1960s. At Manson's command the "family" committed hideous murders. "The Manson crew took their family status seriously. They made what they called 'home movies' of some of their grisly rituals, which involved the killing of various animals, and sometimes of people" (p. 254). Manson attempted to control every aspect of "his children's" lives.

(Continued)

Women were regularly ordered to perform sexual acts with Manson and with various of his friends and cronies; they obeyed him without question. The most minute details of their lives were in Manson's control: One male member wistfully remarked at one point that "Maybe someday Charlie will let us grow beards." They seem to have reveled in obedience as much as they reveled in bloodshed because they were given a community—a sense of literally *belonging* to the family. (p. 255)

The negative alternative family is like an extreme form of the traditional family. Its ideology supports total authority and power invested in the head and total submission by his followers. These dangerous family forms reflect the extent to which individuals will go in order to try to gain a sense of belonging and a semblance of a family. Lindsey warns, "For those of us consciously concerned with creating new forms of family, a look at the negative family can serve as a guide-post for what to avoid—and a warning not to be too smug about what we are doing" (p. 256).

Since this strong group identity does not allow the experiencing and expressing of personal feelings, it is difficult for members to form a very close relationship with another person. A basic requirement for the development of intimacy is disclosure of personal feelings. Kibbutzniks do, however, experience a feeling of comaraderie and security with the group. Dyadic intimacy is replaced by a sense of belonging to a group.

The kibbutz children lack role models for intimacy in their family relationships. The marital relationship of the parents is not likely to be emotionally close, since dyadic intimacy of any kind is minimized. In addition, when children see their parents during their visits, the contact is brief and focused solely on a happy atmosphere. It's doubtful that children see their parents relating intimately—sharing a range of emotions, resolving conflicts, providing emotional support, and engaging in social activities. Personal feelings in communal families tend not to be expressed, and what feelings are expressed tend to be positive.

What scientific evidence do we have that children raised on a kibbutz are less intimate than those raised in more conventional families? Rabin and Beit-Hallahmi (1982) measured the personalities of adult kibbutz children by various research instruments—surveys, questionnaires, and interviews. A moshav was studied as a comparison group. Using an intimacy scale, the researchers found a significant difference between the kibbutz and moshav groups. In evaluating the quality of contacts between best friends, contacts between kibbutz friends were significantly more instrumental than intimate. In terms of intimacy (quality of interpersonal interaction) versus sociability (quantity of interpersonal interaction), "more members of the kibbutz group preferred numerous but superficial friendships compared to the moshav group" (p. 131).

Rabin and Beit-Hallahmi (1982) also analyzed the degree of intimacy in marriage relationships. Since the kibbutz took over all the other functions of the family—production, consumption, and the socialization of children—these researchers expected that the function of marriage would be primarily to provide emotional security. In regard to feelings about marriage, however, the kibbutz couples (compared to moshav couples) expressed less positive feelings toward marriage in general and toward their spouses in particular. Also, the members of the kibbutz group indicated much lower expectations in terms of emotional security from marriage (Rabin and Beit-Hallahmi, 1982). Rabin and Beit-Hallahmi's findings indicate that the kibbutz-reared individuals "may have a different style of relating in marriage, and that their expectations may be different" (p. 141). The results of this study appear consistent with Bettelheim's conclusion that "true intimacy finds no fertile soil to grow on in the kibbutz" (1970, p. 280).

CHAPTER REVIEW

1. Being single as an alternative life-style has become more acceptable in American society in the past couple of decades. But still, most people consider their singleness to be a temporary state. Ironically, those individuals who can accept and enjoy the single state are the least likely to remain single. By contrast, those singles who are uncomfortable about being single, even bitter about it, are unlikely to be found attractive by other people.

2. The fear of intimacy may inhibit a single person from making a commitment; mostly it's a fear of losing one's independence and autonomy in a very close relationship. Friendships are very important to a single person, mostly serving to meet emotional and social needs. Indeed, a close network of friends can actually be considered like "family" itself.

3. Living together is an alternative chosen by couples who do not want the legal obligations of marriage but who still desire the benefits of a close relationship. Cohabitors tend to be less interdependent and to have more liberal gender-role attitudes than married couples. Some cohabitors view their living arrangement as a permanent substitute to marriage; others may see it as a preparatory step to marriage, that is, a "trial marriage." Research has not shown, however, that living together does a better job at preparing couples for marriage.

4. Homosexual couples have not been studied as extensively as heterosexual ones. This stems, in part, from society's reluctance to accept homosexual pairs as legitimate couples and because of some common beliefs about the instability of gay relationships. Gender roles do not govern homosexual couples in the same way that they do heterosexual relationships. The assignment of household tasks between gays, for example, is based on preferences and abilities as opposed to gender.

5. Since females, in general, tend to be more relationship oriented than males, it is not surprising to find lesbians investing a lot of time and energy in building an intimate relationship together. The problems that males generally have in building intimacy may only be magnified when there are two males in a relationship. Same-sex couples, however, seem to enjoy more similar interests than most heterosexual couples. Companionship, therefore, is an important aspect in gay relationships.

6. Dissatisfied with traditional nuclear families, or disillusioned by society as a whole, some individuals set out to create their own communal type of family. In a communal living arrangement, emphasis is on commitment to the group, with the minimization of strong dyadic ties. Intimate bonds between two communal members function as a threat to the survival of the commune. Thus while a commune can provide its members with a sense of community, such a group also tends to limit intimate contact between people and to limit individual freedom.

Difficulties
in Close
Relationships

PHYSICAL VIOLENCE

The Incidence of Physical Violence
Spouse Battering
Child Battering

SEXUAL EXPLOITATION

Description of Sexual Exploitation

Father-Daughter Incest
Other Forms of Incest
Impact of Sexual Abuse on the Victim
Marital Rape

EMOTIONAL ABUSE

NEGLECT

Impact on the Victim
Reasons for Neglect
The Relationship of Abuse to Neglect

CHAPTER REVIEW

Violent
and Abusive
Relationships

Four types of abuse have a significant impact on family relationships. They are *physical violence, sexual exploitation, emotional abuse,* and *neglect.* Public concern about these various forms of abuse is relatively recent. Abuse and neglect of children began to receive widespread attention during the early 1960s and the sexual exploitation of children around the late 1960s and early 1970s. The problem of spouse abuse was brought to the forefront during the 1970s, and more recently marital rape has been defined as a specific problem.

Modern American society now recognizes that these forms of abuse are widespread family and social issues and not simply isolated acts of deviance. There is increased understanding of the damage done to the victims of abuse and growing concern about prevention. The women's movement and the proponents for children's rights have provided the impetus for bringing these problems to the attention of the rest of society.

Some researchers suggest that the family is the most likely setting for abuse to occur. Owing to high levels of stress, the emotionality of conflicts, and shear numbers of interactions, the family is said to be especially prone to violence. Some factors in family relationships that contribute to the potential for violence include the following:

1. *Time at risk*—Many hours of the day are spent interacting with family members.
2. *Intensity of involvement*—The degree of felt injury or hurt in the family will likely be greater than if the offender was someone outside the family.
3. *Age and sex discrepancies*—These differences often result in unequal power among members.
4. *Family privacy*—The privacy of a family insulates it from controls and assistance outside the family in coping with interpersonal family conflict.

5. *High level of stress*—Changes inherent in the family life cycle are important—the birth of children, maturation of children, aging, and retirement—and external changes—work status, income, social expectations.
6. *Extensive knowledge in marriage*—Because marriage exposes each other's weaknesses, verbal assaults on the partner's vulnerable points are easy to launch. (adapted from Gelles and Straus, 1979)

Many of these factors relating to family life serve a dual role. "On the one hand, they contribute toward making the family a warm, supportive, and intimate environment; on the other hand, they suggest reasons why this social group may be especially prone to violence" (Hotaling and Straus, 1980, p. 15).

PHYSICAL VIOLENCE

The definition of "family violence" can vary greatly. It has been narrowly defined to include only those acts directed at another person that cause physical injury such as broken bones, permanent disabilities, or even death. The definition could be extended to include acts that do or could result in not only physical but also emotional injury to the victim. To a certain extent, however, violence and abuse are "in the eyes of the beholder." Also the victims of family violence often accept and tolerate many acts that would be considered unlawful if they occurred between strangers (Gelles, 1980). In addition, some forms of violence fall within socially acceptable levels, such as slapping or spanking children or shoving a spouse.

Family conservatives have sometimes reacted negatively against government agencies that try to intervene and set limits on marital and parenting behavior. Such behaviors were once hidden in the sanctity and privacy of the family. But parents are now being told that they cannot necessarily discipline their children in the same ways that their own parents disciplined them. Wives are now refusing to be treated by their husbands in the same manner that their mothers were treated by their fathers. Both the large numbers of child-abuse cases being reported and of women seeking shelter in domestic-assault facilities testify to the growing intolerance of abuse. Still, some individuals feel threatened by outside intervention; they are afraid that such actions will break up the family as they have known it and violate its traditional roles and values.

"Abuse" refers to recurrent violent patterns of behavior directed by one family member (the abuser) to another (the victim); typically it is a pattern that endures over a considerable period of time (Gelles and Cornell, 1985; Deschner, 1984). But certainly a single violent episode can be devastating to a family relationship and can even result in death. Most violence, however, involves a history of abuse, even though perhaps in other, less noticeable forms.

The Incidence of Physical Violence

The statistics on family abuse are questionable and usually report fewer incidents than in fact take place. There are several reasons for the inaccurate reporting of abuse. First, there is a problem with *recognizing and labeling abuse* on the part of the victim (L. Walker, 1979). Violence against family members is a norm in some subcultures. "It is only when the level of violence in the family rises above the normally tolerated level that people within that family are willing to consider themselves victims" (L. Walker, 1979, p. 147). But some persons may think an abusive

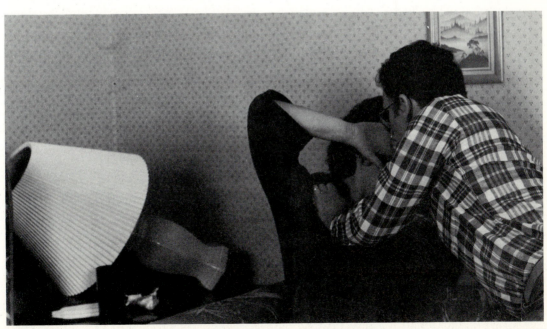

Twenty-eight percent of American couples experience at least one physically violent exchange during the course of their marriages.

or violent act is normal behavior and that the only way to cope with stress or to resolve conflict is through the use of physical force.

Second, traditional respect for family *privacy* tends to inhibit the reporting of abuse; a strong opposition to outside intervention exists. For example, most of the physical violence experienced by wives is never reported to the police. Dobash and Dobash (1979) found that the 100 battered wives they interviewed reported a total of approximately 32,000 assaults throughout their collective married lives. Yet only 517 of these assaults, less than 2 percent, were ever reported to the police.

Third, personal feelings of *guilt* and *shame* over being an abuser or victim may inhibit reporting. The abuser's shame and guilt may also "prohibit him from seeking help for himself and he in turn prevents his wife from revealing the violence to others" (Giles-Sims, 1983, p. 36).

Another problem in reporting accurate statistics is the lack of agreement on the definition of violence and abuse. The variety of definitions used in research efforts make comparisons difficult. Also, definitions change and evolve. For example, marital rape was not even defined as a category of abuse ten years ago or acknowledged to exist. Also, in many studies, population samples are small and are not representative of the population as a whole. For example, women seeking shelter or agency assistance against physical violence may obviously experience much higher rates of violence and in different forms than those not seeking help.

Nevertheless, the numbers of people seeking outside assistance for abusive situations in the family or the numbers coming to the attention of community agencies—such as mental-health, social-service, and law-enforcement agencies—has drastically increased. But it is unclear as to whether these statistical increases are due to an actual increase in physical violence, to an increased public awareness and recognition of the problem, to more broadly defined abusive acts labeled as unacceptable, to changes in the family structure that decrease privacy, or to better public educational programs that identify and intervene in abusive family situations.

Another issue involves the debate as to whether to view family violence the same, legally and socially, as abuse carried out between nonfamily acquaintances or strangers. Often law-enforcement officers and judges will not treat assault by a family member as a criminal offense. The underlying belief is that family relationships are private, and society should not intervene in them. Prosecuting an abusive member may harm the family unit by breaking up what positive bonds do exist. Instead, the court, and increasingly "family courts," will often try to work with the abusive family members through family counseling with the hope of trying to keep the family together.

In reality, of course, victimization by a family member can be very traumatic, with long-term consequences for the victim, because of the unique characteristics of the family (Armstrong, 1983). People expect to be able to trust their family members and to receive positive responses and warmth from them. Thus, more emotional harm can result when one is abused by a significant other as compared to abuse by a stranger. In addition, victimization by a stranger is generally a one-time occurrence. Family victimization is likely to occur several times, during which times the victims must continue ongoing interactions with the abuser. Also, the abuser may be a person on whom the victim is dependent physically, emotionally, and financially. Box 13.1 examines one theory that offers an explanation for family violence.

BOX 13.1

PLEASURABLE TOUCHING AND THE ORIGINS OF VIOLENCE

What does pleasurable touching have to do with violence in society? James Prescott believes there's a connection. He hypothesized that the deprivation of pleasurable touching is a principal cause of violence. Prescott first based his hypothesis on Steele and Pollock's research (1974) showing that parents who abused children were deprived of physical affection themselves. Steele and Pollock's study also found that abusive parents had extremely poor sex lives as adults. Therefore, it was postulated that human societies that provide their infants and children with a great deal of physical affection (touching, holding, carrying) would be less physically violent than human societies that give very little affection to their infants and children.

Prescott (1975) set out to test his proposition by systematically evaluating cultures of 49 primitive societies. He looked at the relationship between certain variables that reflect physical affections (fondling, caressing, and playing with infants) and variables that measure crime and violence (frequency of theft and killing). Societies that ranked either high or low on an Infant Physical Affection Scale were examined for their degrees of violence. The results were that "Those societies which give their infants the greatest amount of physical affection were characterized by low theft, low infant physical pain, . . . and negligible or absent killing, mutilating, or torturing of the enemy" (p. 66). Prescott claims that his data confirm that the deprivation of bodily pleasure during infancy is significantly linked to a high rate of crime and violence. Another interesting finding was that "Societies which inflict pain and discomfort upon their infants tend to neglect them as well" (p. 66).

Although Prescott studied primitive societies, he believes that the relationship between violence and pleasure holds true in modern industrial nations also. To prove this thesis, he surveyed 96 college students. His findings indicate that "Students who have relatively negative attitudes toward sexual pleasure tend to favor harsh punishment for children and to believe that violence is necessary to solve problems" (p. 71).

Spouse Battering

Battering involves repeated physically injurious attacks on a family member. Straus, Gelles, and Steinmetz (1980) conducted a national study of violence in American homes, surveying 2143 family members. They found that 28 percent of American couples experience at least one violent physical exchange during the course of their marriages. Milder acts of violence are far more prevalent, such as pushing, slapping, or shoving. At least 2 percent of all the couples, however, were involved in an ongoing pattern of violent interactions, which included kicking, hitting, severe beatings, and the threat of using, or the actual use, of a knife or gun. "Even a 2 percent minimum figure for battering translates into nearly three million pairs habitually injuring, endangering, and also sometimes killing each other" (Deschner, 1984, p. 6).

These rates of incidence may be low since the sample included only couples currently living together, leaving out those separated or those who are divorcing, possibly owing to physically abusive situations. It is important to recognize that in the study by Straus, Gelles, and Steinmetz (1980) the families are actually living together and tolerating these levels of violence.

When does battering first erupt in a relationship? Roy (1977) found that violence can surface for the first time at any stage of the relationship, although it is most likely to begin in the earlier rather than later stages. A study by Giles-Sims (1983) found that 23 percent of the women increased their commitment to an abusing man—by either moving in to live with him or marrying him—*after* the first violent incident occurred. Of course, as the degree of commitment increases, it becomes more difficult to leave a relationship. Some argue that it is the nature of emotional bonds, legal ties, and resource dependence that creates a situation of "entrapment" for both the victim and the abuser, whereby they cannot dissolve their investment without high emotional and personal costs.

Fagan, Stewart, and Hansen (1983) found that the median length of a battering-spouse relationship was approximately 5 years. But one in five of the battering relationships lasted 11 years or more. Of those relationships lasting 3 years or more, 40 percent involved violence weekly or more often.

Physical batterings have been described by women seeking emergency shelter from their husbands. The residents of these domestic-assault shelters provide an excellent population to pinpoint the forms of abuse that are intolerable. A study of 542 shelter residents by Stacey and Shupe (1983) found slapping, punching, and kicking (usually in combination) to be the most common forms

of violence experienced. Other women were pushed into walls, furniture, or down stairs.

More serious abuse, some of it life-threatening, was not uncommon. In over 10 percent of the cases the man had done such things as crush out lighted cigarettes on the woman's back, neck, face, or arms, throw acid on her, or hold a butane lighter against her hair or body. (Stacey and Shupe, 1983, p. 29)

Victims also reported being cut with razors, stabbed with knives or scissors, shot, and struck with various items such as golf clubs, shoes, drinking glasses, or chairs.

Stacey and Shupe (1983) also found that once physical violence surfaces it does not level off. It tends to escalate, occurring more and more often and resulting in increasingly more serious injuries. The most severely injured women in their study "were also the ones who had been beaten the longest and most frequently. Thus, any woman who has been hit or shoved or hurt physically in any way faces a strong likelihood that in the future such violence will happen more often and may become more serious. . . . Things will not automatically 'take care of themselves' or clear up" (p. 105).

PROFILE OF THE BATTERING SPOUSE. Most battering incidents that come to the attention of law-enforcement or community agencies involve the husband as the batterer and the wife as the victim. Therefore, the woman seeks protection from the violence. Most of the information about batterers comes from asking victims to describe the battering men.

The studies that have attempted to describe the traits of battering men generally have found similar characteristics. *Unemployment* or *underemployment* is one such common characteristic (Stacey and Shupe, 1983; Prescott and Letko, 1977; Fagan, Stewart, and Hansen, 1983). Men who cannot find employment or who are dissatisfied with the lack of success in their jobs often compensate for these frustrations by trying to exert more control or power over their wives with physical force. Apparently, the lack of a job or a ''poor job'' creates feelings of inadequacy as a good provider. Also the diminished or inadequate financial resources resulting from employment problems can contribute to more stress and marital conflict (Prescott and Letko, 1977).

Alcohol or *drug abuse* on the part of the battering spouse appears as a common factor in spouse violence (Stacey and Shupe, 1983; Deschner et al., 1980; Feazell, 1981). Although there is typically a substance-abuse problem, the spouses are not always drinking at the time of the actual incidents of abuse (L. Walker, 1979; Fagan, Stewart, and Hansen, 1983). Thus drinking and family violence appear to have an association but not necessarily a direct causal relationship.

Abusive husbands are also found to have *uncontrollable jealousy* (L. Walker, 1983). Men who are at high risk for being abusive are often insecure and need a great amount of reassurance and nurturance from their wives. It is typical of them to be very possessive of the woman's time.

Finally, *a history of past violent behavior* is often present in the battering spouse's background. He was frequently a victim or witness to physical abuse in his family when he was growing up (L. Walker, 1983; Fagan, Stewart, and Hansen, 1983; Deschner, 1984; Stacey and Shupe, 1983; Roy, 1977). In addition, he was more likely to have committed violent acts as a child, to have been cruel toward pets, to have been in fights as an adolescent, to have put his fist through doors or walls, and to have behaved violently toward women previously. It would indeed be valu-

able to educate women to recognize such behaviors in men before marriage, since the pattern of violence often emerges during courtship (see Box 13.2).

PROFILE OF THE BATTERED SPOUSE. Compared to batterers, battered spouses are less likely to be victims of child abuse or to have witnessed violence between their parents (L. Walker, 1979; Giles-Sims, 1983; Deschner, 1984; Stacey and Shupe, 1983). On the contrary, those who experienced violence in their families of origin seem less tolerant of the violence and quicker to seek outside help (Roy, 1977; Gelles, 1979).

It is very difficult for people in nonbattering situations to understand why battered victims remain in such circumstances and subject themselves to injury. Or why victims supplied with seemingly adequate alternatives to their situations decide to return to battering relationships. The major reason women stay in or return to these relationships is the hope that the batterer will reform (Roy, 1977). Other reasons given include no other place to go; fear of the batterers' retaliation against themselves, children, relatives, and friends; security for the children; economic dependence; fear of loneliness; and the stigma of being divorced. The willingness to escape a battering relationship is most affected by the frequency of the violence, the severity of the violence, and the woman's employment resources. By arresting the abusive spouse, some police departments attempt to end patterns of violence. (See Box 13.3.)

By analyzing the stories of more than 400 battered women, Lenore Walker (1979) developed a theory that explains why women do not leave battering relationships. She has described the battering relationship as a *cycle of violence* consisting of three phases. The first phase is one of *tension building* during which minor battering incidents occur. The victim at

BOX 13.2

COURTSHIP VIOLENCE

It is a startling fact that along with romance, violence is very common in American dating patterns. Studies have found that "between 22 percent and 67 percent of dating relationships involve violence" (Cate, Christopher, and Lloyd, 1982; Henton et al., 1983; Laner, Thompson, and Graham, 1981; Makepeace, 1981, 1983).

One of the most revealing findings from the research on courtship violence is how it is perceived by the individuals involved. Many of the victims, and offenders, interpreted the violence as a sign of love. "This is a scary extension of the elementary school-yard scenario where the young girl recipient of a push, shove, or hit, thinks that it means the boy who hit her likes her" (Gelles and Cornell, 1985, p. 66). Another surprising finding is that the victims were likely to take the blame for helping to start the violence, rather than blaming their partners.

"It is quite clear from the new studies of courtship violence that many of the patterns we find in marital violence emerge long before a person gets married" (Gelles and Cornell, 1985, p. 66). One form of courtship violence is rape; forced sex on a date is probably one of the most common forms of all types of rape. In a study at Kent State University, "More than half the women students surveyed reported sexual aggression in the form of verbal threats, physical coercion, or violence. One in eight indicated they had been raped" (Barrett 1982).

In "date rape" a woman's trust is violated, sometimes by a man she loved or considered a friend. But "Victims of date rape feel a sense of self-blame, that they somehow gave the wrong message, or that he perhaps had some 'right' to expect sex" (Nass, Libby, and Fisher, 1984, p. 244). In one study, college men were presented with various descriptions of dates between "John" and "Mary." They rated forced sex as "more justifiable under some conditions: when the woman initiated the date, when the couple went to John's apartment rather than to a religious function or a movie, or when the man paid for everything" (H. Goodman, 1982, p. 75).

this point attempts to calm the batterer by becoming more nurturing or compliant or simply by staying out of his way. In certain ways she typically takes on some responsibility for his abusive behavior. For example, she will think, "Maybe I did overcook his dinner," or "I haven't kept the house as clean as he likes." She may also look to outside sources for his anger—trouble at work or drinking. But as tension builds, both the vic-

tim and batterer have less control over the batterer's behavior. In response to her passive acceptance, the batterer continues or escalates his abusive behavior. The victim's efforts to calm the abuser become less and less effective over time.

In the second phase, an *acute battering incident* finally erupts when the victim and abuser are unable to control the tensions that have mounted. Sometimes external stress re-

BOX 13.3

ARREST THE WIFE BEATERS!

Each year, about 5 million men in the U.S. physically abuse their wives. And each year the nation's police spend 25% to 30% of their duty time investigating (usually without resolution) such cases. What is the best method the police can practice to prevent men from repeatedly beating their wives or live-in lovers? According to Anthony Bouza, chief of police in Minneapolis, Minnesota, the simple answer is to arrest them.

The Minneapolis Police Department conducted a 16-month study in which its officers responded to about 250 cases of moderate domestic assault by randomly employing one of three methods: arrest, mediation or separation. The preliminary findings of that pioneering study . . . revealed that only 10% of the men who had been arrested for wife-beating repeated that offense within six months, compared to 24% of the men who had been banished from their residences for at least eight hours (separation) and 17% of the men who had been involved in mediation or counseling.

. . .

In Duluth, Minnesota, the police procedure mandates arrest if there is any evidence of physical abuse on the face or figure of the victim. . . . "Duluth's arrest procedure has been in effect since 1982," says Deputy Police Chief Eugene Sisto, "and in the first six months of 1983, repeat phone calls complaining of wife-beating decreased 23%." . . .

SOURCE: Parade Magazine, *October 16, 1983, p. 8.*

lated to the children, work, or finances triggers the explosion of violence. This phase differs from the previous one in that it involves major destructiveness and out-of-control, raging behavior. What may have started out as "teaching the woman a lesson"—without intending to inflict any particular injury on her—ends "when he feels she has learned her lesson," which generally is when she has been very severely beaten.

The acute battering phase is generally followed by a phase of *kindness and contrite, loving behavior* during which the batterer tries to make up for his abusive behavior. During this time the batterer is most charming and will initiate actions to demonstrate his sincerity.

He promises he will never do it again. At some point when the batterer is assured that the victim has forgiven his behavior and will remain in the relationship, the tensions begin to surface again, instigating a repetition of the entire cycle.

It is during the loving-contrition stage, however, that the victims reap rewards from remaining in the relationship. This period of calm and kindness is their reward for accepting the previous violence. In addition, the woman has her most power in the relationship during this final stage. The abuser's neediness and fears that his wife will leave him give her a sense of control, the power of "least interest." He tells her over and over again how much he needs her. And she perceives that she is the only one that can help this poor man; a "rescue fantasy" prevails. If the abuser were truly remorseful, however, he would seek help in changing his behavior. This rarely happens. "I'm sorry" is only a manipulation to continue the relationship.

The woman, if she does seek help, normally seeks it shortly after the acute battering phase. The batterer, however, then immediately courts the victim with loving contrition. He reminds her of all of his positive qualities. He promises her that he will be able to control his behavior. During this phase she sees glimpses of love and intimacy and "chooses to believe that the behavior she sees during phase three signifies what her man is really like" (L. Walker, 1979, p. 68). At this point the emotionally dependent man and the caretaking woman view themselves as a united front against the world. She may realize underneath that the cycle of violence will only repeat itself again, but her great longing for some degree of closeness is met during this loving-contrition stage.

The closeness that these couples experience during this phase is a pseudo-intimacy. It is not an intimacy based on the personal strengths of two partners. It is more a desperate search for security by two weak individuals. They do not exchange as confident, consistent equals. The power and control in the marriage is ever shifting. First, the husband exerts his power and dominates the wife, and then the wife is holding the power of "least interest." They are overly dependent on each other.

The woman bases her decision to stay in the relationship on the behavior she sees in him during the loving-contrition phase, and she hopes that the other two phases can eventually be eliminated. Walker (1979) points to the difficulties facing "helpers" who see the woman during this stage. When the

batterer starts seeing his wife again—showing kindness, love, and contrition—there appears to be almost no way of talking the wife out of going back to him.

> *These women were thoroughly convinced of their desire to stop being victims, until the batterer arrived. I always knew when a woman's husband had made contact with her by the profusion of flowers, candy, cards, and other gifts in her hospital room. By the second day, the telephone calls or visits intensified, as did his pleas to be forgiven and promises never to do it again. He usually engaged others in his fierce battle to hold on to her. His mother, father, sisters, brothers, aunts, uncles, friends, and anyone else he could commandeer would call and plead his case to her. They all worked on her guilt: she was his only hope; without her, he would be destroyed. (L. Walker, 1979, p. 66)*

The woman victim, having experienced several cycles of violence that become a pattern in her marital relationship, can also sink into a state of "learned helplessness" (L. Walker, 1979). She has learned that averting the battering is beyond her control. She feels increasingly helpless and thereafter less able to solve problems or seek out options. She comes to accept the chronic battering with passivity. The process of learned helplessness is similar to brainwashing and takes time to reverse.

CONFLICTS AND STRESSES IN ABUSIVE MARRIAGES. What types of conflict and stress do violence-prone families find overwhelming? Pregnancy seems to be one stress highly correlated with battering incidents (Stacey and Shupe, 1983; L. Walker, 1983; Gelles and Straus, 1979). Jean Giles-Sims (1983) asked battered women to indicate what they considered the most serious problems in their marriages; she found jealousy, the use of alcohol, children, sex, and affection the most frequently mentioned. The presence of other problems such as household tasks, the woman's income or employment, and the man's income or employment were also cited. Giles-Sims concluded that "the picture that emerges from this is of multiproblem marriages" (p. 46).

The number of stressful factors that precipitate violence tends to decrease over time (Giles-Sims, 1983). That is, stress factors may be important in precipitating the first incidents of violence but are not necessary to trigger later incidents. This suggests that "once violence occurs, it may be easier for it to occur again" (p. 55).

Marriages with the greatest potential for ongoing battering are those with extreme imbalances of marital power (Straus, Gelles, and Steinmetz, 1980; Giles-Sims, 1983). "Wife-beating is much more common in homes where power is concentrated in the hands of the husband. The least amount of battering occurs in democratic households" (Straus, Gelles, and Steinmetz, 1980, pp. 192–193). In general, "Family members resort to physical coercion when they have power over family decision-making but have few resources to bring to bear to *legitimize* their position" (Straus, Gelles, and Steinmetz, 1980, p. 193).

Child Battering

The belief that children are best reared with the use of physical punishment has existed since earliest times. Today abundant evidence exists to suggest that physical punishment is one of the poorest ways to educate children (Zaphiris, 1975). But still, parental acts of physical violence directed at children are very common, in fact, far more common than spouse battering. "Most American parents approve of spanking and slapping their children, almost two out of three American parents slap or spank their children in any given year" (Straus, Gelles, and Steinmetz, 1980, p. 72). (See Box 13.4.)

Should spanking a child on his or her bottom or slapping a child's hands or face be labeled as abusive? The parent's intention is often to cause the child to experience negative consequences for his or her behavior. Although such parental actions could result in some form of injury, typically they are more likely to result in emotional abuse, injuring the child's self-concept.

Any repetitive form of physical attack on a child that results in physical injury—welts, bruising, lacerations, broken bones, for example—is unquestionably abusive. As with spouse abuse, a single physical attack against a child, regardless of the motive, can have a far-reaching impact. A few isolated, explosive incidents of violence by a parent can permanently destroy trust in relationships and can cause fear of vulnerability because such acts are so far beyond a child's control. Bodily injuries are most likely to be inflicted by beating the child with the hands, fists, or instruments such as belts, electrical cords, wires, and sticks. Other methods of inflicting injury include kicking, burning, strangling, stabbing, slashing, or poisoning (Gil, 1973). Whereas adult males are usually the primary batterers in spouse abuse, both adult males and females are responsible for the physical abuse of children (Martin, 1983). (See Box 13.5.)

PROFILE OF THE ABUSING PARENT. Agency statistics suggest that there is more child battering in the lower class (Gil, 1973). Financial resources and higher social status, however, probably insulate some families from having reports of child abuse given to public agencies. In reality, abusing parents represent all

BOX 13.4

PHYSICAL PUNISHMENT OF CHILDREN: SWEDEN AND THE UNITED STATES

Many researchers suggest that the cultural support for the use of physical punishment in child rearing contributes to child battering. What often begins as ordinary physical punishment escalates into abuse.

In 1979 Sweden passed a law with the intention of establishing a *norm* to pressure parents away from the use of physical punishment. The new law, which was an addition to previous laws against criminal assault and battery upon children, banned *any form* of physical punishment, even by parents or guardians. This law, however, did not provide for direct penalties, such as jail or fines, but only conviction.

Warren DeLey (1983) conducted a study exploring possible differences between American and Swedish college students in the area of corporal punishment and child abuse. American students were more likely than the Swedes to report "having received physical punishment as children at least 'occasionally'. . . [and] having experienced one or more incidents of physical abuse" (p. 1). The statistics show that almost 90 percent of U.S. students were spanked as children at least "occasionally," while only 44 percent of the Swedish students were. Furthermore, the majority of American students opposed the 1979 Swedish no-spanking law, whereas the majority of Swedish students agreed with it. Thus American cultural norms not only support the acceptability of physical punishment (and its implementation), but also there is strong resistance to changing such practices. There is little doubt that such positive views of physical punishment contribute to the battering of children.

socioeconomic classes. Their education ranges from partial grade school to postgraduate degrees; with IQ variations from borderline to superior ratings; and from those with employment problems to those with stable professional careers. There are various religious affiliations, but there is a tendency to adhere to strong, rigid, fundamentalistic beliefs. Poverty, alcoholism, broken marriages, and racial differences are not significant factors (Steele and Pollock, 1974).

Abusing parents are significantly more likely to have feelings of worthlessness, depression, distrust, and inadequacy as wife and mother or husband and father (Steele and Pollock, 1974). Such parents tend to hold unrealistic expectations for their children. The child from early in infancy is expected to show exemplary behavior and a respectful, submissive attitude toward adult authority. The demand for performance is not only great but premature and beyond the ability of the child to comprehend. Abusive parents deal with the child as if he or she were much older than the child actually is. "With more normal families a child elicits parental protection, care, and concern. The helplessness of a child is no more than a normal period of dependence upon the strength of parents who care for his needs and find happiness in doing so"

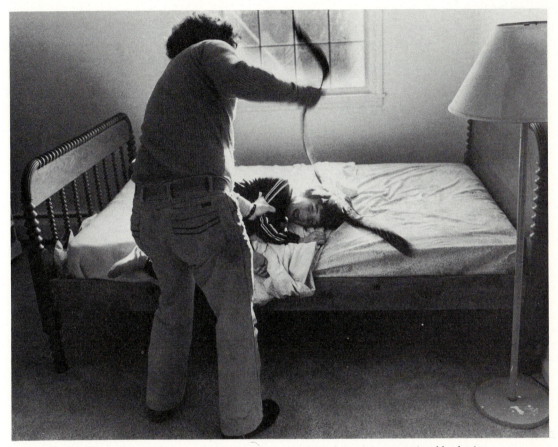

Any form of repetitive physical attack on a child that results in physical injury is unquestionably abusive.

(Young, 1976, p. 55). For the abusing parents, however, the child's dependence is perceived as a situation of exploitation (Young, 1976).

The backgrounds of abusive parents were found by Steele and Pollock (1974) to contain some common elements. All the battering parents in their study had a history of having been raised in the same style that they had been repeating in rearing their own children. Many experienced actual abuse, but for the most part, all had experienced a "sense of intense, pervasive, continuous demand from their parents. This demand was in the

form of expectations of good, submissive behavior, prompt obedience, never making mistakes, sympathetic comforting of parental distress, and showing approval and help for parental actions" (p. 97).

Along with these excessive demands was a "sense of constant parental criticism." The child received the message that his or her behavior was "erroneous, inadequate, inept, and ineffectual." No matter what the abusing parent as a child had tried to do, it fell short of parental expectations. "Inevitably, the growing child felt, with much reason, that he was unloved, that his own needs, desires, and

BOX 13.5

THE CASE OF MARY ELLEN: AN IMPETUS FOR CHILDREN'S RIGHTS

The case of Mary Ellen Wilson, an illegitimate child, is considered by most child welfare experts as a graphic illustration of the turning point in child welfare and concern for abused children. Mary Ellen was an illegitimate child, born in New York City in 1866 and a ward of the New York Department of Charities (Robin, 1982). A charity worker found eight-year-old Mary Ellen beaten and badly abused. Much to the charity worker's chagrin, neither the police nor the New York Department of Charities would provide aid for Mary Ellen. Mary Ellen's plight was brought to court, not by a human service agency, but by the Society for the Prevention of Cruelty to Animals. . . . At this time in history animals were protected by law but children were not. As a consequence of the Mary Ellen case, the Society for the Prevention of Cruelty to Children was formed.

SOURCE: *Gelles and Cornell, 1985, p. 29.*

capabilities were disregarded, unheard, unfulfilled, and even wrong" (Steele and Pollock, 1974, p. 97).

Abusive parents have also been found to have been deprived of love and nurturance when they were growing up. They did not feel a deep sense of being cared for and cared about from the beginnings of their lives. Similarly, the battering parents had difficulty giving emotional nurturance and tender loving care to their own infants. The type of care they did provide was the "mechanical" duties of feeding, dressing, and cleaning the infant. Indeed Steele and Pollock (1974) found the infants in their study to be almost always "well-fed, clean, and well-clothed." But they noted that the "emotional attitudes" of the parent while caring for the infant were "fraught with constant tension and frequent disruptions" (p. 99).

It is apparent that owing to the lack of emotional bonding in their own families of origin, abusing parents have difficulty giving

emotionally of themselves and attaching themselves to their infants and children. If these parents had the capacity to be emotionally close to their infants and children, most likely there would not be any physical abuse. Intimacy and physical violence are incompatible at the same time in a relationship.

What emerges from the lack of emotional bonding is a child lacking confidence and trust in other people. Confidence instilled in a child involves a "belief that others can be looked to for help and oneself is worth helping" (Steele and Pollock, 1974, p. 105). The pattern of lack of confidence originating in early childhood with the parents persists throughout the abusing parent's adulthood. All relationships are rather distant, superficial, unrewarding, and certainly nonintimate. "Thus, the abusing parent tends to lead a life which is described as alienated, asocial, or isolated" (p. 105).

The parent is looking to the infant for gratification of his or her own needs; the child, it is hoped, will replace the love the parent lacked in his or her childhood from his or her own parent. When the infant cries or fusses, the parent perceives that behavior as criticism, the kind he or she received from his or her parent.

> *Quite often abusing parents tell us, ''When the baby cries like that it sounds just like mother (or father) yelling at me, and I can't stand it.'' The perception of being criticized stirs up the parent's feelings of being inferior. It also increases the frustration of his need for love, and anger mounts. At this time there seems to be a strong sense of guilt, a feeling of helplessness and panic becomes overwhelming. (Steele and Pollock, 1974, p. 116)*

HIGH-RISK CHILDREN.   Younger children, particularly those age 3 and under, are the most likely victims of physical abuse (Justice and Justice, 1976). They are also more likely to suffer from serious or fatal injuries (Gil, 1973). Several factors contribute to the young child's vulnerability. First, infants or toddlers, of course, cannot defend themselves as well as an older child. They also can be more easily harmed by the physical punishment because of their underdeveloped bodies.

Second, younger children are more vulnerable to abuse because their dependence increases stress, which can trigger an abusive parent to attack. Infants and young children are naturally more demanding of the parent's time and energy. Parents can feel a great deal of frustration as they try to toilet train a child, to get him to stop crying, or to get her to obey their commands. Third, the very birth of the child may create stress by producing economic hardship or by interfering with professional, occupational, educational, or other plans of the parents (Gelles, 1979).

Children who are different from the normal expectations for a child—ill, handi-

capped, premature, unattractive, overly demanding, or overly active—are at greater risk of being physically abused (Friedrich and Boriskin, 1976). This risk can extend further to children who fail to meet parental expectations in respect to developmental ability and temperament (Kempe and Kempe, 1978; Steele and Pollock, 1974). Battering parents have difficulty understanding or coping with even the normal development of children. Thus, those children who require special care increase the parent's level of stress even more. Approximately one-half of the abusing mothers and fathers of children with physical or developmental deviations stated that they did not love the child, suggesting that the normal *bonding* and *attachments* between parent and child had not developed (Johnson and Morse, 1974). A child who is a product of an unwanted pregnancy, who is a constant reminder of a detested partner, is also more likely to be abused (Steele and Pollock, 1974). The child may also be "the wrong sex."

Another high-risk group for physical violence is teenagers (Straus, Gelles, and Steinmetz, 1980; Gelles, 1979). Although they experience abuse less frequently, the forms of violence are more extreme and have more potential to cause injury. Often when the teenager seeks help or protection from physical abuse, his or her situation is minimized by "helpers." The attitude is often held that the teenager's behavior was so frustrating to the parent that the teenager got what he or she *deserved.*

The potential for child abuse greatly increases when marital partners resort to violence between themselves. Stacey and Shupe (1983) found in their sample of 424 residents of a shelter for battered women that "*almost half* (45 percent) of the children had been physically abused or seriously neglected, often both" (p. 63). The forms of the child abuse were similar to those that the mother had experienced. Looking at just the severity of the battering, the researchers found that "men who battered women more severely were also likely to harm their children" [italics omitted] (p. 65).

IMPACT OF ABUSE ON THE BATTERED CHILD.

What impact does physical abuse by a parent have on the child? Basically the social dynamics that contributed to the parent becoming an abuser are transmitted to the child of the next generation. The child certainly does not experience positive models of parenting. More specifically, two types of somewhat extreme behavioral adaptations are noted in children in response to physical battering—either aggressive, acting-out behavior or a passive acceptance (Zaphiris, 1975).

The aggressive children may express their anger toward others and try to gain an advantage over others in particular situations. Children who act aggressively often define themselves as "bad" and are acting that way so as to gain reactions and attention from others. Behaviors such as defiance, rebellion, tantrums, lying, stealing, and youthful sexual activities are examples of their actions.

Passive acceptance as a reaction to abuse results in the victims resigning themselves to violent behavior as a way of life. Such individuals become passive and obedient. Even in physical pain or discomfort these abused children appear stoic, expressing no feelings (Kempe and Kempe, 1978).

Both adaptations to abuse are based on the individual's sense of worthlessness. The aggressive response attempts to deny vulnerability and generally to lash out because of the abuse. The passive response attempts to make the self invisible, with the hope that no resistance will lessen other people's assaults. Such individuals tend to be both fearful and shy.

Henry Kempe (1978) observed that several behavioral adaptations among abused children continued even after they were removed from the abusive situations. He found that all the children had difficulty trusting adults and sometimes other children as well. "They relapse only too easily into distrust at the slightest sign of disappointment" (p. 38). Even when relationships are going well for the abused child, he or she will relapse into periods of distrust.

Throughout life abused children have difficulty with interpersonal relationships. "They relate indiscriminately, quickly making superficial friendships but ready to discard them at the slightest sign of rejection" (Kempe and Kempe, 1978). Perhaps this stems from a fear of being in a position of vulnerability, a position they frequently experienced as children. The more intimate a relationship becomes, the more they will be required to reveal themselves and the more risk is involved in possibly being hurt. Victims of abuse will avoid taking risks in trusting others. Hence, they will often run away from close relationships that leave them too vulnerable.

But it is important to recognize that even abused children "love" and have some degree of attachment to their parents. The abusive parent is not constantly battering 100 percent of the time. There are periods of tenderness, consideration, and nurturance. Some children, however, grow to believe that physical abuse is part-and-parcel of love and affection. They are not aware that most parents act in any other way. They label abuse as normal and as the way to treat children and to treat others. Other children, aware that their peers are not abused by their families, resort to the denial of their own abuse, intentionally hiding their bodily injuries or lying about how they occurred in order to protect the parent. These children are desperate to hold on to the only family they have, as inadequate as it may be.

The children may even idealize the level of love that exists in their families. Battered children in foster care routinely show what appears to be an illogical desire to return to their abusive parent. "Such children often worry, in the manner of a care-giver, about the parent's welfare or may romanticize about the parent's love as providing much more happiness than the foster family does" (Deschner, 1984, p. 22). Apparently the familiarity and comfortableness of one's family, even though abusive, is enough to pull these children back.

When abused children become adults, their need for love is so great that they will often accept it at any price. They tend not to look too carefully at what they are getting into and what they are getting in return (Kempe and Kempe, 1978). Lacking the experience and the role models for emotional closeness, they have difficulty identifying a partner's potential for an intimate relationship. Even if they do identify a positive mate, they typically feel that they are not worthy of having such a person. In addition, they feel safest when replaying and reenacting a familiar role. It's not surprising that they often end up with mates similar to their parents.

SEXUAL EXPLOITATION

Within the last ten years, public attention has turned to yet another form of child abuse that occurs in families, the sexual abuse of children. Incest—sexual activity between two family members who are not married—has long been an interest of social scientists. It has traditionally been studied from the standpoint of a social taboo. Social scientists have examined why it tends to be a universal taboo and what happens when the taboo is vio-

lated. As reports of children engaged in sexual activity with an older person in their family have increased in recent years, "incest" has taken on a new meaning synonymous with the *sexual exploitation* of children.

In 1980 the National Center on Child Abuse and Neglect indicated that at least 351,000 children were known victims of all forms of child abuse. Of these children, 44,700 acknowledged that they had been sexually exploited, sometimes in connection with other forms of abuse or mistreatment (Gelles and Cornell, 1985). Child sexual abuse involves sexual activities between adults and children or between older children and younger children. Approximately 1 in 5 females and 1 in 11 males report that as a child they experienced sexual activity with a person at least five years older than themselves. The abuser is likely to be someone the child knows, someone from the child's own family, rather than a stranger (Finkelhor, 1979).

Exploitation infers that the child is a victim. There were a few early attempts to argue that children do not necessarily suffer ill consequences when engaged in sexual activities with older partners (Bender and Blau, 1937). It is now generally recognized that children do suffer negative effects from most of these experiences, but because they are primarily emotional in nature, they are not as easy to identify as a bruise or broken bone. An emotional injury may surface in certain behaviors during the childhood years, but it typically does not become fully visible until the victim attempts to establish and maintain a close relationship during his or her adult and parenting years.

Description of Sexual Exploitation

The sexual exploitation of children can be defined more comprehensively as any family member involving a child or adolescent in "sexual activities that they do not fully comprehend, are unable to give informed consent to, and that violate the social taboos of family roles" (Schechter and Roberge, 1976, p. 129). The motivations of the adult for engaging the child in sexual activity, the willingness of the child to participate in the activity, or pleasure derived by either the adult or the child from the sexual behaviors do not lessen the exploitation. The potential for emotional injury is ever present. Because a child does not have the emotional and cognitive development of an adult, he or she cannot interpret the sexual experience on an equal basis with the adult. Children are raised to accept adults in positions of authority. What adults sometimes project as the child's *consent* is actually the child's *submission* to authority.

The sexual exploitation of children can take many forms. Some of the more common forms involve being subjected to seductive speech and conduct, exhibitionism, fondling of the breasts and genitals, oral-genital contact, vaginal and anal intercourse, and the engagement in pornography or prostitution activities.

Sometimes adults tend to minimize the degree of the exploitation because the sexual activity seems minor, such as seductive conduct by the parent. Any of the above sexual behaviors, however, can have an impact on the child equal in intensity to actual intercourse. Adults tend to think of sexual acts on a continuum ranging from the milder activities, associated with sexual foreplay, through a progression of sexual involvement toward sexual intercourse. Adults also attempt to classify the seriousness of sexual acts by taking into account the frequency, duration, and nature of the relationship with the partner. These adult perceptions are superimposed on the child, but they have relatively little effect on the seriousness of the emotional injury suffered by the child.

David Finkelhor (1979) measured the intensity of trauma experienced by victims of child sexual exploitation. He questioned 329 college students who had been sexually victimized as children in order to rate the types and nature of sexual activities they had experienced. He found that their feelings about the kinds of sexual acts, number of times the acts occurred, duration of time over which the sexual activities continued, and "relatedness" of the adult had little correlation with the trauma experienced. Two factors were significant, however—the *degree of force* used by the abuser to coerce the victim and the *age difference* between the abuser and the victim (Finkelhor, 1979).

When sexual exploitation occurs within the family, it is likely to be repeated over a period of time, possibly over several years. This repetition is due to the abuser's opportunity to have access to the child. Despite the proximity of other persons within the family setting, who could discover or terminate the sexual exploitation, access to the victim is rarely cut off. Sexual abuse of the child typically ends when the abuser decides it is no longer in his best interests to continue the abusing, when the child grows up and leaves the home, or when someone intervenes.

Sexual exploitation of the child has a general pattern, although there are unique characteristics within each family. The pattern often consists of five stages (Sgroi, Blick, and Porter, 1983). In the first stage, the *engagement phase,* the adult selects his or her victim, who may be of any age. The adult must have opportunity to be alone with the child, and the child must be "induced" to participate in the sexual activity with the adult. Inducements can be positively presented to the child, such as playing a game, doing something special with the child, or offering gifts or special privileges. Or inducement can be of a more overtly coercive nature, such as implied or actual threats against the child's physical safety or the safety or welfare of those he or she loves.

The second stage is the *sexual interaction phase,* during which the abuser engages the child in sexual activity. It is common for the initial activities to start out with the adult exposing his genitals, along with mild forms of sexual stimulation, such as kissing or fondling. As the relationship continues, the adult may introduce a variety of other sexual acts, progressing toward sexual intercourse, or the sexual activity may level off short of actual intercourse.

After the child is initially engaged in the sexual activity, and for as long as the abuser hopes to repeat the behaviors on future oc-casions, the activity must remain a secret between the adult and the child. This is the *secrecy phase* (Burgess and Homstrom, 1975). The methods used by the abuser are similar to those used to ''induce'' the child in the first place. Sometimes the abuser must resort to more threatening or coercive techniques to maintain the silence of the child, especially if the relationship continues over a number of years and the child outgrows the original inducements.

The family faces its primary crisis when the sexual abuse comes to the attention of other family members or persons outside the family; this is the *disclosure phase*. The sexual exploitation may be disclosed by the victim,

Educating children about sexual abuse tends to help them avoid possible sexual exploitation.

usually when she or he can no longer tolerate the situation. Sometimes the disclosure is accidental; someone sees nonverbalized clues or catches the abuser in the act. It is at this point that the family must decide on how to interpret the sexual transgressions of the abuser and the child. Recently the media have attempted to assist children in disclosing incidences of sexual exploitation. (See Box 13.6.)

It is not unusual for the disclosure to be followed by the *suppression phase,* during which time parents, siblings, and sometimes even the victim, deny or minimize the sexual abuse that occurred. Intensive family therapy may be necessary to help the family resolve its emotional dilemmas.

Father-Daughter Incest

The most commonly *reported* form of sexual abuse in the family occurs between fathers and daughters. Upon discovery, fathers usually try to deny that sexual exploitation has occurred. When pressured to own up to their behavior, abusers resort to blaming other people or other things beyond their control, such as sexual problems with their wife, "a greater need for sex than most men," wanting the child "to have a proper education and introduction to sexuality," or the "girl is a whore at heart and sex at home keeps her off the streets" (Renvoize, 1982, pp. 70–71). One of the most difficult tasks for the sexually abusive father is to assume responsibility for his behaviors. Few are able to recognize their motivations without counseling.

Some common characteristics of sexually abusing fathers include low self-esteem, powerlessness and passivity outside the home, substance abuse (alcohol or drugs), the need for immediate gratification, the tendency to project blame and not take responsibility for one's own actions, and a low degree of guilt.

Such men often seek to have their emotional needs met through sexual activity; they show love through sex. Often uncomfortable with adult sexual relationships, the man turns to his child for gratification (Groth, 1983).

Approximately 80 percent of the incestuous adults in one study felt that the child exploitation was due to a very poor marital relationship (Maisch, 1973). Sgroi and Dana (1983) found two typical marriage patterns where father-daughter incest took place—either dependent husbands with independent wives or dominant husbands with passive wives. Women in both patterns of marriage were "dissatisfied with their roles vis-à-vis their spouses." Typical characteristics of the wives of incest offenders included (1) emotional absence (and sometimes physical absence) from the family unit; (2) failure to provide emotional nurturance, guidance, limit setting, or role modeling for the children (the relationship seemed to be more sibling-like than maternal); (3) impaired communication, or little direct verbal communication with family members; and (4) negative self-perceptions (1983).

Many victims of father-daughter incest come to feel as negatively about their mothers as they do about the abusing father (Tsai and Wagner, 1978). The daughter may view the mother as "inadequate, unable, or unwilling to care for the family in respect to nurturance, guidance, or protectiveness" (Tsai and Wagner, 1978, p. 172). The daughter may feel anger toward the mother, who she perceives could have done something more to protect her but intentionally did not. The mother has failed not only to provide protection for the victim of sexual abuse but has failed the whole family in a more general sense (Sanford, 1980).

In fact, in perceiving the mother as "inadequate, unable, or unwilling to care for the family," the daughter may take over instru-

BOX 13.6

"SPIDER-MAN BATTLES SEX ABUSE"

In a four-page, full-color newspaper comic insert, the creators of the super-hero Spiderman aimed to teach children how to deal with and prevent sexual abuse. Prepared by Marvel Comics and the National Committee for Prevention of Child Abuse, the comic strip was written for both children and parents and attempted to encourage family communication about the topic of sexual abuse. The comic strip showed children in uncomfortable situations and stressed that children are not to be blamed for sexual exploitation.

> "We felt that if we showed Spider-Man is vulnerable as well, it would help ease the burden [for children]," said Marvel's Pamela Rutt, . . . "We agreed that the best way to say to kids that this can happen to anybody—and that if it happens, it's not your fault and you can go on and be strong—was to somehow use this superhero, a figure to whom they can look up. . . ." (N. Rubin, 1985, p. 3F)

When newspapers throughout the United States ran the comic strip, a substantial number of children who were previously silent came forward to report child abusers. Below are three sample frames from the comic strip.

mental parts of the mothering role—making meals, caring for younger children, and cleaning the house (Sanford, 1980). Herman and Hirschman (1977) also found that in families where the mothers were ill, disabled, or overwhelmed by child-care responsibili-

ties, the oldest daughter, who was the victim of incest, assumed major responsibility for housework and/or child care. "Forty-five percent of the women in the incest group, as opposed to only 5% in the comparison group, reported that they took on a maternal role within their families. . . . Providing sexual services to their fathers seemed to develop as an extension of their maternal family role'' (1977, p. 968).

Sexual abuse by *stepfathers, adoptive fathers, foster fathers,* and *live-in boyfriends*—by males who assume the function of a father figure in the home—generally present dynamics similar to the father-daughter incest. Some writers argue, however, that the assumed role of father figure to the child, as opposed to being a biological father, may present factors that *increase* the potential for sexual activity.

Other Forms of Incest

Between 70 and 90 percent of all reported sexually exploitative relationships in the family involve father-daughter incest. The remaining 10 to 30 percent is divided among incestuous relationships between father and son, mother and son, mother and daughter, and between members of the extended family such as grandparents, aunts, uncles, and siblings (Sanford, 1980). Although these other forms of incest are not *reported* as often as father-daughter incest, they still warrant attention since the *actual incidence* of some of these incestuous relationships could be much higher.

FATHER-SON INCEST. It is estimated that about 10 percent of all incest victims are boys, and most are likely to be victimized by their fathers (Herman and Hirschman, 1977). Sex with the son is substituted for other kinds of affection and other normal father-son activities (Sanford, 1980). Although young boys may feel that there is something not quite right about the father's behavior, they may go along with it ''believing it is the only form of affection they will ever know from him'' (Sanford, 1980, p. 194). It is often more dif-

ficult for a male victim to disclose this type of sexual exploitation because of the homosexual overtones. Such activity, however, tends not to be homosexually motivated. The father's feelings of inadequacy motivate his approach to his son. ''Typically, the father is *not* a homosexual'' (Sanford, 1980, p. 195).

Father-son incest has a negative impact on a young boy's self-concept. It is difficult for a boy to grow up interacting with his father and using him as a role model, when his father has exploited him. In addition, confusion over his own sexuality may reduce his self-esteem. ''Their primary sexual experience has been with a man (one who was supposed to guide and protect them) under at least subtly coercive circumstances. They never had the chance to flirt and grope as other prepubescent boys experiment and discover their own sexuality'' (Sanford, 1980, p. 195).

MOTHER-SON INCEST. The reported incidence of mother-son incest is low, at least partly due to the male victims being less likely to admit to its occurrence (Renvoize, 1982). In addition, the types of sexual acts are more subtle. The most usual kind of sexual activity between a mother and son is intense flirting, having the son watch her while she takes baths or gets dressed (Renvoize, 1982). Other activity consists of fondling, but actual intercourse is rare. The activities take such forms as ''washing the child's genitals to stimulation; the boy sleeping in the mother's bed past the age when that is appropriate; [and] massaging the boy to erection'' (Sanford, 1980, p. 191).

The needs of the mother are typically more emotional than sexual (Sanford, 1980). Often the father is absent from the home; perhaps he is deceased, travels with his job, or is divorced from or has deserted the mother. The mother may be looking to the son to fulfill some emotional needs not fulfilled by a husband. A role reversal is also possible with this type of incest. The son could be protecting his mother and pretending to be a "little man" (Sanford, 1980).

> The son wants very much to help his mother to fill the void the father left. To this end, he may begin to sleep with her at night because she is frightened. Attempting to soothe the mother's feelings of rejection, the son escorts her about town. A quasiromance begins. They genuinely enjoy each other's company. The son enjoys making his mother feel better. (Sanford, 1980, p. 192)

The mother often is very possessive of the son (Sanford, 1980). She may attempt to cut him off from his peers, discouraging him from making outside contacts and from growing up or away from her (Renvoize, 1982). Consequently, the "boy will probably feel insecure outside his home and have difficulty in making friends, especially female friends who will arouse in him ambivalent feelings of desire and prohibition" (Renvoize, 1982, p. 132).

MOTHER-DAUGHTER INCEST. Probably the least-reported type of incest is that between mothers and daughters. Again, a major dynamic in this type of incest is role reversal. "The mother has great needs for attention and affection. She may or may not have a husband. She relies on her daughter for emotional support" (Sanford, 1980, p. 195).

It is difficult for the daughter to look to her mother as a role model when her mother is overly dependent and is looking to her daughter for care and support. This becomes quite confusing to the daughter. Much of the daughter's self-concept becomes tied up in taking care of her mother (Sanford, 1980). "The relationship has untold effects on the victim's sexuality. In the mother's possessiveness, she has probably 'sheltered' the daughter from normal sexual exploration appropriate to her age" (Sanford, 1980, pp. 196–197).

EXTENDED-FAMILY INCEST. A few studies have been conducted on grandfather-granddaughter relations, none as far as we know on grandfather-grandson. In a study of 118 sexually molested women, approximately 10 percent said that they had been molested by their grandfathers (Tsai and Wagner, 1978). The age of the grandfather may cause some people to doubt his involvement in incestuous activity. "Older men in this society are thought to be nonsexual" (Sanford, 1980, p. 197). But incest does not necessarily have to relate to sexual needs. The grandfather may be experiencing self-doubts, just like the incestuous father, which are magnified by the problems of aging. He may "not feel as competent or powerful as he once was. . . . He may want companionship, yet fear rejection. His granddaughter offers him affection. She will not judge him weak or make difficult demands on him. With her, he experiences free-flowing warmth that he has missed. . . . It is a special relationship that can easily be exploited if the grandfather is so inclined" (Sanford, 1980, p. 198).

Unfortunately, if the child realizes the inappropriateness of the grandfather's behavior and tries to report it, she may find she is not taken seriously because of his age. Respect and obedience to a grandfather, along with the belief that he is a "harmless old man," also discourage people from taking reports of grandfather-granddaughter incest seriously. But unless stopped, this type of incest can carry "every adverse effect as [much as] any other form of incest" (Sanford, 1980, p. 199).

The impact of extended-family incest on the victim depends to a large degree on the age difference between the victim and the abuser and the living arrangements. "Two cousins, close in age to each other, experimenting with each other on a summer vacation or a weekend visit, is not something to be considered harmful. However, a sixteen-year-old uncle bribing his eight-year-old niece into mutual masturbation is *not* part of the normal growth and development for either person" (Sanford, 1980, p. 197). If the living situation is such that the relative lives in the home of the child and plays a mother or father role, then the dynamics of the incest would be very similar to the parent-child incest. If the child's contact with the relative is occasional and infrequent, the impact will probably be less harmful. "The imbalance of power, knowledge, and resources is still being exploited, yet the child probably does not feel that daily survival depends on the continuation of the incest" (Sanford, 1980, p. 197).

SIBLING INCEST. The largest *incidence* of incest, not the most often reported, occurs between partners of the same generation, between brothers and sisters (Finkelhor, 1979). The harm of this type of incest depends again on the age difference between the siblings and the amount of force or threat used. Siblings are typically more equal in terms of power and resources.

In cases of older brother-younger sister incest, the dynamics can be quite similar to father-daughter incest. The older brother may feel inept at social relations with his peers and so he turns to his younger, less threatening sister to fulfill his needs for affection and sexual exploration (Sanford, 1980). A similar pattern can exist for older sister-younger brother incest. The sister may lack self-confidence in relating to adolescent boys so "she turns to her younger brother to satisfy her curiosity and emotional needs" (Sanford, 1980, p. 200).

In Finkelhor's survey of undergraduates who experienced sibling incest, 30 percent found it positive, 30 percent found it negative, and the rest had no strong feelings about it being either. Those who had been threatened or forced, or whose sibling partners were much older, were four times as likely to find the experience negative as those who were of similar ages or who were not forced. Since girls usually had less choice in the matter, they were more likely to find the experience unpleasant than boys (Finkelhor, 1980).

Finkelhor's study also indicated that the age at which the incest occurred seemed to make no difference in the outcome, as long as the relationship between the siblings was close enough for neither of them to feel exploited. Whether it was a homosexual or a heterosexual sibling experience also did not make a difference. For the most part the sexual activities between young children were mild: exhibiting, fondling, and touching the genitals. Intercourse or attempted intercourse was found more frequently among older children, ages 13 to 17.

Impact of Sexual Abuse on the Victim

Child victims of sexual exploitation appear to suffer many of the same severe consequences as do adult women who have been raped (Burgess and Holmstrom, 1975). Specifically, feelings of confusion, depression, shame, and guilt commonly exist, as well as an awareness of a stigma that endures for some time. It is not unusual to find child sex victims undergoing long periods of therapy. The most common problems for women are ongoing depression and difficulties in relating to men (Finkelhor, 1979).

A large proportion of female drug addicts (Benward and Densen-Gerber, 1975), prostitutes (James and Meyerding, 1977) and adolescent runaways (Weber, 1977) are found to have incest in their backgrounds. "When a child has been sexually abused at an early age, sex becomes a survival skill, a way to get what she or he needs" (S. Butler, 1978, p. 36). It is no surprise, then, to find some victims turning to prostitution as a means of support. "Some who have never learned the difference between sex and love, may repeatedly trade their sexuality for the only touching and affection they have ever received" (S. Butler, 1978, p. 36).

In another study Sgroi (1983) reports the following characteristics commonly found among victims of incest: poor self-image, a lack of social skills, poor or unsatisfying peer relationships, and hostility or depression, with possibly suicide attempts. As adults they may lack satisfactory relationships with their family of origin and have difficulty establishing any sort of intimate relationships. For some, part of this difficulty with emotional closeness may take the form of being sexually unresponsive, or they may experience a sexual dysfunction (Sanford, 1980).

One of the most prominent effects of sexual exploitation is its impact on basic trust. Sexual abuse can be labeled as an "abuse of trust" (S. Butler, 1978). The sexual offender has abused the trust he "has assumed in having taken responsibility for the birth and care of a child, the responsibility he has taken upon himself to provide a safe and loving environment in which his son or daughter can develop into adulthood" (p. 59). There is a sense of betrayal among incest victims (Sanford, 1980).

> As young girls, the victims were taught to trust their fathers. They looked to them for guidance, believing they should never do anything to hurt them. All of society reinforces the concept that fathers are wise, protective, and inherently good. But to incest victims, society has lied. Their fathers did not protect them—they used them. Their fathers were not wise and good. They involved the children in something they did not want or understand. (Sanford, 1980, p. 170)

Obviously such distrust of men hinders the development of intimate relationships. "Some victims can work out their distrust in their daily lives so that they are not suspicious of *all* men" (Sanford, 1980, p. 172). The distrust may arise, however, as they attempt to achieve real closeness and commitment to potential husbands, lovers, or meaningful male friends (Sanford, 1980).

Marital Rape

Wife rape has become a social issue in the 1980s. "Traditionally sex in marriage has been considered a husband's right and a wife's responsibility" (Finkelhor and Yllo, 1983). Only recently have many states changed their laws to include the prosecution of husbands for the rape of their wives. Prior to these changes, rape by a husband was not considered possible in the legal sense. The first published article on wife rape was by Richard Gelles in 1977, in which he introduced marital rape as a problem warranting scientific study.

Rape can be defined in a narrow, legal way as "forced intercourse," vaginal penetration. Feminists prefer a broader definition— any sexual activity forced on one spouse by the other (D. Russell, 1982). Thus, while some researchers have considered only acts involving sexual intercourse to constitute marital rape, others include a wider variety of actions, such as oral-genital contact, fondling, or forced kissing. Theoretically rape can be committed by either men or women, but owing to the physical differences in size and strength between the sexes, rape is predominantly a male crime. Similarly, most of what is known about marital rape involves husband rapists and wife victims.

In a representative sample of 930 women in San Francisco, 14 percent of the women who had ever been married acknowledged an experience of forced sexual activity, such as vaginal, oral, or anal penetration by their husbands (D. Russell, 1982). Approximately one-third of all of the rapes were isolated cases, one-third occurred from 2 to 20 times, and one-third occurred more than 20 times. The degree of physical force ranged from pushing and pinning down (which was the most common) to severe beatings.

Finkelhor and Yllo (1983) divide marital rape into three categories. One category can be described as "typically battered women." Sexual violence for these women was just another aspect of a general pattern of physical and verbal abuse. This is a common occurrence as shown by the high percentages (37) of women in shelters for battered women who describe experiences of marital rape as well as physical abuse (Spektor, 1980; Giles-Sims, 1979; Pagelow, 1980). In the second category, "The forced sex grew more specifically out of sexual conflicts. There were long-standing disagreements over some sexual issue, such as how often to have sex or what were appropriate activities" (Finkelhor and Yllo, 1983, p. 123). A third category involved "bizarre sexual obsessions," such as wanting to produce pornography or needing "rituals" or "force" to become sexually aroused; bondage or sadism, for example.

REASONS FOR MARITAL RAPE. The wife's refusal to have sex is not, in and of itself, the reason for these assaults. Rather, what seems to be important is how the refusal is experienced by the husband (Groth, 1981). Groth explains that sex can be equated with power. When wives refuse, husband-rapists may experience a "pervasive feeling of not being in control of their lives or able to manage marital and other life demands effectively" (p. 178).

Morton Hunt (1979) describes a marital rapist as "a man who still believes that husbands are supposed to 'rule' their wives." This belief carries over to sexual matters: "When

he wants her, she should be glad, or at least willing; if she isn't, he has the right to force her. But in forcing her he gains far more than a few minutes of sexual pleasure. He humbles her and reasserts, in the most emotionally powerful way possible, that he is the ruler and she the subject" (Hunt, 1979). Of course, there are many men in traditional marriages who believe they are supposed to rule their wives but who do not rape them. Nevertheless, Hunt's idea that the typical husband-rapist seeks power over his wife rather than sexual gratification is consistent with other research findings (Groth, 1981; D. Russell, 1982). Of course, sex can also be used by a wife as a means of power by withholding sex as a form of punishment.

Sex may also be equated with love and affection by marital rapists. Since many of these men may not have developed "ways to experience and express closeness and affection in nonsexual ways, such offenders equate getting sex with being loved" (Groth, 1981, p. 178). Hence, their wives' refusals to engage in sex are interpreted by the men as they themselves not being loved. This condition becomes intolerable for husbands who have underlying fears of not being cared for or valued.

> *This is their deepest fear, that they are of no value, that they don't deserve love or respect. For men who are insecure in regard to their feelings about their personal worth, such rejection is devastating. Sex, even if it is forced, is an affirmation of their worth, a defense against such rejection, and proof that their fears about their wives' not loving them are groundless. (Groth, 1981, p. 178)*

Such husbands define love largely in a sexual way. Therefore, forced sex is one way for such men to affirm their self-worth and feel loved.

The rapist-husband may also equate sex with virility and manhood. By having sex with his wife, his manhood is reaffirmed; the denial of sex is emasculating. "For men who are insecure about their masculinity or have few other avenues of personal expression, physical strength and sexual activity become their means of self-assertion" (Groth, 1981, p. 178). Marital rape then becomes the husband's way of eliminating any doubts about his manhood.

Finally, sexual activity may be viewed by rape offenders as a measure of the success of their marriages. That is, if sex takes place, then everything else must be OK. Sex can also be seen as a solution to a marital problem. Sexual intercourse may be the husband's way of "patching things up" after a marital dispute. Therefore, forced sex may be used to assert control, to affirm self-worth, to be reassured of being loved, to prove manhood, or to make up after an argument (Groth, 1981).

While the data show that those committing more general violent crimes tend to be more representative of the lower class, this does not appear to hold true for marital rape. In terms of marital rapists, Russell (1982) found that there is a wide variation in educational level, occupation, income, and race. Also it appears that "the social characteristics of husband-rapists may differ greatly from men who rape women other than their wives" (p. 131).

IMPACT OF MARITAL RAPE ON THE VICTIM. Immediately following an attack, marital rape victims experience feelings similar to those of other rape victims. Fear, shock, disbelief, humiliation, embarrassment, and self-blame are common reactions (Burgess and Holmstrom, 1974). In addition, marital rape can have a direct negative effect on the wife's self-esteem, can result in her developing negative attitudes toward men such as not wanting sexual relations with her partner, and can lead to the increased use of alcohol as a method of dealing with depression (Shields and Hanneke, 1983, p. 140).

The fact that the assailant was not a stranger, but rather a spouse, results in some differing effects on the victim. When a woman is raped by someone whom she trusted, she will reexamine and redefine her relationship with this individual (Weis and Borges, 1973). Trust becomes the key issue for her. While women raped by strangers may go through a long period of being afraid, especially for their physical safety, women raped by their husbands have difficulty trusting again (Finkelhor and Yllo, 1983).

Another major difference in this type of rape is that the victim is living with her assailant; "She is under his scrutiny and surveillance, and he has continual access to her. The person to whom she looks for protection and caring is her victimizer" (Groth, 1981, p. 179). This is a person she is dependent on, emotionally and often financially.

For these reasons, marital rape appears to have a stronger impact on a victim's life than rape by a stranger. Much more is at stake for the victim of wife rape than for a woman who is raped by an unknown assailant. No longer can a woman who was raped by her husband be assured of comfort and safety in her own home. Her choices are to leave the marriage or to live with him and take what happens. Either option may be devastating to her. "Leaving involves all the trauma and readjustment of divorce . . . but staying with someone who has raped you often results in loss of self-esteem" (D. Russell, 1982, pp. 198–199). A wife who is not aware of the alternative of leaving may feel she has to stay in the abusive marriage. Staying in the marriage, however, leaves her vulnerable to repeated sexual assaults by her husband (Finkelhor and Yllo, 1983).

EMOTIONAL ABUSE

Emotional abuse within the family is much more difficult to define than physical or sexual abuse. In general, it occurs when the specific behavior(s) of one family member leads to emotional (rather than physical) harm to another family member. As seen from the previous discussion, it is obvious that the victims of virtually all forms of physical and sexual abuse will experience emotional abuse also. Emotional abuse, however, can exist independently of these other forms of abuse.

Within every family, there are times when individuals do or say things that hurt other family members. If such incidents do not occur too often, allowances are usually made for them. The hurts may, at times, be unintentional and interpreted just that way. Actual emotional abuse, however, focuses on long-term situations in which the intent is to hurt another individual; it occurs repeatedly and in varied forms. In such situations, the victim bases his or her own self-image on the negative treatment and views his or her own behavior as bad or inadequate. The problem is that the victim does not experience enough positive interactions to balance the negative ones.

Emotional abuse can take many forms. There can be a verbal assault—calling someone derogatory names, criticizing continually and excessively, ridiculing behavior or appearance, threatening the personal safety or health of the person, threatening to withdraw love or to abandon the person, or constantly telling the person he or she is bad or worthless. Emotional abuse impinges on a person's perception of himself or herself in relation to others. Hence, it can result in a distorted picture of self and others.

Destructive forms of communication are often found in emotionally abusive families. A double bind is one example of emotionally abusive communication. It exists when "communication has taken place in a contradictory fashion between two people" (Mayhall and Norgard, 1983, p. 160). The tone of voice may communicate disapproval, disbe-

lief, or dislike, while the words themselves actually communicate something else (Faller, n.d.). An abusive parent, for example, may say to the child, "You are wonderful" in a degrading tone. The child then is confused as to which message was meant. The child does not know whether to accept the verbal message at face value or the sarcastic tone of the parent's voice as the real message.

Emotional abuse can also take the form of actions that rob the individual of human dignity, such as confinement—tying the child up to a chair or bed, making him or her stand in a corner for extended periods of time, locking the child in a closet, shutting him or her in a dark basement. Forced humiliating situations, such as eating out of a dog's dish, dressing a boy in girl's clothing, hanging a bedwetter's sheets out the window, sending a child to school in diapers as a form of punishment, all diminish human dignity. These forms of emotional embarassment, humiliation, and harassment are attempts by some parents to control their children. Emotional abuse may also take the form of segregating or excluding a family member from family activities—such as meals, outings, and parties—or from general human contact with other people.

When a child reaches adolescence, the parents may particularly feel a loss of control over his or her behavior. As control issues surface between a parent and the teenager, who is growing more independent, some parents attempt increasingly to "put the youth in his or her place" (Mayhall and Norgard, 1983). Excessive criticism, rejection, or unreasonable restrictions often have a damaging effect on the developing self-image of a teenager.

Sometimes the injury from emotional abuse surfaces in children's behavior along a similar line as the emotional and behavioral adaptations of physically abused children; they become withdrawn and depressed, or they become aggressive and rebellious. With emotional injury, the damage is not easily visible or so easily reversed. Cuts, bruises, and scrapes, typical results from physical abuse, are obvious, and early detection can elicit appropriate help for the child and the parent. But only behavioral symptoms are evident with emotional abuse. To compound the problem, the full effects of emotional abuse may not surface for years, when the victim is crippled in his or her abilities to interact with people, particularly in developing intimate relationships.

The result of growing up in an emotionally abusive home is often a person who lacks basic self-esteem, is emotionally immature, and is incompetent in dealing with the requirements of child rearing later in life.

Children who have poor self-concepts often become adults with poor self-concepts. Children who are emotionally needy may grow to adulthood with the same emotional neediness. As these children become adults and move through the life cycle to become parents, they may look to their children to fill their unmet needs. Role reversal is one distinguishing feature of emotional abuse and neglect. (Mayhall and Norgard, 1983, p. 159)

Thus feelings of insecurity of the emotionally abused make it difficult for them as adults to provide adequately for the emotional needs of a child, much less of a spouse (Mayhall and Norgard, 1983).

Although it is common to think of the most extreme forms of emotional abuse as occurring between parents and children—owing to the "dependency" and "power" imbalances in the relationship—emotional abuse also takes similar forms between marital partners. Lenore Walker (1979) discusses two forms: (1) emotionally depriving a spouse of "adult" rights and responsibilities, in relation to freedom, personal opportunities

for growth, creativity, and satisfaction; and (2) socially battering the spouse by resorting to humiliation, criticism, embarrassment, and belittlement in front of others to undermine his or her self-esteem. Ironically, Walker (1979) found in her research on battered wives that verbal battering was experienced as the most powerful coercive technique by many of the women. Despite their severe physical batterings, most of the women in her sample reported that the "verbal humiliation was the worst kind of battering they had experienced" (p. 172). Abuse can also occur between adult children and their elderly parents—another situation where power imbalances exist. (See Box 13.7.)

NEGLECT

Abuse refers to acts that one person commits against another. There is an element of implied action and intent. Neglect, by contrast, refers to acts that a person *omits* to do for another individual. Leontine Young (1976) states, "If the behavior of neglecting parents toward their children could be summed up in one word, that word would be indifference" (p. 31). The "neglecter" is indifferent toward the victim and avoids ongoing responsibilities and interactions.

Neglect in families is generally focused on the parental treatment of children. The role of parent involves particular obligations to provide for the needs of children, who are dependent by virtue of age, size, abilities, knowledge, and resources. Neglect then occurs when parents do not provide for their children's needs. The neglect can take three basic forms: physical neglect, social neglect, and emotional neglect.

Physical neglect occurs when parents fail to provide for their child's basic physical needs, such as food, clothing, shelter, and supervision. It is neglect to the extent that the child's health, safety, or normal development

BOX 13.7

A HIDDEN TRAGEDY: ABUSE OF THE ELDERLY

Abuse of the elderly across the United States today has become almost commonplace. . . . Most of the abuse of the aged is by members of their own families. . . . More than a million men and women 65 and over are seriously mistreated—physically, psychologically, and financially—every year. . . . One out of every 25 old people is abused. . . . Abuse can take the form of assault, neglect, deprivation, or even rape. The average victim is 75 or older and, more often, a woman. Most victims must rely on others—generally, those who abuse them—for care, food, and shelter. . . .

"The situation is getting worse because people are living longer and are not economically productive anymore. Their families have to care for them and don't know how. Many lose control out of frustration. . . ." [Suzanne Steinmetz quoted by Robinson] The maltreatment takes many forms.

"Resentment at having to tend to a frail, bedridden, incontinent parent can push some people to the breaking point" Howard Segars says. "The situation can . . . trigger some awful form of abuse. These people really want to do right by their parents, but they cannot cope with all the emotional and financial stress placed on them."

Complicating the problem of abuse is the fact that elderly people seldom report incidents to authorities. More than 70 percent of all cases are reported by third parties. Old people apparently are ashamed to say that they've been abused by their own children, don't want to cause trouble for their children, or simply are afraid. . . .

Steinmetz says the one hope is for government agencies to provide counseling *and* financial help to families caring for aged parents.

SOURCE: *Robinson, 1985.*

is jeopardized. Neglect can also include such things as failing to obtain medical care when the child needs it, failing properly to supervise a child playing near a busy street, or, in its most extreme form, it can involve abandonment.

Social neglect stems from the belief that parents have a responsibility to teach and guide their children in learning to conform to the norms and laws of society. In addition, parents are believed to be responsible for teaching their children social skills and behaviors that will help them in interpersonal interactions. Besides teaching them directly, they may provide their children with the opportunities to learn social skills; for example, allowing them to play with neighborhood children or to join clubs or athletic teams.

Emotional neglect involves the failure to provide the emotional support necessary for a child's well-being (Faller, 1981). It is based on the belief that children have common emotional needs. These include such things as "feeling a sense of belonging, having a place and a role within the family, and having a positive self-concept" (Mayhall and Norgard, 1983, p. 157). Affection, approval, consistency, stimulation, encouragement, recognition, and appreciation provided by parents or other caregivers all help to fulfill the child's emotional needs (Mayhall and Norgard, 1983).

The lack of adequate nurturance and the failure to provide appropriate social or cognitive stimulation are also forms of emotional neglect. Specific examples include the parent who rarely talks to or cuddles a baby, rarely takes the infant out of his or her crib, or commonly leaves the infant crying in the crib with his or her bottle propped up instead of being held (Mayhall and Norgard, 1983). The failure to play with a young child or keeping him or her in a playpen all the time are forms of lack of stimulation. The failure to help the child with his or her problems can also constitute emotional neglect (Faller, 1981). A specific example of this type of emotional neglect would be the "parent who persistently fails to respond to a child's fears and worries which are so severe that the child cannot sleep at night" (Faller, 1981, p. 31).

Impact on the Victim

What are some of the harmful effects of emotional neglect on a child? Many of the effects are the same as those found in emotional abuse: developmental lags, low self-esteem, and problems in developing intimate relationships. Withdrawn, depressed, and apathetic behaviors are also common responses among neglected children (Faller, 1981; Mayhall and Norgard, 1983). Aggression is not as common with neglected children as with abused children (Faller, 1981).

Mayhall and Norgard (1983) observed the following behaviors of children experiencing emotional neglect:

behavior problems in the classroom or other setting that requires the child to follow rules

an overconcern (disproportionate to other children of the same age) about conforming to the instructions of the adult

emotional turmoil evidenced by "repetitive rhythmic movements, lack of verbal or physical communication, or an inordinate attention to details" (p. 158)

These behaviors are not necessarily proof that emotional neglect is occurring, but they are possible signals to watch for and to check further (Mayhall and Norgard, 1983).

Neglect can affect a child's growth and development, resulting in drastic physical maladjustments such as nutritional deprivation or failure to thrive. A *nutritional deprivation* can occur "when a parent cannot or does not provide a child with adequate or proper food or drink. These children may appear emaciated, dehydrated, or have a puffy face and feet and a large belly due to inadequate calories" (Faller, 1981). Needless to say, these are extreme cases of neglect, and the parents are likely to be quite emotionally disturbed.

Failure to thrive (FTT) is a lack of normal growth in infants for which there is no organic cause. It is the result of an "environmental" or "maternal" deprivation. Nurturing human contact is missing in the normal care of the child—feeding, bathing, holding, stimulation, for example. Failure-to-thrive babies will begin to grow in a hospital or other environment if the cause is neglect.

Reasons for Neglect

Lack of knowledge and *poverty* are two reasons for parental neglect. Another very common reason is *depression*. Parents who are in a depressed mood will seem "sad, show little animation, rarely smile, complain of being overwhelmed, and may show evidence of an inability to cope" (Faller, 1981, p. 36). Those parents with severe depression may spend the day in bed, not cook meals for the child, or pay little attention to their child's behavior and appearance. *Substance abuse* is a fourth reason for child neglect. Neglect occurs when the drug-addicted or alcoholic parent becomes immobilized, or semiconscious, or passes out and is unable to perform daily tasks (Faller, 1981).

Like abusive parents, neglectful parents are often found to have *feelings of low self-esteem.* "They may think that they are worthless, incompetent, or bad as people. Some neglectful parents neglect themselves as well as their children, and these patterns continuously remind them of what worthless people they are" (Faller, 1981, p. 34).

A lack of an emotional attachment between the parent and infant can also contribute to the potential of neglect. Particular infants are especially at high risk. Those who are born prematurely are at risk owing to a greater possibility of maternal illness or because of the conditions imposed by and associated with prematurity, in particular the hospital separation between the mother and infant (Mayhall and Norgard, 1983). Adopted infants may also be at risk if there has not been sufficient time for an attachment to develop between the parent and child. Also, a parent may have difficulty forming an attachment with an unwanted child, who will then be at risk for neglect. "Certainly, if the attachment between the infant and the parent or caretaker does not form, there is already emotional neglect in that the infant is not getting what he or she needs at that early time in life" (Mayhall and Norgard, 1983, p. 164).

The Relationship of Abuse to Neglect

One issue of abuse and neglect of children is whether they should be regarded as conceptually the same or different phenomena. Most research thus far tends to treat child neglect as different from child abuse. But the causes and results of abuse and neglect are quite similar. In a nationwide survey of reported child abuse, one-third of all parents reported for child abuse were reported for child neglect as well (Gil, 1973).

In looking at the causes of child abuse and neglect, the literature describes the abusive parent in much the same way as the neglectful parent—characterized by immaturity, low self-esteem, powerlessness, lack of knowledge of child development and child care, and a childhood marked by physical and emotional deprivation and/or abuse. Similar environmental stresses such as poverty, unemployment, and social isolation can contribute to both abuse and neglect. An important question for further research is "why some immature, inadequate parents become neglectful, while others become abusive, and still others *both* neglect and abuse" (Zaphiris, 1975, p. 62). A distinction among these types of parents would aid in providing more effective intervention and treatment.

Available data indicate that child abuse is much rarer than child neglect. Even though an overlap in the groups of neglectful and abusive parents exists, obviously the vast majority of neglectful parents are not considered abusive (Zaphiris, 1975, p. 62). In addition, it is not uncommon to find an abusive parent and a neglecting parent in the same family. Typically, when one parent is abusing a child, the other parent ignores the situation or fails to provide protection, emotional support, or medical attention and is therefore neglecting his or her responsibilities in caring for the child.

CHAPTER REVIEW

1. Certain situational factors such as time spent together, intensity of involvement, and family privacy, which contribute to making

the family a place for intimacy, can also make the family prone to violence. Even though family violence is not treated legally and socially as a problem as serious as nonfamily violence, it can have a more debilitating effect on the victim.

2. What is considered to be acceptable physical action varies from family to family and within different cultures and subcultures. Thus, problems in labeling violence make determining its incidence more difficult. Other difficulties regarding the reporting of abuse stem from traditional attitudes of family privacy and feelings of guilt and shame over being an abuser or victim. Regardless of the considerable reluctance to report abuse, however, the amount of reported family violence has increased over recent years.

3. A profile of the battering spouse includes such characteristics as unemployment or underemployment, alcohol or drug abuse, "uncontrollable jealousy," and a history of past violent behavior. The "cycle of violence," consisting of the stages of *tension-building, acute battering,* and *kindness and contrite loving,* explains why wives often remain married to battering husbands.

4. Parents who batter their children represent all social classes, a range of education and intelligence, and a variety of types of occupations. Battering parents often have unrealistic expectations for their children. The parents themselves are likely to come from a family deprived of love and nurturance, and they tend to lack self-confidence. The potentially damaging effects of physical abuse on children is evidenced by their later problems with interpersonal relationships, in particular the lack of trust and the avoidance of intimacy.

5. Since the early 1970s, considerable attention has been given to the problem of sexual exploitation in families. No matter how minor the sexual activity may seem to adults, it can leave emotional scars on children, including poor self-image, lack of social skills, unsatisfying peer relationships, and depression. So prominent is its impact on trust that sexual exploitation has been labeled the "abuse of trust."

6. Only recently has marital rape emerged as a social concern. In fact, rape by a husband is still not legally an offense in some states. Marital rapists often believe that they are supposed to "rule" their wives. Also, sex to these men may be equated with love and affection, and hence any refusal on the part of the wife to engage in sex is interpreted by the husbands as not being loved.

7. Emotional abuse in a family can occur independent of physical or sexual abuse. It can happen when a family member verbally assaults another member or takes actions that rob an individual of human dignity by emotionally embarrassing or humiliating him or her.

8. Neglect refers to acts that a person omits to do for another human being. If such a person is a parent, he or she is indifferent toward the victim and avoids responsibilities for a child's physical, social, or emotional needs. The impact of neglect can be found in developmental lags, physical maladjustments such as nutritional deprivation or failure to thrive, low self-esteem, and adult problems in developing intimate relationships. The reasons for neglect can include poverty, a parent's lack of knowledge, a parent's low self-esteem, or the lack of an emotional attachment between the parent and infant.

The Dissolution of Marriage and Intimacy

The criteria of successful marriages have changed from just the accomplishment of specific traditional roles. They now include such demands as emotional support, sexual gratification, and good communication. This shift is evident in studies examining the reasons given for marital breakups. Previous to the 1965–1975 era, common complaints revolved around the instrumental functions of marriage, such as the inadequacy of the husband in providing for the family or the wife's inadequacy in taking care of the house and children. Increasingly in the last 20 years the complaints of divorcing couples have emphasized expressive functions (Kitson and Sussman, 1982). For example, the very high divorce rate among women with graduate degrees is one indicator that more and more females no longer need men to play the good-provider role but are looking for men who can function in more expressive ways. Hence, a shift to more emotional expectations in marriage, for all social classes, means that the conditions for the dissolution of marriage have also changed.

As individuals begin to expect the development of intimacy in their marriages, such relationships are more likely to dissolve when that goal is not met. Today the emotional bonds of marriage are of primary importance; they serve an essential purpose in an impersonal, urban society. But even intimate marriages are not immune, or totally protected, from dissolution. Under extreme conditions of stress or conflict between the partners or within the family, these bonds, even bonds of closeness, may break down.

Of course, many marriages dissolve before a real emotional closeness has ever developed; in fact, this lack is probably one of the major reasons for dissolution. Not every partner has the individual prerequisites or interpersonal skills necessary to achieve and maintain a high level of intimacy. Nor does everyone have a desire to be emotionally close to someone else, even though he or she may seek marriage as a goal in life. When such a person is paired with a partner who has the ability to be intimate and who has expectations for intimacy in the marriage, dissatisfaction will likely be the result, with a good possibility of eventual dissolution. As dissatisfactions outweigh the rewards of marriage, partners will begin a process of disengaging from each other.

THE PROCESS OF UNCOUPLING

Marital dissolution is not merely an *event* in one's life; it is a *process* with many facets. Emotions, behaviors, and thoughts are all involved. Thus, divorce itself can be viewed as a "complex, multidimensional process" (Hagestad and Smyer, 1982). Dissolution usually occurs after some emptiness, disorder, or turbulence has been in existence in the relationship for some time. A study of divorced individuals found that most dissolutions come about after the marriage has been going badly for at least months but often years. Most people, both men and women, take more than a year to deliberate and make a final decision about divorce.

There is a distinct difference between the emotional breakdown of a marriage and its actual dissolution. In other words, a marriage may have broken down to the point where the partners do nothing with, or say almost nothing to, each other. But such partners may still reside together, as in an empty-shell marriage. Social factors—pressures from those outside the couple—often help to keep the partners together, even though few, if any, emotional bonds exist between the spouses.

The divorce experience can vary greatly among people. A few may view divorce as liberating and fulfilling; others may experience it as a personal trauma with lifetime repercussions. Most people fall between these two extremes or experience a combination of them at different time intervals. But regardless of one's particular reactions, there is a *process* of uncoupling, of *becoming* "unattached" or "unmarried" or "disengaged," which divorcing partners go through. Uncoupling is rarely an orderly and predictable progression of events; more likely it will be "messy, uncontrolled and uncertain" (Duck, 1982). The variety of possible experiences is reflected in a study of couples divorcing during middle age:

> *The respondents showed striking but systematic contrasts in their divorce experiences. Some of them had twenty years in which to prepare marital exits, others had little more than two months. Some of them carefully planned and controlled the marital dissolution, taking one thing at a time. Others had a whole complex of changes thrown at them with no warning: the interruptions of long-standing routines, the severing of emotional bonds, and the legal status change. (Hagestad and Smyer, 1982, pp. 186–187)*

As uncertain and disorderly as the processes of uncoupling may be, there are some behaviors common to withdrawal from a relationship. Such behaviors as negotiating the dissolution of the relationship, reducing indicators of commitment, and building new networks of friends are typical.

The activities of uncoupling usually start with one partner. Rarely will both initiate the disengagement at the same time. More typically one partner finds the marriage satisfactory, while the other finds it inadequate. Social psychologist Steve Duck (1982) thinks that the first phase of uncoupling primarily involves what is going on within the individual partners—their thoughts, interpretations, and expectations. He calls this an "intra-psychic," or "*individual*" *phase*. The uncoupling then moves gradually into a "*dyadic*" *phase* involving interaction between both partners. Another phase involves people outside the dyad, the "*social*" *phase*. It focuses on social and cultural factors, which exert pressure on the marriage. Finally, if the uncoupling continues, there is the *phase of "closing,"* referred to as "grave dressing" by Duck. Similar stages are experienced by nonmarried couples whose relationships break up.

The Individual Phase

In the individual phase at least one of the partners begins to have doubts about the marriage. One may or may not be able to pinpoint the problem exactly, but there is the realization that something is wrong with the relationship; at the very least, "something is missing." Thoughts and feelings about whether to disengage from the marriage may emerge. These may also be reflected in certain behaviors—doing things in hope of "revitalizing" the marriage or perhaps ignoring the marriage by involvement in other things. However, the doubts about the marriage and the possible desire to disengage are not being expressed to the spouse at this point. During this phase the individual is focused on analyzing the partner's behavior, evaluating the costs and rewards of the relationship, and assessing alternatives to the marriage.

EVALUATION OF THE PARTNER'S BEHAVIOR. One early stage toward dissolution involves identifying dissatisfactions with the partner's behavior. The individual thinks about how the partner could be different and about what changes would be needed so that the individual's needs would be satisfied. There may be doubts about the partner's ability to be emotionally close to another person. Often such an evaluation is used to justify feelings of dissatisfaction, for emotional withdrawal, or even for leaving. It's a "justification that satisfies oneself privately and will be used as the basis for subsequently confronting the partner when and if that occurs" (Duck, 1982, p. 18).

ASSESSMENT OF COSTS AND REWARDS IN THE RELATIONSHIP.

Obviously when individuals marry, there are certain things that attract them to the partner. These attractions may include the following: (1) *material* rewards, derived from income and the ownership of property; (2) *symbolic* rewards, obtained from family status and the sharing of similar values and interests; and (3) *affectional* rewards, associated with companionship and sexual enjoyment (Levinger, 1979b). The accumulation of these rewards in a marriage will help to keep the spouses in the relationship, while the lack of them may encourage its dissolution.

Material rewards.

Research indicates that divorce rates are lower for couples with high income levels (Carter and Glick, 1976). But the extent to which income itself serves as a deterrent to marital dissolution is still uncertain. For example, it may be that money or shared income keeps the partners in the marriage. Or it could be that couples with higher incomes do not experience the financial stresses facing other couples and hence experience fewer marital problems.

Those couples who are home owners have a lower divorce rate than do nonowners (Levinger, 1979b). Although that fact may also be a result of higher income or longer lengths of marriage, it makes sense that joint home ownership may "stabilize the marriage tie." Other property acquired as a couple may also help to keep the marriage together; "It symbolizes what they both treasure; joint property would be a strength rather than a weakness of their relationship" (Levinger, 1979b, p. 47).

An exception to this influence of income exists for blacks. While the divorce rate for upper-class blacks is less than for lower-class blacks, the decrease is not nearly as significant as it is among whites (Carter and Glick, 1976). The reasons for this difference are unclear. James Blackwell (1985) speculates that black couples who recently arrive into the middle and upper classes experience extra demands and stresses on their marriages associated with these new life-styles. Furthermore, black women who earn high incomes often marry down, and divorce is more common in marriages where there is a large discrepancy in income, particularly where the wife earns more than the husband.

Symbolic rewards.

Status in one's community can be an important reward for some people, particularly the upper class. Thus partners may be attracted to each other for reasons related to social class. Couples with lower levels of education and lower occupational status are more prone to divorce than those with higher educational and occupational status. But we cannot attribute clear-cut causal effects to occupation and education; other factors may intervene. High education, for example, is associated with better marital communication.

Social similarity may be another type of symbolic reward. Similarities in religion and age help in stabilizing marriages. Homogamous couples may find it easier to communicate with each other, and they are more likely to adhere to the same social norms, which will help avoid friction and possible dissolution. In addition, the status of being a couple is almost universally more valued than that of being single. "Much of our society's life is based on the assumption that people are paired: pairs of people are invited to dinner parties; it is even true that pairs of people are usually the socially negotiable unit that is invited to play tennis and bridge. A single person—one without an appropriate partner—is thus something of a difficulty for *other people* to manage in a vibrant social environment" (Duck, 1982, p. 26).

Affectional rewards.   Affectional rewards can include such benefits as emotional closeness, sexual enjoyment, and companionship. Especially in marriages in the United States, these characteristics are valued. Satisfaction with companionship has been found to be strongly related to measurements of marital adjustment (Blood and Wolfe, 1960).

In summary, these are a few types of rewards—material, symbolic and affectional—that individuals will be assessing as they evaluate their relationship. The more rewards the partner sees in being connected with the other person, in comparison with the costs, the less likely will he or she be dissatisfied. But when the rewards are few, in comparison to the costs, then dissatisfaction is likely to occur. A partner may assess the exchange with the other person as being inequitable, that is, he or she is receiving fewer rewards than the other person is receiving. A wife, for example, may feel that she's given her husband extensive emotional support—empathizing with him, listening to him—but that she receives very little, if any, support in return.

When a partner views an imbalance in exchange, typically it is unlikely that he or she will immediately confront the person. Instead, the individual may brood and think about it a lot, and possibly consult with a confidant. Merely noticing inequity causes some personal dissatisfaction, but doing something about it makes the problem no longer individual but dyadic (Duck, 1982).

ALTERNATIVE ATTRACTIONS.   A partner may also assess alternatives. It is unlikely for a spouse to disengage from a relationship unless some other option seems more attractive.

The alternative can be a relationship with another person or living alone. It may not necessarily involve another woman or another man. A spouse could leave in order to invest himself or herself totally in a career, to pursue an education, or to become involved in other activities that he or she was unable to pursue while being married. These alternative styles of life may be perceived as more rewarding and more contributing to the individual's self-esteem.

Of particular importance are alternative attractions for wives, since they are the ones to initiate the termination of a majority of marriages. Although the husband's actions, or lack of actions, are often the cause for the break, the end of the wife's continuing tolerance of her husband's behavior appears to be the key factor in the application for divorce (Levinger, 1979b). An attractive alternative for the wife may be an independent social and economic status. Perhaps she is tired of economic dependence or feels smothered by a domineering husband. Being divorced may symbolize freedom and new opportunities. Or a partner may feel that another person could provide her with material, status, and affectional rewards that are lacking in her current marriage.

During this stage of deliberation, the person may be quite indecisive about the future of the relationship. Agitation, stress, and ambivalence are common characteristics of people in such quandaries. This phase generally involves a private, personal process, and feelings and thoughts are not directly communicated to the partner. But eventually the person is faced with the decision of whether and how to confront the partner about his or her dissatisfactions (Duck, 1982). It may be that the individual accepts as reality that this is the way marriages are and that the only thing to do is resign oneself to it. But if one wants to pursue a better-quality relationship or if one wants to end the relationship, either way the individual will need to communicate his or her dissatisfactions to the partner. If the issues are expressed to the spouse, then they enter a different phase.

The Dyadic Phase

In the dyadic phase *both* partners are assessing the relationship. This situation may have been brought about by one partner confronting the other or by both bringing up issues after highly conflictual and disturbing interactions. In any event, during this phase dis-

satisfactions with the relationship are expressed. The person who initially questions the relationship may "present a case" regarding his or her feelings and how behaviors in the relationship need to be changed. But primarily "the initiator must bring the other to the point of sharing a common definition of the marriage as 'troubled'" (Vaughan, 1985, p. 431).

The partner who is confronted may point out his or her own costs in the relationship in its present form. He or she, too, may assess the costs resulting from changing the rela-

"Try to forgive me. I'm afraid I haven't been very good company for the past forty-six years."

Drawing by George Price; © 1984. The New Yorker Magazine, Inc.

tionship, the costs of actually disengaging, and the costs of "going public" with a divorce. Sometimes the announcement of the wish to redefine the relationship is dismissed by the partner. The partner may deny such a request ("You don't really mean it"), take it lightly ("It will work out—You'll get over it"), or interpret it as a mere power ploy ("You just want me to give in to you; it's just a threat") (Duck, 1982).

If feelings of dissatisfaction are taken seriously, the couple may, at this time seek marital therapy. Unfortunately, often the counseling is too late, since one partner may have fallen emotionally "out of love." The accumulation of hurts, the feelings of rejection, and the costs of the relationship may have reached a point where one person does not want the relationship anymore. In fact, disengagement may be well underway for this person at the time that he or she first brings up problems in the marriage. (See Box 14.1.)

The person who is already "emotionally divorced" may try to prepare the partner to live alone.

By encouraging the other to make new friends, find a job, get involved in outside activities, or seek additional education, the initiator hopes to decrease the other's commitment to and dependence upon the coupled identity for self-validation and move the other toward autonomy. This stage of preparation is not simply one of cold expediency for the benefit of the initiator, but is based on concern for the significant other and serves to mitigate the pain of the uncoupling process for both the initiator and the other. (Vaughan, 1985, pp. 433–434)

How partners interact during this dyadic stage may further influence the assessment of rewards and costs. For example, on the one hand, a partner's resistance to change or to seeing the reality of the problems in the relationship may lead the initiator to proceed

with the uncoupling. On the other hand, so much stress may be caused by the discussions of possible dissolution that both partners decide not to go through with a divorce. Or a partner's claims to be able and willing to make behavioral changes may effectively "block off" and discourage the other person's intent to dissolve the relationship (Duck, 1982). Typically this stage consists of a lot of "trying." Both partners now share a definition of the marriage as troubled. They each, however, may have different ideas as to how the marriage should be changed.

Both partners could be quite uncertain or ambivalent during this stage. Oscillation can take place as partners move back and forth between attempts at reconciliation and withdrawal. Besides assessing the other's behavior, there is typically an assessment of the relationship itself. Partners often explore what an ideal relationship *ought* to be like. They begin asking themselves some of the following questions: "Is it realistic to expect the relationship to work? Is it the right sort of relationship? Is it, perhaps, unduly stifling or constraining to the partners, such that they would be better out of it after all?" (Duck, 1982, p. 23). The issue confronting them at this stage is "repair versus dissolution." A temporary physical separation may occur during this phase to help the couple make a decision regarding a final dissolution.

If repair of the relationship is rejected as a possibility, the partners begin the final steps of preparation for the relationship's dissolution. This involves "going public" with the plans for a divorce (Duck, 1982).

The Social Phase

Once dissolution has been chosen, the third phase involves facing certain social consequences while implementing the decision and making it public (Duck, 1982). With the initiation of legal proceedings, uncoupling ob-

BOX 14.1

FALLING OUT OF LOVE

Many individuals appear to go through particular stages when falling out of love. While people may not pass through each and every stage outlined below, they usually will experience most of them as they fall out of love.

1. *Illusionary Intimacy.* Not all relationships begin with idealization, but a large number do. In this stage there is an extremely intense emotional and romantic identification based upon imaginary perceptions of the other person. Since this idealization always dies, it is typically replaced by a somewhat more accurate perception of the other's humanness.

2. *Positive Expectations for the Future.* Almost all couples have positive expectations at the time they are ready to make a commitment to each other, or at the time of marriage. They perceive of their love as strong and secure; they truly expect it to last a lifetime. There is an expectation of happiness and positive exchange. This is a period of great anticipatory rewards.

3. *Recognition of Something Missing.* Over time, behaviors and interactions do not generally work out the way they were envisioned. While it is often difficult at this stage to pinpoint the problem exactly, there is a recognition that something is wrong with the relationship. Usually the person will eagerly try new and different patterns of behavior; he or she may attempt to love harder, to give more, or to be sexier.

4. *Reevaluation of Early Expectations.* At this point there is a more realistic analysis of the relationship and of the lack of rewards. The relationship is reevaluated with one of two possible outcomes. (a) The individual may simply accept as reality that this is the way marriages are and there isn't much anyone can do about it. The result is a tempering of expectations and a resignation to a lower-quality relationship. (b) The person does not lower his or her expectations and decides to seek a high-quality relationship including emotional intimacy and personal happiness.

5. *Increased Awareness of Loneliness.* Over time there is a more obvious lack of closeness. Feelings of aloneness, distance, and isolation occur with increasing frequency. At this point an attempt may be made to discuss these feelings with the partner, often to no avail. Or a suggestion may be made to obtain outside help, which is usually vetoed by the partner. The partner typically tends to downplay any issues in the marriage and may state that "We can solve our own problems."

6. *Accumulation of Hurts.* During this stage, feelings of rejection, of not being needed, of being taken for granted, of not being important in the partner's life are common. The person has the perception that his or her own needs are largely ignored or dismissed. This is a time

period when the person may weep a lot. The specific causes of hurts may include such things as the following: "Spouse is too busy or working extensively," "Few fun times are spent together," "Spouse is not there when needed," "Special occasions or dates are missed or ignored," "There is insensitivity."

7. *Increased Anger.* Because of the accumulation of hurts over time, negative emotions are increased. There is growing anger toward the partner and uncertainty about the relationship. The person now has strong doubts about the partner's ability to love that person the way he or she wants to be loved. At this point typically, there is a "lashing out" at the partner or withdrawal or both.

8. *Sexual Behavior Diminishes or Stops.* One of four patterns may exist. (a) One simply refuses sex with the partner or makes various excuses to avoid sexual activity. In this pattern sex is stopped altogether. (b) Sex continues to be carried out but only as "a duty"; it is typically of low quality. (c) Deprivation sex may exist. It may offer the only opportunity for closeness in the relationship, and the individual uses sex to help relieve his or her deprivation of closeness. (d) Because of personal insecurities, the individual continues some sexual activity as a strategy to hold on to the partner.

9. *A Search for Help.* The individual is becoming more desperate at this point. An effort is made to talk to friends or extended family about the relationship. Or individual counseling may be sought as a last resort. At this point the person may not be sure whether he or she wants the marriage or not. The person may not even be sure why he or she is seeking counseling.

10. *Fallen Out of Love.* At this point there are no strong feelings left at all for the partner, either positive or negative. Apathy and indifference best describe the emotions; there is no longer any ambivalence about the relationship. The tears have long since stopped. Some comments that are typical of this stage are: "I don't want to hurt him," "I don't look forward to being with him," "I don't miss him when he is away," "I don't want to go home when he is there," and "I don't look forward to his coming home."

11. *The Final Decision.* Having fallen out of love still leaves decisions to be made. There are three possible choices: (a) to make a move toward getting out of the relationship, to separate or divorce; (b) to try through counseling or other means to rekindle the love that once existed (which, incidentally, is very difficult to accomplish); (c) to resign oneself totally to a nonintimate relationship. Reasons for staying in such a marriage may include any of the following: one's stage in the life cycle, religious convictions, guilt, pity, finances, feelings of failure (which may be greater if there were previous divorces), children, health, or commitment to the institution of marriage.

viously becomes less tentative. But the impact of the dissolution cannot thoroughly be understood without considering the social network in which the personal relationship is embedded.

A network consists of friendships and family relationships of the partners, people to whom the couple's relationship is often important. Thus friends and family members must also adjust to the loss of the couple. "It is usually the case that once we begin a romantic relationship, the people around us develop expectations that we will continue it" (M. Johnson, 1982). In fact, these social expectations—"that one must struggle to maintain a marriage in the face of adversity"—may be one factor working against dissolution.

Friends may disapprove of the divorce because of the effects it will have on their own lives. Members of the couple's social network have typically built patterns of behavior around the couple's "lines of action." A trivial example includes a pair of friends who may have a married couple with whom they frequently play doubles tennis and the dissolution of the marriage will force the friends either to play singles or to search for a new pair of tennis partners (M. Johnson, 1982, p. 56).

In one study of the social aspects of divorce, 42 percent of the respondents' marital network members had been dropped after a marital separation (Rands, 1980). The spouses' relatives were often dropped and replaced with friends and co-workers (M. Johnson, 1982). Networks became smaller after the separation than they were during the marriage. Some of the close relationships in a person's network, however, became even closer, providing more emotional support, greater physical contact, the sharing of more personal feelings, and participation in joint activities.

"The problem is as much an adjustment problem for the network as it is one for the pair themselves within the network" (Duck, 1982, p. 26). Such problems as taking sides, inviting one partner without the other, and accepting a new partner may face the members of the social network. Partners may lose those mutual friends who find it difficult to deal with both partners of a couple after they have become divided by divorce.

> *Questions such as who [sic] to invite to a dinner party become difficult ones. Does one invite the man, the woman, both, neither? Should one hold two separate dinner parties, inviting one former spouse to each? A divorce can cause all kinds of complications for friends, especially when each former spouse tries to convince friends that his or her former spouse is at fault for the marital breakup. (Beal, 1985, p. 2)*

In earlier periods of history social networks exerted much greater pressure than they do today. The power of "barriers" (Levinger, 1979a, 1979b)—family, friends, religion, community disapproval, and the couple's children—to divorce in contemporary society appear to be not nearly as strong as they used to be. We cannot ignore, however, the role that these social factors still play during the negotiation and evaluation processes, when partners are concerned with what to tell neighbors, friends, and relatives. These thoughts may not prevent the couple from eventually breaking up, but they do serve to slow down the process (Duck, 1982). The partners may take a lot of time and careful preparation in developing an explanation of the divorce for the public. The account needs to be "socially valid" at this stage, not merely "personally valid" (Duck, 1982).

The Closing Phase

By the time of the divorce, often the partners' fondness for each other has largely dissipated, at least on the part of one spouse. Faults become clearer; trust gives way to mistrust; anger and the wish for revenge replace nurturance and support (Weiss, 1975). Although some of the emotional work in dissolving the marriage has been completed, one final phase remains. It has to do with putting memories of the relationship to rest, putting it behind you, and going on with your life without this other person.

The goal of this stage is "to create an acceptable personal story for the course of the relationship, its beginning and its end and to tidy up the memories associated with it" (Duck, 1982, p. 25). The broken marriage probably is never totally erased from the partners' memories. But their thinking about it changes, and the relationship assumes a lower and lower priority in their thoughts over time (Harvey et al., 1982). The relationship matters less and less; feelings of caring and concern turn more and more to apathy.

Diane Vaughan (1985) points out that typically linkages between the partners persist despite the formal termination of the relationship. Mutual loved ones—the children, in-laws, grandparents, and so on—are the links between partners. For example, the husband has moved out but still visits with the children once a week. In the early years of the divorce they may still celebrate holidays with the whole family together. A divorced mother and father probably will participate in their daughter's wedding.

BREAKING THE LEGAL TIES

Traditional Divorce Law

Just as attitudes and behavior regarding divorce have changed dramatically in recent decades, so have divorce laws. The traditional divorce law in the United States was based on English and European laws, which required proof of a spouse's adultery, cruelty,

---

COMES THE DAWN

After awhile you learn the subtle difference
Between holding a hand and changing a soul,
And you learn that love doesn't mean leaning
And company doesn't mean security,
And you begin to learn that kisses aren't contracts
And presents aren't promises,
And you begin to accept your defeats
With your head up and your eyes open,
With the grace of a woman, not the grief of a
*   child,*
And learn to build all your roads
On today because tomorrow's ground
Is too uncertain for plans, and futures have
A way of falling down in mid-flight.
After awhile you learn that even sunshine
Burns if you get too much.
So you plant your own garden and decorate
Your own soul, instead of waiting
For someone to bring you flowers.
And you learn that you really can endure . . .
That you really are strong
And you really do have worth.
And you learn and learn . . .
With every goodbye you learn.

ANONYMOUS

---

or other wrongdoing. Divorce laws in the United States typically contained four major elements.

First, they perpetuated the gender-based division of roles and responsibilities found in traditional marriages. The wife was primarily responsible for child-care and homemaking services, and the husband's responsibility was economic support. The divorce law encouraged the continuation of these gender-based roles even after the divorce. The husband was to continue his economic role through alimony and child support, and the wife was to continue to care for the children (Weitzman and Dixon, 1983).

Second, traditional divorce law required grounds for divorce; one party had to prove that the other had committed a "marital offense." Typically only serious marital offenses, such as adultery, cruelty, or desertion, served as legal bases for divorce. Again these grounds were interpreted on the basis of gender-typed expectations of the traditional marriage. For example, when husbands were charged with cruelty, it was usually because they *physically harmed* their wives. Cruelty by wives consisted of *neglecting* their husbands, showing a lack of affection, belittling them, or ignoring domestic duties. Desertion, another common ground for divorce, was also gender based.

> *If a wife refused to live in the domicile chosen by her husband, she was held responsible for desertion in the divorce action. In addition, if the husband moved and she refused to accompany him, she was considered to have deserted him, because he had the legal right to choose the family home. (Weitzman and Dixon, 1983, p. 222)*

Third, spouses were antagonists, pitted against each other like enemies. The purpose of the court proceedings was to punish the guilty spouse. In fact, "If a spouse who was found guilty could prove that the other was also at fault, or that the other had colluded in or condoned his or her behavior, the divorce thus might not be granted in order to punish both parties" (Weitzman and Dixon, 1983, p. 223).

The fourth and final element of traditional divorce law involved the linking of the financial settlement of the divorce to the determination of fault. Important financial consequences stemmed from being found "guilty" or "innocent" (Weitzman, 1981). For example, the awarding of alimony was based on the wife's innocence; a wife guilty of adultery would not receive alimony. A husband guilty of adultery or cruelty, however, could be ordered to pay for his transgressions

with increased alimony. Alimony thus was used as a punishment against a "promiscuous" husband and as a reward for a "virtuous" wife (Weitzman, 1981).

In a similar way, property awards were linked to fault. More than half of the property was awarded to the "innocent" or "injured" party. Heated accusations and counteraccusations of wrongs were commonplace as each party attempted to obtain a better property settlement. In addition, a spouse who did not want a divorce—and if there were no grounds for a divorce—could use the property award as a lever in the negotiations. The other spouse, who very much desired the divorce, was forced to give up more property in order to obtain the divorce. Custody could also be influenced by the finding of fault. "A woman found guilty of adultery or cruelty might be deprived of her preference as the custodial parent—especially if her behavior indicated that she was an 'unfit' mother" (Weitzman and Dixon, 1983, p. 224).

No-Fault Divorce

Although the intentions of the traditional divorce law were noble in their aim for fairness and justice, there were problems with its adversarial nature. In 1970, California instituted the first no-fault divorce law in the Western world, and nearly all states have followed by permitting some form of no-fault divorce. This law completely abolished any requirement of proving one partner at fault to obtain a divorce. *One* party simply had to assert that "irreconcilable differences" existed.

No-fault divorce attempts to reduce the amount of bitterness, hostility, and trauma typical of fault-oriented divorces. In addition, the law seeks to eliminate the hypocrisy, perjury, and collusion that often existed in the courtroom practice under the "fault" system and to lessen the personal stigma attached to divorce. More reasonable and equitable settlements of property and spousal support were also goals. In short, the new laws changed all four elements of traditional divorce law by (1) eliminating the fault-based grounds for divorce; (2) attempting to eliminate the adversary process; (3) basing the financial aspects of divorce more on equity, equality, and economic need than on either fault or gender-based role assignments; and (4) redefining the traditional responsibilities of husbands and wives toward each other and toward their children by instituting a new norm of equality between the sexes.

Standards for child custody are also supposedly gender neutral under no-fault divorce law. Judges are supposed to award custody in the "best interests of the child." Also, both husbands and wives are considered responsible for child support under the new law. So, in essence, the new law has tried "to institutionalize sex-neutral obligations that fall equally upon the husband and wife" (Weitzman and Dixon, 1983, p. 228).

While the no-fault law attempts to make the divorce process more humane and more equitable in terms of property settlement, some weaknesses exist. No-fault divorce is based on a new norm of equality between the sexes, in particular, recognizing the growing ability of women to be self-supporting. "With a reformist zeal, they assumed that the employment gains of women already had eliminated the need for alimony as a means of continued support after divorce" (Weitzman and Dixon, 1983, p. 227). It was assumed that following a divorce a woman could be immediately self-supporting. Although a majority of married women do work, female workers still earn less than men, around 60 percent of what men earn. Thus the reality of the work world and the inadequacy of women's salaries are not consistent with the intent of the new divorce law.

The purpose of eliminating alimony was to encourage formerly dependent wives to assume responsibility for their own support. But it is difficult for women with the custody of young children and for older housewives to become self-supporting. "Clearly one of [the] greatest inequities in the current law is the almost punitive treatment of divorced wives after long-duration marriages. They, like widows, deserve survivors' benefits" (Weitzman, 1981, p. 152).

The new law has recognized, in theory at least, the need for *transitional support*. "Maintenance," a type of alimony, has been adopted by many states. Its function is to provide the dependent person with temporary compensation until he or she becomes self-supporting. Such compensation is typically limited to a couple of years at the most.

Thus, while the aims of the no-fault laws, i.e., equality and sex-neutrality, are laudable, the laws may be instituting equality in a society in which women are not fully prepared (and/or permitted) to assume equal responsibility for their own and their children's support after divorce. (Weitzman and Dixon, 1983, p. 229)

What seems to be needed is public policy that protects the transitional woman but still encourages a new equality (Weitzman and Dixon, 1983). Some states have adopted provisions that specify that the court, in determining temporary maintenance, should take into account the time necessary for a woman to acquire sufficient education or training to enable her to find appropriate employment. For example, a husband whose wife has supported him during his graduate education or professional training may be required to finance her education or training in order to place her in a position similar to his. More recently, the courts have decided to treat a person's professional license (as a medical doctor or psychologist, for example) as joint property from which the spouse must be compensated if there is a divorce.

One concern about no-fault laws is that they make divorce too easy and simple to obtain, which results in a very high divorce rate. Thus some people may believe that no-fault laws are responsible for the great increase in the divorce rate in the 1970s. In actuality the divorce rate has been rising gradually for more than a hundred years, and research suggests that the recent climb in the last two decades has relatively little to do with no-fault laws. Several explanations for the high divorce rate in the United States are examined in Box 14.2.

In sum, traditional divorce law and no-fault divorce define "justice" in two different ways. The traditional law sought to establish a moral justice that rewarded the good spouse and punished the bad spouse for *past behavior* in the marriage. By contrast, ignoring both moral character and moral history as a basis for awards, the no-fault law seeks to deliver a fairness and justice based on financial *needs* and upon equality of the two spouses (Weitzman and Dixon, 1983, p. 228).

Custody Options: Who Gets the Kids?

Divorcing parents today find themselves faced with a number of different options when deciding custody of the children. But such options were not always available. In preindustrial society, for example, fathers were granted sole custody regardless of the circumstances (Luepnitz, 1982; Ware, 1982; Weitzman, 1981). Women and children during this time were treated as property owned and controlled by men.

He [the father] had the primary right to his children's services and, in return, he was

liable for their support and maintenance. Child care was perceived primarily as child training, and fathers were presumed to have superior skills and knowledge (especially where boys were concerned) for this vocationally oriented relationship. (Weitzman, 1981, pp. 99–100)

With industrialization and the move from farm life to factories and offices in cities, mothers increasingly became involved in the full-time responsibility of child care and child rearing. Women were then viewed by lawmakers and judges as the persons who "naturally" should be responsible for their children (Weitzman, 1981). It was believed by the court that "nature had given women a unique attachment to children and that the baby would thus receive better care from its mother," according to Deborah Luepnitz (1982, p. 2).

In the twentieth century, up until the 1970s, the mother was almost invariably granted sole custody. The reasoning used was that the child in most cases had a unique emotional attachment to the mother. The father was given some visitation rights but was not encouraged to play a significant role in parenting. One court decision in 1942 specifically stated that the preference for the mother is "not open to question, and indeed *it is universally recognized that the mother is the natural custodian of her young. This view proceeds on the well known fact that there is no satisfactory substitute for a mother's love"* (Weitzman, 1981, p. 101).

This idea that a child's "best interests" are met by maternal custody has important social and emotional implications for mothers. Weitzman (1981) cites three consequences resulting from this maternal preference. First, custodial mothers are pressured to conform to the traditional and narrow legal ideal of a "good" or "fit" mother. In order for a divorced mother to be defined as "fit"

BOX 14.2

WHY DOES THE UNITED STATES HAVE SUCH A HIGH DIVORCE RATE?

The United States has the highest divorce rate in the world. Recently there has been a slight downward trend in divorce after a steady rise for two decades. The rate is still much higher, however, than in other countries.

Although couples of any age may seek divorces, the peak period of divorce is two to five years after the marriage (Spanier and Thompson, 1984). "Given the time required to make the decision to divorce, separate, file, and wait for a final decree, this peak period reflects evidence of serious marital problems very early in the relationship for most couples who eventually divorce" (Spanier and Thompson, 1984, p. 13).

The following factors help explain the high divorce rate in the United States: higher expectations, economic changes, attractive alternatives, and the declining stigma of divorce.

HIGHER EXPECTATIONS FOR MARITAL HAPPINESS

People now expect more from marriage and are less willing to stay in an unhappy marriage than in the first two-thirds of the twentieth century (Thornton and Freedman, 1983). Years ago people seemed to be satisfied with an intact marriage, but today they expect it to provide intimacy, excitement, and sexual pleasure.

> We can predict a higher divorce rate when the criteria of success in marriage change from family integrity, security, and contentment to happiness in which people are to grasp opportunity and feel vital; when compromise is judged to be a sign of inadequacy; when "doing your own thing" and "getting yours" are legitimized, so that relationships are continued only as long as they gratify one's own needs. (Bardwick, 1979, p. 120)

In fact, social scientists in the past focused on studying "marital satisfaction" or "marital stability." Today's researchers look at "marital happiness." Thus, it is no longer expected that spouses simply be satisfied with a marriage; one must be happy. The rising expectation for happiness in marriage makes it difficult to justify staying in an unsatisfactory marriage (Weitzman, 1981).

Not only is happiness a goal, but Judith Bardwick contends that the modern American definition of happiness is totally unrealistic, based on childish dreams and fantasies. When these dreams and fantasies are unachievable, frustration abounds. When personal growth or happiness is not attained in a marriage, the person often looks elsewhere, either in living the single life or in seeking another partner, who one hopes is more compatible.

The goal of personal happiness is also reflected in the shift away from "staying together for the sake of the children." This shift is illustrated by a study in which 82 percent of women interviewed in 1980 disagreed with

(Continued)

the statement: "When there are children in the family, parents should stay together even if they don't get along." Only 51 percent of these same women disagreed with this statement in 1962 (Thornton and Freedman, 1983, p. 37).

ECONOMIC CHANGES

Women's new economic options have had a tremendous impact on the divorce rate. Since more women work outside the home and are capable of supporting themselves, divorce becomes a more viable alternative to an unhappy marriage. Until relatively recently, marriage was essential for economic security; few economic options were available to divorced women. In addition, married couples in the past had a larger number of children over a greater number of years, which required women to spend more time in the home.

Not only does a woman's employment affect her perception of the economic viability of divorce, but it also changes the husband's perceptions. Unhappy with his marriage, the husband may feel more reassured to take the divorce option if his wife has gainful employment. "Liberalized divorce laws and employed wives have given husbands new opportunities to leave marriage without having to bear a heavy financial burden" (Weitzman, 1981, p. 150).

ATTRACTIVE LIFE-STYLE ALTERNATIVES

Another trend that has contributed to the rising divorce rate has been the increase in various attractive alternatives to marriage. The large number of currently divorced people serve as models for those who are still married. Successful, divorced, middle-aged women can be models for other middle-aged women who may feel stuck in unhappy relationships. A woman resigned to an empty-shell marriage may look with envy at a divorced friend who has an active social life and seems happy with her newly acquired independence.

The possibility of remarriage is also a realistic alternative for those considering divorce, especially for men and for younger people. The vast majority of divorced people do remarry. But remaining single is becoming an increasingly popular and respectable option. "More people are currently remaining in their after-divorce single status for longer periods of time, and a growing percentage of never-married young adults have chosen to maintain their single life-style" (Weitzman, 1981, pp. 147–148).

THE DECLINING STIGMA OF DIVORCE

In general "Negative attitudes toward divorce have been declining as Americans have become more willing to see it as a solution in specific cases" (Thornton and Freedman, 1983, p. 9). The decline of the social stigma of divorce is one of the most striking changes in the social climate surrounding divorce (Weitzman, 1981). Today's acceptance of divorce stands in sharp contrast to the turn of the century, when people who had been divorced were excluded from any social circles, and most divorced people lost respectability to some extent (Goode cited in Weitzman, 1981, p. 146).

In a study by Weitzman (1981), only 26 percent of recently divorced men and 31 percent of the divorced women reported that they felt there was any stigma attached to divorce. In addition, a third of both sexes reported "receiving more favorable treatment or having someone perceive them as more interesting, sophisticated or desirable because they were divorced" (p. 146). Other studies have revealed a similar ascribing of a positive value to divorce. Divorce is "being redefined as a period of personal growth, and divorced people are more likely to be seen as interesting, coping people who are taking control of their own lives" (p. 146).

---

by the court, she needs to devote herself almost entirely to her children. Those mothers who spend a lot of time and energy on careers or who begin dating or living with a new man could be perceived by the legal system as "unfit" and could have their children taken away.

Second, since the maternal preference reinforces the traditional roles of housewife and mother, the woman's dependence on her ex-husband, or on welfare, is therefore increased. It also becomes difficult for such full-time mothers to earn money or to improve their income potential. Thus, a divorced mother may experience a double bind. If she works full time to support her children, she may run the risk of "neglecting" them. But if she becomes a full-time caregiver—and remains at home to devote herself exclusively to child care and homemaking, she thereby isolates herself socially and remains financially dependent on her former husband or on welfare funds. "Thus, the legal system seems to put custodial mothers in the position of having to choose between losing their children and losing their major opportunities to build a new economic and social life" (Weitzman, 1981, p. 118).

Finally, the maternal preference may cause the woman who does not really want custody to feel guilty and deviant. It is simply assumed that all mothers want custody of their children. Hence, there is strong pressure to take on this role even though the mother may not want to. If the woman is brave enough to admit she does not want custody, she is viewed with suspicion by the legal system as well as by society (Weitzman, 1981).

The law's assumption that women can and should bear the full-time responsibility for child care is not in line with the current social situation. In contemporary society there has been a dramatic drop in full-time motherhood, even among mothers of very young children (Weitzman, 1981).

Those fathers who have wanted custody of their children have had to prove the mother "unfit." This necessity has resulted in detrimental consequences for everyone involved. It emphasizes the adversarial nature of the divorce process once again, and it discourages any working relationship between the parents regarding their children after the divorce. "The labeling of one parent as unfit or bad may also create serious conflicts for the child (and may be traumatic for at least one of the adults as well)" (Weitzman, 1981, p. 111).

The courts are now beginning to recognize that there are fathers who are sincerely

BOX 14.3

HOW COURTS DECIDE CUSTODY DISPUTES

One of the most difficult decisions to make in divorce cases is which parent should have custody of the children. No magical formula exists to determine who would be the better custodial parent.

Circuit court judges are required by law to consider 11 factors in determining the custody of children in divorce. These factors vary among states; the ones listed below are for the state of Michigan.

1. The love, affection and other emotional ties between the children and the parties involved. . . .

2. The length of time the child has lived in a stable, satisfactory environment, and the desirability of maintaining continuity. Attorneys will frequently advise divorce clients to stay in the house if they want custody of the children. If there has been a separation, who currently has temporary custody?

3. The capacity and disposition of the parents to give the child love, affection, and guidance, and the continuation of educating and raising of the child in a religion or creed, if any.

4. The capacity and disposition of the parties to provide the child with food, clothing, medical care, and other material needs. In one-income households, fathers frequently are better able to provide for the financial needs of their offspring. As more women enter the job market, this male edge is giving way.

5. The permanence, as a family unit, of the existing or proposed custodial home. Will the children be moved in and out of schools, change neighborhoods, and be forced to lose friends and make new ones?

6. The moral fitness of the parties. Who triggered the break-up of the marriage? Was there a third party involved? Fault is not considered by the courts in granting divorces, but it is a factor in child custody.

7. The mental and physical health of the parties. Physical handicaps or illnesses, which might hinder a parent's ability to do a good job with his or her children, are a consideration. If one parent is an alcoholic, that would be a factor.

8. The home, school, and community record of the child. How well is the child doing at home and in school? Are grades up to abilities? Does the child relate well to others his or her age?

9. The preferences of the child, if the court finds the child old enough to express a preference. Beginning at about age seven or eight, judges rely heavily on the child's stated preferences.

10. The willingness and ability of each parent to facilitate and encourage a close and continuing relationship between the child and the other

parent. Are the parents talking to (not screaming at) each other? Do they question the children about what the other party is doing? Do they make negative statements about the other parent to the child? Does the custodial parent attempt to unfairly block visitation?

11. Any other factor the court considers relevant to a particular custody dispute. This can include a close-knit extended family relationship which includes grandparents, aunts and uncles, or the results of psychological evaluations. (*Detroit Free Press,* 1984, p. 4F)

Recently researchers have designed a test measuring attachment between parent and child, which is used to help resolve custody disputes. A set of 50 questions is presented to the child as a kind of guessing game. The questions measure four aspects of attachment: responsiveness, confidence, security, and hostility. Test questions include the following: "Guess who likes to make up games for you? If you fell down and got hurt, guess who would pick you up? Guess who would still like you a whole lot even if you fight with them? When you do something wrong, guess who would yell at you?"

It has been found that "In most cases, the test shows that a youngster is attached to both mother and father, but that the attachment is stronger to one than to the other" (Roll, 1983, p. 7). Additional information from tests and interviews is used to supplement the attachment test. So far the use of this test has enhanced recommendations to the court in custodial disputes. Roll (1983) concludes that it is not crucial that this specific test be used but that the courts be made aware of the importance of attachment in making custody decisions.

interested in their children's welfare and that a number of factors need to be considered in custody decisions. (See Box 14.3.) The new emphasis is on the parent-child relationship, assuming that the parent could be a father and *not* only the mother. The result is that there are a number of custody options available to divorced parents today.

SOLE CUSTODY TODAY. Sole custody is still the most common type of custody arrangement. The children live primarily with one parent but spend some time with the other parent, as specified in the divorce decree. All legal and final decisions regarding the children's welfare are the responsibility of the custodial parent. In many cases, however, both parents participate in major decisions such as education, religious training, medical care, and vacations (Gardner, 1980).

Most states have now rejected the assumption, at least in theory, that young children are better off living with their mothers as a hard and fast rule, and many more fathers now seek custody of their children. "If the question of custody is disputed, a mother now must prove that she is in fact the principal nurturing parent, or that, for some other reason, the children would best be served by being placed in her custody" (Friedman, 1984, p. 27). So the parent pursuing sole custody must prove that he or she is the more "fit" parent. Still today, however, women obtain sole custody in about 90 percent of the cases that are contested, mostly because of tradition and custom.

In trying to determine the advantages and disadvantages of sole custody, compared to other custody arrangements, a sample of 16 custodial mothers, 16 custodial fathers, 18 parents with joint custody, and 91 children was interviewed (Luepnitz, 1982). How satisfied are parents with the sole custody arrangements? Of the mothers and fathers who were custodial parents, all said they were happy with the arrangement; none was interested in changing the existing situation. Unfortunately Luepnitz didn't interview the noncustodial parents, who might have expressed a different view.

Approximately one-third of the mothers with custody felt that having custody of their children helped them emotionally pull through their divorce. Almost all the mothers indicated that being a single mother meant less conflict than existed in their marriages and that the children were growing up removed from extensive turmoil. Other common responses from custodial mothers included these: "It is personally satisfying to raise them," "With me I know they're in good hands," and "They are good company for me" (Luepnitz, 1982, p. 29). Most of the advantages listed by fathers were similar to those stated by mothers. The only different response was that fathers indicated it was cheaper to raise children in one's own house than to pay the ex-spouse to take care of them.

Regarding the disadvantages of sole custody, 80 percent of both mothers and fathers reported that there were times when single parenting was overwhelming. Such items as exhaustion, worry, and limitations on freedom were commonly mentioned. As one mother complained,

It is lonely being a single parent. It is a heavy responsibility. I used to want to run away right after the divorce; the kids were driving me nuts. I couldn't have a private life. I had to work nights because of them. All I wanted was some time off, yet I felt guilty about sending my son to stay with his father for the summer. (Luepnitz, 1982, p. 30)

The sole-custody fathers stressed the difficulty of carrying on an active social life while raising children alone.

The main disadvantage of having custody is not being able to come and go as you please. Sometimes I would just like to go to a movie at the last minute, or go to join someone for a drink, but with a baby to take care of, it's impossible. It seems like every thing I do socially has to be planned at least a week in advance. (Luepnitz, 1982, p. 31)

In general, the children in the sample were satisfied with their custodial placements. Only 4 of the 91 children expressed a definite wish to change the custodial arrangement, and 19 (21 percent) said they "sometimes wished" they lived with the other parent. The reason given for this wish was not based on a desire to leave one parent but on a desire to be with the other parent also. Simply put, they missed the noncustodial parent.

In terms of visitations, the majority of the children visited their noncustodial parents only occasionally or less. "Noncustodial mothers are much less likely to give up all contact with their children than are noncustodial fathers" (Luepnitz, 1982, p. 34). Primarily two reasons appear to explain the lack of visits by the noncustodial father. "In half of the cases where the noncustodial father visits rarely or never, it is because the children dislike him and have decided not to see him. But in many other cases, custodial mothers reported that their ex-spouse had 'split the

In cases of sole custody, the majority of children visit their noncustodial parents only occasionally or less.

scene' in order to evade support payments" (p. 34). Luepnitz found that 38 percent of the noncustodial fathers who visited rarely or less paid nothing to their ex-wives, whereas *no* father who visited frequently paid nothing. In cases where noncustodial mothers rarely visited, it was usually because they lost interest in the children or the mothers had left town.

Although the noncustodial parents were not interviewed, it's possible that some of them were discouraged from visiting their children by their ex-spouses. Most counselors who work with divorced families are familiar with the many ways in which custodial parents can undermine visitations for the purpose of punishing the other parent.

About half of the children desired more visitation, and half desired the same amount or less. Some of those desiring less felt that the noncustodial parent was placing them in the middle of the parents' differences. These children were often asked questions about the personal life of the custodial parent.

Recent research by Judith Wallerstein and Joan Kelly (1980) found that an important factor in the successful outcome for children of divorce was a stable, close relationship with both the custodial parent and the noncustodial parent. In cases in which the noncustodial parent was irregular in visiting or totally absent, the child felt rejected or rebuffed in addition to having lower self-esteem. They found that "the unvisited or poorly visited child was likely to feel unloved and unlovable" (p. 281).

JOINT CUSTODY. Joint custody is known by a number of different names: joint parenting, co-custody, or shared custody. When joint custody is awarded, *both* parents share legal custody and often physical custody. Joint physical custody can mean that "The children spend approximately equal amounts of time with each parent; tasks related to child rearing are divided between both parents in a way that makes sense to them; and major decisions are made jointly concerning the health and well-being of the children" (Galper, 1980, p. 16). Joint physical custody does not, however, require a strict sharing of the child's time on a 50-50 basis. Actually such joint arrangements can come in various forms—children splitting every week exactly between the two parents, children alternating weeks between the parents, children alternating school semesters between parents, and children alternating holidays.

Joint custody was rarely an option before 1970. But the majority of states have now enacted legislation allowing some form of joint parenting. "Eight states have actual laws declaring joint custody to be the best alternative in every case where both parents are seen to be fit" (Francke, 1983, p. 264).

What impact does joint custody have on

children? A common criticism of joint custody is that it deprives children of a sense of
security and stability; it is said that "the children need one home, one custodian." But
stability need not be limited in meaning to
only one primary parent and one primary
home. "Stability can also mean a relationship
of constancy and permanence with two parents in two separate homes" (Galper, 1980,
p. 71). There is a sense of stability when children continue to have a positive relationship
with both parents and are not pressured into
situations in which they are forced to express
loyalty to one parent over another (Galper,
1980). "Living at two residences allows a
child whose parents have separated to relate
to each of his parents continually and to
know each of them intimately" (p. 76). Thus
in shared custody there is a greater opportunity to maintain close emotional ties with
both parents, whereas sole custody is more
likely to break any tie that had existed with
the noncustodial parent (Galper, 1980).

Nearly all of the joint-custody children
(n=25) in Luepnitz's study were satisfied
with this arrangement. When asked how they
felt about living in two houses, only two children in the study could identify something in
their living arrangement that was confusing.
In her interviews with children, Miriam Galper (1980) found some confusion in the first
few months of establishing a shared parenting
system, but it subsided fairly quickly. A majority of these children described their arrangement as "more fun," "more interesting," or "more comfortable" than did sole-
custody children.

*The children themselves talk about how
much they value their relationships with
both parents and they understand that they
have something special in those relationships. . . .*

*Rebecca told me, "Being with you half
the time and Dad half the time makes me
feel more grateful for both of you." (p. 88)*

In fact, some children reported that they see
more of their parents, especially their fathers,
than they did before the separation took
place. They are also very much aware of the
fact that they spend more time with their
fathers than their friends do who live in intact
families (Galper, 1980).

A couple of major disadvantages do exist
with joint-custody arrangements. First, there
are logistical problems of moving children
back and forth between households. A typical
problem is not having all the necessary items,
such as clothes and toys, at both houses. Another disadvantage is that the divorced parents remain somewhat tied to each other, often owing to the necessity of living in the
same area or school district. Obviously, it is
more difficult for co-parenting to work well
if the two parents live in distant cities.

SPLIT CUSTODY. Split custody involves dividing a multiple number of children between
the two parents. One or more of the children
is awarded to one parent and the remaining
children (or child) to the other parent. "Splitting the children is usually done only when
the children clearly prefer it" (Friedman,
1984, p. 29). Of course, keeping siblings together can provide continuity and stability for
the children themselves when parents have
separated. Unfortunately this sibling continuity is sometimes sacrificed as a negotiated
compromise, or it is done simply as a parental
convenience (Friedman, 1984). "Working on
the principle that 'half a loaf is better than
none,' some parents give serious consideration to this form of custody so that they will
not be deprived completely of living with the
children" (Gardner, 1980, p. 299).

While most professionals may discourage this type of arrangement, it may be advisable in certain cases. In particular, there are some parents who may be so rejecting of or hostile toward a particular child that it is better to have that child live with the other parent. For example, a son may remind the mother of the rejecting husband, and it may work out better for her to have custody of the daughters while the father takes the son.

To conclude our discussion of custody options, it is apparent that the same type of arrangement may not be appropriate for everyone. Among some of the things to be considered when deciding custody are the ages of the children, the needs and desires of the children, their rapport with each parent, the desire of each parent to be a custodial parent, and the amount of cooperation between the parents.

CONSEQUENCES OF DIVORCE

The divorce experience will never be exactly the same for any two persons, even though certain responses seem to be typical for many individuals. Differences in type of reactions, as well as their intensity and duration, depend on such factors as the amount of forewarning of the divorce, the length of time married, the economic situation of each of the individuals, new love relationships, each partner's support network of friends, the quality of the postmarital relationship between the partners, and personal factors (Weiss, 1975).

Loneliness

For some separated and divorced people, loneliness is nothing new; they were lonely even when they were married (Weiss, 1979).

But for the majority of men and women, divorce brings a loneliness that was unknown to them during marriage. Wallerstein and Kelly's study of divorced adults and children revealed that two-fifths of the men and two-thirds of the women described themselves as lonely, about half of them painfully so. Spanier and Thompson (1984) found that very few individuals in their sample escaped feelings of loneliness since their separations. Their loneliness was reflected in such statements as "I just have this overwhelming lack of a sense of belonging," "I really dread being alone," "There's no one to share things with, no one to talk to" (p. 107).

For those who had not remarried, their social lives were often described as "difficult and largely ungratifying" (Wallerstein and Kelly, 1980). What typically occurs is that immediately following the divorce, married friends are supportive and spend considerable time with the recently divorced. These contacts, however, rapidly decline, and the divorced person is on his or her own to build new friendships (Hetherington, Cox, and Cox, 1977).

Women, in particular, feel frustrated with their social lives because the social norms hinder women from initiating social engagements with men and also because of the shortage of available men. Men typically date more frequently than women. The small number of men who do not date at all are either still closely attached to their predivorce family or suffer from severe depression, which hinders their venturing out (Wallerstein and Kelly, 1980).

Although social activities involving other adults were fairly common, a central complaint was the absence of a meaningful relationship that had some continuity. The men and women who were dating, but not yet in a steady relationship, expressed "a weariness

Few individuals escape feelings of loneliness and loss during a divorce.

with the superficiality of the social scene and the succession of individuals who had passed through their lives'' (Wallerstein and Kelly, 1980, p. 156). Most of the female respondents in Wallerstein and Kelly's study were disillusioned by the ''singles scene'' and were longing for a continuous close relationship, ''someone with whom they could talk, share, and be affectionate on a daily basis.'' Apparently, their emotional loneliness could not be remedied until they found a new significant or intimate other.

The presence of children for most divorced individuals does not seem to totally abate the parent's loneliness, even though it may help somewhat. His or her desire is for an adult person to share things with on an equal level. Children, in fact, may sometimes be blamed for their parents' loneliness; the custodial spouse may not feel free to come and go as he or she pleases or to pursue an active social life with the hope of replacing the ex-partner. In fact, one study labeled women who are single parents as the ''true isolates'' because their lives are more severely restricted in terms of opportunities for much social contact with friends (Institute for Social Research Newsletter, 1984). Single adults who live alone tend to establish many more contacts outside the household than do people who live with others. The researchers concluded that the isolation of single parents has ''detrimental consequences'' and that ''these women reveal significantly negative feelings about their life circumstances'' (Institute for Social Research Newsletter, 1984, p. 4).

Economic Stress

Financial problems often exist when there is a divorce. Economic stress occurs for the divorced family because they must maintain two households instead of one. Financial constraints typically become apparent, and a change in life-style may be inevitable.

Divorced women, in particular, often must face financial problems. Since the divorced mother is usually awarded child custody, the ultimate financial burden of the children may fall on her shoulders. Fathers are supposed to contribute child support, but many do not or only pay a portion of it. Baruch, Barnett, and Rivers (1983) found finances to be the single greatest worry of the divorced women in their study. Ironically, many men end up with improved income situations (Weitzman, 1985).

Weitzman's analysis of the no-fault divorce law revealed some startling statistics on the economic consequences of divorce. "When income is compared to needs, divorced men experience an average 42 percent rise in their standard of living in the first year after the divorce, while divorced women (and the children) experience a 73 percent decline" (1985, p. 323). Those who suffer the most economically after divorce are older and longer-married women. After comparing the incomes of men and women who stayed in intact families with the income of divorced men and women, Weitzman concluded *"divorce is a financial catastrophy for most women"* (p. 339). The "feminization of poverty," a phrase coined by Diana Pearce, is one consequence of divorce. The National Advisory Council on Economic Opportunity has declared the feminization of poverty as "one of the most compelling social facts of the decade" (quoted in Weitzman, 1985, p. 350).

Why is divorce so economically devastating for women and not for men? Weitzman offers the following explanations. First, the courts' awards to wives are often inadequate in that they do not take into account women's lower earnings in society and do not honor and reward women's work in the home and their contributions to their husbands and children. Second, there are expanded demands on the wife's resources after divorce. Since women are usually caring for the children after divorce, they need extra support. Third, the husband often has greater earning capacity and the ability to supplement his income. The demands on his income are fewer; he often lives alone, and he is no longer totally responsible for the financial support of his ex-wife and children (Weitzman, 1985).

According to Weitzman (1985), the current legal system can be "refashioned" so that the positive aspects of the no-fault reforms can be retained, but its present economic consequences be altered. She recommends (1) more financial support for children and more effective means of securing the support they are awarded; (2) an equal sharing of all a husband's career assets for long-married older wives; (3) full support for younger mothers with the care of the children so that they are not forced to work; and (4) support for wives in the early years of divorce to maximize their long-range employment prospects.

Of course, not all divorced women are financially desperate. Little anxiety about finances exists among those divorced women in high-prestige jobs; they can command very good salaries. When these well-paid women discuss financial problems, they often talk about "belt-tightening but rarely about survival" (Baruch, Barnett, and Rivers, 1983).

These women are able to escape one of the most serious and distressing effects of the end of a marriage.

Self-Esteem

Despite the distress and disturbing feelings and economic stress associated with divorce, such an experience can ultimately have a potentially positive impact on a person's well-being. Once individuals have dealt with the stress of the divorce process, "They are likely to find their lives after divorce better and more satisfying than they anticipated" (Weitzman, 1985, p. 345). Based on findings from her research, Weitzman (1985) reports,

> Most divorced women along with most divorced men report a rise in competence and self-esteem at some time during the first year after divorce. The majority of respondents (83 percent of both sexes) reported they were now functioning better than during the marriage. They also felt better about themselves (82 percent of the men, 88 percent of the women) and considered themselves more competent in their work (47 percent of the men, 68 percent of the women), more physically attractive (45 percent of the men, 50 percent of the women), and possessed of better parenting skills (48 percent of the men, 62 percent of the women with minor children). (pp. 345–346)

For individuals who were caught in empty-shell marriages or in relationships with extensive negative exchange, divorce itself may be viewed as a positive step. The result of divorce, that is, no longer living in a bad marriage, is what is considered to be positive.

Despite the economic hardship and unfair divorce settlements, longer-married older housewives state that they are "personally" better off than they were during the marriage (Weitzman, 1985). "They are proud of the skills they used to deal with the crisis to marshal a support network, to manage their finances, and to take control of their lives. They also report improved self-esteem, more pride in their appearance, and greater competence in all aspects of their lives" (Weitzman, 1985, p. 346).

Baruch, Barnett, and Rivers (1983) found that many of the women they interviewed also experienced "a strong sense of personal growth and competence after the divorce." These women spoke of having "grown up, of having become a whole person, of taking charge of their own destinies at last" (p. 168). For many, marriage had been a source of anxiety, tension, and reduced self-esteem. "Their ex-husbands had brought out the worst in them" (p. 168). They experienced a process of grieving that immediately followed the breakup of the marriage, but they emerged from this difficult process as stronger and more confident persons (Baruch, Barnett, and Rivers, 1983). Wallerstein and Kelly (1980) also found that divorce served a useful purpose for women in particular. "More than half of the women arrived at better solutions for living their lives, and half of this group had undergone striking and significant positive changes that appeared to have lifelong implications" (p. 193).

Unlike the women, however, men were less likely to utilize the divorce experience to bring about positive change in their lives. In part this could be because fewer men actually sought the divorce initially. The men's "manner of addressing life and relationships was similar to what it had been before the divorce" (Wallerstein and Kelly, 1980, p. 194). The divorce did not change their lives to become "appreciably more productive and gratifying" (Wallerstein and Kelly, 1980).

Children of Divorce

Like adults, children also feel a sense of loss when there is a divorce in their family. Because of their age, their stage of development, and their lack of power, children experience divorce in ways quite different from the ways adults experience it. To understand fully the impact of this stressful event on children, we need to look at how they perceive and think about the world at different stages of development. In addition, we need to keep in mind that divorce involves a series of events, not merely a single event, such as a parent moving out of the house. The child may have to cope with visits from a noncustodial parent, a mother going to work, being placed in a child-care facility, moving to a new residence, or going to a new school. The stresses and strains of divorce and living in a stepfamily can be seen in children's drawings (see Box 14.4).

It is not uncommon for the child to "lose" both parents at the time of a divorce. One parent is typically physically absent, and the other is often not functioning very well emotionally; he or she is unable to be supportive to the child. Thus many children face the tensions and sadness of divorce with little help from their depressed parents or from anyone else. During the critical months following a separation, parental care is often least when it is needed the most. It is not because the parents are necessarily less loving

It is not uncommon for children to lose both parents at the time of divorce—one is absent physically and the other is unsupportive emotionally.

BOX 14.4

DIVORCE AS SEEN THROUGH CHILDREN'S DRAWINGS

Family therapists and counselors sometimes use drawings by children as vehicles to tap children's feelings about their families. Feelings about a divorce and/or remarriage of parents are depicted in the following drawings. The children who made these particular drawings were instructed to draw each family member doing something.

Drawing #1. This is a drawing by a 7-year-old girl whose parents are in the middle of divorce proceedings. Notice how she depicts the stress and strain of the divorce procedure by the scribbling between the two parents. The drawing seems somewhat depressive, even the sun is blacked out and no one is smiling (Burns and Kaufman, 1970).

Drawing #2. This was drawn by a 14-year-old boy with a recently acquired stepfather and two stepsisters. The drawing depicts the forces between the two families. The boy attempts to protect the mother from the intruding father, and the competitiveness between the boy and stepfather is clearly shown. The boy may be feeling somewhat powerless in the situation as the stepfather shields himself from the boy's darts (Burns and Kaufman, 1970).

Drawing #3. This drawing was by an 11-year-old boy whose parents had divorced and whose mother had recently remarried. Notice how he compartmentalizes the family members by drawing lines between people. The boy lives with his mother but would like to move in with his father. He positions himself between his parents, symbolizing this conflict (taken from the authors' files).

or less concerned with their children during a divorce, but because of the dramatic changes in their own lives, they tend to focus their attention on their own troubles (Wallerstein and Kelly, 1980). Whatever the reasons, many parents deny or dismiss the feelings of their children.

Most children want their parents' marriage to continue, no matter how bad it is in the parents' view. An intact home apparently is viewed by children as preferable to a happy single parent or remarried family. This preference is interesting in light of the popular professional opinion that an empty-shell or damaging intact marriage is less healthy for children than a successful divorce.

Recent research on children of divorce has revealed some common reactions. One well-known study conducted by Wallerstein and Kelly (1980) followed 60 divorcing families and their 131 children during the first five years of divorced life. They found that children's reactions varied according to their ages.

REGRESSION AND FEAR OF ABANDONMENT.
Among very young children (preschool age), regression is a common reaction at the time of divorce. Usually for a short time, a few weeks or a few months at most, these children return to their security blankets, recently outgrown toys, whining and crying, eating with their fingers, wetting their beds, and experiencing difficulty in separating from the custodial parent. The child is seeking reassurance and security in much the same form it was provided when he or she was at a younger age (Wallerstein and Kelly, 1980).

Fear of abandonment is another reaction prevalent among younger children. If the divorced spouse experiences feelings of rejection and separation distress, it is not surprising that the child has these feelings also, and

to a greater degree. Also, the child who has already lost one parent becomes fearful of losing the other and being left alone. After their parents have split up, some children refuse to let the custodial parent leave on routine errands, or depart for work, without considerable fuss, whimpering, or crying (Wallerstein and Kelly, 1980).

SELF-BLAME AND GUILT.
Ironically, some young children—preschool and young school-age—assume primary responsibility for the divorce. The child thinks, "Daddy left because I was too noisy" or "He left because I hit my baby sister." These self-accusations are particularly common when no other explanation for the divorce is provided to the youngster.

Feeling responsible for the divorce, many of these children fantasize about how they can bring their parents back together. They think, "If I caused my parents to separate, I can and must get them back together." Some children hold firmly to the fantasy of reconciliation even after the remarriage of one or both parents. The parents may also contribute to this fantasy. Especially when parents are not emotionally divorced or are vascillating between being married and being unmarried, their state provides the child with some hope of their coming back together.

Ridden with guilt, some of these children may behave like a "too-good child." The only way they think they can make things turn out all right is by being relentlessly good. They will attempt to be on their best behavior at all times. Parents and teachers will remark what a "mature" child he or she is, how quiet he or she is, and how well-behaved. Unfortunately, adults often do not see below the surface of this good behavior and how the guilt is gnawing away at the child's self-worth and self-confidence.

ANGER.   Children are often angry at their parents for getting a divorce. While younger children may feel some anger, older children feel it more strongly and they more clearly direct their anger at a particular person. In general, the children are angry at the parent whom they blame for the divorce (Wallerstein and Kelly, 1980).

Some children are outraged that the parent who had been correcting their behavior is behaving in what they consider to be an immoral and irresponsible fashion. Although aware of the serious considerations behind their parents' decision to divorce, many of the teenagers in Wallerstein and Kelly's study "were still angry at their parents and considered them selfish and insensitive for seeking divorce at this time" (1980, p. 87).

The child may keep the anger hidden and become unusually quiet and withdrawn. Or he or she may express the anger in an overtly hostile way. Sometimes it can be handled in both ways depending on the situation. For example, a child may act out his or her anger in school, but when visiting the father, he or she is the "perfect kid." The child may be fearful of expressing hostility toward the father and may look for a safer person with whom it can be expressed. Boys, compared to girls, are more likely to express their anger through outward, obnoxious behavior.

GRIEF AND DEPRESSION.   At any age, signs of grief and depression can appear in children as a result of a divorce. The reaction is similar to losing a loved one through death. In reality, it is emotionally healthy for a child to go through a mourning process, involving the release of feelings of sadness that should not be inhibited by the parents. Wallerstein and Kelly (1980) observed children's pervasive sadness, especially among the 6- to 8-year-olds. "Crying and sobbing were not uncom-mon, especially among the boys, and many children were on the brink of tears as they spoke with us" (p. 66). The impact of the separation was so strong that the children had difficulty coping under the stress. The younger ones did not express quite as much grief; they were still holding to the fantasy that their parents would be reunited.

Adolescents also go through a mourning process. "They reported feelings of emptiness, tearfulness, difficulty in concentrating, chronic fatigue, and very troublesome dreams, all symptoms of mourning" (Wallerstein and Kelly, 1980, p. 86). Teenagers mourn the loss of the family known to them in their childhood. Recent research indicated that the divorce of parents can be traumatic even for college students (Hagestad et al., cited in *Marriage and Divorce Today*, 1984). (See Box 14.5.)

RECOVERING FROM THEIR PARENTS' DI-VORCE.   How do children function a year or two after their parents' divorce? In following their sample, Wallerstein and Kelly found that most of the children and adolescents had changed for the better 18 months after the divorce. Thus for the majority of children the emotional response to the stress of divorce was short-lived. A significant minority, however, appeared to be under just as much stress, or even more stress, than previously.

The most common problems for this minority were depression as well as feelings of helplessness and hopelessness. Feelings and behavior included "pervasive sadness, poor self-esteem, school performance well below potential, difficulty in concentrating, preoccupation with the parental divorce, play inhibition, social withdrawal, self-blame for the divorce, some petty stealing, compulsive overeating to the point of obesity, chronic irritability, and sexual promiscuity" (Wallerstein and Kelly, 1980, p. 170). There was an obvious need for professional counseling (Wallerstein and Kelly, 1980). Probably the key factor accounting for the differences between children who were coping well and those who weren't was "a profound sense of rejection by one or both parents" (p. 171).

The researchers were surprised to find a higher incidence of intense loneliness at the five-year follow-up than at the 18-month mark.

> *These children complained of coming home to empty houses after school to await the return of the working parent. On weekends, these youngsters often felt ignored because of the social life of both divorced parents. Several also complained of loneliness following the remarriage, while recognizing ruefully that the newly-married adults wanted privacy and time away from curious children. (Wallerstein and Kelly, 1980, p. 212)*

One recent study of children of divorce by Glynnis Walker attempted to ascertain the feelings of adult children about their parents' divorce through an extensive questionnaire. Most of the respondents' parents had been divorced for at least several years. The researcher discovered that children are quite resilient, are not "emotionally scarred" by divorce, and often cope with divorce much better than the adults around them (G. Walker, 1986). In the majority of the respondents, "negative feelings such as rejection and abandonment were replaced over time with feelings such as contentment, satisfaction, and relief" (G. Walker, 1986, p. 136). Seventy-six percent of the respondents said they would not have preferred that their parents had stayed together.

In general, the major complaint of Walker's respondents was the way in which their parents handled, or mishandled, the divorce,

not the fact that the divorce occurred. If parents can better carry out the job of obtaining a divorce, according to Walker, children will not experience as many adversive feelings. (See Box 14.6.)

REMARRIAGE AND THE STEPFAMILY

Of those individuals who divorce, about 75 percent remarry. In fact, almost half (45 percent) of the marriages registered each year are remarriages, for at least one spouse (*Monthly Vital Statistics*, February 29, 1984). To put it another way, one in five existing households maintained by married couples involves a remarriage. About one-half of all divorced men and women remarry within three years of the dates of their divorces. Divorce today is considered to be a "transitional" process rather than a "terminal" event in most people's lives (Furstenberg and Spanier, 1984). Second marriages provide individuals with another chance to find intimacy.

Remarriage is not new. It was fairly common in the early history of the United States because high mortality rates ended many marriages prematurely (Furstenberg and Spanier, 1984). Remarriage is occurring less and less frequently as a result of death today; in 1974 the number of divorces in a given year exceeded the number of deaths of married persons for the first time (Glick, 1980). In addition, divorce takes place at an earlier point in the life cycle, compared to death. The typical divorced woman today is in her late 20s (Furstenberg and Spanier, 1984). The earlier age of divorce, compared to marriages ended by the death of one partner, allows more time for individuals to remarry.

Are marriages the second time around more stable than first marriages? According

BOX 14.5

ADULTS ARE HURT BY PARENTS' DIVORCE, TOO

Too often in the past we have looked at divorce as having a detrimental impact on young children, ignoring the effects it has on adult children, also. But researchers are currently finding that the impact of parental divorce on children away at college or those leading independent lives is much greater than was previously thought.

Common reactions include anger, mourning, shame, and disillusionment. Adult children are angry at the loss of an intact family. For even as adults we have certain fantasies about getting together as a family for holidays, both parents attending our college graduation, or both parents sharing the joy of a birth of a child. These fantasies are shattered when parents divorce (Engel, 1984). Divorce also raises questions and doubts about the true state of the family in the past.

Many adult children feel burdened by their parents' need for emotional support during this time (Hagestad et al., cited in *Marriage and Divorce Today,* 1984). Since the children are old enough to empathize with their parents, they may become a valuable source of support for them. But Hagestad warns, "In providing empathy for troubled parents, young adults may be placing themselves in a more vulnerable position. The emotions their parents share may become as real for the young adults, making it seem as if they are actually experiencing the divorce themselves" (p. 1). Some adult children express shame regarding their parents "promiscuous" behavior after the divorce. "It's embarrassing to see your 60-year-old father running around with a woman young enough to be your sister" (Francke, 1983).

One positive effect is the young adults' improved relationships with their peers. Their parents' divorce seems to sensitize them to the quality of their own relationships. It makes them more careful about making hasty commitments (Hagestad et al., 1984).

---

to the data, they're not. Divorce rates are actually slightly higher among the remarried than among the first married. The difference is not large, however: a couple of percentage points. Using divorce registration, the data show that 47.4 percent of first marriages eventually end in divorce compared to 48.9 percent of remarriages (Weed, 1980).

Various explanations have been offered to explain this slightly higher divorce rate among remarried couples. Andrew Cherlin

(1978) suggests that it's the special challenges that accompany remarriage. Lack of clearly defined norms, a complex family structure, and the presence of stepchildren are adjustments not typical of first marriages. Furstenberg and Spanier (1984) argue that remarried couples are more willing to terminate a marriage that is a failure, primarily because they have had previous experience with divorce. Knowledge that one has survived the divorce situation once may make it more likely that

BOX 14.6

HOW PARENTS CAN HELP CHILDREN DURING A DIVORCE

Children are bound to have hurt feelings and feel intense pain at the time of divorce. But there are actions parents can take to help alleviate the stress in their children's lives. In her book, *Growing Up Divorced* (1983), Linda Francke offers numerous suggestions on how parents can help their children deal with divorce. The following eight suggestions are derived from her book.

1. *Present the divorce carefully to the children.* Telling the children about the impending separation a week or two *before it actually happens* gives them time to adjust to the shock. It also allows them to spend time talking with the parent who is leaving and gaining some reassurance that he or she will continue to be his or her parent. Unfortunately, many separations are not well planned but take place quite spontaneously, usually after a heated argument. It's been estimated that 80 percent of the children have no warning at all, no chance to prepare for the pending separation.

2. *Tell children about the divorce together.* Parents are well advised to try to sit down with their children during a period of calm and tell their children about the divorce together. Not only does this procedure reassure the children that they still have both parents but it doesn't make one parent out to be the "bad guy." "Admit to the children that the parents are sorry that they can no longer live happily together" (Francke, 1983, p. 86).

3. *Reasons for the divorce should be spelled out in terms the child can understand.* Giving no reason at all leaves it up to the child's imagination as to what went wrong. Often this results in the child thinking he or she is at fault and did something wrong to cause the parent to leave. Therapist Richard Gardner recommends telling children a specific reason, not something vague like "we don't love each other anymore," but explaining the reasons in terms the children can understand.

4. *Provide them with concrete, specific, step-by-step projections of what is going to happen to them.* Giving children information should help alleviate their worries. Tell them specifically who will be taking care of them and where they will live. Francke offers these examples— "Mommy (or Daddy) is going to take care of you," and "Nice Mrs. Jones next door will take care of you in the afternoons after nursery school because Mommy is going to get a job" (p. 86). Routines such as eating dinner with one parent or reading bedtime stories should be mentioned to reassure the child of some consistency. But don't be afraid to admit that there may be some confusion at times until these changes fall into place.

5. *Provide infants and young children with consistency.* Especially during the first couple of years, children have difficulty with numerous separations and need a consistent environment. For this reason, a baby under 2 should not be moved back and forth between the homes of the divorced parents. Instead the baby should stay put in one place and have the parents visit. Not only is a familiar face important, but the familiar physical surroundings of the crib, toys, and bedroom walls help the baby feel secure.

6. *If the parent is too preoccupied or depressed, have someone help care for the baby or child.* Sometimes divorce can immobilize a parent to the point of being unable to effectively care for a baby or young child. Eliciting help from a friend or relative may relieve some of the burden until the single parent is ready to take on full-time parenting responsibilities.

7. *Parents should do their best to remain parents during and after the divorce.* A child's reaction to divorce mirrors the way the parents are handling it. Any tension between the parents after the divorce is felt by the child. The child who sees parents put behind the anger, bitterness, and fighting and rebuild their lives will be better able to do likewise.

   What is really devastating, according to Francke, is when one parent disappears by choice from a child's life. Some parents not only divorce their spouse but their children also. To help deal with a parent's absence, the custodial parent may want to involve the child with someone who could be another role model.

8. *Avoid unloading too much criticism of the other parent.* It is easy for parents to allow their marital antagonisms to spill over into their roles as parents. Unfortunately, the children are often the ones to be hurt. For example, it is difficult for a child to develop a close and loving relationship with a parent who is being totally degraded and put down by the other parent. Teenagers in particular will idolize their parents as role models to follow. The denigration of one parent by the other not only strains the teen's sense of loyalty to both but undermines his or her development of a positive self-concept. Francke concludes, "What is essential for the parents to do is to reestablish a sense of continuity and caring in the separate households as soon as possible" (1983, p. 88).

---

the individual will allow it to happen again. Remarriers may be less committed to marital continuity for its own sake in an institutional sense.

Since 60 percent of the remarriages involve an adult with physical custody of one or more children, the majority of remarriages result in stepfamilies. Approximately 15 million children in the United States are living with remarried parents (Visher and Visher, 1979). With continuing high divorce rates, about half of the children born during the 1970s will experience broken families, and most of these will eventually become step-

Since 60 percent of remarriages involve adults with physical custody of one or more children, the majority of remarriages result in stepfamilies.

children (Einstein, 1982). A general and simple definition of a stepfamily is "a family in which at least one of the couple is a stepparent" (Visher and Visher, 1979, p. 4).

Recently stepfamilies have been referred to by other terms such as "reconstituted," "blended," "acquired," "recoupled," "refamilied," and "binuclear." The term *stepchild* has traditionally meant "a bereaved child or orphan." The term *step* came into use at a time when it was usually the death of a biological parent, rather than a parental divorce, which led to the remarriage. Some people prefer not

to use this term because it carries negative feelings and places the stepfamily in a second-rate status (Einstein, 1982). Unfortunately, American society has yet to provide other agreed-upon terms to describe such family members or various forms of families.

Challenges in Stepfamilies

What particular aspects of stepfamilies help or hinder members in becoming close to one another? What exactly is it about the makeup of stepfamilies that makes them inherently different from other nuclear families? Factors that must be considered in answering these questions relate to expectations, interactions with the former family, rules and guidelines for stepfamilies, competition, and the support from outside the family.

UNREALISTIC EXPECTATIONS. Beginning a new family often brings with it high expectations and hopes. With at least one of the partners having prior adult experience in marriage and family life, many stepparents mistakenly believe that this time things will be easier and perhaps better. Also, if the stepparents feel as though they failed with their former families, the pressure and expectations to succeed with the next family will be even greater. Unfortunately, such high expectations may be one of the stepfamily's greatest stumbling blocks.

In general, people hold unrealistic expectations that a stepfamily will be like an intact family. But most of the members of a stepfamily have experienced, some perhaps recently, a divorce or death. Children may have difficulty trusting a new stepparent because of a previous loss of a biological parent. The child may withdraw and build a "wall" between him or her and the new stepparent. Any attempts at showing affection by the stepparent may be met with resistance and hostility on the child's part (Visher and Visher, 1979). Also, the bonds between a biological parent and child were formed through a history of contact and continuity. This history is typically missing from a stepparent-stepchild relationship.

"Instant love" is another unrealistic expectation. "As soon as we marry, I will of course love these children, and they will return my love." Visher and Visher (1979) contend that a time period of at least 1 1/2 to 2 years is required for stepfamilies to develop a "sentimental order" of their own. Unprepared for such a long period of adjustment, many families become frustrated and impatient. But trying to speed up the process may set the family back. Not only does the "instant love" expectation disappoint the stepparent, but the child may have the same fantasy. He or she can also be disappointed when the stepparent does not instantly love him or her.

INTERACTIONS WITH THE FORMER FAMILY. Remarrying does not always totally cut off ties with a former family. A noncustodial parent may still pay child support and visit his or her children. Another difficulty exists when a parent leaves the children of a previous family to become a stepparent in a new family. The stepparent often feels guilty for leaving his own children to go and live with unrelated children. His own children may be angry about the fact that they have to visit their parent while these other children live with him or her full time (Francke, 1983).

In such stepfamilies, children from the previous marriage may visit on weekends or for vacations. Visher and Visher (1979) describe a "superdad" phenomenon in which a father overcompensates by trying to make up for all the days or months that he has not been there when his children needed him. Another way the parent may relieve some guilt is by letting his or her children "get away with murder" when they come to visit, in front of the stepchildren no less.

In addition, some remarried couples have not completed an emotional recovery from their former marriages. As a result, the new stepfamily may be the target of some hostility and bitterness linked to the former spouse and/or children. In other words, stepfamily members can pay for the "sins" of family members from a previous relationship.

LACK OF RULES AND GUIDELINES. The roles of stepparent and stepchild have not been clearly defined in American society. Adult partners may have widely differing ideas about their roles, differences that can lead to arguments, confusion, and feelings of disappointment (Visher and Visher, 1979).

Stepparents may feel uncertain about the amount of involvement that they want to, or should, invest in somebody else's children (Francke, 1983). "Children are equally confused about how they should regard a stepparent. 'It makes me confused,' says ten-year-old Adam. 'Sometimes I think of her like a friend, sometimes a sister, sometimes an aunt. I don't know what a stepmother is supposed to be' " (Francke, 1983, p. 196).

Discipline is one of the most common areas of confusion for stepparents and parents. The amount of disciplining that a stepparent should do often remains undefined. In intact families, parents can work out their differences in methods of discipline slowly as the child grows. In remarriages the couple is typically faced with instant decisions. Decisions are sometimes made without the opportunity to check out the feelings of the other spouse first.

In addition, the children may not be very receptive to discipline from the stepparent and may refuse to cooperate. Out of frustration from useless attempts to discipline the children, the stepparent may finally give up and defer all responsibility to the natural parent. In other situations the stepparent may want to discipline the children, but the natural parent blocks him or her, either out of the habit of being totally responsible for the children or to relieve the stepparent of the responsibility. Such latter actions weaken the stepparent's position with the children and further cloud role responsibility (Francke, 1983).

COMPETITION AND JEALOUSIES. Competition can occur between a number of different family members. For example, a former spouse will usually continue to have contact with the children. This situation can pose a threat to the stepparent of the same sex who is trying to be accepted by the stepchildren. Because of this threat the stepparent may try to be a better parent than the real parent. "The prize is the love of the children" (Einstein, 1982, p. 87). This competition is likely to be more intense between a stepmother and a biological mother than between their male counterparts. Motherhood is often a more central role to a woman's identity. "It is difficult for a mother to accept that another woman is filling the role she considered hers alone—even when she was the one who chose to end her marriage" (p. 87).

A barometer of this rivalry between the noncustodial parent and the stepparent is the child's use of names to refer to the new stepparent. Noncustodial parents are often surprised when their children refer to their stepparents by a term the parents felt was reserved for themselves. Noncustodial parents may actually prohibit the child from referring to their stepparent as Mom or Dad (Furstenberg and Spanier, 1984).

A stepparent, on the one hand, may feel envious of the natural parent's freedom from child-care responsibilities. The stepparent often feels burdened by rearing someone else's children while the biological parent pursues a career or other interests. The biological parent, on the other hand, may be longing for more time and rapport with his or her child and may be jealous of the closeness between the stepparent and the child. Societal disapproval of giving up one's children, especially for women, weighs heavily and only compounds a parent's guilt.

If the stepparent and natural parent are

not competitive or threatened by each other, the children have a much easier time going back and forth between families. The children can then avoid being caught in no-win loyalty conflicts. By treating each other with respect, the adults can be positive models for the children in these families and help to strengthen the stepfamily.

A competitive situation can also occur between two ex-spouses who still are angry or bitter over the divorce. The two biological parents may be competing for their children's affections, often taking the form of who can outdo the other in gift giving. A lot of damage results from verbal putdowns of the missing parent in front of the children. These do less harm, however, to the rapport between the children and the ex-spouse than they do to one's own relationship with one's own children. "When parents defame their former mates, they actually erode the respect they command from their children. Oddly enough, children tend to idealize the absent parent, and putdowns simply double the pain" (Einstein, 1982, p. 90).

It is common for rivalry and jealousy to exist among stepsiblings also. Children may view stepsiblings as competitors for their own parents' attention and ask, "Who is loved the most?" (Visher and Visher, 1979). "Sibling rivalry can become serious in stepfamilies because diverse personalities and histories, coupled with rivalry for the parents' attention, make compatibility difficult" (Einstein, 1982, p. 111). If resources such as money and time are scarce, the rivalry may be greater. Surprisingly, a new baby born to the remarried couple can help to create harmonious relationships between stepsiblings.

Finally, there may be competition between a child and a stepparent for a spouse's attention. When a parent remarries, children at least temporarily lose some of the parent's attention. Even when the noncustodial parent remarries, the children may see far less of the parent. Visitations become fewer and last for shorter periods of time (Francke, 1983).

Children may also feel that they are being replaced by this new spouse. After a divorce an older child may take the place of the ex-spouse in the single-parent family. When the parent remarries, this child may feel the new spouse is invading his or her "turf" and trying to take over a role he or she has played. For example, a son may take over as the man of the house when his mother divorces. He may enjoy the attention he gets from his mother for babysitting his younger siblings, cleaning the house, and being her confidant. When his mother remarries, the new husband becomes the man of the house and receives the mother's attention. The son is threatened by him and feels now that he has to compete with him for his mother's attention.

Likewise, a stepparent may be jealous of the spouse's children. For example, a stepmother may view her teenage stepdaughter as another woman competing for her husband's affections. As a stepdaughter blossoms into adolescence, her physical appearance can heighten the jealousy and competition.

INADEQUATE SUPPORT FROM OUTSIDE THE STEPFAMILY. The uniqueness of stepfamily relationships is generally not acknowledged by other institutions in society. Cultural norms and expectations still are based on the assumption that most families consist of two parents and their biological children. "Boy Scouts, churches, and most community organizations are not yet structured to deal easily with stepfamilies" (Visher and Visher, 1979, p. 126). Hence, the stepfamily faces more obstacles. A school, for example, may give children only two tickets for the band concert or honors assembly, not recognizing the fact that the child has three parents. In essence, the stepparent is often ignored or isolated from the rest of the family.

Extended-family members can also either support or discourage harmonious stepfamily relationships. Grandparents of divorced and remarried couples often react negatively for various reasons. It may be difficult for them to cope with the breakup of the offspring's marriage, and then when remarried, they often do not know what their particular role or relationship should be to their new step-grandchildren. Many fear losing contact with their own grandchildren, especially in situations where the in-law is awarded custody of the children. Fearful that the parent will not allow them the right to visit their children, some grandparents have gone to court. More than half the states have enacted laws permitting grandparents to petition the court for visiting rights (Einstein, 1982). An additional difficult challenge is accepting stepgrandchildren to whom one has no biological tie. Inequitable gift giving, which is common, reflects this reluctance to accept new children into the kin network.

Also, in-laws can influence the acceptance of a new stepparent. Since the in-laws may have trouble accepting a new stepparent, at times they may encourage the stepchildren not to accept him or her either. Some in-laws may even compete with the new stepparent and try to retain power over the children through manipulation.

Instead of pulling the stepfamily apart, extended-family members could be used to help support stepfamily relationships. They could help by providing child care or other assistance. Black stepfamilies perhaps have an advantage in this area since the extended family plays a more integral role in black families. The black family uses members of the extended family to fill gaps, to step in during a crisis, or to take in children, tem-

porarily or permanently (R. Hill, 1972; Blackwell, 1985; J. Dodson, 1981; Hines and Boyd-Franklin, 1982). Hence, the extended-family relationships provide warmth and support during the transition to stepfamily living.

Strengths of Stepfamilies

Is living in a stepfamily destined to be chaotic and troublesome? Can anything be gained by living in a stepfamily arrangement? Despite the many challenges that stepfamilies must face, benefits can develop from such an arrangement. And as research on stepfamilies brings more insight into their workings, it is to be hoped that stepfamilies will be able to handle the many obstacles. The following are some of the potential benefits of a stepfamily.

ADDITIONAL ROLE MODELS. Increasing the extended kin through remarriage may be a way to offset the trend toward the smaller family size that has occurred in recent decades. "People may have fewer relations by blood, but they may acquire a greater number through marriage" (Furstenberg and Spanier, 1984, p. 137). Another way of looking at this is to say that a smaller number of children are being shared by a greater number of adults. This may result in relatives competing for the rights to the children, but it also means that a greater number of kin will feel obligated to care for and support the child.

Having more than two parents provides stepchildren with more adult role models than a child from an intact nuclear family would have. A stepchild can learn skills and attitudes from both stepparents and natural parents. An extra parent figure can also be another adult to provide emotional support to the child; he or she may serve as a sounding board for a child or teenager. One teenager told Einstein, "I like having two mothers. I can ask the same question of both, get two opinions from people who care about me, and make up my own mind" (1982, p. 187).

Stepsiblings can also be additional role models. "For an only child who becomes a stepchild, brothers and sisters and a large family are an exciting bonus" (Einstein, 1982, p. 188). Stepsiblings can teach each other about give-and-take, sharing, and companionship. Older stepsiblings may teach the younger children new activities that they may not have encountered otherwise. Younger children can learn social skills from the older ones. Learning to get along with people within the family also aids in exchanging with those outside the family. Faced with different sets of views and ways of doing things, stepchildren develop an ability to see several points of view. "Their exposure to the stepfamily's complex network of relationships may make it easier to accept new people with diverse ideas and values" (Einstein, 1982, p. 188).

"RECYCLED FATHERS." Visher and Visher (1979) found that if a man felt he had failed as a father in his first marriage, he may become more committed to being a stepfather in his next marriage. The "recycled father" may feel that he missed out on raising his biological children and therefore he shows more interest in his stepchildren. A stepfather may be somewhat less concerned about how his stepchildren are going to turn out. Hence, he can approach them in a more relaxed manner and can be more accepting of their behavior. This acceptance can help the children grow in self-confidence and self-esteem. Other stepfathers feel a sense of failure with the first family and may try "too hard" to make the stepfamily "turn out right" (Visher and Visher, 1979). This pressure creates resentment and resistance from the stepchildren.

In addition, given the fact that the stepfather may be approaching middle age at the time he is parenting in the stepfamily may also make a difference. It was noted in Chapter 11 that men during middle age tend to "mellow" in terms of showing their feelings and being more intimate. The stepfather may now feel more comfortable in developing a close relationship with children. If the man has already been successful in his career and no longer must devote all his time to his work, he can turn his energies toward the family.

In summary, what factors can be singled out as contributing to the success of stepfamilies? Hetherington, Cox, and Cox in a six-year longitudinal study looked at stepchildren who were functioning better than those in single-parent families or conflict-ridden intact families. The study concluded that the following factors contributed to the success of stepfamilies: (1) The natural parent had encouraged the active involvement of the stepparent in the new family, (2) the stepparent was not only authoritative but warm, and (3) the children's natural parents maintained close relationships with the children (Hetherington, Cox, and Cox, 1981).

Much of the success of these families depends on parents being able to resolve past relationships, to put behind them the prior attachment to the divorced partner. "The extent to which the adults are able to deal with the children in terms of the children's needs separate from their marital battles and the divorce the more likely the children will be able to share in the benefits of the remarriage" (Wallerstein and Kelly, 1980, p. 301).

CHAPTER REVIEW

1. Marital dissolution, or the dissolution of any close relationship, involves a process of uncoupling. It usually starts with an individ-

ual phase, moves gradually into a "dyadic" phase, then involves a social phase, and finally ends with a phase of "closing."

2. Divorce law has changed over recent years with no-fault divorce attempting to make the process more humane and more equitable. In its attempt to be more equitable, however, it has resulted in economic hardship for many divorced women. Since the economic position of women is still much lower than that of men in the world of work, many divorced women are struggling to support themselves and their children on inadequate incomes.

3. Divorcing parents now have various custody options from which to choose. Joint custody is becoming increasingly popular. It has certain advantages over sole custody in that the responsibilities of parenting do not fall totally on one parent, the children have extensive contact with both parents, and the financial support of the children is more likely to be shared by both parents. Disadvantages may involve logistical problems of moving the children back and forth, as well as the requirement that ex-spouses live in the same area or school district.

4. While divorce affects individuals in different ways, certain consequences such as separation distress, sadness, depression, loneliness, and economic stresses are common. Divorce may ultimately result, however, in some positive consequences for a person's well-being. Children also feel similar emotions when parents are divorcing—sadness, depression, and loneliness. Their age, stage of development, and lack of power, however, make their experience of divorce quite different from that of the adult.

5. Since most divorced individuals remarry, the stepfamily is becoming a more common family form in American society today. Stepfamilies, however, often face the challenges of unrealistic expectations, of dealing with former families, of the lack of rules and guidelines, of competition and jealousies, and of inadequate outside support. But stepfamilies may provide advantages of additional role models for children and the greater involvement of "recycled fathers."

Close Relationships in the Future

15

Prospects for Change in Close Relationships

The search for human closeness is not an easy one. Even though most people desire intimate relationships, or at least one, American society has not focused on a socialization or educational process to make it easier to achieve this goal. There are few organized efforts to help produce close relationships, either within marriage, among family members, or between friends. Even though people indicate that "a happy marriage" and "a good family life" are among the most important domains in their lives (see Table 15.1), society still focuses more on instrumental rather than emotional needs in terms of training.

In this final chapter we want to look at the prospects for change in marriage, family, and friendships as we move toward the twenty-first century. Today the number of intimate marriages is still small compared to all types of marriages. What can be done to increase closeness in marriage? How can young people be taught about the realities of love, and how can they learn to be intimate others? In addition, will friendships become increasingly important as sources of emotional closeness, particularly if divorce rates remain high over an extended period of time? In a society that has traditionally not emphasized friendships in a formal way, can we teach people to invest in more meaningful nonmarital relationships? And what is the importance of family or kinship relationships? What are the differences between nonkin friendships and friendships with family members?

TABLE 15.1

DOMAINS OF RELATIVE IMPORTANCE IN LIFE

Aspect of life	Percentage of respondents who indicated this was "extremely important" or "very important"
Being in good health and in good physical condition	94%
A happy marriage	91
A good family life—having family members you can enjoy being with	91
Having good friends, and the right number of friends	70
An interesting job	70
A house or apartment that you like to live in	69
Things you like to do when you are not working—hobbies and things like that	42
A large bank account, so that you don't have to worry about money	35
Organizations you want to belong to	11

SOURCE: *Adapted from Campbell, Converse, and Rodgers, 1976*

MARRIAGE

The traditional marriage was clearly organized for the purpose of survival. Such marriages were based on a hierarchical system of fixed gender roles leading to confining and stifling relationships, with few possibilities for growth or change. Husbands held almost all of the power, and good wives were quiet and obedient. This led to a very stable system of social order, which provided ready-made answers to almost any questions that were likely to arise.

The traditional couple didn't have to struggle with many problems resulting from personality differences, and there was no need to be concerned with each other's inner thoughts. People learned to wear masks in order to hide their true selves, to project images that made good impressions, and to be pleasing to the point of being dishonest and hypocritical. Since the husbands made all the major decisions, there was no concern for either the ability to communicate or the skills to make decisions. In reality, a husband was close to neither his wife nor his children; simply put, he played the role of disciplinarian, authority figure, and economic provider (Mace, 1982).

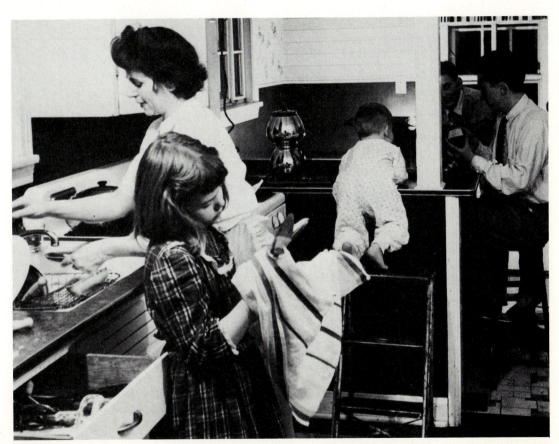

Traditional marriages are based on a hierarchical system of fixed gender roles.

Traditional marriages are still common today. Over the past couple of decades, however, most specifically since the mid-1970s, there has been a growing recognition of a new style of marriage stressing the equality of the two sexes. The trend is for marriage to be increasingly held together by *internal cohesion*, in contrast to the traditional type of marriage held together by *external cohesion*—"social pressures imposed mainly by religion, law, and the resulting public opinion" (Mace, 1982, p. 42). Table 15.2 shows a comparison of some traits of this new style of intimate marriage and the traditional marriage.

David Mace (1982) calls the growing equality of men and women "the most significant event of the twentieth century" having an impact on intimate relationships. In addition, the increasing desire for marital closeness exists among all social classes, even among blue-collar couples. Growing affluence in the general population over the last half of this century has meant that survival needs are no longer dominant in marriage. A new key function of marriage relates to emotional satisfaction. More and more people believe that their marriage should be happy and "fun."

TABLE 15.2

MARRIAGE: THE OLD AND THE NEW

Traditional	Intimate
One-vote system—husband makes all major decisions	Two-vote system—decisions jointly made by husband and wife
Fixed roles—husband's and wife's roles clearly differentiated by gender	Fluid roles—roles based on personal choice and competence with little emphasis on gender difference
Husband-provider—wife-homemaker	Flexible division of provider and homemaker functions
Husband initiates sex—wife complies	Sex initiated by either husband or wife
Basic concept—marriage a hierarchy	Basic concept—marriage an equal partnership
Issues settled with reference to legalistic principles and rules	Issues settled with reference to personal and interpersonal needs
Wife close to children, husband disciplinarian and authority figure	Husband and wife both close to children, both represent authority
Husband assumes role of religious head of family	Religious functions of family shared by husband and wife
Further education important for husband, not for wife	Further education equally important for both
Husband's vocation decides family residence	Family residence takes account of both husband's and wife's vocation

SOURCE: *Adapted from Mace, 1982, p. 16.*

There is now the acceptance of a philosophy that states that people do not have to remain in very unhappy marriages. The negative stigma attached to being divorced has almost completely disappeared. Unhappily married couples, more than ever before in history, are looking either for ways to get out of their commitments or for help to try to "breathe new life and closeness" into their relationships through marital therapy and marital enrichment programs (Mace, 1982).

For a married couple to be close the two partners do not necessarily have to carry out the exact *same* behaviors or to carry out the *same* tasks equally. But it is important that the power in the relationship be roughly equal. Whether this is power determined by "objective" resources or a "subjective," behind-the-scenes power, or more commonly a combination of both, is really not the issue. What is most important is whether the two individuals feel that they *are* equal partners. Of course, most women are going to feel that they have more power if they have an income-producing job. But still, some women can focus on the jobs of child care and homemaking, have high self-esteem, and view themselves as equal partners—and also be viewed by their husbands as equal.

Transitional Marriages

Transitional marriages are those that can no longer be accurately described as traditional; neither have they reached a high enough degree of emotional closeness to be described as intimate. These are marriages experiencing extensive confusion as the old roles are discarded and new desires for personal happiness in marriage become more and more prominent. In these situations the foundations of the traditional marriage have been shaken, but the vast majority of people do not know how to have an intimate marriage. There is extensive conflict between existing

socialization and expectations for a new type of marriage.

The chaos that the transition brings is reflected in heightened fantasies of lifelong happiness, illusionary intimacy, high divorce rates, and an unawareness of what it really means to have an emotionally close marriage. The switching to a two-vote marital system brings with it the potential for a lot more conflict, disagreement, and strife. Unless couples develop "interpersonal competence" in the complex art of negotiating disagreements, their marriages will probably end up in trouble. So while having a 50-50 marriage sounds really great, the problem is that most people have not been taught how to function in such a marriage (Mace, 1982). And even though more and more women are demanding to be equal partners, still a significant number of men are unable to bring themselves to treat women this way. Somewhere these men have been taught that they are supposed to be "in control."

Most couples who are involved in transitional marriages do not even have a clear understanding of the problems that they face. Most have anticipations of effortless harmony, at least when they are first married. The rude discovery that their expectations do not match reality concerns them deeply. Furthermore, the majority of people are ashamed to admit that they are "having problems" (Mace, 1982). It is estimated that only about 5 to 10 percent of all marriages are intimate relationships with a very high level of mutual happiness (Mace, 1982).

It is easy to understand why the family conservatives are so upset. "Our disturbingly high rates of marital and family breakdown are interpreted by some religious groups as manifestations of moral corruption and it is reasoned that the only way to avoid disaster is to go back to a literal reconstruction of the past, to the 'good old days' when virtue abounded" (Mace, 1982, p. 44). In reality,

Drawing by George Price; © 1984. The New Yorker Magazine, Inc.

the old days were not as good as we think they were, and our nostalgia would probably quickly evaporate if we could actually return to spend some time in the past (Mace, 1982).

Requisites for Building Intimate Marriages

MOTIVATING MEN TO BECOME INTIMATE. For intimacy to develop in more marriages Michael McGill in his study *The McGill Report on Male Intimacy* (1985) believes that men will have to be convinced that it is to their advantage to become emotionally close to their wives. But McGill found that the majority of

men in his research did not see any reason to be more disclosing with their wives. Since most men are satisfied with their marriages the way they are, why would they want to change? McGill suggests three reasons as to why it is in the best interests of men to become more intimate.

McGill gives as a first reason the fact that a growing body of evidence suggests that social relationships have a significant impact on both the physical and mental health of people. Also, the number one and number two causes of death for men are heart disease and cancer, both of which are said to have links to stress. The third leading cause of death for men is suicide.

It appears to be a possibility "that if men become more self-disclosing and expressive of themselves in their relationships with others, they will be better able to deal with the stressors that are associated with disease" (McGill, 1985, p. 237). Thus, one motivation that could be used to induce men to seek intimacy is the possibility of improved mental and physical health. A key factor involved in stress management is emotional support from others, derived from active participation in close relationships (McGill, 1985).

A second reason why it is advantageous for men to become more intimate is that they will find it to be a more effective approach to decision making and problem solving. A man who tries to "go it alone," avoiding and shunning the help of others, will limit his problem-solving capabilities. Thus, because many men are reluctant to share their problems with others, they miss out on the opportunity to see the many different ways in which their problems might be solved (McGill, 1985).

Particularly in their interactions with other men, males often avoid "helping" relationships. Many men resist turning to other men "for advice, counsel, or an extra hand, no matter how complex the problem or weighty the task" (p. 240).

In part, this solitary behavior derives from the belief that a real man can and should handle his own affairs. In part, it is because the shallow relationships men have with others do not provide a context for asking for help. In part, it is because men do not ask for help due to uncertainty about what they might be obligating themselves to do in return. Any one or all of these reasons may keep a man from reaching out to others when he is confronted with problems. (McGill, 1985, p. 240)

The message is that men can act much more effectively "if they will first act more intimately" (p. 244).

A third reason why greater intimacy is in the best interests of men is that it increases their own self-awareness. Nonintimacy for a man increases alienation from himself. "The man who is alone—and in the absence of intimate relationships, most men are—does not know who he is. Alienation literally means separation. To alienate is to make something foreign, strange" (p. 246). To discover oneself one must reveal oneself to others and then read the verbal and nonverbal reaction of others.

A man will not be able easily to determine what he wants to *be* or what he wants to *do* "without testing his priorities against those held by others" (p. 252). McGill argues that the social separateness experienced by many men gives rise to anomie, a feeling of isolation. Furthermore, anomie is often given as one of the most common reasons for suicide. Men who experience anomie "do not see that the way to connect with society is to connect with a caring other" (p. 254). McGill concludes:

Should men be more intimate because their wives and families want it? Yes. Should men be more intimate, more loving because it will improve their mental and physical health? Yes. Should men be more intimate because they will be able to act more effectively? Yes. Should men be more loving because it will make them more self-aware? Yes. Will men change their intimate behavior for these reasons? Probably not. (p. 254)

In the final analysis McGill believes that men will become more intimate only if they come to see that through self-disclosure to others in close relationships they become *empowered* rather than *emasculated*. "A man will get close if he believes that getting closer means getting control" (p. 255). But many men claim that they really do not know how to get close to others, that they don't have the slightest idea of how to achieve intimacy (McGill, 1985).

Sometimes a man's plea for help to become more intimate does not win a receptive response from females. Many women just can't believe that what comes so naturally for them is something that must be taught to men. A man's statement that "I want to be emotionally closer to you but I don't know how" is sometimes viewed by women as just one of many excuses, since knowing and expressing feelings come easily and effortlessly for most women. Some women actually become angry at the suggestion that they help their husbands with this problem. McGill ar-

gues that there is a dual agenda; "Men do need help in learning how to be intimate, and women need help in learning how to help them" (p. 258).

Women can play an important role in encouraging male openness. Their own responses to men's self-disclosures can either reinforce men to continue to reveal feelings or reinforce them to close up. In reality, women may be the best teachers for men to learn the skill of self-disclosing. Box 15.1 offers suggestions for making these changes.

No man will seek to become more intimate unless he is motivated to do so, but there are some specific things that can be

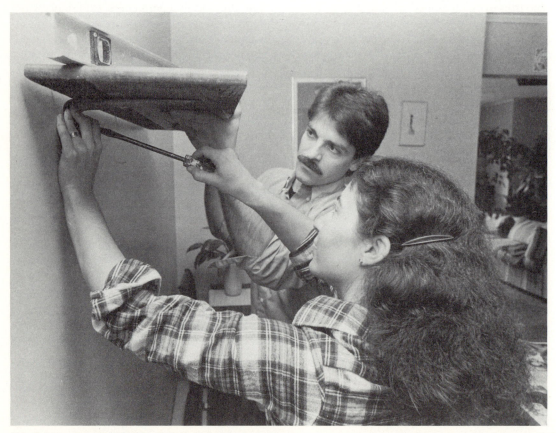

The division of work in families is becoming more equitable.

BOX 15.1

TEACHING MEN TO OPEN UP

Men may need some extra help from their wives and women friends if they are going to learn to disclose their feelings. According to Steven Naifeh and Gregory Smith (1984), "The inner man wants to be freed, but needs someone else to make the first move, to extend a hand, to unlock the door of masculine stereotypes and dispell the fears of dependence that keep him closed" (p. 103). Indicated below are 10 suggestions given by Naifeh and Smith for helping a man become more intimate.

1. *See the problem from his perspective.* The first step is to understand why he's inexpressive. This may be difficult because many men are adept at concealing their problems. But a woman must begin to see "a man's insecurities from his perspective." If, for example, the problem is anxiety, he may be fearful of losing his own identity if he reveals himself to you.

2. *Set the right example.* The woman should model the practice of being open, showing vulnerability, and risking rejection. "If a woman is comfortable with her emotions and expresses them easily, she's proof that it can be done" (p. 109). But while candor begets candor, its best "to strike a balance between candor and consideration" (p. 110).

3. *Let him "feel" for himself.* "Sometimes a woman inadvertently keeps a man closed by assuming all of the emotional 'duties' herself. . . . By refusing to be automatically responsible for emotional behavior, the woman sends a non-threatening signal: 'It's your turn to show emotion,' instead of 'I demand that you show me some emotion'" (pp. 110–111). Part of the problem is often that the woman assumes that the man "can't talk," so she talks for him—and the man assumes he doesn't have to talk, so he keeps quiet.

4. *Don't force the issue.* Because the fear of intimacy stems from deep-rooted insecurities, "any effort to pry him open will only trigger a defensive reaction" (p. 111). A woman should let up "on trying to make him open up, but not on communicating her desire that he open up. . . . She has to convince him that if he opens up he'll still be desirable, that he can be both vulnerable and exciting, both dependent and masculine" (p. 112). A man has to be convinced that it's more than *good* for him to show emotion; he has to be convinced that it's *appealing.*

5. *Find common ground.* "A woman who wants her man to talk to her must make sure they have something to talk about" (p. 116). Shared actions and experiences bring two people closer to each other. Men, particularly, are more "willing and able to establish intimacy by sharing their feelings about some common shared interest. . . . A

(Continued)

woman can take advantage of this willingness to get a man in the habit of discussing his feelings" (p. 117). By talking about a sporting event, a book, a movie, or a television show, this provides a non-threatening emotional dialogue.

6. *Teach him how to express himself.* Since women are more likely to be aware of their feelings and, in general, are better at articulating them, they "may have to teach a man the skills necessary to express himself" (p. 117). One of the best ways of doing this is with I-statements—"I believe . . . ," "I feel . . . ," "I want . . ." "The point is for men to learn to distinguish things they think and things they feel" (p. 118).

7. *Exchange secrets.* "The token of intimacy that a man may be most willing to give is a secret" (p. 119). The way to get a man to tell secrets about his life is to tell him secrets from your own past, not just the things you *want* him to know but the ones you don't want him to know. If you tell some things you're embarrassed about, he will know that you trust him and he will more likely trust you with his secrets.

8. *Be a good listener.* Listening requires attention and concentration; it's more important than talking "because you need to give the speaker the confidence to continue" (p. 120). Convey interest, look straight at him, attempt to show that there is nothing more important than what he has to say. By creating the right environment a woman makes opening up easier.

9. *Be prepared for his openness.* Women sometimes unknowingly discourage emotional openness because of their reactions to particular attempts at the sharing of feelings by a man. They may act shocked or surprised, laugh, or hear something they didn't want to hear. His first emotional stirrings must be treated with necessary care and positively reinforced. And she should not be "verbally promiscuous" and tell everything her husband told her to other friends.

10. *Look behind the words.* "Part of the good listener's job is to look behind a person's words and behavior and try to understand what they mean. . . . Where is he coming from? What is he *really* trying to tell me?" (p. 122). Also study his nonverbal communication and his body signals; listen to what his body says.

---

done to help create motivation. McGill suggests four conditions that can create the motivation in men to be more intimate—coercion, anxiety, disconfirmation, and psychological safety.

Coercion, or what might better be termed *confrontation,* is one technique for encouraging men to be intimate. In this approach, conditions are created involving great potential costs for the man unless certain changes are made. The confrontation must include the threat of the loss of something really important to the male. The most important fear of most men is the loss of their spouses and families. So wives must be made strong enough to get across a powerful message that says, in essence, "If my needs for closeness with you are not met there will not be a marriage!" McGill (1985) quotes a woman he interviewed who used confrontation successfully:

> It's terrible to think that you have to threaten someone to love you "or else," but I honestly don't think that he would have heard me any other way. When I finally did say "love me or I'm leaving" he started listening and now he's started changing. (p. 262)

This is indeed a high-risk strategy, one less likely to be made by very dependent women with young children. It's also obvious that threats against a man may result in his making threats in return. Also, the woman making threats must be prepared to follow through if change is not forthcoming. Threats without follow-through are empty and ineffectual (McGill, 1985).

Anxiety can also be a powerful motivator for change. A man who finds that he does not have the resources to handle a personal crisis and who does not have friends may try to build a closer relationship with someone if he feels enough pain. The unresolved pain of an illness, separation, divorce, or death of a loved one may cause a man to reach out and become more intimate. Box 15.2 gives an example of how an illness led to emotional closeness.

A third suggestion for motivating men to be intimate involves *disconfirmation* between goals and behavior. The idea behind this approach is that people will change their behavior if they realize that their current behavior is not producing the results they want. Disconfirmation is a good motivator because it requires no goal change. We know, for ex-

ample, that men desire to be viewed as manly by others. Writes McGill:

> If men were suddenly to perceive that the way to be manly was to be open, self-disclosing, and loving, they would behave in those ways. They don't need to set aside the goal; it remains important to them. They have only to change their behavior. If, on the other hand, men were asked to give up the goal of being manly, we can predict that there would be very little in the way of change. (1985, p. 266)

The use of disconfirmation starts with what men value or what they consider their goals. Typically if men value control, they will not self-disclose feelings that may be a threat to control. If, however, men can be shown that being close to someone increases their self-awareness, and therefore their control, they can be motivated to carry out more intimate behavior.

A fourth way that men can be motivated to seek more intimacy is through *psychological safety*. This situation is one in which there are either no risks associated with change or any risks that there might be are very manageable. The crux of the matter is that men must believe that the risks are largely within their control. As long as men see potential harm in self-disclosure, they will resist opening up. Those who are the helpers of nonintimate men might suggest to them that they can handle whatever risks might be associated with greater emotional closeness. McGill thinks that any or all four of the above approaches to motivating a man to seek intimacy *can* be effective (McGill, 1985).

Still, a significant percentage of men insist that they can't disclose themselves because they say that they honestly don't know themselves well enough to say how they feel. Although many men use ignorance of their

BOX 15.2

INTIMACY MOTIVATED BY ANXIETY

Dear Ann Landers: This is a plea to "Exit in Toronto," the 41-year-old who has learned he has a terminal case of liver cancer.

Exit has a wife and two children. He has told no one about the diagnosis and is determined to keep it a secret in order to spare his family the agony of watching him wither away day by day. His plan is to leave home, drop out of sight and die alone.

You told Exit his plan was neither wise, humane nor realistic and pleaded with him to stay with his family and allow them to give him the love and emotional support so vital during the final days of a terminal illness.

If he won't listen to you, Ann, perhaps he will listen to me. My husband has had terminal cancer for eight months. "Tim's" illness has brought our family closer together than it ever was before. He was never a man who could express his feelings but the realization that his days are numbered has made him much more accepting of my love for him. He has opened up to me and other members of our family in a way that I never dreamed possible. It is wonderful to see the change in Tim, but it is sad, too, that this had to happen before we could achieve this beautiful feeling of oneness. This may sound crazy but we have never felt closer or appreciated each other more.

There is a lesson here for all husbands and wives. Please don't wait until some awful tragedy strikes before you open up to one another. Tim and I wasted too many years living along parallel lines, our lives never touching. Now that he has been stricken with cancer, every day is precious.

Please, Mr. Whoever-you-are, don't run away. Stay with your family and share the time that is left. It could be the best part of your life.—**Voice of Experience Somewhere in the Middle West**

SOURCE: Detroit Free Press, *November 29, 1986.*

feelings as an excuse, many others in reality do not know how they feel (McGill, 1985). The authors have found in counseling that about one-half of the men with intimacy problems are aware of their difficulties with self-disclosure and intimacy, and about one-half are not even aware that they have a problem with closeness. Obviously for the second group the learning of intimacy is going to be more of a challenge because there is not even any conscious awareness of a problem. McGill says of such men, "Years of

suppressing their feelings and hiding them from others have resulted in men being cut off from their own emotional responses" (1985, p. 275). When one is not aware of one's own feelings and therefore is incapable of revealing them to others, it prevents other people from providing needed emotional support (see Box 15.3).

Men often intellectualize and analyze so as to avoid an emotional response; therefore, feelings are often removed from their consciousness. For feelings to emerge slowly over

BOX 15.3

THE ART OF GIVING EMOTIONAL SUPPORT

When partners trust each other with their feelings, they are able to fit into place another building block of mutual growth: the exchange of emotional support. That exchange—the promise that you will "be there" when needed, that you will not only accept your partner's feelings but also help him or her to deal with them—should be implicit in an intimate relationship. It is vital to have what you are, what you think, what you feel, and what you do confirmed by the person who is closest to you. This is not to say that emotional support always implies agreeing with one's partner. Constructive criticism can be supportive in its own way. But emotional support does imply a mutual respect between partners that allows them to sanction, if not endorse, each other's thoughts and actions. This is not primarily an intellectual exercise. The operative word in "emotional suppport" is "emotion."

A woman who placed her ailing seventy-six-year-old mother in a nursing home is plagued by guilt for having "abandoned" her. "My husband keeps telling me that Mother will get better care there than we could give her. I suppose that's true, but his saying so doesn't stop me from feeling bad. Logic doesn't help. If only my husband would just put his arms around me and hold me and say I didn't do anything wrong!"

A young attorney recalls the "loneliest moment" in his life: "It was when I graduated from law school and Diane, my fiancée, wasn't there to share the thrill with me. Her sister had just had an operation and Diane felt she should be at the hospital. I said I understood, and I tried to. But I've always felt she let me down."

Almost everyone has had the experience of feeling let down emotionally by the failure of someone we love to be with us in a time of joy or to support us in a time of trouble. Sometimes we may want only the sense of physical closeness: a handclasp, an embrace. At other times we may need the psychological sustenance of a sympathetic listener, or objective advice to help us make a difficult decision, or just someone to stand by our side and comfort us. It hurts when the emotional support we seek is lacking. "You weren't there when I needed you," we say—or think. And for some people the aftereffects of that disappointment can last a lifetime. A successful novelist cannot forget that when his early manuscripts were regularly rejected, his wife kept urging him to give it all up and get a job. "She didn't show any faith in my ability to make it as a writer," he says. . . .

Giving emotional support to a partner is a complex skill that requires sensitivity to his or her needs. For example, it is not easy to know what particular *kind* of support he or she wants, how much to offer, or when to offer it. A large part of the problem is that the person expected to provide emotional support frequently does not get any clear signals from the person

(Continued)

seeking it. Most of us tend to feel that if we have to ask (or even hint) for encouragement or comfort, it somehow makes the response less authentic, less meaningful. Indeed, one of the most staunchly held beliefs—and one of the most erroneous—is that "if you loved me you'd *know* what I need!" . . .

Giving unsolicited advice or offering "better" solutions for a partner's problems is a common response when two emotionally close people use each other as sounding boards. It's a bad habit—but an understandable one, for it usually reflects the listener's concern, as well as his or her desire to be a helpful partner. There are some people who find it hard to hear about a problem without offering their analysis of the situation. That doesn't necessarily mean they feel the other person is incompetent. It is more a sign of their own emotional need to be supportive, to make everything run smoothly. Usually they don't realize their attitude is annoying until it has already begun to cut off communication.

The best solution is to announce at the outset what kind of response you are hoping for. If you mainly want a sympathetic ear while you get your troubles off your chest, say so. If you want to share information or feelings, announce that ahead of time too. By telling your partner exactly how you would like him or her to listen to you, you stand a better chance of getting the kind of emotional support you want or need. (Some of us also have unrealistic ideas about the ways in which emotional support should be provided. Frequently, we feel that unless our partner comes through absolutely on target—unless he or she meets *exactly* the unspoken specifications we've set up in our own minds—then whatever support is offered is little better than none at all.)

It is difficult for many of us to offer emotional support even when we would like to. . . . Here are guidelines that can help to enhance the ability to be supportive:

1. Try to be alert for the clues that indicate when your partner needs support but cannot openly ask for it. With some people this can mean irritability, silence, physical withdrawal, even a sudden eating or drinking or spending splurge.

2. Listen attentively. This can often be more supportive than any words we can say.

3. Being supportive does not mean totally subordinating your own values or good sense. Nor does it mean overreacting and being overly solicitous and sympathetic or joining in to fuel the flames of a partner's hurt or anger.

4. Essentially, giving support is a matter of being able to share the feelings of those we love.

SOURCE: *Lasswell and Lobenz, 1983, pp. 199–203.*

time, habitual, automatic responses need to be restrained. In addition, since much of men's behavior has been "conditioned by 'shoulds'—what a man *should* be, how a man *should* behave—they often look for the 'feeling' shoulds. This behavior is frequently encouraged by women, who expect that men should feel as they themselves do. When confronted by a situation, a man may struggle so hard over how he should feel that he doesn't attend to how he *does* feel" (McGill, 1985, p. 276). Feelings simply *are;* they are not right or wrong, good or bad. As one respondent told McGill,

The most difficult thing of all is that it all feels so awkward. That's the incredible paradox: when you get closest to what you really are, it doesn't feel like it's you because it's so strange. When you get to where you are dealing with your feelings, it feels uncomfortable because you're in strange territory. Add to that the sense of vulnerability, really feeling defenseless, and it takes a lot of guts to hang in there and change. I truly feel that it is the most courageous thing I have ever done in my life. (McGill, 1985, pp. 277–278)

Where men have been motivated to become more intimate they usually credit women for getting the needed message of change across to them, as well as for helping them to change. A man is not likely to continue increasing his intimacy unless he receives positive reinforcement for new behaviors from his partner. But what is *the woman's* reward? Her reward is the emotional closeness that she so much desires with her husband. Says one woman:

Sometimes Gil and I will be together talking, really talking now about important personal things, and I will think about how

different things are for us now that he is so much more caring, and my eyes will fill with tears. Gil asks why I am crying and I tell him it's because I feel that he loves me so much, and he smiles and starts crying too. You can't know what it means to me to see my husband cry because of the love we have. I can truly say that his tears are my reward for whatever part I had in helping him open up. (McGill, 1985, pp. 280–281)

NONINTIMATE WOMEN.   Not only men have problems with emotional closeness. Women too, although not nearly so often as men, can fear vulnerability, can be afraid of disclosing feelings, and can try to avoid intimacy. Typically such women come from families with no models of intimacy, families in which one or both parents were "cold" and did not show much emotion. Female nonassertiveness, in itself, makes intimacy impossible.

Nonintimate women will usually have to learn the skills of intimacy from a therapist or from a female friend, particularly if their spouse is also nonintimate. One of the most difficult situations exists when both the husband and wife have nonintimate personalities. But even in such cases, if motivation is high, such couples can learn to become emotionally close.

Implementing Programs to Build Intimacy

David and Vera Mace (1986) argue that just receiving *information* about close relationships is not enough; it is only a start. For information to be of value it has to be processed by the brain into *knowledge,* meaning that it has to be understood. Then knowledge is transformed into useful *insight,* which can be utilized in a practical way to improve a relationship. But even having insight is meaningless unless it is acted on in the form of *experimental actions.* Such actions are not complete in themselves, however; they must lead to *behavior changes* that exemplify ongoing commitment. Both members of the dyad must move through these stages together. The key to building an intimate marriage involves a commitment to change. Attitudes and words must be transformed into behavioral changes (1986).

EDUCATION ABOUT INTIMACY. When marriages end in divorce, the partners usually feel a sense of failure. Actually, however, it is American society that has failed to help people build good relationships. Most individuals receive little, if any, formal education about how to build an emotionally close marital relationship. What high schools offer in terms of family-life courses seems to be wholly inadequate. Premarital counseling, typically done by the clergy, is often weak in effort and quality (Mace, 1982). Evidence evaluating whether such counseling has a significant impact on the couple suggests that these interactions are of quite limited value (Olson, 1976).

One study (Guldner, 1971) "found that premarital couples generally were in a state of 'bliss'—an emotional detachment from reality, which rendered them not very teachable. This condition, it was found, continued into the early months of marriage. Not until the sixth month after the wedding had most of the couples come to see themselves in very realistic terms" (Mace, 1982, p. 192). Around the sixth month many couples needed help, help that they were previously often closed to in premarital counseling. But most important, these six-months-married couples indicated that the help they needed at that time "actually couldn't have been provided before marriage, because they just weren't ready for it then. They needed first to have

actual *experience* of married life" (Mace, 1982, p. 192).

Seldom does just information in itself provide the necessary motivation for couples to make changes to improve their relationships. Therefore, college courses in marriage and the family for unmarried undergraduates probably would also have limited value. Students may obtain knowledge that may generate some insight, which some may use as they imagine themselves as spouses and parents in the future. "However, unless they are already married, there is little possibility of direct experimental action, except in the distant future, by which time most of what they learned will probably have been forgotten" (Mace, 1982, p. 67). In addition, writes Mace:

> If some of them are *married, unless their spouses are also taking the course,* the chances of both developing the same insight together are probably poor; and if the insight is not shared, the motivation for experimental action will be one-sided and will probably fail. The chances of behavioral change, now or later, are probably quite remote. (1982, p. 67)

Other forms of education come from self-help books and popular magazines. Often such knowledge creates a desire for change in a marriage on the part of the wife; she is the one who is much more likely to read such material. Whatever fantasies for a different kind of relationship the wife may have, the husband typically does not respond enthusiastically. He may resist reading or just skim over the material; but more usually the whole matter is dropped. "The evidence is that it takes an unusual combination of favorable circumstances to bring an isolated married couple to the point of working through a self-help book together and really acting on it.

There is a possibility, but a rather remote one'' (Mace, 1982, p. 67).

NEW PROGRAMS TO BUILD INTIMATE MARRIAGES.

The movement from traditional to intimate marriages has resulted in a need for revolutionary changes in terms of education. Today most people have expectations for marriage that are much different from and higher than those in the past. And people have been given the wrong kind of preparation or practically no preparation at all for this new type of marriage.

We have seen that the informational approach is of very limited value *before* the actual experience of being married is under way. Mace and Mace (1986) indicate, ''It is rather like giving children classroom teaching about swimming—but offering no help when they get into the water'' (p. 24). The Maces suggest three limited goals for premarital couples:

1. *Get them to know each other* in depth by opening up their detailed life histories to each other. Each should try to learn as much as he or she can about the other.

2. *Help them to find out what they have in common* and what they don't have in common. Get them to understand their capacities to tolerate differences in values.

3. *Get them to share* in depth *their expectations of marriage. (Mace and Mace, 1986, p. 24)*

The focus here is on examining the marriageability of the two people as individuals and their compatibility as a potential married couple. A valuable instrument that is helpful in these areas is ''PREPARE,'' a questionnaire developed by David Olson.

This enables a couple, by each of them checking a series of questions, to get back a computerized evaluation of areas in the relationship in which they will have to work hard if the future marriage is to be successful. A two-year follow-up study has shown these predictions to be over 80 percent accurate. (Mace and Mace, 1986, p. 25)

There are also some things that can be taught to young people in schools or special classes that could be of value to them in their future marriages. ''It is never too early for children to learn the basic skills for communication with others, for empathic acceptance, for handling anger creatively, for making creative use of conflicts, and for negotiating disagreements'' (Mace, 1982, p. 191). Why such skills are not currently taught in elementary and high schools remains a mystery to the authors.

Mace (1982) argues, however, that the most important time to help couples is in the first year of marriage. Ironically this period has been when the least help has traditionally been available. Most people believe in letting the couple ''go it alone'' without outside interference; the feeling is that each marriage should be kept private. Isolated couples typically act as if everything is fine, and they hide any problems that they may be having, most of which they are poorly equipped to deal with anyway. Mace indicates that people play a curious game in the United States, ''pretending that we all have great marriages, although we know quite well that this is far from the truth'' (p. 198). Mace thinks it is time we gave up this charade and begin ''to *offer help* to newlywed couples *when they are having the experience of marriage*'' (p. 198).

There is considerable evidence that the first year in the marriage is critical (Guldner, 1971; Bader, 1980). In one study one-third of divorced people interviewed ''admitted that their marriages were already in serious trouble by the time they reached their first wedding anniversary'' (Mace, 1982, p. 198). One plan suggested by Mace has already been put into operation in Kansas City, since 1979, under the name of Growth in Marriage for Newlyweds program. It involves a six-week marriage-enrichment experience designed especially for newlyweds. Clergymen persuade the couple to commit themselves to the program before they are married. This approach focuses more on *preventive* than remedial services. Other types of programs would be possible during the newlywed period.

Another time period when young couples often need extra help is when a child arrives, particularly the first child. Typically this is a period of dramatic stress on the marital dyad. Because of myths surrounding this ''blessed happy event,'' the reality of the negative pressure on the marriage is usually hidden. Frequently there is a marital crisis, or the baby becomes the turning point that ultimately leads to the end of the marriage.

While four-fifths of all spouses share in the training for the birthing experience, few of these birthing groups continue *after* the baby is born. It would be possible to organize support groups for young mothers and fathers to help share and cushion the impact of a baby on a marriage. One example of such a group is called MELD, the Minnesota Early

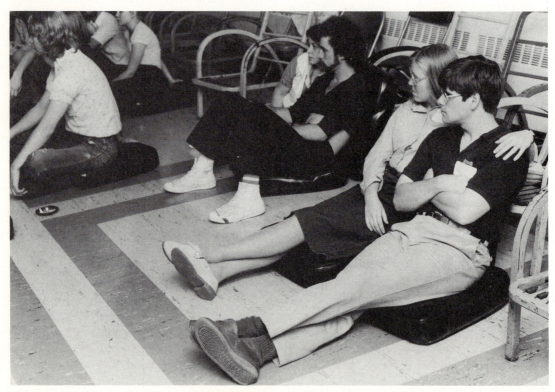

Various organizations are beginning to offer new programs on building intimacy to couples.

Learning Design. Couples join together during the second trimester of pregnancy and meet in groups for up to two years. The groups have access to whatever expert help they feel they need (Mace and Mace, 1986).

FAMILIES

What are the prospects for close relationships among other family members beyond the marital dyad? Mace (1982) argues that in an intact nuclear family when the quality of the marriage is high, there will usually be good-quality relationships between the parents and children also. Thus, if husbands and wives work to improve the degree of closeness in their marriages, their efforts will have a profoundly positive impact on their children as well. For example, new insights and relational skills tend to be shared with children. Mace thinks that "attempts on the part of one parent (usually the mother) to change patterns of interaction with the children, when the other parent is not participating, are hard to sustain" (1982, p. 48). But the development of an intimate marriage can help facilitate other intimate dyads in the nuclear family.

Children constantly observe their parents' interactions. Some parental behaviors are warm and pleasant; others involve arguing or the lack of skills in conflict resolution and crisis management. While intimate communication between the spouses usually occurs when they are alone, it can also occur in front of the whole family. The open sharing of feelings can thus come to be seen as a normal pattern of behavior. "Parents, however, also suggest something of their capacity for intimate communication in indirect ways. The way they look at each other, touch, sit close, exchange barely perceptible nods—there are a host of ways that children learn a

deep level of human communications, one that need not even be verbal" (J. Lewis, 1979, p. 79).

Thus, there are many ways in which parents can model intimacy. Besides directly sharing private feelings and thoughts, parents can create an *atmosphere of openness* where communicating in-depth emotions is a desirable process. "Whether the children are aware of the content of the parents' communication is probably not as important as their being conscious that it occurs" (J. Lewis, 1979, p. 79).

Kinship and Closeness

PARENTS AND ADULT OFFSPRING. The interaction between adult offspring and parents has been characterized by Bert Adams (1980) as one involving *positive concern.* Contrary to popular opinion, frequent contact between such intergenerational kin is common. Weekly or more frequent interaction exists if they live close by; those separated by large distances will typically communicate by telephone or mail at least monthly. Substantial mutual aid is exchanged as part of this positive concern.

There is also typically an *emotional bond* involving strong affectionate ties, which encourages frequent contact and an obligation to be there in time of need. The mother-daughter role is typically closer than mother-son, father-daughter, or father-son. Mothers and daughters are more likely than the other three dyads to play similar roles (wife and mother). "Thus, role convergence, coupled with the generally greater social emotional involvement of females with all sorts of kin, forms the basis for an extremely close relationship between adult daughters and their mothers" (B. Adams, 1980, p. 329). The other three parent-offspring relationships, however, are still among the closest of all kin relationships.

ADULT SIBLING RELATIONS. Adams uses the terms *interest* and *comparison* to describe the relations between adult siblings. *Interest* relates to the feeling that one should know what one's siblings are doing with their lives, how they are getting along, but typically there is no need for regular contact or mutual aid as there is with parents. In fact, financial aid can become a bone of contention or even the cause for a breakoff in relations.

The term *comparison* relates to sibling rivalry that does not end when brothers and sisters leave home. The point is that in a success-oriented society such as that in America, brothers and sisters compete and compare.

> That is, the question "How am I doing?" can well be answered by noting how one's achievements compare with those of one's siblings. . . . When the kin of orientation (adult offspring and their parents) get together, conversation is likely to turn—sometimes subtly, sometimes openly—to how well brother George or sister Susan is doing professionally or to how their marriages are going. (B. Adams, 1980, p. 330)

Thus, for example, there can be a great deal of emotional alienation between two brothers who have had widely differing degrees of success in their occupations. Women, in general, feel as though they would like more contact with their siblings, although they may not have the power to bring it about. They typically feel a greater obligation to keep kinship contacts going. On the whole, women in adulthood are more likely to try to be close not only to the nuclear family they helped to establish, but to their kin of orientation—parents and siblings—as well.

Some sibling dyads do involve extreme closeness in adulthood, but "best friends" as a label for a sibling relationship is more of an exception than the rule.

SECONDARY KINSHIP. Included in secondary kin are cousins, aunts, uncles, grandparents, and others. Adams uses the terms *circumstantial* and *incidental* to describe these relations. Such relations "seldom involve frequent contact, common interests, mutual aid, or strong affectional or obligatory concern. Yearly contact—the Christmas card, for example, or perhaps a kin reunion at holidays or during a vacation—frequently suffices" (1980, p. 331). One way to describe the circumstantial side of these relatives is that they may commonly be brought together by a marriage or death of a mutual family member. Most people in American society are not bothered by the weakness of secondary kinship relations (Adams, 1980).

There are two exceptions to the incidental nature of most secondary kin relations. One is grandparents, who actually, along with women, often form the hub of kin activity and involvement. The other exception is many ethnic groups. "Their activities—originally means for ensuring mutual survival—are now more likely to be means for achieving individual success" (p. 231). Jewish and black families would be examples.

IN-LAW RELATIONS. In-laws are relatives gained by marriage. Earlier studies (Komarovsky, 1962) found most in-law troubles took place between the husband and the wife's parents, possibly because of the traditional need for the man to control. Later studies have found more in-law conflicts between the wife and the husband's mother. Three factors mentioned by Adams that affect in-law relations are age of spouse, proximity to in-laws, and dependence on in-laws.

In terms of *age,* younger wives have more in-law troubles than older wives. Having children, however, is likely to improve relations between the two mothers. In terms of *proximity,* it appears that there are fewer troubled in-law relations when the young married couple lives a long distance away from the in-laws. Finally, a young husband's or wife's degree of emotional *dependence* on his or her own mother or father has an impact on in-law problems. For example, a "momma's boy" dependence often results in the wife and mother-in-law competing for the young man's time and interest, particularly if both have controlling personalities.

It is important to point out that publicity about the "meddlesome, troublesome mother-in-law" often results in mothers-in-law doing everything they can to avoid being a problem. It also appears that good in-law relations are associated with happier marriages. Judson and Mary Landis (1963) found that two-thirds of the people with good in-law relations also said that they have very happy marriages, whereas only 18 percent with fair or poor in-law relations reported that their marriages were very happy (B. Adams, 1980).

Kinship and Friendship

Lillian Rubin (1985) asked 300 men and women she interviewed what differences they saw between friends and family. One key difference was found to be self-disclosure. Most said that it was easier to share private information about themselves with a friend than with kin; a friend tended to be less judgmental. Repeatedly the comment was made that friends "accept me as I am." People said they tend to censor themselves to their families (L. Rubin, 1985; R. R. Bell, 1981; and B. Adams, 1968).

Friendships and family are indeed different types of relationships, and they involve differences in closeness. For example, people seem to be nicer to their friends and to risk more conflict with family than with friends. Family seems better equipped to survive stormy situations, partly because we tend to view family with a high sense of permanence. It may be because of this greater sense of security that people feel they have a greater sense of entitlement with kin than with a friend; they can behave in ways that would be unacceptable outside the family (L. Rubin, 1985).

But Rubin also found a tendency for people to protect family members compared to friends from hurt that they may be personally experiencing. When an individual experiences a painful event, he or she is more likely to seek out friends, whereas people will try to protect family from the depth and intensity of their misery. Still, if people are desperate, they tend to feel that they can always count on family; friendship is more likely to be experienced as a conditional relationship, whereas family is unconditional. As Robert Frost wrote in 1915, "Home is the place where, when you have to go there / They have to take you in" (L. Rubin, 1985).

Thus friends can *choose* or *choose not* to do what family is obligated to do. "There's no obligation to take a friend or to keep one; we're free to choose" (L. Rubin, 1985, p. 23). This quality of friendship is both its strength and its weakness. The freedom to choose and become involved means that one can be "unchosen" as well (L. Rubin, 1985).

Friendships can die by unilateral decision or by a shared decision. But most often they primarily drift apart by mutual consent. In contrast, family relations don't fall apart with little notice. Family relationships are based on "a blood tie" and "a shared history"; family doesn't end except by death. And shared experiences become part of the foundation of family solidarity. For many of us, kinship seems to fall more into the category of the sacred and friendship is in the area of the secular. While we have to fulfill the obligatory demands of family, friends typically have to be more understanding as they wait in the wings for us to finish our family responsibilities (L. Rubin, 1985).

In the final analysis the relative importance of family versus friendship is not easy to pinpoint. For example, certainly adult children and often other kin provide older people with extensive help, emotional and otherwise (Wood and Robertson, 1978). But it seems that to many of the elderly, friends are more important than family. "Several studies (Philblad and Adams, 1972; Anling, 1976; Wood and Robertson, 1978; Perlman et al., 1979) have examined the contribution of kin and friends to life satisfaction and loneliness and these studies consistently show that friendships contribute more to morale than do relations with kin" (Dickens and Perlman, 1981, p. 120). Perhaps contact with family members persists for older people, but the enjoyment gained from such interaction lessens. Rosow (1967) has argued that frequent contact between the elderly and their children may be ritualistic, based on obligation rather than on warmth or closeness (Dickens and Perlman, 1981).

FRIENDSHIPS

The statement that "blood is thicker than water" has traditionally been true in American society. In the United States friendship is strictly a private affair, with no public ceremonies or rituals existing as in other countries.

In Germany, for example, there's a small ceremony called Duzen, *the name itself signifying the transformation in the relation-*

ship. The ritual calls for the two friends, each holding a glass of wine or beer, to entwine arms, thus bringing each other physically close, and to drink up after making a promise of eternal brotherhood with the word Bruderschaft. *When it's over, the friends will have passed from a relationship that requires the formal* Sie *mode of address to the familiar* Du. (L. Rubin, 1985, p. 4)

No clear lines mark either the beginning or the end of a friendship in America. Also, the one word *friend* is used to describe a wide range of relationships involving varying degrees of closeness (L. Rubin, 1985).

Most people value having friends so much that it is considered to be a sign of a personality weakness if one does not have them. Even small children are tormented about the lack of friends. Most of all teenagers fear being unpopular. But it is only recently that the social sciences have started to study the topic of friendship. The reason is that our primary focus on marriage and the family has "blinded us to the meaning and importance of friendship in our lives. Until the soaring divorce rate pointed so sharply to a crisis in marriage, we still expected that all our needs for emotional intimacy, social connectedness and intellectual stimulation would be met there" (L. Rubin, 1985, p. 9). Friends have traditionally been secondary in our lives to marriage and romantic love. Today there is increased awareness of the importance of friendship. It is now recognized that even married people need friends, and the single, divorced, and widowed need them even more (L. Rubin, 1985; R. R. Bell, 1981).

For friends we tend to choose people like ourselves; one study showed that friends "were alike in social and demographic characteristics as well as in attitudes, interests, intelligence, and personality traits" (R. R.

Bell, 1981, p. 19). Age is one of the most powerful characteristics friends have in common. Since people of any age group are likely to be similar also in terms of personal and social resources, the relationship is more likely to be equal and exploitation is less likely. Friendships between the same sex particularly have this characteristic.

Bell (1981) states that friendships usually come from one's own social class, again because it is the nature of friendship to be based on social equality. Allan (1977) found, however, that friendships differ somewhat in various social classes. Middle-class individuals form friendships with others met in a wide variety of contexts. Working-class friendships, by contrast, are mostly restricted to neighbors and workmates but primarily to kin. Thus, while family makes up the most significant social friends of the working class, they seem not to do so in the middle class (Allan, 1977; Hendrix, 1979; B. Adams, 1970). Among the working class, nonkin are rarely entertained at home, a place reserved for kin.

Friendships do infer rights and obligations, even though these are not spelled out explicitly. To make such responsibilities explicit causes the relationship to become formalized, and such formalization is not typical of friendship in the United States (R. R. Bell, 1981). Friendships obviously will vary greatly in intimacy, ranging all the way from proximity friends and selected friends to significant others and intimate others. The quality of any friendship relates to needs of the partners, what they are willing to put into it, or what they need to receive from a friendship. (See Table 15.3.)

Friendship over the Life Cycle

Typically, individuals do not just have a single friendship that serves their needs throughout their lifetimes. The usual pattern is that "new friends are added and old friends drop off" (R. R. Bell, 1981, p. 21). Also we seem to need somewhat different kinds of friends over time; they vary with our stage in the life cycle.

Dickens and Perlman (1981) have summarized studies of friendship over the life cycle. In general, the number of friends that adult people have tends to decline with age, especially for men (Fischer, 1979). The frequency of contact with friends also declines with age. For example, Stueve and Gerson (1977) found that "73 percent of young single friends were seen at least weekly whereas the corresponding figure for people in the post-parental stage of the family life cycle dropped to 39 percent" (Dickens and Perlman, 1981, pp. 110–111). Intimacy with friends also declines slightly with age (Stueve and Gerson, 1977); men particularly have fewer confidants as they grow older (Fischer and Phillips, 1982).

Declining friendships can partly be explained by marriage and parenthood (Dickens and Perlman, 1981). For example, more friendships are reported by single individuals, an intermediate number by childless couples, and fewest by parents (Shulman, 1975; Fischer and Phillips, 1982). It seems that as people grow older, "they appear content with their old friends and seem to lack initiative in forming new relationships" (Dickens and Perlman, 1981, p. 111). But older women have larger friendship networks than older men. In addition, the quality of older female friendships is deeper; they are more likely to have confidantes or intimate others (Lowenthal and Haven, 1968; Powers and Bultena, 1976). Also women seem to have more stringent criteria as to what constitutes a friend. Highest intimacy is reported with childhood friends, while relationships with workers and neighbors tend to be less intimate. "As an

TABLE 15.3

INGREDIENTS OF FRIENDSHIP

More than 40,000 people participated in *Psychology Today*'s 1979 survey on friendship in America. The following list summarizes responses to the question, "How important to you is each of these qualities in a friend?" The numbers represent the percentage of respondents who said a quality was "important" or "very important." Note that those near the top of the list are more likely to be intimacy-related items than those near the bottom of the list.

Keeps confidences	89%
Loyalty	88
Warmth, affection	82
Supportiveness	76
Frankness	75
Sense of humor	74
Willingness to make time for me	62
Independence	61
Good conversationalist	59
Intelligence	57
Social conscience	49
Shares leisure (noncultural) interests	48
Shares cultural interests	30
Similar educational background	17
About my age	10
Physical attractiveness	9
Similar political views	8
Professional accomplishment	8
Abilities and background different from mine	8
Ability to help me professionally	7
Similar income	4
Similar occupation	3

SOURCE: *Adapted from Parlee, 1979, p. 49.*

overall generalization, contact with friends declines during the adult stage of the life-cycle while contact with kin increases" (Dickens and Perlman, 1981, p. 113).

Gender Differences in Friendship

In her book *Just Friends* (1985) Lillian Rubin indicates that more than 75 percent of the single women she interviewed had no problem identifying a best friend. Those who didn't have a best friend were often looking for one. In contrast, more than two-thirds of the single men interviewed could not name a single best friend. Most of the men shrugged the question off and said, "Best friends are for kids." In addition, for the single men who did name a best friend the person named was much more likely to be a woman than a man. Most of these men talked about how hard it was to develop a close relationship with a man. Said one man, "Nobody likes to feel they've been vulnerable to another man" (p. 63).

According to Robert Bell in his book *Worlds of Friendship* (1981), gender is the most important social factor regarding friendship variations. He found that women who had a variety of friends overwhelmingly formed dyadic paired relationships, not groups of three or more persons. The friendships of men, in contrast, often do include three-or-more-person groups. "For women, the limiting of each friendship to two persons is often a reflection of the intensity of involvement. In general, the more we will reveal or commit ourselves interpersonally, the fewer the people with whom we are willing to enter into that kind of relationship" (Bell, 1981, p. 64).

There is a pattern toward same-gender friendships already among children. Boys have a desire for autonomy, and they look for group support in that search. In contrast, girls develop sets of close friends seemingly because of their particular concern with emotional intimacy. Girls depend on friends for emotional support and as confidantes, not as allies in rebellion. "Even little girls are far more inclined than boys to share secrets, gossip, giggle together, and simply *talk*. As they grow up, girls usually develop and expand their friendships, which often are based on the simple willingness of one person to reveal herself to another" (Novak, 1983, p. 62).

In a study of American fifth graders, sociologist Janet Lever found that girls tended to feel most comfortable when they were with a single best friend. There often was an open show of affection, physically with hand holding and verbally with "love notes," both of which reaffirmed how special each was to the other. Even when girls did get together in groups, the tone was more likely to be one of closeness than of rebellion. A 12-year-old girl reports, for example, "Naomi had a party on Saturday (sleep over). We had true confessing and everyone told their secrets. Then we felt so close! We hugged each other and said we loved each other. Some people cried" (Z. Rubin, 1980, pp. 107–108).

It is difficult to imagine boys behaving in this way. Boys, however, can also have best friends, but these friendships usually are less expressive and intimate than those between girls. For example, hand holding and love notes are virtually nonexistent among boys; they are more likely to share "group secrets" than personal thoughts and feelings. Girls also tend to be more exclusive than boys; "They are less likely to expand their two-person friendships to include a third person. Girls appear to have a more acute appreciation than boys of the fragility of intimate relationships and of the ways in which one friendship may sometimes threaten another" (Z. Rubin, 1980, p. 108).

Traditionally, adult female friendships have been seen as inferior, trivial, and frivolous as compared to those of men. Throughout the world historically men's friendships have been considered more important. For example, in China and among the middle class in Mexico, women are not supposed to have "friends"; they have family and neighbors. Thus Robert Bell writes, "In many societies men have friends and women have relatives" (1981, p. 59).

Bell strongly believes that the traditional view that women's friendships are rather insignificant is wrong. The research evidence indicates that women's friendships typically are of a higher quality and greater depth than men's friendships. Women are both more self-revealing and accepting in their close relationships; typically men's friendships are defined in terms of doing things together. "Women more typically come from within themselves in their friendships with other women while men typically . . . reveal little about what is going on inside them'' (1981, p. 61).

In the United States women usually have an easier time forming friendships than men. In addition, women more actively seek out others as potential friends, "and because women are more willing to reveal parts of themselves, they set up a situation where the intimacy of friendship can develop" (R. R. Bell, 1981, p. 61). The wife is often a man's only confidante (R. R. Bell, 1981).

Women, unlike men, tend to make clear distinctions between important friends and a mate. Typically a woman does not think of her husband as her best friend. Said one woman in Lillian Rubin's sample, "I love my husband and my kids, but they cannot give me what I get from my women friends" (1985, p. 66). Men say they don't need best friends, particularly if they have a wife. The difference between the two sexes is "what an intimate relationship with someone of the same sex means to each of them" (p. 66).

Female friendships are probably more important today than in previous history, particularly for women beyond their 40s. While men who divorce in middle age or later are very likely to remarry, that is not true for women. Women who do not remarry are commonly supported emotionally in their lives by a friendship network of women of a similar marital status and age. "The friends provide the means for a social and interpersonal life without a husband. It also seems clear that women are better able to adapt to not having a husband than is the man to not having a wife" (R. R. Bell, 1981, p. 70).

In terms of social class, lower-status women have fewer friendships than higher-status women. Also, lower-class women are more likely to develop a greater proportion of their friends from the neighborhood. "By contrast, higher-status housewives first met a

Since women who divorce in middle age are less likely to remarry than men, female friendships become very important to them.

greater percentage of their close friends at clubs and organizations and through their husbands' work and their children's school. When contrasted with working-class women, those women in the middle class have a wider community from which to draw their friends" (R. R. Bell, 1981, p. 70). Working-class wives tend to maintain close ties with old girlfriends and family. Thus, for these women, emotional and social support has not traditionally come from their husbands but rather from same-sex friends and family. Women who work outside the home are more likely to develop occupationally based friendships than men are. Men seldom establish close friendships with co-workers because typically they are in competition or in contact with people of differing power. "The women's movement encouraged women to see each other more as allies than as competitors, and this, in turn, paved the way toward much stronger friendships among women" (Novak, 1983, p. 62).

Some studies indicate that men have more friends than women, but "this has more to do with men's propensity for naming as friends anyone with whom they have some ongoing association—co-workers, neighbors, tennis partners, members of the bowling team—while women tend to use the term 'friend' more selectively. Generally, women's friendships with each other rest on shared intimacies, self-revelation, nurturance and emotional support" (L. Rubin, 1985, p. 61). As one of Rubin's female respondents said,

> *There are a lot of people I can play with, but the people I call my real friends are the ones I can talk to also. I mean, they're the people I can share* myself *with, not just my time. (1985, p. 61)*

Men tend to *do* together rather than *be* together.

Lillian Rubin (1985) argues that some men do have some emotional ties between them, which would not be categorized as intimacy. It involves what she calls "bonding" between males. She writes, "Men, I believe, can be quite deeply bonded to each other without the kind of sharing of thought and feeling that is so much a part of women's friendships and that we associate with the word 'intimacy' " (p. 68).

Only when bonding is distinguished from intimacy can the friendships among buddies that are seen among men in the United States, especially in the working class, be fully understood. These are relationships where particular men seem very intensely connected but there is little, if any, deep, verbal expression. Writes Rubin,

> *By the time I finished talking with those few [cases of bonding] I encountered, I came to believe that the nights of drinking together that are so common among these men come not so much out of a desire to carouse but, at least in part, out of [a] . . . wish*

> *to relax some of the constraints that bind them in their human relationships. (1985, p. 72)*

It is argued by Fasteau (1975) that drinking allows men to say things to their friends for which they are not truly responsible. Men can then reveal deeper feelings, exchange confidences, and even show empathy and emotional support for another man. "Often what is revealed or displayed in a drunken exchange is not to be brought up when both friends are sober" (R. R. Bell, 1981, p. 83).

Rubin believes that such bonding relationships exist among men in the middle class also. According to her, "There's comfort for men in the very nonverbal quality of their friendships that women decry—comfort in the belief that intimacy can be there without words" (1985, pp. 73–74). But she argues that bonding is not intimacy. "Intimacy requires some greater shared expression of thought and feeling than these friendships exhibit, some willingness to allow another into our inner life, into the thoughts and feelings that live there" (1985, p. 74). Rubin found 10 percent of the males she interviewed, mostly men who were not married or living with a woman, "who told of friendships with other men that included the kind of intimacy and sharing of self that, when it exists at all, usually is reserved for women" (1985, p. 74).

Robert Bell points out that men often fake or kid about something that is really emotionally important to them because they cannot deal with presenting their feelings in a straightforward manner. Ironically, men may even call each other nasty names as a form of endearment. Often, in the locker room particularly, one male will tell another that he sure is "an ugly son-of-a-bitch"; actually this is considered to be a sign of affection. Rarely is this type of talk taken literally.

Male bonding involves emotional ties between men but lacks an in-depth sharing of feelings.

Also, rarely would women make such insulting exchanges to each other (Bell, 1981). Bell found that the majority of men had never told their best friend that they like him. If they did so, they did it negatively and jokingly—"You dumb bastard, you're okay."

Working-class men reveal less about themselves to their friends than do middle-class people. But working-class men are much less competitive in their work situations than middle-class men, so working-class men will have more work-related friends. These friendships, as mentioned, however, are seldom expanded to the home in the form of entertaining.

Are men making changes in their friendships? Bell argues that he does not see much change in the quality and acceptance by men of new levels of male friendship. Such a change "would mean the development of new relational skills that would call for changes in men's views about competition, sexism and its values about male supremacy, and especially about fears of homosexuality" (1981, p. 92).

Cross-Gender Friends

Throughout history, friendships have generally been limited to persons of the same sex. The idea that men and women could be friends in nonsexual ways, other than in courtship, has not typically been considered a realistic possibility. This appears to be a universal pattern (R. R. Bell, 1981).

The pattern that has existed in the twentieth century in the United States has permitted a high level of cross-gender interaction but mainly among the young and nonmarried. Once marriage is entered into, relationships with the other sex are drastically restricted. Adult cross-sex needs are expected to be met primarily within marriage (R. R. Bell, 1981).

Even among the unmarried, friendships are typically not the goal; seeking a marriage partner is. In fact, when one single person tells a person of the other sex that he or she is liked as a friend, it typically is not taken as a compliment. Robert Bell notes that it is a common belief that men and women can be lovers but not just friends. It is also a common belief that men will exploit cross-gender friendships sexually (Bell, 1981).

In Bell's research both men and women viewed same-sex friendships differently from other-sex friendships. "In general, respondents said they would reveal more to a same-sex friend than to an opposite-sex friend" (p. 99). As one business woman respondent in Bell's study said:

> With women I can share and relate. . . .
> Men don't know how to be companions.
> They don't have the ability to just be. They
> have got to have a purpose and be doing
> things. But basically with my women
> friends we all know where we are coming
> from—but with male friends there is always
> a part that is unknown. (1981, p. 99)

In terms of social class the general pattern is for the working class to have greater sex segregation than the middle class. Cross-gender friendships in the lower class are also less likely because of the stronger "machismo" values among males, who in general devalue women and any relationships with them, other than sexual. Many men who view women as inferiors would try to avoid cross-gender friendships because such relationships are viewed as "socially and personally demeaning, inappropriate, or wrong" (R. R. Bell, 1981, p. 103).

What do men and women want from cross-gender friendships? Men are more likely to focus on sexuality. "They see a particular woman, or even a given time with a woman, as having only sexual significance—they show little or no interest in interpersonal involvement" (R. R. Bell, 1981, p. 104). "While they turn to women as sexual partners, that may be for no more than a few minutes a week. Sometimes it is just long enough for the man to establish a sense of heterosexuality. For many men, women are good to sleep with but not to stay awake with" (R. R. Bell, 1981, p. 78).

Largely it is women rather than men who tend to be more interested and appreciative of other-gender friendships.

> Often then, men and women come from
> different directions in what they want from
> cross-sex friendships, and the potential for
> conflict is great. . . . Because women have
> traditionally been treated as inferior, they
> sometimes enjoy friendships with men because that represents some acceptance by
> men as to their being equal and worthwhile
> partners and companions. (R. R. Bell,
> 1981, p. 104)

The biggest deterrent to cross-gender friendship is the sexual dimension, even among the unmarried. But there are some close male and female friendships among singles that are strongly influenced by sexual activity. Such a relationship, however, is difficult to maintain in many societies, including American society. "The social pressures are such that if the two people like each other as friends and are also sexually involved, they generally feel compelled to move into a romantic relationship" (R. R. Bell, 1981, p. 105).

It appears to be quite difficult to have a male-female friendship without sexual involvement. In fact, often "a sexual relationship is assumed to exist between friends who keep their friendship private, whether or not it is actually the case" (R. R. Bell, 1981, p. 105). Women complain about sexual pressure in their cross-gender relationships. Some feel that sex will inevitably interfere and threaten the relationship. A 26-year-old female law student says,

Some of my male friendships have had to end because of attempts to move it into the bedroom. I have never had one male friend who accepted the friendship without wanting to move into sexual involvement. (R. R. Bell, 1981, p. 106)

Thus it is not uncommon for sex to end the friendship. But some friendships can survive after the sexual involvement has ended. "Some men and women find it easier to become good friends after they have stopped being lovers or spouses. This was often the case when sexual tension had been the cause of problems—without it, the friendship was closer" (R. R. Bell, 1981, p. 106). But when the sexual, or love, dimension ends in a relationship, "It was found that where a rejected woman might be able to redefine her relationship with her former boyfriend from 'love' to 'friendship,' a rejected man found it much more difficult to accomplish such a redefinition" (Bell, 1981, p. 107).

The potential for sexuality particularly complicates friendships where one or both of the partners are married. A cross-gender "friendship often implies to others that something must be missing from their respective marriages, because it is generally assumed that couples will get all they need in cross-sex friendship from their spouse" (R. R. Bell, 1981, p. 108). A husband would not typically be as threatened if his spouse had a close female friend, but he would if the friend were a man.

There will always be people who will say close cross-gender friendships "cannot successfully coexist with a couple's own intimate relationships" (Lasswell and Lobsenz, 1983, p. 151). To say the least, society tends to discourage such relationships. In the business world, however, cross-gender friendships are increasing as more women have careers. Still people gossip and act out petty jealousies. Such relationships are often misunderstood, and many such participants fear sexual involvement will become a reality—the same fear their spouses have (Lasswell and Lobsenz, 1983).

Third parties of either sex who become intimate friends can indeed damage a marriage. The revealing of private information about the marital dyad to a person outside the marriage—regarding sex, money, children, secrets of any sort—could be viewed as a form of betrayal by the spouse. The friend hearing about such private matters may also be uncomfortable. "Accepting a friend's confidences may also involve you and your partner in the problems they represent" (Lasswell and Lobsenz, 1983, p. 150).

Some career women find that male friendships may help them advance professionally. Most of these women attempt to keep these friendships platonic; they see the friendships as too valuable to risk sexual involvement. "In short, though office romances are usually recognized as being hazardous to one's occupational health, office friendships are seen as valuable assets" (Lasswell and Lobsenz, 1983, p. 153). But platonic cross-gender friendships typically are not easily formed. Men and women will have to learn how to make friends with each other. Few of us are taught to view someone of the other gender as a potential friend (Lasswell and Lobsenz, 1983). Lasswell and Lobsenz have four suggestions for developing cross-gender friends:

1. Don't conceal being married; this helps to make your intentions clear.

2. Allow the relationship to develop slowly. Don't self-disclose too freely in the beginning.

3. If sexual overtones develop, clear this up with frank discussions. Discuss any feelings of jealousy your spouse may have; silence helps to increase suspicion.

4. Know what you expect from such a cross-gender friendship. It is dishonest to have the secret aim of sexuality.

To avoid the sexual overtones of cross-gender friendships, some women seek friendships with gay men. Contrary to the view that homosexual men dislike women, more than two-thirds of gay men are found to have women friends (Bell and Weinberg, 1978). Straight women state that they feel more like an equal with a gay man. Many women genuinely like gay men; they are said to offer several qualities that heterosexual men do not. Included is the belief that homosexual men are more empathic than straight men; they are less conditioned by traditional stereotypes of male behavior. Also, homosexual men are much less likely to judge women by their looks. Since they don't relate to women only in terms of physical appearance, they are more likely to appreciate other traits such as intelligence, humor, or personality. But the most important reason why straight women and gay men can be friends is the fact that these men do not come on sexually to women (Malone, 1980).

Women who have male gay friends tend to be more accepting of, and enlightened about, homosexuality. Most are so open and frank that they can discuss their own emotional and sexual lives with their gay friends. About two-thirds of the women studied by Malone said ''that they 'let down their hair' with gay men as much as they did with their female friends'' (Malone, 1980, p. 27). And they certainly are more open with gay men than they are with straight male friends. It should be noted that gay men and straight women have a common emotional interest, namely a physical interest in men. Straight women also indicate that they share other interests with gay men, such as the ballet, the opera or the theater; dancing; shopping; and cooking. Also, straight men are often angry toward and fearful of gay men, just as many are of feminists. So straight women and gay men may have an understanding of straight male hostility in common.

Married Couples and Their Friends

Most social relationships among married couples take place with other married couples. It is doubtful, however, that friendships between two married couples provide the same sort of privacy and exclusiveness found in a close dyadic relationship. Obviously the emotional needs and demands of four people would be much harder to meet than those of just two persons. Of course, the purpose of couple friends may be more for play and activity than for satisfying emotional need. Often a friendship involving two married couples is subdivided into two dyadic relationships—between the two wives and two husbands. In such instances the cross-gender interactions are superficial and ritualistic (R. R. Bell, 1981).

Married Americans have usually viewed their friendships on a ''couple basis,'' two by two, in linked pairs. Foursomes have been formed, at least in traditional marriages, but it has never been easy to do so. ''The women must like each other, the men must like each other, and each man and woman must be able to get along reasonably well with the partner of the opposite sex. Instead of two linkages, eight must be worked out. The complexity of the friendship pattern often proves a source of conflict" (Lasswell and Lobsenz, 1983, p. 148).

It is possible, however, for a couple to become too involved, too close in their friendships with other couples. Some spouses avoid dyadic intimacy with their own partners through the technique of having another couple or couples always around. Obviously if outsiders are usually present, a couple has little time to have fun alone together or to develop closeness. Also, couples who have many difficulties in their marriages will sometimes spend all their time with other people to camouflage their unhappiness (Lasswell and Lobsenz, 1983).

The husband has traditionally been the initiator of couple friendships. Typically a male friend from before the marriage or a work associate serves to bring the two couples together. Sometimes the wives do not take to their husband's male friends very well, particularly in the lower class. Lillian Rubin (1976) found that many young wives among the working class try to break their husbands' attachments to high school friends. By the same token the husband usually complained about the friends (and their husbands) that the wife tried to bring into the marriage. On the whole, men seem to be less willing to try out possible new friendships. But with more women working outside the home today, they will be trying to bring more friendships into the marriage in the future.

Single Parents and Friendships

Divorce practically always brings a change in friendship patterns. While friendships from the marriage may not entirely be lost, they typically fade in importance. If there is on-going contact with married friends, it is usually with the spouse of the same gender as the divorced person. But by and large the old

married community is gone; "The single parent no longer fits in" (Weiss, 1979, p. 174).

No matter whether single parenthood came about through either death or divorce, there is a need to make new friends and modify other old friendships. The individual should develop a new sense of community, and until that is accomplished there will be feelings of emptiness, isolation, and marginality to earlier friendship networks (Weiss, 1979). It is difficult for many single parents, however, to construct this new friendship community. "There is a sense of personal inefficiency, a questioning of self-worth, that makes rejection seem a thoroughly plausible anticipation" (Weiss, 1979, p. 177).

Various kinds of friendships are maintained by single parents. "There will be friends to go out with . . . friends with whom to do things with the kids, and friends who are intimates, with whom it is possible to talk about worries, moods, plans, and hopes" (Weiss, 1979, p. 178). Most important in this network are one or two intimate others. "These are the friends to whom the single parent feels closest, who are regularly used as confidants, whose understanding and support play critical roles in maintaining the single parents' emotional equilibrium" (p. 180). But even intimate friends will have limitations on their time. It is generally understood by such intimate others that work, children, family demands, and probably even a new boyfriend take precedence over their friendship (Weiss, 1979).

Single-parent friendships tend to differ in a number of ways from interactions with kin. The helpfulness of friends is more spontaneous and less obligatory. Still, favors have to be returned for favors given; failure to reciprocate is exploitation and grounds for ending the relationship. While kin may be more likely to help without reciprocation, this is too much to ask in most friendships. The reciprocity need not be exact, however; true friends do not keep a running count of who has done what for whom. Friends tend to be less judgmental after a divorce than kin. This is one reason people turn more to friends than to kin when going through a divorce. Women often receive material support from families, emotional support from friends (R. R. Bell, 1981).

Weiss (1975) indicates that a few partners remain good friends after a divorce. They may talk regularly by telephone, consult with each other about various problems, or spend holidays or a child's birthday together. But most couples have mixed feelings about such a friendship; it is a bittersweet relationship, which is both painful and rewarding. "It carries unhappy memories and is itself a reminder that things might have been different, and better, if only the couple had been able to be friendly earlier" (Weiss, 1975, p. 91).

THE FUTURE OF INTIMATE RELATIONSHIPS

The 1980s have seen more interest in the topic of intimacy than ever before in history. People's goals have changed from finding personal happiness through *individual* fulfillment in the human potential movement to finding happiness through *relationships.* Most Americans have come to realize in the 1980s that the so-called ideal of the independent self of the 1970s was in reality a way of avoiding vulnerability by not expressing a need for others. There has never been a human being so independent that he or she did not need someone. "To be split off from relationships and to define ourselves solely by our separateness is . . . pathological" (Bardwick, 1979, p. 128).

But it is also pathological to define *all* that we are, or *ever may be,* in terms of a relationship. It is unhealthy for a person to base his or her total self-worth only on the role played in a relationship. Having a sense of self-esteem, however, does not negate the simultaneous need for commitment. "Relationships are healthy when the individuals within them are neither solely dependent upon the relationship for identity nor so resistant that they prevent intimacy" (Bardwick, 1979, p. 129). What has really changed between the 1970s and the 1980s is that fewer people now deny their dependence.

The traditional hallmark of mature human development in the United States has been the possession of traits that involve a person's ability to *separate* from relationships—from mother, from siblings, from family of orientation. Adult maturity is said to be found in economic success, independence, autonomy, self-reliance, and self-actualization. These traits have been held up as signs of mental health by much of American society. This model was developed by men and primarily for men. Women too have tried this model, but have more recently found it to be lacking in many respects (Frieden, 1981). (See Box 15.4.)

In contrast to the model that stresses the "self" and "independence," men and women in the future need to be taught a "healthy" dependence. The more a person feels that he or she can legitimately call upon others for help and the more a person feels others are listening and caring, the more worthy that person will feel and the higher that person's self-esteem will be. Women also have a need to be listened to and affirmed, just as they have listened to and affirmed their men, children, and friends. If their emotional needs are not met and they have to continue to provide for others, they will grow to resent the demands that are continuously made on them (Stiver, 1984). The authors have found this to be one of the most common reasons that women emotionally divorce their hus-

BOX 15.4

THE TRAP OF SELF-ACTUALIZATION

The quest for self-fulfillment borrows its forms of expression from whatever sources are most convenient. Unfortunately, the materials closest to hand have been an odd combination of the psychology of affluence, reinforced by an outlook whose interwoven tenets proclaim: live for the moment, regard the self as a sacred object, be more self-assertive, hold nothing back.

Where did those assumptions come from?

Early in the postwar quarter-century, the ideas of "more of everything" and the "primacy of self" merged in a school of thought that may be called "self" psychology. Self psychology received its most influential expression in the work of the psychologists Abraham H. Maslow, Carl Rogers, and Erich Fromm. Their thinking spread throughout the culture, with the help of self-help movements such as est and books with titles such as *Looking Out for No. 1, How to Be Your Own Best Friend,* and *Pulling Your Own Strings.*

In particular, the theories of Maslow ingeniously combine a psychology of affluence with a vision of inner development. In the 1950s, Maslow posited a hierarchy of human needs that has become part of the conventional wisdom of our time. According to the hierarchy, people who are preoccupied with meeting "lower-order needs" for food, shelter, and economic security have little energy left for pursuing the "higher-order needs" of the spirit. Vital energies are released to the search for "self-actualization" only when the lower-order needs have been met. We move up the hierarchy of needs in an orderly fashion, on an escalator of increasing affluence.

There is obviously some sense in which human priorities do function according to a hierarchy. When we are sick, all that counts is getting well. When our survival, physical or economic, is threatened, it powerfully concentrates the mind (as Samuel Johnson observed about the prospect of being hanged). But the idea that self-actualization—the highest achievement of which human beings are capable, according to Maslow—presupposes our ascension through various stages of economic well-being is a peculiarly self-congratulatory philosophy for a materialistic age.

In Maslowism, the self-actualized person who steps off at the top of the escalator is a particular personality type. He or she is assumed to be a creative, autonomous self, virtually independent of culture. The theme of the creative individual, independent of culture, is to be repeated over and over again in the literature of self psychology and its pop psychology progeny. One of Wayne Dyer's books speaks glowingly of the theory that "You are the sum total of your choices."

By now, millions of Americans have garnered extensive—and painful—experience in personal struggles with the new, Maslow-inspired duty-to-self ethic. It has, to be sure, some benefits to offer the individual, but the core idea is a moral and social absurdity. It gives moral sanction to desires that do not contribute to society's well-being. It contains no principle for synchronizing the requirements of the society with the goals of the individual. It fails to discriminate between socially valuable desires and socially destructive ones, and often works perversely against the real goals of both individuals and society. It provides no principle other than hedonism for interpreting the meaning of the changes and sacrifices we must make to adapt to new economic-political conditions.

SOURCE: *Adapted from Daniel Yankelovich, 1981.*

bands. Even the most eager to please and unselfish person will feel some resentment if need fulfillment is not reciprocated.

In reality, both sexes need the same thing: emotionally enriching relationships. At this time in history, the role of "supplying connections between people has been by and large assigned to women and carried by women for everyone" (Miller, 1986b). They have been responsible for those specific "connections which will foster and enhance well-being and especially the growth or enlargement of others" (Miller, 1986b). This has been the traditional definition of the mother and also the "good wife" (Miller, 1986b). In contrast, males are not raised to believe that a primary goal in life is the enhancement of others in relationships—a process, incidentally, which will simultaneously enhance themselves. Certainly from day one our cultural teachings for males do not focus on learning how to do everything possible to enlarge and strengthen others and most particularly women (Miller, 1986b).

For these new kinds of empowering relationships to exist, each individual has to be able to communicate his or her experience as he or she really is. And the partner must be able to hear these experiences. But the partner must not only hear out of a sense of obligation, but must *want* to hear these experiences. This is "the best and truly the only way that we find out about *ourselves* and allow ourselves then to grow. Growth occurs

only in interaction— nobody grows in isolation!" (Miller, 1986b).

While attempting to understand the other person's experience, something new is acknowledged in ourselves and we are touched by that experience (Jordan, 1986). From exchanges based on increasingly authentic interactions, people go on to increasing intimacy. We feel close to "people who have engaged with us in ways that make us feel expanded as opposed to contracted or diminished" (Miller, 1986b). We also feel close to the people whom we have engaged in a manner so that they expand. This is why we feel close to our spouses and our children and close to our friends, if we are lucky enough to find this intimacy in relationships outside our families (Miller, 1986b).

Our culture does not provide purposeful training in close relationships. Americans do not learn a "relational mode" for living and acting. But this, says Miller, "is basic to everything" (1986a, p. 2).

Either we deal with the feelings which are inevitably present by turning to each other—or we turn away from others. If we turn from others without conveying recognition of the existence of their feelings, we inevitably lead the other person to feel diminished. (Miller, 1986a, p. 13)

When one grows in a relationship one is connected with another person through feelings, thoughts, and behaviors. When the partners build a relationship, something exciting happens. Something new is shared. The connection or the relationship does not belong to one or the other but rather to both. Yet each will feel that the relationship is "his" or "hers" because it is part of him or her and because each has contributed to the new creation. And the relationship itself has contributed to each of the partners, for both are now *more* than they were before the relationship began (Miller, 1986a).

CHAPTER REVIEW

1. While traditional marriages are still common, more and more people are seeking intimacy in their relationships. The growing equality of women is probably the most important factor influencing this turn to emotional closeness. Most marriages today, however, are probably best described as "transitional marriages"; they no longer involve rigid gender roles, but neither have they reached a high degree of emotional closeness.

2. In order to develop more intimacy in marriages, men will have to be convinced that it is to their benefit to share deep feelings with their wives. It is advantageous for men to become more intimate because it may improve their physical and mental health, because they may be able to make better decisions, and because it will create more self-awareness. Four conditions that can help men to be more intimate include confrontation, anxiety, disconfirmation, and psychological safety.

3. New educational programs, before and after marriage, are needed to teach such skills as empathy, the creative handling of anger, conflict management, and the negotiation of disagreements. But probably the most crucial time for providing help is during the first year of marriage, after the newlyweds have had some experience in marriage and when illusionary intimacy is declining.

4. The key to a close family life is a high-quality marriage. The degree of closeness among husbands and wives will have an impact on parent-child dyads. Also parents are the models of intimacy for their children. Contrary to popular beliefs, intergenerational (parent and adult offspring) contact remains strong in American society. Relations with secondary kin (such as cousins, aunts, and grandparents) are typically incidental, with the possible exception of grandparents and some ethnic groups such as blacks and Jews.

5. Friendships have gained more importance in recent years because of high divorce rates. Women tend to have more intimate friends, and men mostly have activity friends with little meaningful self-disclosure. Cross-gender friendships are difficult to achieve; they often become complicated by sexual activity. Friends among straight women and gay men, however, are not uncommon.

Family Research Methods and Techniques

1. Surveys

Surveys are used more than any other method by family researchers. People are asked about their attitudes, feelings, behavior, thoughts, and values. Usually only a sample of a larger population is taken. The goal simply is to have every person in the larger population have an equal chance of being chosen in the sample. Such a sample would then be representative of the larger population on particular variables such as age, marital status, gender, and social class.

ADVANTAGES

1. The researcher can obtain large amounts of data from a small sample and generalize to the whole population.
2. The data can easily be analyzed with the use of computers.
3. Trends over time can be determined by asking the same questions in repeat studies.

DISADVANTAGES

1. Survey data are usually not in-depth and lack richness of feeling.
2. If questions are too personal (sexual practices, spouse abuse, extramarital sex), respondents may not answer honestly.
3. Responses to survey questions are sometimes so structured that a respondent's real answer is not among the available choices.

Example: A national survey of marital happiness among husbands and wives by Veroff, Douvan, and Kulka (1981), *The Inner American.*

2. Interviews

An interview is usually conducted as part of a verbal conversation in which one person attempts to obtain information from another. The questions asked can be either "fixed" (structured) or "open-ended" (unstructured). Unstructured interviews allow more probing with more follow-up questions and they obtain more in-depth information because they don't force answers into a small number of alternatives. Interviews can be carried out face to face or over the telephone. The most truthful responses come when the interview dyad is matched in terms of race, gender, age, and ethnic and religious backgrounds. A survey design may or may not be combined with the interview technique.

ADVANTAGES

1. The researcher can search and probe for underlying motives for behavior.
2. Interviewers can offer clarification of questions or restate questions.
3. Personal interaction allows for the possibility of picking up dishonesty in the respondent.

DISADVANTAGES

1. The method is expensive and time consuming.
2. Various interviewers may ask questions differently and particular characteristics of the interviewers may influence answers in the same research project.
3. Extremely personal information and feelings may be kept hidden because of face to face embarrassment.

Example: An interview study of decision making and power within the marital dyad by Blood and Wolfe (1960), *Husbands and Wives.*

3. Questionnaires

Questionnaires are often combined with survey techniques. The questions asked and the choice of answers are precise; that is, they are usually structured rather than open ended. Questionnaires can be given personally to individuals or groups, or they can be sent through the mail. The respondent can be identified or remain anonymous.

ADVANTAGES

1. This is one of the least expensive methods of obtaining information, particularly for large samples.
2. Both quick and easy tabulation and computer analysis are possible because of standardized questions.
3. If the respondent is allowed to remain anonymous, then honest answers are more likely.

DISADVANTAGES

1. Questions could be misinterpreted when the questionnaire is self-administered.
2. A structured questionnaire may be very inflexible in terms of choice of responses.
3. Respondents may fear that they could be identified in some way and that the information provided could be used against them.

Example: A questionnaire study of body image, physical appearance, and self-esteem done by Berscheid, Walster, and Bohrnstedt (1983) for *Psychology Today.*

4. Participant Observation

In participant observation the researcher actually takes part in the activities of, or joins or lives with, the group being studied. The group may or may not be told of the reasons for the researcher's participation. Sometimes there are difficulties in gaining admission into a group for the purpose of observing their behavior. Informal interviews are usually conducted with selected members. The goal

of this approach is to obtain as complete a picture as possible of the life-style of a group over a period of time.

ADVANTAGES

1. The researcher can gain deep insight and understanding about a group, including emotions and beliefs that are often hidden.
2. A more realistic view of a population may be obtained because they are studied in their natural environment.
3. Many more aspects of a group's life can be studied than in a structured research design.

DISADVANTAGES

1. The researcher's presence could possibly change the behavior of the group.
2. The approach is very subjective, and different researchers studying the same group could come up with different findings.
3. The findings from one group cannot be generalized to other groups or settings.

Example: A study done on homosexual activity in public restrooms by Humphreys (1975), *Tearoom Trade.*

5. Case Studies

Case studies allow researchers to probe deeply into both behavior and emotions. A great variety of types of cases may be studied. A "case" could be an individual, a marriage, a family, an extended family, a teenage group, a feminist organization, a community, or any specific event. Particular techniques that can be utilized in conducting a case study include analyzing existing records, intensive interviews, and participant observation. A case may or may not have a lot in common with other cases.

ADVANTAGES

1. Such research can provide for the analysis of a multiplicity of details about a case.
2. The research can delve deeply into feelings and motivations about behavior.

DISADVANTAGES

1. Single cases may be atypical, and therefore generalizing to the larger society may be impossible.
2. The findings will need to be tested by more general survey methods to be more scientifically meaningful.

Example: Studies done on the community of Middletown in the 1920s, 1930s, and 1970s.

6. Clinical Studies

In the field of marriage and the family, clinical data can be very revealing to social scientists. While clinicians (marriage counselors, psychologists, and social workers, for example) are generally not scientists themselves, scientific methods can be utilized in analyzing clinical information. Clinical data often provide the most meaningful insights into behavior, emotions, and motivations. Clinical studies are particularly valuable in connection with the following types of problems: marriage difficulties, sexual problems, family conflict, incest, rape, spouse abuse, chemical dependencies, and adjustment to divorce. In addition, clinical information can be utilized for developing hypotheses for survey studies, for concept development, and for theory building.

ADVANTAGES

1. Respondents are likely to be very open and honest, since they initiated therapy to attempt to get help.

2. The depth of understanding that comes out of clinical studies helps in explaining behavior and motivations.
3. The data are usually collected over time, not just on a one-shot basis.

DISADVANTAGES

1. The individuals studied may not be typical of the general population, since they are likely to have some problem that brought them to therapy.
2. Clinical studies are not generalizable.
3. The observations may overly reflect the clinician's perspectives since they were not made with research objectivity in mind.

Example: Data collected by Masters and Johnson (1970) from clients who had sexual dysfunctions, *Human Sexual Inadequacy.*

7. Secondary Data Analysis

The technique of secondary data analysis involves the use of existing information, and there is no direct contact between the researchers and the persons, behavior, or events being studied. Information for such research can be obtained from such sources as census data, marriage license applications, divorce decrees, birth and death certificates, or autobiographies. The research findings and data from the work of other social scientists can be combined, compared, or re-analyzed.

ADVANTAGES

1. The researcher can obtain information at little or no cost or investment of time.
2. The researchers can combine the findings of many studies together and analyze them.

DISADVANTAGES

1. Relying on data collected for other purposes may not provide the researchers with exactly what he or she needs.
2. Any problems with the original research methodology are apt to be perpetuated.

Example: Emile Durkheim's study (1897) of suicide statistics in various countries, *Suicide.*

8. Content Analysis

The content-analysis method involves examining such sources as magazines, newspapers, songs, proverbs, speeches, diaries, church records, or books. A particular topic is chosen, and changes regarding that topic over time are studied. This content analysis utilizes existing written material in a systematic way to test hypotheses.

ADVANTAGES

1. It is an easy way of conducting research at low cost.
2. The method is good for studying trends over time.

DISADVANTAGES

1. The data may not lend themselves to making broader generalizations with changes in content.
2. Changes in language or terminology may be confused.

Example: Friedan's analysis (1963) of sex roles in women's magazines, *The Feminine Mystique.*

9. Comparative Studies

Data on groups or societies are compared so as to look at similarities and differences in attitudes, behavior, norms, feelings, or motivations. Examples of specific topics that could be studied include divorce, problems of adolescents, romantic love, kinship organizations or extended-family patterns, courtship, and extramarital sexual practices. Such studies could be conducted on existing societies or on subgroups within a society. Groups could also be compared over historical time periods.

ADVANTAGES

1. The method allows for a broader perspective beyond one's own cultural experience.
2. It avoids mistaking cultural patterns as inborn or inherent biological traits.

DISADVANTAGES

1. The same questions may be interpreted differently in various cultures or subcultures.
2. Apparent differences (or similarities) may just represent language or communication differences.

Example: Harold Christensen's (1973) comparative study of attitudes toward extramarital intercourse in nine cultures.

10. Experiments

Experiments are one of the least-used research techniques in the family field, although they are one of the best ways of determining cause and effect. Usually conditions are as highly controlled as possible, either in a laboratory or in field research. In the laboratory the subjects are brought into an artificial environment. Field experiments take place under more natural conditions, such as in a household, at a teenage hangout, or at a feminist meeting. In a typical experiment an independent variable is introduced and its effect on a dependent variable is noted. Ideally the population is divided into two matched groups; one is introduced to the independent variable and the other (a control group) is not.

ADVANTAGES

1. There is a high degree of control, precision, and reliability.
2. The researcher can determine cause and effect.
3. There is relatively low cost and experiments can usually be repeated easily.

DISADVANTAGES

1. People may behave differently in an artificially contrived environment or situation.
2. The presence of researchers can "contaminate" the results.
3. Subjects are often selected by availability rather than representativeness.

Example: Experiments by Rausch, Barry, Hertel, and Swain (1974) on marital communication and conflict, *Communication, Conflict and Marriage.*

B

Researching Human Sexuality

Freud: Clinical Case Studies

Sigmund Freud (1856–1939) was one of the first to study human sexuality. A Viennese physician, he developed a theory of psychoanalysis in which he emphasized the significant role that sexuality plays in human development. He argued that a person's innermost drives and conflicts are related to sex. Like others during the Victorian period, Freud viewed sex as a dangerous force that had to be kept under control.

Freud promoted the idea that sexuality begins in infancy. Needless to say, his ideas of infant and childhood sexuality shocked the scientific world in 1905. Freud stated, "The capacity for sensate experience develops very early in life, beginning prenatally. What the child lacks is opportunity, not capacity" (quoted in Katchadourian, Lund, and Trotter, 1979, p. 153). Freud was often criticized and condemned for his frank talk about human sexuality. He relied on clinical case studies for his research; his data came from his analysis of disturbed and unhappy patients and an in-depth analysis of himself (Offir, 1982).

Although Freud was correct in stating that sexuality begins in early childhood, many of his other ideas were either empirically untestable or later proved to be incorrect. Some of his views regarding female sexuality have been labeled as sexist and invalid. For example, he viewed women as anatomically inferior because they lack penises. He also made the distinction between clitoral and vaginal orgasms and believed that women who were incapable of vaginal orgasm were psychologically immature. All in all, Freud did not advance sexual knowledge to a great extent, but no one can deny the impact his contributions have had on bringing sex out in the open and making it an area of study and research.

The Kinsey Reports: Interviews

Alfred Kinsey and his associates—Wardell Pomeroy, Clyde Martin, and Paul Gebhard—used survey methods to study human sexuality on a large scale. Their work was one of the first major, systematic attempts to study and classify human sexual behavior in the United States. In the 1940s and early 1950s Kinsey and his colleagues collected more than 16,000 histories from people of diverse backgrounds and geographic areas across the country. The Kinsey reports were published in two books—*Sexual Behavior in the Human Male* (1948) and *Sexual Behavior in the Human Female* (1953). These books prompted a great deal of discussion and criticism and had a powerful impact on sexual knowledge by bringing the subject into the open.

Kinsey's research involved interviewing each subject personally, either by Kinsey himself or one of his three co-workers. The interviewing techniques were highly regarded by other social scientists. The interviewers made every attempt to establish rapport with the people they spoke to. They were skillful in phrasing questions in language that was easily understood. They worded questions to encourage subjects to be quite open in reporting anything sexual they had done. For example, instead of asking, "Have you ever masturbated?" the interviewers asked, "At what age did you begin masturbating?" (Hyde, 1982).

Other techniques were used to elicit accurate and honest information. Methods were utilized for cross-checking a subject's report for any false information. Strict precautions were taken to ensure that responses were anonymous and would remain that way. Although the interviewing techniques were probably successful in minimizing deception, problems of memory in a self-report do remain.

But the major shortcoming of the Kinsey studies is the lack of a random sample. Kinsey's respondents did not represent the American population as a whole. His sample was made up primarily of college students, young people, the well educated, Protestants, urban dwellers, and residents of Indiana and the northeastern states. Kinsey, along with other sex researchers, also faced a problem with volunteer bias. There may be large differences between those people who would volunteer information of such a private nature and those who would not. Nevertheless, Kinsey and his associates made sex a legitimate area of study in the twentieth century.

Masters and Johnson: Laboratory Observations

William Masters, a physician, and Virginia Johnson, a behavioral scientist, believed that to understand the complexities of human sexuality people must understand sexual anatomy and physiological response patterns. They set up a laboratory to measure changes in the heart rate, the muscular contractions, and the physiological responses of the vagina during the various stages of the sexual response cycle. Subjects engaged in sexual behavior while physiological changes were carefully observed, measured, and recorded. The observations included both intercourse and masturbation.

Masters and Johnson were able to recruit normal subjects from the general population for their research. Most subjects were obtained from the local community simply by word of mouth (Hyde, 1982). All subjects were screened in initial interviews for any individuals with emotional problems. In all, 694 people participated in the laboratory studies—276 married couples and 142 single men and women. More than 10,000 episodes

of sexual activity were observed from beginning to end. In 1966 Masters and Johnson published their findings in the book *Human Sexual Response.*

The subjects were volunteers and, of course, not a random sample of the population. But that was not an important concern with Masters's and Johnson's work because they were focused on the physiological processes taking place during sexual relations, assuming that the processes work essentially the same way in all people. They could not, however, make statistical conclusions based on their observations or generalize to the rest of the population (Hyde, 1982).

The Hunt Study: Questionnaires

During the early 1970s a survey was conducted by Morton Hunt and its findings published in the book *Sexual Behavior in the 1970's.* He attempted to collect data comparable in some respects to Kinsey's in order to determine possible changes in sexual behavior from the 1940s to the 1970s. But he explored certain areas in more detail than Kinsey. For example, he focused more on the emotional and psychological aspects of sex than Kinsey, who was concerned mostly with behaviors.

Hunt's study was sponsored by the Playboy Foundation, but the purpose was not to question solely readers of *Playboy* magazine. Respondents were 2026 males and females residing in 24 cities in the United States; an extensive self-administered questionnaire (more than 1000 items) was used to gather the data. Hunt recruited his subjects by first choosing names at random from telephone directories and asking these people to participate anonymously in small-group discussions of changing sexual behaviors in America. Approximately 20 percent of those originally invited agreed to join the groups. The participants were asked to fill out a questionnaire after the discussions.

The Hite Report: Open-Ended Questionnaires

Shere Hite conducted a study on female sexuality, which was published as *The Hite Report* (1976). Her goal was not to find out specifically how *many* people engaged in particular sexual acts but to determine *how* women experienced sex and how they actually felt about it. She distributed her questionnaires to women's groups (including chapters of the National Organization for Women), abortion-rights groups, and women's centers on college campuses. The sample was heavily weighted with young, educated, and profeminist women (Francoeur, 1982). She mailed out 100,000 questionnaires and had only slightly more than 3,000 returned—a remarkably low rate of 3 percent. Thus only people who were willing to make their sexual behavior known were included as subjects (Hyde, 1982).

The major focus of Hite's research was to provide information regarding how women go about sexual activity. For example, she explains how they masturbate, where they touch themselves, what kind of stimulation they use, and what kind of fantasies they indulge in. Unlike most surveys, Hite phrased her questions in an open-ended way as opposed to structured multiple-choice questions. *The Hite Report* does provide extensive quotations with detailed examples of a wide variety of sexual expressions. Many of the women in her study repeatedly expressed that the process and quality of a sexual encounter were more important than orgasm (Sandler et al., 1980).

In 1981, Hite published a second report, *The Hite Report on Male Sexuality*. The respon-

dents were 7200 men, ages 13 to 97. In this study Hite took great pains to try to make her sample of men representative of the general population. She tried to match age, race, and other factors in her sample as closely as possible to the general male population in the United States. Although this study also suffered from a poor rate of return on the questionnaires, the book contains extensive case material, suggesting that there is much more variability in male sexuality than was previously thought (Offir, 1982).

The *Redbook* Studies: Magazine Surveys

Redbook magazine conducted a survey of their female readers in 1974. The study covers attitudes and behavior related to premarital, marital, and extramarital sex, and was published in *The Redbook Report on Female Sexuality.* Carol Tavris and Susan Sadd, the survey researchers, received questionnaires from 100,000 women. While this is an impressive number of respondents, it amounted to only 1 percent of the 10 million claimed readership (Katchadourian et al., 1979). The readers of *Redbook* magazine are largely young, married, Protestant, politically moderate, white women with a high school or some college education, who enjoyed a middle to high income (Francoeur, 1982).

In 1977, Tavris surveyed 40,000 men for the same magazine. These men resembled the 100,000 women of the previous study but were slightly older and better educated (Francoeur, 1982). In 1980, Philip and Lorna Sarrel conducted another survey for *Redbook* dealing with the quality of sexual relationships. Twenty thousand female readers and 6000 of their male partners were surveyed. It was found that the topics most often discussed and argued about by partners included how often to make love, the quality of lovemaking and specific behaviors, such as oral sex. Many of the findings seemed to connect the duality of emotional intimacy in a marriage with sexual satisfaction.

The *Cosmo Report*: A Magazine Survey

Another magazine, *Cosmopolitan*, conducted a survey of their readership, leading to the *Cosmo Report* (1981). One hundred and six thousand women between the ages of 14 and 80 responded to this survey conducted by Linda Wolfe. This sample of "self-selected" respondents was asked to comment on various sexual practices and to assess how they felt about the sexual revolution. Interestingly, the author found that close to 50 percent of the women felt content about today's more sexually free atmosphere, and a little more than 50 percent felt that things had gone too far (Wolfe, 1981). Many of the latter women said that they were disillusioned with their sexual freedom—finding that they didn't receive from their sexual encounters the kind of happiness they imagined they would (Wolfe, 1981). Many respondents indicated a desire for an emotionally intimate relationship as opposed to a purely sexual one.

Sexually Transmitted Diseases

Chlamydia

Chlamydia is the most prevalent of all sexually transmitted diseases (STD) and has been coined the "disease of the 80's" (Wallis, 1985). Named for the tiny bacterium (*Chlamydia trachomatis*) that causes it, chlamydia strikes between 3 million and 10 million Americans each year (Wallis, 1985). Chlamydia is a generally mild form of genital infection, which causes inflammation of the urinary tract in men and vaginal inflammation in women. It is also the cause of as many as one out of two cases of pelvic inflammatory disease (PID), a painful, sometimes sterilizing infection that affects about 1 million American women each year (Wallis, 1985). Like herpes, chlamydia is rapidly becoming a common STD of the middle class; up to 10 percent of all college students are afflicted with it.

The symptoms of chlamydia are sometimes subtle and easily misinterpreted. Men with chlamydia can experience a burning sensation during urination and a mucus discharge. In women, chlamydia causes a vaginal discharge and painful urination (Wallis, 1985). It is usually contracted through sexual activity. Once chlamydia is diagnosed, it is easy to treat. Repeated doses of the antibiotics tetracycline or erythromycin over a period of at least one week are required to eliminate it (Wallis, 1985). Chlamydia is so widespread now that many doctors have begun administering antibiotics to suspected patients even before the tests are in.

If not treated, complications can occur, particularly in women. The infection can spread throughout the reproductive tract. The bacteria may travel through the uterus into the fallopian tubes, which become inflamed and eventually scarred. It could also lead to a potentially life-threatening condition known as tubal ectopic pregnancy. Women who contract chlamydia during a normal pregnancy can transmit the disease to their babies, who are infected while passing through the birth canal. There is some evidence that chlamydial infection during pregnancy increases the risks of premature and stillborn births (Wallis, 1985).

Young, sexually active persons with multiple sexual partners experience the greatest risk for chlamydial infection. Recent findings indicate that the risk of chlamydia increases with the use of oral contraceptives. A barrier birth-control method (for example, the diaphragm or condom) would prevent exposure to bacteria from the partner.

Gonorrhea

Gonorrhea is the second most common STD. It is a bacterium (*Gonococcus*) that can enter the body by way of warm, moist tissues. It can be transmitted during penile-vaginal intercourse, during anal intercourse, and when the penis comes in contact with the upper throat (Offir, 1982). The cervix is the most common site of infection.

The symptoms of gonorrhea include frequent and painful urination in men, and the urine may contain thick pus or there may be a milky discharge from the penis. If gonorrhea is transmitted by anal intercourse, a discharge may occur from the rectum. A greenish or yellow-green vaginal discharge is the primary symptom in women. As many as 80 percent of infected women, however, show no symptoms at all.

If untreated, gonorrhea can spread and lead to serious and painful infection of the pelvic area, leading to pelvic inflammatory disease. A woman's fallopian tubes may become infected, and scarring in the tubes can cause permanent sterility. Likewise, untreated gonorrhea can invade the male's reproductive system. Scarring of the male's epididymides can cause permanent sterility (Offir, 1982).

The usual treatment for gonorrhea is high doses of penicillin or doses of other antibiotics if the person is allergic to penicillin. Over the past 25 years, new strains of gonorrhea have emerged, which are resistant to penicillin (Crowe, 1984). Other medications are being prescribed.

A pregnant woman with gonorrhea can infect the baby's eyes as it passes through her birth canal. The infection causes blindness unless it is treated with drops of silver nitrate, a treatment required by all states for all babies (Crowe, 1984). The prevalence of gonorrhea in the general population has remained relatively stable at a high level.

Herpes

Herpes is caused by the *herpes simplex* virus (HSV), "a tiny primitive organism whose nature is still more or less a mystery." There are two types of herpes simplex viruses: Type I (HSVI), which is usually characterized by cold sores or fever blisters on the lips, face, and mouth, and Type II (HSVII), which most often involves sores in the external genitals, inside the vagina, in the urethra, on the cervix, around or in the anus, and on nearby skin areas such as the thighs and buttocks.

Herpes is transmitted during vaginal, anal, or oral sex with someone who has an active infection. It can also be spread from the mouth to the genitals via the fingers. Some experts contend that direct contact with the affected area is not always necessary (Offir, 1982). For example, it can be spread through linens and towels, although this rarely happens.

The symptoms usually occur 2 to 20 days after exposure, although some people may not have symptoms or may not be aware of them until much later (Crowe, 1984). The sores start out as tiny, itchy, fluid-filled blisters, which change into small, round, painful ulcers that last two or three weeks. While the sores are active, urination may be painful, and a dull ache or sharp burning pain may occur in the entire genital area. During the first outbreak, the person may experience headaches, fever, or pelvic pain. Until the sores disappear the disease is highly contagious (Offir, 1982). The initial outbreak takes the longest to heal (two to six weeks) and is usually the most painful.

Usually the herpes virus goes underground, hiding in nerve cells, and then reemerges at any time for another attack, although some people never experience a second outbreak of herpes. But for most (75 percent) a recurrent episode occurs 3 to 12 months later and in the same area of the body. No one knows for sure what brings on recurring episodes. At the time this text was written there was no medical cure for herpes. There are some soothing ointments and pain relievers that a physician can prescribe to help alleviate the pain.

Complications can emerge with herpes. It can be spread via the hands to the eyes, damaging the eyesight. Among women with herpes there seems to be an increased risk of cancer of the cervix, a five times greater risk. Pregnant women with herpes have a higher risk of miscarriages and premature delivery. If the herpes is active during birth, the baby can contract it during passage through the birth canal. This can cause brain damage, blindness, and even death. In men there is a possible link with prostatic, penile, and testicular cancer (Francoeur, 1982).

Syphilis

Syphilis is an STD caused by a small, spiral-shaped bacterium, a spirochete. It is transmitted through sexual or skin contact with someone who is in an infectious stage, usually the early stages of the disease. After the bacteria enter the body, the disease goes through four stages. The *primary stage* is when a painless sore called a chancre (pronounced "shanker") shows up. It may look like a pimple, a blister, or an open sore, and it appears from 9 to 90 days after the bacteria enter the body. Usually the sore appears on the genitals or near the place where the bacteria entered. The chancre disappears in one to five weeks, naturally, without treatment, but the disease is still present.

By the *secondary stage,* which occurs anywhere from a week to six months later, the bacteria have spread all through the body. They produce a rash, flulike symptoms, mouth sores, or patchy hair loss. During this stage the disease can be spread by simple physical contact, including kissing, because bacteria are present on the exposed body (Crowe, 1984). This stage lasts weeks or months, but symptoms can come and go for several years.

The third stage, the *latent stage,* may last 10 to 20 years, during which there are no outward signs. At this time the bacteria may be invading the inner organs, including the heart and brain. After the first few years of the latent stage the disease is no longer infectious. In the *late stage* serious effects appear. "Depending on which organs the bacteria have attacked, a person may develop serious heart disease, crippling, blindness and/or mental incapacity" (Crowe, 1984, p. 278). With the present ability to diagnose and treat syphilis, reaching this stage is rare.

Penicillin or, if a person is allergic to penicillin, a substitute antibiotic is used to treat this disease. The first three stages can be completely cured with no permanent damage. In late syphilis, destructive effects can be stopped from going further but cannot reverse the organ damage that has already oc-

curred. Unlike most disease bacteria, syphilis bacteria can pass through the placenta during pregnancy and infect the fetus in the womb. If the baby does not die, it is born with important tissues deformed or diseased, symptoms of secondary or even late syphilis.

AIDS (Acquired Immune Deficiency Syndrome)

AIDS is the deadliest STD. The cause of AIDS is a virus (HIV) that breaks down the body's ability to fight off certain diseases such as pneumonia, hepatitis and cancer. The number of cases of AIDS is doubling every year. The incubation period is considered to extend to about 10 to 15 years after exposure. Many individuals may carry the AIDS virus without having any symptoms at all and can pass the AIDS virus on to others.

There are currently two tests for AIDS; both involve screening for the AIDS antibody. It is estimated that 10 to 20 percent of the persons who are antibody positive will develop AIDS within two years. Also, such antibody-positive persons are contagious. "There is no known treatment for AIDS. No one has recovered from the disease. It appears to be 100 percent fatal. A vaccine, if possible at all, is thought to be 10 to 15 years away" (Crenshaw, 1986, p. 3). It must be stressed that AIDS is not just a homosexual disease. It can also be transferred to heterosexuals—young and old alike. "It is estimated that over 25 percent of the prostitute population in New York is positive for AIDS antibodies. The AIDS virus has been found in many body fluids, including blood, semen, pulmonary secretions, saliva, and recently tears" (Crenshaw, 1986, p. 3).

While there is no known cure for AIDS, it can be prevented. Here are some suggestions:

1. Do not have casual or anonymous sex.

2. Do not have sex with prostitutes.

3. Be sexually conservative. Develop one primary relationship and attempt to establish exclusivity. The only dependable way of avoiding AIDS is to be monogamous with a monogamous partner who is not already infected.

4. Avoid exchange of body fluids.

5. Use condoms. Use of condoms is not sufficient to prevent transmission of the AIDS virus. Condoms have a 10 percent failure rate for pregnancy. A virus is much smaller than a sperm and, consequently, the risk of being exposed to the virus is at least 10 percent.

6. Do not use illegal intravenous (I.V.) drugs, or share needles.

7. Get periodic blood tests for the AIDS antibody for you and your sexual partner(s).

8. Improve personal hygiene.

9. Do your part to educate spouses, friends, lovers, and children. *Only education* can arrest this epidemic at this time.

10. Keep up with new information as it is published. Aggressive research in progress will provide additional information in time. Keep informed. (Crenshaw, 1986, p. 7)

Trichomoniasis

Trichomoniasis is a one-celled parasite found in some men and 50 percent of all women (Francoeur, 1982). Often there are no symptoms. Close to 3 million cases are estimated annually, and trichomoniasis is now considered to be a major STD. Most often the infection is transmitted sexually, but it can also be transmitted by moist towels, bathing suits, underwear, wash cloths, and toilet seats.

Males rarely show symptoms but can be carriers. If symptoms appear, a male with trichomoniasis may experience a feeling of irritation deep in the urethra, especially during urination or ejaculation. Women with the infection usually have a foamy, bad-smelling vaginal discharge that is gray or yellowish in color and vaginal irritation. It often flares up just prior to or during menstruation.

An oral medication (Flagyl) is used to treat trichomoniasis. To limit further spread of the disease, sexual partners should be treated at the same time. Some doctors may advise special douches for women. Complications can occur if the disease is not treated. Repeated infections may be linked to cervical cancer in women. Males can experience a urethral blockage.

Venereal Warts

Venereal warts are warts that appear on the genitals. They are caused by a virus, *papillomavirus* (HPV), which also causes common skin warts. The virus is transmitted through direct contact with warts through vaginal, anal, or oral sex. They are more common in uncircumcised men than in circumcised men. Until recently, HPV-caused infections have not been associated with serious complications, but studies now show that women with HPV-caused lesions on the cervix probably have a higher-than-normal risk for developing cervical cancer (Crowe, 1984).

Genital warts can appear from three weeks to three months after exposure. During this time, warts can be very contagious. They are not painful, but they may spread. They look like regular warts, starting as small, painless, hard spots. In women, they appear on the bottom of the vaginal opening, on the vaginal lips, inside the vagina, on the cervix, or around the anus, where they can be mistaken for hemorrhoids. In men, warts usually occur toward the tip of the penis, sometimes under the foreskin, and occasionally on the shaft of the penis or scrotum. Use of a condom can help prevent the spread of warts.

Warts can be treated by a solution or

ointment of podophyllin. They can also be frozen or burned off by cryotherapy (dry ice treatment) or acid. In cases of large warts, surgery may be necessary to remove them. If not treated, warts can spread enough to block vaginal and/or rectal openings. Possible transmission can occur to an infant during delivery if warts are located on the cervix or in the vagina (Francoeur, 1982).

Pubic Lice

Pubic lice, or crabs, are tiny yellowish gray parasites that like to live in genital hair. They attach themselves to the skin to suck their host's blood (Offir, 1982). Sexual contact is not necessary for transmission. Any skin-to-skin physical contact or mattresses, bed linens, couches, chairs, clothing, or toilet seats can also transmit the lice. Intense itching, pinhead blood spots on underwear, and a possible rash are some symptoms of pubic lice (Francoeur, 1982). Various creams, lotions, and shampoos will kill the lice and any of their eggs. If untreated, secondary infections can occur due to scratching. No dangers to an unborn infant are known.

D

Family Financial Planning

Financial planning is an important skill that is often neglected in terms of knowledge and education. Money can be the source of considerable conflict in marriage, even though other, larger issues typically underlie disagreements over finances. People tend to vary in their attitudes regarding money. Some individuals are very conservative and frugal; they watch every penny and take care to see to it that their money is well spent. Many of these persons end up with a very restrictive life-style. For other persons money tends to "burn a hole in their pocket," and they spend impulsively. These individuals lack planning skills, and they often end up with substantial debt. Either way, most couples, particularly young married couples, do not manage their money very well. Typically no one has bothered to provide the couple with training in financial planning.

In the final analysis how one handles money is related to one's philosophy of life. People who gain more rewards in life external to themselves are more likely to spend recklessly and accumulate considerable debt. People in extrinsic marriages usually follow such a pattern, if both partners have the same attitudes toward spending. But there can be real problems if the two spouses have very different philosophies on how money should be spent. In traditional marriages usually the husband was the basic breadwinner, and he tended to maintain control over all the money. Often the wife did not even know how much the husband made. Partners in an intimate marriage are most likely to share jointly their financial resources. Typically there are no hidden secrets about money and joint decisions are made on expensive purchases.

FINANCIAL PLANNING OVER THE LIFE CYCLE

Since life involves continuous changes, financial planning is a must if we are going to live comfortably throughout our entire lives. Obviously, our income and expenditures will vary during different stages of the life cycle, depending upon whether we are a young single person, a partner in a childfree marriage, part of a family with dependent children living at home, a partner living in an empty-nest situation, retired, or living as a divorced or widowed person. In addition, there will, more than likely, be general economic cycles—recessions and inflationary periods. All of these variations mean that we need to plan ahead in terms of our money needs.

Single Life

Young people typically stop being financially dependent on their parents when they get their first full-time jobs. Then income usually increases up until the time of retirement. Young singles are typically only responsible to themselves, which often results in a temptation to overspend. If people are on their own, there is also the necessity, maybe for the first time in their lives, of providing for food, shelter, transportation, clothes, and medical care, as well as many other expenses.

The stage of single life is actually the best time to begin financial planning. Contact with financial institutions is more extensive at this time as checking and saving accounts are opened. The repayment of educational loans may be under way, or new loans—to buy a car, for example—may be taken out. Insurance may become more important—including automobile, medical, and disability insurance. Life insurance is typically not necessary at this point if the single person has no dependents. Higher risks in terms of financial investment may be tolerable, since extra funds may be available for the single person.

Childfree Marriages

Marriage for most people usually follows a few years after working at a full-time job.

Early in the marriage both spouses usually work, and the couple may do well financially. There will be considerable pressure, however, to spend money, and conflicts over spending may occur if one or both partners lack financial self-control. If children are anticipated in the future, planning for this inevitable expense should begin because of the high cost of raising children. Life insurance at this point is still a low-priority item because both of the spouses are probably self-supporting.

Marriage with Children

A marriage with children is the most expensive of the whole life cycle. Expenses become greater and greater until college is finished or the children leave home. This is usually also the time period when major purchases, such as buying a house, take place. While total income may be increasing, there often tends to be little money left over for investments. More and more the trend is for both spouses to continue to work, even though the wife and mother may be out of the labor force for periods of time. Life insurance and an up-to-date will are now essential for the family's protection in the event something should happen to one of the spouses.

The Empty Nest

When the children move out and become self-supporting there will be more money available to save or invest. Income may be the highest it has been over the entire life cycle. The couple may already have accumulated most of the material things desired, and house payments possibly are decreasing. It is during this period that the couple should earnestly plan for retirement. Estate planning and low-risk investments are important, as well as a review of life-insurance policies.

Retirement

Upon retirement, income typically declines, and the couple begins to draw on their savings. No one knows how long he or she will live, which makes budgeting extremely important, as well as difficult. Social security by itself tends to provide for a minimum standard of living; pensions provide for additional income. Risky investments need to be minimized during these years. Unfortunately, many people experience a lowered standard of living upon retirement. The equity provided by home ownership is often a big part of the couple's total wealth. Renting or buying a smaller house or condominium is an available option. Since medical expenses usually increase, it is important that the couple have a good plan of health insurance. Often health insurance is an individual responsibility after retirement, when it is no longer offered as a fringe benefit of employment.

Widowhood

Besides the emotional crisis of a spouse's death there may be a decrease in income and possibly living style. Advice may be needed on estate planning and again in preparing a will. Often housing arrangements will change.

FINANCIAL PLANNING BY A COUPLE

Most couples in American society will earn more than $1 million in their lifetimes. This money will be stretched, on the average, over about 75 years. Besides everyday expenses— house, children, food, social activities—there also can be unpredictable financial disasters. The possible loss of one's job, a house fire, or a debilitating illness would be crises that make financial planning a must. It should be emphasized that money management is not a one-time affair, but rather it is a *process* that should continue throughout one's entire life. Financial planning by a couple involves the distribution of family resources to meet agreed-upon goals.

Goal Setting

Before financial planning can begin—before a budget can even be developed—goals must be set. Goal setting, however, is an ongoing process, since a family's needs may change somewhat over the life cycle. Budgets need to be tailored to specific needs based on particular life-styles and the particular stage of the life cycle the couple is passing through. A budget is a means to an end (a goal), not an end in itself.

Developing a Budget

Most couples resist developing budgets for one reason or another. A lot of resistance is the result of just not knowing what a budget is supposed to accomplish. Actually a budget allows a couple to achieve their financial objectives. Many couples not guided by a budget spend their money in haphazard ways. A budget allows each person in the family (including children) to have an awareness of how his or her money should be utilized.

The first step in preparing a budget involves taking stock of the total amount of money coming into the family—from wages, interest or dividends, or extra jobs, for example. Next, expenses of various types should be determined. This can be accomplished partly by keeping track of all expenditures for several months. The expenses should be put into different categories. If checks are written as much as possible during this period, it will help facilitate keeping

track. It is *not* necessary to account for every penny.

There are two general types of expenses—fixed and flexible. Fixed expenses are those that must be met on some regular basis—house or rent payment, car payment, utilities bills. Fixed expenses that are not paid monthly, such as car or life insurance, tuition, or taxes, should be prorated monthly. Fixed expenses are typically beyond the couple's control and would be difficult to change.

A personal allowance for each family member should be part of the fixed expenses. In addition, a savings program, typically 5 to 10 percent of the family's net income, should be a regular part of the budget. People who try to save just what is left over usually don't save very much. Savings should be a regular budget item, even if they are only 1 percent of the income. Savings are important even if they function only as an emergency fund. Some people have a certain amount automatically deducted for savings from their pay check each month.

Flexible expenses are those that a family can control a little more—including such items as food, clothes, household furnishings, gifts, contributions, and recreation. It is primarily in these areas that a family can cut back if expenses are exceeding income. What exactly is cut relates to each couple's goals and the goals of the family as a whole. An effort could also be made to increase income by one person getting a second job or by other family members going to work. A budget should be flexible and adapt to various changing conditions, such as the birth of a new baby, the wife going back to work, or the children leaving home.

Saving

Most people in American society today do not keep the money that they have saved under their mattresses. Americans have for-mal institutions for savings, including com-mercial banks, savings and loan associations, credit unions, and brokerage firms.

Banks provide opportunities for savings as well as checking accounts. A host of other services can be included—the use of 24-hour banking machines, bank credit cards, the au-tomatic transfer of funds between savings and checking accounts, and other services, at no extra charge. Most banks are insured by the federal government. While interest on savings varies somewhat among different banks, the interest is generally lower than that obtained through other financial institutions.

Savings and loan associations generally give slightly higher interest rates on savings. Such organizations typically do not provide as many services as banks; their primary focus is the saving and lending of money. Many home mortgage loans are handled through such institutions. Like banks, savings are in-sured by the federal government up to $100,000. More and more, savings and loan organizations are beginning to offer extra free services similar to those of banks. Interest-earning checking accounts and money-mar-ket accounts (with higher interest rates) are now usually available at savings and loans.

Credit unions are nonprofit organizations in which workers involved in similar occu-pations can pool their money. Deposits are also insured to $100,000. Credit unions usu-ally offer checking accounts, low-interest loans, long-term certificates of deposit, and other services. Somewhat higher interest rates than in banks and savings and loans are usually offered.

Investment firms, usually brokerage houses, typically offer higher interest rates than any of the above organizations. The con-sumer can put money into money-market ac-counts or cash-management accounts. The money is invested in stocks, bonds, or Trea-sury bills or all three. There is usually greater risk involved with these investments, and there is no insurance on deposits. Another disadvantage is that usully large deposits are required. It is also often more difficult to withdraw money quickly.

Borrowing Money

Money can be borrowed in a variety of ways. Use of credit cards is a common and conve-nient way of borrowing money, sometimes too convenient. Credit cards make carrying large sums of cash unnecessary. Their advan-tage is that if one pays off one's account within a certain number of days after billing, there is no financial charge for the use of the card. Broader credit is most commonly used on big-ticket items such as a house, car, or appliances.

Credit is provided by all financial insti-tutions—banks, savings and loans, credit unions, and others. Credit cards are often easy to obtain for young married couples. But the use of "plastic money" often brings a host of problems. Many couples go into debt way over their heads and end up paying a much higher price for purchased items when inter-est is included. Some couples, no matter how much they earn, seem to be always in debt. Credit counselors are often needed when couples can no longer deal with their debts. Sometimes a declaration of bankruptcy may be necessary in order to become solvent again.

Major Purchases

HOUSING. Housing is usually the biggest sin-gle investment a couple will make. Com-monly the question is raised as to whether to rent or own housing. Owning a home is probably a better economic bargain in the long run, but some people never have the money necessary for a down payment to buy a home.

Rental housing can offer certain advantages. In some apartment complexes certain amenities such as swimming pools, tennis courts, meeting rooms, or saunas are available. Also, renters usually do not have to spend their time cutting grass, shoveling snow, or making home repairs. In addition, an apartment complex can offer social benefits, particularly if the residents are of the same age (such as young singles or older, retired people). Neither do people have to tie up large amounts of income when they are renting. On the whole, however, long-term renting is not recommended. There is a general rule of thumb that a person should not pay more than 25 percent of his or her gross income for rental expenses.

Buying a home or condominium is often a hedge against inflation. In terms of taxes, home buyers can deduct mortgage interest and property taxes that are paid; renters cannot deduct rent payments. The home buyer is also building up equity in the house over time, which will provide the couple with cash value should they sell their home. Look at many, many houses before you make a final decision.

The rule of thumb on buying a house is that the total monthly payments (mortgage, taxes, utilities, and insurance) should not exceed 25 to 30 percent of the average gross monthly income of the buyers. The couple will need cash to make the down payment on the house (usually 10 to 20 percent), and they will have to qualify for a mortgage loan to finance the remaining balance of the purchase price. Current interest rates on mortgages are a big factor in determining monthly cost. By making payments every two weeks instead of monthly, much can be saved in terms of interest payments. Also different lenders may offer somewhat different mortgage rates, so it is to the advantage of the buyer to shop around.

At one time a standard fixed rate on 20- or 30-year mortgages predominated. Today many mortgages are variable-rate mortgages. In this situation the interest rate charged rises or falls with overall market interest rates. In general, a fixed-rate mortgage is preferable; if interest rates go lower, one can always refinance the mortgage at a lower rate.

OTHER BIG-TICKET ITEMS. Besides buying or renting a house, most couples will buy a car and a number of other durable items such as television sets, washers and dryers, furniture, or a home computer. Of these items, buying a car, particularly if it is new, is probably the most expensive. You should check the magazine *Consumer Reports* for a comparison of various makes of cars in terms of mileage, safety, and maintenance. Also, you should shop around, since there is often a wide variation in prices for both new and used cars from different dealers.

It is a good idea to have in mind what you are looking for and the options you want on a car—air conditioning, automatic transmission, stereo, power brakes—before actually bargaining on a price. This way high-pressure salespersons will be less likely to influence you in buying something you don't want. It is also a good idea to test drive many different types of cars. If you are going to trade in your old car on a new one, check on the blue-book value of your car before you take it to the dealer. You can usually get a better price, however, if you advertise and sell your old car yourself. It is also better to make a deal for your new car before your old car is brought into the picture.

Don't be in a rush to buy a new car; high-pressure salespersons will take advantage of your eagerness. Be patient in making a decision, since you may be making payments on your decision for three to four years. Obtain your final total costs *in writing,* since some dealers try to add on extra costs when you come to pick up your new car.

In a similar fashion, buying major appliances and furniture requires some research, comparison, and shopping around. Again it is good to check *Consumer Reports.* Often, there are certain times of the year when better deals are available. Furniture stores usually have sales in February and August, for example. Energy-efficient appliances should be considered. The length of warranties should also be compared.

Family Insurance Protection

Among the various types of insurance that it is advantageous to carry are life insurance, health insurance, and property and liability insurance.

LIFE INSURANCE. Life insurance is particularly important for the family economic provider or providers. Its purpose is to protect the survivors from heavy financial burdens should the wage earner or wage earners die. Besides ongoing living expenses, there will be funeral costs and probably estate taxes and probate costs. The goal of each provider is to make possible a comfortable life-style for his or her family through life insurance. A married person's life-insurance needs depend on whether he or she has children who need financial support and whether his or her spouse has employable work skills. Life-insurance needs vary throughout the marital life cycle.

There are three general types of life insurance—term insurance, whole-life insurance, and universal life insurance. *Term insurance* has become more popular in the last 20 years. Coverage is provided for a specific period of time, usually five-year periods. The insurance ends after this period unless you choose to renew it. Seldom can term insurance be renewed after age 65.

Term insurance usually is more economical than other types of insurance. It tends to be very cheap for a young person and becomes more expensive with age. If a person has a *renewable policy,* he or she has the right to continue the policy without taking a physical examination to provide insurability. If a policy is *convertible,* the insured individual has the right to change the policy to some form of permanent insurance that is not limited to a short time period. The lower cost of term insurance is its most important advantage; it provides the greatest protection for the least money. The biggest disadvantage of term insurance is that its costs go up as a person grows older.

In *whole-life insurance* there is a death benefit, which is the value of the policy. In addition, this policy provides a form of savings, commonly referred to as the cash value of the policy. This cash value is determined by the total premiums paid plus interest. Because of the savings aspect of this type of policy, there are higher premium costs.

The value of a whole-life policy in case of death stays the same throughout the life of the policy. The cost of whole-life tends to be lower the earlier in life one takes it out, and the premiums remain the same throughout the life of the policy. If you take out this type of insurance when you are very young, however, you will pay many more years into the policy. Generally speaking, life insurance should be taken out when it is most needed; young people tend to have very low death rates.

One of the advantages of whole-life insurance is that you can recover an amount invested *before you die.* You can also borrow money on your insurance at a very low interest rate. The biggest disadvantage of whole-life is that it is very expensive compared to term insurance. Also the amount of return on the cash value of whole-life is low because of very low interest on your money paid by insurance companies. Usually the money put into whole-life insurance could be invested elsewhere with a greater interest return. The greater your life-insurance needs in terms of the amount of money, the more advantageous term insurance is over whole-life.

A relatively new type of life insurance is *universal life*. It combines features of both term insurance and whole-life. Universal insurance provides permanent life coverage as well as a higher rate of interest (based on prevailing rates) on the money put into the policy. This type of policy allows you to make adjustments when needs change during the life cycle. Coverage can be raised or lowered, and thus the premium payments can be raised or lowered also. In essence, universal life allows you to have a term insurance program as well as being part of an investment fund with a good rate of return.

HEALTH INSURANCE. While some insurance is optional, everybody should have health insurance. The cost of health care can be one of life's major expenses, a burden that few families can handle without insurance. The most expensive item is usually hospital care. Thus hospital expenses for laboratory tests, X-rays, drugs, and operating room use, for example, are all charges that should be covered by a health-insurance plan. The cost of surgery is usually included as part of hospital insurance plans. What is often referred to as basic health insurance coverage includes hospital, surgical, and physician's expenses.

Another type of health insurance is called major-medical expense insurance. This type of insurance is designed for extended illnesses

or a major injury, items that basic health insurance is not designed to cover. Most major-medical policies have deductibles, which the individual must pay before the policy will begin. Comprehensive major-medical insurance includes in a single policy both basic and major-medical coverage. Such insurance is usually offered in group plans through your employer.

Disability-income insurance functions to replace some percentage of a person's income if illness or an injury prevents the person from working. You can receive anywhere from 50 to 80 percent of regular earnings if you are disabled. There are short-term disability policies that provide for up to a year or two and long-term disability policies that apply for much longer periods.

A relatively new type of health protection is offered by health-maintenance organizations (HMOs). They provide a host of services for yearly payments from subscribers. Health-maintenance organizations have their own staff of physicians, surgeons, and other professionals, who provide for almost all of a person's health needs for a fixed fee. HMOs also include regular checkups at no extra cost, and they provide preventive health care. One drawback of this type of health care is that you usually cannot choose your own physician.

Other sources of health protection are found in Worker's Compensation, Social Security, Medicare, and Medicaid. Every state has some form of Worker's Compensation, which provides benefits to a person who was injured or who has contracted an illness as the result of work on the job. Each business is required by law to provide such benefits for their employees. Typically companies buy Worker's-Compensation insurance. Such a program provides for such things as disability income, doctor's expenses, rehabilitation costs, and hospital costs. Being included in such a program does not mean that you should not still.have personal health insurance.

Most people believe that Social Security benefits are received only after retirement. Actually there are a number of programs under Social Security, including benefits to your dependents should you die and benefits to you yourself should you become physically or mentally disabled. Children under 18 are eligible for benefits, as well as a spouse who is taking care of children under 18.

The federal government also provides a health-insurance program called Medicare. People who are age 65 or older are eligible for this program, as well as those under 65 who have some form of disability. If you have Social Security, you automatically can receive Medicare, or you can subscribe to the program by making monthly Medicare insurance payments. This insurance will cover doctors' services, hospital costs, some nursing-home care, and the cost of a visiting nurse. Unfortunately, Medicare covers only a small portion of nursing-home care; many individuals needing this type of care must pay privately or be eligible for Medicaid, a program for very low-income people only. Since Medicare does not cover all health expenses, personal health insurance should still be maintained.

LIABILITY AND PROPERTY INSURANCE. Liability, car, and home insurance should also be part of a person's total insurance program. Both home owners and renters should protect themselves from theft, fire, storms, and wind damage. Property insurance protects your home. Under most home owner's policies, personal belongings and household furnishings are covered. Every home owner or renter should keep an inventory of all personal property; if possible photographs of each room of the dwelling should be taken. It is best to keep these items in a safe-deposit box. A good policy will also cover living expenses for you and your family should your house be destroyed.

Home owners, renters, and condominium owners all carry different kinds of policies. But no matter which type of dwelling you live in, you should have personal liability insurance. This type of insurance protects you from lawsuits or any claims filed against you or a member of your family, or even against your pet. Even if you, in reality, did no wrong, it can cost you substantial amounts in legal fees just to protect yourself. Most property-insurance policies typically include liability coverage.

Most home owner's coverage does not completely pay for replacement costs, should the whole structure be destroyed. To receive actual replacement costs for your dwelling unit, you must insure your home for at least 80 percent of the actual replacement costs. Only 80 percent is necessary since the property and the foundation of the structure will still be in existence. The way your home is constructed (brick, wood frame, for example) will affect your insurance payments. Many people neglect the factor of inflation when insuring their homes. It is advantageous to review your policy regularly and increase coverage as the house increases in value.

If you own an automobile, it is important that you maintain insurance coverage. Probably most important is liability insurance covering body injuries, which protect you against other people's injury or death claims, as well as the cost of legally protecting yourself. Property-damage liability insurance protects you from being held responsible for the damage you may have caused in an auto accident, as well as any legal costs involved.

Medical-payments insurance covers medical and funeral expenses for anyone involved in an automobile accident, regardless of who is at fault. Uninsured-motorist insurance provides you with benefits even if the other driver in an accident had no insurance. Collision insurance covers damage to your own car regardless of who is at fault in an accident. If your car is quite old and of little value, perhaps collision insurance is not necessary. Comprehensive insurance protects against losses that are not the result of a collision, such as fire and theft. Since claims are limited to the cash value of the car, again if your car is old, you may not want to carry this type of insurance.

The cost of automobile insurance is greatly affected by the age of the drivers. The highest rates are paid by males under age 30. Your driving record in terms of accidents and tickets can also increase the cost of automobile insurance. Married drivers have lower rates than single individuals. The type of car is also important; high-performance sports cars are the most expensive to insure. Generally, if the deductible is higher ($250 versus $100 or less) your insurance will cost less.

Glossary

Abstinence The standard by which premarital intercourse is considered wrong for both men and women, regardless of circumstances.

Abuse Recurrent violent patterns of behavior directed by one family member (the abuser) to another (the victim).

Accommodation style of handling conflict Actions in which an individual neglects his or her own needs in order to satisfy the concerns of the partner.

Acquaintances Persons one recognizes and acknowledges but with whom interaction is quite superficial and restricted.

Aggressiveness The tendency to harm another person either physically or verbally.

AIDS (acquired immune deficiency syndrome) A sexually transmitted disease that is caused by a virus (HIV) that breaks down the body's ability to fight off serious diseases.

Alternative attractions Alternative lifestyles, opportunities, or partners that a spouse may think are more attractive than the current partner or relationship.

Altruistic love A type of love in which one voluntarily rewards another person without expecting any reward in return or any reduction of costs.

Ambisexuals Enduring bisexuals, or people who continue to have sexual contact on an ongoing basis with both genders.

Androgynous The quality of having both traditionally masculine and feminine characteristics in one person.

Annoying modes of delivery Vocal properties and speech mannerisms that annoy the listener. Examples include fast talk, slow talk, over talk, under talk, singsong speech, monotone speech, and stuttering.

Anticipatory socialization The learning of the expectations of a social role before assuming it.

Anxious attachment Lack of a complete and secure attachment between a child and a caregiver.

Assertiveness The tendency to make one's self-interests and wishes known without degrading or putting down the other person.

Assertiveness training Program designed to make individuals more assertive in standing up for their rights or in saying no to people.

Attachment An emotional connection that results from extensive positive involvement and interaction.

Authoritarian parent The type of parent who values order and obedience and uses punitive, forceful disciplinary measures.

Authoritative parent The type of parent who is not overly indulgent but is nurturant, offers a high degree of positive reinforcement, and seldom uses punishment.

Avoidance style of handling conflict Actions in which the partners avoid pursuing their own concerns as well as those of the other person. The style is nonassertive, passive, and low in cooperation.

Baby boom A period of time following World War II up until about 1965 with exceedingly high birth rates.

Battering Repeated physical harm that one individual inflicts on another.

Biosocial theory of gender roles A theory that suggests that the differences in behavior between the genders are a result of both biological influences and cultural learning.

Blue-collar worker A manual worker whose work is primarily physical and who deals mostly with things rather than people.

Brinkmanship in courtship The skill needed to avoid dangerous situations that may cause a relationship to break up.

Caregiver The primary person who provides for the emotional and physical needs of a child. Could be either the mother, the father, a relative, or a nonrelative.

Celibacy The state of remaining unmarried.

Chlamydia A genital infection that causes inflammation of the urinary tract in men and vaginal inflammation in women.

Clingers Persons who disclose too much to others and have a desperate need to attach themselves to someone.

Closing phase of uncoupling The final stage of uncoupling when partners put the relationship behind them, go on with their lives without the partner, and develop indifferent attitudes toward the relationship.

Collaboration style of handling conflict Actions in which two people work creatively to find new solutions that will maximize rewards for both.

Commune A group living arrangement where property is held in common and all aspects of life are shared, including children.

Compadrazgo A form of friendship between godparents and godchildren and between godparents and biological parents.

Companionship The experience of two people doing things together in shared enjoyable activities.

Comparison level of alternatives The situation in which a person compares the current level of rewards from a partner with perceived potential rewards from an alternative relationship.

Compensatory exchange Making up for the lack of physical beauty in a relationship with some other desirable attribute, such as money.

Compensatory training Additional training provided to each gender to offset certain biological tendencies.

Competitive style of handling conflict Actions in which the partners show aggressiveness and a low degree of cooperation. There is a focus on one's own concerns at the expense of the other person.

Complementary needs theory The theory that most people prefer partners with personalities that complement their own.

Complex marriage A practice in the Oneida Community in which individuals had sex with other husbands or wives besides their own.

Compromise style of handling conflict Actions in which each person recognizes that he or she cannot totally have what each wants so each person gives in a little to achieve some of what each wants.

Conflict resolution A process of collaboration in which a conflict is clearly defined, each person's desires and needs on the issue are fully made known, many solutions are considered, and finally one solution is agreed to by all and is implemented.

Conflict theory The perspective that views conflict as a natural and inevitable part of human interaction. Conflict itself is not considered as either good or bad.

Conjoint marital therapy Counseling in which the therapist meets with the husband and wife together.

Contemporary pattern of courtship A pattern in which two young people make a joint decision to marry on their own and then announce it to their parents.

Content communication The part of communication that focuses on *what* is communicated, or the information itself.

Coupling process The process that relationships go through as they move from first glimpse to marital commitment. The process includes (1) initial attraction, (2) investigatory exchange, (3) trust development and attachment, and (4) committed reciprocity.

Cunnilingus Oral stimulation of the female genitals.

Cutaneous person A sexually mature adult whose entire skin surface is sensitive to touch.

Cycle of violence The three phases of a battering relationship including tension building, an acute battering incident, and kindness and contrite loving behavior.

Decoding The process by which the receiver of a message puts it back into feelings, thoughts, or images that mean something to him or her.

Dependency love A type of love in which lonely people need someone badly. It involves love-prone individuals, who often are "in love with being in love."

Developmental theory The perspective that focuses on family relationships over the life span or life cycle.

Dilemma of love The situation in which a person is under pressure to give evidence of love to a partner, but if he or she does so too readily, the value of his or her affection will decrease.

Disclosure flexibility The ability of an individual to adjust his or her disclosure levels according to the interpersonal and situational demands of the moment.

Double messages The communication of a thought or feeling in a nonverbal manner that contradicts the spoken message.

Double standard The norm by which certain forms of sexual behavior are considered acceptable for men but not for women.

Dyad A relationship involving two persons—a pair or couple.

Dyadic phase of uncoupling A period when both partners are assessing the costs of a marital relationship and where a common definition of the marriage as troubled is shared. The partners may oscillate between attempts to reconcile or to withdraw in this phase.

Emotional abuse Such forms of mistreatment as calling someone derogatory names, criticizing excessively, ridiculing, threatening a person's personal safety, threatening to withdraw love or to abandon the person, telling the person that he or she is bad or worthless, or forcing humiliating situations that rob the person of human dignity.

Emotional loneliness A feeling of loneliness or isolation that occurs when a person is missing an attachment figure—a significant or intimate other.

Empathy The ability to imagine oneself in another's position and to understand what that person is experiencing.

Empty-nest syndrome A condition traditionally thought to be experienced by mothers who live for and through their children and who experience depression, sadness, and despair when the children leave home.

Empty-shell marriage   A marriage that lacks fun, stimulation, and emotional closeness. The marriage is an accommodation and resignation for people who are committed to the institution of marriage, even though they are very unhappy.

Encoding   Putting feelings, images, or thoughts into words or symbols so that others can understand them.

Enlightened self-interest   Attaining one's own self-interests by taking the self-interests of others into account and cooperating with these people.

Equity of disclosure   A situation in which each person feels that he or she is revealing similar amounts of self-information.

Equity of rewards   A situation in a relationship where there is a sense of equality in terms of the giving and receiving of rewards.

Erection difficulties (impotence)   A sexual difficulty in which the man is not able to maintain an erection during sexual intercourse.

Erogenous zones   Areas of the human body that are the most sexually sensitive to touch.

Erotica   Movies, books, tapes, pictures, stories, or strip-tease shows intended to arouse sexual desire.

Estrogen   A feminizing hormone which is produced primarily in the ovaries.

Evaders   Persons who try to present the appearance of not needing anybody, but who underneath are very needy and lonely.

Exchange theory   The perspective that involves the evaluation of human interaction in terms of costs and rewards.

Exploitative relationships   A behavior pattern in which one person takes much more than he or she gives in a relationship.

Expressive roles   Roles carried out within the family that provide nurturance, affection, and emotional satisfaction.

Extended family   Relatives beyond the nuclear family, such as aunts, grandparents, cousins.

Extrinsic marriage   A marriage in which the partners are focused on material things or activities with groups of people outside the marriage.

Extrinsic rewards   Rewards given from the outside or externally to the individual.

Familial love   A type of love involving positive feelings, thoughts, and caring behavior toward the members of one's family.

Family conservatives   People who are opposed to homosexual rights, pornography, sexual permissiveness, abortion, the feminist movement, and ERA; known as the ''pro-family group.''

Family liberals   People who believe that many types of families exist today and that the decline of the traditional nuclear family from the past is a good thing.

Faultfinding   Indiscriminate criticism where the criticizer cannot distinguish between what is important and what is not important. The individual finds fault with seemingly minor actions; nit-picking.

Feelings   Internal subjective reactions to perceived costs or rewards in the external world, used synonymously with emotions.

Fellatio   Oral stimulation of the male genitals.

Feminization of poverty   The economic consequences for women of no-fault divorce, which lowers their standard of living to the poverty level. It results from women's lower earnings in society and their increased financial responsibility for their children.

Flextime   Scheduling that allows the worker to adjust his or her own starting and finishing times at work, as long as a fixed number of work hours per week are completed.

Free love The practice of participating in sexual activity with any other member of a group.

Friendship love A type of love, usually found outside of marriage, that is relaxed and not filled with intense passion or emotions. There is an implicit, informal commitment.

Functionalism The theory that looks at the contribution something (for example, *providing for nurturance* or the *good provider role*) makes for the maintenance of the family institution in society as a whole or to a particular family.

Gender norms The particular expectations of behaviors, goals, and attitudes for each sex.

Gender roles Behaviors that are consistent with gender norms.

Generalized other The general values, attitudes, and expectations held by a group which influences one's behavior and beliefs.

Gonads Glands that secrete sex hormones—ovaries in women, testicles in men.

Gonorrhea A sexually transmitted disease involving frequent and painful urination and a milky pus discharge from the penis. This disease often has no symptoms in women except for a possible yellow-green vaginal discharge.

Good-provider role The breadwinning role developed for men as a result of the Industrial Revolution in the nineteenth century.

Gunnysacking Behavior in which marital complaints (usually unresolved) are carried along quietly for a length of time and then are brought out from time to time for convenient use in arguments.

Herpes A sexually transmitted disease that can involve blisterlike sores on the genitals, inside the vagina, in the urethra, on the cervix, around the buttocks, or in the anus.

Homogamy The theory that people like others who are similar to themselves, or that "likes marry likes."

Housewife syndrome An illness identified by mental health professionals to describe the unhappiness of women who feel trapped and bored as wives and mothers with no outside employment.

Human contact A public type of activity that is typically very fleeting and involves little or no physical or emotional interaction.

Hurried child A child who is pressured to dress like, act like, and carry out the responsibilities of, an adult.

Ideal type A conceptualization of a group of characteristics used for the purpose of social analysis.

Idealistic love A type of love based on false or naively optimistic views of the partner, self, or relationship. Illusion and infatuation are common.

Identification theory A theory of gender roles that suggests that males are socialized to be "independent" and females are socialized for "interdependence."

Illusionary intimacy The feeling of being an emotionally close couple which is based on false perceptions of the partner. It is often experienced before marriage and/or just after marriage.

Individual phase of uncoupling A period when one spouse has doubts about the marriage and has thoughts and feelings about disengaging from it but does not yet express them to the partner.

Individual prerequisites to intimacy Personality characteristics that are needed in order for intimacy to develop.

Inequitable exchange A situation in which one partner perceives that he or she is receiving fewer rewards from the relationship than the other person is receiving.

Infatuation   The state of being possessed by extreme. passion and feelings of attraction toward another person.

Institutional commitment   A commitment to a marriage such that even if it is unfulfilling, the partner will treat the marriage as an unbreakable covenant.

Instrumental roles   Roles relating to the physical support of the family, such as the good-provider role.

Intermediary pattern of courtship   Behavior in which both the kin group and the young couple participate in the mate-selection process. Many items are bargained over and "courtship" involves a lengthy process.

Interview   The gathering of information through conversation between an investigator and an informant.

Intimate others   People who provide persons with emotional closeness.

Intimate relationship   A relationship involving an emotional bond with proven mutual commitment and trust between two people that provides personal and relationship security and rewards.

Intimate sexuality   Sexual activity in a committed, monogamous relationship involving trust, mutual empathy, interdependence, sensitive self-disclosure, warmth, and abundant touching carried out for its own sake.

Intrinsic rewards   Rewards given to oneself from within or internally.

Irretrievable investments   Certain investments in a marriage—time, money, personal disclosures, emotional support and so on—that cannot be recovered if the relationship breaks up.

Joint custody   An arrangement in which both parents share legal custody and often physical custody of children. Major decisions are made jointly concerning the health and well-being of the children.

Kegal exercises   A series of exercises recommended by sex therapists to help women become orgasmic.

Learned helplessness   A feeling of being increasingly helpless and therefore less able to solve problems or seek out options.

Lecturing   Giving a long speech or sermon without allowing the other person to get a word in edgewise.

Leveling   Expressing one's feelings, wants, and desires openly and honestly without putting the other person down or putting him or her on the defensive.

Low sexual desire (LSD)   A common sexual difficulty in which men and women have abnormally low sexual appetites.

Marital rape   Sexual activities of various kinds that are forced on one partner by another. In some states this is now a crime.

Marriage enrichment   Programs for married couples (who are not seriously troubled) where such skills as expressing feelings, communicating, and resolving conflicts are taught.

Marriage gradient   The tendency of men to marry down in terms of education and income.

Marriage mandate   The cultural expectation for women to marry.

Masturbation   Self-stimulation of the genitals.

Matching hypothesis   The idea that persons tend to pair off with someone equal to their own desirability level, including physical beauty.

Matriarchal family   The form of family organization in which the mother is dominant and the formal head.

Metapelet   A nurse–house mother who is the primary caregiver for the children on a kibbutz.

Midlife transition   A time when many men and women make changes in their work and family roles.

Mind reading   The assumption by one person that he or she knows what another person is thinking or feeling without asking that person.

Mortality rate The frequency of death in a given population.

Motherhood mandate The cultural expectation for women to have babies and become mothers.

Mourning process The release of feelings of sadness after losing a loved one through divorce or death.

Mutual empathy The state in which two people imagine themselves in each other's position to the degree that they understand what the other person is experiencing.

Negative exchange An ongoing pattern of hurtful interaction between two people involving the reciprocal giving and receiving of costs.

Negative-exchange marriage A marriage with almost constant conflict and fighting, the expression of anger and bitterness, and faultfinding and nit-picking.

Neglect Failure to perform acts for another person that normally are expected. Three basic forms of neglect include physical neglect, social neglect, and emotional neglect.

No-fault divorce law Law that permits a divorce without requiring that one spouse must be proved to be at fault; one party simply asserts that "irreconcilable differences" exist.

Non-accepters Individuals who have trouble accepting acts of kindness, praise, or compliments from other people.

Nonejaculation A sexual difficulty in which the man is not able to ejaculate.

Nonmarital cohabitation The practice of a man and woman living together without legal marriage.

Norms Generally accepted rules about expected behavior.

Nuclear family A kinship group in which natural parents and their child(ren) live together in one household.

Orgasmic difficulties A sexual problem in which the woman is unable to experience orgasm.

Overgeneralizations and absolute statements Statements that are too broad and inclusive; absolute or unqualified statements.

Patriarchal family The form of family organization in which the father is the official head.

Permissive parent The type of parent who is nonpunitive and allows the child extensive freedom to govern his or her own activities. No particular standards of behavior are asked for or required.

Permissiveness with affection The norm permitting premarital intercourse for both men and women in a stable relationship characterized by love or strong affection.

Permissiveness without affection The norm permitting premarital intercourse for both men and women regardless of the amount of affection present.

Personal-fulfillment movement The movement in the 1965–1975 period stressing "growth," "autonomy," "self-actualization," "freedom," "independence," "new experiences," and "human potential."

Pheromones Substances or odors given off by one gender that are sexually stimulating to the other gender.

Pleaser A person who is focused on almost continuous giving to another individual whether or not he or she receives much in return.

Polyfidelity A condition in which a group of people live together, have sexual access to all the members of the other sex but no sexual involvement with others outside of the group, and a lifetime commitment is intended.

Positive communication A situation in which positive comments outweigh negative ones. Also, communication that shows respect for people; supports their self-esteem or self-worth; and includes praise, compliments, and good manners.

Positive exchange The reciprocal giving and receiving of rewards between two people. The interactions are much more rewarding than costly.

Power The ability to obtain what one wants even if it is against the will of others.

Premenstrual syndrome (PMS) Any of the numerous symptoms (tension, depression, irritability, crying spells, anxiety, fatigue, etc.) that occur from two weeks to three days before the onset of menstruation.

Prenuptial agreement A contract made between two parties before their marriage regarding such items as money, property, inheritance to children from a prior marriage, child-custody arrangements, and household responsibilities.

Principle of least interest The concept that indicates that the partner with less interest in the relationship has more power.

Protestant work ethic The view perpetuated in American society that encourages individuals to pursue their work as though they have no other commitments.

Proximity friends People who become friends simply as the result of close physical location, such as neighbors, professional colleagues, and students in the same class.

Proximity theory of attraction (propinquity) The idea that the closer two individuals are geographically, the more likely it is that they will be attracted to each other.

Pseudo-intimate marriage A marriage that may appear idyllic and intimate from the outside, but in reality is a facade of a marriage, hiding discontent and conflict—none of which is made public.

Psychic arousal Erotic thoughts that originate in the brain and then proceed down the neural pathways to the spinal cord and then to the genitals.

Puberty The stage of development in which a person becomes physiologically capable of sexual reproduction.

Pubococcygeal (PC) muscle The large muscle surrounding the vagina, which contracts during orgasm.

Put-downs Blaming, attacking, or criticizing another person with the intent to inflict hurt, to punish, or to seek revenge.

Putting the other on the defensive Assuming a superior, know-it-all attitude and regularly putting the other person in the position of having to defend himself or herself.

Questionnaire A research instrument using a series of questions on a form, which are to be filled out by respondents.

Quick ejaculation A sexual difficulty that occurs when a man has inadequate control over the ejaculatory reflex.

Radiating effect The effect of positive qualities that are transferred from a beautiful woman to a man she dates or with whom she associates.

Random sample A sample of a larger population such that each person has an equal chance of being chosen in the sample.

Reciprocal sensitive disclosure The giving and receiving of personally private information in a sensitive manner between two people in a relationship.

Reciprocity of liking The tendency to like people who like you, but only if you like yourself.

Recycled father A stepfather who feels he missed out on raising his biological children and shows greater interest in his stepchildren.

Reference group A group to which a person relates that helps determine his or her own values, beliefs, and behaviors.

Reflexive arousal A form of reflex sexual response that can occur automatically, without the person being cognitively aware or in immediate control of the response.

Regression A coping mechanism in which a child returns to behaviors of an earlier stage of development such as needing a security blanket, whining and crying, and bed-wetting in order to seek assurance and security from a caregiver.

Relationship communication   That part of communication which indicates how the communicating persons are related, such as the way parents and children or employers and employees talk to each other.

Renewable marriage   A type of marriage that would require a commitment of only a limited duration—for three, five, or ten years. At the end of the period the couple decide if they want to recommit themselves to the marriage or end it.

Rescue fantasy   The thought that one can change a partner who has a host of personal problems. The "rescuer" believes that if he or she just "loves" this partner enough the problems will disappear.

Role cycling   The attempt to coordinate one's individual career cycle with the natural cycle of the family.

Role overload   A situation in which a person is committed to more roles than he or she can manage effectively in the time available.

Romantic love   A feeling, artificially heightened by the media and usually combined with sexuality, that tends to be the basis for marriage in American society.

Romeo and Juliet effect   A pattern of behavior often followed by parents in which they try to discourage a romantic relationship among teenagers. Such an approach typically results in the young couple developing an even closer relationship.

Sarcasm   Statements, passed off as humorous but usually meant to hurt, in which speakers actually mean the opposite of what they say.

Secondary reward value   The benefit derived from mentally reliving past rewards and happy events. Such good times are not lost and they help partners further to commit themselves to the marriage and to expect rewards in the future.

Selected friends   Persons with whom we *choose* to work or play. These friendships are usually quite segmented in that contact is usually restricted to certain activities.

Self-awareness   Being conscious of one's total self—one's feelings, thoughts, and behaviors.

Self-concept   A subjective view of oneself as a result of interaction with others and one's impressions of how others view oneself.

Self-disclosure   The sharing of personal feelings, ideas, thoughts, opinions, and values with another person.

Self-esteem   A personal assessment of the extent to which one is worthwhile, lovable, capable, and confident.

Sexual exploitation   Sexual activity in which an older, more powerful person forces a younger individual into such activity.

Sexually permissive cultures   Cultures in which some formal sexual prohibitions exist but they tend to be very loosely enforced. These cultures *tolerate* sexuality.

Sexually repressive cultures   Cultures that view sexuality as extremely dangerous and that generally *deny* human sexual needs.

Sexually restrictive cultures   Cultures that are focused on the *limitation* of sexuality.

Sexually supportive cultures   Cultures in which sexuality is openly *encouraged* and is seen as necessary for human happiness.

Significant others   Important friends, spouses, or other family members who supply some degree of emotional support and who tend to be available when needed.

Similarity theory of attraction   The idea that people like people similar to themselves on a number of traits, or that "likes marry likes."

Socialization The lifelong interactive process by which one learns the attitudes, values, and expectations of others in society and through which one acquires a personality.

Social loneliness A feeling of loneliness or isolation resulting from the lack of a social network of friends with whom to do things.

Social phase of uncoupling The stage in which the decision to divorce is implemented and made public.

Sole custody The arrangement by which a child lives primarily with one divorced parent who makes all legal and final decisions regarding the child's welfare. The other parent spends some time with the child and in many cases participates in decisions dealing with education, religious training, medical care, and vacations.

Split custody The arrangement by which a number of children are divided between two divorced parents.

Stepchild A child whose biological parents' marriage ended in divorce or death and at least one of the parents has remarried.

Stepfamily A family in which at least one partner is a stepparent, that is, not the biological parent of a child. Such a family is sometimes referred to as ''reconstituted,'' ''blended,'' or ''binuclear.''

Stranger anxiety A behavior pattern that infants have acquired by the ninth month of life that shows that they have developed an attachment to a caregiver.

Structure The organization of positions or roles in a family.

Survey A systematic study of the attitudes, feelings, behavior, thoughts, or values of a population.

Swinging Simultaneously shared extramarital sex, or adultery, on the part of the husband and wife.

Symbolic interactionism The theory that looks at family interaction as an ongoing process, using symbols to understand behavior.

Syphilis A disease transmitted through sexual or skin contact with someone who is in an infectious stage. There are four stages to the disease, each with more damaging effects on the body.

Systems theory The perspective that views each family as a system in itself, which has boundaries that define and separate it from the outside world.

Tactfulness The ability to be sincere in communication while at the same time showing respect for the other person's feelings and taking care not to hurt him or her unnecessarily.

Tactile expressiveness The ability to give and receive holding, caressing, cuddling, and touching behavior.

Temperament An in-born variation in terms of behavior patterns. For example, there are easy babies, slow-to-warm-up babies, and difficult babies. Some temperament traits can exist into adulthood.

Testosterone A type of androgen, which is known as the masculinizing hormone.

Theory A set of interrelated assumptions, principles, and concepts organized to explain relationships among facts.

Total love A type of love that exists when an individual makes a voluntary, recognized, public pledge of commitment to another person.

Touching Expressing one's feelings through such means as stroking, caressing, holding, brushing, hugging, kissing, and squeezing.

Toughlove A program for parents who are troubled by their teenagers' antisocial or uncooperative behaviors.

Traditional divorce laws Laws that require proof of a marital offense and that perpetuate a gender-based division of roles and responsibilities. The guilty spouse is punished and the financial settlement is linked to the determination of fault.

Traditional marriage A marriage in which the husband is dominant and plays the good-provider role and the wife is subordinate to the husband and plays the role of nurturer, caregiver, and homemaker.

Traditional pattern of courtship Mate selection involving bargaining between two kin groups or the parents of the two young individuals. The bargain achieved results in an "arranged marriage."

Transitional bisexual A bisexual person who finally switches from one sexual preference to another, usually from heterosexuality to homosexuality.

Transitional support A type of temporary maintenance provided for a dependent spouse. Limited compensation is given until the individual can become self-supporting after a divorce.

Transition marriages Those marriages that can no longer be accurately described as traditional but that have not reached a high enough degree of emotional closeness to be described as intimate.

Transitory bisexual A person who experiments with bisexuality but returns finally to his or her preferred sexual choice.

Trust Reliance on another person to follow through with certain behavior. It also involves faith that the other person will not purposely try to hurt the trusting individual.

Turning the other cheek Declining an invitation to argue by reacting in a reasonable, concerned, and tactful manner, such as continuing the conversation without retaliating or changing the subject.

Typology A system of classification of ideal types.

Vaginismus A sexual difficulty in which the muscles surrounding the vagina close tightly as a result of an involuntary muscle spasm.

Verification feedback Checking on whether one has correctly understood the speaker's feelings, opinions, or desires by repeating back what one thought one heard in one's own words.

Voluntary commitment A decision to maintain a relationship only so long as it provides personal happiness, or more satisfaction is not perceived of as coming from an alternative relationship.

Vulnerability The ability to disclose personal feelings, initiate investments in others, and make commitments—all with the possibility of being rejected by other people.

Wake-sleep cycles The biological clocks of individuals, which lead them to be either "morning persons" or "night persons."

Widow A woman who has lost her husband by death and who has not remarried.

Widower A man who has lost his wife by death and who has not remarried.

Working class A category of skilled and unskilled manual workers, often including low-paid, white-collar individuals such as clerical workers.

Bibliography

ADAMS, BERT N. 1968. *Kinship in an Urban Setting.* Chicago: Markham.

ADAMS, BERT N. 1970. "Isolation, function, and beyond: American kinship in the 1960's." *Journal of Marriage and the Family* 32: 575–597.

ADAMS, BERT N. 1980. *The Family: A Sociological Interpretation.* Skokie, Ill.: Rand McNally.

ADAMS, BERT N., AND RONALD CROMWELL 1978. "Morning and night people in the family: A preliminary statement." *Family Coordinator* 27: 5–13.

ADAMS, MARGARET 1981. "Living singly." In Peter J. Stein, ed. *Single Life: Unmarried Adults in Social Context.* New York: St. Martin's Press, pp. 221–234.

ADE-RIDDER, LINDA, AND TIMOTHY H. BRUBAKER 1983. "The quality of long-term marriages." In Timothy H. Brubaker, ed. *Family Relationships in Later-Life.* Beverly Hills, Calif.: Sage.

ADLER, RONALD B., AND NEIL TOWNE 1984. *Looking Out/Looking In: Interpersonal Communication.* 4th ed. New York: Holt, Rinehart and Winston.

AINSWORTH, MARY E., M. C. BLEHAR, E. WATERS, AND F. WALL 1978. *Patterns of Attachment: A Psychological Study of the Strange Situations.* Hillsdale, N.J.: Erlbaum.

AINSWORTH, MARY E. 1973. "The development of infant-mother attachment." In Betty M. Caldwell and Henry N. Ricciuti, eds. *Review of Child Development Research.* Vol. 3. Chicago: University of Chicago Press.

ALLAN, GRAHAM 1977. "Class variations in friendship patterns." *British Journal of Sociology* 28: 389–393.

ALTMAN, IRWIN, AND DALMAS TAYLOR 1973. *Social Penetration: The Development of Interpersonal Relationships.* New York: Holt, Rinehart and Winston.

ALWIN, DUANE F.; PHILIP E. CONVERSE; AND STEPHEN S. MARTIN 1983. "Living arrangements and social integration." Ann Arbor: University of Michigan, Institute for Social Research.

AMERICAN BAR ASSOCIATION 1983. *Law and Marriage: Your Legal Guide.* Chicago: ABA Press.

ANDREWS, LORI B. 1985. "The truth about PMS (premenstrual syndrome)." *Parents,* Jan., pp. 51–56.

ANN ARBOR NEWS 1984. "More married

couples collect two checks, census report says." Apr. 2, pp. C1–C2.

ARIES, PHILIPPE   1962. *Centuries of Childhood: A Social History of Family Life.* Robert Baldick, trans. New York: Random House.

ARLING, G.   1976. "The elderly widow and her family, neighbors and friends." *Journal of Marriage and the Family* 38: 757–768.

ARMSTRONG, LOUISE   1983. *The Home Front: Notes from the Family War Zone.* New York: McGraw-Hill.

ARONSON, E.   1961. "The effect of effort on the attractiveness of rewarded and unrewarded stimuli." *Journal of Abnormal and Social Psychology* 63: 375–380.

ARONSEN, E.   1969. "Some antecedents of interpersonal attraction." In William J. Arnold and David Levine, eds. *Nebraska Symposium on Motivation.* Lincoln: University of Nebraska Press.

ATHANASIOU, R., AND R. SARKIN   1974. "Premarital sexual behavior and postmarital adjustment." *Archives of Sexual Behavior* 3: 207–225.

ATKINSON, TI-GRACE   1969. "The oppressed majority demands its rights." *Life,* Dec. 12.

ATWATER, LYNN   1982. *The Extramarital Connection.* New York: Irvington.

AXELSON, L.   1970. "The working wife: Differences in perception among negro and white males." *Journal of Marriage and the Family* 32: 457–464.

BACH, GEORGE R., AND PETER WYDEN   1968. *The Intimate Enemy.* New York: Avon Books.

BADER, EDWARD; GISELE MICROYS; CAROLE SINCLAIR; ELIZABETH WILLETT; AND BRENDA CONWAY   1980. "Do marriage preparation programs really work?: A Canadian experiment." *Journal of Marital and Family Therapy* 6 (Apr.): 171–179.

BAILYN, L.   1970. "Career and family orientations of husbands and wives in relation to marital happiness." *Human Relations* 23: 97–113.

BALKWELL, CAROLYN   1981. "Transition to widowhood: A review of the literature." *Family Relations* 30 (Jan.): 117–128.

BALLWEG, JOHN A.   1967. "Resolution of conjugal role adjustment after retirement." *Journal of Marriage and the Family* 29: 277–281.

BANK, STEPHEN P., AND MICHAEL D. KAHN   1982. *The Sibling Bond.* New York: Basic Books.

BARBACH, LONNIE GARFIELD   1975. *For Yourself: The Fulfillment of Female Sexuality.* New York: New American Library.

BARDWICK, JUDITH M.   1979. *In Transition.* New York: Holt, Rinehart and Winston.

BARFIELD, ASHTON   1976. "Biological influences on sex differences in behavior." In Michael S. Teitelbaum. *Sex Differences.* Garden City, N.Y.: Doubleday (Anchor Books), pp. 62–121.

BARKAS, J. L.   1980. *Single in America.* New York: Atheneum.

BARNES, HOWARD   1985. "Marital satisfaction not predicated on good communication, researcher." *Marriage and Divorce Today* 10 (Jan. 14): 1.

BARNES, HOWARD L., AND DAVID H. OLSON   1984. "The Family Communication Scale." *Family Circle,* Oct., p. 7.

BARNES, HOWARD L., AND DAVID H. OLSON   1985. "Parent-Adolescent Communication Scale" in David Olson et al., eds. *Family Inventories,* University of Minnesota.

BARRETT, KAREN   1982. "Date rape." *Ms.,* Sept., pp. 48–51.

BAR-TAL, D., AND L. SAXE   1976. "Perceptions of similarity and dissimilarly attractive couples and individuals." *Journal of Personality and Social Psychology* 33: 772–781.

BARTELL, GILBERT D.   1971. *Group Sex.* New York: Wyden.

BARUCH, GRACE; ROSALIND BARNETT; AND CARYL RIVERS   1983. *Lifeprints: New Patterns of Love and Work for Today's Women.* New York: New American Library.

BAUMRIND, DIANE   1968. "Authoritarian

versus authoritative parental control." *Adolescence* 3: 255–272.

BAUMRIND, DIANE   1971. "Current patterns of parental authority." *Developmental Monographs* 4.

BEAL, EDWARD   1985. "The ripple effect of divorce: Loss of friends." *Marriage and Divorce Today* 10 (Apr. 29): 2.

BELL, ALAN P., AND MARTIN S. WEINBERG 1978. *Homosexualities.* New York: Simon & Schuster.

BELL, ALAN P.; MARTIN S. WEINBERG; AND SUE KIEFER HAMMERSMITH   1981. *Sexual Preference.* Bloomington: Indiana University Press.

BELL, RICHARD Q.   1971. "Stimulus control of parent or caretaker behavior by offspring." *Developmental Psychology,* 4: 63–72.

BELL, RICHARD Q.   1974. *The Effect of the Infant on Its Caregiver.* In Michael Lewis and Leonard A. Rosenblum, eds. New York: Wiley, pp. 1–19.

BELL, ROBERT R.   1975. "Swinging: Separating the sexual from friendship." In Nona Glazer-Malbin, *''Old Family/New Family'' Interpersonal Relationships.* New York: Van Nostrand, pp. 150–168.

BELL, ROBERT R.   1981. *Worlds of Friendship.* Beverly Hills, Calif.: Sage.

BELL, RUTH DAVIDSON   1978. "The middle years." In the Boston Women's Health Book Collective, eds. *Ourselves and Our Children.* New York: Random House, pp. 69–86.

BELSKY, JAY   1985. Quoted in Glen Davis. "You, me and baby makes . . . happiness." *Detroit Free Press,* Jan. 8, p. 1B.

BELSKY, JAY; RICHARD M. LERNER; AND GRAHAM B. SPAINER   1984. *The Child in the Family.* Reading, Mass.: Addison-Wesley.

BENDER, LAURETTA, AND ABRAM BLAU 1937. "The reactions of children to sexual relations with adults." *American Journal of Orthopsychiatry* 7: 500–518.

BENWARD, J., AND J. DENSEN-GERBER 1975. "Incest as a causative factor in antisocial behavior: An exploratory study."

Paper presented at the American Academy of Forensic Sciences, February.

BERGER, BRIGITTE, AND PETER L. BERGER 1983. *The War over the Family.* Garden City, N.Y.: Doubleday (Anchor Books).

BERGER, PETER L.   1963. *Invitation to Sociology.* Garden City, N.Y.: Doubleday.

BERGMAN, JERRY   1978. "Licensing parents: A new age of child-rearing." *The Futurist* 12, pp. 290–299.

BERNARD, JESSIE   1981. "Facing the future." *Society,* Jan.–Feb. 18: 53:59.

BERNARD, JESSIE   1981. "The good-provider role: Its rise and fall." *American Psychologist* 36: 1–12.

BERNARD, JESSIE   1982. *The Future of Marriage.* New Haven: Yale University Press.

BERSCHEID, ELLEN, AND ELAINE HATFIELD WALSTER   1974. "Physical attractiveness." In Leonard Berkowitz, ed. *Advances in Experimental Social Psychology.* New York: Academic Press, pp. 158–216.

BERSCHEID, ELLEN, AND ELAINE HATFIELD WALSTER   1978. *Interpersonal Attraction.* Reading, Mass.: Addison-Wesley.

BERSCHEID, ELLEN; ELAINE WALSTER; AND GEORGE BOHRNSTEDT   1973. Seminar presented at the annual meeting of the American Sociological Association.

BERSCHEID, ELLEN; K. DION; ELAINE HATFIELD WALSTER; AND WILLIAM G. WALSTER   1971. "Physical attractiveness and dating choice: A test of the matching hypothesis." *Journal of Experimental Social Psychology* 7: 173–189.

BETCHER, R. WILLIAM   1981. "Intimate play and marital adaptation." *Psychiatry* 44: 13–33.

BETTLEHEIM, BRUNO   1970. *The Children of the Dream.* New York: Avon Books.

BIENVENU, M. J., SR.   1970. "Measurement of marital communication." *The Family Coordinator* 19: 26–31.

BIRCHLER, G. R.; ROBERT L. WEISS; AND J. P. VINCENT   1975. "Multi-method analysis of social reinforcement exchange in maritally distressed and nondistressed spouse and stranger dyads." *Journal of*

Personality and Social Psychology 31: 349–360.

BIRD, CAROLINE.   1979. *The Two-Paycheck Marriage*. New York: Pocket Books.

BLACKWELL, JAMES E.   1985. *The Black Community: Diversity and Unity*. 2nd ed. New York: Harper & Row.

BLAU, PETER M.   1964. *Exchange and Power in Social Life*. New York: Wiley.

BLOOD, ROBERT O., AND DONALD M. WOLFE 1960. *Husbands and Wives*. New York: Free Press.

BLUMSTEIN, PHILIP, AND PEPPER SCHWARTZ 1977. "Bisexuality: Some social psychological issues." *Journal of Social Issues* 33 (Spring): 30–45.

BLUMSTEIN, PHILIP, AND PEPPER SCHWARTZ 1983. *American Couples*. New York: Morrow.

BLUSTEIN, JEFFREY   1982. *Parents and Children: The Ethics of the Family*. New York: Oxford University Press.

BODIN, JEANNE, AND BONNIE MITELMAN 1983. *Mothers Who Work*. New York: Ballantine Books.

BORNEMAN, ERNEST   1982. "Progress in empirical research on children's sexuality." Paper presented at the Sixth World Congress of Sexology. Washington, D.C., May 25.

BOTWIN, CAROL   1985. *Is There Sex After Marriage*. Boston: Little, Brown.

BOWLBY, JOHN   1963. *Child Care and the Growth of Love*. London: Pelican.

BOYD, ROSAMONDE R.   1978. "The valued grandparent: A changing social role." In J. Ross Eshleman and J. N. Clarke, eds. *Intimacy Commitments and Marriage: Development of Relationships*. Boston: Allyn & Bacon.

BRAIKER, HARRIET B., AND HAROLD H. KELLEY   1979. "Conflict in the development of close relationships." In R. L. Burgess and Ted L. Huston, eds. *Social Exchange in Developing Relationships*. New York: Academic Press.

BRANDEN, N.   1969. *The Pscyhology of Self-Esteem*. New York: Bantam Books.

BRECHER, EDWARD M., AND THE EDITORS OF CONSUMER REPORTS BOOKS   1984. *Love, Sex and Aging*. Boston: Little, Brown.

BRIDDELL, DAN W.; DAVID C. RIMM; GLENN R. CADDY; GIL KRAWITZ; DAVID SHOLIS; AND ROBERT J. WUNDERLIN   1978. "Effects of alcohol and cognitive set on sexual arousal to deviant stimuli." *Journal of Abnormal Psychology* 87 (Aug.): 418–430.

BRIM, ORVILLE G., JR.   1976. "Theories of the male mid-life crisis." *The Counseling Psychologist* 6: 2–9.

BRIM, ORVILLE G., JR.   1976. "Male mid-life crisis: ·A comparative analysis." In Beth Hess, ed. *Growing Old in America*. New Brunswick, N.J.: Transaction Books.

BURCHINAL, LEE G.   1964. "The premarital dyad and love involvement." In Harold Christensen, ed. *Handbook of Marriage and the Family*. Skokie, Ill.: Rand McNally.

BURGESS, ANN W., AND LYNDA L. HOLMSTROM   1974. "Rape trauma syndrome." *American Journal of Psychiatry*, 131: 981–986.

BURGESS, ANN W., AND LYNDA L. HOLMSTROM   1975. "Sexual assault of children and adolescents: Pressure, sex and secrecy." *Nursing Clinics of North America* 10 (Sept.): 551–563.

BURGESS, ERNEST W., AND PAUL WALLIN 1943. "Homogamy in social characteristics." *American Journal of Sociology* 49: 109–124.

BURGESS, ERNEST W., AND PAUL WALLIN 1953. *Engagement and Marriage*. Philadelphia: Lippincott.

BURGWYN, DIANA   1981. *Marriage Without Children*. New York: Harper & Row.

BURNS, ROBERT C., AND HARVARD S. KAUFMAN   1970. *Kinetic Family Drawings* (K-F-D). New York: Brunner/Mazel.

BURR, WESLEY R.   1970. "Satisfaction with various aspects of marriage over the life cycle: A random middle class sample." *Journal of Marriage and the Family* 26 (Feb.): 29–37.

BURR, WESLEY R.; REUBIN HILL; F. IVAN NYE; AND IRA L. REISS, EDS.   1979. *Con-*

temporary Theories about the Family. New York: Free Press.

BUTLER, ROBERT 1984. "Today's senior citizens: Pioneers of new golden era." Interview in *U.S. News & World Report.* July 2, pp. 51–52.

BUTLER, SANDRA 1978. *Conspiracy of Silence: The Trauma of Incest.* New York: Bantam Books.

CALDERONE, MARY S. 1983. "Fetal erection and its message to us." In *Siecus Report* 11 (May–July): 9–10.

CAMPBELL, ANGUS; PHILIP E. CONVERSE; AND WILLARD L. RODGERS 1976. *The Quality of American Life.* New York: Russell Sage.

CAPLOW, THEODORE; HOWARD M. BAHR; BRUCE A. CHADWICK; REUBEN HILL; AND MARGARET HOLMES WILLIAMSON 1982. *Middletown Families.* Minneapolis: University of Minnesota Press.

CARDEN, MAREN LOCKWOOD 1971. *Oneida: Utopian Community to Modern Corporation.* New York: Harper & Row.

CARGAN, LEONARD, AND MATTHEW MELKO 1982. *Singles: Myths and Realities.* Beverly Hills, Calif.: Sage.

CARTER, HUGH, AND PAUL C. GLICK 1976. *Marriage and Divorce: A Social and Economic Study.* Cambridge, Mass.: Harvard University Press.

CATE, RODNEY M.; F. S. CHRISTOPER; AND SALLY LLOYD 1982. "Premarital abuse: A social psychological perspective." *Journal of Family Issues* 3 (Mar.): 79–90.

CHAFETZ, JANET S. 1974. *Masculine/Feminine or Human?: An Overview of the Sociology of Sex Roles.* Itacca, Ill.: F. E. Peacock.

CHELUNE, G. J., ED. 1979. *Self-disclosure: Origins, patterns, and implications of openness in interpersonal relationships.* San Francisco: Jossey-Bass.

CHERLIN, ANDREW J. 1978. "Remarriage as an incomplete institution." *Journal of Sociology* 84: 634–650.

CHESS, STELLA; ALEXANDER THOMAS; AND HERBERT G. BIRCH 1965. *Your Child Is a Person.* New York: Viking Press.

CHODOROW, NANCY 1978. *The Reproduction of Mothering.* Berkeley: University of California Press.

CHOPRA, G. S. 1969. "Man and marijuana." *International Journal of Addictions* 4: 215–247.

CHRISTENSEN, HAROLD T. 1973. "Attitudes toward marital infidelity: A nine culture sample." *Journal of Comparative Family Studies.* 14 (Autumn): 197–214.

CLANTON, GORDON 1984. "Social forces and the changing family." In Lester A. Kirkendall and Arthur E. Gravatt, eds. *Marriage and the Family in the Year 2020.* Buffalo: Prometheus.

CLANTON, GORDON, AND LYNN G. SMITH, EDS. 1977. *Jealousy.* Englewood Cliffs, N.J.: Prentice Hall.

CLARK, A. C. 1952. "An examination of the operation of residential propinquity as a factor in mate selection." *American Sociological Review* 27: 17–22.

CLINEBELL, HOWARD J., AND CHARLOTTE H. CLINEBELL 1970. *The Intimate Marriage.* New York: Harper & Row.

COLE, K. C. 1982. "Couples that play." *Psychology Today,* Feb., pp. 33–37.

COLEMAN, SAMUEL 1983. *Family Planning in Japanese Society.* Princeton, N.J.: Princeton University Press.

COMSTOCK, G.; S. CHAFFEE; N. KATZMAN; M. MCCOMBS; AND D. ROBERTS 1978. *Television and Human Behavior.* New York: Columbia University Press.

CONNECTICUT MUTUAL LIFE INSURANCE CO. 1981. *The Connecticut Mutual Life Report on American Values in the '80's: The Impact of Belief.* Hartford.

COOLEY, CHARLES HORTON 1902. *Human Nature and the Social Order.* New York: Scribners.

COOMBS, ROBERT H., AND WILLIAM F. KENKEL 1966. "Sex differences in dating aspirations and satisfactions with computer-selected partners." *Journal of Marriage and the Family* 29: 470–479.

COSER, ROSE LAUB, AND GERALD ROKOFF 1974. "Women in the occupational world: Social disruption and conflict." In

Rose Laub Coser, ed. *The Family: Its Structures and Functions.* 2nd. ed. New York: St. Martin's Press.

COZBY, PAUL C.   1973. "Self-disclosure: A literature review." *Psychological Bulletin* 79: 73–91.

CRENSHAW, THERESA LARSEN   1983. *Bedside Manners: Your Guide to Better Sex.* New York: McGraw-Hill.

CRENSHAW, THERESA LARSEN   1986. *AIDS.* Handout presented to the American Association of Sex Educators, Counselors, and Therapists, April 1986, Los Angeles, Calif.

CRÉPAULT, C., ET AL.   1977. "Erotic imagery in women." In R. Genne and C. C. Wheeler, eds. *Progress in Sexology.* New York: Plenum, pp. 267–283.

CROSBY, JOHN F.   1985. *Illusion and Disillusion: The Self in Love and Marriage.* 2nd. ed. Belmont, Calif.: Wadsworth.

CROWE, MARY   1984. "Sexually transmitted diseases." In The Boston Women's Health Book Collective, eds. *The New Our Bodies, Ourselves.* New York: Simon & Schuster.

CSIKSZENTMIHALYI, MIHALY, AND REED LARSON   1984. *Being Adolescent: Conflict and Growth in the Teenage Years.* New York: Basic Books.

CUBER, JOHN, AND PEGGY HARROFF   1965. *Sex and the Significant Americans.* Baltimore: Penguin Books.

CURRAN, DELORES   1983. *Traits of a Healthy Family.* Minneapolis: Winston Press.

CURRIER, RICHARD L.   1981. "Juvenile sexuality in global perspective." In Larry L. Constantine and Floyd M. Martinson, eds. *Children and Sex.* Boston: Little, Brown, pp. 9–19.

DANIELS, PAMELA, AND KATHY WEINGARTEN   1981. *Sooner or Later: The Timing of Parenthood and Adult Lives.* New York: Norton.

DAVIDSON, BERNARD; JACK BALSWICK; AND CHARLES HALVERSON   1983. "Affective self-disclosure and marital adjust-

ment: A test of equity theory." *Journal of Marriage and the Family* 45: 93–102.

DEFLEUR, M. L.   1964. "Occupational roles as portrayed on television." *Public Opinion Quarterly* 28: 57–74.

DELEY, WARREN W.   1983. "Physical punishment of children: Sweden and the U. S. A." Presented at the Annual Meeting of the National Council on Family Relations, St. Paul, Minnesota, October.

DELORA, JOANN S.; CAROL A. B. WARREN; AND CAROL RINKLEIB ELLISON   1981. *Understanding Sexual Interaction.* Boston: Houghton Mifflin.

DEMARIS, ALFRED, AND GERALD R. LESLIE   1984. "Cohabitation with the future spouse: Its influence upon marital satisfaction and communication." *Journal of Marriage and the Family* 46: 77–84.

DEMOS, JOHN   1970. *A Little Commonwealth: Family Life in Plymouth Colony.* New York: Oxford University Press.

DEMOS, JOHN   1974. "The American family in past time." *American Scholar* 43: 422–446.

DENFIELD, D.   1974. "Dropouts from swinging: The marriage counselor as informant." In James R. Smith and Lynbn G. Smith, eds. *Beyond Monogamy.* Baltimore: Johns Hopkins University Press.

DENTAN, R.   1968. *The Semai.* New York: Holt, Rinehart and Winston.

DERLEGA, VALERIAN J.; BONNIE DURHAM; BARBARA GOCKEL; AND DAVID SHOLIS   1981. "Sex differences in self-disclosure: Effects of content, friendship and partner's sex." *Sex Roles* 7: 433–447.

DERLEGA, VALERIAN J.; BARBARA A. WINSTEAD; PAUL T. P. WONG; AND SUSAN HUNTER   1985. "Gender effects in an initial encounter: A case where men exceed women in disclosure." *Journal of Social and Personal Relationships* 2: 25–44.

DESCHNER, JEANNE P.   1984. *The Hitting Habit: Anger Control for Battering Couples.* New York: Free Press.

DESCHNER, JEANNE P.; C. GEDDES; V. GRIMES; AND E. STAUCUKAS   1980.

"Battered women: Factors associated with abuse." Arlington: University of Texas at Arlington Graduate School of Social Work (duplicated).

DETROIT FREE PRESS 1984. "How courts decide disputes." Nov. 18.

DEUTSCHER, IRWIN 1973. "Socialization for postparental life." In Marcia Lasswell and Thomas Lasswell, eds. *Love, Marriage, Family: A Developmental Approach.* Glenview, Ill.: Scott, Foresman, pp. 510–517.

DICKENS, WANDA J., AND DANIEL PERLMAN 1981. "Friendship over the life cycle." In Steve Duck and Robin Gilmour, eds. *Personal Relationships 2: Developing Personal Relationships.* London: Academic Press, pp. 91–122.

DION, K. L.; ELLEN BERSCHEID; AND ELAINE WALSTER 1972. "What is beautiful is good." *Journal of Personality and Social Psychology* 24: 285–290.

DOBASH, R. EMERSON, AND RUSSELL DOBASH 1979. *Violence Against Wives.* New York: Free Press.

DOBSON, CYNTHIA 1983. "Sex-role and marital-role expectations." In Timothy Brubaker, ed. *Family Relationships in Later Life.* Beverly Hills, Calif.: Sage, pp. 109–126.

DODGE, D., AND W. MARTIN 1970. *Social Stress and Chronic Disease.* South Bend, Ind.: University of Notre Dame Press.

DODSON, FITZHUGH 1981. *How to Grandparent.* New York: New American Library.

DODSON, JUALYNNE 1981. "Conceptualizations of black families." In Harriette P. McAdoo, ed. *Black Families.* Beverly Hills, Calif.: Sage, pp. 23–36.

DOHERTY, WILLIAM J., AND BRIAN J. WALKER 1982. "Marriage encounter casualities: A preliminary investigation." *American Journal of Family Therapy* 10 (Summer): 15–25.

DORESS, P. B. 1978. "Society's impact on families." In Boston Women's Health Book Collective, eds. *Ourselves and Our Children.* New York: Random House, pp. 186–221.

DOUDNA, CHRISTINE, AND FERN MCBRIDE 1980. "Where are the men for the women at the top." *Savvy,* Feb.

DOUVAN, ELIZABETH, AND JOSEPH ADELSON 1966. *The Adolescent Experience.* New York: Wiley.

DOYLE, JAMES A. 1983. *The Male Experience.* Dubuque, Iowa: Brown.

DOYLE, JAMES A. 1985. *Sex and Gender: The Human Experience.* Dubuque, Iowa: Brown.

DUCK, STEVE 1982. "A topography of relationship disengagement and dissolution." In Steve Duck, ed. *Dissolving Relationships,* vol. 4 of *Personal Relationships.* London: Academic Press, pp. 1–30.

DUCK, STEVE 1983. *Friends, for Life.* New York: St Martin's Press.

DURDEN-SMITH, JO, AND DIANE DE SIMONE 1983. *Sex and the Brain.* New York: Arbor House.

DURKHEIM, EMILE 1897/1951. *Suicide.* New York: Free Press.

DUVALL, EVELYN 1971. *Family Development.* 4th ed. Philadelphia: Lippincott.

EDWARDS, MARIE, AND ELEANOR HOOVER 1974. *The Challenge of Being Single.* New York: New American Library.

EICHENBAUM, LOUISE, AND SUSIE ORBACH 1983. *What Do Women Want?: Exploding the Myth of Dependency.* New York: Coward, McCann & Geoghegan.

EINSTEIN, ELIZABETH 1982. *The Stepfamily.* New York: Macmillan.

ELKIND, DAVID 1981. *The Hurried Child: Growing Up Too Fast Too Soon.* Reading, Mass.: Addison-Wesley.

ELWIN, V. 1968. "The duration of marriage among the Aboriginals of the Maikal Hills." *Man In India* 22: 11.

ENGEL, TAMARA 1984. Quoted in *New York Times.* (n.d.)

ENGLISH, COREY W. 1985. "Job sharing gains grounds across U. S." In *U.S. News & World Report,* Oct. 14, p. 76.

FAGAN, JEFFREY A.; DOUGLAS K. STEWART; AND KAREN V. HANSEN 1983. "Violent men or violent husbands? Background factors and situational correlates." In David Finkelhor, Richard J. Gelles, Gerald T. Hotaling, and Murray A. Straus, eds. *The Dark Side of Families.* Beverly Hills, Calif.: Sage, pp. 49–67.

FALICOY, CELIA JAES 1982. "Mexican families." In Monica McGoldrick, John K. Pearce, and Joseph Giordano, eds. *Ethnicity and Family Therapy.* New York: Guilford Press, pp. 134–163.

FALLER, KATHLEEN COULBORN Undated. "Parent-child interaction in child abuse and neglect: Assessment and treatment." Paper.

FALLER, KATHLEEN COULBORN, ED. 1981. *Social Work with Abused and Neglected Children.* New York: Free Press.

FASTEAU, MARC FEIGEN 1975. *The Male Machine.* New York: Dell (Delta Books).

FEAZELL, C. S. 1981. "Status of services for men who batter their living partners with suggested implications for program development." Unpublished thesis, University of Texas at Arlington.

FELDMAN, H. 1961. "Development of the husband-wife relationship: A research report." Ithaca, N.Y.: Cornell University (mimeographed).

FENDRICH, MICHAEL 1984. "Wives' employment and husbands' distress: A meta-analysis and a replication." *Journal of Marriage and the Family* 46: 871–879.

FINDLAY, STEVEN 1985. "Jobs sap couples' craving for sex." *USA Today*, May 8, p. 1D.

FINKELHOR, DAVID 1979. *Sexually Victimized Children.* New York: Free Press.

FINKELHOR, DAVID 1980. "Risk factors in the sexual victimization of children." *Child Abuse and Neglect* 4: 265–273.

FINKELHOR, DAVID 1980. "Sexual socialization in America: High risk for sexual abuse." In Jean Marc Samson, ed. *Childhood and Sexuality.* Montreal: Editions Etudes Vivantes, pp. 641–648.

FINKELHOR, DAVID, AND KERSTI YLLO 1983. "Rape in marriage: A sociological view." In David Finkelhor, Richard J. Gelles, Gerald T. Hotaling, and Murray A. Straus, eds. *The Dark Side of Families.* Beverly Hills, Calif.: Sage, pp. 119–130.

FIRESTONE, SHULAMITH 1970. *The Dialectic of Sex.* New York: Bantam Books.

FISCHER, CLAUDE S. 1979. "Friendship, gender and the life cycle." University of California, Berkeley, Institute of Urban and Regional Development.

FISCHER, CLAUDE S., AND SUSAN L. PHILLIPS 1982. "Who is alone? Social characteristics of people with small networks." In Letitia Anne Peplau and Daniel Perlman, eds. *Loneliness: A Sourcebook of Current Theory. Research and Therapy.* New York: Wiley, pp. 21–39.

FISHER, ROGER, AND WILLIAM URY 1981. *Getting to Yes: Negotiating Agreement Without Giving In.* Middlesex, England: Penguin Books.

FISHER, SEYMOUR 1973. *The Female Orgasm.* New York: Basic Books.

FISHER, WILLIAM A. 1983. "Gender, gender-role identification, and response to erotica." In Elizabeth Rice Allgeier and Naomi B. McCormick. *Changing Boundaries.* Palo Alto, Calif.: Mayfield, pp. 261–284.

FORD, CLELLAN S., AND FRANK A. BEACH 1951. *Patterns of Sexual Behavior.* New York: Harper & Row.

FOSTER, GEORGE M. 1972. "The anatomy of envy: A study in symbolic behavior." *Current Anthropology* 13: 165–202.

FRANCKE, LINDA BIRD 1983. *Growing Up Divorced.* New York: Linden Press.

FRANCKE, LINDA 1984. Quoted in *New York Times.* (n.d.)

FRANCOEUR, ROBERT T. 1982. *Becoming a Sexual Person.* New York: Wiley.

FREEMAN, DEREK 1983. *Margaret Mead and Samoa: The Making and Unmaking of an Anthropological Myth.* Cambridge, Mass.: Harvard University Press.

FREEDMAN, JONATHAN L. 1978. *Happy People.* New York: Harcourt Brace Jovanovich.

FREUD, ANNA, AND SOPHIE DANN 1976. "An experiment in group upbringing." In Arlene Skolnick, ed. *Rethinking Childhood.* Boston: Little, Brown, pp. 287–317.

FRIEDAN, BETTY 1963. *The Feminine Mystique.* New York: Dell.

FRIEDAN, BETTY 1981. *The Second Stage.* New York: Summit.

FRIEDMAN, JAMES T. 1984. *The Divorce Handbook.* New York: Random House.

FRIEDRICH, OTTO 1983. "What do babies know?" *Time,* Aug. 15, pp. 52–59.

FRIEDRICH, W. N., AND J. A. BORISKIN 1976. "The role of the child in abuse: A review of literature." *American Journal of Orthopsychiatry* 46: 580–590.

FRIEZE, IRENE H.; JACQUELYNNE E. PARSONS; PAULA B. JOHNSON; DIANE N. FUBLE; AND GAIL L. ZELLMAN 1978. *Women and Sex Roles.* New York: Norton.

FURSTENBERG, FRANK F., AND GRAHAM B. SPANIER 1984. *Recycling the Family: Remarriage and Divorce.* Beverly Hills, Calif.: Sage.

GAGNON, JOHN H., AND CATHY S. GREENBLAT 1978. *Life Designs: Individuals, Marriages and Families.* Glenview, Ill.: Scott, Foresman.

GALENSON, ELEANOR, AND HERMAN RIOPKE 1974. "The Emergence of genital awareness during the second year of life." In Richard C. Friedman, ed. *Sex Differences in Behavior.* New York: Wiley, pp. 223–231.

GALINSKY, ELLEN 1981. *Between Generations.* New York: Berkley Books.

GALPER, MIRIAM 1980. *Joint Custody and Co-Parenting.* Philadelphia: Running Press.

GARDNER, RICHARD A. 1980. *The Parents' Book About Divorce.* Toronto: Bantam Books.

GARFINKEL, PERRY 1983. "The best 'Jewish mother' in the world." *Psychology Today,* Sept., pp. 56–60.

GELLES, RICHARD J. 1977. "Power, sex and violence: The case of marital rape." *Family Coordinator* 26 (Oct.): 339–347.

GELLES, RICHARD J. 1979. *Family Violence.* Beverly Hills, Calif.: Sage.

GELLES, RICHARD J. 1980. "Violence in the family: A review of research on the seventies." *Journal of Marriage and the Family* 42: 873–885.

GELLES, RICHARD J. 1983. "An exchange/social control theory." In David Finkelhor, Richard J. Gelles, Gerald T. Hotaling, and Murray A. Straus, eds. *The Dark Side of Families.* Beverly Hills, Calif.: Sage, pp. 151–165.

GELLES, RICHARD J., AND CLAIRE P. CORNELL 1985. *Intimate Violence in Families.* Beverly Hills, Calif.: Sage.

GELLES, RICHARD J., AND MURRAY A. STRAUS 1979. "Determinants of violence in the family: Toward a theoretical integration." In Wesley R. Burr, Reuben Hill, F. Ivan Nye, and Ira L. Reiss, eds. *Contemporary Theories About the Family.* New York: Free Press.

GERSON, M. 1966. "On the stability of the family in the kibbutz." *Megamont* 14: 395–408 [Hebrew].

GERSTEL, NAOMI, AND HARRIET GROSS 1984. *Commuter Marriage.* New York: Guilford Press.

GIBB, JACK R. 1973. "Defensive communication." In John Stewart, ed. *Bridges, Not Walls: A Book about Interpersonal Communication.* Reading, Mass.: Addison-Wesley, pp. 73–80.

GIBSON, ROSE 1983. "Research on the black elderly focuses on work, retirement, coping strategies." *Gerontology at Michigan.* Ann Arbor, Mich.: Institute of Gerontology.

GIL, DAVID G. 1973 (1970). *Violence Against Children: Physical Child Abuse in the United States.* Cambridge, Mass.: Harvard University Press.

GILBERT, SHIRLEY J. 1976. "Self-disclosure, intimacy and communication in families." *The Family Coordinator* 25 (July): 221–230.

GILES-SIMS, JEAN 1979. "Stability and

change in patterns of wife-beating: A systems theory approach." Ph.D. diss., University of New Hampshire.

GILES-SIMS, JEAN   1983. *Wife Battering: A Systems Theory Approach.* New York: Guilford Press.

GILMARTIN, BRIAN G.   1978. *The Gilmartin Report.* Secaucus, N.J.: Citadel Press.

GLENN, NORVAL D.   1975. "Psychological well-being in the postparental stage: Some evidence from national surveys." *Journal of Marriage and the Family* 37: 105–110.

GLICK, PAUL C.   1977. "Marrying, divorcing and living together in the U. S. today." *Population Bulletin* 32: 3.

GLICK, PAUL C.   1980. "Remarriage: Some recent changes and variation." *Journal of Family Issues* 1: 455–479.

GOETTING, ANN   1983. "Divorce outcome research: Issues and perspectives." In Arlene S. Skolnick and Jerome H. Skolnick, eds. *Family in Transition.* 4th ed. Boston: Little, Brown, pp. 367–387. [Reprinted from *Journal of Family Issues* 2 (Sept.): 350–378.]

GOLD, A., AND M. ANGE   1974. "Development of sex role stereotypes in black and white elementary school girls." *Developmental Psychology* 10: 461.

GOLD, DOLORES   1983. Quoted in Marion Long, "Do working women make good moms?" *Family Weekly,* May 8: pp. 4–5.

GOLDBERG, HERB   1979. *The New Male.* New York: New American Library.

GOLDBERG, HERB   1982. *The New Male Female Relationship.* New York: Morrow.

GOLEMAN, DANIEL   1978. "Special abilities of the sexes: Do they begin in the brain." *Psychology Today,* Nov., pp. 48–49, 120.

GOLEMAN, DANIEL   1980. "Leaving home: Is there a right time to go?" *Psychology Today* 14 (Aug.): 52–61.

GOLEMAN, DANIEL   1984. "Senility—debunking the myth." *Ann Arbor News,* Feb. 27, pp. B1–B2.

GOODE, WILLIAM   1959. "The theoretical importance of love." *American Sociological Review* 24 (Feb.): 38–47.

GOODE, WILLIAM J.   1961. "Family disorganization." In Robert K. Merton and R. A. Nisbet, eds. *Contemporary Social Problems.* New York: Harcourt Brace Jovanovich.

GOODMAN, HAL   1982. "Assertiveness breeds attempt." In *Psychology Today,* Dec., p. 75.

GOODMAN, MARY ELLEN, AND ALMA BEMAN   1971. "Child's-eye views of life in an urban barrio." In Nathaniel N. and Marsha J. Haug, eds. *Chicanos: Social and Psychological Perspectives.* St. Louis: Mosby.

GORDON, SUZANNE   1976. *Lonely in America.* New York: Simon & Schuster.

GORSKI, R. A.; J. H. GORDON; J. E. SHRYNE; AND A. M. SOUTHAM   1978. "Evidence for a morphological sex difference within the medical preoptic area of the rat brain." *Brain Research* 148: 333–346.

GOTTMAN, JOHN   1982. Quoted in Anthony Brandt, "Avoiding couple karate: Lessons in the marital arts." *Psychology Today,* Oct., pp. 38–43.

GOTTMAN, JOHN; CLIFF NOTARIUS; JONNI GONSO; AND HOWARD MARKMAN   1976. *A Couple's Guide to Communication.* Champaign, Ill.: Research Press.

GOY, ROBERT W.; W. E. BRIDSON; AND W. C. YOUNG   1964. "Period of maximal susceptibility of the prenatal female guinea pig to masculinizing actions of testosterone propionate." *Journal of Comparative Physiological Psychology* 57: 166–174.

GRAHAM, S., AND L. REEDER   1972. "Social factors in chronic disease." In H. Freeman, ed. *Handbook of Medical Sociology.* Englewood Cliffs, N.J.: Prentice-Hall.

GRAHAM, VICTORIA   1983. "In China, someone is always watching, and often informing," *Ann Arbor News,* Apr. 20, p. F5.

GREENGLASS, ESTHER R.   1982. *A World of Difference: Gender Roles in Perspective.* Toronto: Wiley.

GREER, GERMAINE   1971. *The Female Eunuch.* New York: McGraw-Hill.

GROSS, L., AND S. JEFFRIES-FOX 1978. "What do you want to be when you grow up, little girl?" In G. Tuchman, A. Daniels, and J. Benet, eds. *Hearth and Home*. New York: Oxford University Press.

GROTH, A. NICHOLAS 1981. *Men Who Rape: The Psychology of the Offender*. New York: Plenum.

GROTH, A. NICHOLAS 1983. "The incest offender." In Suzanne Sgroi, ed. *Handbook of Clinical Intervention in Child Abuse*. Lexington, Mass: Lexington Books.

GUERNEY, BERNARD G. 1977. *Relationship Enhancement*. San Francisco: Jossey-Bass.

GULDNER, CLAUDE A. 1971. "The postmarital: An alternative to pre-marital counseling." In *Family Coordinator* 20 (Apr.): 115–119.

GUNDERSEN, BJORN HELGE; PER STEINER MELAS; AND JENS E. SKAR 1981. "Sexual behavior of preschool children." In Larry L. Constantine and Floyd M. Martinson, eds. *Children and Sex*. Boston: Little, Brown, pp. 45–61.

GURIAN, ANITA, AND RUTH FORMANEK 1983. *The Socially Competent Child*. Boston: Houghton Mifflin.

GURIN, GERALD; JOSEPH VEROFF; AND SHEILA FELD 1960. *Americans View Their Mental Health*. New York: Basic Books.

GUTMANN, DAVID 1974. "Parenthood: A key to the comparative study of the life cycle." In Nancy Datan and Leon H. Ginzberg, eds. *Life Span Developmental Psychology Normative Crisis*. New York: Academic Press.

HAAN, NORMA 1981. "Common dimensions of personality development: Early adolescence to middle life." In Dorothy H. Eichorn, John A. Clausen, Norma Haan, Marjorie P. Honzik, and Paul H. Mussen, eds. *Present and Past in Middle Life*. New York: Academic Press, pp. 117–147.

HACKER, HELEN MAYER 1981. "Blabbermouths and clams: Sex differences in self-disclosure in same-sex and cross-sex friendship dyads." *Psychology of Women Quarterly* 5 (Spring): 385–401.

HAGESTAD, GUNHILD D., AND MICHAEL A. SMYER 1982. "Dissolving long-term relationships: Patterns of divorcing in middle age." In Steve Duck, ed. *Dissolving Relationships*, vol. 4 of *Personal Relationships*. London: Academic Press, pp. 155–188.

HAGESTAD, GUNHILD D.; MICHAEL A. SMYER; T. COONEY; AND R. KLOCK 1984. "New pilot study: Parents' divorce has major impact on college students." *Marriage and Divorce Today* 10 (Aug. 20): 1.

HARDYMENT, CHRISTINA 1983. *Dream Babies: Three Centuries of Good Advice on Child Care*. New York: Harper & Row.

HARKINS, ELIZABETH 1978. "Effects of empty nest transition on self: Report of psychological and physical well being." *Journal of Marriage and the Family* 40: 546–556.

HARVEY, JOHN H.; ANN L. WEBER; KERRY L. YARKIN; AND BONNIE E. STEWART 1982. "An attributional approach to relationships' breakdown and dissolution." In Steve Duck, ed. *Dissolving Relationships*, vol. 4 of *Personal Relationships*. London: Academic Press, pp. 107–126.

HATFIELD, ELAINE; MARY K. UTNE; AND JANE TRAUPMANN 1979. "Equity theory and intimate relationships." In Robert L. Burgess and Ted L. Huston, eds. *Social Exchange in Developing Relationships*. New York: Academic Press, pp. 99–134.

HAYS, WILLIAM E., AND CHARLES H. MINDEL 1973. "Extended kinship relations in black and white families." *Journal of Marriage and the Family* 35: 51–57.

HEIDER, K. G. 1976. "Dani sexuality: A low energy system." *Man* 2: pp. 188–201.

HEIMAN, JULIA P. 1975. "Physiology of erotica: Women's sexual arousal." *Psychology Today*, April, pp. 90–94.

HELFER, RAY E., AND C. HENRY KEMPE, EDS. 1974. *The Battered Child*. Chicago: University of Chicago Press.

HENDRICK, CLYDE, AND SUSAN HENDRICK 1983. *Liking, Loving, and Relating.* Monterey, Calif.: Brooks/Cole.

HENDRIX, L. 1979. "Kinship, social class and migration." *Journal of Marriage and the Family* 41: 399–407.

HENTON, J. R.; RODNEY CATE; J. KOYAL; SALLY LLOYD; AND S. CHRISTOPHER 1983. "Romance and violence in dating relationships." *Journal of Family Issues* 4 (Sept.): 467–482.

HERMAN, JUDITH, AND LISA HIRSCHMAN 1977. "Father-daughter incest." *Signs: Journal of Women in Culture and Society* 12: 735–756.

HETHERINGTON, E. MAVIS; MARTHA COX; AND ROGER COX 1977. "The aftermath of divorce." In J. H. Stevens, Jr., and M. Matthews, eds. *Mother-child, Father-child Relations.* Washington, D.C.: NAEYC.

HETHERINGTON, E. MAVIS; MARTHA COX; AND ROGER COX 1981. "Divorce and remarriage." Paper presented at the meeting of the Society for Research in Child Development, Boston.

HILL, CHARLES T.; ZICK RUBIN; AND LETITIA ANNE PEPLAU 1976. "Break-ups before marriage: The end of 103 affairs." *Journal of Social Issues* 32: 147–168.

HILL, ROBERT 1972. *The Strengths of Black Families.* New York: Emmerson Hall.

HINDE, ROBERT 1979. *Towards Understanding Relationships.* New York: Academic Press.

HINES, PAULETTE M., AND NANCY BOYD-FRANKLIN 1982. "Black families." In Monica McGolderick, John K. Pearce, and Joseph Giordano, eds. *Ethnicity and Family Therapy.* New York: Guilford Press, pp. 84–107.

HIPGRAVE, T. 1981. "Childrearing by lone fathers." In R. Chester, P. Diggory, and M. B. Sutherland, eds. *Changing Patterns of Child-bearing and Child Rearing.* London: Academic Press, pp. 149–166.

HITE, SHERE 1976. *The Hite Report: A Nationwide Study of Female Sexuality.* New York: Macmillan.

HITE, SHERE 1981. *The Hite Report on Male Sexuality.* New York: Ballantine.

HOEBEL, E. A. 1960. *The Cheyennes: Indians of the Great Plains.* New York: Holt, Rinehart and Winston.

HOFFERTH, S. 1981. *Effects of number and timing of birth on family well-being over the life cycle.* Washington: Urban Institute.

HOFFMAN, LOIS W., AND MARTIN L. HOFFMAN 1973. "The value of children to parents." In James T. Fawcett, ed. *Psychological Perspectives on Population,* New York: Basic Books, pp. 19–76.

HOFFMAN, LOIS; ARLAND THORNTON; AND J. B. MANNIS 1978. "The value of children to parents in the United States." *Journal of Population* 2: 91–131.

HOLLISTER, L. E. 1975. "The mystique of social drugs and sex." In M. Sandler and D. L. Gessa, eds. *Sexual Behavior: Pharmacology and Bio-Chemistry.* New York: Raven Press.

HOLMSTROM, LYNDA L. 1972. *The Two-Career Family.* Cambridge, Mass: Schenkman.

HOTALING, GERALD T., AND MURRAY A. STRAUS 1980. "Culture, social organization and irony in the study of family violence." In Murray A. Straus and Gerald T. Hotaling, eds. *The Social Causes of Husband-Wife Violence.* Minneapolis: University of Minnesota Press.

HOWARD, JANE 1978. *Families.* New York: Simon & Schuster.

HUMPHREYS, LAUD 1975. *Tearoom Trade.* Hawthorne, N.Y.: Aldine.

HUNT, MORTON M. 1959. *The Natural History of Love.* New York: Knopf.

HUNT, MORTON M. 1974. *Sexual Behavior in the 1970's.* Chicago: Playboy Press.

HUNT, MORTON 1979. "Legal rape." In *Family Circle,* Jan. 9, pp. 24, 37–38, 125.

HUPKA, RALPH B. 1981. "Cultural determinants of jealousy." *Alternative Lifestyles* 4 (Aug.): 310–356.

HUSTON, ALETHA C. 1983. "Sex-typing." In Paul H. Mussen, ed. *Handbook of Child*

Psychology. 4th ed. New York: Wiley, pp. 387–467.

HUSTON, TED, AND ROBERT L. BURGESS 1979. "Social exchange in developing relationships: An overview." In Robert L. Burgess and Ted L. Huston, eds. *Social Exchange in Developing Relationships.* New York: Academic Press, pp. 3–28.

HYDE, JANET SHIBLEY 1982. *Human Sexuality.* New York: McGraw-Hill.

INSTITUTE FOR SOCIAL RESEARCH NEWSLETTER 1984. "Living alone: Do today's independent lifestyles reflect a trend toward social isolation and a consequent threat to health and well being?" Ann Arbor: University of Michigan, Aug., pp. 3–4.

JACKLIN, CAROL N., AND ELEANOR E. MACCOBY 1984. Quoted in *Marriage and Divorce Today,* Apr. 30, p. 1.

JAMES, J., AND J. MEYERDING 1977. "Early sexual experiences as a factor in prostitution." *Archives of Sexual Behavior* 7: 31–42.

JOHNSON, BETTY, AND HAROLD A. MORSE 1974. "Injured children and their parents." In Jerome E. Leavitt, ed. *The Battered Child.* Morristown, N.J.: General Learning Corporation, pp. 18–23.

JOHNSON, MICHAEL P. 1978. "Personal and structural commitment: Sources of consistency in the development of relationships." Paper. Pennsylvania State University, Department of Sociology.

JOHNSON, MICHAEL P. 1982. "Social and cognitive features of the dissolution of commitment to relationships." In Steve Duck, ed. *Dissolving Relationships,* vol. 4 of *Personal Relationships.* London: Academic Press, pp. 51–74.

JONES ELISE F.; JACQUELINE DARROCH FORREST; NOREEN GOLDMAN; STANLEY K. HENSHAW; RICHARD LINCOLN; JEANNIE I. ROSOFF; CHARLES F. WESTSOFF; AND DEIRDRE WULF 1985. "Teenage pregnancy in the United States." *Family Plannning Perspectives* 17 (Mar.–Apr.): pp. 53–63.

JONES, HARDIN B., AND HELEN C. JONES 1977. *Sensual Drugs.* New York: Cambridge University Press.

JOURARD, SIDNEY 1971. *The Transparent Self.* New York: Van Nostrand.

JUSTER, F. T. (In press). "A note on recent changes in time use." In F. T. Juster and F. Strafford, eds. *Studies in the Measurement of Time Allocation.* Ann Arbor, Mich: Institute for Social Research, pp. 397–422.

JUSTICE, BLAIR, AND RITA JUSTICE 1976. *The Abusing Family.* New York: Human Services Press.

KADUSHIN, ALFRED 1970. "Single-parent adoption: An overview and some relevant research. *The Social Service Review* 44: 263–274.

KAGAN, JEROME 1976. "The psychological requirements for human development." In Nathan B. Talbot, ed. *Raising Children in Modern America: Problems and Prospective Solutions.* Boston: Little, Brown, pp. 86–97.

KAIN, EDWARD L. 1984. Quoted in "Rise of singlehood a myth, says demographer." *Marriage and Divorce Today Newsletter,* Aug. 6, p. 4.

KALISCH, P., AND B. KALISCH 1984. "Sex-role stereotyping of nurses and physicians on prime-time television: A dictionary of occupational portrayals." *Sex Roles* 109: 533–553.

KANIN, E. J.; K. D. DAVIDSON; AND S. R. SCHECK 1970. "A research note on male-female differentials in the experience of heterosexual love." *Journal of Sex Research* 6: 64–72.

KANTER, ROSABETH MOSS 1968. "Commitment and social organization: A study of commitment mechanisms in utopian communities." *American Sociological Review* 44: 499–517.

KANTER, ROSABETH MOSS 1972. "'Getting it all together': Communes past, present, future." In Louise Kapp, ed. *The Future of the Family.* New York: Simon & Schuster, pp. 311–325.

KANTER, ROSABETH MOSS 1973. *Commitment and Community: Communes and Utopias in Sociological Perspective.* Cambridge, Mass.: Harvard University Press.

KANTER, ROSABETH MOSS 1974. "Oneida, community of the past." In Rose Laub Coser, ed. *The Family: Its Structures and Functions.* 2nd ed. New York: St. Martin's Press, pp. 541–549.

KANTER, ROSABETH MOSS 1977. *Men and Women of the Corporation.* New York: Basic Books.

KAPLAN, HELEN SINGER 1974. *The New Sex Therapy.* New York: Brunner/Mazel.

KAPLAN, HELEN SINGER 1979. *Disorders of Sexual Desire.* New York: Simon & Schuster.

KATCHADORIAN, HERANT A.; DONALD T. LUNDE; AND ROBERT TROTTER 1979. *Human Sexuality.* New York: Holt, Rinehart and Winston.

KATZ, A. M., AND REUBEN HILL 1958. "Residential propinquity and marital selection: A review of theory, method and fact." *Marriage and Family Living* 20: 327–335.

KEETING-GROEN, N. 1977. "Marital, Satisfaction and Retirement." Ph.D. diss., Syracuse University.

KELLEY, HAROLD H. 1983. "Love and commitment." In Harold H. Kelley; Ellen Berscheid; Andrew Christensen; John H. Harvey; Ted L. Huston; George Levinger; Evie McClintock; Letitia Anne Peplau; and Donald R. Peterson, eds. *Close Relationships.* San Francisco: Freeman, pp. 265–314.

KELLY, GARY F. 1980. *Sexuality: The Human Perspective.* Woodbury, N.Y.: Barron's.

KEMPE, RUTH S., AND HENRY C. KEMPE 1978. *Child Abuse.* Cambridge, Mass.: Harvard University Press.

KEPHART, WILLIAM 1967. "Some correlates of romantic love." *Journal of Marriage and the Family* 29: 470–479.

KEPHART, WILLIAM M. 1982. *Extraordinary Groups: The Sociology of Unconventional Lifestyles.* 2nd. ed. New York: St. Martin's Press.

KERCKHOFF, ALAN C. 1964. "Husband-wife expectations and reactions at retirement." *Journal of Gerontology* 19: 510–516.

KERCKHOFF, ALAN C., AND KEITH E. DAVIS 1962. "Value consensus and need complementarity in mate selection." *American Sociological Review* 27: 295–303.

KERSTEN, LAWRENCE K., AND KAREN K. KERSTEN 1981. *The Love Exchange.* New York: Fell.

KIDD, VIRGINIA 1977. "Happily ever after." *Human Behavior* 6 (June): 64–68.

KILMANN, PETER R. 1984. *Human Sexuality in Contemporary Life.* Boston: Allyn & Bacon.

KINSEY, ALFRED C.; WARDELL B. POMEROY; AND CLYDE E. MARTIN 1948. *Sexual Behavior in the Human Male.* Philadelphia: Saunders.

KINSEY, ALFRED C.; WARDELL B. POMEROY; CLYDE E. MARTIN; AND PAUL H. GEBHARD 1953. *Sexual Behavior in the Human Female.* Philadelphia: Saunders.

KITSON, G. C., AND MARVIN B. SUSSMAN 1982. "Marital complaints, demographic characteristics and symptoms of mental distress in divorce." *Journal of Marriage and the Family* 44: 87–101.

KOFF, WAYNE C. 1974. "Marijuana and sexual activity." *Journal of Sex Research* 10 (Aug.): 194–204.

KOLODNY, ROBERT C. 1980. "Adolescent sexuality." Paper presented at the Michigan Personal and Guidance Association Annual Convention, Detroit, November.

KOMAROVSKY, MIRRA 1967. *Blue Collar Marriage.* New York: Random House.

KOMAROVSKY, MIRRA 1976. *Dilemmas of Masculinity.* New York: Norton.

LAMB, M. E. 1977, "Father-infant and mother-infant interaction in the first year of life." *Child Development* 48: 167–181.

LAMB, MICHAEL 1982. "Why Swedish fathers aren't liberated." *Psychology Today,* Oct., pp. 47–77.

LAMB, MICHAEL; M. OWEN; AND L. CHASE-LANSDALE 1979. "The father-daughter relationship: Past, present, and future." In C. Kopp and M. Kirkpatrick, eds. *Becoming Female.* New York: Plenum, pp. 113–140.

LANDIS, JUDSON T., AND MARY G. LANDIS 1963. *Building a Successful Marriage.* Englewood Cliffs, N.J.: Prentice-Hall.

LANDY, D., AND H. SIGALL 1974. "Beauty is talent: Task evaluation as a function of the performer's physical attractiveness." *Journal of Personality and Social Psychology* 29: 299–304.

LANER, M. J.; J. THOMPSON; AND R. GRAHAM 1981. "Abuse and aggression in courting couples." Paper presented at the annual meeting of the Western Social Sciences Association, San Diego.

LASSWELL, MARCIA E., AND THOMAS E. LASSWELL, EDS. 1973. *Love, Marriage, Family: A Developmental Approach.* Glenview, Ill.: Scott, Foresman.

LASSWELL, MARCIA, AND NORMAN M. LOBSENZ 1976. *No Fault Marriage.* New York: Ballantine Books.

LASSWELL, MARCIA, AND NORMAN M. LOBSENZ 1980. *Styles of Loving.* Garden City, N.Y.: Doubleday.

LASSWELL, MARCIA, AND NORMAN M. LOBSENZ 1983. *Equal Time.* Garden City, N.Y.: Doubleday.

LEDERER, WILLIAM J., AND DON D. JACKSON 1968. *The Mirages of Marriage.* New York: Norton.

LEIK, ROBERT K., AND SHEILA A. LEIK 1977. "Transition to interpersonal commitment." In Robert L. Hamblin and John H. Kunkel, eds. *Behavioral Theory in Sociology.* New Brunswick, N.J.: Transaction Books.

LEIN, LAURA 1979. "Male participation in home life: Impact of social supports and breadwinner responsibility on the allocation of tasks." *The Family Coordinator* 28 (Oct.): 489–495.

LEMASTERS, E. E., AND JOHN DEFRAIN 1983. *Parents in Contemporary America: A Sympathetic View.* 4th ed. Homewood, Ill.: Dorsey Press.

LENSKI, GERHARD E. 1966. *Power and Privilege.* New York: McGraw-Hill.

LESHAN, E. 1975. *The Wonderful Crisis of Middle Age.* New York: Warner Books.

LEVER, J. 1976. "Sex differences in the games children play." *Social Problems* 23: 478–487.

LEVINE, S., AND N. SCOTCH 1970. *Social Stress and Illness.* Chicago: Aldine.

LEVINGER, GEORGE 1964. "Note on need complementarity in marriage." *Psychological Bulletin* 61: 153–157.

LEVINGER, GEORGE 1979a. "A social exchange view on the dissolution of pair relationships." In Robert L. Burgess and Ted L. Huston, eds. *Social Exchange in Developing Relationships.* New York: Academic Press, pp. 169–193.

LEVINGER, GEORGE 1979b. "A social psychological perspective on marital dissolution." In George Levinger and O. C. Moles, eds. *Divorce and Separation: Context, Causes and Consequences.* New York: Basic Books, pp. 37–60.

LEVINSON, DANIEL J.; CHARLOTTE N. DARROW; EDWARD B. KLEIN; MARIA H. LEVINSON; AND BRAXTON MCKEE 1978. *The Seasons of a Man's Life.* New York: Knopf.

LEWIS, JERRY M. 1979. *How's Your Family?* New York: Brunner/Mazel.

LEWIS, OSCAR 1951. *Life in a Mexican Village: Tepoztlán Restudied.* Urbana, Ill.: University of Illinois Press.

LEWIS, OSCAR 1960. *Tepoztlán, Village in Mexico.* New York: Holt, Rinehart and Winston.

LIEF, HAROLD 1977. "What's new in sex research? Inhibited sexual desire." *Medical Aspects of Human Sexuality* 7 (July): 94–95.

LINDSEY, KAREN 1981. *Friends as Family.* Boston: Beacon Press.

LIPMAN, AARON 1961. "Role conceptions and morale of couples in retirement." *Journal of Gerontology* 16: 267–271.

LIPMAN, AARON, AND CHARLES F. LONGINO 1983. "Gender roles in later life: An introductory statement." Paper presented at the annual meeting of the American Sociological Association, Detroit, September.

LIVSON, FLORINE B. 1981. "Paths to psychological health in the middle years: Sex differences." In Dorothy H. Eichorn, John A. Clausen, Norma Haan, Marjorie P. Honzik, and Paul H. Mussen, eds. *Present and Past Middle Life.* New York: Academic Press, pp. 194–220.

LOCKE, H. 1951. *Predicting Adjustment in Marriage.* New York: Holt, Rinehart and Winston.

LONG, LYNETTE, AND THOMAS LONG 1983. *The Handbook for Latchkey Children and the Parents.* New York: Arbor House

LONG, MARION 1983. "Do working women make good moms?" *Family Weekly,* May 8, pp. 4–5.

LOPICOLLO, JOSEPH 1986. "Advances in integrated treatment of sexual dysfunction." Paper presented to the American Association for Marriage and Family Therapy, Orlando, Fla., October.

LORING, ROSALIND 1972. "Love and women's liberation." In Herbert A. Otto, *Love Today: A New Exploration.* New York: Dell, pp. 73–85.

LOWEN, ALEXANDER 1972. "The spiral of growth: Love, sex and pleasure." In Herbert A. Otto, *Love Today: A New Exploration.* New York: Dell, pp. 17–26.

LOWENTHAL, MARJORIE FISKE, AND CLAYTON HAVEN 1968. "Interaction and adaptation: Intimacy as a critical variable." *American Sociological Review* 33: 20–30.

LOWENTHAL, MARJORIE FISKE; MAJDA THURNHER; DAVID CHIRIBOGA; AND ASSOCIATES. 1976. *Four Stages of Life.* San Francisco: Jossey-Bass.

LOWENTHAL, MARJORIE FISKE, AND BETSY ROBINSON 1976. "Social networks and isolation." In Robert H. Binstock and Ethel Shanas, eds. *Handbook of Aging and the Social Sciences.* New York: Van Nostrand, pp. 432–456.

LUEPNITZ, DEBORAH ANNA 1982. *Child Custody.* Lexington, Mass.: Lexington Books.

LYNCH, JAMES J. 1977. *The Broken Heart: The Medical Consequences of Loneliness.* New York: Basic Books.

LYND, ROBERT, AND HELEN LYND 1929. *Middletown.* New York: Harcourt Brace Jovanovich.

LYND, ROBERT, AND HELEN LYND 1937. *Middletown in Transition.* New York: Harcourt Brace Jovanovich.

McADOO, HARRIETTE 1978. "The impact of upward mobility of kin: Help patterns and the reciprocal obligations in black families." *Journal of Marriage and the Family* 4: 761–776.

McCALL, MICHAEL M. 1966. "Courtship as social exchange." In Bernard Farber, ed. *Kinship and Family Organization.* New York: Wiley, pp. 190–200.

McCLELLAND, DAVID C.; C. A. CONSTANTIAN; D. REGALADO; AND C. STONE 1978. "Making it to maturity." *Psychology Today,* Dec., 42ff.

MACCOBY, ELEANOR E., AND CAROL N. JACKLIN 1974. *The Psychology of Sex Differences.* Stanford, Calif.: Stanford University Press.

McCORMACK, PATRICIA 1982. "Present that Pet the Day After Christmas." *Detroit Free Press,* Dec. 24, p. 1B.

MacDONALD, A. P. 1982. "Research on sexual orientation: A bridge that touches both shores but doesn't meet in the middle." *Journal of Sex Education and Therapy* 8: 9–13.

McEWEN, BRUCE S. 1976. "Endocrine effects on the brain and their relationship to behavior." In W. Albers et al., eds. *Basic Neurochemistry.* Boston: Little, Brown, pp. 737–764.

McGILL, MICHAEL E. 1985. *The McGill Report on Male Intimacy.* New York: Holt, Rinehart and Winston.

McKENRY, PATRICK E. 1984. "Men in transition: The male family role at midlife." Paper presented at the Midwestern Society for Research on Lifespan Development, Akron, Ohio, May 17.

McWHIRTER, DAVID P., AND ANDREW M. MATTISON 1984. *The Male Couple: How Relationships Develop.* Englewood Cliffs, N.J.: Prentice-Hall.

MACE, DAVID 1982. *Close Companions.* New York: Continuum.

MACE, DAVID 1983. *Love and Anger in Marriage.* Grand Rapids, Mich.: Zondervan.

MACE, DAVID, AND VERA MACE 1986. "Marriage enrichment: Developing interpersonal potential." In Paula W. Dail and Ruth H. Jewson, eds. *In Praise of Fifty Years: The Groves Conference on the Conservation of Marriage and the Family.* Lake Mills, Iowa: Graphic.

MACE, N., AND P. RABINS 1981. *The 36-Hour Day.* Baltimore: Johns Hopkins University Press.

MACKLIN, ELEANOR D. 1983. "Cohabitation in the United States." In J. Gipson Wells, ed. *Current Issues in Marriage and the Family.* New York: Macmillan, pp. 62–78.

MAHONEY, E. R. 1983. *Human Sexuality.* New York: McGraw-Hill.

MAISCH, H. 1973. *Incest.* New York: Stein & Day.

MAKEPEACE, JAMES M. 1981. "Courtship violence among college students." *Family Relations* 30 (Jan.): 97–102.

MAKEPEACE, JAMES M. 1983. "Life events—stress and courtship violence." *Family Relations* 32 (Jan.): 101–109.

MALATESTA, VICTOR J.; ROBERT H. POLLACK; TERRI D. CROTTY; AND LELON J. PEACOCK 1982. "Acute alcohol intoxication and female orgasmic response." *The Journal of Sex Research* 18 (Feb.): 1–17.

MALATESTA, VICTOR J.; ROBERT H. POLLACK; W. A. WILBANKS; AND HENRY E. ADAMS 1979. "Alcohol effects on the orgasmic-ejaculatory response in human males." *The Journal of Sex Research* 15 (May): 101–107.

MALINOWSKI, B. 1929. *The Sexual Life of Savages in North-Western Melanesia.* New York: Harcourt Brace Jovanovich.

MALONE, JOHN 1980. *Straight Women/Gay Men.* New York: Dial Press.

MARCUS, PHILIP M. 1977. "Courtship as knowledge and bargaining power." In Jacqueline P. Wiseman, ed. *People as Partners.* San Francisco: Harper & Row (Canfield Press).

MARGOLIN, GAYLA 1981. "Behavior exchange in distressed and nondistressed marriages: A family cycle perspective." *Behavior Therapy* 12: 329–343.

MARGOLIN, GAYLA 1982. "A social learning approach to intimacy." In Martin Fisher and George Stricker, eds. *Intimacy.* New York: Plenum, pp. 175–201.

MARLIN, EMILY 1984. *Taking a Chance on Love.* New York: Schocken Books.

MARMOR, J., ED. 1980. *Homosexual Behavior.* New York: Basic Books.

MARSHALL, MEGAN 1984. *The Cost of Loving.* New York: Putnam.

MARTIN, JUDITH 1983. "Maternal and paternal abuse of children: Theoretical and research perspectives." In David Finkelhor, Richard J. Gelles, Gerald T. Hotaling, and Murray A. Straus, eds. *The Dark Side of Families.* Beverly Hills, Calif.: Sage, pp. 293–304.

MARTINSON, FLOYD M. 1981. "Family intimacy and affection: A sociology of positive affect." Paper presented at National Council on Family Relations Pre-Conference: Theory Construction and Research Methodology, October 14.

MARTINSON, FLOYD M. 1982. "Sensory/erotic development: Embryo, fetus, infant, child." Paper presented at the Sixth World Congress of Sexology, Washington, D.C., May 24.

MASLOW, ABRAHAM H. 1970. *Motivation and Personality.* 2nd ed. New York: Harper & Row.

MASNICK, G., AND M. J. BANE 1980. *The*

Nation's Families: 1960–1990. Boston: Auburn.

MASTERS, WILLIAM H., AND VIRGINIA E. JOHNSON 1966. *Human Sexual Response.* Boston: Little, Brown.

MASTERS, WILLIAM H., AND VIRGINIA E. JOHNSON 1970. *Human Sexual Inadequacy.* Boston: Little, Brown.

MASTERS, WILLIAM H., AND VIRGINIA E. JOHNSON 1973. "Emotional poverty: A marriage crisis of the middle years." Paper presented at the American Medical Association Congress of Quality of Life, Chicago, March 3.

MASTERS, WILLIAM H., AND VIRGINIA E. JOHNSON 1975. *The Pleasure Bond.* New York: Bantam Books.

MASTERS, WILLIAM H., AND VIRGINIA E. JOHNSON 1979. *Homosexuality in Perspective.* Boston: Little, Brown.

MASTERS, WILLIAM H.; VIRGINIA E. JOHNSON; AND ROBERT C. KOLODNY 1980. Unpublished observations.

MASTERS, WILLIAM H.; VIRGINIA E. JOHNSON; AND ROBERT C. KOLODNY 1982. *Human Sexuality.* Boston: Little, Brown.

MATHISON, D. L., AND P. K. TUCKER 1982. "Sex differences in assertive behavior." *Psychological Reports* 46: 943–948.

MAY, ROLLO 1972. *Power and Innocence.* New York: Norton.

MAYHALL, PAMELA D., AND KATHERINE EASTLACK NORGARD 1983. *Child Abuse and Neglect: Sharing Responsibility.* New York: Wiley.

MEAD, GEORGE HERBERT 1934. *Mind, Self, and Society.* Chicago: University of Chicago Press.

MEAD, MARGARET 1950. *Sex and Temperament in Three Primitive Societies.* New York: New American Library (Mentor Books).

MEHRABIAN, ALBERT 1968. "Communication without words." *Psychology Today,* Sept., pp. 52–55.

MEHRABIAN, ALBERT 1971. *Silent Messages.* Belmont, Calif.: Wadsworth.

MESSENGER, J. C. 1971. "Sex and repression in an Irish folk community." In Donald S. Marshall and Robert T. Suggs, eds. *Human Sexual Behavior.* New York: Basic Books, pp. 3–37.

MEYENDORF, RUTH 1971. "Infant depression due to separation from siblings, syndrome or depression, retardation, starvation, and neurological symptoms: A re-evaluation of the concept of maternal deprivation." *Psychiatrica Clinica* 4: 321–335.

MILLER, JEAN BAKER 1986a. "What do we mean by relationships?" Work in progress, mimeographed by the Stone Center for Developmental Services and Studies, Wellesley College, Wellesley, Mass., pp. 1–23.

MILLER, JEAN BAKER 1986b. "Love, intimacy and sexuality." Speech given to the American Academy of Psychoanalysis, November 8.

MILLER, SHEROD; ELAM W. NUNNALLY; AND DANIEL B. WACKMAN 1976. "Minnesota couples communication program (MCCP): Premarital and marital groups." In David Olson, ed. *Treating Relationships.* Lake Mills, Iowa: Graphic, pp. 21–39.

MIRANDE, ALFREDO 1977. "The Chicano family: A reanalysis of conflicting views." *Journal of Marriage and the Family* 39: 747–756.

MONEY, JOHN 1976. "Childhood: The last frontier in sex research." *The Sciences* 16: 12–15.

MONEY, JOHN, AND ANKE A. EHRHARDT 1972. *Man and Woman: Boy and Girl.* New York: New American Library (Mentor Books).

MONEY, JOHN, AND PATRICIA TUCKER 1975. *Sexual Signatures: On Being a Man or Woman.* Boston: Little, Brown.

MONTAGU, ASHLEY 1953. *The Meaning of Love.* Westport, Conn.: Greenwood Press.

MONTAGU, ASHLEY 1971. *Touching: The Human Significance of the Skin.* New York: Columbia University Press.

MONTAGU, ASHLEY   1974. *The Natural Superiority of Women.* New York: Macmillan (Collier Books).

MONTAGU, ASHLEY, ED.   1975. *The Practice of Love.* Englewood Cliffs, N.J.: Prentice-Hall.

MONTAGU, ASHLEY   1983. *The Dehumanization of Man.* New York: McGraw-Hill.

MONTAGU, ASHLEY, AND FLOYD MATSON   1979. *The Human Connection.* New York: McGraw-Hill.

MOORE, KRISTIN A., AND ISABEL V. SAWHILL   1984. "Implications of women's employment for home and family life." In Patricia Voydanoff, ed. *Work and Family: Changing Roles of Men and Women.* Palo Alto, Calif.: Mayfield, pp. 153–171.

MORGAN, MARABEL   1973. *The Total Woman.* Old Tappan, N.J.: Revell.

MORRIS, DESMOND   1973. *Intimate Behavior.* New York: Bantam Books.

MOSHER, D. C.   1973. "Sex differences, sex experience, sex guilt, and explicitly sexual films." *Journal of Social Issues* 29: 95–112.

MOSHER, WILLIAM D., AND CHRISTINE A. BACHRACH   1982. "Childlessness in the United States: Estimates from the national survey of family growth." *Journal of Family Issues* 3 (Dec.): 517–543.

MURSTEIN, BERNARD I.   1974. *Love, Sex and Marriage Through the Ages.* New York: Springer.

MURSTEIN, BERNARD I.   1980. "Mate selection in the 1980's." *Journal of Marriage and the Family* 42: 777–792.

MURSTEIN, BERNARD I.; M. GOYETTE; AND M. CERRETO   1974. "A theory of the effect of exchange orientation on marriage and friendship." Manuscript.

NADELMAN, L.   1974. "Sex identity in American children: Memory, knowledge and preference tests." *Developmental Psychology* 10: 413–417.

NAIFEH, STEVEN, AND GREGORY WHITE

SMITH   1984. *Why Can't Men Open Up?* New York: Warner Books.

NASS, GILBERT D.; ROGER W. LIBBY; AND MARY PAT FISHER   1984. *Sexual Choices.* Belmont, Calif.: Wadsworth.

NEUGARTEN, BERNICE L.   1968. "Adult personality: Toward a psychology of the life cycle." In Bernice Neugarten, ed. *Middle Age and Aging.* Chicago: University of Chicago Press, pp. 137–147.

NEUGARTEN, BERNICE L., AND KAROL K. WEINSTEIN   1973. "The changing American grandparent." In Marcia E. Lasswell and Thomas E. Lasswell, eds. *Love, Marriage, Family: A Developmental Approach.* Glenview, Ill.: Scott, Foresman, pp. 505–509.

NEWSON, JOHN, AND ELIZABETH NEWSON   1976. "Cultural aspects of child rearing in the English-speaking world." In Arlene Skolnick, ed. *Rethinking Childhood,* Boston: Little, Brown, pp. 325–346.

NICHOLS, S., AND E. METZEN   1980. "Impact of wives' employment upon husbands' housework." *Journal of Family Issues* 3: 199–216.

NOVAK, WILLIAM   1983. *The Great American Man Shortage.* New York: Rawson, Wade.

O'BRIEN, JOHN E.   1975. "Violence in divorce-prone families." In Suzanne K. Steinmetz and Murray A. Straus, eds. *Violence in the Family.* New York: Dodd, Mead, pp. 65–75.

OFFIR, CAROLE WADE   1982. *Human Sexuality.* New York: Harcourt Brace Jovanovich.

OLDS, SALLY WENDKOS   1978. "How to stay close in love without losing your self." *Redbook,* Apr., pp. 107, 164, 166, 168.

OLSON, DAVID H. L.   1976. *Treating Relationships.* Lake Mills, Iowa: Graphic.

OLSON, DAVID H.; DAVID G. FOURNIER; AND JOAN M. DRUCKMAN   1984. "The couple communication scale." *Family Circle,* October, p. 5.

OLSON, DAVID H.; DAVID G. FOURNIER; AND

JOAN M. DRUCKMAN 1985. "ENRICH Marital Communication Scale." In David H. Olson et al., eds. *Family Inventories,* University of Minnesota.

O'NEILL, NENA, AND GEORGE O'NEILL 1972. *Open Marriage.* New York: Evans.

OTTO, HERBERT A. 1972. *Love Today: A New Exploration.* New York: Dell.

PAGELOW, M. D. 1980. "Does the law help battered wives? Some research notes." Madison, Wis.: Law and Society Association.

PARADE 1983. "Arrest the wife beaters!" Oct. 16, p. 8.

PARKE, ROSS D. 1981. *Fathers.* Cambridge, Mass.: Harvard University Press.

PARKE, ROSS D., AND SANDRA E. O'LEARY 1976. "Family interaction in the newborn period: Some findings, some observations and some unresolved issues." In Klaus F. Riegel and John A. Meacham, eds. *The Developing Individual in a Changing World. II. Social and Environmental Issues.* The Hague: Mouton.

PARKE, ROSS D., AND D. B. SAWIN 1977. "Fathering: It's a major role." *Psychology Today,* November, p. 111.

PARLEE, MARY BROWN 1979. "The Friendship Bond." *Psychology Today,* Oct., pp. 42–55.

PARSONS, JACQUELYNNE ECCLES 1982. "Biology, experience, and sex-dimorphic behaviors." In W. R. Gove and G. R. Carpenter, eds. *The Fundamental Connection Between Nature and Nurture.* Lexington, Mass.: Lexington Books, pp. 137–169.

PEPLAU, LETITIA A.; ZICK RUBIN; AND CHARLES T. HILL 1977. "Sexual intimacy in dating relationships." *Journal of Social Issues* 33: 86–109.

PERRY, JOHN D., AND BEVERLY WHIPPLE 1981. "Pelvic muscle strength of female ejaculators: Evidence in support of a new theory of orgasm." *Journal of Sex Research* 17: 22–39.

PETERSON, JAMES A. 1973. "Anticipation of things to come." In Marcia E. Lasswell and Thomas E. Lasswell, eds. *Love, Marriage, Family: A Developmental Approach.* Glenview, Ill.: Scott, Foresman, pp. 524–530.

PHILBLAD, D. L., AND D. L. ADAMS 1972. "Widowhood, social participation and life satisfaction." *Aging Human Development* 3: 323–330.

PINES, AYALA, AND ELLIOT ARONSON 1981. "Polyfidelity: An alternative lifestyle without jealousy?" *Alternative Lifestyles* 4 (Aug.): 373–392.

PLECK, E. H., AND J. H. PLECK 1980. *The American Man.* Englewood Cliffs, N.J.: Prentice-Hall.

PLECK, JOSEPH H. 1977. "The work-family role system." In *Social Problems* 24 (Apr.): 417–427.

PLECK, JOSEPH H. 1985. *Working Wives/ Working Husbands.* Beverly Hills, Calif.: Sage.

POGREBIN, LETTY COTTIN 1980. *Growing Up Free: Raising Your Child in the 80's.* New York: McGraw-Hill.

POGREBIN, LETTY COTTIN 1983. *Family Politics.* New York: McGraw-Hill.

POHLMAN, E. H. 1969. *Psychology of Birth Planning.* Cambridge, Mass.: Schenkman.

POLICOFF, STEPHEN P. 1985. "Bottle Babies." *New Age,* Oct., pp. 54–60.

PORCINO, JANE 1982. "The need for intimacy." *Ms.,* Jan., p. 104.

POWERS, EDWARD A., AND GORDON L. BULTENA 1976. "Sex differences in intimate friendships of old age." *Journal of Marriage and the Family* 38: 739–747.

PRESCOTT, JAMES W. 1975. "Body pleasure and the origins of violence." *The Futurist,* Apr., pp. 64–73.

PRESCOTT, SUZANNE, AND CAROLYN LETKO 1977. "Battered women: A social psychological perspective." In Maria Roy, ed. *Battered Women.* New York: Van Nostrand Reinhold, pp. 72–96.

PRESTON, SAMUEL H., AND JOHN McDONALD 1979. "The incidence of divorce with cohorts of American marriages contracted since the Civil War." *Demography* 16: 1–25.

PROCHASKA, J., AND J. PROCHASKA 1978. "Twentieth century trends in marriage and marital therapy." In T. J. Paolino and B. S. McCrady, eds. *Marriage and Marital Therapy.* New York: Brunner/Mazel, pp. 1–24.

PYEN, CHONG 1984. "Unwed: Living without the ties that bind." *Ann Arbor News,* Dec. 9, p. G1.

QUEEN, STUART A.; ROBERT W. HABENSTEIN; AND JILL S. QUADAGNO 1985. *The Family in Various Cultures.* New York: Harper & Row.

RABIN, ALBERT I., AND BENJAMIN BEIT-HALLAHMI 1982. *Twenty Years Later: Kibbutz Children Grown Up.* New York: Springer-Verlag.

RADIN, NORMA 1982. "Primary caregiving and role sharing fathers." In Michael E. Lamb, ed. *Nontraditional Families: Parenting and Child Development.* Hillsdale, N.J.: Erlbaum, pp. 173–204.

RAINWATER, LEE 1960. *And The Poor Get Children.* New York: Quadrangle.

RAINWATER, LEE 1965. *Family Design: Marital Sexuality, Family Size and Contraception.* Chicago: Aldine.

RAINWATER, LEE 1969. "Sex in the culture of poverty." In Carlfred Broderick and Jessie Bernard, eds. *The Individual, Sex and Society.* Baltimore: Johns Hopkins University Press, pp. 129–140.

RAINWATER, LEE 1971. "Marital sexuality in four 'cultures of poverty.'" In Donald S. Marshall and Robert C. Suggs, eds. *Human Sexual Behavior.* New York: Basic Books, pp. 187–205.

RAMEY, JAMES W. 1978. "Multi-adult household: Living group of the future?" In Jerald Savells and Lawrence J. Cross, eds. *The Changing Family.* New York: Holt, Rinehart and Winston, pp. 355–363. Re-

printed from James W. Ramey, 1976, *Intimate Friendships.* Englewood Cliffs, N.J.: Prentice-Hall, pp. 147–158.

RANDS, M. 1980. "Social networks before and after marital separation: A study of recently divorced persons." Ph.D. diss., University of Massachusetts.

RAUSCH, HAROLD L.; W. A. BARRY; R. K. HERTEL; AND M. A. SWAIN 1974. *Communication, Conflict and Marriage.* San Francisco: Jossey-Bass.

REBELSKY, R., AND C. HANKS 1974. "Fathers' verbal interaction with infants in the first three months of life." In F. Rebelsky and L. Dorman, eds. *Child Development and Behavior.* New York: Knopf, pp. 145–148.

REECE, REX 1979. "Coping with couplehood." In Martin P. Levine, ed. *Gay Men: The Sociology of Male Homosexuality.* New York: Harper & Row, pp. 211–221.

REEDY, MARGARET N. 1977. "Age and sex differences in personal needs and the nature of love: A study of happily married young, middle-aged and older adult couples." Ph.D. diss., University of Southern California, Los Angeles.

REINISCH, JUNE M. 1981. "Prenatal exposure to synthetic progestins increases potential for aggression in humans." *Science* 211 (Mar.): 1171–1173.

REISS, IRA L. 1960. *Premarital Sexual Standards in America.* New York: Free Press.

REISS, IRA L. 1966. "The sexual renaissance: A summary and analysis." *Journal of Social Issues* 22: 123–137.

REISS, IRA L. 1980. *Family Systems in America.* New York: Holt, Rinehart and Winston.

REISS, IRA L. 1986. *Journey Into Sexuality: An Exploratory Voyage.* Englewood Cliffs, N.J.: Prentice-Hall.

RENSHAW, DOMEENA C. 1982. *Incest: Understanding and Treatment.* Boston: Little, Brown.

RENVOIZE, JEAN 1982. *Incest: A Family Pattern.* London: Routledge & Kegan Paul.

RICE, F. PHILIP 1978. *The Adolescent: Devel-*

opment, Relationships and Culture. 2nd ed. Boston: Allyn & Bacon.

RICHER, STEPHEN 1968. "The economics of child-rearing." In *Journal of Marriage and the Family* 30: 462–466.

ROBERTS, ELIZABETH J.; DAVID KLINE; AND JOHN GAGNON 1978. *Family Life and Sexual Learning.* Cambridge, Mass.: Population Education.

ROBERTSON, JAMES 1983. Quoted in Marion Long, "Do working women make good moms?" *Family Weekly,* May 8, pp. 4–5.

ROBERTSON, JOAN F. 1978. "Women in midlife: Crisis, reverberations, and support networks." *The Family Coordinator* 27: 375–382.

ROBINSON, DONALD 1985. "How can we protect our elderly?" *Parade,* Feb. 17, pp. 4–7.

RODIN, MIMI 1985. "The world of single." In James Henslin, ed. *Marriage and Family in a Changing Society.* 2nd ed. New York: Free Press, pp. 261–269.

ROELOFS, SUE 1985. "Premenstrual syndrome and intimacy." Paper.

ROGERS, CARL R. 1961. *On Becoming a Person.* Boston: Houghton Mifflin.

ROLL, SAMUEL 1983. "Ties that bind." *Psychology Today,* Sept., pp. 6–7.

ROLLINS, BOYD C., AND KENNETH L. CANNON 1974. "Marital satisfaction over the family life cycle: A reevaluation." *Journal of Marriage and the Family* 36: 271–282.

ROLLINS, BOYD C., AND HAROLD FELDMAN 1970. "Marital satisfaction over the family life cycle." *Journal of Marriage and the Family* 26: 20–28.

ROLLINS, JUDY 1983. "A conceptual and theoretical differentiation between loneliness and aloneness." *Family Perspectives* 17: 29–34.

ROLLINS, JUDY (n.d.) "Loneliness versus aloneness: An empirical differentiation." Paper, Kansas State University, Department of Family and Child Development.

ROSENBLATT, PAUL C. 1977. "Needed research on commitment in marriage." In George Levinger and Harold Rausch, eds. *Close Relationships: Perspectives on the Meaning of Intimacy.* Amherst: University of Massachusetts Press.

ROSENTHAL, R.; D. ARCHER; M. R. DI MATTEO; J. H. KOIVUMAKI; AND P. L. ROGERS 1974. "Body talk and tone of voice: The language without words." *Psychology Today,* Sept., pp. 64–68.

ROSOW, IRVING 1967. *Social Interaction of the Aged.* New York: Free Press.

ROSSI, ALICE S. 1968. "Transition to parenthood." *Journal of Marriage and the Family* 30: 26–39.

ROSSI, ALICE 1984. "American Sociological Association, 1983 presidential address." *American Sociological Review* 49: 1–19.

ROSSI, ALICE S. 1985. "Gender and parenthood." In Alice Rossi, ed. *Gender and the Life Course.* New York: Aldine, pp. 161–191.

ROWE, MARY P. 1978. "Choosing childcare: Many options." In Rona Rapoport and Robert Rapoport, eds. *Working Couples.* New York: Harper & Row, pp. 89–99.

ROY, MARIA, ED. 1977. *Battered Women: A Psychosociological Study of Domestic Violence.* New York: Van Nostrand Reinhold.

RUBENSTEIN, CARIN 1982. "Real men don't earn less than their wives." *Psychology Today,* Nov., pp. 36–41.

RUBENSTEIN, CARIN, AND PHILIP SHAVER 1982. *In Search of Intimacy.* New York: Dell (Delacorte Press).

RUBENSTEIN, PAUL, AND HERBERT F. MARGOLIS 1971. *The Group Sex Tapes.* New York: McKay.

RUBIN, J.; F. PROVENZANO; AND Z. LURIA 1974. "The eye of the beholder: Parents' views on sex of newborns." *American Journal of Orthopsychiatry* 44: 512–519.

RUBIN, LILLIAN BRESLOW 1976. *Worlds of Pain: Life in the Working-Class Family.* New York: Basic Books.

RUBIN, LILLIAN BRESLOW 1979. *Women of a Certain Age: The Midlife Search for Self.* New York: Harper & Row.

RUBIN, LILLIAN BRESLOW 1983. *Intimate Strangers.* New York: Harper & Row.

RUBIN, LILLIAN BRESLOW 1985. *Just Friends.* New York: Harper & Row.

RUBIN, NEAL 1985. "Spider-man battles sex abuse." *The Detroit Free Press,* Feb. 17, p. 3F.

RUBIN, ZICK 1969. "The social psychology of romantic love." Ph.D. diss., University of Michigan, University microfilms No. 70-4179.

RUBIN, ZICK 1970. "Measurement of romantic love." *Journal of Personality and Social Psychology* 15: 265–273.

RUBIN, ZICK 1973. *Liking and Loving: An Invitation to Social Psychology,* New York: Holt, Rinehart and Winston.

RUBIN, ZICK 1980. *Children's Friendships.* Cambridge, Mass.: Harvard University Press.

RUBIN, ZICK 1984. "Are working wives hazardous to their husbands' mental health?" In Ollie Pocs and Robert H. Walsh, eds. *Marriage and Family Annual Editions, 84/85.* Guilford, Conn.: Dushkin Publishing Group, pp. 203–204.

RUDY, A. J., AND R. PELLER 1972. "Men's liberation." *Medical Aspects of Human Sexuality* 6 (Sept.): 84–85.

RUSSELL, CANDYCE SMITH 1974. "Transition to parenthood: Problems and gratifications." *Journal of Marriage and the Family* 36: 294–302.

RUSSELL, DIANA E. 1982. *Rape in Marriage.* New York: Macmillan.

RUSSELL, G. 1978. "The father role and its relation to masculinity, feminity, and androgyny." *Child Development* 49: 1174–1181.

RUSSO, NANCY 1976. "The motherhood mandate." *Journal of Social Issues* 32: 143–153.

RYDER, ROBERT G. 1973. "Longitudinal data relating marriage satisfaction and having a child." *Journal of Marriage and the Family* 35: 604–606.

RYFF, C. D. 1983. "The subjective experience of life-span transitions." Paper presented at the Thematic Session on Gender Comparisons in Life-Span Transitions at the annual meeting of the American Sociological Association, Detroit.

SAFILIOS-ROTHSCHILD, CONSTANTINA 1970. "The study of family power structure: A review 1960–1969." *Journal of Marriage and the Family* 32: 539–552.

SANDLER, J.; M. MYERSON; AND B. N. KINDER 1980. *Human Sexuality: Current Perspectives.* New York: Mariner Publishing Co.

SANDS, MELISSA 1981. *The Making of the American Mistress.* New York: Berkley Books.

SANFORD, LINDA TSCHIRHART 1980. *The Silent Child: A Parent's Guide to the Prevention of Child Sexual Abuse.* New York: McGraw-Hill.

SANIK, M. 1981. "Division of household word: A decade comparison: 1967–1977." *Home Economics Research Journal* 10: 175–180.

SAUL, CAROL P. 1984. "Gram." In Ralph La Rossa, ed. *Family Case Studies: A Sociological Perspective.* New York:: Free Press, pp. 223–228. Reprinted from "Coming home," by Carol P. Saul from *Aging: An Album of People Growing Old.* New York: Wiley.

SAXTON, LLOYD 1986. *The Individual, Marriage, and the Family.* Belmont, Calif.: Wadsworth.

SCANZONI, JOHN 1983. *Shaping Tomorrow's Family.* Beverly Hills, Calif.: Sage.

SCANZONI, LETHA D., AND JOHN SCANZONI 1981. *Men, Women and Change: A Sociology of Marriage and Family.* New York: McGraw-Hill.

SCARF, MAGGIE 1982. "Husbands in crisis." In Lawrence R. Allman and Dennis T. Jaffe, eds. *Readings in Adult Psychology.*

2nd ed. New York: Harper & Row, pp. 108–113.

SCHAFFER, KAY F. 1981. *Sex Roles and Human Behavior.* Cambridge, Mass.: Winthrop.

SCHAFFER, RUDOLPH 1977. *Mothering.* Cambridge, Mass.: Harvard University Press.

SCHECHTER, MARSHALL D., AND LEO ROBERGE ROBURG 1976. "Sexual exploitation." In Ray E. Helfer and C. Henry Kempe, eds. *Child Abuse and Neglect: The Family and the Community.* Cambridge, Mass.: Ballinger, pp. 127–142.

SCHNALL, MAXINE 1981. *Limits: A Search For New Rules.* New York: Potter.

SCORESBY, A. LYNN 1977. *The Marriage Dialogue.* Reading, Mass.: Addison-Wesley.

SEGAL, JAY 1984. *The Sex Lives of College Students.* Wayne, Penn.: Miles Standish Press.

SEGAL, M. W. 1974. "Alphabet and attraction: An unobtrusive measure of the effect of propinquity in a field setting." *Journal of Personality and Social Psychology* 309: 654–657.

SELTZER, VIVIAN 1981. Quoted in *New York Times,* Dec. 7.

SGROI, SUZANNE M.; LINDA C. BLICK; AND FRANCES S. PORTER 1983. "A conceptual framework for child sexual abuse." In Suzanne M. Sgroi, ed. *Handbook of Clinical Intervention in Child Sexual Abuse.* Lexington, Mass.: Lexington Books, pp. 9–38.

SGROI, SUZANNE M., AND NATALIE T. DANA 1983. "Individual and group treatment of mothers of incest victims." In Suzanne M. Sgroi, ed. *Handbook of Clinical Intervention in Child Sexual Abuse.* Lexington, Mass.: Lexington Books, pp. 191–214.

SHIELDS, NANCY M., AND CHRISTINE R. HANNEKE 1983. "Battered wives' reactions to marital rape." In David Finkelhor, Richard J. Gelles, Gerald T. Hotaling, and Murray A. Straus, eds. *The Dark Side of Families.* Beverly Hills, Calif.: Sage, pp. 131–148.

SHOPE, D. F., AND CARLFRED B. BRODERICK 1967. "Level of sexual experience and predicted adjustment in marriage." *Journal of Marriage and the Family* 29: 424–427.

SHULMAN, N. 1975. "Life-cycle variations in patterns of close relationships." *Journal of Marriage and the Family* 37: 813–921.

SIEGAL, SIDNEY, AND LAWRENCE FOURAKER 1960. *Bargaining and Group Decision Making.* New York: McGraw-Hill.

SIGALL, H., AND D. LANDY 1973. "Radiating beauty: Effects of having a physically attractive partner on person perception." *Journal of Personality and Social Psychology* 28: 218–224.

SILVERMAN, I. 1971. "Physical attractiveness and courtship." *Sexual Behavior,* Sept., pp. 22–25.

SIMENAUER, JACQUELINE, AND DAVID CARROLL 1982. *Singles: The New Americans.* New York: New American Library.

SIMMEL, GEORG 1950. *The Sociology of Georg Simmel.* Kurt H. Wolff, ed. New York: Free Press.

SINGER, IRVING 1974. *The Goals of Human Sexuality.* New York: Schocken Books.

SINGER, JOESPHINE, AND IRVING SINGER 1972. "Types of female orgasm." *Journal of Sex Research* 8 (Nov.): 255–267.

SINNOTT, J. D. 1977. "Sex-role inconstancy, biology and successful aging: A dialectical model." *The Gerontologist* 17: 459–463.

SKINNER, DENISE A. 1984. "Dual-career family stress and coping." In Patricia Voydanoff, ed. *Work and Family: Changing Roles of Men and Women.* Palo Alto, Calif.: Mayfield, pp. 261–271.

SKIPPER, JAMES K., AND GILBERT NASS 1966. "Dating behavior: A framework for analysis and an illustration." *Journal of Marriage and the Family* 28 (Nov.): 412–420.

SKOLNICK, ARLENE 1979. "Public images,

private realities: The American family in popular culture and social science." In Virginia Tufte and Barbara Myerhoff, eds. *Changing Images of the Family.* New Haven: Yale University Press, pp. 297–315.

SMITH, JAMES R., AND LYNN G. SMITH 1970. "Comarital sex and the sexual freedom movement." *Journal of Sex Research* 6 (May): 131–142.

SMITH-ROSENBERG, CARROLL 1975. "The female world of love and ritual: Relations between women in nineteenth-century America." *Signs* 1 (Autumn): 1–29.

SPANIER, GRAHAM 1983. "Married and unmarried cohabitation in the United States: 1980." *Journal of Marriage and the Family* 45: 277–288.

SPANIER, GRAHAM B. 1986. "The changing American family: Demographic trends and prospects." In Paula W. Dail and Ruth H. Jewson, eds. *In Praise of Fifty Years: The Groves Conference on the Conservation of Marriage and the Family.* Lake Mills, Iowa: Graphic, pp. 86–93.

SPANIER, GRAHAM B., AND LINDA THOMPSON 1984. *Parting: The Aftermath of Separation and Divorce.* Beverly Hills, Calif.: Sage.

SPEKTOR, P. 1980. Testimony delivered to the Law Enforcement Subcommittee of the Minnesota House of Representatives, February.

SPERRY, ROGER 1982. "Some effects of disconnecting the cerebral hemispheres." *Science* 217: 1223–1226.

SPITZ, RENE A. 1945. "Hospitalism: An inquiry into the genesis of psychiatric conditions in early childhood." *Psychoanalytic Study of the Child* 1: 53–74.

SPITZ, RENE A. 1945. "Hospitalism: A follow-up report." *Psychoanalytic Study of the Child* 2: 113–117.

SPOCK, BENJAMIN 1946. *Baby and Child Care.* New York: Duell Sloan.

STACEY, WILLIAM A., AND ANSON SHUPE 1983. *The Family Secret: Domestic Violence in America.* Boston: Beacon Press.

STAPLES, ROBERT 1972. "Research on black sexuality: Its implication for family life, education and public policy." *The Family Coordinator* 21: 183–188.

STEELE, BRANDT F., AND CARL B. POLLOCK 1974. "A psychiatric study of parents who abuse infants and small children." In Ray E. Helfer and C. Henry Kempe, eds. *The Battered Child.* Chicago: University of Chicago Press, pp. 89–133.

STEIN, PETER 1976. *Single.* Englewood Cliffs, N.J.: Prentice-Hall.

STEIN, PETER J. 1975. "Singlehood: An alternative to marriage." *The Family Coordinator* 24: 489–503.

STEPHENS, WILLIAM 1963. *The Family in Cross-Cultural Perspective.* New York: Holt, Rinehart and Winston.

STERN, DANIEL 1977. *The First Relationship: Mother and Infant.* Cambridge, Mass.: Harvard University Press.

STEVE, C. A., AND K. GERSON 1977. "Personal relations across the lifecycle." In Claude S. Fischer, ed. *Networks and Places: Social Relations in the Urban Setting.* New York: Free Press.

STEWART, JOHN 1973. *Bridges Not Walls: A Book About Interpersonal Communication.* Reading, Mass.: Addison-Wesley.

STIVER, IRENE P. 1984. "The meanings of 'dependency' in female-male relation ships." Work in progress, mimeographed by the Stone Center for Developmental Services and Studies, Wellesley College, Wellesley, Mass., pp. 1–12.

STRAUS, MURRAY A.; RICHARD J. GELLES; AND SUZANNE K. STEINMETZ 1980. *Behind Closed Doors: Violence in the American Family.* Garden City, N.Y.: Doubleday.

STREIB, GORDON F., AND R. W. BECK 1980. "Older families: A decade review." *Journal of Marriage and the Family* 42: 937–956.

STRONG, JOHN R. 1983. *Creating Closeness: The Communication Puzzle.* Ames, Iowa.: Human Communication Institute.

SULLIVAN, JOYCE 1981. "Family support

systems paychecks can't buy." *Family Relations* 30 (Qct.): 607–613.

TAMIR, L. M.   1982. *Men in Their Forties: The Transition to Middle Age.* New York: Springer-Verlag.

TAVRIS, CAROL   1982a. "Anger defused." *Psychology Today,* Nov., pp. 25–35.

TAVRIS, CAROL   1982b. *Anger: The Misunderstood Emotion.* New York: Simon & Schuster.

TAVRIS, CAROL, AND SUSAN SADD   1977. *The Redbook Report on Female Sexuality.* New York: Dell.

TEDESCO, N. S.   1974. "Patterns in prime time." *Journal of Communication* 24: 118–124.

THIBAUT, JOHN W., AND HAROLD H. KELLEY   1959. *The Social Psychology of Groups.* New York: Wiley.

THOMAS, EDWIN J.   1977. *Marital Communication and Decision Making: Analysis, Assessment and Change.* New York: Free Press.

THOMAS, KENNETH, AND RALPH KILMANN   1975. "The social desirability variable in organizational research." *Academy of Management Journal* 41: 413–420.

THOMAS, SANDRA; KAY ABBRECHT; AND PRISCILLA WHITE   1984. "Determinants of marital quality in dual-career couples." *Family Relations* 33 (Oct.): 513–521.

THOMPSON, KEN   1980. "A comparison of black and white adolescents' beliefs about having children." *Journal of Marriage and the Family* 42: 133–139.

THORNTON, ARLAND, AND DEBORAH FREEDMAN   1983. "The changing American family." *Population Bulletin* 38 (Oct.): 1–44.

THORNTON, ARLAND, AND DEBORAH FREEDMAN   1985. "Changing attitudes toward marriage and single life." In Ollie Pocs and Robert H. Walsh, eds. *Marriage and Family 84/85: Annual Editions.* Guilford, Conn.: Dushkin, pp. 22–28. Reprinted from *Family Planning Perspectives* 14 (Nov.–Dec.).

TIEFER, LEONORE   1979. *Human Sexuality: Feelings and Functions.* New York: Harper & Row.

TIMASHEFF, NICHOLAS S.   1946. *The Great Retreat.* New York: E. P. Dutton.

TROLL, LILLIAN E.   1983. "Grandparents: The family watchdogs." In Timothy H. Brubaker, ed. *Family Relationships in Later Life.* Beverly Hills, Calif.: Sage, pp. 63–74.

TROLL, LILLIAN E.; SHEILA J. MILLER; AND ROBERT C. ATCHLEY   1979. *Families in Later Life.* Belmont, Calif.: Wadsworth.

TROPMAN, JOHN E.   1986. *Cultural Dissonance: American Culture and Social Welfare.* Unpublished manuscript. Ann Arbor: University of Michigan, School of Social Work.

TSAI, M., AND N. WAGNER   1978. "Therapy groups for women sexually molested as children." *Archives of Sexual Behavior* 7: 417–427.

UHLENBERG, PETER   1980. "Death and the family." *Journal of Family History,* Fall, 313–320.

U.S. BUREAU OF THE CENSUS   1983. "Marital status and living arrangements." *Current Population Reports,* Series P-20, No. 389, Mar. Washington, D.C.: U.S. Government Printing Office.

U.S. BUREAU OF THE CENSUS   1985. "Households, families, marital status, and living arrangements." *Current Population Reports,* Series P-20, No. 402, Mar. Washington, D.C.: U.S. Government Printing Office.

U.S. DEPARTMENT OF HEALTH AND HUMAN SERVICES: NATIONAL CENTER FOR HEALTH STATISTICS   1984. *Monthly Vital Statistics Report* 32 (Feb. 29).

VANCE, E. B., AND N. N. WAGNER   1976. "Written descriptions of orgasm: A study of sex differences." *Archives of Sexual Behavior* 5: 87–98.

VAUGHAN, DIANE   1985. "Uncoupling: The social construction divorce." In James H.

Henslin, ed. *Marriage and Family in a Changing Society.* 2nd ed. New York: Free Press, pp. 429–439.

VEROFF, JOSEPH; ELIZABETH DOUVAN; AND RICHARD A. KULKA 1981. *The Inner American.* New York: Basic Books.

VIORST, JUDITH 1975. "What is this thing called love?" *Redbook,* Feb., p. 12.

VISHER, EMILY B., AND JOHN S. VISHER 1979. *Stepfamilies: A Guide to Working with Stepparents and Stepchildren.* New York: Brunner/Mazel.

VOYDANOFF, PATRICIA 1984. *Work and Family: Changing Roles of Men and Women.* Palo Alto, Calif.: Mayfield.

WAHLROOS, SVEN 1983. *Family Communication.* 2nd ed. St. Louis: Mosby.

WAKIN, EDWARD 1983. "Marriages of climbing executives," *Today's Office,* Aug., pp. 42–50.

WALKER, GLYNNIS 1986. *Solomon's Children: Exploding the Myths of Divorce.* New York: Arbor House.

WALKER, LENORE E. 1979. *The Battered Woman.* New York: Harper & Row.

WALKER, LENORE 1983. "The battered women syndrome study." In David Finkelhor, Richard J. Gelles, Gerald T. Hotaling, and Murray A. Straus, eds. *The Dark Side of Families.* Beverly Hills, Calif.: Sage.

WALLER, WILLARD W. 1937. "The rating and dating complex." *American Sociological Review* 2 (Oct.): 727–734.

WALLER, WILLARD 1938. *The Family: A Dynamic Interpretation.* New York: Holt, Rinehart and Winston.

WALLER, WILLARD W. 1938. *The Family: A Dynamic Interpretation.* New York: Dryden Press.

WALLER, WILLARD, AND REUBEN HILL 1951. *The Family.* New York: Dryden Press.

WALLERSTEIN, JUDITH, AND JOAN BERLIN KELLY 1980. *Surviving the Breakup.* New York: Basic Books.

WALLIS, CLAUDIA 1985. "Chlamydia: The silent epidemic." *Time,* Feb. 4, p. 67.

WALSH, ANTHONY 1981. *Human Nature and Love.* Washington, D.C.: University Press of America.

WALSTER, ELAINE, AND G. WILLIAM WALSTER 1978. *A New Look at Love.* Reading, Mass.: Addison-Wesley.

WALSTER, ELAINE; V. ARONSON; D. ABRAHAMS; AND L. ROTTMANN 1966. "Importance of physical attractiveness in dating behavior." *Journal of Personality and Social Psychology* 4: 508–516.

WALSTER, ELAINE; G. WILLIAM WALSTER; AND ELLEN BERSHEID 1978. *Equity: Theory and Research.* Boston: Allyn & Bacon.

WALSTER, ELAINE; G. WILLIAM WALSTER; J. PILIAVIN; AND L. SCHMIDT 1973. "Playing hard to get: Understanding an elusive phenomenon." *Journal of Personality and Social Psychology* 26: 113–121.

WARE, LIJI 1982. *Sharing Parenthood After Divorce.* Toronto: Bantam Books.

WATERS, EVERETT; J. WIPPMAN; AND L. A. STROUFE 1979. "Attachment, positive affect and competence in the peer group: Two studies in construct validation." *Child Development* 509: 821–829.

WATSON, JOHN B. 1928. *Psychological Care of Infant and Child.* New York: Norton.

WATSON, ROY L. 1983. "Premarital cohabitation vs. traditional courtship: Their effects on subsequent marital adjustment." *Family Relations* 32 (Jan.): 139–147.

WATZLAWICK, PAUL; J. BEAVIN; AND DON D. JACKSON 1967. *Pragmatics of Human Communication.* New York: Norton.

WEBER, ELLEN 1977. "Incest: Sexual abuse begins at home." *Ms.,* Apr., pp. 64–67.

WEED, J. A. 1980. "National estimates of marriage dissolution and survivorship: United States." Vital and Health Statistics: Series 3, Analytic Statistics, No. 19 DHHS Publication No. (PHS) 81-1403. Hyattsville, Md.: U.S. Department of Health and Human Services; Public Health Services; Office of Health Research, Statistics and Technology; National Center for Health Statistics.

WEIS, K., AND S. BORGES 1973. "Victimology and rape: The case of the legitimate victim." *Issues in Criminology* 8: 71–115.

WEISS, ROBERT S. 1973. *Loneliness: The Experience of Emotional and Social Isolation.* Cambridge, Mass.: MIT Press.

WEISS, ROBERT S. 1975. *Marital Separation: Managing After a Marriage Ends.* New York: Basic Books.

WEISS, ROBERT S. 1979. *Going It Alone.* New York: Basic Books.

WEITZMAN, LENORE J. 1981. *The Marriage Contract.* New York: Free Press.

WEITZMAN, LENORE J. 1985. *The Divorce Revolution.* New York: Free Press.

WEITZMAN, LENORE J., AND RUTH B. DIXON 1983. "The transformation of legal marriage through nofault divorce." In J. Gipson Wells, ed. *Current Issues in Marriage and Family.* 3rd ed. New York: Macmillan, pp. 217–231.

WHITE, JOSEPH 1972. "Towards a black psychology." In Reginald L. Jones, ed. *Black Psychology.* New York: Harper & Row, pp. 43–50.

WHITING, B., AND C. P. EDWARDS 1973. "A cross-cultural analysis of sex differences in the behavior of children aged three through eleven." *Journal of Social Psychology* 91: 171–188.

WIEST, W. 1977. "Semantic differential profiles of orgasm and other experiences among men and women." *Sex Roles* 13: 399–403.

WILL, J. A. 1978. "Neonatal cuddliness and maternal handling patterns in the first month of life." *Dissertation Abstracts International* 38: 5128B–5129B.

WILLIAMSON, JOHN B.; ANNE MUNLEY; AND LINDA EVANS 1980. *Aging and Society.* New York: Holt, Rinehart and Winston.

WILLIE, CHARLES V. 1985. *Black and White Families: A Study in Complementarity.* Bayside, N.Y.: General Hall.

WILMOT, JOYCE H., AND WILLIAM W. WIL- MOT 1978. *Interpersonal Conflict.* Dubuque, Iowa: Brown.

WINCH, ROBERT F. 1952. *The Modern Family.* New York: Holt, Rinehart and Winston.

WINCH, ROBERT F. 1958. *Mate Selection: A Study of Complementary Needs.* New York: Harper & Row.

WINN, MARIE 1983. *Children Without Childhood.* New York: Pantheon Books.

WITELSON, SANDRA F. 1976. "Sex and the single hemisphere: Specialization of the right hemisphere for spatial processing." *Science* 193: 4251.

WOLFE, LINDA 1981. *The Cosmo Report.* New York: Arbor House.

WOOD, V., AND J. F. ROBERTSON 1978. "Friendship and kinship interaction: Differential effect on the morale of the elderly." *Journal of Marriage and the Family* 409: 367–375.

WRONG, DENNIS 1961. "The oversocialized conception of man in modern society." *American Sociological Review* 26: 183–193.

YANKELOVICH, DANIEL 1981. "New rules in American life." *Psychology Today,* Apr., pp. 35–92.

YANKELOVICH, DANIEL 1982. *New Rules.* New York: Bantam Books.

YORK, PHYLLIS; DAVID YORK; AND TED WACHTEL 1982. *Toughlove.* New York: Bantam Books.

YOUNG, LEONTINE 1976. *Wednesday's Children: A Study of Child Neglect and Abuse.* New York: McGraw-Hill.

ZAPHIRIS, ALEXANDER G., ED. 1975. *Protective Services to Abused and Neglected Children and their Families.* University of Denver, Graphics Department.

ZELDITCH, MORRIS, JR. 1964. "Family, marriage, and kinship." In Robert E. Lee Faris, ed. *Handbook of Modern Sociology.* Chicago: Rand McNally, pp. 680–733.

ZELNICK, MELVIN, AND JOHN F. KANTER 1980. "Sexual activity, contraceptive use and pregnancy among metropolitan area teenagers: 1971–1979." *Family Planning Perspectives* 12 (Sept.–Oct.): 230–237.

ZEROF, HERBERT G. 1978. *Finding Intimacy.* Minneapolis: Winston Press.

ZILBERGELD, BERNIE 1978. *Male Sexuality.* New York: Bantam Books.

ZILBERGELD, BERNIE, AND C. R. ELLISON 1980. "Alternatives to couples counseling for sex problems: Group and individual therapy." *Journal of Sex and Marital Therapy* 6: 3–18.

ZUBE, MARGARET 1982. "Changing behavior and outlook of aging men and women." *Family Relations* 31: 147–156.

ZUCKER, SHEVA 1983. "Never Go Out With Anyone Who . . ." In William Novak. *The Great American Man Shortage.* New York: Rawson, pp. 194–195.

Text and Illustration Credits

We gratefully acknowledge the use of the following quotations, illustrations, and photographs:*

Chapter 1 Photo, p. 3, Eastern Michigan University, Office of Public Information & Publications. Photo, p. 14, EKM-Nepenthe. Quoted material in text, p. 18, from Jessie Bernard, "The Good-provider Role: Its Rise and Fall," in *American Psychologist,* 1981, *36,* 2–5; copyright © 1981 by the American Psychological Association. Reprinted by permission of the publisher and author. Quoted material in text, p. 19, from Carroll Smith-Rosenberg, "The Female World of Love and Ritual: Relations Between Women in Nineteenth-Century America," in *Signs* (Autumn 1975), *1,* 1–29; reprinted by permission of The University of Chicago Press. Photo, p. 20, EKM-Nepenthe. Photo, p. 21, Brown Brothers. Photo, p. 29, Shumsky, The Image Works.

Chapter 2 Photo, p. 39, Carey, The Image Works. Song lyrics, p. 42, "I Am a Rock," copyright © 1965 Paul Simon, used by permission. Figure 2.2, p. 47, adapted from: LOOKING OUT/LOOKING IN, 4/e, by Ronald B. Adler and Neil Towne. Copyright © 1984 by CBS College Publishing. Copyright © 1981, 1978 by Holt, Rinehart and Winston. Copyright © 1975 by Rinehart Press. Reprinted by permission of Holt, Rinehart and Winston, Inc. Figure 2.3, p. 49, after Shirley Gilbert, "Self-Disclosure, Intimacy and Communication in Families," *The Family Coordinator, 25* (July 1976), p. 228. Copyrighted © 1976 by the National Council on Family Relations, 1910 West County Road B, St. Paul, Minnesota 55113. Reprinted by permission. Photo, p. 49, © 1981, Menzel, Stock, Boston. Photo, p. 50, Gaylord, Jeroboam. Photo, p. 55, Hill, Jr., Menzel, Stock, Boston.

Photo, p. 59, Carey, The Image Works. Cartoon, p. 60, Cathy Gendron (artist), from McCormack, "Pets Can Promote Health, Well-Being . . . even Parenthood." Reprinted with permission of United Press International, Copyright 1984. Photo, p. 63, Carey, The Image Works.

Chapter 3 Photo, p. 69, © Palmer, The Picture Cube. Photo, p. 71, Stock, Boston. Photo, p. 75, Vandermark, Stock, Boston. Quoted material in text, pp. 78–79, Lori B. Andrews, "The Truth about PMS (Premenstrual Syndrome)," *Parents,* January 1985, pp. 51–56. Reprinted by permission. Quoted material in text, p. 80, Susan Roelofs, "Premenstrual Syndrome and Intimacy," unpublished paper, pp. 1–3. Reprinted by permission. Photo, p. 86, © Siluk, EKM-Nepenthe. Quoted material in text, pp. 88–89, Alice S. Rossi, "American Sociological Association, 1983 Presidential Address," *American Sociological Review,* 49, pp. 1–19. Reprinted by permission. Photo, p. 91, Forsyth, Monkmeyer. Figure 3.2, p. 92, Baruch, et al.: *Lifeprints: New Patterns of Love and Work for Today's Women.* Adaptation of figure from page 37. Copyright 1983 McGraw-Hill Book Company. Used with permission.

Chapter 4 Photo, p. 97, Weisbrot, Stock, Boston. Song lyrics, p. 102, "Show Me," by Alan Jay Lerner and Frederick Loewe. Copyright © 1956 by Alan Jay Lerner and Frederick Loewe. Copyright renewed, all rights administered by Chappell & Co., Inc. International copyright secured. All rights reserved. Used by permission. Photo, p. 105, © 1980, Kroll, Taurus. Photo, p. 110, © 1980, Spratt, The Image Works. Photo, p. 115, EKM-Nepenthe.

* An attempt has been made to obtain permission from all sources of poems, lyrics, and other quotations used in this edition. Some sources have not been located, but permission will be requested from them upon notification to us of their ownership of the material.

Poem, p. 121, "There's a Me," by Althea Scott. Quoted material in text, pp. 124–125, Ralph B. Hupka, from "Cultural Determinants of Jealousy," in *Alternative Life-styles, 4,* 1981, pp. 310–356. Photo, p. 126, © Bates, The Picture Cube.

Chapter 5 Photo, p. 131, Dratch, The Image Works. Quoted material in text, p. 132, from pp. 252–254, 490–491, 493, 495, 498. Bernard I. Murstein, *Love, Sex and Marriage Through the Ages,* 1974. Reprinted by permission of Springer Publishing Company, Inc. Figure 5.1 and caption, p. 133, Figure 1.2 from E. R. Mahoney, *Human Sexuality,* p. 10, 1983. Reprinted by permission of the publisher, McGraw-Hill Book Company. Photos, p. 134 (left), Brown Brothers; p. 134 (right), UPI/Bettmann Newsphotos. Quoted material in text, pp. 135ff, from Floyd M. Martinson, "Sensory Erotic Development: Embryo, Fetus, Infant, Child," paper presented at the Sixth World Congress of Sexology, 1982. Reprinted by permission. Figure 5.2, p. 142, Figure 4.4 in Morton G. Harmatz and Melinda A. Novak, *Human Sexuality,* p. 72, 1983. Reprinted by permission of the publisher Harper & Row, Publishers, Inc. Figure 5.3, p. 143, Figure 4.9 in Morton G. Harmatz and Melinda A. Novak, *Human Sexuality,* p. 80, 1983. Reprinted by permission of the publisher, Harper & Row Publishers, Inc. Photo, p. 140, Bodin, Stock, Boston. Poem, p. 140, "There is something I don't know," from *Knots* by R. D. Laing. Copyright © 1970 by R. D. Laing. Reprinted by permission of Pantheon Books, a Division of Random House, Inc. Figure and caption, p. 146, from William H. Masters and Virginia E. Johnson, *Human Sexual Response,* Boston: Little, Brown, 1966. Copyright © 1966 by William H. Masters and Virginia E. Johnson. Reprinted by permission. Quoted material in text, pp. 148ff, from Gilbert Nass, Roger Libby, and Mary Pat Fisher, *Sexual Choices,* 2nd Edition. Reprinted by permission of the present publisher, Jones and Bartlett Publishers, Inc. Quoted material in text, pp. 151–152, from William R. Fisher, "Gender, Gender-role Identification, and Response to Erotica," in Elizabeth Rice Allgeier and Naomi B. McCormick, *Changing Boundaries,* Palo Alto, Calif.: Mayfield, pp. 261–284. Reprinted by permission. Photo, p. 152, Carey, The Image Works. Quoted material in text, pp. 153ff, from William H. Masters, Virginia E. Johnson, and Robert C. Kolodny, *Human Sexuality,* pp. 237, 246–247, 250, 251–252, 298, 320–322, 422. Copyright © 1982 by William H. Masters, Virginia E. Johnson, and Robert C. Kolodny. Reprinted by permission of Little, Brown and Company. Quoted material in text, pp. 158ff, from Elise F. Jones et al., "Teenage Pregnancy in Developed Countries: Determinants and Policy Implications." *Family Planning Perspectives,* 17:53, 1987. Reprinted by permission of the publisher, The Alan Guttmacher Institute. Figure 5.5, p. 166, after Alfred C. Kinsey, Wardell B. Pomeroy, and Clyde E. Martin, *Sexual Behavior in the Human Male,* Philadelphia, Saunders, 1948, p. 638. Reprinted by permission of The Kinsey Institute for Research in Sex, Gender, and Reproduction. Photo, p. 168, © Eckert, Jr., EKM-Nepenthe. Quoted material in text, pp. 168ff, from

Philip Blumstein and Pepper Schwartz, "Bisexuality: Some Social Psychological Issues." *Journal of Social Issues,* 33 (Spring 1977), pp. 30–45. Reprinted by permission of the publisher, The Society for the Psychological Study of Social Issues.

Chapter 6 Photo, p. 179, © 1983, Hazel Hankin. Quoted material in text, pp. 180ff, from Michael M. McCall, "Courtship as Social Exchange," in Bernard Farber (ed.), *Kinships and Family Organization,* 1976, pp. 190–200. Reprinted by permission of the publisher, John Wiley & Sons. Quoted material in text, pp. 182–184, from Bernard I. Murstein, "Mate Selection in the 1980's." *Journal of Marriage and the Family, 42,* 1980, pp. 777–792. Reprinted by permission of the National Council on Family Relations. Photo, p. 185, © Bates, The Picture Cube. Photo, p. 189, © Kroll, Taurus. Quoted material in text, pp. 191ff, from Ellen Berscheid and Elaine Hatfield Walster, *Interpersonal Attraction,* Second Edition, 1978. Reprinted by permission of Random House, Inc. Quoted material in text, p. 192, adapted from Sheva Zucker, "Never Go Out with Anyone who . . ." Excerpted from William Novak, *The Great American Man Shortage.* Copyright © 1983 William Novak. Reprinted with the permission of Rawson Associates, a division of Macmillan, Inc. Photo, p. 196, AP/Wide World. Quoted material in text, pp. 202ff, from William Novak, *The Great American Man Shortage.* Copyright © 1983 William Novak. Reprinted with the permission of Rawson Associates, a division of Macmillan, Inc. Photo, p. 204, Carey, The Image Works. Figure 6.1, p. 207, diagram from p. 33 of *The Future of Marriage,* by Jessie Bernard, © 1982 Yale University Press, New Haven, Conn. Reprinted by permission of the publisher.

Chapter 7 Photo, p. 213, Carey, The Image Works. Quoted material in text, pp. 217–218, "Ten Myths About Marriage," taken from *Love and Anger in Marriage* by David R. Mace. Copyright © 1982 by The Zondervan Corporation. Used by permission. Quoted material in text, pp. 219ff, from *Close Relationships* by Harold H. Kelley et al. Copyright © 1983 W. H. Freeman and Company. Reprinted with permission. Quoted material in text, p. 219, from "Needed Research on Commitment in Marriage," in George Levinger and Harold Raush (eds.), *Close Relationships: Perspectives on the Meaning of Intimacy,* 1977, Amherst, University of Massachusetts Press, pp. 74–75, 79. Copyright © 1977 by George Levinger and Harold L. Raush. Reprinted by permission. Quoted material in text, pp. 221ff, from *American Couples* by Philip Blumstein, Ph.D., and Pepper Schwartz, Ph.D. Copyright © 1983 by Philip Blumstein and Pepper Schwartz. By permission of William Morrow & Company, Inc. Quoted material in text, pp. 221–223, American Bar Association, *Law and Marriage: Your Legal Guide,* 1983, Chicago, ABA Press, pp. 9–13. Reprinted by permission. Photo, p. 225, Carey, The Image Works. Quoted material in text, pp. 228ff, from *Worlds of Pain: Life in the Working-Class Family* by Lillian Breslow Rubin. Copyright © 1976 by Lillian Breslow Rubin. Reprinted by permission of Basic Books, Inc., Publishers. Photo, p. 229, Photo Trends. Photo, p.

237, Boughton, Stock, Boston. Photo, p. 242, Cheney, EKM-Nepenthe. Photo, p. 244, © Takatsuno, The Picture Cube. Quoted material in text, pp. 248–250, from Naomi Gerstel and Harriet Gross, *Commuter Marriage*, 1984, pp. 54, 67, 74, 121, 132. Reprinted with permission of The Guilford Press, publisher.

Chapter 8 Photo, p. 253, Karp, Omni-Photo Communications. Quoted material in text, pp. 254–255, from John Stewart, *Bridges Not Walls: A Book About Interpersonal Communication*, 1973, pp. 20–21. Reprinted by permission of the publisher, Random House, Inc. Photo, p. 259, © Brilliant, The Picture Cube. Quoted material in text, pp. 263–265, from Carol Tavris, "Anger Defused," *Psychology Today*, November 1982, pp. 25–35. Copyright © 1982. Reprinted with permission from Psychology Today Magazine; Carol Tavris, from *Anger: The Misunderstood Emotion*, 1982, pp. 134–135, 223, 226. Copyright © 1982 by Carol Tavris. Reprinted by permission of the publisher, Simon & Schuster, Inc. Quoted material in text, p. 272, from Marcia Lasswell and Norman M. Lobsenz, *Equal Time*, 1983, pp. 150, 151, 153, 199–203. Reprinted by permission of the authors. Photo, p. 273, Gans, The Image Works. Photo, p. 274, Mercado, Jeroboam. Poem, p. 275, "Touch Me," by Anonymous. Photo, p. 275, © Bates, The Picture Cube. Quoted material in text, pp. 276–277, from David H. Olson, David G. Fournier, and Joan M. Druckman, "The Couple Communication Scale," *Family Circle*, October 1984, p. 5; from Howard L. Barnes and David H. Olson, "The Family Communication Scale," *Family Circle*, October 1984, p. 7; Barnes and Olson, "Parent-Adolescent Communication Scale," in Olson et al., *Family Inventories*, University of Minnesota, 1985. Used by permission. Figure 8.1, p. 281, from R. H. Kilmann and K. W. Thomas, "Interpersonal Conflict—Handling Behavior As Reflections of Jungian Personality Dimensions," *Psychological Reports*, 1975, pp. 37, 971–980, Fig. 1. Reprinted with permission of the authors and the publisher, Psychological Reports.

Chapter 9 Photo, p. 291, © Alper, Stock, Boston. Quoted material in text, pp. 292ff, from Morton M. Hunt, *Sexual Behavior in the 1970's*, reprinted with permission from PLAYBOY Enterprises, Inc., from "Sexual Behavior in the 1970's" by Morton Hunt. Copyright © 1974 by Morton Hunt. Photo, p. 297, Karp, Omni-Photo Communications. Quoted material in text, pp. 299–301, from Lee Rainwater, "Sex in the Culture of Poverty," in Carlfred Broderick and Jessie Bernard (eds.), *The Individual, Sex and Society*, 1969, p. 135. Reprinted by permission of the publisher, Johns Hopkins University Press, Baltimore. Photo, p. 303, Siteman, Stock, Boston. Quoted material in text, pp. 304ff, from Helen Singer Kaplan, *The New Sex Therapy*, 1974, pp. 258, 260–261, 262, 263, 290–291, 292, 296, 384, 397–398, 399, 410. Reprinted by permission of the publisher, Brunner/Mazel, New York. Photo, p. 305, © 1985, Siteman, EKM-Nepenthe. Quoted material in text, pp. 311ff, from Helen Singer Kaplan, *Disorders of Sexual Desire*, 1979, pp. 62–63, 68, 79, 83–85, 88, 90–91, 92, 183. Reprinted by permission of the publisher, Brunner/Mazel, New York.

Quoted material in text, p. 312, Steven Findlay, "Jobs Sap Couples' Craving for Sex," *USA Today*, May 8, 1985. Copyright, 1985 USA TODAY. Reprinted with permission. Quoted material in text, pp. 315–318, from Lynn Atwater, *The Extramarital Connection*, 1982, pp. 58, 60–61, 62, 63, 65, 66, 68, 69, 70, 71. Reprinted by permission of the publisher, Irvington Publishers. Poem, p. 316, "Secret Meetings," by Judith Viorst, from *How Did I Get to Be 40 & Other Atrocities*. Reprinted by permission of the author's representatives, Lescher & Lescher, Ltd. Quoted material in text, pp. 320–321, from Melissa Sands, *The Making of the American Mistress*, 1981, pp. 179, 180, 181, 187, 188. Reprinted by permission of Roslyn Targ Literary Agency, Inc. Copyright © 1981 by Melissa Sands.

Chapter 10 Photo, p. 325, © 1984, Hazel Hankin. Photo, p. 329, © 1983, Arms, Jeroboam. Quoted material in text, pp. 330–331, from Jerry Bergman, "Licensing Parents: A New Age of Child-Rearing?" *The Futurist*, December 1978. Reprinted, with permission, from THE FUTURIST, published by the World Future Society, 4916 St. Elmo Ave., Bethesda, Maryland 20814. Quoted material in text, pp. 332–333, from E. E. LeMasters and John DeFrain, "Folklore about Parenthood," in *Parents in Contemporary America*, by E. E. LeMasters and John DeFrain. © 1983 by The Dorsey Press, Chicago. Reprinted by permission of the publisher. Photo, p. 337, Vandermark, Stock, Boston. Photo, p. 339, © Keillor, Jeroboam. Photo, p. 341, © Hazel Hankin. Photo, p. 344, Carey, The Image Works. Figure 10.1, p. 345, from Mihaly Csikszentmihalyi and Reed Larson, *Being Adolescent: Conflict and Growth in the Teenage Years*, 1984, p. 160. Copyright © 1984 by Basic Books, Inc. Reprinted by permission of Basic Books, Inc., Publishers. Photo, p. 351, Grossman, The Picture Cube. Quoted material in text, p. 352, from Susan Ferraro, "Hotsy Totsy," *American Way*, April 1981, p. 61. Reprinted by permission of *American Way*, inflight magazine of American Airlines, copyright 1981 by American Airlines. Photo, p. 355, Strickler, Monkmeyer. Photo, p. 357, Karp, Omni-Photo Communications. Quoted material in text, p. 359, from Michael Lamb, "Why Swedish Fathers Aren't Liberated," *Psychology Today*, October 1982, p. 74. Reprinted with permission from Psychology Today Magazine. Copyright © 1982 American Psychological Association.

Chapter 11 Photo, p. 363, Stock, Boston. Figure 11.1, p. 364, illustration from *Family Development*, 2d ed., by Evelyn Duvall. Copyright © 1957, 1962 by Evelyn Duvall. Used with permission. Photo, p. 366, Chidester, The Image Works. Photo, p. 368, Carey, The Image Works. Figure 11.2, p. 371, after Boyd C. Rollins and Kenneth L. Cannon, "Marital Satisfaction over the Family Life Cycle: A Reevaluation," *Journal of Marriage and the Family* 36, 1974, p. 275. Copyrighted 1974 by the National Council on Family Relations, 1910 West County Road B, Suite 147, St. Paul, Minnesota 55113. Reprinted by permission. Photo, p. 374, Carey, The Image Works. Photo, p. 379, Myers, Stock, Boston. Quoted material in text, p. 379, from Aaron Lipman and Charles F. Longino,

Jr., "Gender Roles in Later Life: An Introductory Statement," paper presented at the 78th annual meeting of the American Sociological Association, Detroit, Michigan. Reprinted by permission. Quoted material in text, pp. 383–386, from Carol P. Saul, "Coming Home," in Shura Saul (ed.), *Aging: An Album of People Growing Old,* 2nd ed. Copyright © 1983, reprinted by permission of the publisher, John Wiley & Sons, Inc. Quoted material in text, p. 394, from Robert R. Bell, *Worlds of Friendship,* 1981, Sage, Beverly Hills, Calif. Reprinted by permission of the publisher. Photo, p. 395, © Pacheco, EKM-Nepenthe.

Chapter 12   Photo, p. 399, © Scherr, Jeroboam. Photo, p. 401, Hankin, Stock, Boston. Quoted material in text, pp. 403–405, from Leonard Cargan and Matthew Melko, *Singles: Myths and Realities,* 1982, pp. 193–202. Reprinted by permission of the publisher, Sage, Beverly Hills, Calif. Photo, p. 409, Strickler, Monkmeyer. Quoted material in text, p. 414, from Chong W. Pyen, "Unwed: Living Without the Ties that Bind," the *Ann Arbor News,* December 9, 1984, p. G1. Reprinted with permission of the author. Photo, p. 416, Skytta, Jeroboam. Quoted material in text, pp. 426–427, from Ayala Pines and Elliot Aronson, "Polyfidelity: An Alternative Life-Style Without Jealousy," *Alternative Lifestyles,* April 1981, pp. 373–392. Reprinted by permission of the publishers, Human Sciences Press, Inc., 72 Fifth Avenue, New York, NY 10011. Photo, p. 428, Wolinsky, Stock, Boston.

Chapter 13   Photo, p. 435, Antman, The Image Works. Photo, p. 437, © Bryan, Southern Light. Quoted material in text, p. 443, from "Arrest the Wife Beaters!" *Parade* Magazine, October 16, 1983, p. 8. Reprinted by permission. Quoted material in text, pp. 446–449, from Brandt F. Steele and Carl B. Pollock, "A Psychiatric Study of Parents Who Abuse Infants and Small Children," in Ray E. Helfer and C. Henry Kempe (eds.), *The Battered Child,* 2nd Edition, 1974, pp. 97, 99, 105, 116. Reprinted by permission of the publisher, The University of Chicago Press. Photo, p. 447, Kalman, The Image Works. Photo, p. 453, © Barnes, Southern Light. Quoted material in text, p. 464, from "How Can We Protect Our Elderly?" *Parade* Magazine, February 17, 1985, pp. 5–6. Reprinted by permission from Parade Magazine and the author.

Chapter 14   Photo, p. 469, © 1978, Kliewe, Jeroboam. Quoted material in text, p. 471, from Gunhild D. Hagestad and Michael A. Smyer, "Dissolving Long-Term Relationships: Patterns of Divorcing in Middle Age," in Steve Duck (ed.), *Personal Relationships: Dissolving Relationships,* 1982, pp. 155–188. Reprinted by permission of the publisher, Academic Press, Orlando, Florida. Quoted material in text, pp. 472–475, from Steve Duck, "A Topography of Relationship Disengagement and Dissolution," in Steve Duck (ed.), *Personal Relationships: Dissolving Relationships,* 1982, pp. 18, 23, 26. Reprinted by permission of the publisher, Academic Press, Orlando, Florida. Quoted material in text, pp. 474–475, from Diane Vaughan, "Uncoupling: The Social Construction of Divorce," in Howard Robboy and Candace Clark (eds.), *Social Interaction: Readings in Sociology,* 2nd ed., 1985.

Reprinted by permission of the publisher, St. Martin's Press. Quoted material in text, p. 478, from Edward Beal, "The Ripple Effect of Divorce: Loss of Friends," *Marriage and Divorce Today,* April 29, 1985, p. 2. Reprinted by permission of ATCOM, Inc., 2315 Broadway, New York, NY 10024. Quoted material in text, pp. 480ff, from Lenore J. Weitzman and Ruth B. Dixon, "The Transformation of Legal Marriage Through No-fault Divorce," in J. Gipson Wells (ed.), *Current Issues in Marriage and Family,* 3rd ed., 1983, pp. 222–224, 227, 229. Reprinted with permission of Macmillan Publishing Company. Copyright © 1983 by J. Gipson Wells. Quoted material in text, pp. 486–487, from "How Courts Decide Disputes," *Detroit Free Press,* November 18, 1984, p. 4F. Reprinted by permission. Photo, p. 489, © 1983, Siteman, Stock, Boston. Photo, p. 492, © 1983, Kahn, Stock, Boston. Photo, p. 495, © Takatsuno, The Picture Cube. Drawings, pp. 496–497, from Robert C. Burns and S. Harvard Kaufman, *Kinetic Family Drawings (K-F-D): An Introduction to Understanding Children Through Kinetic Drawings,* 1970, Figures 42 and 49, pp. 117, 131. Reprinted with permission of the author, Robert C. Burns. Photo, p. 504, © 1982, Hedman, Jeroboam.

Chapter 15   Photo, p. 513, © Herwig, The Picture Cube. Table 15.1, p. 514, from Angus Campbell, Philip E. Converse, and Willard L. Rodgers, *The Quality of American Life: Perceptions, Evaluations, and Satisfaction.* Table 3-4, p. 84. Copyright © 1976 by Russell Sage Foundation. Reprinted by permission of Basic Books, Inc., Publishers. Photo, p. 515, Brooks, Monkmeyer. Quoted material in text, pp. 515ff, from David Mace, *Close Companions,* 1982, pp. 42, 44, 48, 67, 191, 198; table on p. 16. Reprinted by permission of the publisher, The Continuum Publishing Corporation, New York. Quoted material in text, pp. 518ff, from Michael E. McGill, *The McGill Report on Male Intimacy,* 1985, pp. 237ff. Reprinted by permission of the publisher, Henry Holt and Company, Inc. Photo, p. 520, Weisbrot, Stock, Boston. Quoted material in text, p. 524, from Ann Landers, "Cancer Patient Told to Stick by His Family," November 29, 1986, in the *Detroit Free Press.* Copyright © 1986 by Ann Landers, Los Angeles Times Syndicate. Reprinted by permission. Quoted material in text, pp. 525–526, from Marcia Lasswell and Norman M. Lobsenz, *Equal Time,* 1983, pp. 150, 151, 153, 199–203. Reprinted by permission of the authors. Photo, p. 530, Spratt, The Image Works. Quoted material in text, pp. 533–534, from Lillian Rubin, *Just Friends,* 1985, pp. 4, 9, 23, 61, 63, 66, 68, 72, 73–74. Copyright © 1985 by Lillian B. Rubin. Reprinted by permission of Harper & Row, Publishers, Inc. Quoted material in text, pp. 534–536, from Wanda J. Dickens and Daniel Perlman, "Friendship over the Life Cycle," in Steve Duck and Robin Gilmour, *Personal Relationships 2: Developing Personal Relationships,* 1981, pp. 110–111, 119, 120. Reprinted by permission of the publisher, Academic Press, Orlando, Florida. Quoted material in text, pp. 534ff, from Robert R. Bell, *Worlds of Friendship,* 1981, pp. 21ff. Reprinted by permission of the publisher, Sage Publications, Inc. Table 15.3, p. 536, from Mary Brown Parlee, "The

Friendship Bond," *Psychology Today,* October 1979, table, p. 49. Reprinted with permission from Psychology Today Magazine, copyright © 1979 American Psychological Association. Photo, p. 538, © 1979, Gardner, The Image Works. Photo, p. 540, Albertson, The Picture Cube. Quoted material in text, pp. 546–547, from Daniel Yankelovich, "New Rules in American Life," in *Psychology Today,* April 1981, pp. 46–47. Reprinted by permission of Yankelovich, Skelly and White, 575 Madison Avenue, New York, NY.

Appendix C Quoted material in text, pp. 563–564, from Theresa Crenshaw, *AIDS,* 1986, mimeographed from presentation to *AASECT* annual meeting. Reprinted by permission of the author.

Name Index

Subject Index